PAULI MURRAY

Other Books by Pauli Murray

Proud Shoes: The Story of an American Family
Dark Testament and Other Poems

Pauli Murray

The Autobiography
of a Black Activist,
Feminist, Lawyer,
Priest, and Poet

The University of Tennessee Press
Knoxville

Formerly titled "Song in a Weary Throat: An American Pilgrimage"

Reprinted in paperback in 1989 by The University of Tennessee Press, Knoxville, by arrangement with Harper & Row, Publishers, New York

LIBRARY OF CONGRESS CATALOGING-IN-PUBLICATION DATA

Murray, Pauli, 1910–
  [Song in a weary throat]
  Pauli Murray : the autobiography of a Black activist, feminist,
lawyer, priest, and poet / by Pauli Murray.
      p.   cm.
  Originally published: Song in a weary throat. New York : Harper &
Row, © 1987.
  Includes index.
  ISBN 0-87049-596-8 (pbk. : alk. paper)
  1. Murray, Pauli, 1910– . 2. Afro-Americans—Biography.
  3. Feminists—United States—Biography.   I. Title.
[E185.97.M95A3 1989]
973'.0496073024—dc19
[B]   88-20728
                                                            CIP

TO MAIDA

Incomparable companion, critic,
and guide on the pilgrimage

Hope is a crushed stalk
Between clenched fingers.
Hope is a bird's wing
Broken by a stone.
Hope is a word in a tuneless ditty—
A word whispered with the wind,
A dream of forty acres and a mule,
A cabin of one's own and a moment to rest,
A name and place for one's children
And children's children at last . . .
Hope is a song in a weary throat.

From *Dark Testament and Other Poems*

Contents

A section of photographs follows page 212

Introduction

Why should the life of Pauli Murray matter to those who never felt her effervescence? Pauli's achievements foreshadowed dramatic changes during her lifetime. But history—and her own prescient determination—placed her just ahead of her time, removing her from the spotlight of those changes when they occurred.

Yet hers is a life worth examining because it is so remarkably instructive. It is not simply what Pauli became and overcame as poet, lawyer, writer, teacher, and priest, it is her purposeful creation of a life full of adventures in achievement that fascinates, inspires, and teaches. Pauli's life makes us understand why biography and autobiography are different from fiction; they compel an inescapable identification. When the life is extraordinary, as Pauli's was, we probe to find why and how it branched away from the common experience. Unintended lessons emerge.

For most of us life is a series of accidents that we piece together, trying to make them coherent and whole. To be sure, this often means active intervention to make things go one way rather than another. But perhaps more often it means going along with the natural stages of life, taking events in turn, and making the best of them. Against the usual standard, Pauli's life is a singularly wrought act of self-creation, yielding one unusual achievement after another. If Pauli did not become everything she wanted to be, she surely became everything it was possible for her to be. She overcame the limitations imposed on her as a black and a woman through strength of will and through sheer toil. What she could not altogether change was the reception society would give the talent she so painstakingly cultivated.

It is that cultivation—the constant doing and redoing to make it better, the insistent striving and climbing not merely to reach but to become the unattainable—that guided her life. It began not with her pioneering efforts that broke race and sex barriers, but when she was a child alone with only her aspirations as the standard against which to measure herself.

When Pauli Murray drew sustenance from sources outside herself, they often were close to home. Orphaned as a child, she nevertheless makes us understand family love and pride as a source of personal strength. Pauli's upbringing in an extended family, that equipped her so well, reveals how crucial family is. In her willful way, she sought her family at its roots, in the stories of her aunts and other relatives and in the records of a heritage of black and white forebears so typical of black Americans. Just as she created her own life with purpose and determination, Pauli re-created her family, writing about her ancestors in her book *Proud Shoes: The Story of an American Family.*

Pauli's life may be seen as her triumph in a series of tests she deliberately set for herself. What distinguishes her goals is a studied selectivity, a bias toward goals for which she was in some sense disqualified—whether by race, sex, or preparation. She was at once disheartened and motivated by her rejection when she sought admission to the highly competitive Hunter College of the 1930s in New York City. In order to overcome the deficiencies of her segregated Southern education and gain entry to Hunter, she returned to high school for a year in New York, where she matriculated as the only black among 4,000 students. The same competitive spirit took hold when her Berkeley graduate law advisor insisted that limitations in her background would keep her from passing the difficult California bar. Pauli took such assessments as challenges. She focused her intelligence and energy and passed the California bar even though she had only three weeks in which to prepare.

Pauli was just as determined when confronted by barriers that could not be overcome by work and will. She applied to do graduate work at the University of North Carolina and received a letter rejecting her on the basis of race. Years later she received a similar letter from Harvard Law School rejecting her on the basis of sex. In middle age, when discrimination bars were no longer common, she would revisit barriers that were not ready to fall when she was young.

The obstacles came in even more formidable varieties. It was one thing to risk self-esteem applying to schools which had never before admitted people like her. It was quite another to risk life and limb in sit-in demonstrations against discrimination and in Southern jails in the 1940s when both the law and the prevailing mood of the country were set against racial change. I was fresh from sitting-in when I met her at Yale in the 1960s, and I marveled at the nerve and bravery of this little woman who had already done what we were only beginning to do; she did not have the safety and protection of the full-blown movement and reformist national mood that cushioned our risk.

Fascinated by Pauli's pioneering incursions, I used information from her meticulous files to write a major paper for a graduate history course in 1963, and titled the paper "World War II and the Beginnings of Non-Violent Action in Civil Rights." I was thrilled to have use of the original papers of an original civil rights protestor and to be the beneficiary of the detailed files she collected and carted around with her wherever she moved. (Following her death, twenty years later, a copy of that paper, neatly labeled using her filing system, was sent to me!) Later, though I could not foresee it then, I would be the beneficiary of the work she did almost single-handedly in keeping a prohibition against sex discrimination in a law I would be appointed to administer—Title VII of the 1964 Civil Rights Act. The memoirs that follow here, with their conscientious attention to the names, conversations, and details of Pauli's past, confirm what I learned firsthand from her files. In effect, she recorded her life not at the end but as she went along, keeping records and notes of events small and great. It is a testament to her need to remember, her regard for history, and her insistence to learn from her past.

But Pauli never lived in the past. She lived on the edge of history, seeming to pull it along with her. She was a civil rights activist before there was activism, and a feminist when feminists could not be found. She practiced at a major law firm and earned a renowned professorship at a major university before blacks or women did either.

Yet Pauli was not simply the sum total of her work and her pathbreaking feats. She had poignant friendships and personal experiences. Her brief marriage gently ended when the couple realized that they had been too young and hasty. She had dear friends and two aunts who were like a nuclear family. Her description of the feelings and loyalty she felt for relatives and friends alike shows the spirit of a woman who experienced deep and caring love. The extraordinary love she had for her father comes through not only in her observations of him in his prime, but in her graphic description of his brutal murder in a mental institution and of her eerie affinity to him as he lay dead and disfigured.

But perhaps the most fascinating relationship in this book is her friendship with Eleanor Roosevelt, which began with a letter from Pauli. The correspondence and many meetings between them over most of Pauli's adult life were deeply affectionate, but Pauli never hesitated to cajole and strenuously criticize President Roosevelt and Eleanor Roosevelt herself on national issues, especially race. Their friendship thrived on prickly issues and deep and mutual affection. It was a remarkable friendship between the best-known woman in the world and the equally energetic black woman who became a central figure in Mrs. Roosevelt's conscience on race.

Pauli was always insatiable and restless for more life and more challenges. She never put down roots for long. She was like a mountain climber whose stamina increases with each new climb. Energized by her own achievements she was always in search of new peaks. When she decided to study to be an Episcopal priest, it was the act of a woman determined to consummate her life, not simply to let it end. She had been always in search of life's meaning. Over and over again, right until the end, when she worked on these lovely memoirs, she found it. Characteristically, Pauli has had the last word on herself.

—ELEANOR HOLMES NORTON

Washington, D.C.

Editor's Note

Special recognition is due Casey Miller and Kate Swift, writers of unusual sensitivity, intelligence, and talent, for their indispensable editorial contribution to Pauli Murray's final manuscript of *Song in a Weary Throat*. This book could not have been published without their help.

—TERRY KARTEN

CHAPTER 1

Daughter of Agnes and Will

To be small, afraid, and silent
among the eternal spheres . . .
From a Poet's Notebook

M Y first memory is of standing on the floor of our kitchen in Baltimore when I was around three, entangled in my mother's billowing white skirts to which I clung as she went about her work. I cannot remember her face or her voice, only her movements and the warm fragrance of her body. My only memory of my father when he was alive is a brief visit to him in the hospital when I was eight. I never used the familiar words "Mamma" and "Papa" when I was growing up; I always spoke of my parents as "my mother" and "my father."

Aside from these fleeting encounters, almost everything I knew about my parents came from their pictures, the few letters and books they left behind, and the recollections of my aunts, grandparents, and other people who knew them. Because they were the unchanging reality of my identity, fixed points of reference in my confused world of uncertain boundaries, I clung to these borrowed images with desperate single-mindedness. No detail of my parents' lives was insignificant. When I was a small child I pestered my elders with endless questions about Will and Agnes Murray and fed voraciously on the remembrances of others to fill the void of their physical absence. Their mystical nearness, especially during my earliest years, blurred the mystery of separation between the living and the dead as they came alive in my imagination. Stories of my mother and father, always told in love with an undertone of sadness, had a remarkable influence on my development. Their striving to achieve filled me with pride and incentive, while their misfortunes left a legacy of mournfulness hovering like a gray mist over my early childhood. From a realm beyond my senses they both inspired and gave me my first stern lessons in the meaning of adversity.

1

My father, William H. Murray, was a public school teacher in Baltimore. My mother, Agnes Fitzgerald Murray, was a graduate of the Hampton Training School for Nurses. I was the fourth of their six children, born shortly after noonday on Sunday, November 20, 1910, in our home at 1330 Argyle Avenue, a Baltimore street of attached brick houses with white marble front steps. In 1910, Argyle Avenue was a well-kept neighborhood of rising young professional people of color who were buying their own homes and paying ground rent to the City of Baltimore for the land on which their houses were built. By 1952, when I made my first pilgrimage back to the house in which I was born, 1330 still retained features of its original structure, and the woman who then lived there allowed me to walk through the six-room house and identify the front upstairs bedroom where I first saw life, the rooms in which the Murray brood spent their infancy and earliest childhood, the study where my father kept his books and papers, and the small backyard where my mother grew rosebushes. In 1980, the house had become a grimy slum, the basement had been sealed off, the backyard was an unsightly dump, and the half-blind woman who lived in the house was the victim of an absentee landlord, living in poverty and ill health. The 1300 block of Argyle Avenue had become the target of rehabilitation efforts which had not quite reached number 1330.

When I became old enough to be interested in the historical events which surround one's beginnings, I learned that I was born during the presidency of William Howard Taft, in the same year that Halley's Comet returned to the vicinity of planet Earth, not to appear again for seventy-six years, and that the great Russian novelist and advocate of nonviolence, Leo Tolstoy, author of *War and Peace,* died within twenty-four hours of my nativity. As I grew up and embraced nonviolence as a way of life, this last fact was to spark recurring fantasies about the transmigration of souls.

Because I was born into a family of "colored" people, as we were then designated, it has also been of increasing significance to me that my life and development paralleled the existence of the two major continuous civil rights organizations in the United States, both of which were founded around the time of my own beginnings—the National Association for the Advancement of Colored People (NAACP) in 1909, and the National Urban League in 1910. It was in the year and month of my birth that the great protagonist of civil rights causes, W. E. B. Du Bois, published the first issue of *The Crisis,* which is still the official organ of the NAACP.

According to Aunt Pauline, my godmother and my mother's oldest sister, who later adopted me, I entered the world during a stormy period in my parents' lives. Before I was conceived, my mother and father had had one of their brief but periodic separations. My mother had fled to her parents' home in Durham, North Carolina, where her family urged her to seek a divorce. She had returned to Baltimore with that intention, or so her family thought. Instead, there was a passionate reunion between my parents, and I, not a divorce, was the result.

Aunt Pauline said that in spite of my rocky start in life I was an unusually happy baby and a very cheerful small child, always in perpetual motion even, she maintained, when sleeping. As the person chiefly responsible for my upbringing, she always encouraged me to have high expectations of myself. She told me that being born on Sunday was a good portent, and she would quote the familiar rhyme "And a child that is born on the Sabbath day/Is fair and good and wise and gay." She, too, had been born on a Sunday, in 1870, and I knew she had become the respected eldest member of her generation, looked up to by all her younger relatives. All of this had a powerful effect on my image of self as I was growing up. Increasingly I saw myself through her eyés as a child of reconciliation conceived in love.

Aunt Pauline could not gloss over the unhappy facts of family disruption which had made me an orphan, but in response to my insistent questions, her telling of my parents' private tragedy turned a tale of ordinary folk into a drama of heroic proportions. Their passionate devotion to one another throughout the perplexities of their nearly eleven years of married life invested them with an aura of legendary, star-crossed lovers. They had begun their life together under the most promising circumstances, it seemed, favored with good looks, vitality, education, and ambition. Each had come from a strongly knit family of hardworking people who were independent-minded, thought well of themselves, and had high ideals and strong religious values. Notwithstanding the handicaps of racial status in the early twentieth century, their success had seemed assured.

My father, a Marylander, was born in Reisterstown, Baltimore County, in 1872, the oldest of four children. In 1881, his family migrated to Baltimore City, where his father, Nelson Murray, worked as a waiter and later as a church sexton, while his mother, Annie Price Murray, washed the fine linens of wealthy white people to help earn the family's living. William grew up carrying his mother's laundry back and forth from her customers, waiting table, and doing odd jobs to get himself through school. He and his younger brother, Lewis Hamilton Murray, fifteen years his junior, had a scholarly bent, and both entered the teaching profession. His parents' second son, Joseph, remained a waiter most of his life, and their one daughter, Rosetta, dropped out of school and soon married a "sporting man," Will Shipley, who was valet to an army officer. Will Shipley liked good whiskey, cardplaying, and betting on horse races, all of which offended his brother-in-law William's Victorian code of respectability.

Aunt Rose later explained that she left school and married early because she was an unusually fat girl, and the other children made fun of her. Few opportunities for development existed for young colored women of her time and place, and when her marriage did not work out she came home again to live in the shadow of her menfolk, haunted by a deep sense of inferiority over her lack of formal education.

Education beyond elementary school for people of color was extremely hard to come by, of course, and it was a measure of my father's tenacity in pursuing this elusive goal that he graduated from the Howard University college preparatory department in 1899 at the age of twenty-seven. His achievement automatically placed him among the more privileged of Baltimore's colored population, and he was appointed to teach in the Baltimore Colored Schools. In time, he became principal of the Carey Street School and followed a pattern familiar to the public school teachers of his day—toiling in the classroom all winter and attending teachers' institutes in the summer to add to his academic credentials. He married a young Baltimorean named Florence Gray, but lost his wife and their infant in childbirth. When he first met my mother, he had been recently widowed.

Agnes Fitzgerald was one of the five daughters and one son born to Robert George and Cornelia Smith Fitzgerald, who farmed and made bricks in Orange and Durham counties, North Carolina. Grandfather Fitzgerald, a Union Army veteran, had fought at Petersburg, Virginia, and had returned South after the War Between the States embued with the mission of the church-related movement to establish schools for former slaves. His assignment took him to Orange County, North Carolina, where he met and married Cornelia Smith in 1869. Grandmother Cornelia, the daughter of a white lawyer, Sidney Smith, and his family's part-Cherokee slave, Harriet, had been raised by Sidney's unmarried sister, who interrogated the young schoolteacher-suitor to her satisfaction before approving the marriage.

My grandfather was convinced that the Reconstruction era opened up new opportunities for ambitious colored people. In the same year that he married, he persuaded his landowning parents, his younger brother Richard, a brickmaker, and his teenage sisters, Mary Jane and Agnes, to move from their Pennsylvania farm to Durham, North Carolina. He continued to teach school until blindness overtook him and then, to earn a living, turned to brickmaking and farming with the aid of his wife and children.

My mother, Agnes, who was my grandparents' fifth child, was born on Christmas night in 1878 at the farm near Chapel Hill that my grandmother had inherited from her aunt and former owner, Mary Ruffin Smith. Everyone loved "Aggie" for her beauty and winsome ways. Like her sisters, she grew up learning to drive and ride horses, plow fields, sow and harvest crops, trade cows and pigs at market, pitch hay, and toss bricks, as well as to cook, sew, and keep a spotless house. When she was old enough to go to school, my grandmother sent her to Saint Augustine's School in Raleigh, where her older sisters Pauline and Sallie had studied, but Agnes had no desire to follow them into teaching; nor did she want to emulate her sister Maria, who had gone to Hampton to learn the dressmaking and tailoring trade. Agnes had a mind and will of her own and felt that healing was her true calling; she wanted to become a nurse.

In those days nursing was not favored as a profession for young women, and my grandparents vigorously opposed her ambition, fearing it would expose their daughter to too many indignities and physical hardships. Agnes had been a frail, delicate child, and although she had held her own in heavy farmwork, they drew the line at the rigors of bedside duty as unfitting and too hazardous. Yet Agnes was as persistent as she was persuasive, and her opportunity came when she went to visit her oldest sister, my Aunt Pauline, who had married a young graduate of Howard University Law School named Charles M. Dame and gone to live and teach in Hampton, Virginia, where her husband was trying to establish his law practice. During her visit my mother had an opportunity to see Dixie Hospital, and she immediately wrote home for permission to enter the Hampton Training School for Nurses. With Aunt Pauline's support she eventually won her parents' still reluctant consent.

My mother met my father while she was a student nurse and he was attending Hampton summer school. Aunt Pauline and Aunt Sallie were also enrolled in the summer school that year and were in some of "Mr. Murray's" classes. As a child I loved to hear them vie with one another in telling the story of my parents' romance. The young couple, they recalled, had been introduced to one another by Sadie Fitzgerald, my mother's cousin, on a crowded streetcar late one evening coming back to Hampton from a dance at Buckroe Beach. Mr. Murray had escorted Sadie to the dance, but Agnes and Sallie had gone without escorts, a daring thing for young women to do in those days. My mother looked stunning in a pink dotted-swiss dress she had made for the occasion, her hair brushed back and her long, dark curls tied with a pink bow at the nape of her neck. My father watched her all evening but did not ask her for a dance; instead he timed his departure to coincide with hers, and they were among those who caught the last streetcar to leave the beach that night. Once aboard, he maneuvered the unsuspecting Sadie Fitzgerald through the car until they came face to face with Agnes and Sallie. He said later that he did not walk up and introduce himself at the dance, or ask Sadie to introduce him, because he was president of the campus YMCA and did not want to appear "frivolous." As for my mother, she was horrified to discover, on her return to Aunt Pauline's, where she was staying, that she had worn her pink dress inside out!

Such quaint embarrassments hardly mattered, for once Will Murray met "Miss Agnes," he never had eyes for anyone else and promptly wrote Aunt Pauline a note requesting permission to visit her younger sister. By all accounts it was a betrothal made in heaven. When my father returned to Baltimore, my parents' courtship continued through letters, and after my mother graduated from nursing school in the class of 1902, he came down to Durham to meet my grandparents and ask their consent to marry her.

The wedding of William and Agnes Murray, one of the most popular unions in the three branches of the transplanted Fitzgerald family, took place in Durham on July 1, 1903. It was a day in our family history as notable for the dramatic entry into the world of little Gerald (Jeff) Jeffers, Aunt Maria's only son, as it was for the marital event itself. Maria, my grandparents' second daughter, had lost her husband from "galloping consumption" after a brief marriage, and she had come home, widowed and pregnant, to await the birth of her child.

My father had come down from Baltimore in grand style, bringing an entourage of young men headed by his best man and adoring younger brother "Hampt," as Uncle Lewis was called, and the groom's party was already at Emmanuel Church waiting for the bride to arrive when little Jeff made his bid for life. Aunt Maria, who had made my mother's wedding gown but was too close to term to attend the ceremony, was putting the finishing touches on the bride's finery minutes before Agnes was due at the church, when severe labor pains warned that Jeff's arrival was imminent. While my father agonized over the unexplained delay, my mother quickly laid aside her wedding dress and assumed her role as nurse, assisting the hastily called physician in a difficult birth in the midst of a sudden thunderstorm that raged overhead. Her coolheadedness in the crisis was largely responsible for saving the baby's life in a situation where the mother's survival had to be the doctor's principal consideration. Several hours later the wedding was performed and the reception was shifted from my grandparents' home to Great-uncle Richard's house. Though all had eventually gone well, the interruption seemed a portent of the crises that awaited my parents.

Before the bad times came, the Murray home in Baltimore was a center of bubbling activity and excitement for my mother's sisters whenever they came to visit, which was often. My father was a much beloved brother-in-law in whom they took delight, my parents a fun-loving pair who attracted a large circle of friends and made everyone feel at home.

Active in settlement house work and other community services, they were devoutly religious and apparently my mother had no difficulty converting my father to her denomination. The records of Saint James Episcopal Church, a leading black parish then under the rectorship of the Reverend George F. Bragg, show that six months after my parents were married, my father, a former Methodist, was confirmed an Episcopalian. He later served as lay reader at Saint James, where we children were baptized as we came along. (I was christened there on July 9, 1911, named Anna Pauline Murray for my father's mother, Annie, and my godmother, Aunt Pauline.)

Many people thought my handsome parents looked like brother and sister. They were of similar ethnic background, the products of several generations of a generous intermixture of African, European, and Native American stocks. My father was a slight, wiry, quick-moving man of boundless energy, who in Aunt Pauline's words "dressed immaculately and looked as if he just stepped from a bandbox." My mother's delicate talisman-rose coloring, flashing dark eyes, and masses of dark wavy hair made her such a strikingly beautiful woman that people often stopped and stared at her on the street. She had a gift of wry humor and a capacity to laugh at herself, and often when her sisters came to visit she would shrug off her endless household chores, saying, "I'm giving everything a lick and a promise today," and take them downtown on a shopping spree. Like Grandmother Cornelia, she was high-spirited and quick-tempered; when roiled she flashed sparks of anger, but her sudden storms quickly subsided and she did not hold grudges.

I did not know that I had inherited this trait from my mother until nearly thirty years after her death. I was on a speaking tour to raise funds for the defense of Odell Waller, a sharecropper convicted of first-degree murder, and in Los Angeles made a fiery speech refuting the charge that the Workers Defense League, which sponsored my tour, was a Communist organization. It seemed to me an insult to my intelligence and belief in American democratic values to suggest that I needed a foreign ideology to enable me to speak out against the poll tax system, which denied voting rights to millions of black and white sharecroppers and other poor citizens in eight states in the South. The speech brought a heavy round of applause, and afterward a woman whom I had never seen before came to the platform, looked at me searchingly, then asked if by any chance I was the daughter of Agnes Murray from Baltimore. Astounded, I wanted to know how she knew. She smiled and said, "I knew your mother many years ago, and as you spoke I could see her spirit flashing in your eyes." She was Mrs. Hugh McBeth, Sr., from an old Baltimore family who had been friends of my parents before the McBeths moved to Los Angeles.

From my father I inherited a restless energy that in his case sought many outlets. He composed music, dabbled in poetry, played the piano (with a particular flair for the marches of John Philip Sousa), and for a time played the flute in a local band. He was also a sportsman who, in addition to hunting and fishing, sometimes raised carrier pigeons, which he kept in a coop in the backyard. In his youth he played catcher and was captain of a local semiprofessional baseball team. In school, he supplemented his pupils' academic training with practical skills; each year he had them clear a vacant lot to learn vegetable gardening, and I found pictures of him with a fellow teacher in a crude laboratory where his classes conducted scientific experiments.

My father's most marked characteristic, however, was a passionate desire to improve his own education and excel in his profession. At home, he would work all hours of the night in his study, poring over his books and keeping himself awake with strong coffee and cigarettes, a trait I discovered in myself years later. I was able to understand more fully my father's relentless effort to achieve excellence when I began to read the social history of the first decade of the twentieth century, in which he lived and worked. He had to carry on his duties as a teacher of Negro boys and girls in the face of a racial ideology of black people's inherent inferiority, which dominated public opinion, disparaged their aspirations for advancement through education, and doomed the entire race to a permanently degraded status. This absolute racial view not only pervaded every aspect of communication in American life, but was reinforced and perpetuated in the authoritative writings of white scholars at the most prestigious universities.

How utterly damning this literature was to the hopes of people like my father came home to me when I ran across a study entitled *Social and Mental Traits of the Negro*. It had been published the year I was born, in the 1910 volume of the *Columbia University Studies in History, Economics and Public Law*. The author, Howard W. Odum, a sociologist who later became a professor at the University of North Carolina, had based his findings upon his examination of Negro life in southern states. Odum's principal theme was that "the races have different abilities and different potentialities" and that those who wished to help the Negro should "not expect too much of him, either in demanding his results or in offering him the completed ideals of white people." The best education for the Negro child, he concluded, would be those influences which "lead him to an unquestioning acceptance of the fact that he is a different race from the white, and properly so; that it has always been and always will be." Odum summarized the differences he perceived as immutable limitations on a Negro child's development:

Back of the child, and affecting him both directly and indirectly, are the characteristics of the race. The Negro has little home conscience or love of home, no local attachment of the better sort. . . . He has no great pride of ancestry, and he is not influenced by the lives of great men. The Negro has few ideals and perhaps no lasting adherence to an aspiration of real worth. He has little conception of the meaning of virtue, truth, honor, manhood, integrity. He is shiftless, untidy, and indolent. The migratory and roving tendency seems to be a natural one to him, perhaps the outcome of an easy-going indolence seeking freedom to indulge itself and seeking to avoid all circumstances which would tend to restrict its freedom. The Negro shirks details and difficult tasks; he is incapable of turning his mind toward any other subject when once morbid curiosity holds his attention. He does not know the value of his word or the meaning of words in general. . . . He recognizes no causal relation between stability and prosperity . . . is improvident and extravagant; lazy rather than industrious . . . lacks initiative . . . is often dishonest and untruthful. He is over-religious and superstitious. The Negro suspects his own race and the white race as well; his mind does not conceive of faith in humanity—he does not comprehend it.

Odum dismissed evidence that contradicted his dismal findings with the assertion that individual Negroes, "however excellent they might be in character, are nevertheless of a race that cannot share the communal life of the whites."

Dr. Odum modified his views in later years and by the late 1930s had become a strong voice for improved race relations in the South. Nevertheless, the philosophy of his earlier study, which permeated the racial policies of the early twentieth century, were unchallenged in my father's time. I can only surmise that my father's obsession with study and self-improvement stemmed from a determination to demonstrate, almost single-handedly and in his own person, the falsity of a blanket racial indictment which undermined his influence as a teacher and threatened to destroy the ambitions of girls and boys he sought to inspire.

Ultimately, my father was a casualty of an unequal struggle that engulfed him. Several summers before I was born, he had fallen victim to typhoid fever aggravated by what was probably encephalitis, although it was then known as "brain fever." My mother had begged him to take a vacation, but he had continued his grueling pace and was worn out from overwork. Fortunately, Aunt Pauline was with my mother in the ensuing crisis, and they fought together to save his life. For two weeks he was not expected to live, and his survival was largely the result of my mother's faith and nursing skill. She called in Baltimore's top specialists for consultation with their family physician, a Dr. Wright, and when she was assured that my father would recover, "barring unforeseen troubles," she wrote to her anxious parents, reporting on his condition:

> All the other members of the family seemed so hopeless about Will, I waited until after the consultation was over before telling you more. . . . neither money nor labor has been spared in treating Will's case. It has been the finest and best that money could secure. Everything one could get in the best hospitals. Now I have made for myself a city wide reputation among both white and black, for every one seems anxious and worried about Will. The fine white physicians are delighted with such efficient work for a colored, and said I must have had a great experience in nursing Typhoid fever.

But though my father recovered, he was never the same after that illness. Weak from the effects of the fever, he nevertheless insisted on returning to school, and while he continued to teach, he soon began to have unpredictable attacks of depression and violent moods. My mother lived in a continual state of anxiety and often feared for the safety of her family. At such times, she would gather up her children and flee to my grandparents' home in Durham, but she would barely have arrived before she would begin to worry about my father, cut short her stay, and return to Baltimore. On two occasions while she was in Durham my father was hospitalized, and she hurried back to have him released. As his violent outbursts became more frequent, her family urged her to have him committed to an institution, but she flatly refused and told them, "I would rather *die* with my Will than *live* without him."

Aunt Pauline was a citadel of strength during the turmoil of those years. She was devoted to both of my parents, had lived with them when she taught in Baltimore County one year, spent her summer vacations with them, and was their loyal ally in many crises. My father revered her and restrained his violent behavior when she was present. When I was fifteen months old, Aunt Pauline took a bold step which foreshadowed my future. My mother had brought her four children—Grace, Mildred, Willie, and me—to Durham for a visit and while there discovered she was pregnant with her fifth child, Rosetta. As we were leaving to return to Baltimore, Aunt Pauline literally plucked me off the train while it was standing in the station. She announced that four small children with another on the way were too many for my mother to cope with alone and that she was keeping me with her until after the new baby was born. I stayed behind while all my clothes went along in my mother's luggage, and Aunt Pauline had to buy me new clothes to wear. During the nine months she kept me, Aunt Pauline said I became so attached to her that when she brought me back to Baltimore my parents had to woo me to regain my affection.

Many years later, reading the poignant letters my mother wrote during my stay in Durham, I realized how wise Aunt Pauline had been. My mother revealed her failing strength, growing hardships, and fear of another pregnancy. She wrote:

> If I can keep on my feet and keep my family on theirs, I will be thankful. My little baby [Rosetta] is so frail and tiny. . . . I am working to keep her well, for I was so sick myself before she was born, she has not a strong foundation to build on. . . . Pauline, is little Pauline still using her diapers? I do hope you will train her to use the chamber [pot] for all these children require so much to be done for them, and I am not so strong. . . . I let Mrs. Dial go, as times are so extremely hard, and I need that money so bad, to get so many needful things. . . . Mrs. Waller comes to see me quite often. . . . She heard me say I needed a coat for my baby so she fixed her baby's coat and sent it to me. She is one true friend worth having.
>
> . . . What a world of good it would do if you could only talk to me for a while. I believe it would lift Will's spirits could you appear on the scene and have an old chat with him. . . . The bell has just rung and when I went to the door it was the old tin woman, who buys shoes and exchanges them for tin. I had the baby in my arms and she said, "You have another little girl and she [is] a sickly baby, and you are going to have another one soon. Your face shows it. You can't help it, it's for you." Tell mamma she knew that old tin woman who told me when Pauline would be born and that I would have another baby soon. This came true, but I certainly hope she made a mistake about the next one.

But the old tin woman was right, and baby Rosetta was less than fourteen months old when little Robert Fitzgerald (named for his grandfather) was born at Johns Hopkins Hospital, so frail that my mother could not bring him home, and he had to stay there for the first six months of his life.

The strain of too frequent pregnancies and my father's mental condition took their toll. My mother collapsed on the stairs one morning in late March 1914, as my father was leaving the house for school with two of the older children. He heard her cry out, rushed back, picked her up, and sent for the doctor, but it was too late. She had suffered a massive cerebral hemorrhage, then called apoplexy, and died within an hour. At the time she was thirty-five years old and in the fourth month of her seventh pregnancy.

I had been recovering from chicken pox, isolated from the other children, when my mother died. The only recollection I have of that fateful time is of being alone in a room, seated on a trunk and banging my heels against its side. It is as if a protective shield of forgetfulness was drawn over the shock and confusion that enveloped our household, a burden too great for my memory to bear. I am told that at the time, however, I startled my elders with the declaration, "You just wait till my Aunt Pauline comes. She'll straighten things out."

Aunt Pauline came up for the funeral, and after my mother was buried in the family plot at Laurel Cemetery, she went to Johns Hopkins Hospital and brought little Robert Fitzgerald home, a child so pale and fragile he was not expected to survive. That he lived for nearly seventy-two years, the father and grandfather of a large brood, was testament of the stubborn tenacity with which he clung to life.

With my mother's death our family was shattered; my father was too stricken to cope with the future of six children ranging in age from nine years to six months, and so we had to be separated. The three oldest, Grace, Mildred, and Willie, stayed on at home with him. His sister, Aunt Rose Shipley, and his unmarried brother, Uncle Lewis Murray, who lived on West Lanvale Street, a short distance from our house, took the two infants, Rosetta and Robert. Although Aunt Rose wanted to keep me also, so that all six children would be close together, my fate was decided partly by my mother's wish and partly by my own choice. As if she had a premonition of her death, my mother had just written Aunt Pauline, saying: "If anything happens to me, I want you to have little Pauline. She is not like the other children and I'm afraid they will ruin her disposition."

Young as I was, a few months past three years of age, Aunt Pauline let me make my own decision, a pattern she would follow in the years ahead. On the day of our separation, when Aunt Rose was putting the two babies into the perambulator to take them home with her, Aunt Pauline asked me if I wanted to go with them or stay with her. She told me that I answered, "I want to stay with you, Aunt Pauline," then burst into tears. That moment forecast the many painful choices I would be called upon to make as I grew into womanhood.

Three years after Aunt Pauline took me back to North Carolina with her, my father was committed to Crownsville State Hospital, where he was confined until his death in 1923. Aunt Rose and Uncle Lewis took over the job of rearing the other Murray children. It was well for me that I was living far enough away from Baltimore to be spared the full impact of this latest calamity. In those days, it was a stigma to have one's parent in an "insane asylum," and in the case of our family this stigma was intensified by the careless gossip of adults who circulated a cruel rumor that our mother had committed suicide. My brothers and sisters, living on the scene, grew up having to face the taunts of children who jeered, "Your daddy went crazy and your mother killed herself!" The net effect of that kind of talk was to instill in us a dread of hereditary insanity, which cast a shadow over our lives far into adulthood.

Fortunately for me, I did not hear the devastating rumor of suicide until Aunt Pauline took me to Baltimore for my first reunion with my brothers and sisters, five years after my mother's death. When I told her what was being said, she was furious. "There's not a word of truth in it," she stormed, explaining that the doctor had showed her the purple streak on my mother's temple where a blood vessel had hemorrhaged. Nothing could make Aunt Pauline or any of my mother's people in Durham believe that "our Aggie," who had such a love for people and life, would do away with herself. Yet, since I could not know what actually happened on the morning of my mother's death, the rumor planted an element of doubt in my mind which reappeared to haunt me over the years.

All of this left me with a deep, unspoken grief over the loss of my parents and the unhappy circumstances which cut short two lives that had held such great promise. It was my blessing that Aunt Pauline understood and silently shared my grief. She took pains to cushion its effect, not by concealing the sorrow that marked the closing chapter of my parents' life together but by keeping before me their courage in adversity and the ideals they sought to uphold—giving me a reassuring picture of my heritage which helped me at an early age to face the baffling reality of human bereavement. Only a caring and compassionate spirit long attuned to the inexpressible needs of small children could have accomplished so delicate a mission.

CHAPTER 2

Aunt Pauline

Aunt Pauline's decision to adopt me was a significant departure from her traditional role in the Fitzgerald family. I learned afterward that she had taken the step in the face of dire warnings and admonitions from friends and relatives. As the oldest of six children of a blind father and a high-strung mother, she had been the workhorse, the person to whom everyone looked to keep things going through all emergencies. The wishes and needs of her parents had been her paramount concern. Around 1899, she had escaped this role briefly when she married and embarked on a life of her own, but that bleak venture was marked by an unrelieved struggle for existence and by the loss of both her children in infancy. After only a few years, the marriage foundered on an issue of principle.

The future seemed promising enough when Pauline Fitzgerald married young, blond, blue-eyed Charles Morton Dame, fresh from Howard University Law School, but they had not reckoned with the formidable barriers to the successful practice of law by a colored man. Racial lines, which had been blurred to some extent during Reconstruction, were now being drawn ever tighter by the wave of segregation laws enacted by southern states in the wake of the 1896 *Plessy* decision, which validated the doctrine of "separate but equal." The best young Dame could do was to earn a few dollars surreptitiously writing wills and deeds for white attorneys, income supplemented by his wife's meager earnings as a teacher. The young couple moved from Virginia to West Virginia in search of opportunities, but Dame seemed unable to establish himself at the bar.

Some of the white men for whom he worked told him flatly that he would never get anywhere as a colored lawyer. "You're as white as any white man," Aunt Pauline remembered one saying, "and you'll have a better chance if you cross the line."

During the first half century after Emancipation, thousands of near-whites exercised this option to escape racial oppression, and the temptation to end a grubbing existence finally overpowered Charles Dame. He told his wife what he had decided to do and tried to persuade her to join him. She, too, looked indistinguishable from a Caucasian, and the two of them would have had little difficulty fading into the white background.

Aunt Pauline's refusal brought an end to their marriage and ultimately led to a divorce. Charles Dame disappeared from her life, and there were rumors that he became a very successful lawyer in a neighboring state. Aunt Pauline returned home to slip into her accustomed harness, and it was taken for granted that she would have no further life of her own. Thus it was with some consternation that her relatives and close friends viewed her proposal to adopt me as a first step toward renewed independent action. They told her that taking a three-year-old child was too great a responsibility for a lone woman of forty-three who already had two aging parents. "It's a mistake to raise somebody else's child, particularly a girl," they said. "It's too full of heartaches." "She'll bring you nothing but trouble."

Their concern was genuine. When I came to Durham to live, the household included my Fitzgerald grandparents, who were frail and in their late seventies, Aunt Pauline, and Aunt Sallie, then thirty-six and unmarried. Both sisters taught in local public schools and were away for most of the day. Aunt Pauline's chief problem in those early days was what to do with me when she was not at home. It was too much to expect my grandparents to try to cope with an active, mischievous child. There were no nursery schools for working parents. Her appointment to the city system required her to teach all winter and attend school each summer in order to raise the grade of her teacher's certificate.

A teacher in a small town then combined the functions of instructor, social worker, truant officer, psychiatrist, counselor, adult education specialist, and community leader. Aunt Pauline was up at five every morning and was usually at school before seven-thirty. She got home late in the afternoon, prepared supper, and then returned to night school to conduct literacy classes for the hardworking parents and grandparents of her day school pupils. If a child was absent, she visited the child's home after school to discover the reason. She was expected to attend all community gatherings in addition to teachers' meetings and parents' meetings. On Sundays she usually went to church twice: morning service at her own Saint Titus Episcopal Church and evening service at the neighborhood Second Baptist Church, which many of her students and their parents attended.

My coming not only introduced considerable hubbub into a household of settled adults but also presented her with a continual problem of child care. For all her stolid exterior, Aunt Pauline had a timid streak and shrank from all contention. She would give in on many issues to keep peace in the family, and in most of her decisions she deferred to her parents' wishes. But on the issue of my future she was resolute. If she ever had any misgivings about taking me to live with her, she never voiced them.

There were obvious reasons for her decision, of course. I was her namesake and her godchild, and it was my mother's last request that Aunt Pauline have me. I also filled a void left by the deaths of her own infant children. But I think there were other reasons she could not put into words. Aunt Pauline was inarticulate in expressing her inner feelings to adults, but she had no difficulty communicating with small children. She had the unerring intuition of a great teacher and master artisan. To her, teaching was not merely imparting knowledge; it was building character, molding and shaping the future. Whether a child was pliable and responsive or wooden and inflexible, she sensed the possibilities. She envisioned the finished product, the fine grain of wood beneath a rough and splintered exterior.

Although she did not use these words in talking to me about her decision in later years, I think that in adopting me she was fulfilling what to her was a sacred trust which required the fullest measure of her devotion and teaching skills. I was the window through which she glimpsed other children, also not her own but entrusted to her care for a short while. Her effort to give me freedom to grow while instilling a sense of responsibility and discipline in me may have helped her to understand the hundreds of children who came under her supervision during her long years in the classroom.

Aunt Pauline's sturdy ally but strong competitor in her new undertaking was my Aunt Sallie. Although she married two years after I came to live in my grandparents' home, moved away, and had children of her own, never in the more than forty years I knew my aunts did she relinquish her rivalry with Aunt Pauline for my affection. Aunt Sallie often reminded me that she was my mother's "pal sister" and that she was as close blood kin as Aunt Pauline. She also got great satisfaction from the fact that I resembled her so closely I might have been her own child.

Seldom were two individuals less compatible than my two aunts, and yet they were fiercely loyal to each other to the end of their lives. Aunt Pauline was a doer, a woman of few words, who was intensely practical and who seldom smiled. She was strict, never allowed me to dawdle over my chores or to evade responsibility for misdeeds, but she was always kind and never unjust. She had a methodical mind and plodded through the most difficult task until it was done. Aunt Sallie was imaginative and entertaining. She had a contagious laugh, a sense of humor, and an endless repertoire of engaging stories, but she tended to be disorganized and followed a pattern of stops and starts. She sang, played the piano, read widely, had great intellectual curiosity, and was a ready conversationalist. Aunt Pauline's singing was a little off key and she had less of an artistic bent. If one arrived hungry, in a matter of minutes Aunt Pauline would have a meal of plain food on the table. With Aunt Sallie a meal was a work of art; if one could contain one's hunger for the hours it took her to put it together, one sat down to a feast. I could always talk out my troubles with Aunt Sallie, but in any emergency requiring action I automatically turned to Aunt Pauline. Their contrasting personalities were my strongest maternal influences, and I grew up absorbing characteristics from each.

My schooling began in a somewhat unorthodox manner, when I was four or five. Since Aunt Pauline was determined not to burden my aging grandparents with caring for me, she decided to enroll me formally in school. She taught at West End, a six-grade public school housed in a weather-beaten two-story wooden building on Ferrell Street across the road from the long, low Liggett & Myers tobacco warehouses near the Southern Railroad tracks. Although West End had no kindergarten, it had three levels of first grade. A child normally progressed from one level to the next, and it usually took three years to reach second grade. While this was a slow system, the teachers were dedicated and their methods were thorough. A child received a good foundation in reading before going on.

Aunt Pauline taught the highest section, 1-A, but she obtained the principal's permission to place me with other beginners in Miss Hattie Jenkins' class, 1-C. For more than two generations, Miss Hattie's reputation terrified first graders and sixth graders alike. She was a short, plumpish, brown-skinned woman with snapping dark eyes and the voice and manner of a military drill sergeant. One learned in her class not only because she was a good teacher but also from fear of her displeasure. She never married, and teaching was the central purpose of her life. After she retired, she taught in a nursery school until a few years before her death, when she was well into her eighties.

My career in Miss Hattie's class was short-lived. Within a few weeks my presence had stirred up a controversy among parents, who complained that if "Mis' Dame" could put her child in school before the legal age of six, they had the same right. Mortified, Aunt Pauline immediately withdrew me from formal enrollment, but having no alternative, she continued to bring me to school with her every day, keeping me in her own classroom. The older children adopted me as class mascot, and under Aunt Pauline's watchful eye I was permitted to sit with them at their desks and to look on while they recited. In order to avoid criticism, however, I was not allowed to participate in class games or to be anything more than an onlooker.

In those days, the most common classroom game in the lower grades was one in which children recited their reading and spelling lessons standing in line side by side. When a child made a mistake, the next child, upon reciting correctly, took his or her place. The line was constantly changing, the objective being to reach the head of the class. Children who misbehaved forfeited their place in line and were sent to the foot of the class. It was a harsh game for slow learners, but the faster learners loved it.

Toward the end of the school year, Aunt Pauline was surprised to see me standing in line with the other children, something she had never allowed me to do. In spite of her sternness she was gentle with children and I never knew her to single one out for humiliation. She simply ignored me and was about to pass over me to the next pupil when she heard me say, "I can read, Aunt Pauline."

Without waiting for her to reply, I seized the book of the child next to me and began to read out loud. When the class was over, Aunt Pauline called me to her desk. She reached in her drawer and pulled out a book I had never seen before.

"Let me see you read this book," she said. She had assumed that in my earlier performance I had been mimicking the other children and speaking words from memory. When I read the new book without making a mistake, she realized that all the time I had been in her class I was learning whatever she taught the others. From then on, study was as natural to me as breathing, and the classroom was my second home.

Aunt Pauline also took me back and forth with her to night school. Her adult pupils had never had an opportunity to learn to read and write. I became her small apprentice, and she kept me happily occupied erasing the blackboard, cleaning erasers, handing out copybooks, and sometimes even helping her elderly students with their lessons.

School was so much a part of me that it dominated my fantasies at play. Once when I had whooping cough and was bedridden for several days, I stayed under the covers only until Aunt Pauline left the house each morning. As soon as she was out of sight, I dragged my box of battered dolls from under the bed, lined them up on the pillows, and sat cross-legged in front of them with a book in my hand. I gave each doll its own voice and reading level, and I alternately assumed the roles of students and teacher, reciting or praising and scolding. When Aunt Pauline came home from school I was lying meekly in bed, of course, without a doll in sight.

I grew up a thin, wiry, ravenous child, overly active and eager to please but strong-willed and irrepressible. Although living in a household of settled adults was lonely at times, I never lacked affection. People had loved my mother, Agnes, and as her child I inherited the bounty of love that had been hers. I was my grandmother's favorite, and she used to tell me that I had my "mother's eyes and her sunny ways." Everyone in the family learned that telling me I was like my mother would call forth my best efforts.

After Aunt Sallie married the Reverend J. E. G. Small and moved to the Saint Titus Church rectory on Pine Street, I graduated from a little white iron crib in the hallway to share Aunt Pauline's bedroom upstairs under the steeply sloping roof. It served as both sleeping quarters and workshop, and was sparsely furnished with a large bed, a marble-topped bureau, a washstand holding a basin and water pitcher, a small oval-shaped tin stove, a trunk, and an oil lamp which stood on the mantelpiece. Since we had no closet, our clothes hung on pegs on the back of the door. Between the two low windows were Aunt Pauline's chair and the desk where she prepared her lesson plans and worked on her monthly reports. When I got older, my "desk" was a wooden kitchen table near the bed, which held my books and a lantern. For fear of fire, Aunt Pauline never allowed me to use the oil lamp after she had gone to bed, so I did my late-night reading by lantern light.

Of the six rooms in my grandparents' house, I liked the parlor best. It had a touch of elegance and was seldom used except on formal occasions. As I was growing up, it became a sanctuary where I could withdraw to read or study. I would close the door, spread my books and papers on the floor, and lie on my stomach on the matting in front of the iron grate in the fireplace. There was not much furniture: a three-piece parlor set upholstered in red brocade, a tall brass table lamp with a pale-green globe, and a bookcase of four shelves overburdened with books and magazines, which sagged in a corner. When I began taking music lessons, a piano filled the wall space opposite the fireplace.

A wooden cross stood in the center of the mantelpiece as a reminder of our faith, and a tall red candle graced each end. On the wall above the cross hung Miss Mary Ruffin Smith's painting of a mother-of-pearl fountain cascading from a silver basin. Grandmother Cornelia gave this painting an honored place in our household as testimony to the strong bond of affection that had existed between her and the antebellum woman who had been both her blood relative and her legal owner. The other walls held family pictures of four generations, including one of the Murray family taken when I was around two. There was even a photograph of Aunt Pauline's dead infant son, Morton Dame, laid out on a table in his white burial dress. The picture I cherished most was one of my mother in her nurse's uniform when she was in her early twenties. When I was small, the presence of so many dead ancestors staring down at me from their pictures was disconcerting, but they became familiar companions as I grew older and spent long hours in the parlor working my way through the small collection of books in the bookcase.

I read indiscriminately, devouring the contents of such incongruous volumes as *Dying Testimonies of the Saved and Unsaved; Stoddard's Lectures; Works of Paul Laurence Dunbar; Chambers's Encyclopedia; The Remarkable Advancement of the Afro-American Negro from the Bondage of Slavery, Ignorance and Poverty to the Freedom of Citizenship, Intelligence, Affluence, Honor and Trust,* published in 1899; and Booker T. Washington's *Up from Slavery.* Aunt Pauline also had a set of English literary works and a ten-volume series on American history, which included four novels based on the major wars the United States had then fought. I skipped the history text and read the novels many times. I also read the few novels I found by Gene Stratton Porter, Ellen Glasgow, and Zane Grey.

When I had exhausted our slender supply of books, I began to make trips to the Durham Colored Library, a small one-room collection in a building at the corner of Fayetteville and Pettigrew streets near the Southern Railroad tracks. Mrs. Wooton, the librarian, steered me toward the children's books and I gobbled up *The Bobbsey Twins, The Five Little Peppers and How They Grew, The Boy Allies* series, and the nature-story books *Frank the Young Naturalist, Frank in the Woods,* and *Frank on the Prairie.* One year I won first prize among the colored children for having read the most books in the library. The prize, a fountain pen, was presented to me by General Julian S. Carr, a man my folks called a "true Southern aristocrat." The presentation ceremony and General Carr's words of praise made me feel very proud of my achievement.

At home, I read the Bible to Grandmother, and although I skipped over many difficult names and failed to understand a great deal of what I read, Grandmother seemed to enjoy it. We both loved the Psalms, which I read to her over and over again. World War I broke out by the time I was in the second grade, and Grandfather required me to read the war news to him from the *Durham Morning Herald.* When the colored soldiers went off to war, Grandmother took me down to Union Station to see them go, and I was very excited over the parade of hundreds of colored men smartly dressed in new khaki uniforms and broad-brimmed hats. (Someone gave me one of those hats when the war was over, and I wore it everywhere except to church, where Aunt Pauline drew the line.) Because our immediate family had no men in uniform the war touched us only remotely, but I well remember the rationing. We had to use black molasses as a substitute for sugar, and our meat came in large mustard-colored square tins containing slabs of salted pork. In time, I began to notice Gold Star certificates hanging in the windows of homes in the neighborhood, indicating that a family had lost a son or husband in France. The flu epidemic that followed the war was so fierce the schools were closed. Old Whitted High School was turned into a temporary hospital during the crisis, and Aunt Sallie worked there as a volunteer nurse.

While my family was not penniless, making ends meet involved a continual struggle. My Fitzgerald grandparents owned their house, on its acre of land behind Maplewood Cemetery, free and clear, but Grandfather's tiny pension from his Civil War service was little more than enough to keep up the taxes. Grandmother's hundred-acre farm near Chapel Hill gave her a strong sense of independence, but taxes also ate up the little cash she got each fall from the tenant farmer who rented it from her. After Aunt Sallie married and moved to Saint Titus rectory, Aunt Pauline's salary of about fifty dollars a month was our mainstay.

In one generation the Fitzgeralds had made the transition from farmers and small tradespeople to town dwellers whose main occupation was teaching, but they had managed to preserve their tradition of self-sufficiency. My grandparents had brought up their five daughters and one son to do whatever work would help them remain independent. It was part of Grandfather's philosophy that everyone should have at least two trades to fall back on when times were hard. The three aunts I knew as a child could sew and work with handicrafts in addition to their teaching. Aunt Sallie and Aunt Maria (who called herself Marie because, she said, she did not like the way people said Ma-rye-ah) were very talented in tailoring and dressmaking, which at times was their chief source of income.

Since cash was scarce, we had to supplement what little we had with our own labor. After our cow died we seldom had milk, but the chickens we kept furnished us with eggs and much of our meat. Our acre of ground had strawberry and blackberry patches, a grape arbor, and a small orchard of apple, peach, pear, plum, and cherry trees. Aunt Pauline even cultivated a fig tree near the back door. Each spring we planted a garden of vegetables and put in a crop of sweet potatoes. Every summer Aunt Pauline and Grandmother canned dozens of jars of fruit, jellies, corn, beans, okra, tomatoes, blackberry mash, and grape juice to tide us over the winter.

Grandfather's blindness did not prevent him from contributing to the family enterprises. Grandmother would sort out old stockings and scraps of colored cloth, which he plaited into braids. She would then sew the braids into oval scatter rugs for the house. In the spring he would prune the grapevines so that each new crop of grapes would be large and juicy. Grandmother made patchwork quilts and knitted woolen scarves and shawls. Aunt Pauline, though not a fancy dressmaker, made over her old clothes and cut down adult dresses for me.

My own talents never included handicrafts—I was much more at home with a pencil than a needle—and the division of labor in our household was such that I did not learn to cook. I would have enjoyed working with a hammer and tools, but cooking and sewing seemed beyond me, and at school I regularly exasperated my domestic science teachers. One year we girls were required to make dresses and wear them in a fashion show. My pattern was simple enough—a straight blue dress with a white Peter Pan collar and white cuffs on the short sleeves. I tried hard, but when I finished the hem was uneven, the collar was lopsided, and I looked like a beanpole in a potato sack, as Grandmother would have said. Having to wear the dress in a public ceremony was so humiliating it put an end to my efforts on the sewing machine.

At home, my awkwardness in household arts was not a problem. There were too many other jobs that needed young hands and swift feet. We had running cold water in those days but no inside plumbing or electricity. Our house was lighted by oil lamps and heated by wood-and-coal stoves and open fireplaces. My duties were to split and stack endless loads of wood and kindling, keep all rooms supplied with scuttles of coal in cold weather, feed the chickens twice a day, clean wicks and chimneys and fill the oil lamps and lanterns, scrub out the outhouse and keep it supplied with lime, whitewash the trees and fences in spring, hoe the garden, cut down weeds and grass with a small sickle, and dig sweet potatoes in the fall. Since we had no telephone, I ran many errands to kinsfolk, neighbors, or the grocery store, and I was on call to guide my grandfather when he wanted to go to town or to see his sisters and his brother.

As I grew older, Aunt Pauline encouraged me to earn my own money, but she allowed this privilege only on condition that I had already completed all my household chores. I had my first paying job by the time I was eight. On Saturdays, after I had helped Aunt Pauline carry home the grocery order and had swept and scrubbed the wooden floors and dusted the furniture in our house, I was allowed to walk a mile across town to Aunt Sallie's house to sweep, dust, and mop her five rooms. When this was done I had earned a quarter. In my family there was no such thing as an allowance.

At ten, I branched out into a business career, selling subscriptions to *Ladies' Home Journal, Saturday Evening Post,* and *Country Gentleman.* Then I got a newspaper route on Saturday afternoons, carrying the *Carolina Times,* Durham's Negro weekly newspaper, later published by Lewis E. Austin. I earned two cents on each five-cent paper sold, and considered that I had had a good day when I counted up my share on Saturday night and found I had earned as much as $1.30. I kept my newspaper route through high school and earned enough money to buy my own skates and bicycle, pay for carfare and lunches, and purchase my class ring. During the summer I sometimes made extra money selling some of my surplus garden vegetables.

My newspaper route took me all over the West End section of Durham, up and down the dirt roads, the steep hills, and the Bottoms, where the colored people lived. After I got my bicycle I could cover the whole area during a Saturday afternoon. Few colored families lived on paved streets with sidewalks, and in bad weather the roads were muddy in summer and slippery in winter. Some of my customers bought the paper only to encourage me, for a nickel in those days was a large sum to poor people. The prosperous folk lived in neat cottages and bungalows, and some had fenced-in lawns and flower beds. Many others lived in rented, unpainted two- or three-room shacks with no running water and only a pump in the yard. Their bare walls were pasted over with brown-colored rotogravure newspapers, which served as decoration and as covering for the cracks. What I noticed most about those houses was that there were never any books and scarcely any furniture.

One of Aunt Pauline's big problems was how to fill the bottomless pit in my stomach. She could not understand how so scrawny a child could eat so much and stay so skinny. I had three passions—beefsteak, molasses, and macaroni and cheese. I had embarrassed her once when I was very small and we met Mr. John Sprunt Hill, one of the town's leading citizens, on the elevator in a business building downtown. He gave me a dime and then asked me what I was going to do with it. "Buy beefsteak," I promptly replied.

We had macaroni and cheese almost every Sunday and molasses was cheap, but steak was usually beyond Aunt Pauline's pocketbook. She would buy a few ounces, just enough to flavor thick flour gravy, and provide hot biscuits as a filler. I would gobble up the gravy, sopping it with biscuits, and for dessert I would finish off any remaining biscuits soaked with molasses and butter melted on the stove.

The only times in those early years I rebelled against Aunt Pauline's discipline involved food. Once she cooked buttermilk pancakes, served Grandfather, and put one tiny pancake on my dish.

"How come you give Grandfather *three* pancakes and me only one?" I complained. I must have been five or six at the time and always remember the incident as my first protest against what I believed to be inequality.

The other incident was more serious because it embarrassed Aunt Pauline when we were away from home. We had been invited to dinner at the home of Dr. Charles Shepard, members of whose family were among Aunt Pauline's most admired friends and whose five-year-old daughter, Dorothy, was about my age. Aunt Pauline was very anxious for me to be on my best behavior.

All went well at the dinner table until I asked for another piece of meat. Aunt Pauline said no, but I insisted. "Let her have it, there's plenty," Mrs. Shepard said, but Aunt Pauline believed that good discipline required firmness, and she explained that I had to learn that no meant No! I continued to ask for meat and finally she threatened to take me down from the table and give me a whipping if I asked again. She almost never whipped a child and this to her was the most drastic thing she could do. Her warning had not the slightest effect; I stubbornly clung to my request.

The inevitable happened. Aunt Pauline took me into another room and gave me one of the few whippings of my life. I was in disgrace when we came back to the table, but my first words were "I want more meat, Aunt Pauline." I didn't get it, of course, but the incident made such a deep impression on me that after that I always saved the meat on my plate to eat last.

Aunt Pauline's method of home training was a remarkable blend of firm discipline and freedom to make my own choices and live with the consequences, however bizarre some of them might be. This unorthodox approach collided with the more traditional methods used at school, and during the five years I attended West End, Aunt Pauline was in the unhappy position of being both my parent and the colleague of fellow teachers who found me too self-assertive, "too fast," and "too womanish" for my own good. She seldom was spared a detailed report from them of my slightest misdeed, with the implication that a teacher's child was expected to be a model of good conduct and not a ringleader of mischief. Their complaints were never that I was insolent or deliberately disobedient, but that I had too much energy for one child, was continually bobbing up and down in my seat, waving my hands to recite, talking, passing notes in class, and perpetrating other little infractions of discipline which add to a teacher's harassment.

Once when I did disobey the rules the incident ended in near-disaster. On rainy days we had to spend recess in the school basement, a poorly lighted dungeon full of heating ducts from the furnace and square brick columns which supported the upper floors. When a hundred or more children were crowded into this narrow space there was scarcely room to move about, and we were sternly forbidden to play running games. That day we broke the rules by playing a tag game called Policeman, and chose Mary Frances Joyner, who was the biggest girl in school and who could not run fast, to be the policeman. In the heat of the game Mary Frances and I crashed into one another, and I was thrown against the sharp corner of one of the brick columns, which sliced open my right temple to the bone. Blood spattered everywhere, and everybody thought I had been killed. When they called Aunt Pauline, she kept a cool head and closed the wound with adhesive plaster after the bleeding had stopped. The cut healed, but I never lost the scar.

In the lower grades my teachers used various schemes to keep me under control. One of the teachers, my cousin Ethel Clegg, whom I adored, felt that she had to be extraordinarily severe with me so that the other second graders would not complain of favoritism. Her solution was to make me sit apart from the class at a corner desk near hers in the front of the room, where she could keep her eye on me. It was the lingering remnant of the "dunce stool," and Cousin Ethel could not have contrived a more embarrassing symbol of disgrace.

Miss Martha Hester, my third-grade teacher, would take me along with her whenever she left the room on an errand, explaining to other teachers that she dared not leave me behind or I would have the class in an uproar by the time she returned. I alternated between loving the fun we had in Miss Hester's class and fearing her voluble wrath. She was a tall, rawboned brown woman with fiery eyes and large, protruding lips. When she was displeased she bellowed her disapproval. What she lacked in gentleness she compensated for through her energy and imagination. She was dedicated to her work, and always looked for new ways to bring fresh experiences to children who lacked the most rudimentary visual aids to learning. We had no radio, television, movies, or picture slides in those days. We had only our pencils and tablets, a few scratched-up books, and the inventiveness of our teachers.

My worst ordeals at West End came in the fourth grade, under Miss Louise Bullock, a massive woman who ruled by instilling naked fear, sometimes cuffing a child without warning. Once when we were standing in line she thought I had created a commotion. Without saying a word, she slapped my face so hard she left the red print of her fingers on my cheek for all to see. My problems with Miss Bullock were complicated by the fact that along with Christine Taylor and Lucille Johnson, I was one of three "light-skinned" pupils in a class of darker hues, a minority within a minority. That Lucille and I also had parents who taught in the school system did not add to our popularity. We seemed to be the prime targets of Miss Bullock's ire.

Sneaking off during school hours to a little grocery store a few doors from our school building was a forbidden pleasure. The storekeeper kept a big barrel of vinegar pickles in the back of his store, which he sold for a nickel each. Wedging ourselves between rows of piled-up cans and cartons, we would fish around in the barrel with a long-handled fork for the biggest cucumber we could find, then buy a penny's worth of sour balls, bite off the end of the cucumber, insert the candy, and suck the sweet and sour combination until the pickle gradually disappeared. This indulgence was my supreme joy, but it was also once my misfortune to have Miss Bullock catch me with a half-eaten pickle in my desk. She not only gave me a thrashing, but she did it before the entire class.

My worst crime occurred one day when Chris Taylor and I pulled some rotten wooden palings off the school fence to make a springboard. When Miss Bullock found out about it, she marched us to the principal's office, carrying a tough green switch with her. Chris was craftier than I was; at the first stroke she began to holler and shed great tears, promising she would never do it again. As a result, she got off lightly. When it was my turn, I stood there dry-eyed and silent. The more Miss Bullock applied the switch, the more determined I was not to cry. Our encounter ended in mutual frustration; for all her bulk, Miss Bullock was unable to cow me, while I was painfully aware that the matter was not ended and that she would report it to Aunt Pauline.

On such occasions, Aunt Pauline would look at me steadily through her rimless glasses, a sadness in her eyes and deep disappointment apparent in her low, even voice. She would sigh when I brought home my report card each month with a string of A's in scholarship marred by the column labeled "Conduct," which wavered from A to D. I would feel more remorseful than if she had given me a second whipping, because I knew that I had brought her disgrace. (Apart from the incident at Dr. Shepard's, I remember only two times in my entire childhood when Aunt Pauline whipped me. One was for lying and the other for disobeying and stopping to play on the way home from school. In each instance my punishment was by appointment. When I was ready for bed, Aunt Pauline applied the business end of her hairbrush to my bare rump. I was so ashamed that I never repeated either offense.)

At the end of that year, Miss Bullock was promoted with her class to teach the fifth grade, and I was horrified. Fortunately for me, our principal, Professor Clyde Winslow, was a wise, gentle man whose ideas about dealing with children were more modern than Miss Bullock's. Quietly, he had Christine, Lucille, and me promoted at midyear to sixth grade, which he taught, and for the remainder of the school term my conduct improved. I had survived, and yet the years of being a high achiever in scholarship and a low achiever in deportment made me ambivalent about myself. I desperately sought approval, and my inability to measure up to my teachers' expectations made me feel there was something wrong with me.

I was also made to feel different from most people because I was left-handed. In the years when I was going to elementary school, it was not uncommon for teachers and other adults to try to force left-handed children to use their right hands, and while I stubbornly resisted these efforts, just enough disapproval was involved to make me feel self-conscious. "You're doing it all wrong," my folks used to tell me. On my own I learned to write with either hand, but I suspect my efforts to conform took their toll.

Another difference I felt in those early years was not having parents and sisters and brothers I could talk about as naturally as other children did. It must have been my need for a visible parent that finally led me to ask Aunt Pauline if I might call her "Mother." To her credit, she tried to fill my need while being very careful not to usurp my own mother's place in my memory. She did not try to shield me from painful truths, and she answered endless questions about my parents. So strong was the fusion of need and reality that I lived with two symbols of motherhood. On Mother's Day, when people wore flowers in tribute to their mothers, I could not decide whether to wear a white flower in memory of my real mother, Agnes, or a red flower in recognition of Aunt Pauline. It was characteristic of my way of resolving dilemmas that I wore both.

CHAPTER 3

Learning About Race

ALTHOUGH I did not live with my sisters and brothers, I did not lack close relatives. At least a dozen households of Fitzgerald kinsfolk—Cleggs, Dodsons, Reynolds, Yarboroughs, Fawcetts—lived within a few minutes' walk from our house. When the whole family, including my great-aunts, great-uncle, and second and third cousins of all ages, assembled, it looked like a United Nations in miniature, ranging from fair-skinned, blue-eyed, red-haired, freckle-faced types through various shades of peach and olive to those with Indian copper skin, dark eyes, and heavy black hair.

Some of my North Carolina relatives worked for themselves as small tradespeople, doing carpentry, running a dressmaking shop, operating a grocery store, a pharmacy, or engaging in the hauling business. Others were clerks in the Negro-owned North Carolina Mutual Insurance Company or teachers in the public schools. My grandmother's Smith relatives —the Morphis, Kirby, and Toole families—had remained on the land and were farmers in Orange and Chatham counties. Close to their farming origins, they believed that owning land made one more independent. Most of them owned their homes outright or were paying off the mortgages.

The Fitzgeralds and Cleggs (the family of Great-aunt Agnes Fitzgerald and her husband, Robert Clegg) were very close to their in-laws. There was much visiting back and forth, and the children ran around in groups as their parents had done before them. In those days the generations mingled closely, and age and experience rated highly within the family. I had to show proper deference to each degree of kinship. Outside my immediate household, the authority of my grandfather's brother and two sisters—Great-uncle Richard Fitzgerald, Great-aunts Mary Jane Fitzgerald and Agnes Clegg—was supreme. Their children, who were my second cousins and members of my mother's generation, had to be obeyed as uncles and aunts. I was also expected to defer to older third cousins and seldom went anywhere that I was not under the watchful eye of some adult relative. While this web of intricate relationships kept me under constant supervision, it also gave me an identity and an expanding world to which I belonged by right of birth.

My grandfather was highly esteemed by all the family as the oldest and most educated of the four Fitzgeralds who came South with their parents after the Civil War, but my Great-uncle Richard was catered to as the wealthiest. He had more of everything than the others—more children, more property, and more money. By sheer nerve and persistence, he had become one of Durham's leading businessmen without regard to color. He owned a large brickyard as well as rental property all over town. Back in 1884, he was listed in the Durham Directory as having orders on hand for 2,500,000 bricks. Later he had helped to organize Durham's first Negro-owned financial institution, the Mechanics and Farmers Bank; he was its first president and a large stockholder.

Great-uncle Richard's home, The Maples, where he lived with his wife, Great-aunt Sallie Fitzgerald, and two daughters, the youngest of their twelve children, was the most imposing house in our part of town. Located at the end of Wilkerson Avenue and surrounded by the houses of white neighbors, it came close to being an estate. He had defied custom and bought the property in the face of fierce opposition from white people. It was said in the family that a white businessman named Tom Walker had fallen out with some of his associates and settled his grudge by selling his home to a colored man.

In my eyes, this awesome slate-roofed eighteen-room house, with its circular tower, attic, piazza, and portico over a carriage driveway, seemed like a small castle. The Maples sat in a park of maple and magnolia trees separated from the outside world by a tall, thick hedge and surrounded by white gravel driveways. In front of the house was a goldfish pond partly covered with lily pads, and near the Wilkerson Avenue entrance was a broad arbor of cultivated scuppernong grapes. We children would ramble through the park picking up red magnolia seeds, or climb the arbor to stuff ourselves with scuppernongs.

Behind the house were the big red barns and stables where Great-uncle Richard kept his cattle and hay, several horses and wagons, a fringe-topped surrey, and a black buggy with bright-red spoked wheels. Beyond the barns he had built his brickyard on a red-clay hillside which sloped down to a brook. I loved to watch the bricks being transported to the loading wagons from the kilns in little cars on pulleys, which ran on a miniature track.

As the family showplace, Great-uncle Richard's house was the seat of wedding receptions and other family gatherings. Whenever I went to visit with my grandparents or Aunt Pauline, I was awed by the spaciousness of everything: the two stairways, the front and back parlors, the library, the inside toilets and bathrooms. While the older folks talked, I would sit and stare at the heavily stuffed furniture, the brilliant chandelier overhead, the great fireplace with its brass andirons, and the massive Swiss music box that stretched from floor to ceiling.

No holiday was complete without stopping by The Maples for lemonade or hot chocolate, cookies and tiny sandwiches. Every Christmas we would cut down our own small tree from the hillside near our house, but the big treat of the day was the huge Christmas tree at Great-uncle Richard's. Long before dawn on Christmas morning, we would be awakened by a troop of cousins singing Christmas carols. When I was old enough, I was permitted to join them and we would go from house to house gathering up relatives and neighbors' children until a small army of young people arrived at The Maples for eggnog in the big parlor before a roaring fire.

There was even a Fitzgerald family church. Emmanuel Methodist Church on old Chapel Hill Road (now Kent Street) was built with Great-uncle Richard's bricks, and he held title to it. His youngest daughter, Irene, was organist, and Fitzgerald children and grandchildren sang in the choir or filled the Sunday school pews. My parents were married there, and most of our family funerals were held there, although the family divided its affiliations among the Presbyterian, Methodist, and Episcopalian denominations.

Despite the fact that Great-uncle Richard's family was referred to as the "rich Fitzgeralds" and my grandfather's family as the "poor Fitzgeralds," the family bond was a countervailing force against the view that colored people were inferior. All about me among my own kin was evidence that a Fitzgerald was *somebody*. My consciousness of the world beyond the family developed on two planes—"the race of colored people" and "the white people." My aunts were "race women" of their time. They took pride in every achievement of "the race" and agonized over every lynching, every black boy convicted and "sent to the roads," every insult to "the race." I would hear: "The race is moving forward!" "You simply can't keep the race down!" "The race of colored people is going to show the world yet!"

I grew up with copies of *The Crisis* in our home, the NAACP publication which I knew had produced its first issue in the year and month of my birth. When I was around five, my aunts belonged to a group that put on a little play entitled *Fifty Years of Freedom.* I loved it because I had four lines of a jingle to speak in the opening scene. All I can remember now is "Jubah dis and Jubah dat, and Jubah killed a yaller cat!" Later I found an earlier version of the play, called *Thirty Years of Freedom,* which my people had put on in the 1890s.

Paul Laurence Dunbar was our favorite poet, both at home and in school. The 1907 edition of Dunbar's *Works* was the most worn book in our home library. My Aunt Roberta, who had died of typhoid fever before I was born, had used the title of his poem "Ships That Pass in the Night" as the theme of her high school graduation valedictory. His "Crust of Bread and a Corner to Sleep In," "Little Brown Baby with Sparklin' Eyes," and "Oh, Dere's Lot of Keer an' Trouble" were my bedtime nursery rhymes. At school, a child who could recite from memory "The Party" and "An Ante-Bellum Sermon" was in demand for all school programs. My classmate Betty Hicks was the best reciter in our school and might have been a great dramatic actress had anyone discovered her talent and encouraged her to develop it.

In our segregated world, we had a sense of identity and a sense of racial pride, fragile though they might be. We were close to the roots of our immediate past because of the many elderly people still alive who had been born in slavery. To those of my generation reared in the South, it has always been somewhat bewildering to observe young blacks seeking an identity that we already had half a century earlier.

Surrounding and intersecting our segregated world at many points was the world of "the white people." It was a confusing world to me because I was both related to white people and alienated from them. I learned an intricate racial code listening to and watching the older members of my family, and I knew that not all white people were alike. According to this code, there were "white aristocrats," whom my family admired, "nice white people," toward whom they were charitable in their thoughts, and "mean, prejudiced white Rebs," a classification corresponding roughly to the more recent "Whitey" or "Honkie." My family had nothing but contempt for this last group.

While this discriminating assessment of the white population prevented me from developing a blanket hatred of *all* white people, there was a threshold reserve which applied to the white world generally. For example, I knew that I was not to greet white people on their porches, although in my small town everybody knew everybody else in the neighborhood, and the natural impulse upon seeing a person was to say "Howdy." Since white and colored people often lived side by side on the same street, I would have to stifle this impulse when I passed a white person sitting out front, even though I had sung out cheerfully to the

colored person next door. Having been taught to be polite and deferential
to all older people, I nevertheless had to freeze when the older person had
a white skin. I learned to throw my eyes off focus whenever I passed a
white person, so that I would not see the face or the expression.

Segregation was another matter. It could not be entirely avoided, but
as I grew older and came to understand what it meant, I carried on my
own private protest. I walked almost everywhere to stay off the Jim Crow
streetcars and I would not go downtown to the theaters because that
meant climbing the back stairs to the colored "peanut gallery." But sometimes even family solidarity fell victim to the color bar. Once, when a
fair-skinned relative from the North came to visit and took me to town one
day for company, she made me stand outside while she went into the
stores on Main Street. She said they would give her better service if they
did not know she was colored. Aunt Pauline was furious when she heard
about this and would not let me go anywhere with that relative again.

Unavoidable contacts with white people often built up silent resentment. There was the school superintendent who came to our annual
exercises, stood on the rostrum beaming with affability, and made a speech
praising us for our progress. We children sat taut waiting for the chilling
moment when he smiled condescendingly and said, "You people" or
"You're a credit to your race." (In later years I would quip, "Be a credit
to your space.") We knew without turning our heads that our teachers had
also stiffened. It was also quite common for the white supervisor to visit
our classrooms and find an opportunity before she left to address our
teacher by her first name. If our teacher had responded as she felt, she
would have been fired on the spot.

Here and there, individuals slipped through the wall of segregation.
They had names and faces and were not just a blur of whiteness. There
were the Couch cousins, for instance, who delivered the mail on our route
for many years. Their gray-blue uniforms of the U.S. Post Office and their
association with letters from relatives far away made them seem somewhat different from other white people in my eyes. The older Mr. Couch
was tall, thin, and pale; his cousin was robust and ruddy. Both were
friendly, and they liked to stop and pass the time of day with my grandfather. "Passing the time of day" between a Fitzgerald and a white person
was a delicate operation requiring great skill. If the white person forgot
himself and said *"Mister* Fitzgerald," he would swallow air and get red in
the face. If he followed custom and said "Fitzgerald," or addressed my
grandmother as "Cornelia" or "Aunt Cornelia," *my* side would get red in
the face, and the warmest conversation would sink into a chasm of freezing silence. Over the years, the Couches found a workable compromise.

It was "M-m-m-m Fitzgerald," never quite saying "Mr." or "Mrs." and never quite leaving it out.

There were others, like the succession of newsboys who delivered the *Durham Morning Herald* and were usually saving money to go to college. They were "nice boys" or "dirty little rascals," depending upon whether they were careful to throw our paper on the porch or merely chucked it on the grass, where it got soaked with dew, or whether they took off their caps when they came to the house to collect on Saturdays. If they were "nice boys," Aunt Pauline would ask them all about their schoolwork. If they were the other sort, she would hand them the money in silence and shut the door.

The white boy I remember best, although I never knew his name or where he lived, was a woebegone little creature of six or seven, several years younger than I, whom I met in the dirt road of Cameron (now Carroll) Street one morning as I was going to the store. He spoke first.

"Do you want a puppy?" he asked.

He pushed a shoebox into my hands and I found myself holding a tiny muff of brown dog with long, drooping ears and sorrowful eyes. He told me he was trying to find a home for the puppy because his father said he could not keep a dog. I never forgot the tearful small face and trusting eyes which looked into mine as the shoebox passed from white hands to brown.

And there were a few other individuals whose humanity overrode their whiteness. Once, when I was about seven, Aunt Pauline sent me downtown to pay her tax bill. Later the tax collector laughed heartily as he told her how he heard a grown-up little voice but couldn't tell where it was coming from until he leaned over the counter and found me. Then there was Mr. Pritchard, of Pritchard and Jones Shoe Store, where Aunt Pauline always took me to buy my shoes. I loved the store because I could watch a little mechanical man in the window stepping stiffly over shoes arranged in a circle to advertise Walk-Overs. Mr. Pritchard showed great interest in me and used to tell Aunt Pauline I was an intelligent little girl and should have freedom to express myself fully.

A family named Greenberg kept a grocery store on Proctor Street, just up the hill from the rectory on Pine Street where Aunt Sallie and her husband, the Reverend Small, lived. They traded at the Greenbergs' store and found them very friendly. The Reverend Small could read Hebrew, which made a bond between him and the Jewish family, and Aunt Sallie's teaching experience made her interested in young people. The Greenbergs told her all about their son, Henry, who had won a Shakespeare contest in high school and was now away at college. Years later, as an attorney in New York City, I appeared in a case before Justice Henry Clay

Greenberg of the New York Supreme Court without realizing until the case was over that our families had lived only a few doors apart in the same North Carolina town. The Greenbergs also had a very brilliant daughter, and Aunt Sallie would tell them about her little niece who had won a prize for reading the most books in the colored library.

Most of the white people I knew well enough to speak with in my childhood were men, since women were not insurance salesmen, letter carriers, or tradespeople with whom one had to transact business, and since no one in my home worked in a white person's house. In fact, the only white woman I got to know was an old, grimy, wrinkled one who lived alone in a junk-filled shack on the edge of Forest Hills woods, which we passed on our way to Hillside High School. The neighborhood children called her "crazy," but she took a liking to me and she never saw my color. Her white hair reminded me of my own grandmother, and I would stop by to talk and to do little kindnesses for her.

My meager contact with white people was paradoxical, since the two races lived close together, and, within the limits of the strict racial code, considerable familiarity existed in their dealings with one another. My family, however, preferred never to cross the gulf that separated us from white people unless we could do so without losing our dignity and pride. It was a straitjacket existence, which became more oppressive as I grew older. Each of us had to deal with it as best we could. Some were ultimately destroyed, some led crippled lives, some endured, and some fled the South, as I did later. Some took comfort in the occasional escape by "passing," and of those who could do so, some moved back and forth between the two worlds with comparative ease.

It was no secret that my fairer-skinned relatives indulged in casual "passing" when it suited their convenience, particularly when they were traveling. In their pragmatic view, it was not disloyalty to "the race." Curiously enough, my relatives from the South did not bother to pass where segregation was most oppressive, but they sometimes did so in the North, where they were unknown and jobs were at stake. For several years before the end of World War I, my Aunt Maria—who had changed her name to Marie—lived in Harlem and worked as a highly paid (white) draper in Lady Duff Gordon's salon on Fifth Avenue in New York City. After the war she came home again and took up where she had left off, teaching in the colored county schools in winter and working as a dressmaker in summer.

"Passing" had its humorous side, and my relatives used to tell wry jokes about it. Most of their stories were about our Burton and Valentine cousins, my grandfather's people who still lived in or around Chester County, Pennsylvania, where the Fitzgeralds had settled before they came South.

Some of the girls married Italian men and disappeared completely from the colored race. Others "passed" sporadically, working in white-collar jobs in Philadelphia, coming home to visit and, finally, to be buried in the family graveyard. One distant cousin who was employed as a clerk in a Philadelphia store used peroxide on his hair to lighten its color. He was so attractive to young ladies they could not leave him alone. Once some white girls came unannounced to visit him and, discovering he was colored, exposed him. He lost his job. Another Pennsylvania cousin was fair-skinned but had kinky hair. He wore a wig to work, but one day a stiff breeze blew off the wig, and with it went his job.

Sometimes passing was inadvertent. The story I liked best was that of another distant cousin, Amos Burton. Amos was the son of a barber, Nory Burton, whose family held a corner on the barber's trade in Toughkenamon, Pennsylvania, for a century or more. Amos was more interested in baseball than barbering and may have been the first known colored man to play on a professional baseball team. He was catcher for the Kennett Square Mohican Baseball Club when it won the Chester County League title in 1895 by defeating West Chester thirteen to twelve, and it was Amos's home-run ball in the ninth inning that broke the tie. The *Sports Digest* for Southern Chester County, reporting the pennant-winning game, said that by the time Burton rounded third base, "Kennett Square fans were heaping money on home plate for him." Amos was still catcher for the Chester County League Champions of 1912 when the pitcher was Herb Pennock, Kennett Square's representative in baseball's Hall of Fame.

The Kennett Square people all knew that Amos was a colored man and it didn't bother them at all, but playing away from home was a problem. Even though Amos looked Italian and the team kept its collective mouth shut when not playing in its own park, word eventually got out. Once that happened, Amos was required to eat at a separate table in the hotel dining room when the team went to Philadelphia.

One morning a party of white guests came into the dining room and sat at the same table with the solitary ballplayer. "I hear they've got a yurdy on the ball team," one of the guests remarked, laughing heartily. (Apparently "yurdy" had the same connotation as "nigger" in his vocabulary.)

"Yes, I guess we have," replied the noncommittal Amos, and he kept right on eating. The friendly guests finished their meal and departed without ever knowing they had been eating and chatting with the "yurdy."

Learning about race did not for the most part come in terrifying shocks, although there were those too—especially news of lynchings, which, frequently unreported in the newspapers, traveled by word of mouth. More often race was the atmosphere one breathed from day to day, the pervasive irritant, the chronic allergy, the vague apprehension which made one uncomfortable and jumpy. We knew the race problem was like a deadly snake coiled and ready to strike, and that one avoided its dangers only by never-ending watchfulness. The problem had a way of intruding itself at moments of family crisis when normal routines were upset and one was most vulnerable. Then the intrusion was unbearable, for no one had time to deal with it or to adopt the special behavior the racial code demanded. When piled on top of other troubles, race could be the sharp curve rising suddenly in the darkness, the blind railroad crossing, the fatal accident that happened when habitual wariness was momentarily relaxed. I was to learn this lesson the summer of my first visit back to my native Baltimore.

CHAPTER 4

Between Two Worlds

THAT FIRST unnerving encounter with the race problem happened during a family emergency when I was nearly nine. Aunt Pauline and I were in Baltimore on an extended visit to the Murray side of my family when our trip was cut short by a telegram from Durham urging Aunt Pauline to come home at once; Grandfather Fitzgerald had taken ill suddenly and was in critical condition. We got the telegram late in the afternoon and there was barely time to catch the only evening train that would take us south.

Earlier that day, a severe thunderstorm accompanied by torrential rains had swept through the area and washed out part of the Southern Railroad tracks south of Washington, and we learned to our dismay that we would have to detour to Norfolk and change trains there for Durham. In addition to this roundabout route, Aunt Pauline could not get Pullman reservations on short notice and we would have to ride in a dirty, stuffy, half-baggage, half-passenger Jim Crow car next to the engine and exposed to a stream of flying cinders.

In Baltimore we had no transportation and had to walk nearly a mile to the station. Two of my sisters came with us to help with our heavy bags and bundles. As we were rushing across a cobblestoned square near the B & O tower, Aunt Pauline slipped on a wet spot and crashed to the pavement, shattering her glasses. Some glass fragments embedded themselves in her cheek. Blood spurted from her cuts, her packages were scattered in the street, and she was so stunned she could not move for several moments. Frightened, we children looked about frantically for help. Two white men sat on the curb nearby, watching us passively. They

37

continued to sit without moving, and when we turned toward them they looked the other way. Somehow we got Aunt Pauline to her feet. Her face was swelling and she could hardly see anything without her glasses, but she was determined to catch the train, and we staggered on to the station. Though badly shaken by her fall, she said nothing about her pain. I knew how deeply she had been hurt in another way when she sighed, "To think, those two white men saw how helpless I was and sat right there. They never made a move to lend a hand."

Our ride to Norfolk seemed endless, and when we arrived there, late at night, the station was almost deserted and no one was about to help carry our baggage. The ticket window was far off at the other end of the waiting room, so Aunt Pauline had to leave me near the entrance to watch our things while she went to inquire about our train connections to Durham. She was gone a long time and I began to get nervous standing there by myself in the dimly lighted station.

Suddenly I looked up to see a huge, red-faced white man towering over me. After he had stared at me awhile, he scratched his head, then beckoned to someone. I found myself surrounded by a circle of white faces, all regarding me intently and turning to look at one another. Not a word was said, just stares, shrugs, and head scratchings. I was too frightened to scream; I stood frozen with terror for one long, awful moment. Just then Aunt Pauline appeared out of the semidarkness and, sizing up the situation, calmly took me by the hand. Ignoring the group of men, she said, "Come on, darling. Our train is waiting on the track and we can go aboard now." We gathered up our baggage and she hustled me as fast as she could along the passageway, out to the tracks, and into the Jim Crow car. We had barely settled in our seats when the door opened and the white stranger who had first scrutinized me in the station pushed into the car. He strode past us, looking us up and down, and Aunt Pauline stared right back at him. Finally, he dropped his eyes and without a word hurried from the car.

After the man had gone, we sat uneasily until the train pulled out of the station and the conductor came to collect our tickets. We had no way of knowing whether the man was aboard the train and might return. When some time had passed and he did not reappear, Aunt Pauline explained to me in a low voice what had happened. Without her glasses and in unfamiliar surroundings, she had set me down with the bags in the White waiting room. She had not realized her mistake, for it had been many years since she had been in Norfolk, and in those days the waiting room had not been segregated. Since she was fair-skinned, her presence did not attract attention, but when the white men saw a child standing alone they became curious and came over to investigate. I was a borderline racial type and in the poorly lighted station they were trying to determine whether I was colored, and therefore out of place, or some foreign mixture. Before they could decide, Aunt Pauline had appeared and they were even more confused, so the ringleader had followed us out to the train to make sure of our racial identity.

We were the only passengers in the Jim Crow car, and riding alone after that unspoken threat made us so fearful that we sat tense through the night, not daring to sleep and jerking our heads around each time the conductor opened the car door behind us. The incident awakened my dread of lynchings, and I was learning the dangers of straying, however innocently, across a treacherous line into a hostile world.

The encounter had come as the final blow in a day already filled with misery, and it left me overwhelmed with unhappy memories of the first reunion with my family in Baltimore. For months I had looked forward to seeing my father and being with "my very own sisters and brothers." I could not remember them but felt as if I knew them through our family group pictures taken more than five years earlier and through the many stories Aunt Pauline had told me about them. She had promised me the trip as soon as she saved enough money for it, and when the day had finally come I was so excited I could hardly endure the suspense of the overnight journey from Durham. I could not eat the fried chicken Grandmother had fixed especially for our lunch and, wide-eyed in anticipation of a joyous homecoming, had rolled and tossed all night in an upper berth on the Pullman car as our train rumbled northward.

Baltimore was the first large city I had ever seen and everything was strange to me—the blocks and blocks of paved streets, the rows and rows of identical brick houses joined together without porches or lawns, only marble steps leading to the sidewalks, and the alleyways out back where children romped among garbage cans and trash. When we got to the Murray household nothing was as I had imagined it would be. My siblings lived with our father's sister and brother in a big house across from the Baltimore City Armory. Their home, which consisted of three floors and a basement, was elegantly furnished and kept like a showplace. They lived well, dressed well, and were more in tune with the latest fashions than my Fitzgerald relatives.

Red-haired, freckle-faced Aunt Rose Murray Shipley was a woman of enormous bulk whose shrill voice unsettled me, accustomed as I was to Aunt Pauline's quiet monotone. Because of her great weight, Aunt Rose moved about as little as possible and would yell her orders to the older children from whatever room she happened to be sitting in. Uncle Lewis Murray, who taught school, was tall, thin, and bespectacled. Fastidious in his dress and in everything else he did, he kept me under such constant, critical scrutiny that I felt uncomfortable in his presence. My sisters and brothers were not at all as I had pictured them. Grace and Mildred, the oldest, were no longer little girls with short curls; they had grown tall and had long braids swinging down their backs. They seemed aloof, removed from me by the superiority of age. Willie, only fifteen months my senior, hardly noticed me. He gave me the once-over when we first arrived, then went back to riding his bicycle with other boys in the street. Although I could ride as well and play as hard as he could, I was a mere girl and beneath his consideration. Rosetta, seven, and Robert, six, were much smaller and less hardy than I was; they inspected me shyly but stayed close to Aunt Rose, and I was there for some time before they ventured to play with me in the backyard. I felt ill at ease and overwhelmed by a houseful of strangers whose only links to me seemed to be our common name and a strong family resemblance.

Although I never entirely got over the strangeness, there were fleeting moments when I felt part of the family. I loved evenings on the Murray front stoop when the family relaxed under the glow of the street lamp. Then my older sisters, free of household chores, seemed more sociable and actually talked to me a bit. Willie even let us smaller children join with his street pals in a game called Liftstick, a variant of baseball played with a short flat stick and a broom handle. The high point of the evening was a tinkling bell announcing the arrival in our block of the pushcart man who sold ices of many flavors in little paper cups, for two cents each.

Sunday morning breakfast was another happy time, when we all sat together at the long table in the dining room. Aunt Rose would bake hot rolls and serve fried chicken with creamy potatoes or liver and bacon with hominy grits floating in butter, along with plenty of milk and buttermilk. On those occasions I was awed by the presence of Great-grandmother Spriggs, oldest member of the Murray family, a tiny, mahogany-colored woman with frizzy white hair. She was then 100 and lived to be 104. I had never seen anyone so ancient and, not daring to speak to her, I would walk around her chair gazing at her in wonderment.

Despite these blissful moments, an underlying tension plagued our visit and ultimately created a feeling of alienation in me that took years to overcome. My loyalty to Aunt Pauline made me wary when Aunt Rose introduced me to her friends—in Aunt Pauline's presence—as "another one of my children, the one that's been living down South." Also, I had been there only a short time before I discovered the attitude Aunt Rose had adopted toward my parents, and it turned my wariness into resentment and finally open rebellion. I first sensed something was wrong shortly after we came, when I overheard Aunt Pauline telling Aunt Rose what a fine job she and Uncle Lewis had done with the children and how happy and proud Will and Agnes would be now if they could see us all together. To my surprise, Aunt Rose cut her short.

"We don't talk about the past in this house, Pauline," she snapped. "I don't want my children hearing sorrowful things that can't be helped. The two little ones don't know anything about the past, and that's the way I want it to be."

"But there's nothing wrong in children knowing about their parents," Aunt Pauline protested. "Little Pauline knows all about her father and mother. I've never tried to hide anything from her."

"Well," Aunt Rose retorted, "you can say anything you please to little Pauline, since you've got her, but these five are *my* children and I don't want you upsetting them by talking about anything that's happened in the past when you're around them."

Aunt Pauline didn't argue. She was a guest and did not want to make a scene, but her face got very red and I knew she was fuming inside. I was shocked. It was unthinkable not to speak of my parents. Ever since I could remember, Aunt Pauline had talked of them and made them real to me. She told me that sometimes I was like Agnes and sometimes I was like Will. It almost became a game; I would say, "Who am I like today, Aunt Pauline?" and she would answer, "Oh, you've got your mother's sweet disposition today," or she might say, "As I watched you reciting a piece, you looked just like your father. I saw Will Murray all over again."

I noticed that my parents' names were never mentioned in the Murray household and that all of their pictures and our family group pictures had been hidden away or destroyed. Aunt Rose had forbidden the three older children to speak of our parents in the presence of Rosetta and Robert, who believed Aunt Rose was their natural mother. Robert's name had been changed to Raymond, in effect obliterating his Fitzgerald connection, since he had been named for our mother's father. It was as if William and Agnes Murray had never existed.

Aunt Rose could not know how important my family identity was to me, and in her effort to protect the younger children she unwittingly threatened my sense of self by pushing *my* parents into oblivion and usurping my mother's place. My resentment against her heavy-handed silence and deception was bound to explode into defiant anger. It came one day while Rosetta, "Raymond," and I were playing in the backyard and they questioned our family relationship. They were obviously perplexed; they wanted to know why, if I was really their sister, I called Aunt Pauline "Mother" and *their* mother "Aunt Rose."

"You see," I tried to explain, "our *real* mother is dead and Aunt Pauline adopted me just like Aunt Rose adopted you. Aunt Rose is really your aunt, the same as she is my aunt."

My cruel logic dealt a crushing blow to my little brother and sister, who howled their disbelief. Finally, I burst out impatiently, "How can Aunt Rose be your *real* mother when she is your *father's* sister?" In my anger, I also told my little brother his real name. My small siblings' world fell apart, and weeping bitterly, they ran inside to tell Aunt Rose the horrible things I had said. In her fury, she would have struck me if Aunt Pauline had not been there to intervene.

"No, Rose, I can't let you punish her for telling the truth," Aunt Pauline said firmly.

Aunt Rose and I glowered at each other, my will mobilized against her will, my anger blazing back at hers. She could not get me to apologize, so she ordered me to go upstairs to bed. When I got to the top floor I slammed the bedroom door shut with all my might and cried myself to sleep. Hours later, when she sent the children to call me downstairs to dinner, the door had stuck fast and Aunt Rose had to drag her heavy body up three flights of stairs and smash the door open to get me out. After that episode, the distance between Aunt Rose and me widened, and while my dislike of her abated as I grew to womanhood, we remained strangers. I never lost the feeling of being an outsider in the Murray home and carried about with me an unsatisfied longing for the family I loved but could not wholly embrace.

This rupture in our family relations was especially painful on the sensitive issue of our father's illness. My spunky, twelve-year-old sister Mildred was fiercely loyal to our father and unafraid to speak freely about him to me when Aunt Rose was not around. I learned from her that after our mother died, he became increasingly hostile toward Aunt Rose and Uncle Lewis, said they were meddling in his affairs, and would not let them come near his house. Things got so bad that one of the Spriggs relatives had him picked up by the police in January 1917 and he was eventually committed to Crownsville State Hospital, where he had been for the past two and a half years. None of the family had been to see him since his commitment.

Aunt Pauline had promised that we would visit my father while we were in Baltimore, and Mildred was eager to go with us. She was already determined to become a nurse like our mother and was bitterly disappointed when, just as we were leaving for the hospital, Aunt Rose flatly refused to let her go. So Aunt Pauline and I set off alone that stiflingly hot Sunday in late July, bound for Crownsville and carrying a basket of fruit, loaves of freshly baked bread, a bag of cupcakes, and packages of cigarettes for my father. We did not know then that our visit to my Murray relatives would end abruptly later that afternoon, when the telegram arrived telling us of Grandfather Fitzgerald's illness.

Although she did what she could to prepare me for seeing my father, Aunt Pauline did not know what to expect. She told me that even though he was not sick in bed, he would have to stay in the hospital until the doctors thought he was well enough to be discharged; she could not say how soon that would be but felt our visit would cheer him up immensely. I could not wait to see him; I knew exactly how he would look and I knew he would remember me because people said I looked so much like him and had his quick mind. I was bursting to tell him all about school and that I was on the Honor Roll in my class.

We took an electric train to Crownsville, near Annapolis, and walked from the station along the track toward the hospital, following the crowds of people who were also going to visit relatives. On the way I saw two bedraggled, shabbily dressed women who were not part of the crowd but hobbled along by themselves, stopping to pick up discarded orange peels and chewing on them as they went. Aunt Pauline said they must be patients from the hospital. When we got there we were shown into a small, gloomy waiting room where people were sitting on rows of rough wooden benches to wait for the patients they had come to see. Pretty soon a stream of men dressed in clean blue overalls filed into the room. Each joined his family group, laughing and talking with his kinsfolk. Then one by one the groups went outside to walk about the grounds, until Aunt Pauline and I were left alone in the stuffy room, listening to the murmur of voices drifting in from the open windows. She sat stiffly on the backless bench holding the basket in her lap, pressing her lips hard against her teeth in the way she did when she was worried. We sat there a long time and I began to think my father wasn't coming. Every few seconds I would jump up, go to the door, and peer down the hallway to look for him.

Finally, the door opened and an old man shuffled in. He was wearing worn, discolored overalls patched here and there; his shoes were cracked, his hair was scraggly, his eyes were dull, and his face was unshaven. He resembled the wandering creatures we had seen along the track, neglected and forgotten.

He came forward uncertainly and Aunt Pauline gasped as she rose to meet him.

"It's Will, isn't it?"

"Yes, it's what's left of me," he said. "Pauline, they didn't tell me it was you. I almost didn't come. You haven't changed a whit since I saw you five years ago."

"He doesn't look like *my* father," I blurted out to Aunt Pauline, who squeezed my shoulder hard and pushed me toward him. I stood like a block of wood staring at my father stupidly, my tongue paralyzed. He looked at me without recognition and turned to Aunt Pauline.

"Which one is this? I haven't seen any of my children in so long, I don't know if I'd recognize them."

"This is little Pauline, Will. You know, the one you let me take with me."

"Oh, yes, I remember. She was so little when I last saw her. You have her with you down in Durham. I'm glad."

I cannot remember whether he hugged me or not. I remember only gaping at him incredulously, unable to speak. He looked down at his clothes apologetically.

"I'm sorry you had to see me like this. They let us wear our new overalls when we have visitors, but I got into an argument with one of the fellows on my ward this morning and this is my punishment. If I'd known you were coming, I'd have tried to stay out of trouble. You know what a quick temper I have. Nobody ever comes to see me, and I'm always getting into scrapes."

"How do they treat you here?" Aunt Pauline asked.

My father glanced about quickly, then sat down on the bench, leaned close to her, and dropped his voice. "To tell you the truth, in a place like this you never know what's going to happen. I have to watch every move. The guards are worse than the patients. I want to get out of here and they tell me I'm ready to go, but there's nobody to have me signed out."

Aunt Pauline did not know what to say, so she changed the subject. "I brought you some things," she said, handing him the basket. "Rose remembered how you like cupcakes and baked some for you, and Mrs. Brooks out near Cedar Hill where I used to teach baked you some yeast bread when she heard I was coming to see you."

He took the basket mechanically, looked it over, and saw the cigarettes. His eyes brightened a bit.

"I'm glad you brought me some smokes. It's the only comfort I have around here. Time passes you by in a place like this and one day is just like another."

He did not ask about the other children or about Aunt Rose and Uncle Lewis. He sat there silently, his face working as if there was something important he wanted to say. Before he could get it out, a uniformed guard came in.

"Visiting hours are over, Murray. You'll have to go now."

My father grasped Aunt Pauline's hands and held them tight. "You'll never know how glad I am that you came. I'll never forget you," he said, choking a little, then he kissed her cheek, patted my head, picked up the basket, and moved haltingly toward the door without looking back, his shoulders drooping and his head bowed.

Aunt Pauline's glasses were misty and I thought she was going to cry, but she bit her lip and said, "Let's go, child." I followed her silently out of the hospital grounds past the old dilapidated buildings. I could see people inside, pressing their faces against the windows and screaming at us as we went by, but I was too heavy with the things I had come to say and had not said to my father to pay much notice. He was only forty-seven at the time, a little younger than Aunt Pauline, and I was trying to understand how this forlorn, old-looking man I had just seen could be the same as the dapper gentleman in my parents' photographs or the brilliant teacher Aunt Pauline had talked about. She had explained to me that an adult relative could have my father discharged from Crownsville, and I remember saying over and over to myself, "When I get to be twenty-one I'm going to take my father away from this awful place."

As if to match the somberness of that visit, the skies threatened as we waited for the train, and on our way back to Baltimore we were overtaken by the same violent thunderstorm that washed out railroad tracks south of Washington. Aunt Pauline was terrified of lightning, and I had absorbed her fears. We were traveling through a woods when a bolt of lightning struck the car we were riding in. Although no one was injured, the train was stalled on the track for almost an hour while the storm raged overhead. We could see people running among the trees in panic and someone told us later that a boy riding a bicycle through the woods had been struck and killed by lightning. We sat almost petrified in the eerie darkness between the blazes of fire until the storm passed, and then had to abandon our car and move forward to another before the train could continue.

When we finally reached Baltimore, the telegram about Grandfather Fitzgerald's sudden illness was waiting for Aunt Pauline, and in the face of this new emergency my anguish over my father's plight had to yield to the urgency of packing our bags and getting the train to Norfolk. I had time only for a whispered conversation with Mildred, telling her what I had seen that day, and in the telling, the pain of knowing that we children were powerless to help our father in his abandonment became a bond between us. Our one consolation was a mutual vow to have him released when we reached the age of majority. We parted, not knowing that our desperate pact was doomed and that we would not see each other again until our father's death brought me back to Baltimore four years later.

CHAPTER 5

Loss and Change

GRANDFATHER Fitzgerald died in August 1919, a few days after Aunt Pauline and I had hurried back from Baltimore, and with his passing the gloom of deep mourning settled over our house. Grandmother and Aunt Pauline were now the only adults left, and the old homeplace seemed shrunken and lonely. Grandmother and Grandfather had shared a stormy but durable partnership for fifty years, and now she was torn loose from her moorings and cast adrift by his death. Despite Grandfather's blindness and frailty, his presence in our household symbolized stability and security, and without him Grandmother began to relive the fears of her past, rooted in the turmoil of Reconstruction and its aftermath.

In the early days of their marriage, when my grandparents were struggling to establish a foothold, Grandmother often stayed alone on her farm near Chapel Hill. Grandfather was working in his brickyard in Durham, twelve miles away, until he was able to build the family home there, and their children were often in Durham helping him. It was a time when the Ku Klux Klan in Orange County sought to run colored farmers off their land, and Grandmother's isolated cabin in the woods was an easy target. Late at night she would be awakened by the thudding of horses' hooves as night riders, brandishing torches and yelling like banshees, swept into the clearing and rode round and round her cabin, churning the earth outside her door. She never knew when they might set fire to the place, burning her to death inside, and some nights she was so terrified that she would get out of bed in the middle of the night, creep through the woods to the roadway, and trudge the twelve miles to Durham, preferring the dark, lonely but open road to the risk of being trapped at the farm.

Now her old terrors of the night resurfaced with increasing intensity, and she was so overwrought that Aunt Pauline could no longer do her schoolwork in peace. To get some rest, she went to stay with Aunt Sallie at the rectory on Pine Street for a while that fall, leaving me alone with Grandmother, to keep her company. Grandmother's obsession that Ku Kluxers or robbers might break in on us at night made me dread the approach of darkness, especially because our house, which was behind Maplewood Cemetery, was in deep shadows, isolated from other houses in the neighborhood and far from the protective glow of street lamps. Every evening at dusk, Grandmother and I would begin to fortify the downstairs, locking and bolting all the doors and windows and securing them with crossbars. Then we would set an oil lantern on the stair landing and carry a slop jar, a pail of water, food, and dishes upstairs to Grand-mother's bedroom. Once inside it, we barricaded the door and windows from floor to ceiling by piling barrels, chairs, tables, and baskets of clothing against every opening. Sealed in as we were, we would never have gotten out alive if there had been a fire.

Grandmother always kept Grandfather's Civil War musket, bayonet, and saber, along with an ax, under the bed, and she hid a pearl-handled revolver under her pillow. She had no ammunition for the guns, but it seemed to comfort her to have them there. When she had completed her defenses, she would cook our supper in the fireplace, usually potatoes roasted in the ashes, greens boiled with salt pork, and cornmeal bread fried in a black iron skillet. By that time I was so scared I had lost my appetite and would force down a few mouthfuls, undress quickly, dive into the big double bed, burrow down in the feather mattress, and pull the covers over my head. I wanted to go to sleep while Grandmother was still stirring about; also I hoped that by sleeping I could avoid the ordeal I knew was coming.

It never worked. Sometime after midnight I would be awakened by heavy thuds and scrapings on the bare floor under the bed. Grandmother, convinced that an intruder was breaking in downstairs, was dragging the ax back and forth and pounding on the floorboards. "You get away from my window, you devil!" she would shout. "If you don't, I'm going to pour a kettle of scalding water down on your head." She would listen for a few seconds, then the draggings and thumpings would continue until she was exhausted and fell into bed. Pretty soon I would hear her snoring and would lie there trembling, listening to the creaking of the walls as the old house settled and jumping up in bed when a tree limb scraped against the porch roof. Too frightened to go back to sleep, I would wait until I could see the first hint of dawn through the window barricades, then throw on my clothes, pull the barriers from the doors, and flee from the house into the morning twilight.

The only place I dared go at such an early hour without being questioned by an adult was the home of two schoolmates my age, Ruby and Ethel Green, who had no mother or father and who lived with an older brother in a two-room frame house at the northern end of Maplewood Cemetery. Their brother left at dawn each morning for his job at the tobacco factory, and they fended for themselves. Scooting up the rugged hillside along the Bottoms to arrive at their house after he had gone, I would climb a ladder to the loft where they slept, and snuggle down beside them, gradually shedding my fright. The Greens had a tall honey locust tree near their front porch, and when the long purplish pods were ripe I would clamber onto the tree from the loft and gather handfuls of pods. We would bite into them and suck out the sticky sweet fruit, which was sometimes the only breakfast we had before going to school.

We always went to school early because I knew Aunt Pauline, who arrived an hour before classes started, would want to inspect my appearance since she was not at home to oversee my dressing. She was unaware of my bizarre morning routine until the day I had an accident with my dress. On our way to school that morning we had found a big rope, which we dragged along with us to use for jump rope at recess. I was running down a steep red-clay hillside to jump across a brook, when my feet got tangled in the rope. I stumbled and fell into the water. My white dress and my shoes and socks were mudstained. Afraid to face Aunt Pauline in such a state, I hurried to school, sneaked down into the basement, washed the dress, and hung it on the steam pipes to dry. When Aunt Pauline saw me later, she was aghast to find me wearing a rough-dried garment streaked with faint reddish stains. She began to question me and the truth about my early morning activities came out. Aunt Pauline did not punish me for ruining my dress, but soon after that she was back home to stay. My dawn visits to the Greens ended abruptly, and Grandmother's stormy midnight vigils gradually subsided.

The Episcopal Church and its struggling colored missions were, like the schoolroom, a natural extension of my home life when I was growing up. Aunt Pauline and Aunt Sallie were prime movers in the formation of Saint Titus, our mission church in Durham. When I was a child it was a tiny frame chapel at the corner of Pine and Proctor streets. (It is now a parish church located in "Hayti," the chief Negro section of town.) Aunt Sallie's fine singing voice and her devotion to the rituals had attracted the new vicar, the Reverend J. E. G. Small, and they were married when I was around five. The rectory next door to the church became my second home.

The new suffragan bishop of North Carolina, the Right Reverend Henry B. Delany, was a close family friend whom my aunts looked upon as an older brother as well as pastor and priest. As a very young man he had taught them at Saint Augustine's School in Raleigh. He officiated at Aunt Sallie's wedding ceremony and confirmed me when I was nine years old. He was one of the first two colored bishops to serve the Episcopal Church in the continental United States, having been consecrated at the age of sixty as 298th in its succession of bishops. He served for ten years, until his death in 1928. I knew him as a gracious old gentleman with kindly eyes, a man who loved children and took the time to answer my many questions.

The Delanys were a remarkable family. Of Bishop and Mrs. Delany's ten children—four daughters and six sons—two were teachers, two lawyers, two dentists, one an undertaker, one a music teacher, one a photographer, and one a physician. Their daughter Bessie E. Delany—the first woman dentist I had ever known—took care of my teeth when I was a college student. A son, Hubert T. Delany, became a distinguished judge in New York City. In the 1930s, the Delanys' professional successes were beacon lights to younger people like me.

My uncle-in-law, the Reverend John Ethophilus Grattin Small, was all that his name implied. British to the core, he was a native of Barbados who came to this country and trained for the ministry at Princeton Theological Seminary. When I first knew him, he was in his forties, dark-skinned, balding, solidly built, round-faced, with a drooping mustache and trim goatee. He was a learned man, and his marked West Indian accent and undisguised disdain for most things American set him apart as a foreigner, to be treated with reserve. I never heard any member of my family address him by his Christian name, not even Aunt Sallie. To her, he was always "Father Small"; to everyone else, he was "Reverend Small." He clung to his British citizenship until his death, as did many West Indians of his time, because it was felt to accord a higher status than the second-class citizenship of native American Negroes. And indeed, it seemed that his accent and haughty bearing exacted a grudging respect from many white people.

Aunt Sallie was nearly forty when they married, and I doubt that she would have married at all but for the Reverend Small's dogged persistence. She loved her teaching and her independence. I think she finally consented because of her sense of mission and because she was one of those women in the Episcopal Church who would have entered the or-

dained ministry had it been possible in her time. As it was, she answered
her call to service by becoming a minister's wife. She gave up teaching to
have their first child and did not return to it until after her husband died
and she was in her sixties.

The Smalls had three sons, the first of whom was stillborn. Two years
later, a few days after Grandfather Fitzgerald's funeral, James Fitzgerald
Small was born. Joshua Ethophilus followed in 1922, and at the age of
eleven I became his godmother. Although I was much older than my
cousins, they were like my little brothers and they looked upon me as a
sister.

I loved visiting the rectory on Pine Street, especially after James was
born. It had conveniences we did not enjoy at home. It was a five-room
cottage built on one level, surrounded by other houses on a paved street,
and at night it was bathed in the cheerful glow of the streetlight on the
corner. It had a bathroom, a flush toilet, electricity, and gas for cooking,
supplied by feeding quarters into a meter. Aunt Sallie, who was as jolly as
Aunt Pauline was grave, kept me entertained with stories. The rectory was
also the center of activities connected with the church, and Aunt Sallie had
a busy life working with the Altar Guild, the Women's Auxiliary, the
Sunday school, and the choir.

All this changed when the Reverend Small accepted a post as vicar of
three small rural mission churches in southern Maryland, under the jurisdiction of the Diocese of Washington. Saint Simon's, located in Croom,
about twenty-five miles southeast of Washington, had a rectory where the
family would live. Saint Philip's, at Aquasco, was fifteen miles south of
Croom, and Saint Mary's, at Charlotte Hall, was another fifteen miles
beyond Aquasco. The diocese would supply the vicar with an automobile
—a rare privilege in those days—to travel the circuit holding services and
visiting his parishioners scattered over Prince George's and Saint Mary's
counties. The diocese also offered him a higher salary than he earned in
Durham. It was an advancement for my uncle, although it entailed hard
work and long hours. But for Aunt Sallie it meant being uprooted from the
hometown where she had lived all her life and being isolated in the
country, where her days would be filled with drudgery.

When the Smalls moved to Maryland in the summer of 1921, Aunt
Pauline let me go with them to help Aunt Sallie settle into her new home.
It was the first of many summers and holidays I would spend with them
until I was grown. For a ten-year-old it was a great adventure. We took
the train to Washington and stayed overnight at the new and, to me,
luxurious Whitelaw Hotel at Thirteenth and T streets, N.W. The next
afternoon we rode the Baltimore train and got off about halfway, at Bowie,
where a spur railroad ran on a single track south to Brandywine. The train

had only two cars; one was for white passengers and the other—typically partitioned in the middle—was both the baggage car and the coach for colored passengers.

The train tunneled through patches of undergrowth and swampy land and let us off at Croom station, where a man met us with a horse-drawn surrey and drove us to our destination, three miles away. The white sandy road climbed steadily uphill, wound past a few scattered farms and through the village of Croom, a cluster of dwellings around Duley's General Store and Post Office. At a fork a half mile from the village, Croom Road (now Route 382) curved right and went southward through the hills toward Naylor, Horsehead (designated by a wooden horse's head on a post at a crossroad), and Aquasco. We took the road to the left, curving downhill around Saint Thomas Church and churchyard and turning into the lane of Saint Simon's, which led to the rectory.

It was almost dark when we got there, but the church people who were waiting to welcome us had prepared a dinner that made my eyes bulge. I could not remember having seen so much food on one table—large platters of golden fried chicken, plates of steaming yellow corn, hot biscuits and butter, a mountain of potato salad, dishes of thick-sliced tomatoes, cucumbers, pickles, a yellow cake with chocolate icing, and buckets of lemonade.

My introduction to southern Maryland was a child's delight and influenced the way I saw it during my growing years, for to me it represented a vacation in the country, plenty of good food, space to run about, and trips through the countryside in my uncle's car. While Croom never ceased to hold a certain charm for me, I gradually realized how lonely it must have been for Aunt Sallie, cut off from all active community life and, as she put it, "buried in the sticks." She was so isolated that even a crow cawing in the woods, or a buzzard soaring into the air from its perch on a dead forest tree, or a cow mooing in the meadow, was a welcome diversion in the monotony of her days.

The rectory stood by itself several hundred yards from the road, a two-story frame house surrounded by open fields. One could look for miles over rolling hills and tobacco farms to the south. Some distance beyond the house was a dilapidated building called The Hall, which stood in ghostly solitude on the edge of a thick wood. It had long since fallen into disrepair and its only occupant was the local blacksmith, Mr. Ross, who had a shop down near the road across the lane from Saint Simon's and spent his evenings at The Hall producing mournful sounds on his saxophone. Sometimes he held rehearsals with a five- or six-piece band which practiced only one tune—"I nev-er knew I could love a-ny bo-dy, hon-ey, like I'm lov-in' you." The band seldom got beyond the first two lines without floundering in sour notes, and they would break off to begin all over again. This endless repetition of discordant sounds supplied our only musical entertainment.

The Butlers, our nearest neighbors, who lived at the bend in Saint Thomas Road, were within sight but not within calling distance. They supplied us with butter and eggs, and I made the trip across the field twice a day to get a pail of milk from them. The Butlers were good neighbors but not the visiting kind. They were Roman Catholics, and they were also known as Wesorts—very fair people of mixed white, Indian, and colored ancestry. The Wesorts were caught between the races, rejected by white people and refusing to be identified as colored. Unlike the Fitzgeralds and many others of mixed heritage who had long ago dedicated themselves to the advancement of the colored race, the Wesorts tended to keep to themselves and to intermarry.

The only other neighbor was Mrs. Henry, the director of a school for delinquent Washington girls that was situated in a cluster of small buildings near the road a short distance beyond Saint Simon's Church. Mrs. Henry was a large, distinguished-looking woman with soft gray hair. She traveled back and forth from Washington, but when she was in Croom she was Aunt Sallie's only outlet for conversation. Her daughter, Miss Myrtle Henry, a quiet young woman in her early twenties, was working on her doctorate and would become a professor of English at Howard University.

We used oil lamps and cooked on a three-burner kerosene stove. There was no bathroom and the outhouse was down in the field some distance away. We got our water from a fifty-foot well close to the house, which had two buckets on a pulley under cover in a well shed. When Aunt Sallie did her weekly wash, my job was to draw and carry enough water to fill five large tin tubs.

The nearest store was Duley's General Store, a mile away, and the nearest telephone was owned by Dr. Gibbons, the local physician, who lived on Croom Road a half mile from our house. In emergencies, a telegram was telephoned to Dr. Gibbons, who would send a note to the rectory. The nearest shopping center was in Washington, and we seldom saw a newspaper. And of course in those days there was no radio or television. Apart from the church services, people had very little social life. They lived far apart, traveled by horse and buggy, and seldom visited at night.

There had once been an active community life around the church. Saint Simon's, the rectory, the school, and The Hall were all built on the same property. During a controversy that arose some years before the Smalls came to Croom, the church separated from the school and The Hall fell into disrepair. Now the only contact between the school and the church was the common use of the well. Mrs. Henry's girls made several trips a day to get water.

I think Aunt Sallie was so starved for companionship she saved her conversations all winter until I came in the summer. Then, as we worked, she would talk nonstop, telling me all the things that had happened in my absence. My uncle was away a good deal of the time, carrying on his pastoral duties among the three churches. Our chief entertainment at night after the supper dishes were washed was to sit on the front porch and count the headlights of cars that passed along Croom Road, which we could see across several fields. Cars were so scarce we seldom counted more than a dozen before bedtime. On some nights the northwestern sky glowed with the reflection of the lights of Washington. Due north was the fainter glow of Baltimore, and to the northeast, that of Annapolis.

For me the isolation in southern Maryland made the atmosphere seem freer than that of Durham. The absence of stores and restaurants and other aspects of close city life meant fewer reminders of racial segregation. On the whole, our infrequent contacts with white people were friendly. But there was one visual symbol of the separation of the races which we were compelled to look at daily.

The two Episcopal churches in Croom, both visible from the rectory, were so close together they might have been part of the same property. Saint Thomas, for white Episcopalians, stood in a grove of trees at the top of the hill, a stately red structure dominating the countryside, it seemed to me then, its churchyard filled with vaults and tombstones befitting its historical significance. Its bell, which tolled for services and funerals, had a deep, mellow sound. Down the hill, across the road from the churchyard, was Saint Simon's, the church for colored Episcopalians, a small frame chapel on a grassy plot barren of trees. Like the other two churches my uncle pastored, it had been established during Reconstruction when the white people would no longer tolerate former slaves as members of their congregations. Its high, shrill bell was more like a dinner bell than a church bell, and the few graves behind the chapel were marked by weather-beaten wooden crosses with no other sign of identification. The main cemetery for Croom's colored population was in the woods back of The Hall.

The people who attended the two churches were intimately acquainted with one another's families, and the easy familiarity common to rural life marked their daily interchange. But on Sunday they inhabited different worlds, although they sang the same hymns and worshiped from the same prayer book, within sight and sound of one another. These symbols of separation made the deepest impression on me during my visits to Croom. When I was a child, the gulf was so wide that it would have been unthinkable for me even to enter the gate of Saint Thomas Church. The only white person I knew of in Croom who showed special interest in colored people was a Miss Wills, a wraithlike, aging woman whom I saw at a distance and who was considered eccentric. A member of an old family, she had once been a benefactor of Saint Simon's and still maintained a lively interest in the nearby school.

When I went back to Croom more than forty years later, Saint Simon's and the rectory were gone, as was the old Hall. The school had become the private home of one of the girls who had lived there when I was a child, now Mrs. Kitty Pinkney and a grandmother. The congregations of the two churches had been "integrated," and Saint Thomas was the church for both races. When I attended the morning service I was surprised to see how small Saint Thomas was inside. In its remoteness to me during those earlier years, it had seemed like a cathedral church. But while the symbols of separation had been torn down, the reality remained. I saw only one other Negro worshiper in the congregation and learned that the colored people had felt so keenly those years of rejection that when the two congregations merged, most of them withdrew and joined the black Methodist church.

What I enjoyed most about those summers of my childhood were the trips with the Reverend Small in his open Model T Ford touring car when he held services in Aquasco and Charlotte Hall. An automobile in those days was not only a mark of status but also a source of adventure. To go more than thirty miles an hour was to travel at high speed. We drove along sandy roads full of blind curves and so narrow that we had to be watchful of overhanging bushes and tree limbs which brushed against the sides of the car as we passed. When we met another car or a horse-drawn vehicle, we had to back up until we found a grassy shoulder where we could pull off the road to let it go by. In a sudden downpour, we had to stop and fasten on the side curtains. Sometimes the swamps would overflow and we would plow through small torrents, praying that the motor would not stall and leave us stranded in water up to our knees. If we got stuck in the mud, as we often did after a rainfall, we had to wait until a team of horses or mules came along and pulled us out. Then my uncle had to crank the motor by hand to get us started again.

Sometimes we covered all three churches on a single Sunday. We would leave Croom at dawn to travel the thirty miles to Saint Mary's at Charlotte Hall for early Communion. The people would wait at the church until we got there, however long it took us. Then we would come back to Aquasco for the eleven o'clock service at Saint Philip's, and after church a family would invite us to dinner, loading the car with fresh vegetables from their garden before we left. We would get back to Croom in time for evensong at Saint Simon's.

The high point of the summer vacation was a trip to Washington. We would drive over to Upper Marlboro and take the state highway into Pennsylvania Avenue, turning off to park at Union Station, the only place in downtown Washington where we could get a meal. Lunch at Savarin's Restaurant was then a grand occasion—several courses served on snowy tablecloths by waiters in white jackets. After lunch, while the Reverend Small went off on church business, Aunt Sallie and I walked about the station with the two little boys, then sat out front by the fountains and gazed at the great white dome of the Capitol. Sometimes we would stroll about the Capitol grounds and I felt awe at being so close to important national events. It was during President Coolidge's term in the White House, and I remember how sad we were when his son, young Calvin, Jr., died from an infected blister. When we got back home to Croom, it was difficult to believe that the nation's capital was only twenty-five miles away.

I was spending my third summer at Croom when we got word of my father's death. One morning in June, Dr. Gibbons sent over a message from Aunt Rose in Baltimore saying that Brother Willie had died and she was expecting me for the funeral. I was now nearly thirteen, and four years had passed since I had last seen my sisters and brothers. When Aunt Sallie moved to Croom, she had hoped Aunt Rose would let the children come out for a visit; but the two families had remained as distant as ever, separated by their different views about my parents.

I made the trip to Baltimore alone, and learned when I got there that my father had been killed at Crownsville State Hospital and that his body was being shipped home for burial. His death was still not very real to me; the only sign of it was the lavender crape on the Murrays' front door.

Aunt Pauline had been notified and was coming for the funeral from Hampton Institute, where she was attending summer school. I felt immense relief to know that she would be there soon, for in spite of my joy at seeing my sisters and brothers again, I could not get over the feeling of being more a visitor than a member of the family. My wariness of Aunt Rose had not changed, and I felt uncomfortable when she continued to introduce me to her friends as one of her children. I knew that Aunt Pauline had applied for and received letters of adoption for me shortly after our first visit to Baltimore, so that there could be no question of her custody. But I did not feel at ease until she arrived the day before the funeral.

That same afternoon, my father's body arrived from Crownsville in a gray casket. I am sure that if the adults had known in advance what to expect, they would have had the coffin sealed. We children had no preparation for the effects of violent death. The body we saw was not recognizable as my father, even in the sorrowful state he had been in when I last saw him. His face was purple and swollen, his head was shaven, and his skull had been split open like a melon and sewed together loosely with jagged stitches crisscrossing the blood-clotted line of severance.

Aunt Rose placed a handkerchief over his face to soften the horror, but it did not help. Again and again I was drawn to the coffin, slipping into the parlor when no one else was around to lift the handkerchief and stare at the puffed eyelids, the battered face and lips, the butchered skull, until it was indelibly engraved in my memory. Nothing seemed to link this body to the human race except the hands, which were soft and almost alive. I remember reaching down under the coffin lid, touching them and holding them, trying to convince myself that the wretched thing I saw in its ill-fitting suit was in fact my father.

That night I heard the details of my father's death as they had been related to Aunt Pauline, and they did not vary essentially from the official summary I obtained many years later from the hospital authorities. He had been murdered by a hospital guard, a man of Polish origin named Walter Swiskoski, known as a "floater"—that is, someone not trained to work in mental institutions but hired temporarily when the hospital was short of staff—whose only qualification for the job seemed to be physical brawn. This was the official summary:

> On June 18, 1923 a Mr. Swift or Mr. Swiskoski, who seems to have been known also under a number of other names, was teasing Mr. Murray by putting a piece of fly paper on his face. Mr. Murray took this off and put it on the attendant's face. There ensued a skirmish which was terminated by Mr. Murray going to his place of employment in the Industrial Shop and by the attendant saying he "would get him later." On Mr. Murray's return to the ward he was taken to a basement and there beaten with an instrument resembling a baseball bat over the buttocks and over the head. This was done in the presence of some other patients and was also witnessed by another attendant. Following the blow on the head Mr. Murray was taken to the hospital infirmary where attempts at resuscitation were futile and he died.

The hospital completed the carnage of disfiguration by performing a clumsy autopsy on the brain at the order of the coroner upon the request of the superintendent. Then they kept the body on ice for two days before shipping it home. What the official summary did not report, but I heard the night before my father's funeral, was Swiskoski's threat, "I'll get that nigger later." I always believed that my father was a victim of racial antagonism.

The Reverend George F. Bragg conducted my father's funeral as he had my mother's nearly ten years earlier, and my father was buried in the same grave as my mother in a family plot in Laurel Cemetery. The plot was enclosed by a cement curbing and marked by a slab on which the name MURRAY was engraved. But their children were not to have even their burial place for remembrance. Some years later, when we were adults, Laurel Cemetery went into bankruptcy. Most of the descendants of the people buried there had moved away and the grounds had been so vandalized and overgrown with thicket we could not find our parents' gravestone. It seemed to be the final insult. The grounds were sold and a developer erected a shopping center on the spot.

Swiskoski was tried, convicted of manslaughter, and sent to prison for ten years. While he was there, he apparently lost several fingers in an industrial accident, and he wrote to Uncle Lewis Murray, appealing for assistance in obtaining parole. My uncle actually went to see him in prison, but observed that during their entire interview Swiskoski did not once express regret for having killed my father. My uncle took no action, and parole was denied. We never knew what happened to the man. Uncle Lewis filed a claim against the Industrial Accident Commission on behalf of the children of William H. Murray, deceased, but the ruling was unfavorable because my father was held to be not an employee of Crownsville State Hospital at the time of his death.

It took many years for me to get over the shock of my father's murder. My grief over the loss of a parent whose image I had adored and whom I had hoped to restore to his family was aggravated by an overwhelming sense of helplessness and frustration in an unsuccessful struggle against time and fate. Mildred and I, who had determined to have him discharged from Crownsville when we reached the age of majority, now realized sadly that the urgency we had felt had been fully justified. It was an awareness that made his death all the harder to bear.

The raw wound of bitterness was so painful that for many years I stiffened whenever I saw or heard a name ending in "ski." And I was horrified to find myself thinking automatically, "A Pole killed my father," when I heard the news in 1939 that Hitler's armies had marched into Poland. Fifteen years had passed, and yet I was reacting as if a whole people thousands of miles away were responsible for the private act of an individual here in America. The more lasting effect on me was a vulnerability to human sorrow, especially when it was the result of human violence. I totally identified with the children of John F. Kennedy, Robert F.

Kennedy, and Martin Luther King, Jr. And while I could not always suppress the violent thoughts that raged inside me, I would nevertheless dedicate my life to seeking alternatives to physical violence and would wrestle continually with the problem of transforming psychic violence into creative energy.

The effects of this experience lingered in more private ways. I developed an irrational fear of being hemmed in or struck from behind, as my father had been. I always tried to get an aisle seat when going to the theater and to sit in the last row in the movies, at church, or other public places. My father's death had left the question of hereditary insanity unanswered, and I was never entirely free from apprehension that I might go berserk and do harm to people around me. In our youth this fear hung over my family like a curse. It was small comfort to us as middle-aged adults finally to discover that our father's hospital record showed no definite indication of a major mental illness. What was noted when he was examined shortly after his admission to Crownsville State Hospital was only a diagnostic impression of "anxiety neurosis." There was further irony in the fact that fully two years before he was murdered, a Mental Status Examination indicated a state of good mental health and a fair prognosis for the immediate future, and the examiner recommended parole. It would be another half century before the American Civil Liberties Union made the nation aware of the rights of mental patients, who for so long had been forgotten.

CHAPTER 6

Separate and Unequal

OLD WHITTED HIGH SCHOOL for colored students, a wooden firetrap, burned down mysteriously the year before I entered the eighth grade, and it had to be replaced. Later the same fate overtook West End and East End, our two elementary schools, and it was rumored that the fires were not accidental but rather that the only way to get decent schools for colored children was to burn down the old buildings.

My class became the first to spend four years in the new Hillside High School, a fine, red-brick building which stood on Umstead Street at the top of Pine (now Roxboro) Street hill in the Hayti section of town. Although the state continued to spend much more money per child on white schools than on colored, our new high school was a vast improvement over any building we had previously attended. It had the freshness of new beginnings and included a large auditorium that doubled as a gym, a cafeteria, a library, science labs, playgrounds, playing fields, and all-new equipment. Our principal, Mr. W. G. Pearson, also recruited a corps of new teachers who were recent graduates of Talladega College and Howard, Fisk, and Wilberforce universities. They were young and energetic, and they brought with them advanced ideas which helped to raise our sights.

Our faculty began to institute innovations utterly new to colored high school students in our town. A traveling art exhibit visited our school, and we had a debating team, a glee club, organized baseball, boys' and girls' basketball teams, a school newspaper, and a yearbook. Chemistry and commercial courses were added to the curriculum, and an eleventh grade had been added to the previous ten grades of the colored school system. Our sports teams and debating team competed with those of other high schools in the state, and it was the first time that colored students in Durham had an opportunity to travel to other cities and expand our horizons. These modest advances were important milestones for us. They sustained our hope and gave us a sense of achievement at a time when the prevailing view that Negroes were inherently inferior remained unchallenged.

Hayti, separated from the downtown business district by the Southern Railroad tracks, was the cultural center of Durham's colored community. Along Fayetteville Street, its main thoroughfare, were the library, the two fashionable churches—White Rock Baptist and Saint Joseph A.M.E.—the Negro college, numerous colored-owned business enterprises, Lincoln Hospital, and the spacious homes of many of the leading colored families— Moores, Spauldings, Whitteds, Merricks, Pearsons, Scarboroughs, Shepards, and others. Hayti's most prominent residents included officials of the North Carolina Mutual Life Insurance Company, the Mechanics and Farmers Bank, and the Bankers Fire Insurance Company, as well as lawyers, college professors, teachers and principals, physicians, dentists, ministers, undertakers, and tradespeople. We had no lack of role models for successful business and professional careers.

Going to school in Hayti, however, presented me with the problem of status. The older Fitzgeralds had come to Durham in the Reconstruction era, before Hayti existed, and had settled in West End near clay deposits for their brickyards. Durham Station, as it was called then, was little more than a whistle stop between Greensboro and Raleigh. My aunts, mother, and older cousins were among the most popular young women of their growing community and pioneered in its cultural beginnings. They had helped organize the Volkemania Literary Club, a tennis club, and a drama group. By the time I grew up, the older Fitzgeralds had died, many of their daughters had married and moved away, and the center of social activity had shifted to Hayti. Since we did not own a car, or even a horse, we were cut off from Hayti unless we walked several miles or took the streetcar downtown, which carried us only part of the way. Our distance from the hub of cultural life and our lack of mobility made me acutely conscious of living outside the elite circle.

One day I came home and said something to Aunt Pauline about "the rich children in Hayti." It was one of the few times I ever saw her lose her temper. "Don't you ever let me hear you talking about 'rich children in Hayti' again," she stormed. "Your family stands with the best. It's not what you have but what you *are* that counts."

This was a hard lesson for me to learn. I felt very much out of things when I made the basketball team and we played night games on our home court. There was no one from our side of town to take me to the game or bring me home from the social held afterward. Aunt Pauline would not think of letting me go alone, and my basketball career hung in the balance until I convinced her to let me take my younger cousin Adeline Reynolds, who lived on old Chapel Hill Road not far from our house, with me. After we grew up, Adeline often teased me about acting as my chaperone at the age of seven.

Aunt Pauline set a stern example of not trying "to keep up with the Joneses" in other ways. She thought it was better to do without than to go into debt, and she followed this principle throughout her life. Until we saved the money to get what we wanted, we waited. We were almost the last people in our neighborhood to install inside plumbing and electricity, and Aunt Pauline was around sixty-five before she owned a car. Yet, although she never had a large income, she always had a little spare cash to help us out in an emergency. Some of her thriftiness rubbed off on me. When she gave me money for carfare to school on cold or wet days, I would plod to school on foot and save the cash toward buying a bicycle. And when I was older and on my own, I learned to convert orange crates into storage cabinets and make attractive bookshelves from plain boards and cast-off bricks.

Hillside High was nearly three miles from my house, and until I had saved enough to buy a bicycle, I walked to and from school each day. Later I sometimes got a ride in the mornings with Mrs. Mary Lawson Newby, a neighbor who drove a Ford and would drop me off on her way to teach in the county school. Her husband, the Reverend Dangerfield Newby, had been a widower and was considerably older than she was. In his seventies when I first knew him, he was a cabinetmaker by trade, tall, spare, amber-colored, with white curly hair, and almost deaf. He carried himself with great dignity and was very much respected by my family. What I did not discover until after I had gone to college was that he was the oldest son of Dangerfield Newby, the freeborn mulatto who had joined John Brown's raid and been killed at Harpers Ferry in 1859.

High school provided outlets for much of the nervous energy that had gotten me into trouble in the lower grades. Girls and boys played sandlot baseball together, and I was considered a good catcher as well as a fairly good hitter for my spindly size. I was much better at basketball, and was one of the two regular forwards on the girls' team. We practiced with the boys' team and also played boys' rules, which allowed us to move all over the court instead of being confined to fixed zones, as in girls' rules. Managing our basketball team, editing the school newspaper, and preparing for inter-high-school debates on the debating team, along with classwork and my Saturday newspaper route, kept me well occupied.

Grandmother made a down payment on a piano when I was thirteen so I could take music lessons. I began under Mrs. McCoy, who lived on Umstead Street near the high school, and although I desperately wanted to learn music, my progress was slow. Mrs. McCoy was very strict and would unnerve me by giving me a sharp rap across the fingers with her pencil whenever I made a mistake. Since I had started late, most of her pupils my age had been taking piano lessons for several years when I began. I was especially self-conscious when Mrs. McCoy gave her annual recitals and I had to appear in public playing very simple pieces in a group with students who looked half my size. About all I retained from three years of study under Mrs. McCoy was the ability to play a few simple hymns and to substitute as church organist at Saint Titus when Miss Julia Truman, our regular organist, was away.

Grandmother was eighty when her last illness came upon her. One cold afternoon during the winter after my father died, she had a hemorrhage while we were working in the backyard. I saw her drop the coal scuttle, go down on her knees, and begin vomiting blood. When we got her into the house and the doctor came, he told us she had stomach ulcers and would have to stay in bed on a diet of liquids and soft foods. By spring Grandmother was up again but still very weak.

When I left for Croom in June that year, I did not know that I would never see Grandmother again. I was gone only a few weeks when Aunt Pauline wrote that she had had a setback and was in bed again. That evening at dinner, while Aunt Sallie was discussing plans to go to Durham to see Grandmother, I suddenly got up from the table and went out on the back porch, leaving my plate untouched. I sat there alone for a long time as dusk fell, feeling awful, although I had no pain anywhere. Late that evening the message came that Grandmother had died at seven o'clock. I always believed that I had felt her spirit passing.

Then came the hardest decision of my thirteen years: not to go home for Grandmother's funeral but to stay in Croom to take care of my two small cousins so that Aunt Sallie would be able to go. I loved my grandmother more than anyone else in the world, I think. She was the one person I remember who rocked me in her arms when I was little, who called me "Baby" and petted me. Her death marked the end of my childhood.

Back home that fall, I threw myself with increased intensity into school activities to help me endure the loneliness at home without Grandmother. I was now in the tenth grade, and in addition to academic subjects I enrolled in the new commercial program, which offered typing, bookkeeping, and shorthand. Some classmates ridiculed this heavy schedule. "You're crazy to carry such a load!" "You'll flunk out!" they warned. I did not argue with them but set my jaw and immersed myself in the extra work. Instead of flunking out, I learned from that challenge that what is often called exceptional ability is nothing more than persistent endeavor.

The immediate advantage of the commercial program was that I was able to get summer employment. For several summers the North Carolina Mutual Life Insurance Company hired a number of junior and senior high school students in a crash program to type replacement schedules of policies in force. This experience provided an incentive to enter the business world, and several of my classmates made their careers in the company. The longtime advantage for me was considerable; my secretarial skills helped me earn my way through college and professional school, and knowing the rudiments of record-keeping was of enormous benefit in the management of my personal affairs.

Unfortunately, despite my heavy involvement in academic and extracurricular activities, my record in conduct never matched my scholastic performance, and eventually one of my lapses caused me to suffer a public embarrassment I never forgot. My English teacher senior year was Mrs. Louise Whitted Burton, known to be a terror; as the oldest teacher in the school, she was its unofficial vice-principal. Mrs. Burton was a member of one of Durham's old, prestigious families—her father, Mr. James Whitted, was the town's first colored postman. She had Aunt Pauline's ear, and the fact that her niece had married my cousin made me particularly vulnerable to her eagle-eyed supervision. Although I managed to avoid mishap until spring, I got embroiled in an eraser fight one day late in March when Mrs. Burton was out of the room. She returned just as I was raising my arm to fire back at an assailant, promptly reported me to my homeroom teacher, and that month's C in conduct spoiled my record.

The C would not have hurt so much if the school had not held a big ceremony during commencement week to award Certificates of Distinction to students who had excelled in scholarship, attendance, and conduct. The entire school assembled in the auditorium to witness the awards, and Mr. Pearson, the principal, called out the name of each honoree, who then walked proudly to the platform to receive the prized certificate. I felt so bad about the one low mark that kept me off the list that on the day of the ceremony I sneaked into the auditorium and sat in the last row instead of in front with my senior classmates.

Suddenly I heard Mr. Pearson call out my name. My homeroom teacher had apparently not thought one bad mark serious enough to destroy an otherwise good record and had included me on the list. But I felt sure it was a mistake and sat quite still. Other students began nudging me out of my seat, heads turned around, and finally I had no alternative but to walk to the rostrum. When I got there, Mr. Pearson smiled at me, held out a certificate with my name on it, and shook my hand. As I turned to leave the platform, I caught sight of Mrs. Burton hurrying down the aisle, an angry look on her face. She met me at the bottom step and in the presence of the stunned assembly snatched the certificate from my hand. I had to walk the entire length of the auditorium, empty-handed and publicly disgraced. Nothing which happened after that, not even the fact that I graduated first in my class and won a scholarship to attend Wilberforce University in Ohio, could erase the bitter memory of that humiliation.

Graduation from Hillside High School was not an inconsiderable achievement for the class of 1926. We had lost many members along the way, especially among the boys. Of the forty students who received diplomas, only three were male. One of our number, Hassie Vanhook, was a woman in her twenties who had had no opportunity for education when she was younger. She persevered and ultimately became one of the finest teachers in the county schools. Our class would face the Great Depression when we were scarcely out of our teens, and all our lives we would be vulnerable to poverty and ill health. When we held an impromptu fiftieth anniversary reunion in May 1976, we discovered that at least fifteen of our classmates had died. Seventeen of those still living had remained in the Durham area. Given the handicaps of segregated education in a small southern town in the 1920s, we had nevertheless managed to contribute some stalwart recruits to the cause of racial advancement and to the never-ending struggle for survival with dignity. We were part of a generation who had held body and soul together in discouraging times to create the base for spectacular racial breakthroughs in the 1950s and 1960s. Most of the graduates who settled in Durham owned beautiful homes. Many had married and their children had achieved graduate and professional degrees at major universities. Against the odds, our class had produced a number of college graduates including teachers and office workers, a confidential legal secretary, a lawyer, and two or three college professors.

Going to college after graduation from high school was not an automatic decision for me. There was no money to send me away to school, and since the Wilberforce scholarship barely covered tuition for one semester, I turned it down. Aunt Pauline's salary was among the lowest in the school system, for even though she had been teaching since she was fifteen years old, she had gone to school back in the 1880s, when Saint Augustine's offered little more than high school training, and her educational qualifications did not meet the new uniform standards. She had only a C-grade teaching certificate, in contrast to graduates from accredited colleges, who automatically got A-grade certificates. By going to summer school almost every year, she finally raised her certificate to B-grade, but before she could raise it to the maximum she had reached retirement age.

Meanwhile, on her pitifully low salary she was trying to pay off the mortgage on our homeplace, which she had bought at auction in the settlement of Grandmother's estate to prevent it from passing to strangers. The only hope for me to go to college, it seemed, was to matriculate at the North Carolina College for Negroes in Durham.

Since I was determined not to attend a segregated college, this prospect prompted my first overt stand against racial segregation. For a year I had been thinking about going to school in New York City. Aunt Pauline had taken me on my first visit there the previous summer to see Cousin Maude, who lived with her husband and three small sons in Richmond Hill, Queens. She was the oldest daughter of Grandfather Fitzgerald's sister, Agnes Clegg. We had motored north with the Reverend Eugene L. Henderson, our vicar, who had replaced the Reverend Small at Saint Titus. Reverend Henderson and his wife, Lula, were a childless couple who were very fond of me and did whatever they could to widen my horizons.

That first trip to New York had been the most exciting experience of my young life. U.S. Route 1, the main north-south highway in those days, was then a graveled washboard road for much of the way, although it was in the process of being widened and paved. To get from New Jersey to New York City we had to take a ferry across the Hudson River. I was astounded by almost everything I saw in New York, particularly the skyscrapers, the Statue of Liberty, the amusements at Coney Island, the theaters on Broadway, the double-decker buses on Fifth Avenue, and the Automat, where one could put nickels in a slot and get out dishes of hot food. Most of all I was impressed because we could sit anywhere we chose in the subway trains, buses, and streetcars, and there was no special section for colored people in the movies. I knew then that someday I would live in New York.

Aunt Pauline heard me out when I told her I did not want to go to any college in the South, that I wanted to attend Columbia University in New York City. I knew nothing about the school or its policies. I knew only that I had seen one of my favorite teachers at Hillside High—a Miss Nash—wearing a red coat sweater with a *C* on one sleeve. When I asked her what it stood for, she told me Columbia, and not realizing she meant Columbia Teachers College, I forthwith decided that Columbia University was the school for me. In keeping with her desire to let me make my own decisions, Aunt Pauline was willing to go to New York to see if anything could be worked out. So she wrote to Cousin Maude.

Here again I was the beneficiary of loving family ties. Cousin Maude thought the sun rose and set on Aunt Pauline, and she had dearly loved my mother when they were growing up together in Durham. She had three sons, then eleven, nine, and five years old, but she had longed for a daughter ever since her little Ethel, who would have been about my age, died in infancy. I think she saw in me the possibility of a surrogate daughter who would be a companion for her. She replied to Aunt Pauline's letter by inviting us to come for another visit to explore possibilities.

Cousin Maude's family lived in a two-story frame house several blocks from the Lefferts Avenue El station, the terminal point of the Brooklyn-Queens Fulton Street elevated line. Their home, separated from the neighboring house on each side by a narrow walkway, was one among blocks and blocks of similar dwellings put up during the building boom of the 1920s. Most of the home owners in the area were first- and second-generation European immigrants—Irish, German, Italian, Polish, Armenian—who had strange-sounding names. There were only two other colored families in the entire Richmond Hill area, since most colored people lived farther east in Jamaica. Cousin James, Maude's husband, was a doting spouse who left everything to "Mother." He was almost totally deaf and miraculously held on to a responsible job in a Brooklyn garage because he was able to renew his driver's license by mail without revealing his handicap. Riding with him was a scary experience, however, since he could not hear car horns, and in those days people in heavy traffic depended largely on blowing their horns to avoid collisions.

My first disappointment came when Aunt Pauline took me to the registrar's office at Columbia. Columbia did not admit women, and we were referred to Barnard College, across the street. When Aunt Pauline talked with someone in the admissions office there, it became evident that I had neither the money nor the qualifications to enter that institution. The woman at the desk looked at the transcript of my school record Aunt Pauline had brought along, and she must have seen the dejected expression on my face as we turned to go. Calling us back, she suggested that Aunt Pauline try to get me into Hunter College. She pointed out that it was a city school and that I would not have to pay tuition if I could meet entrance and residence requirements. She thought it was worth a trip over to Hunter to investigate, and wrote down directions for us to get there. Aunt Pauline thanked her and we left.

Neither of us had ever heard of Hunter College, but if it had free tuition it might solve our problem, so we found our way to the main building, at Park Avenue and Sixty-eighth Street. Hunter was not at all what I had hoped for—a residential school with a campus. Being a nonresidential school, it had no campus at all. The main building was a single structure which, with its wooden annex, covered a city block. A tiny patch of lawn at the Park Avenue end constituted its only greenery. The other end fronted on Lexington Avenue like any business building. Furthermore, Hunter was a women's college then, and I had wanted to go to a coeducational institution. To go to Hunter, it seemed to me, would be to swap segregation by race for segregation by sex. In my naïveté, I did not know that it was the largest women's college in the world, that it was dubbed "the poor girl's Radcliffe," and that its academic standards were so high it scooped off the top-level women students of New York City's high schools.

I was soon jolted into reality. The difficulties of getting into Hunter mocked my scruples. I could not meet the entrance requirements. The eleven-grade curriculum of Durham's colored schools did not provide me with sufficient high school credits, and I would need another year of English, Latin, and French as well as a formidable list of subjects I had not taken. Even to meet their admission standards would require a year and a half to two years of additional study. Also, only legal residents of New York City were eligible for admission, and since I was a minor from another state, I could not establish a legal residence on my own. Despite these barriers, however, the admissions people at Hunter did not turn us away without hope; they sat down with Aunt Pauline and worked out a curriculum of the courses I would need for admission provided she could resolve the problem of residence. They recommended that I try to complete my education in a New York City high school and receive a diploma which would be accepted automatically by Hunter College.

At first the obstacles were so disheartening that it seemed to Aunt Pauline there was nothing she could do but take me back to Durham. But the difficulties aroused my competitive spirit, and I immediately put aside initial reservations about Hunter in my determination to meet entrance requirements in *one* year if I could possibly do so. We went back and told Cousin Maude what we had learned, she talked it over with Cousin James, and they volunteered to keep me for a year and let me attend Richmond Hill High School. Later they went to the trouble of getting letters of adoption so that I could meet legal residence requirements for attendance at a free city college. Aunt Pauline arranged to pay them a small monthly sum to help out with my board. Then we went over to Richmond Hill High School to see about my admission.

In those days New York City high schools were rated among the best in the nation, and almost invariably colored children from southern schools were put back one or two grades. Knowing this, I approached Richmond Hill High with more than a little apprehension, but the principal, Matthew L. Dann, immediately put me at ease. As I think of it now, it must have been Aunt Pauline's quiet dignity and experience as a teacher that opened so many doors for us. People seemed to go out of their way to help. Incredibly, after Mr. Dann heard our story and my plan to enter

Hunter College, he arranged to have me admitted unconditionally to fourth year high school, giving me full credit for all subjects taken at Hillside High but explaining that I would have to take certain statewide Regents examinations in order to receive a diploma.

The big problem in working out a schedule of required courses for admission to Hunter was how to complete the list of subjects within a single year, since the total exceeded the maximum load I was allowed to take. Mr. Dann turned me over to an adviser, Maurice D. Hopkins, a young teacher who took a special interest in me and arranged to let me sit in on the extra courses without being formally enrolled. The understanding was that if, at the end of the year, I passed the Regents exams in these subjects with a grade of at least 75, I would receive class credit for them. So now I had been given every opportunity the school system could legally allow, and the rest was up to me.

When school opened a few weeks later, I was thrust into a strange world, the only colored person among four thousand students. My complexion and southern accent made me something of a curiosity, but I felt no hostility; in fact, the other students were very friendly, and my teachers seemed especially anxious to give me all the help possible. In spite of the pleasant atmosphere, however, I could not throw off the anxiety that dogged me during those first months. I had never competed with white children before, and however much I tried to suppress it, I could not overcome the nagging fear of failure, which I felt would be charged not to circumstances but to inherent racial inferiority. My anxiety increased when I received my first school grades. Only a few months earlier, in Durham, I had been voted the most studious member of my class and had finished with top honors. Now I had dropped to a mortifying 65 in Latin, 77 in French, and, for me, only so-so marks in other subjects. Significantly, I made high marks in physics and American history, neither of which required a foundation.

For the next several months I embarked on a regimen of round-the-clock study. I would fall asleep over my books and have a recurring nightmare that I had disgraced myself in class and was made to look stupid by being unprepared when called upon to recite. I began to realize that Cousin Maude was disappointed in me. Since her two sons of school age were doing very well in their classes, she could not understand why I had to shut myself up in my room with my books. She had hoped for a girl who would help her with the housework. She was a compulsive housekeeper who could not tolerate a speck of dust or any object out of place; her life was a continual round of sweeping, mopping, and dusting, and I was no help at all. I failed to hang up my own clothes or keep my dresser drawers in order, and Cousin Maude felt she was getting very little out of the bargain.

Through no fault of my own, I was also embarrassing to Cousin Maude's family in another very important respect. When they had moved from Brooklyn to Queens a few years earlier, only two houses stood on the block in a vast area of empty space. By the time I came to live with them, houses had been built by the dozen, and they were surrounded by white neighbors. I knew the color problem had affected members of my family in different ways. Some tried to ignore it, some did battle with it, and some tried to escape it. I don't think Cousin Maude's family had any thought of passing for white when they bought their home in Richmond Hill. They were looking for relief from the crowded city and a place where their children could play comparatively free from the hazards of city traffic. But they were so fair they blended into the new neighborhood mix and were accepted as another foreign family. They drifted into a suburban environment isolated from their former friends in Brooklyn, who found it inconvenient to make the long trip by elevated train to visit them.

It was an ambiguous situation in which their denial of their racial origins was more a matter of silence than of a contrary assertion. Although Cousin Maude was darker than the rest of her family, her beaked nose and hazel eyes gave her an indeterminate identity. When I came along, with my unmistakable yellow-brown skin, kinky-curly hair, and southern accent, the family's identity was no longer taken for granted. Although the neighbors were nice enough, Cousin Maude saw the questions in their eyes and hinted that my presence made the difference. In spite of everything she did for me, I could not help feeling that I was a stranger who had upset the delicate balance in neighborhood relationships. I kept to myself and made no friends my age on the block. My only acquaintance was little Eleanor Goldberg, several years younger than I, who lived next door and did not seem to care about my color.

This was the most difficult part of my stay with Cousin Maude. At home in Durham, Aunt Pauline had taught me pride in race and set an example in racial achievement. Her whole life had been dedicated to the development of men and women of color who would take their place in society. At Cousin Maude's I was being made to feel ashamed of my color, a message conveyed not by the outside world, as in the South, but by the members of my own family. In later years I came to realize the terrible cost of such an existence. Given the choice of passing, it was easy to drift into the anonymity of the white background and settle for self-imposed mediocrity, working at less than one's capacity. It was a life without bitter struggle, it is true, but it was also a life without an extra challenge, the incentive to excel.

My only answer to Cousin Maude's way of looking at things was to show that one need not take the easier route. I did not win any points that year as a helper in the house, but I graduated with honor, one of twenty-five students in a class of more than two hundred to do so. My grades were not good enough to be among the nine who finished with high honor, but at least I did not need to be ashamed of my record. And Cousin Maude was proud of me. I had not only done well in scholarship but had also won my chevrons in basketball.

Although the way had been opened for my admission to Hunter College, actual attendance was still far away. I had to drop out of school and work for a year. Back home in Durham, after spending the summer as janitor, typist, and reporter for the *Carolina Times,* I got a job as junior stenographer at the Bankers Fire Insurance Company on Fayetteville Street. The staff was small—about ten people in all—and the entire enterprise was carried on in one large room. Two of the senior staff members, Felicia and Catherine Miller, took a special interest in me and trained me in office procedures, filing, and the use of business machines. Felicia, the older of the two sisters and my immediate supervisor, was someone I admired tremendously although she seldom handed out compliments and rode me unmercifully when I made mistakes. I did not realize how much she thought of me until I was ready to leave for college at the end of the following summer. She had persuaded the manager to give me a raise retroactively in a lump sum, which helped greatly in meeting my initial school expenses.

While I was home that year, Bishop Delany became ill and Aunt Pauline took me to Raleigh to visit him before he died. He was confined to bed and very weak, but he seemed overjoyed to see us, and before we left we had prayers with him. During his prayers he blessed me, and later he said to me, "You are a child of destiny." Those words were to have a lasting impact on my life. As long as she lived, Aunt Pauline reminded me that I had been blessed by a bishop on his deathbed. The solemnity of this act and the prophetic quality of Bishop Delany's words would follow me through the years.

CHAPTER 7

Survival

In SEPTEMBER 1928, I returned to live with Cousin Maude in Richmond Hill and entered the freshman class of Hunter College at the Brooklyn Annex, located in a tall business building at 66 Court Street in downtown Brooklyn. It was the only carefree year I would have in college. The Brooklyn Annex drew students from the city's largest borough and from Queens, and hundreds of us rode back and forth on the Fulton Street El. Pretty soon I was one of a crowd of teenage girls who took the train every afternoon, running through the cars and letting off steam in high-pitched shrieks. The group would dwindle as the train dropped off passengers on its way to Queens, and by the time it reached the last stop, I was the only one left. We students lived great distances from one another and most of our visiting was done on the train. It was about then that I adopted Pauli as my official name.

That year I also learned to use the term "Negro." Our political science professor, Dr. Elsa de Haas, required us to read the *New York Times* daily and I discovered that the *Times* capitalized "Negro" and used it interchangeably with "colored." In the South it was always printed with the ignominious lower-case *n*. I was immediately attracted to the capitalized version, which gave dignity to my racial identity. It remains my preference for designating people of African descent, and I am uncomfortable with lower-case "black."

I made two lifelong friends that first year at Hunter—Lula Burton (later Bramwell) and Pauline Diner. Lula was the only other Negro in the freshman class at the Brooklyn Annex. In the late 1920s Negro enrollment at Hunter College was so small that there were only about a hundred of

71

us among five thousand or more students. I first met Lula in an English composition course. She was a tall, slender, olive-skinned girl with large expressive hazel eyes in a round face. Her low voice had the music and cadence of poetry even in casual conversation. She lived with her widowed mother, her grandmother, and her older sister, Gerry, in a brownstone house on Decatur Street. Gerry was as tiny as Lula was tall, but in spite of her fragile appearance she became an outstanding physician. Lula was headed for the teaching profession and became principal of one of New York City's junior high schools.

Lula's presence in the class was a great boost to my morale. She was the first Negro other than myself I had seen in a class with white students, and my conditioning in the South had been such that I still needed reassurance that Negroes could compete favorably. Lula was one of the brightest students in our class and carried her fluency in language and her knowledge of literature with unselfconscious grace. Watching the ease with which she related to other students, I began to gain confidence. Our friendship was crucial to my academic adjustment during those first months at Hunter. Although I loved to write, there were many gaps in my educational background and I was having a rough time in English composition. My weekly essays, required by our professor, Catherine Reigart, came back marked C-minus and D. I seemed to have flashes of originality, but my grammar was poor and my imagery too stilted. Unsupervised reading in childhood had left me with a limited vocabulary and only a smattering of general knowledge. Lula began to introduce me to poetry. Sitting on the front steps of her house on Decatur Street, she would read aloud from Sara Teasdale, Robert Frost, Carl Sandburg, Edna St. Vincent Millay, Lola Ridge, Carl Carmer, and other modern American poets. She also exposed me to the Harlem Renaissance through the published works of Negro poets Claude McKay, Countee Cullen, and Langston Hughes. Until then I had read only Paul Laurence Dunbar.

My English compositions improved only slightly until Miss Reigart invited Lula and me to have tea with her one weekend around Thanksgiving. My self-consciousness began to dissolve in the warm, informal atmosphere of her studio apartment, and I found myself laughing in uninhibited glee when Miss Reigart described how she had "lost her college education in the Bosporus." She was teaching at a girls' school in Turkey, and the trunk containing all her college textbooks and notebooks went down when the freighter transporting them was sunk. That visit had an amazing effect; unobtrusively, Miss Reigart had communicated to me my worth as a person quite apart from my poor academic performance. I tried harder, and my papers improved slowly but steadily. The last assignment I handed in that semester was an essay on my Grandfather Fitzgerald, and it came back marked A-minus. I got a B in the course, a victory over discouragement that I would never forget. The essay on Grandfather Fitzgerald contained the germ of my book *Proud Shoes*, published twenty-eight years later.

During the spring semester I met Pauline Diner, a diminutive girl with gentle eyes and a caring nature, who was in my German class. I have never had any aptitude for foreign languages and was completely out of my depth in a course in which bright German-Jewish students set the pace. Pauline was an excellent student in German and noticed the difficulties I was having. She also rode the Brooklyn El to school and began to coach me as we traveled back and forth on the train. I would leave home an hour earlier in the mornings and meet her on the platform of her station. We would sit on a bench as the trains clattered past while she drilled me in German verbs and vocabulary. We often followed the same routine coming home in the afternoon. Without Pauline's help I would have flunked the course; as it was, I barely squeezed through with a D. Her more lasting contribution to my growth was the appreciation she gave me for Jewish life and culture. I experienced my first seder in Pauline's home and learned then the significance of the Jewish Passover and its close relationship to the Christian Passion season. After college days I lost track of Pauline, and we did not meet again until 1974. She had gone into social work, married, had four sons, and moved to California. After nearly forty years, except for graying hair and a few wrinkles, she had not changed in appearance and her kindness still glowed in her eyes.

My life in Richmond Hill that year was still pretty isolated, and except for Lula and Pauline I had no visitors my age. On Sundays I attended All Saints Episcopal Church with Cousin Maude's family and sang in the choir. The rector, the Reverend Henry Armstrong, was a graduate of General Theological Seminary, and All Saints Church was strongly Anglo-Catholic. With my "low church" background it took me quite a while to get used to the "high church" liturgy—the chants, incense, bells, and elaborate vestments—but I grew to love the pageantry without any understanding of its sacramental significance.

The opportunity to leave Richmond Hill and strike out on my own came in the spring of my freshman year, when Cousin Susie Elliott came out to visit us. I felt especially close to Cousin Susie because she was another link with my parents. As a teenage girl in Baltimore, she had often stayed with them and helped take care of the children. She remembered my mother as a sympathetic young matron in whom she could confide her affairs of the heart, and her love for "Miss Agnes" continued in a strong maternal feeling for the Murray children. After Cousin Susie graduated from Pratt Institute she taught home economics in various institutions, including the Negro college in Durham where she was teaching when I was a small child. Some of the happiest times of my childhood were the occasional weekends Aunt Pauline let me spend with her on campus. She was now house director of the Emma Ransom residence at the West 137th Street YWCA in Harlem.

Cousin Susie must have sensed my loneliness at Cousin Maude's, and during her visit casually asked if I would like a job as relief girl on the Y switchboard and elevator one night a week. The work shift ran from five o'clock to midnight, and I could sleep over in her apartment and take the subway to school in Brooklyn next morning. I jumped at the chance to escape from dull routine, and within a few weeks after taking the relief job I moved to the Harlem YWCA and commuted to Brooklyn for the rest of the school term. Fortunately, I landed a full-time position working afternoons and evenings as dishwasher and steam table runner in the Y cafeteria, which paid expenses and tided me over the summer. I think Cousin Maude was as relieved as I was over the change.

That summer at the YWCA was a heady experience for an eighteen-year-old—no schoolwork to burden me, no accounting to anyone for my goings and comings, no restraints on time as long as I was in by midnight, and a whole city to explore in my free hours. When Cousin Susie left during the summer to head the Home Economics Department of Tuskegee Institute, I was fully on my own. With a bicycle borrowed from the Y recreation director, I rode all over Manhattan—up to the Cloisters, down Riverside Drive along the Hudson River, through Central Park, down Fifth Avenue to Washington Square and Greenwich Village, to Battery Park and South Ferry, and along Delancey and Orchard streets on the Lower East Side. During those adventures I got knocked off the bicycle five times in traffic, but miraculously I escaped serious injury and the bike was not damaged.

My room at the Y was on the fourth floor rear, facing the back windows of the Abyssinian Baptist Church, whose young assistant minister at the time was the future congressman Adam Clayton Powell, Jr. Although I attended Saint Philip's Episcopal Church on West 134th Street, I found myself in partial attendance at Abyssinian as well: whenever I was in my room during their church services, the choir and organ so filled the room that I had to stop whatever I was doing to listen.

Living at the Y brought me into association with other young women who were working and going to school, and it supplied the warm friendships one missed by not attending a residential college. At the same time, close contact with Y leaders and professionals gave me role models in the pursuit of excellence: white-haired, youthful Cecilia Cabaniss Saunders, the executive director of the West 137th Street branch, whose leadership and efficient management had attracted a top-notch staff; Anna Arnold Hedgeman, the membership secretary, who moved on to pioneer in politics and public administration; Margaret Douglas, a teacher and summer camp director, who was the first Negro woman to become assistant superintendent in the New York City public schools; Viola Lewis Waiters, who transferred her YWCA experience to the problems of working women in industry as a consultant to management during World War II; Dorothy Height, who followed the tradition of Mary McLeod Bethune as president of the influential National Council of Negro Women, becoming an important force in national affairs. And there were many others. None of these women would have called themselves feminists in the 1930s, but they were strong, independent personalities who, because of their concerted efforts to rise above the limitations of race and sex and to help younger women do the same, shared a sisterhood that foreshadowed the revival of the feminist movement in the 1960s.

There was also a spiritual dimension in these associations which contributed to my growth. I recall a single encounter that made a lifelong impression. One night while I was running the elevator, a tall woman, perhaps thirty years old, whom I had never seen before got on and gave her floor number. As she got off she handed me a small case containing a pocket-sized comb exquisitely painted in a Japanese design. "I'd like to offer you a little present," she said without introduction. "You see, I just lost my temper downstairs, and whenever I lose my temper I must do penance," she explained. "I want someone to have something I cherish very much." She flashed me a lovely smile and was gone before I could recover from my astonishment. I learned later that she was Juliette Derricotte, National Student Secretary for the YWCA and a former delegate to the convention of the World's Student Christian Federation. Before I had a chance to speak to her again, she left New York to become dean of women at Fisk University, but I never forgot the touch of greatness in her gesture to a stranger. Two years later she was in an automobile accident in the South and died while being carried to a Negro hospital miles away. The local white hospital had refused to give her emergency treatment.

When I began my sophomore year in September 1929 at the Thirty-second Street Annex of Hunter College, I was working after school on West Forty-sixth Street as a dinner waitress in one of the Alice Foote MacDougall restaurants. They were famous for their colorful Italian or Spanish decor, their coffee, and their broiled half chicken or filet mignon dinners. We worked a five-hour shift six nights a week for a weekly wage of four dollars exclusive of tips. Except for its executives and its hostesses and cashiers, the chain was entirely staffed by Negroes, and like other downtown restaurants in those days it drew the color line. Once when a

Negro couple was refused service the entire kitchen crew and waitress staff walked out in a spontaneous protest, but the policy did not change. The color line extended to our own meals. White hostesses and cashiers were served in the dining room from the regular menu; we ate on bare tables in the basement and were given leftovers so tasteless we invariably threw them into the garbage can. If we ate at all on the job, it was because of our skill in ordering an extra chicken dinner and stealing it from the tray between kitchen and dining room without getting caught.

In spite of racial humiliations, the dinner job was considered a boon for working students. The popular menu and efficient service drew long waiting lines of theatergoers, and when I began working there, tips were good. However, after the stock market crashed in October 1929, I became one of those marginal workers who felt the first shocks of the Depression. The long waiting lines soon dwindled and tips fell off. One might work all evening without earning a cent and so have to borrow carfare to get home. My weekly wage was insufficient to cover room rent at the YWCA, and often I had to deposit my weekly pay at the Y desk on Saturday night, then make up the balance in dribs and drabs from meager tips, reserving only ten cents each night for coffee and carfare to school next morning. After school I would walk to work and have my first meal of the day—coffee and a handful of tea sandwiches one of the afternoon waitresses had managed to sneak off her tray and save for me.

By the end of my sophomore year I had lost fifteen pounds and was suffering from malnutrition, and things continued to grow worse. That fall I was laid off from the restaurant and had to stop school to look for work. With so many thousands of people unemployed in New York City alone, finding a job that would even cover bare living expenses was almost impossible. Downtown along Sixth Avenue (now the Avenue of the Americas), storefront employment offices were besieged by hundreds of men scrambling for a half-dozen jobs posted in hastily scrawled handwriting on a bulletin board out front, only to be erased seconds later. Seldom were any jobs posted for women. For a short time I worked as a typist for fifty cents an hour at the headquarters of the Congregational and Christian Churches, but this source of income soon dried up. Although I had no experience in household work, I was so desperate I tried a position as part-time housekeeper for a professional woman who lived in a studio apartment in Greenwich Village. My major responsibility was to prepare and serve her dinner, for which she supplied the menu. After she tasted my first meal, she paid me for the day and let me go.

Until that fall I had given no thought to marriage. Then I met Billy, a young man who was also a stranger in New York trying to work and go to school. He earned a pittance as caretaker of a women's residence and slept in the basement where he worked. We were drawn together by our mutual loneliness and rootlessness, sharing whatever small pleasures we could find that did not cost money. When matters began to get serious and my straitlaced upbringing was a barrier to premarital sex, we got married secretly, fearing I would lose my room at the Y if our marriage became known. We were both twenty at the time, and Billy lied about his age in order to get the marriage license, saying he was twenty-four.

It was a dreadful mistake. We were so poor that we spent our honeymoon weekend in a cheap West Side hotel. Both of us were sexually inexperienced, and the bleak atmosphere aggravated our discomfiture. We had no money to begin housekeeping and no place where we could meet in privacy. After several months of mounting frustration, we gave up in despair. Billy left the city, and some years later we had the marriage annulled.

Around that time a job suddenly materialized in a downtown office through a peculiar circumstance. The Y employment bureau received a telephone call from The Open Road, Inc., a travel agency at 11 West Forty-second Street. The agency would like to hire "an intelligent colored girl" as switchboard operator and stenographer, but wanted to hear her voice over the telephone before interviewing her. The salary was twenty dollars a week, five dollars more than I had ever earned. The agency was apparently satisfied with my telephone voice and employed me without interviewing anyone else. Such hiring was unique in the early thirties; clerical jobs for Negro women in downtown white business firms were virtually nonexistent.

The experiment lasted only a few months. In an economy move, The Open Road merged with World Tourist Agency, a group that arranged tours to the Soviet Union, and when the merger was completed I was out of work again. Those few months on my employment record were sufficient, however, to create difficulties for me years later in a federal security clearance check. Although I knew almost nothing about the agency beyond answering the telephone and taking occasional correspondence, the FBI apparently suspected it of Communist leanings and raised insinuating questions about my association with it.

Losing the job at The Open Road was the last straw in a series of disappointments. My goal to save money and return to school seemed further away than ever. I needed a change of luck and began thinking of hitchhiking to California to make a fresh start. Since I had already done some hitchhiking in New England with a friend, Dorothy Hayden, the potential dangers of traveling alone across the continent did not occur to me.

Fortunately, I got to California that spring without having to hitchhike.

A friend of Dorothy Hayden's who had driven to New York was returning home to Vallejo and was glad to take me along to help with the driving. Leaving my few belongings in Dorothy's care, I started out blithely with only a few dollars and no idea what I would do when I reached the Coast. We crossed the country on U.S. Route 30, and although the trip was recklessly conceived, my discovery of the changing face of the vast United States soon dwarfed the troubles I had left behind. Each hour was filled with wonderment over the miles of flatland with their oceans of waving green wheat, the breathtaking mountain passes in the Rockies, the thousands of sheep clogging the highway in Utah as herdsmen drove them to their spring feeding grounds, and the silence of the Great Salt Lake Desert. Before we reached California I had scribbled what became my first published poem, "Song of the Highway."

The attempt to begin a new life in California did not survive my arrival in Vallejo, where I was to stay a few days with my friend's family. A letter from Aunt Pauline, forwarded from New York, was waiting for me and brought me back to reality. She had written that she was ill, and since I was not in school she wanted me to come home to Durham as soon as possible. I had not told her of my plan to go to California for fear she would veto it, and now I had to wire her revealing my financial predicament. Aunt Pauline wired back that she had no money for my return fare. It was typical of her to let me take the consequences of my choices even though she was worried almost out of her mind, as she told me later. I realized I would have to extricate myself from this scrape through my own efforts and that cross-country traveling, which at first had seemed a lark, was now an awesome necessity: awesome because the immense expanse of the continent I had seen was no longer an appealing prospect for hitchhiking. As I recalled those long stretches of deserted highway where farms were miles apart and we seldom saw another car, the thought of being stranded alone was unnerving. At best, hitchhiking was unpredictable and I had no idea how long it would take to get back to New York.

My hosts finally suggested that if I had the guts to try it, I could ride fast freights going east and make the trip in about two weeks. Hopping freights was a more terrifying thought than thumbing rides on a lonely road. I had never forgotten a gruesome experience in Durham when I was a sixth grader. We schoolchildren had sneaked into the freight yards and were walking along the tracks looking for lumps of tar to chew, when we came upon a burlap sack covering the decapitated body of a man who had just been killed by a moving train. His brains were strewn along the roadbed.

The urgency of getting home finally overruled my dread, and less than a week after arriving in Vallejo I set out for the Southern Pacific Railroad freight yards in Oakland. I did not know in that spring of 1931 that I was about to join an estimated 200,000 to 300,000 homeless boys—and a smattering of girls—between the ages of twelve and twenty, products of the Depression, who rode freights or hitchhiked from town to town in search of work. Thousands lived in "jungles" near railroad tracks, constituting the "tragic army" which aroused the alarm of the Children's Bureau, U.S. Department of Labor, and created a national problem which eventually led to the establishment of the Civilian Conservation Corps. These young people were part of a larger army of nearly three million homeless unemployed men who also rode the rails and lived in jungles. One railroad official reported that some ten thousand transients per month were traveling through the Southern Pacific freight yards in 1931. In the same year, 831 were killed on the arterial highways and dozens met their deaths under freight trains.

It was well for me that I was ignorant of these conditions and also that my sex was not immediately apparent to the hundreds of rough men and boys I encountered during the trip. I carried a small knapsack containing minimum camping equipment, and my attire—scout pants and shirt, knee-length socks, walking shoes, and a short leather jacket—together with my slight figure and bobbed hair made me appear to be a small teenage boy like thousands of others on the road. No one questioned me about my gender and I soon discovered that my boyish appearance was a protection. Also, a single-mindedness that has often led me to overlook obvious difficulties and make costly mistakes was in this case beneficial. The imperative of getting home made me ignore hazards which upon sober reflection would have forced me to abandon the journey.

Hoboes faced the ever-present risk of being shot by armed railroad guards in the big railroad divisions where the freight trains were assembled. When the long trains pulled out of the yards, we had to choose between two dangers. If we ignored the guards who shouted warnings to stay off the train as they ran along the walkways on top of the cars, we became targets for their bullets. If we waited for them to get off, the train had picked up such speed that we risked being thrown under the wheels trying to swing onto a fast-moving boxcar. Another hazard was the fierce cold of windy nights, which forced us to try to keep warm by riding too close to the engine, in the path of hot cinders that blew back upon us. One night the only shelter from the wind I could find was on a flatcar loaded with bridge timber. I crawled into a crevice covered by long wooden beams and went to sleep. Next morning I discovered that the heavy beams shifted every time the train lurched and this shifting had provided my crevice; a strong enough lurch would have dislodged some of the heaviest beams and crushed me to death.

Crossing the country, I learned to ride cattle trains, fruit-butter-and-egg trains, "hot shots" (fast express freights), and "manifestos" (nonstop express freight trains). When refrigerator cars carried citrus fruit, the narrow ice chests, or "reefers," at each end of the car were left empty. The hobo's haven was an open reefer which could be entered through the small trapdoor at the top of the empty ice chamber. The upraised door was held by a jack, and if one was small enough to wriggle through the opening one could slither down inside the steel-plated cell floored with wooden slats and ride in comfort out of sight of railroad "bulls."

Along with a thin migrant worker called "Oklahoma," I managed to scramble down into one of these empty cells, and we rode across the desert and through the mountains for eighteen hours. We had no food or water with us, but the car was carrying crates of oranges, and our hunger and thirst drove us to explore every inch of our cell for an opening to the fruit. We loosened the slats on the floor of our compartment, worked our fingers underneath the partition and through to the crates on the other side. Oklahoma succeeded in ripping open the end of a crate, I stuck my hand through, and after much scraping and bruising reached the oranges. We collected fifteen apiece, quartered them with our knives, and gobbled them down. When we finished, we covered our theft by wrapping the peelings in the tissue covers and throwing them out the trapdoor over the side of the car. I did not know until later that if the steel jack had collapsed and the trapdoor fallen, we would have been sealed inside. People were known to starve to death in sealed ice chests because no one knew they were there and they could not make themselves heard.

The one time my sex proved to be an advantage was near the end of the trip, two days away from New York. I had caught a train alone, spent the night inside an open reefer, and awakened next morning to find the train standing still. I climbed out, right into the arms of a yard policeman who had taken his position on top of the car I was riding in without knowing I was there. I told him my hard-luck story about getting home, which he seemed to believe. But he did not believe I was female and sent for a woman officer to examine me. When he was finally satisfied, he escorted me back to the reefer and cautioned me to stay hidden until the train reached its termination point in the Jersey City yards.

Incredibly, aside from being banged against the sides of boxcars a few times when hopping onto moving freights, I made the trip without a single unpleasant experience and in only ten days. Later I shuddered when reading news accounts of a girl who had lost her legs under the wheels of a freight and of a man who survived six days in a refrigerator car without food or water and within sight of crates of fruit he could not reach. I learned also that around the same time I was riding freights, nine Negro boys were taken off a freight in Scottsboro, Alabama, and charged with raping two white female hoboes who were riding on the same train. I believed that Aunt Pauline's prayers helped to bring me through safely, just as years later I believed her prayers helped me through my bar examinations.

Twenty-four days after leaving New York, I arrived back at Dorothy Hayden's apartment, so cinder-blackened that I resembled a chimney sweep. It took three successive soakings in a hot bath to get me clean.

CHAPTER 8

Making It Through College

THE harrowing trip from California was shock therapy for me. The national toll caused by unemployment, which I glimpsed in the faces of hordes of men and boys who haunted freight yards and lived in hobo jungles, and the struggle for survival I had experienced briefly on the road, made my own problems seem comparatively mild. The adventure was one I never wanted to repeat, but at least it had satiated my wanderlust and now my sole objective was to finish college.

Miraculously, my fortunes improved. Aunt Pauline's health was not nearly as bad as I had imagined it to be three thousand miles away, and that summer of 1931 I landed a job as waitress at the Montauk Hotel on the oceanfront in Asbury Park, New Jersey. To save the expense of room rent I slept on a cot in the laundry room at the hotel and banked my weekly wage of ten dollars together with most of my tips. By the end of the summer I had accumulated $165, which seemed like a huge sum at the time but quickly melted away after I had repaid some loans and bought clothes for school.

Back in New York, I was lucky enough to meet Louise E. Jefferson, a talented young commercial art student from Washington, D.C., who was taking courses at Hunter and looking for a roommate to share expenses. Lou was small, birdlike, and incredibly efficient, with a sharp tongue and rapier wit. She had had polio as a child, and her legs were badly crippled, but she was able to walk without braces and was one of the most agile people I ever knew. Her dogged determination to overcome a physical handicap had made her a local swimming champion and certified lifeguard, and her dedication to her craft had made her a professional artist at the age of twenty-four.

I got a job waiting on tables at another of the Alice Foote MacDougall restaurants. Lou's main source of income when we met was a standing assignment from the West 137th Street branch of the YWCA to make posters as needed to advertise Y activities. We found a furnished room with two cots for six dollars a week in an apartment above a funeral parlor near the Y, and I was in high spirits when I began my junior year at the Sixty-eighth Street building of Hunter College. Three weeks after school began, however, I lost the waitress job and had exactly $2.50 left of my savings, not even enough to pay my share of the week's rent. In desperation, I hurried down to see Harriet L. Loewenstein, the kind, motherly woman who directed Hunter's Bureau of Occupations. Mrs. Loewenstein's optimism and cordial manner helped to dispel my panic. She kept on her wall a motto which impressed me deeply. It read: "No work is dirty save that which soils the soul."

Mrs. Loewenstein beamed when she learned I had secretarial experience and told me she had a few openings for clerical work at the college. She placed me in the Journalism Office, where I worked part time for six dollars a week. Lou and I agreed that my wage would be allocated to our rent so that we could be assured of shelter. For food and other expenses we depended upon Lou's somewhat irregular flow of assignments from the Y. Kindness from another source also helped tremendously. From time to time Miss Mattison, assistant to the dean at Hunter, called me into her office, where she kept a stock of clothing donated by faculty members to assist needy students. She let me take my pick of attractive skirts, suits, and sweaters, and for the remainder of my career at Hunter I was well dressed.

Lou and I managed to weather those two years by scrimping and pinching, sometimes going without meals and walking most places we had to go uptown. But we had the resiliency of youth, and most of the young people we knew were no better off. The Great Depression was felt by Negroes in Harlem at least a year before the stock market crash of 1929. By 1930, one out of every five workers there was unemployed. Negro women domestic workers were so desperate to earn money they would stand on a street corner in the Bronx dubbed the "Bronx Slave Market" and sell their labor to white women as day workers for as little as ten cents an hour. (As late as 1940, three out of every five black women workers were engaged in household employment.) By the end of 1932, an estimated million and a half Negroes in the nation were jobless. Of those who were employed, less than 5 percent earned two thousand dollars a year or more, compared with 25 percent of all white workers. By 1935,

42 percent of the nonwhite population in New York City was on relief.

We were living in the heart of Harlem's Black Belt, where close to 200,000 people were crowded into an area of approximately two hundred city blocks. Robert G. Weaver's study *The Negro Ghetto* estimated that in 1930, over 40 percent of the Negro families in Harlem had to take in from one to four lodgers to pay their rent. Our landlady, Mrs. West, had three young male roomers in addition to us, and this put a strain on bathroom and kitchen facilities. To avoid traffic jams, we had to plan our meals and baths very carefully. The kitchen was our biggest problem, but we solved it by buying food in small amounts, cooking at odd hours, and eating in our room. When we could afford to we ate out. Lou earned seventy-five cents for each poster she made for the Y, and when business was good— four or five posters a week—we splurged and went across the street to the Monterey Luncheonette, where we could get a blue-plate dinner of broiled mackerel, french fried potatoes, lettuce and tomatoes, hot biscuits and butter, for thirty-five cents each. One poster allowed us to have dinner and leave a nickel tip. When business was slow we were often reduced to a meal of hominy grits and butter, seasoned with salt purloined from the landlady's kitchen. Once we had to live on hominy grits for a week, until Lou got another order for a poster.

There were bright spots mixed with the hard times. We loved to ramble through the secondhand bookshops on Fourth Avenue and often spent our food money on a book of poetry or an old art magazine. Occasionally we scraped together enough cash to go to the theater downtown, but our regular amusement was going to the Apollo Theater on West 125th Street, where we could sit in the balcony for twenty-five cents and see the great Negro entertainers in the heyday of their youth—Ethel Waters, Jackie (Moms) Mabley, the one-legged dancer Peg Leg Bates, tap dancers Pete, Peaches, and Duke, comedian Galley de Gaston, and the great bands led by such extraordinary musicians as Duke Ellington and Cab Calloway.

Sharing a room with Lou Jefferson was an important formative experience for me. Her passion for order, her precision in her work, and her deliberateness were steadying influences on one inclined to be harum-scarum and impulsive. Some years later Lester B. Granger of the National Urban League, writing of the only Negro art director and production assistant in the American publishing industry, said of her:

Young Negro Americans who . . . bemoan their lack of opportunity would never enjoy the company of Louise E. Jefferson—nor even receive her sympathy. Jaunty to the point of "cockiness," restlessly energetic, a perfectionist in everything she does or tries to do, Louise Jefferson, in the course of less than a dozen years, has nonchalantly stepped over barrier after barrier marked "it can't be done" and attained a distinctive place in the publishing field in New York City. . . . Miss Jefferson must, first of all, be an artist. . . . Her associates will not think of her as "a Negro artist," nor will she think of herself as "an unusual Negro." She will accept the challenge of her responsibility. She will do her job as best she knows how and that best will be good indeed, for Lou Jefferson is an artist at doing her best.

In those days I accepted the burden of race as something to be endured because there seemed little one could do about it. Although I was acutely aware of the help-wanted newspaper columns that advertised jobs for "White Only," "Colored," or even "Light Colored Girls," unemployment and poverty were so widespread that I did not associate my precarious economic condition with racial discrimination. The cosmopolitan atmosphere of New York City was freer than anything I had known in the South, but there were sharp reminders of inferior status. On those rare occasions when I could afford to go downtown to the theater, my seat was likely to be behind a post or way off to the side. Outside Harlem, service to Negroes in places of public accommodation was always uncertain; even on 125th Street in Harlem, Child's Restaurant refused to serve Negroes until lawsuits were brought in the 1930s. Whenever I went with my college classmates to a soda fountain on Third Avenue near Sixty-eighth Street, I sat tense with apprehension, never assured that I would be served until a glass of water or a menu was placed in front of me.

My one bad experience with race at Hunter College was a year-long American history course. I was the only Negro in the class, and as far as my professor was concerned I did not exist. She was not openly insulting, but she never once suggested that colored people played any role in the nation's development other than as abject objects of the national controversy over slavery. Her treatment of slavery, the Civil War, and Reconstruction made me shrivel in my seat in the back row, feeling shame and resentment. I knew from my own family history that her presentation was one-sided but was too unsure of myself to challenge her in class. Unable to mount an effective protest against her bias, I performed so indifferently in the course that I got only passing grades in a subject in which I had always excelled. That ordeal, however, spurred me to become a passionate student of Negro history after leaving college.

The experience also led me to take my first tentative steps toward activism. Distressed over the general invisibility of Negro students at Hunter and the scant attention given to Negro life in our courses, I began to discuss the problem with another student, Elizabeth McDougald, whom I admired greatly and whose mother, Gertrude Ayers, became the first Negro principal in New York City's public school system. Betty was strikingly tall and regal-looking, knowledgeable, self-assured, and she had great leadership ability. After informal talks with other Negro students, she drafted a plan for an organization intended to create greater self-awareness among the Negro students at Hunter through the study of Negro culture and achievements. The group would hold weekly discussions, and membership would be open to the entire student body. Our modest plan would seem tame indeed to a generation of militants in the late 1960s, who took over college buildings to dramatize their demand for Black Studies. We had neither the numerical strength nor the political climate to support a proposal that our legitimate concerns become part of the school's curriculum, but in 1932 our groping efforts were a beginning, a radical step for those times.

Our plan alarmed some of the leading white students, who feared that a separate organization would reflect adversely upon Hunter's reputation as an inclusive institution. The largest and most active organization in public affairs, International Student, which was affiliated with the National Students League of America, came forward with a counterproposal, an interracial plan. Betty McDougald and I were selected to meet with their leaders in the spring of 1932 to discuss the alternative proposals. They recommended that instead of creating a new organization, the Negro students incorporate their program into that of International Student, which would undertake a special "study of the social and cultural as well as the political status of the Negro" through "special readings, bibliographies, historical surveys, [and] the securing of the best Negro speakers, writers, economists, and social workers." The program would be launched in the fall semester, would take the form of weekly discussions, and would follow the syllabus outlined in Betty's proposal. International Student's executive board would be enlarged to include Negro students.

Both plans were presented to the Negro students as well as to the executive board of International Student for consideration. Betty McDougald had strong misgivings about a joint venture because she was aware of the struggles for power within International Student between members of the Young People's Socialist League and the Young Communist League, and she feared that our program would become a political football between warring factions. I had no political experience and was inclined to go along with the interracial approach, which was ultimately accepted. I graduated just after the program got under way at the end of the fall term, but I learned later that Betty's fears were justified and the Negro students eventually withdrew from International Student to set up their own program.

Meanwhile I had begun to focus on my long-simmering ambition to become a writer. The English Department, then headed by Dr. Blanche

Colton Williams, was considered elite and carefully screened all applicants for the English major. My academic record was so spotty that I barely made the grade point average required for admission to the English Department in my junior year. A C grade in the history of English literature was typical of my uneven performance. Although capable of making A's in courses that permitted the exercise of imagination, I had found the survey course unexciting. Being an English major, however, brought me into contact with Hunter's most articulate students and leading writers and stimulated my own efforts to write.

In the last term of my senior year, I was elected to Sigma Tau Delta, a national professional English fraternity, and I received a tremendous boost that semester when Ruth M. Goldstein, associate editor of the college magazine, *Echo*, invited me to contribute and accepted for publication in the Christmas 1932 issue my article "A Working Student." Lou Jefferson broke through in the same issue with cover and frontispiece illustrations. Ruth Goldstein was one of the most brilliant young women in my class. She was a member of Phi Beta Kappa, an acknowledged leader in publications and drama, and she graduated summa cum laude in June 1933. While my job and studies kept me from getting to know her well, I was aware of her warm sympathy and encouragement. After my graduation we lost contact for forty years, and during that time Ruth never knew how much she had contributed to my writing career in its infancy. True to her calling, she had gone on to become a teacher of English, nurturing among her students future poets, writers, and actors whom she first encountered in New York City's high schools. We finally found one another in 1974 through a clipping about me someone had sent on to Ruth, who was then retired and living in Florida.

Although my tight working schedule at Hunter gave me little time to develop friendships with students who were not in my English classes, Edna Lisle, a science major, was an exception. We met accidentally because we happened to have neighboring lockers, and a spontaneous relationship grew out of our hurried conversations when our paths crossed before we dashed off to class or to work. Under Edna's influence I took an introductory course in anthropology with Dr. Dorothy L. Keur, a young professor about whom Edna was wildly enthusiastic. I look back upon that course as the crucial academic experience of my college days because it gave me a new perspective on my multiracial heritage. Dr. Keur required us to make weekly field trips to the American Museum of Natural History, and through the exhibits of African and American Indian villages I began to see the non-European strains of my ancestry as part of the great human drama of existence on earth. Anthropology gave me some understanding of human development, supplied me with an antidote to the poisonous notion of superior and inferior races, and enabled me to appreciate the infinitely rich variety of human cultures.

Edna was a blond, blue-eyed Caucasian, and while our friendship made all racial barriers seem ridiculous, once beyond the boundaries of school we had to accept the painful reality that we inhabited different worlds. Edna learned that the downtown YWCA had openings for college girls as summer waitresses at Summit Lake, a Y camp, and suggested that we apply. We knew, of course, that the YWCA maintained two camps in Bear Mountain Park—Summit Lake for white women and Fern Rock for Negro women—but it never occurred to us that the hired help was also segregated. Edna was accepted but I was turned down after a soul-searching meeting of the Y board and staff, who decided the time was not ripe to take such an unusual step. This unexpected blow coming from the YWCA hurt more keenly than a rejection from a commercial business that made no pretense to having ideals.

Fortunately, we had better luck at school when Edna graduated before me and recommended me as her replacement to run the Hunter College switchboard in the evenings. The job was a godsend because it paid eleven dollars a week, almost twice what I was then earning.

Looking back on those days at Hunter, I realize how much we lived in a segregated world of women while at school and how little intellectual and social interaction we had with our young male contemporaries. Yet there were certain compensating factors that I learned to appreciate in time. Hunter's tradition for excellence was so strong that in later years I was surprised to find how often I could recognize a Hunter-trained woman by the thoroughness with which she approached her work. Less obvious was the fact that the school was a natural training ground for feminism. Having a faculty and a student body in which women assumed leadership reinforced our egalitarian values, inspired our confidence in the competence of women generally, and encouraged our resistance to subordinate roles.

Toward the end of my junior year I flirted briefly with a project that seemed to be the opportunity of a lifetime. A group of young Negro intellectuals from the United States was being invited to the Soviet Union to make a film depicting Negro life in America. To be called "Black and White," it would undoubtedly be a powerful propaganda weapon against racial discrimination. The project attracted a number of prominent young Negroes from Harlem whom I knew, among them Mildred Jones, a newspaperwoman, reporters Ted Poston and Henry Lee Moon, the poet Langston Hughes, and Loren Miller, a future judge in California. The group was to depart in June after my classes were over and I could join it if I could raise initial expenses of approximately $150. It was a tempting proposition, especially since communism was beginning to attract Negro intellectuals, and a visit to Russia offered a chance to see the social experiment in action. After an inner struggle I decided not to go, because I had at least another semester in school and feared that I would never complete college if I allowed one more interruption.

Although I was downcast over forgoing the trip, it turned out to be a wise decision. Some three months after the group of twenty-two Negroes arrived in the Soviet Union, the film project was abandoned, leaving them stranded. The group split into pro-Communist and anti-Communist factions. Ted Poston and Henry Lee Moon charged in a signed article published in the United States that the film was abandoned, in their words,

> ... upon demand of certain American business interests desirous of establishing accord between the U.S.S.R. and the United States. . . . These interests declared that the production of such a film would be viewed in America as "meddling in internal affairs" and stated the action might retard recognition of the Soviet Union by the American government and influence the latter's position in the Far East situation.

Poston and Moon promptly left Russia and were back in the United States four months after they had departed on their hopeful odyssey. Langston Hughes, on the other hand, stayed on for almost a year, and the remaining members of the group slowly drifted back to the United States.

Ted Poston had been my idol among young writers in Harlem since I first met him when I was twenty and he wrote under his own byline for the *Pittsburgh Courier,* an accomplishment that made him a deity in my eyes. He was tall, lanky, and dark-skinned, with huge ears, full, sensitive lips, and eyes that smiled but hinted sadness. His self-deprecating wit and infectious sense of humor masked his deep compassion, and his graceful prose never failed to catch the human drama in the news stories he wrote. I foolishly asked him once if being so dark wasn't a great handicap. But although Ted never pitied himself, he sometimes betrayed his sorrow when telling an uproariously funny tale about his adventures in a voice that ran the scale from high-pitched laughter to a whisper that was half sob.

Ted was so chained to deadlines that we had to develop a lunch counter friendship. If he saw me in the Monterey Luncheonette, he would whiz in for a cup of coffee between assignments and we would twirl on our stools, chatting a few minutes, before he rushed away. His almost fatherly interest in my writing efforts masked his need for time to work on his own short stories. When we first met, he wrote a short verse about the occasion for his news column, expressing the pathos of feeling old because "she was only twenty while I was twenty-four." The undercurrent of sadness I sensed in Ted's personality foreshadowed his future career. He became one of the "lonely firsts," the first black reporter and editorial writer on a white metropolitan daily newspaper. For more than three decades he covered the turbulent civil rights struggle for the *New York Post,* while the creative talent that sparkled in his whimsical short stories about his childhood in Hopkinsville, Kentucky, was never permitted to flower.

Some time after Ted returned from Russia he introduced me to Maysie Stone, a talented sculptor who had just completed a bust of him. Maysie's family had a Russian background of Socialist tradition. She spoke the language fluently and was an informed critic of Soviet communism. When she was not working with clay, she assisted her father, Dr. Nahum Stone, with the translation of Russian documents, including a book for Columbia University. Maysie's studio was on the top floor of a five-story commercial building with a creaky elevator at 96 Fifth Avenue. The building also had a second entrance, at 2 West Fifteenth Street. Maysie seemed more at home there, surrounded by her clay figures, than she did in the apartment she shared with her father uptown near Columbia University. The studio had a northern skylight, workbenches, and shelves for her art materials, and she had furnished it with a daybed, a coffee table, a two-burner gas stove, some chairs, and a few of her cherished books.

Maysie was looking for a model who could sit during daylight hours, and she said she would love to do a bust of me if I could spare the time. I was impressed with the head she had modeled of Ted; she had caught the essence of his personality, and Ted in clay seemed as alive as Ted in the flesh. Since I would be graduating soon and my days would be free, I readily consented. Maysie seemed amused at my brash naïveté when I added that I knew all artists were temperamental but was prepared to put up with it.

It turned out to be the reverse, and Maysie had to exercise great patience with me, for I was a fidgety model. It was sheer agony to sit motionless for any length of time, and we had to take frequent breaks. During the spring and summer of 1933 I sat for Maysie two or three times a week while she slowly produced what she called "The Girl of a Thousand Faces." She told me that I was one of the most difficult subjects she had ever tried to sculpt; my face was so mobile and my expressions changed so rapidly she often had to tear down what she had done and begin all over again.

The slow evolution of the clay from what resembled an emaciated stocking-masked bandit to a recognizable portrait mirrored our growing friendship. Our mutual enthusiasm for Ted was an enduring bond, but we also shared a love of poetry and literature. Maysie had a marvelous imagination and a wonderful gift for storytelling, and she punctuated her accounts with quotations from her favorite authors. She introduced me to the Uncle Remus stories, mimicking the various animals in hilarious dialect. Until that time I had steadfastly refused to read or listen to anything about Uncle Remus because I considered the stories a takeoff on Negro speech; I'd never asked myself why I accepted so readily Paul Laurence Dunbar's poems in dialect while rejecting Joel Chandler Harris's prose. With Maysie, however, the wit, wisdom, and cunning of the various Uncle Remus characters came through so unmistakably that I got over my prejudice and began to delight in the quaint expressions that were part of authentic American folklore—a big step forward for me.

When Maysie was not concentrating too deeply on a facial expression, she would often draw me out about myself and my background. I found myself talking about my family and giving her sketches of my aunts and grandparents which she thought were fascinating. By the time the bust was finished she was convinced that I had a family story well worth writing. She was perhaps the first person to suggest the book which eventually became *Proud Shoes*.

CHAPTER 9

Among the Unemployed

I GRADUATED from Hunter College in the class of January 1933, one of four Negroes in a group of 247 women. In my yearbook I wrote that it was my first successful milestone, although early 1933 was the worst possible time to come out of school and try to begin one's career. An estimated sixteen million people were out of work. Hundreds of homeless unemployed women were reported to be sleeping in Chicago's parks because the shelters were full and they had no place to go. Some seven thousand men, including some well over seventy, were on the streets of New York trying to make a few cents shining shoes at a nickel a shine. Dozens of others were arrested almost daily for sleeping in subways, and they were happy to go to jail, where they would have a bed and a hot meal.

College graduates were hit as hard as other groups. Six months before I got my degree, the *New York Times* reported an estimated ten thousand unemployed college graduates in New York City alone, and the figure was increasing. Some of my classmates were able to get temporary jobs teaching in the public schools. Others were lucky if they were taken on as salesclerks at Macy's. One could spot several women on any floor at Macy's wearing the Hunter College ring—that is, if they were white. Negroes were limited to elevator and cleaning jobs whether they had a degree or not. For many college graduates the future seemed to hold only two alternatives. One either sat on one side of a desk as a social investigator for the Temporary Emergency Relief Administration or sat on the other side of the desk as an applicant for relief. My friend Edna Lisle was in the first category, which determined her entire career. She never left the Department of Welfare, and when she retired she was administrator of one of the largest public welfare districts in Brooklyn.

My graduation had come just a few weeks before the inauguration of President Franklin D. Roosevelt and the national bank holiday that followed, but I did not share the enthusiasm many people had for the coming New Deal. I had cast my first vote in the election of 1932, and it was a vote of protest. Since I would not vote Republican and, having lived under the *apartheid* of Democratic rule in the "solid South," could not bring myself to vote for a Democrat, I had voted for the Socialist candidate, Norman Thomas.

With no immediate job prospects after graduation, I considered briefly the possibility of getting a master's degree in English and signed up for two courses in the spring term at Columbia University. One classroom session in the philology course—a dry technical lecture—was enough to discourage me, and I withdrew. I had stubbornly resisted the idea of teaching and had avoided all education courses at Hunter not required for my degree. In my blind optimism about a writing career, I was ignorant of the fact that only a few thousand people in the entire country were able to earn a living as writers. Fortunately, I could continue to work evenings at Hunter, using the time when the switchboard was quiet to write poetry. The job left my days free to pose for Maysie Stone.

In the fall of 1933, the field representative of *Opportunity* magazine, house organ of the National Urban League, resigned to get married, and I got the job as her replacement. My assignment gave me the chance to travel and to earn fifteen dollars a week building the circulation of the magazine by promoting it at various social work conferences. When I visited the larger Urban League branches I also sold subscriptions to League supporters at $1.50 a year. My boss was Lester B. Granger, the magazine's business manager, who eventually became executive director of the League.

Opportunity's slogan, "Not alms but opportunity," impressed me greatly, and my enthusiasm for promoting the journal was heightened by the fact that it not only covered social work among Negroes but was an organ of cultural expression as well. Elmer A. Carter, editor of the magazine from 1928 to 1942, followed the tradition of encouraging promising young Negro artists and writers by publishing their work. Several of my poems were first published in *Opportunity*, and Lou Jefferson's cover illustrations drew attention to her early work. Elmer Carter also intensified my interest in Negro history and the continuity of tradition. He was very proud of the fact that as a youth in Auburn, New York, he had known Harriet Tubman, the great abolitionist and conductor on the Underground Railroad. His interest in my writing was genuine; whenever he met me in later years he would ask me about it. No matter what else I might be doing at the time, he would wave it aside and say, "You must get back to your poesy." When I finally was able to send him a copy of *Dark Testament and Other Poems,* published in 1970, he was too ill to reply.

Lester Granger was the kind of boss whose lovable personality inspired total devotion and whose willingness to let me use my own imagination and initiative made me work doubly hard to merit his confidence. He was one of those rare human beings with whom I felt free to disagree sharply about matters on which we both had passionate convictions, knowing that our debates would not affect the deep affection and respect we had for each other.

Selling subscriptions to *Opportunity* gave me a chance to move around and meet people socially, something I had been unable to do while in college. I bought a used Chevrolet sports roadster to get about quickly in the cities and to avoid Jim Crow travel in the South. On long trips I usually drove at night, when traffic was light, falling in behind a trailer truck, which lighted the way ahead, and staying just close enough to keep its red taillights in view. When I got sleepy, I would stop at a filling station, buy some gas, pull off to the side of the road, and take a nap before continuing my journey.

While on that job I had a drastic experience which saved me many embarrassments in later years. Up to that time my social drinking had been limited to ginger ale. When I was a child, we had plenty of grape wine at my house, but whiskey and brandy were used only for emergencies in case of chill or shock. My family impressed me with the idea that a drunken woman was a repulsive sight, and not wanting to become a spectacle, I avoided liquor when I grew up.

On this occasion I was out with a small group of friends in a saloon in Pennsylvania, and when I ordered my customary ginger ale my companions began to razz me unmercifully and dared me to get drunk. Smarting under the taunt that I was a "cream puff," I foolishly ordered and drank in quick succession several jiggers of straight whiskey without a chaser. My friends were astounded at my aplomb, but at least I had stopped their teasing. Nothing unusual happened until sometime later. The minute I went to bed, the ceiling came down to meet me and the walls began to tilt. Next morning when I awoke, the lopsided ceiling and dancing walls were still with me. That one bout with drinking was enough. It gave me a permanent distaste for whiskey and cured me of any temptation to indulge in more than one comparatively mild drink.

Before I had been on my new job twelve months, the years of marginal living caught up with me, and that fall when I returned to New York I came down with a bad attack of pleurisy. My physician, the legendary Dr. Mae E. Chinn, who had seen me through the recurring spells of malnutrition that plagued my school career, now warned me that I was in serious danger of tuberculosis. She insisted that I resign my job, take a rest, and spend the winter in the sun, preferably in Florida or California. Since this solution was virtually impossible, I had to face the prospect of long-term confinement in a sanatorium. Dr. Chinn began to make some inquiries and fortunately discovered an alternative—Camp Tera, a camp for unemployed women, which had been established in the Bear Mountain area of New York State. She thought it would be a fair substitute for a winter in the sun since it provided outdoor life under regulated conditions. One had to be unemployed to meet the entrance requirement.

So I resigned my job and became one of the hundreds of jobless women to participate in the program set up under the direction of Hilda Smith by the Federal Emergency Relief Administration at the urging of Eleanor Roosevelt. Camp Tera was one of the twenty-eight women's camps established by the New Deal to provide a female counterpart to the CCC camps. It was little more than a recreational camp for adult women at the time I was there, since it offered no work experience beyond our camp duties and was only one step removed from the dole. Yet for me, as for most of the other women in the camp, it provided a sanctuary from the pressures of unemployed city life. It was our first experience of the outdoor camp life that we had missed as children. And thanks to an enlightened social policy, it was unsegregated. Such camps were of special interest to Mrs. Roosevelt during her first years in the White House. She had helped to plan the program, and she looked upon Camp Tera as a model for other camps.

The camp was ideal for building up run-down bodies and renewing jaded spirits. There were more than forty women in residence when I arrived, and as sleeping facilities became available, the numbers increased. We slept in a winterized barracks, two women in each room, eating our meals and carrying on other indoor activities in the large main hall. A staff of young, well-trained counselors planned a wide variety of recreational pursuits—dramatics, arts and crafts, hiking along marked trails, rowing, and, when winter set in, sledding, skiing, and ice skating. The outdoor life gave me a tremendous appetite; I got over my cough and began to gain weight.

One of the first persons to greet me on my arrival at Camp Tera was an old friend and hiking companion from the YWCA, "Pee Wee" Inness, whom I had not seen for some time. We were assigned to share a room in the barracks, and having Pee Wee for a roommate made camp life easier for me. Our room, like all the others, was a narrow cubicle which accommodated only two cots, a dresser, and our foot lockers, but we respected one another's need for privacy and fell into a companionable friendship marked by long silences, reserving most of our conversations for the outdoors, when we were hiking. Pee Wee did not talk much about her childhood, but I got the impression that she was an orphan who had grown up the hard way. She had come to the United States from Trinidad when she was sixteen, and her only relatives in this country were a married half-brother and his family. She had little formal training beyond secondary school, but she was thorough in whatever she did and through sheer grit inched toward her goal of becoming a recreation worker. Until the Depression deprived her of employment, she had made it on her own, working as a utility girl in a beauty salon and living in a tiny furnished room crowded with her belongings and her bicycle, meanwhile taking advantage of all the free courses in sports and crafts she could find.

Pee Wee had an amazing sense of her own worth, and she feared no one. Her strong convictions about civic responsibilities led her to write long letters to public officials when she was aroused over some social injustice. Mrs. Roosevelt was a favorite target for her broadsides, written in her distinctive narrow, perpendicular script. She had no qualms about poor syntax and was not deterred by the thought that the letter of an ordinary citizen might receive only scant official consideration. She was solely interested in communicating her concerns. I owe to Pee Wee's example my later habit of writing to newspapers and public figures on social issues, letters I came to call "confrontation by typewriter."

Among the counselors, I especially liked Peg Holmes, who was in charge of hiking and other outdoor activities. Peg and I were about the same age and her intellectual curiosity matched my own. We also had a common interest in poetry, and after I overcame my shyness about my writing I showed her some of my work. Peg seemed utterly without racial or class prejudice although she was the daughter of a banker and came from conservative Putnam County, New York. When she read my poems she told me she was amazed that I could write with such compassion. "I would be bitter if I were a Negro," she said.

My idyllic existence at Camp Tera lasted only three months because of a personality clash with the camp's director, Miss Mills. She was a raw-boned, gray-haired, authoritarian person who had driven an ambulance in World War I and attempted to run the camp on semimilitary lines. She resented my cockiness as much as I resented her patronizing attitude, and I was not prepared to give her the servile deference she demanded. Miss Mills also discouraged any social contact between campers and counselors outside of scheduled activities, despite the fact that we were all adult women and in some instances had intellectual interests in common.

I ran afoul of the director on the occasion of Mrs. Roosevelt's first visit to the camp. One Sunday afternoon in the late fall we saw a far from new coupe driving up with the nation's First Lady at the wheel. She had brought along her secretary and a man I assumed was a secret service agent. It was my first glimpse of Mrs. Roosevelt in person, and during the flurry of excitement that always attended her comings and goings, I slipped away to my bunk, scrubbed my face and hands, brushed my short, unruly hair, and put on a clean blouse in her honor. Miss Mills met her and escorted her around the premises. When the party came through the long corridor of the common hall where several of us were seated, I felt that tremor of excitement I was to experience many times later when coming into Mrs. Roosevelt's presence. I dropped my eyes and pretended to read a newspaper to keep from staring as she passed. Later she spoke to us briefly in assembly before she left.

After Mrs. Roosevelt's departure I was called to Miss Mills' office and was stunned by her verbal assault. She accused me of showing disrespect for Mrs. Roosevelt by failing to stand at attention when she passed through the corridor. The charge seemed ridiculous; we were not being introduced, and I thought I was doing the proper thing by making myself as inconspicuous as I could. I stood my ground with Miss Mills, arguing that Mrs. Roosevelt did not want obsequious behavior from people and that I had paid her the highest compliment of which I was capable when I cleaned up my appearance upon her arrival. Miss Mills did not see it that way, and from then on I was under surveillance.

Some weeks later Miss Mills called me into her office again. This time she declared angrily that she would not have Communists in her camp and that my presence was no longer desirable. I was completely dumbfounded, since I knew almost nothing about communism at the time. Then I recalled that among the books I had brought along to read in my spare time was a copy of *Das Kapital* by Karl Marx. I had owned the book since college days, when it was assigned reading for a course in political philosophy, but had never had time to read it. My interests had run to poetry and literature, but now that I had some leisure it had seemed a good idea to inform myself on an issue of such international significance. Miss Mills had doubtless seen the book in my cubicle during her periodic inspection and had drawn her own conclusion. Since I did not know the contents of the book when she assailed me, I could meet her charge only with a heated denial. I would not have hesitated to say so if I had in fact been a Communist, but I doubt that anything I could have said would have changed Miss Mills' mind. She seemed convinced that I had come to the camp for the express purpose of organizing a Communist cell. After our stormy session I left Camp Tera, determined to educate myself on communism and find out why Communists were so hated and feared.

Living was more precarious than ever back in the city. I sold my car and used the money sparingly to stretch it as far as possible. I could not afford a room, and Maysie Stone let me sleep in her studio at night. The building was never locked, and because it contained only offices and studios, it was almost deserted after business hours. I washed myself and my hose and underwear in the women's public rest room after the tenants had left for the day or before they arrived in the morning. I carried water from the tap in a pail which I kept in the studio for drinking and cooking, and prepared my skimpy meals on a two-burner gas outlet. In the mornings I went through the futile ritual of studying the help-wanted ads or made an equally futile trip to the state employment service office.

On days when Maysie worked in the studio, I spent my time reading in the American History Room of the New York Public Library at Forty-second Street, or walking about the streets, or killing several hours in a fifteen-cent movie. Although enforced idleness was demoralizing, at least I had a roof over my head and only one person to worry about. My difficulties were minor compared to the hardships of many people during the Great Depression. The *New York Times* regularly reported stories of destitution and instances of actual starvation, like the woman and her sixteen-year-old daughter who were found living under a strip of canvas in a patch of woods near Danbury, Connecticut. They had existed for five days on wild berries and apples.

Living from hand to mouth was less devastating to those of us who were just beginning our careers. Many had never known stable employment, and being without a job in those restless times was so common that it permitted us the freedom to travel about in ways that were not otherwise socially acceptable. Hitchhiking about the countryside was one way of relieving the monotony of having nothing to do. That spring of 1935, my friend Peg Holmes, the counselor from Camp Tera, came into New York and we embarked on a five-week hitchhiking trip to Nebraska and back. We discovered that if we did not have to pay for lodgings and used a little ingenuity, we could see the country as inexpensively as we could live in one place. We carried light knapsacks and the equipment we needed for cooking outdoors, traveled at a leisurely pace, avoided large cities, and never accepted a ride that left us on the road at night. Around dusk we would stop off in a town or village and seek free shelter from the local police or the Salvation Army. We were bedded in jails, courthouses, hostels, and once in a hotel at the town's expense. Often we were given breakfast before we left in the morning.

When a free breakfast was not forthcoming, we usually earned it by walking through the town and finding a front lawn that needed attention. We would then present ourselves to the woman of the house, tell her we were hiking through and would like to cut her lawn in return for our breakfast. Whether the woman responded to the novelty of our request or because of compassion for two neatly dressed but hungry wanderers, our scheme worked almost every time. We insisted upon earning our meal and prided ourselves upon leaving the lawn well manicured and the edges neatly trimmed. Our reward was invariably a big breakfast of fresh eggs with bacon or ham, large slices of bread and butter, and plenty of hot coffee. Sometimes our benefactor would be so pleased with the job that she gave us a little money.

After our return to New York that year, I was introduced to my first picket line. Never having worked in a unionized shop, I knew very little about labor disputes, but my interest was aroused when Ted Poston was arrested for picketing the *New York Amsterdam News*, a Negro weekly paper in Harlem. He and other employees had organized a local unit of the American Newspaper Guild, and the management had responded to the demand for recognition of the Guild as bargaining agent by locking out the union members. I telephoned Ted in dismay after reading of his arrest and asked what I could do to help out.

"You can come up here and get on the picket line," was his breezy reply. "I'll be right up," I said automatically.

For all my bravado, deeply engrained notions of respectability filled me with distress. It was one thing to ride freights anonymously or sleep in jails in strange towns where I was unknown. It was quite another to carry a picket sign in the heart of Harlem, where many people knew me. I felt as if I had been asked to parade in public undressed, and was extremely self-conscious when I first joined the line and faced a crowd of onlookers. The sight of Ted and his fiancée, among other friends, was reassuring, and pretty soon Heywood Broun, the famous columnist, came up and took his place at the head of the line. We marched back and forth in single file, singing labor songs in a jovial mood, and I was just beginning to shed my anxiety when a squad of police and several paddy wagons drove up. Although our behavior was above reproach and we were not blocking the sidewalk, we were arrested, herded into the police wagons, and hauled downtown to the old Jefferson Market jail on Sixth Avenue near Eighth Street.

We sat or stood for several hours in crowded cells, the men on one side of the jail and the women on the other. Most of us had never been arrested before, and I was worried about having a police record. Late that night we were bailed out and instructed to appear in Magistrate's Court the next morning. Fortunately, we had a sympathetic judge who promptly dismissed the case against us, and within the hour I was back on the picket line. Although Ted Poston and some of his union comrades lost both the labor dispute and their jobs, it was an important step in my gradual transformation to social activism.

When the Works Progress Administration got under way that fall of 1935, I was among the thousands of jobless New Yorkers processed for employment. The test for getting on WPA was eligibility for Home Relief, and I was amazed to find how many of us, although clearly eligible for Home Relief, had scrambled for existence and hung on until we could get paid employment on WPA. The disparaging reference to WPA workers as "boondogglers" was unjustified. Most of us were only too glad to be doing something useful after months of feeling worthless despite ourselves.

WPA rescued a generation of men and women from despair because it provided the margin between the shame of being on the public dole and the pride of earning one's living, and it allowed one to retain some dignity and self-respect. While the numerous federal projects helped many thousands of people for whom the Depression was a calamity, they were a special boon to Negroes living under permanently depressed conditions, who had never had a decent wage and had been shut out of many professional fields that opened to them for the first time through WPA projects. I remember that my salary of $23.86 per week—the same salary all other workers in my classification were receiving—was the highest wage I had earned up to that time. Hundreds of young Negroes were given creative opportunities they had never had before, and these opportunities on the federal writers', art, and theater projects stimulated a flowering of black writers, playwrights, artists, and actors who made significant breakthroughs in the 1940s and 1950s. The preservation of the Negro cultural heritage was another important aspect of WPA activity. Interviews conducted with many former slaves preserved their firsthand stories before they passed from the scene. A written history of Negro Harlem was another major accomplishment.

WPA made innovative contributions in other ways. My initial assignment was as a teacher on the WPA Remedial Reading Project, the first effort to introduce instruction of that kind on a broad scale to the New York City public schools. Remedial reading was then such a new concept that the few available specialists in the field who qualified for WPA under the test of need were put to work training those of us who had no previous experience, before we were sent into the schools. Printed materials were virtually nonexistent, and we had to construct our own visual aids and make up our own testing devices.

I was assigned to Public School 8 on King Street near Sixth Avenue, several blocks south of Greenwich Village in a largely Italian neighborhood. Ironically, I had rejected a teaching career during college days, but now I threw myself into the new job with enthusiasm. I liked the work because it involved individual instruction and I had only two or three children in my classroom at any one time. Each child was tested for his or her particular reading disabilities, and then I constructed a set of reading materials for that child's individual use. The exercises were treated as games and the children did not have to compete with each other, only with their own records. By concentrating on a specific problem of word recognition or comprehension, and mastering it, a child would begin to experience progress and to gain self-confidence. What had been an ordeal in a large class now became an exciting game which the child could occasionally win. The result was often spectacular. Sometimes children who had tested several years below their class reading level gained a whole year within a few months. The experience I got on that job was invaluable to me thirty years later when, as vice-president of Benedict College in Columbia, South Carolina, I encountered the low reading levels of Negro college freshmen.

The room I rented in the Village so as to be within walking distance of the school was also in a section where many people of Italian descent lived. Once or twice that year of 1935–36 I had to make my way nervously through pro-Mussolini street demonstrations during the height of the crisis over the Italo-Ethiopian war. Crowds of partisans straggled along behind a horse and cart carrying a crude gallows from which dangled a grotesque effigy of the Ethiopian emperor, Haile Selassie. The effigy's close resemblance to pictures I had seen of lynchings in the South made my stomach churn. On the other hand, several of the children assigned to me for remedial instruction were recent arrivals from Italy whose fathers had emigrated with their families to escape military service in the war against Ethiopia. Their educational level was fifth or sixth grade, but they understood little English and I knew no Italian. We had to communicate through pantomine and press other children into service as interpreters. Occasionally my improvisations were successful in helping them to learn English.

On the whole, the year produced mixed results. The most difficult part of the job was my almost total isolation from professional contact with the regularly appointed teachers. The lot of the solitary WPA worker in a public elementary school was an unhappy one. Remedial instruction had not won wide acceptance and, in addition, the stigma of WPA status attached to one's work as well as one's person. Both were treated with indifference; only a few teachers bothered to assign children to the program, and some used it to get rid of disciplinary problems. My lower-caste professional standing was so demoralizing that at the end of the school year, in spite of highly satisfactory ratings, I transferred to the WPA Workers' Education Project. Not only was my new post unrelated to the public schools, but it enabled me to have closer professional contact with my colleagues.

CHAPTER 10

Saved by the WPA

WHEN I joined the WPA Workers' Education Project in 1936, I was thrust into a bewildering situation for which I had little preparation. Hundreds of thousands of workers were being organized in the mass-production industries under the stimulus of the National Labor Relations Act and the leadership of the CIO. Leaders of workers' education saw an urgent need for these new union members to learn about trade union organization, collective bargaining, and the practical details of how to run union meetings and use grievance procedures. The few specialists in the field had the dual task of training raw recruits in labor education while convincing union officials, whose chief concerns were negotiating contracts, running strikes, or conducting union elections, of the ultimate value of educating their membership.

At the same time, the burgeoning unions had become the battleground for the growing Socialist and Communist movements, which saw workers' organizations as the driving force to replace the capitalist system with a socialist society, and both groups were making determined efforts to gain leadership positions within the unions. A lack of trade union experience and ignorance of ideological movements of the Left constituted a severe handicap in this volatile situation.

In many trade unions, members of the Communist party were especially active in the effort to influence or control union policies. They were well organized, hardworking, and highly disciplined, and they used great skill in getting party members into key positions. They came early to meetings and stayed late, often committing a union to a position that followed the party line by raising an issue and having it voted upon after most of the members had gone home. Their influence was far out of proportion to their usually small numbers, and when they were unable to outvote their opposition they sometimes tried to discredit dissenters by labeling them "social fascists."

I was saved from being sucked unwittingly into the morass of party influence by my instantly negative reaction to the principal Communist party slogan directed to Negroes in the 1930s: "Self-Determination for the Black Belt"—by which was meant a separate state carved from areas in the South in which Negroes were most heavily concentrated and where they outnumbered the local white population. To people like me who had lived under Jim Crow and who wanted citizenship rights like other Americans, this slogan not only was wholly unrealistic but seemed to offer merely another form of racial segregation.

I discovered that the most intelligent opposition to the Communist party came from a small group of former Communists who had been expelled from the party in the late 1920s because of differences over strategy and tactics to be applied in the United States. Members of this opposition group were known as Lovestoneites and were based largely in New York City. Intellectual radicals, they were followers of Jay Lovestone, who had been the general secretary of the Communist Party USA before being ousted and who in later years became director of international affairs of the AFL-CIO. The group's expulsion from the Third International grew out of their theory of "exceptionalism"—that is, the belief that capitalism did not follow the same pattern of development in every country, that a party line fashioned by Soviet Communists could not be transferred mechanically to every country in which Communists were active, and that American Communists, for example, should be free to develop strategies most suitable to the peculiar conditions of the United States. Although the Lovestoneites continued to think of themselves as revolutionary Socialists, the logic of their position drove them further and further away from official communism, and they became some of the party's most brilliant critics. I took some courses at their New Workers School, and from men like Ben Davidson, a former teacher who later became executive director of the Liberal party of New York, Bertram Wolfe, Will Herberg, and Lovestone himself, I got a thorough grounding in the fundamentals of communism, differences among the various Socialist and Communist factions, and a critique of the strategy and tactics of the Communist Party USA. It was a valuable learning experience, which equipped me to hold my own in future encounters with Communist party members who joined various liberal organizations with which I was associated.

An ideological orientation was especially important to my work on the WPA Workers' Education Project in New York City, which had to function in a highly political atmosphere. The project itself was an outgrowth of the New Deal's sympathetic attitude toward labor unions, and it had the active support of Mrs. Roosevelt, who had worked for years through the Women's Trade Union League to improve the conditions of workers. Headed by Hilda Smith in Washington, this small WPA operation employed about a thousand teachers throughout the country to cooperate with union officials and community leaders in organizing and conducting classes in workers' and consumers' problems. The actual teaching had to be adapted to the special needs and interests of the adults who joined the classes, and so ranged in subject matter and complexity from instructing Mississippi sharecroppers in simple arithmetic or foreign-born workers in elementary English to leading discussions on unemployment, social security, collective bargaining, the rise of Nazism and Fascism, and the threat of war in Europe.

Our New York office was one of the larger units, with a staff of about eighty people, more than half of whom were assigned to teach in trade union halls, labor centers, fraternal organizations, settlement houses, churches, and Y's. Our managing supervisor, Isabel Taylor, was a mild-mannered woman whose background included settlement house work in the tradition of Jane Addams and working with coal mining families in Pennsylvania. One of her ablest assistants was my schoolmate Agnes Martocci (Douty), a Hunter College graduate with a strong labor background, who supervised teacher training and curriculum building.

It was a hectic assignment, full of challenge and frustration. Our teaching staff had a strong commitment to labor education, and we were imbued with the idea that we were breaking new ground in a much needed area. On the other hand, our training and experience varied widely. Some of us had college degrees and backgrounds in education or social work, although we knew little about unionism. Others had emerged from the labor movement but had little professional training. This mix presented serious problems of teacher training and job performance. In addition, we had to struggle against the demoralizing effect of insecurity and disparagement. Our attempt to develop a program that would have continuing impact was undermined by persistent rumors that the project would be discontinued shortly and by shrill public charges that the WPA was an unnecessary waste of taxpayers' money and that WPA workers were parasites. Some detractors even demanded that persons on work relief be denied the right to vote.

Our critics might have been astonished to know how deeply dedicated we were to our work and how many hours in excess of a normal work week we spent voluntarily in preparation and in teacher training sessions. We had few guidelines and we learned as we taught, pooling our experience through detailed weekly reports and analyses of our classes. We had to acquire teaching techniques and develop teaching materials that would meet the needs of adults of highly diverse backgrounds and levels of education. To accommodate these differences we had to learn to teach on several levels simultaneously. We also had to familiarize ourselves with the immediate problems of clothing workers, Pullman car porters, domestic workers, transport workers, sales clerks, the unemployed, or whatever groups we were assigned to. We had to be well informed on contemporary social, economic, and political issues to satisfy a popular demand among workers for discussions of political events. Since our program was voluntary, attendance was one of the best indicators of our effectiveness. When it dropped we had to reexamine our approach; when it held steady we felt we were doing a good job.

Like many WPA efforts, our Workers' Education Project was significant as a pilot program and a training ground. It stimulated a number of unions, which used our teachers to set up their own educational departments in order to continue the work we had begun. Some of our staff members went on to important careers in the U.S. Department of Labor and other government agencies. Others rose in the ranks of the trade unions as organizers and educational directors. Some went back to teaching, or moved into other professions. Still others moved into positions of leadership in civil rights organizations. I had my first serious involvement with labor organization through the WPA program, then moved toward civil rights activity, and finally into law.

Although a blue-collar worker in the service trades during my college days, I had never worked in a factory or a unionized establishment. Soon after joining the Workers' Education Project, I took a short leave of absence to get more labor background and obtained a scholarship to study at Brookwood Labor College, a small residential school in Katonah, New York, established for trade unionists and supported by the American Federation of Labor and some of the larger unions. For several months I took crash courses in the history of the labor movement, principles of unionism, labor economics, and labor journalism. Most of the thirty-five to forty students in residence were industrial workers sent there by their trade unions because they had shown promise as future union leaders. I was one of three women and two Negroes in the student body, the other Negro being a young teacher from Mississippi who had worked among sharecroppers.

It was an intensive experience. One encountered in the labor movement of the late 1930s an almost religious fervor, which would be seen two decades later in the civil rights movement and in the women's movement of the early seventies. We sang labor songs, thrilled to Earl Robinson's

"Ballad for Americans," and loudly applauded lectures given by the Reuther brothers and other visiting labor dignitaries. We threw ourselves into the Automobile Workers' general strike in early 1937, working as volunteer organizers at the Tarrytown plant and helping to put out a local strike newspaper. We became emotionally involved in the Spanish Civil War when several of the men from Brookwood left to fight for the Spanish Republic. Later we got word that some of our schoolmates had been killed in action.

One of the students at Brookwood was a young, red-haired auto worker from Georgia, who had never been away from his native South before and had never eaten with or talked with Negroes as equals. Sometimes I would catch him staring at me in the dining hall with an expression that was more perplexed than hostile. He questioned me about my background and seemed surprised to learn that I had grown up in the South and had worked my way through college. He said to me, "You know, my mother had a colored laundry woman who worked for us for ten years. She had six children and we didn't pay her much, but you know she put every one of those children through school while she was working for us. I just don't understand how she could do it when I never got to go to college."

"Red" was never able to adjust to Brookwood, and he finally withdrew and returned to Georgia. I often wondered if my presence had triggered a deep conflict in him which he could not resolve. I suspected that he had bolstered his self-esteem through a blind belief in the superiority of his skin color and that his fragile security was shattered when he was forced to recognize that there were Negroes who had achieved a superior education in spite of barriers. I felt very sorry for Red, and for the first time saw clearly how racism could cripple white as well as black people.

If Red had been damaged by reliance upon a racial myth, I had been crippled in other ways. My own self-esteem was elusive and difficult to sustain. I was not entirely free from the prevalent idea that I must prove myself worthy of the rights that white individuals took for granted. This psychological conditioning along with fear had reduced my capacity for resistance to racial injustice. It had not occurred to me that a system of oppression draws much of its strength from the acquiescence of its victims, who have accepted the dominant image of themselves and are paralyzed by a sense of helplessness.

As I became more immersed in workers' education, my conceptions of racial identity and of injustice began to undergo a significant change. I had never thought of white people as victims of oppression, but now I heard echoes of the black experience when I listened to white workers tell their personal stories of being evicted, starved out, beaten, and jailed when they tried to organize a union to raise their miserably low wages. Reading the history of employers' use of violence, labor spies, court injunctions, yellow dog contracts, blacklisting, and other repressive devices to prevent the unionization of workers, I could not fail to see that lynching reached a peak during the same historical period and was the ultimate weapon to discourage Negroes from trying to improve their economic condition. I also discovered that the poll tax initiated in many southern states to bar Negroes from voting disenfranchised millions of poor white people as well.

The study of economic oppression led me to realize that Negroes were not alone but were part of an unending struggle for human dignity the world over. In fact, Negroes held an honorable place in the history of this struggle, having demonstrated the spiritual resiliency to survive two hundred years of enslavement and to continue advancing toward the goal of full humanity in the face of countless barriers. Seeing the relationship between my personal cause and the universal cause of freedom released me from a sense of isolation, helped me to rid myself of vestiges of shame over my racial history, and gave me an unequivocal understanding that equality of treatment was my birthright and not something to be earned. I would be no less afraid to challenge the system of racial segregation, but the heightened significance of my cause would impel me to act in spite of my fears. Such thinking is so commonplace in today's world, where the idea of human liberation has become sufficiently compelling to engage the serious attention of theologians as well as politicians, that it is difficult to understand how revolutionary it seemed in the 1930s. For a Negro to act on this conviction was considered almost suicidal in many parts of the South, and generally such action was assumed to be Communist-inspired.

Actually, world events were breeding a new militancy in younger Negroes like me. One did not need Communist propaganda to expose the inescapable parallel between Nazi treatment of Jews in Germany and the repression of Negroes in the American South. Daily occurrences pointed up the hypocrisy of a United States policy that condemned Fascism abroad while tolerating an incipient Fascism within its own borders. I was also aware of the growing restlessness of African and Asian colonial peoples under British and French imperialism. Watching the increasing disillusionment of many liberals with the Russian "experiment" they had embraced so hopefully, I became convinced that the alternative to communism was a democracy that could be made to work for all its people, including Negroes. From time to time I scribbled my thoughts in a notebook, and the following paragraph has some bearing on my later actions:

> It seems to me that the testing ground of democracy and Christianity in the United States is in the South; that it is the duty of Negroes to press for political, economic and educational equality for themselves and for disin-

herited whites; that it is the responsibility of socially-minded Negro and white Southerners to work out this problem; and that the job of interpretation and leadership falls to those of both races with a knowledge of the problems and an understanding of the tremendous task to be accomplished.

These thoughts influenced my decision to apply for admission to the University of North Carolina in 1938, but I doubt if I would have taken such a step at that time if it had not been for the additional motivation of my personal circumstances. I had returned to the Workers' Education Project in New York after attending Brookwood Labor College and was teaching classes at the Brotherhood of Sleeping Car Porters, Saint James Presbyterian Church, the West 137th Street YWCA, and the Henry Street Settlement House. Although I continued to study and to write poetry during my spare time, the uncertainty of my future and my living situation made me restless and unhappy. Knowledge that WPA would soon go out of existence and the prospect of limited career opportunities made my need for advanced training evident.

On my WPA wages I could afford only a small furnished room in Harlem, invariably a cramped space into which I had to crowd my few personal belongings—piles of books, cartons of papers, a hot plate, an ironing board, my typewriter, a worktable, and two battered trunks. Entertaining in such cramped quarters was out of the question, and sooner or later my landlady would object to the clackety-clack of my noisy typewriter. One year I had to move three times because of it, and I lived in continual fear of eviction.

At the same time I wrestled with the problem of my obligation to Aunt Pauline and my guilt over an unwillingness to return South to live and work. Although I had been in New York for more than ten years, she had not become reconciled to my living away from home: I was in the position of an unmarried daughter who is expected to take care of older members of her family, whatever adjustments in her career plans this entails. Aunt Pauline was then sixty-eight, and she continued to plod to school each day, hoping that she could hang on to her job until the school system adopted a retirement plan. Her health was uncertain, and she had taken on the additional burden of providing a home for Aunt Sallie and her two sons. Some years earlier, the Reverend Small, who had suffered a stroke in Croom, brought his family back to Durham to stay with Aunt Pauline while he took treatments at Duke University's medical center. There he had died, leaving his family with little means of support.

I was torn between the strong pull of family obligation and my increasing inability to endure the system of segregation. How could I explain to those who had managed to live with it every day of their lives that for me to accept this intolerable injustice was to participate in my own degradation and to undermine my self-respect? I dreaded my periodic bus trips home, which involved the ordeal of traveling Jim Crow south of Washington. The bus was the quintessence of the segregation evil, because there the separation of the races was merely symbolic. The intimacy of the bus interior permitted the public humiliation of black people to be carried out in the presence of privileged white spectators, who witnessed our shame in silence or indifference.

It was not the fact of separation that hurt so much; it was, as everybody knew, the fact that the overriding purpose of segregation was to humiliate and degrade colored people. Even if one quietly accepted being forced to sit in the back of the bus, there was apt to be some white driver whose contemptuous treatment of Negro passengers, combined with his uniform and swaggering manner, gave him a striking resemblance to a Nazi storm trooper. Once I saw a Negro mother with her baby in her arms compelled to stand for miles, trying to keep a precarious balance as the bus lurched around curves, while seats in the front of the bus remained vacant. White passengers had spread all over the bus and the driver refused to reassign them to forward seats so that the Negro woman could sit down in the rear. I would never forget my own humiliation when I had an urgent call to use the rest room while the bus was at a rest stop in southern Virginia. I was not permitted to use the facilities for white women, and the bus driver unconcernedly directed me to relieve myself in an open field in full sight of the highway. My alternative was to ride in sheer agony for the remaining two hours of the journey.

Incidents like these had made me passionately opposed to racial segregation in any form; yet I knew I could never change the system by brooding about it in New York, and that I could never avoid it entirely as long as Aunt Pauline continued to live in Durham. When my obligation to try to change the system and my family obligation came together in my mind, I began to think seriously of returning South to live. It struck me that there might be a possibility of doing graduate study at Duke University in Durham or at the University of North Carolina in Chapel Hill. There were no graduate schools for Negroes in the state, and in view of the fact that these two institutions had done considerable work in race relations, they might be receptive to the admission of a Negro graduate student. It could do no harm to apply, and if I was admitted I could live at home with Aunt Pauline while completing requirements for a graduate degree.

In mid-November 1938, I wrote to both universities requesting application forms, and finally I decided to apply to the University of North Carolina, where I could study with sociologists Guy Johnson and Howard

W. Odum, both considered outstanding in the field of race relations. (Professor Odum's racial attitudes had advanced considerably since the publication in 1910 of his devastating study, *Social and Mental Traits of the Negro.*) When the UNC application form arrived, I noticed that additional lines requiring me to supply "Race" and "Religion" had been typed in.

As far as I knew, only one other Negro had applied to the University of North Carolina for graduate or professional training. Raymond Hocutt, who graduated from Hillside High School a year after I did, had sought admission to the UNC School of Pharmacy at Chapel Hill, was rejected, and brought suit. His NAACP attorneys were Conrad O. Pearson and Cecil McCoy of Durham and young, Harvard-trained William H. Hastie, who ended his career years later as chief judge of the United States Court of Appeals for the Third Circuit. I knew that Hocutt had lost his case on the technical ground of failing to comply with the university's requirement that he present satisfactory evidence of "scholastic qualifications." Dr. James E. Shepard, ultraconservative president of the North Carolina College for Negroes in Durham, had refused to supply UNC with a transcript of Hocutt's undergraduate record at the Negro institution. Since I was confident that the university would be unable to raise a similar argument in my case or question the academic standing of a Hunter College degree, I sent off my application and waited for developments.

At the time, I did not consider my action significant and did not confide what I had done to anyone, so that I would not be embarrassed if nothing came of it. In fact, the whole episode would have remained in obscurity but for two public events that followed immediately and gave my application an importance I could not have foreseen. The first was the national publicity focused on the University of North Carolina when President Roosevelt visited the campus on December 5, 1938, to receive an honorary degree of Doctor of Laws. The second was the Supreme Court precedent-making decision in the *Gaines* case one week later, on December 12.

The details of President Roosevelt's visit and the full text of his acceptance speech were prominently featured in the *New York Times.* He hailed the university as a great liberal institution of learning, "thinking and acting in terms of today and tomorrow, and not in the tradition of yesterday." The thrust of his address was the necessity for social change. "We live in a world of change," he declared. "There is change whether we will it or not." Recognition of this philosophy of change had made the University of North Carolina "representative of liberal teaching." Asserting that the future of democracy rested upon "affirmative action which we have taken in America," the President emphasized that he was referring to "the maintenance of successful democracy at home. . . . Because we live in an era of acceleration we can no longer trust to the evolution of future decades to meet these new problems. They rise before us today and they must be met today." Mr. Roosevelt spoke of the importance of young people in current affairs, which entailed "change through recognized processes of government" to meet new social and economic needs, and concluded, "I am happy and proud to become an alumnus of the University of North Carolina, typifying as it does American liberal thought and American tradition."

Reading his address next day, I reflected upon the contradiction between President Roosevelt's high-sounding phrases and the realities. It seemed to me that he spoke as if the local Negro population did not exist. The "liberal" university that he had embraced so warmly had never admitted a Negro student. The only reference to Negro participation in the ceremonies which honored him was that a Negro choir from Durham had sung spirituals. The jovial tenor of his remarks revealed his trait of side-stepping unpleasant issues. During the six years he had been in the White House, I had become increasingly dismayed over his apparent coziness with white supremacy in the South, his silence on civil rights, and his refusal to speak out for a federal antilynching bill, which the NAACP had modestly proposed. On a moral issue of such magnitude I could not accept Mr. Roosevelt's political expediency based on his reputed fears that a southern filibuster on the bill against lynching would delay the New Deal legislation he deemed essential and that condemnation of racial discrimination would cost him the support of conservative southern leaders in Congress.

I had never had the temerity to address a letter to the President of the United States before, but I sat down immediately and poured out my indignation to President Roosevelt on behalf of Negroes, "the most oppressed . . . and most neglected section of your population":

12,000,000 of your citizens have to endure insults, injustices, and such degradation of the spirit that you would believe impossible . . . the un-Christian, un-American conditions in the South make it impossible for me and other young Negroes to live there and continue our faith in the ideals of democracy and Christianity. We are as much political refugees from the South as any of the Jews in Germany. We cannot endure these conditions. . . .

You said yesterday that you associated yourself with young people, and you emphasized their importance in the current affairs of the nation. . . . Do you feel as we do, that the ultimate test of democracy in the United States will be the way in which it solves its Negro problem? . . . Have you raised your voice loud enough against the burning of our people? Why has our government refused to pass anti-lynching legislation? And why is it that the group of congressmen so opposed to the passing of this legislation are part and parcel of the Democratic Party of which you are leader?

Yesterday, you placed your approval on the University of North Carolina as an institution of liberal thought. You spoke of the necessity of change in a body of law to meet the problems of an accelerated era of civilization. You called on Americans to support a liberal philosophy based on democracy. What does this mean for Negro Americans? Does it mean that we, at last, may participate freely, and on the basis of equality, with our fellow citizens in working out the problems of this democracy? Does it mean that Negro students in the South will be allowed to sit down with white students and study a problem which is fundamental and mutual to both groups? Does it mean that the University of North Carolina is ready to open its doors to Negro students seeking enlightenment on the social and economic problems which the South faces? Does it mean, that as an alumnus of the University of North Carolina, you are ready to use your prestige and influence to see to it that this step is taken toward greater opportunity for mutual understanding of race relations in the South?

Or does it mean that everything you said has no meaning for us as Negroes, that again we are to be set aside and passed over for more important problems?

Since I doubted that the President would ever see my letter, I sent a copy of it to Mrs. Roosevelt with a covering note. I did not know her personally at the time and had never written to her before. I admired her greatly but was still somewhat ambivalent in my attitude toward her. She was more forthright on civil rights than the President and had worked behind the scenes for the antilynching bill, but her public statements on race were still cautious and as far as I knew, she had not condemned racial segregation. I did know, however, that she showed great compassion for individuals who sought her help. When my friend Pee Wee Inness had returned from Camp Tera and was trying to find employment and training opportunities in recreation, she had written to Mrs. Roosevelt and had received so concerned a response that I felt emboldened to write her myself.

My letter to the President was eventually referred for reply to the WPA Workers' Education office, since I had identified myself as a teacher on that project. Mrs. Roosevelt, however, answered under her personal signature, saying:

I have read the copy of the letter you sent me and I understand perfectly, but great changes come slowly. I think they are coming, however, and sometimes it is better to fight hard with conciliatory methods. The South is changing, but don't push too hard. There is a great change in youth, for instance, and that is a hopeful sign.

Mrs. Roosevelt's admonition not to "push too hard" naturally did not ease my impatience, but her graciousness in taking the time to reply impressed me. I was also encouraged by her recent symbolic protest against segregation at the inaugurating meeting of the Southern Conference on Human Welfare, in Birmingham, Alabama. Faced with a local ordinance requiring separate seating of the delegates, which was enforced by the local police, Mrs. Roosevelt had moved her chair to the center aisle, midway between the white and colored sections. In that atmosphere it was an act of no mean courage on the part of the First Lady. It moved the *Afro-American,* a Negro weekly, to comment: "If the people of the South do not grasp this gesture, we must. Sometimes actions speak louder than words."

CHAPTER 11

"Members of Your Race
Are Not Admitted . . ."

MY APPLICATION pending before the University of North Carolina was suddenly transformed into a public controversy by the surprising and far-reaching decision of the United States Supreme Court in *Missouri ex rel Gaines* v. *Canada.* The case had moved slowly through the courts for three years without attracting public notice and I was wholly unaware of it, but it could not have been more timely for my purpose. Lloyd Gaines, a twenty-five-year-old Negro of Saint Louis, had been rejected by the University of Missouri School of Law in 1935 solely on the ground of race. A state statute provided for segregation in public- and state-owned schools, but there was no law school at Lincoln University, the state's Negro institution. With the help of the NAACP, Gaines brought suit, charging denial of equal protection guaranteed by the Fourteenth Amendment. His case was directed by Charles Hamilton Houston, a brilliant graduate of Harvard Law School and former dean of Howard Law School, who acted as special counsel for the NAACP.

On December 12, 1938, the Supreme Court ruled in a historic six-to-two decision that the State of Missouri must provide Lloyd Gaines with facilities for legal education substantially equal to those which the State provided for white students or it must admit him to the University of Missouri School of Law. The Court declared that Gaines's right was a personal one and did not depend upon whether other Negroes had sought the same opportunities. It also said: "The question here is not the duty of the State to supply legal training, or of the quality of the training which it does supply, but of its duty when it provides such training to furnish it to the residents of the State upon the basis of an equality of right." The

Court held further that the State could not discharge its constitutional obligation to Gaines by providing tuition fees for him to attend law school in another state, as had been the custom in several southern states when faced with a demand by Negro students for graduate or professional education.

The *Gaines* decision sent shock waves through the South, affecting sixteen states, including North Carolina, which barred Negroes from attending its state universities. The ruling was the first major breach in the solid wall of segregated education since the Supreme Court announced the "separate-but-equal" doctrine in the *Plessy* case of 1896. It would take many hard-won court battles to reach the *Brown* decision of 1954, but for Negroes, *Gaines* was the beginning of the end of compulsory school segregation.

I could hardly contain my joy. Miraculously, it seemed to me, the Court had spoken on a matter in which I had an immediate personal stake. I did not have to wait long for a reaction. Two days after the *Gaines* decision was announced, the University of North Carolina rejected my application solely on racial grounds. On December 14, 1938, the dean of the graduate school wrote me the following letter:

Dear Miss Murray:

I write to state that I am not authorized to grant you admission to our Graduate School. Under the laws of North Carolina, and under the resolutions of the Board of Trustees of the University of North Carolina, members of your race are not admitted to the University. It has long been the social policy of the State to maintain separate schools for the whites and Negroes. It is expected that the Legislature of the State will make provision for graduate instruction for Negroes. At the present time the precise form which this provision will take has not been announced, although a commission appointed by the Governor of the State has submitted a report. Most of us expect that positive action will be taken in the next session of the General Assembly.

Very cordially yours,
W. W. Pierson
Dean

The rejection was not unexpected, but seeing the reason in black and white was infuriating. I wrote immediately to Dr. Frank P. Graham, then president of the university, calling attention both to the Supreme Court's ruling in the *Gaines* case and to President Roosevelt's recent address commending the school's liberal tradition. "It would be a victory for liberal thought in the South if you were favorably disposed toward my application instead of forcing me to carry the issue to the courts," I told him.

I also informed him that I was a product of North Carolina, had grown up in Durham and attended its public schools, and I requested an interview with him to discuss the matter further. Even then, I was only dimly aware of the wider implications of this correspondence. Several months later Glenn Hutchinson, a white southern liberal writing on my case in *The Crisis* of April 1939, would say: "When Miss Murray submitted her application to the graduate school she was not merely submitting it to President Graham and a few university officials. In reality she was submitting it to the South, and especially to the State of North Carolina. The University administration is powerless to follow a policy which is specifically prohibited by the Constitution of the State, unless it were in turn over-ruled by a higher court."

President Graham was away from Chapel Hill for several weeks and referred my letter to Dean Pierson for reply. The dean conveyed Dr. Graham's message that "the important matter you raise is for the State to decide." He assured me that Dr. Graham would submit a report to the General Assembly, which would meet in January 1939, and that the Commission on Higher Education for Negroes appointed by Governor Clyde R. Hoey would also submit a report and recommendations to the legislature. "In the meantime," he wrote, "I suggest that you file with this office a transcript of your undergraduate record and information concerning your citizenship and residence."

The tone of Dean Pierson's letter was cordial and it seemed to me that the university expected mine to be a test case and wanted its records to be complete. I complied with his request, and then sent copies of the correspondence to Walter White, executive secretary of the NAACP, asking for advice as to next steps. The correspondence was referred to Thurgood Marshall, then the assistant special counsel of the NAACP, who later became the first Negro appointed to the Supreme Court of the United States.

I had barely mailed the material to the NAACP when, on January 5, 1939, the story of my application broke in Chapel Hill and was quickly picked up by the local press and radio and by the national news services. The story originated from the university and seemed deliberately timed to appear on the very day Governor Hoey was delivering his biennial message to the state legislature in Raleigh and recommending that graduate and professional schools be established at the two Negro state colleges, Agricultural and Technical College in Greensboro and North Carolina College for Negroes in Durham. The *Daily Tar Heel*, the university's student newspaper, carried banner headlines—OFFICIALS FACED BY NEGRO APPLICATION . . . ADMINISTRATION IS CONFRONTED WITH "LIBERALISM" ISSUE—and a detailed account. How quickly President Roosevelt's words had come home to roost was revealed by student reporter Lafitte Howard's lead paragraph:

> An application for admission to the University now lying on Dr. Frank Graham's desk may turn out to be an eight ball large enough to hide all Carolina liberalism and the progressive philosophy of the University president should a Negro woman now living in New York City be determined to push her demands to enter the graduate school.

Campus opinion, according to Howard, seemed to be "that this was probably part of a similar movement forming in all Southern states as a result of the recent Supreme Court decision granting Lloyd Gaines, Missouri Negro, the right to attend University of Missouri law school if equal facilities were not provided for colored law students in the state." This opinion assumed, of course, that the timing of my application was a result of the *Gaines* case rather than a coincidence. Then followed an account of student threats, chilling in their implications:

> Campus opinion took on an antebellum note yesterday as one man declared, "I think the state would close the University before they'd let a Negro in. I've never committed murder yet but if a black boy tried to come into my home saying he was a 'University student' . . ."
>
> Students hearing of the movement vowed that they would tar and feather any "nigger" that tried to come into class with them.

It was well for my peace of mind that I did not see this story until a week or so later, when I began reading copies of the student paper. The *Daily Tar Heel* came by mail to the office of the *Spectator,* Columbia University's counterpart, and friends of mine on the editorial staff saved it for me. It was also fortunate that the university did not disclose my name in the initial stories, and so I remained anonymous. My personal identity was not important to the southern white press; it was my race that constituted the affront to established custom. Next day the *Durham Morning Herald* headlined its story NEGRESS APPLIES TO ENTER CAROLINA, and the *New York Daily News* carried an Associated Press dispatch headed COLORED, TRIES TO ENTER CAROLINA U. Within ten days, however, the Negro weekly newspapers had discovered my name and for several weeks the Norfolk *Journal and Guide,* the Baltimore *Afro-American,* and the Durham *Carolina Times* carried detailed stories, pictures, and editorials. My effort to enter North Carolina's state university was the first to receive wide publicity, but within a month Negroes had filed applications with officials of the universities of Georgia, South Carolina, Kentucky, Arkansas, West Virginia, and the School of Journalism at the University of Missouri.

The days immediately following the first press stories were anxious ones for me. I had touched the raw nerve of white supremacy in the South, and the outcry reverberated for weeks. A rash of stinging comments and editorials appeared in the daily press, which were not surprising but which cut deeply when one saw them in print. Governor Hoey told the General Assembly: "North Carolina does not believe in social equality between the races and will not tolerate mixed schools for the races, but we do believe in equality of opportunity in their respective fields of service, and the white race cannot afford to do less than justice for the Negro." Such talk was mild enough when compared to what happened years later at the University of Mississippi and the University of Alabama, but at the time it was sufficiently intimidating to prevent any organized effort among Negroes in North Carolina.

The *Durham Morning Herald* thought that the application "by a Negress now living in New York has the appearance of a move to accentuate the Negro graduate and professional school issue while the legislature is in session," and that while it need not be disturbing, "we would call it ill-timed." Continuing with what it considered a reasonable analysis of the issue, the *Morning Herald* said:

> Rational members of both races understand that the policy of segregation of races with respect to schools is a fixed one in this part of the country. No one in his right mind favors trying to abandon or materially amend that policy at this juncture. . . .
>
> It is no credit to the state that it waited until confronted with the force of a supreme court decision to move to discharge its full educational obligations to its Negro citizens. But it is too late to argue about that now. The task now is to face the problem as it is and try to deal with it realistically.
>
> How best can we, as a state, go about that task? First off, we can't turn in and build at one stroke a fullfledged graduate school, a medical school, a law school, a school of pharmacy and other schools that might attract one or two Negro students. If we could do that, it would be perfect foolishness to do so. . . .
>
> What North Carolina can do and ought to do this year is to add modest graduate school facilities to established Negro schools. . . . There is no occasion for bitter controversy and no necessity of a tremendous outlay, to start with.

The *Daily Tar Heel* at Chapel Hill published a long editorial entitled "Mills of the Gods," which defended student opposition to the admission of Negroes to the university. Commenting upon student threats, including the report that a few students had joined a "lynching" posse, the paper declared:

> If that social distinction between races rooted in Southern minds and customs grows out of hollow prejudices and expresses itself unjustly toward individual members of the Negro race who have surpassed their racial heritage, it is nevertheless a real and persistent prejudice that cannot be ignored.
>
> So if the University opens its doors officially to the Negro applicant from New York against the will of the student body, it will deny the right of a supposedly democratic social unit to make up its mind. . . . Prejudices in Southern minds can never be removed if they are suppressed and denied by external forces from without. For, the roots of prejudice grow healthier when the branches are clipped.

These initial reactions from white spokespersons were bad enough, but I was even more disheartened by the widely quoted statement of Dr. James E. Shepard, president of the North Carolina College for Negroes and a deeply respected friend of my family, that "Negroes could do their best work only in their own schools." Dr. Shepard urged a graduate school for Negroes in Durham, pointing out that enlargement of existing facilities at his institution would give increased opportunities to competent Negro educators. He envisioned a graduate school that would be guided at the beginning by nearby Duke University and the University of North Carolina, a situation that many younger Negroes saw as a continuation of white paternalism.

Aunt Pauline sent me all the clippings from the Durham newspaper, along with a letter telling me how frightened she was by the storm my application had stirred up. My Aunt Rose Murray Shipley's death in Baltimore of a heart ailment that same week increased my concern over the possible effect of undue strain on Aunt Pauline, who had written:

> Please be careful what you do about all this, for you can make it very uncomfortable for me. You are away and don't hear it. I've said nothing to anyone about this, though I suppose every one who knows you . . . may think it's you. . . . I too am working and hoping for the teachers' retirement pension and return of the pre-war salaries. Don't do anything rash, please. You know it will take time to change the South. You see you may hurt Dr. Shepard's cause for a [separate] university by beginning the fight. . . . I think the State of N.C. wants this.

When I telephoned Aunt Pauline after receiving her letter, I found that she was terrified of the possibility that aroused whites might burn our house down. She was also afraid that she would be dropped from her school before the pension plan was adopted, since she was overage and had no tenure.

Aunt Pauline's letter and her apprehensions alarmed me greatly. I faced the dilemma of one who spearheads an unpopular struggle and finds that whatever course one pursues is agonizing. There is the risk that one's family may be victimized in retaliation or that one's cause may suffer a setback through one's own unwise move. There is the realization that no deep-seated injustice can be uprooted without overturning traditions, making people uncomfortable, and becoming, oneself, the target of angry criticism. The issues are seldom clear-cut and sometimes there seems to be an element of justice on both sides of a question. In this case, however, my role was primarily that of a catalyst. The whole episode remained in the realm of public debate, and my apprehensions subsided as more favorable sentiment appeared and no further threats were reported. I received no hostile letters after my name and address became known; one anonymous white North Carolinian who had followed the case and apparently was acquainted with my correspondence with Dr. Graham wrote me that "your thinking has been sound and your bravery in daring to express yourself commendable."

Dr. Shepard was the only public figure among Negroes to urge the establishment of separate graduate schools. Roy Wilkins of the NAACP, then editor of *The Crisis,* stated: "We have opposed separate schools for the races since the beginning of the NAACP thirty years ago, because all surveys and statistics show conclusively that there does not exist in America a so-called equal school system." Walter White added: "These conditions force us to the inevitable conclusion that the only method of securing equal opportunity in public education is for the Negro to hold as an ideal the attendance at the same institutions with whites."

Aside from Dr. Shepard, the *Daily Tar Heel* was able to find only one other Negro willing to be quoted as opposed to admitting Negroes to the university. Kennon Cheek, president of the Janitors' Association on the Chapel Hill campus, said in an interview:

As I see it now, it is not advisable for Negroes to enter the university. . . . The masses of our group have not developed to the place where we can classify them from an educational standpoint. Neither have the masses of Negroes had the background and time to develop to the extent of enjoying social equality with the white folk. We must have time to develop culture for the whole group.

All during the months of January and February, while the state legislature was deliberating on the issue, lively discussion continued at the University of North Carolina. The campus newspaper published almost daily items on opinion polls, forums, panel discussions, and comments from faculty and students. Jonathan Daniels, editor of the *Raleigh News and Observer,* on campus to make a speech, got headlines when he declared: "I don't see how anybody can object to taking a graduate course with a Negro." The *Daily Tar Heel* reported a poll conducted among graduate students, who voted eighty-two to thirty-eight in favor of admitting Negro students to the graduate school. (The paper later repudiated the poll as nonrepresentative.) John Alan Creedy, student editor of the *Carolina Magazine,* devoted the February issue almost entirely to the question of graduate and professional training for Negroes in the South, using articles by Negro and white educators. He wired me for permission to include my published poem "Song of the Highway," explaining in a letter he sent me later that "reading it, I feel—and I hope others will feel—acutely just what sort of student we are missing by excluding Negroes from the University." In New York, two recent alumni who had been following the case, George C. Stoney and Don McKee, looked me up and offered to organize a movement among distinguished graduates of the university in support of my cause.

Dr. Howard K. Beale of the History Department wrote a long article, published in the *Daily Tar Heel,* taking issue with the newspaper's editorial stand and pointing out:

> There are among both faculty and students those who feel it would be of value to our white students as well as to the Negro students to admit Negroes at the graduate level, and that to exclude one properly qualified who has applied would endanger the University's leadership in liberalism. . . . Liberalism cannot be pursued in all other categories and then denied whenever the Negro appears. Sooner or later Southern liberals must choose between their liberalism and their own or their neighbors' emotions over the Negro.

Louis Harris, the future pollster, who was then an undergraduate, reported on an interracial panel discussion which brought together students and professors from both Chapel Hill and several Negro colleges. More than a hundred people attended the meeting, which adopted the following resolution to send to the legislature:

> It is the consensus of opinion that in view of the already limited funds for education in North Carolina, and in view of the fact that setting up separate institutions in professional and advanced training would undoubtedly deter the future progress of education and in racial relations in the South, that the legislature consider a policy whereby qualified and carefully cho-

sen Negro students could be educated in graduate and professional levels by the means and forces already existing in the state.

President Frank Graham, long regarded as a liberal in race relations and one of the founders of the Southern Conference on Human Welfare, was careful to say nothing that deviated from traditional views on segregation. When he discussed my application with the press, he reaffirmed his long-held position that the state should provide equal graduate education at the two Negro state colleges as "a wise answer to the question gradually to be worked out." Since I had no access to the local white press, I wrote to Dr. Graham directly, reminding him that Raymond Hocutt, who had attended a state Negro college, was found ineligible on academic grounds to be admitted to a professional school at the University of North Carolina: "This very fact proves the assertion that Negro schools have not been given the facilities which would place them on an equal footing with white schools. Furthermore," I wrote, "accepting your premise that further segregation in the graduate schools is a 'wise long-range solution,' what guarantee have the Negro students of North Carolina that their graduate schools will be any higher in quality than their undergraduate schools?"

This was the embarrassing question which the white hierarchy dared not answer in view of the record of past performance. The Negro press carried stories of pending suits to compel equalization of Negro teachers' salaries. An article by Jefferson E. Grigsby, a Negro high school principal in Charlotte, charged that although the North Carolina Constitution provided that separate schools must offer Negroes equal treatment, Negroes were discriminated against in every phase of public education. He included statistics showing that while the state's school population was one-third Negro, Negroes received only one-eighth of the amount invested in school buildings for whites, one-tenth of expenditures for school buses, one-twenty-third of the money spent for maintenance of school libraries; and that Negro teachers were paid only 60 percent of the amount paid to white teachers in the same classifications.

Dr. Graham's response to my letter was a restatement of the legal position that southern states would attempt to hold against the stepped-up attacks on segregation during the next fifteen years. He asserted that the only way to obey both the North Carolina Constitution requiring separation of the races in public education and the United States Constitution as interpreted by the Supreme Court "is to make adequate provision in the separate institutions." Taking this into account, he wrote:

I have pledged as far as my lawful responsibility permits, the cooperation of the University of North Carolina [with the two Negro state colleges] toward a more adequate provision for Negroes in the public schools, higher standard Negro undergraduate colleges, and a substantial beginning in the provision for graduate and professional work. This may seem to you to be an inadequate and minimum program, but it is going to take the cooperation and struggle of us all to bring it about. The present alternative is a throwback against whose consequences we must unceasingly be on guard in the best interests of both races, who after all go up or down together.

In reply to Dr. Graham I wrote:

The Constitution of North Carolina is inconsistent with the Constitution of the United States and should be changed to meet the ideals set forth by the first citizens of our country. . . . We of the younger generation cannot compromise with our ideals of human equality. We have seen the consequence of such compromise in the bloody pages of human history, and we must hold fast, using all of our passion and our reason.

Both letters were published in the Negro press.

The matter boiled down to whether the legislature would act quickly enough to establish separate graduate education that could withstand a court contest. Meanwhile I was pleased to see that the *Daily Tar Heel* had published for student reaction ten questions I raised with Dr. Graham. This encouraged me to respond directly to the editorial "Mills of the Gods," and excerpts from my response were also published in the campus newspaper. I wrote:

We Negroes, who ponder over the relations between the races in the South, have never been able to understand your definition of "social equality." You sit on the same seat with your Negro nurse as a child, you come to her to pour out all your childish woes, you depend upon her for sympathy and advice when you are in trouble, you eat the food she prepares with her own hands, and yet if that same Negro nurse decides that she too is a human being and desires to study under the same group of professors and with the same equipment as you, you go into tantrums, organize "lynching parties" and raise the old cry of Ku Klux Klan.

Why not be honest with yourselves? You share our songs, our contributions to the field of entertainment and music . . . and yet you resent our intelligence and our determination to better ourselves.

If a young woman from North Carolina, as native as any of you, as aware of the deep emotional prejudices and misunderstandings on the part of both races as you are, happens to feel that you have one of the best Public Welfare and Social Science Departments of any university in the country, . . . if she feels that one cannot study a social and economic problem realistically off the scene, are you so intellectually ungenerous as to resent her desire to gain this information through normal channels—just because she is a Negro?

My greatest supporter close to the scene was Lewis E. Austin, editor of the *Carolina Times* in Durham. I had known him since my early teens, when I sold his paper on Saturday afternoons. A thin, tense man whose high cheekbones and cavernous cheeks made him look emaciated, he used to boast that Nat Turner was one of his forebears, and the restless energy with which he pursued a fearless campaign for racial justice seemed to bear out his tradition.

From the beginning, the *Carolina Times* reflected my own dilemma —how not to oppose Negro universities per se while simultaneously exposing as unrealistic, and perhaps even cynical, the state's attempt to set up separate graduate schools. It feared that the State would establish "makeshift graduate schools for its Negro citizens." It declared that of the two courses open to the state, "the most sensible and economical is to admit Negroes to the University of North Carolina, and thereby save the taxpayers of the state from having to dig down into their own pockets for additional funds." The newspaper pointed out that it was debatable whether the state would be willing or even able to undertake the "mammoth task" of establishing separate graduate education for Negroes that would come close to meeting the requirements. Facing the issue of my application, the *Carolina Times* concluded:

> Naturally a majority of North Carolina Negroes prefer graduate courses at their own schools by members of their own race who will profit from the salaries paid, at least. But Negroes in this state will not be satisfied with graduate courses that will not meet the standard already set by those the state operates for its white citizens. If such is the intention of the legislature now in session, North Carolina will do well to regard the application of the young Negro woman from New York as having the support of a majority of thinking Negroes in the state. There will be many more to follow from points much closer.

When the *Durham Morning Herald* complained that it did not understand why a Negro woman "should want to enter a school where she would be the only member of her race," the *Carolina Times* replied:

> Is the *Herald* not aware of the fact that there is now a lone Chinese girl attending, as a full-fledged student, the University of North Carolina? Surely, a native-born American Negro woman whose parents and foreparents have borne their share of the tax burden to help maintain the university would feel as much at home as a Chinese girl whose native tongue,

habits and customs are different from those with whom she now finds herself in contact?

There was greater irony in my situation than these editorial comments suggested. Few white people in the South wanted to acknowledge blood ties between the races created by the slave-owning class during slavery. Yet from early childhood I had been aware of the family history which linked me to the University of North Carolina. My grandmother Cornelia Smith Fitzgerald was the granddaughter of Dr. James S. Smith of Chapel Hill, a member of the U.S. House of Representatives from 1818 to 1820 and a former member of the board of trustees of the university. Her white father, Sidney Smith, and his brother, Francis Jones Smith, had attended that university in their youth, and their sister, Mary Ruffin Smith (who raised my grandmother), had left part of her sizable estate to the university to create a permanent trust fund for the education of students there. The fund was known as the Francis Jones Smith Scholarships.

Predictably, the North Carolina legislature made such a feeble gesture toward resolving the issue of graduate education for Negroes that even the conservative *Durham Morning Herald* was moved to express dissatisfaction. By early March 1939, the state body adopted an enabling act that provided for graduate courses and professional training for Negroes when and as they were required, or became necessary, or were demanded. Said the *Herald:* "It seems appropriate to remind the members of the legislature at Raleigh that it takes more than a law authorizing graduate facilities for Negroes to bring them into existence. . . . As we understand the situation, neither the enabling act nor the general appropriation bill fashioned by the [finance] committee provide the wherewithal to finance the additional facilities for Negroes." The Norfolk *Journal and Guide* disclosed that the North Carolina legislature not only failed to appropriate funds for graduate facilities but also went further and slashed the recommended sixty thousand dollar appropriation for North Carolina College for Negroes by almost one-third. The Negro weekly commented: "The conservative Negro leadership of the State, of which President [James E.] Shepard is an important symbol, may now ponder how an undergraduate college can be operated with a State subsidy of $44,000, and how graduate schools may be established and operated without money."

Having done what many of us expected it would do, the state legislature adjourned for two years, and the way seemed clear to begin legal action. It appeared to me that there should be little difficulty in convincing the courts that North Carolina had failed to meet the standard required by the *Gaines* case. When I went to see Thurgood Marshall, however, I suffered my worst disappointment. The NAACP counsel had studied my case and had decided not to undertake a court action on my behalf. Mr. Marshall explained to me that the Association had to select test cases with extreme care because they could not risk losses after expensive litigation. They chose their candidates after meticulous scrutiny into background, training, and personal circumstances. They now wanted an "airtight" case which would square on all counts with the *Gaines* decision, and the circumstances of my case presented too great a risk. Although I apparently could meet the test of academic qualification, I was vulnerable on the question of residence. In *Gaines,* the Supreme Court had ruled on the duty of a state to provide equal education to Negro and white residents of that state. Since my residence was in New York, North Carolina might defend successfully on the ground that the state had no constitutional duty to provide nonresidents with graduate training.

I tried to argue with Mr. Marshall that if the state permitted nonresident white students to attend its educational institutions, it had a similar obligation under the Fourteenth Amendment to admit Negroes, but I was not a lawyer and my logic did not persuade him. I was suggesting an extension of the *Gaines* rule which the NAACP was not prepared to argue at that time. During those years its successes came through cautious and modest advances within the framework of the "separate but equal" principle. It concentrated on the "equal" side of the segregation equation and tried to show in each case that in fact the separate facilities were unequal.

I had no alternative but to accept defeat. Conrad O. Pearson, the Durham attorney who had worked on the Hocutt case, wanted me to go ahead and start legal action on my own, but I had no money for litigation and I also felt it would be unwise to ignore the wisdom of the national NAACP staff. Equally disappointing was the unsuccessful effort to find another candidate who would be suitable for a test case. Carl DeVane, a young Negro graduate of Shaw University in Raleigh who wanted to go to law school, had been following my case and writing me regularly. At my suggestion he sent his credentials to Thurgood Marshall, but he wrote me later that Mr. Marshall "has informed me that since Shaw is a class B school the graduates of this school might meet some technicalities. [Johnson C.] Smith and Bennett [College] are the only A-rated private schools in the state and I don't know anybody at present from either of them who would press the issue."

That spring, while I was in Durham during the Easter vacation, I went over to the University of North Carolina to satisfy myself that I was not afraid to appear on the campus, and I was surprised at the cordial reception I got from a number of students and faculty members. I was assured that there was not enough opposition within the university to worry about. Some of the students who had apparently built up a monstrous image in their minds as a result of all the publicity were astonished that I was the candidate. One professor told me that a number of the university staff had met and had decided to support any further action for the admission of Negroes if the state legislature did nothing. In his opinion the legislative provision was inadequate, and he thought a court test might be a good thing now. When I told him of my problem of residence, he agreed that it might cloud the issue and urged me to find another person willing to bring court action. In Durham, Dr. Shepard was gleeful over the plans of his college to set up graduate courses in seven areas, including law. He told me smugly that the situation was settled as far as North Carolina was concerned and that while he did not think a court case would do any harm, he believed it would be useless.

Ironically, the first effort to set up a Negro law school at North Carolina College for Negroes ended in failure. The school was given an appropriation of fourteen thousand dollars and a law library, and professors from Duke University and the University of North Carolina were recruited to teach. It opened on September 25, 1939, and closed five days later because only one student had enrolled. The student was Logan Drummond Delany, grandson of the late Bishop Henry B. Delany. Another strange twist was that Lloyd Gaines disappeared before he could enter the University of Missouri School of Law, and he was never heard from again.

With my failure to go forward, the second round in the battle against segregation in North Carolina was lost by default. Ultimately a law school and graduate school were set up at North Carolina College for Negroes (now North Carolina Central University) in Durham, a development that caused Lewis Austin to joke, "Every time Pauli Murray writes a letter to the University of North Carolina they get a new building at the Negro college in Durham."

Several more Supreme Court decisions were handed down before North Carolina finally yielded to a federal appeals court order in 1951. Floyd McKissick, future civil rights leader and director of the Congress of Racial Equality (CORE), and several of his fellow law students became the first Negroes to be admitted to the University of North Carolina. One of these young men was William Alston, son of my Durham schoolmate Christine Taylor Alston; it had taken the better part of a generation to win the battle. When I met McKissick some years later, he told me that he had almost completed his legal training at the separate law school in Durham when the court order was issued, but he enrolled at the university anyway, "because I wanted to prove to myself I could meet the competition with

white students." He was a public school student at the time of my application to the graduate school, but he remembered it just as I had remembered Raymond Hocutt's fight for admission.

Talking with Floyd McKissick, I saw my own role in a new light. I was
part of a tradition of continuous struggle, lasting nearly twenty years, to
open the doors of the state university to Negroes, a struggle marked by
modest beginnings and several bitter defeats before the victorious breakthrough of McKissick and his friends. Each new attempt was linked with
a previous effort, which, although unsuccessful, nevertheless had an impact on the forward movement. I had dared because Hocutt had tried and
failed, and while I did not experience a personal triumph, at least my
application to the university had forced public discussion of an alternative
to the system, which had seemed impregnable to attack. Once begun, this
debate would not be silenced until the system of enforced segregation was
outlawed everywhere in the land.

At the time, however, what I felt was the galling disappointment of
personal defeat, and it was only later that I made a surprising discovery.
Much of my life in the South had been overshadowed by a lurking fear.
Terrified of the consequences of overt protest against racial segregation,
I had sullenly endured its indignities when I could not avoid them. Yet
every submission was accompanied by a nagging shame which no amount
of personal achievement in other areas could overcome. When I finally
confronted my fear and took a concrete step to battle for social justice, the
accumulated shame began to dissolve in a new sense of self-respect. For
me, the real victory of that encounter with the Jim Crow system of the
South was the liberation of my mind from years of enslavement.

The final irony of my role in this controversy came many years later,
when the University of North Carolina at Chapel Hill decided to award
me an honorary degree at commencement in 1978. Early that year I was
formally notified of the proposed award by the chancellor, Ferebee Taylor, who had been a first-year student on campus in 1938 and 1939, when
my application for admission had created such a furor. Chancellor Taylor
was ecstatic over the university's gesture of recognition after so many
years, and so was I. To me, it was more than an academic honor; it was
a symbol of acceptance stretching back to my Grandmother Cornelia and
her relationship to the Chapel Hill Smiths, whose position as benefactors
of the university from which I was excluded had intensified my feeling of
being disinherited. My enthusiastic letter of acceptance conveyed to
Chancellor Taylor the special significance of this honor to me.

To my dismay, several weeks later an acrimonious dispute between the
University of North Carolina and the Department of Health, Education,
and Welfare surfaced in the press. Under pressure of a federal court order

to enforce the desegregation provisions of the civil rights law more vigorously, HEW threatened to cut off federal funds to the University of North Carolina, charging it with failure to produce and implement an acceptable plan for fully dismantling the historic legacy of segregation on the sixteen campuses of its statewide system. North Carolina officialdom, including the governor, defied HEW and girded for a stiff court battle. The matter was at an impasse when the university got in touch with me for final arrangements preparatory to public announcement of commencement honorees.

I had anxiously followed the controversy, urging mediation of the issues, but without success. With the challenge I had raised forty years earlier still not fully resolved, I found myself in an untenable position. To accept an honor from the university at this point would be interpreted as acquiescence in its unwillingness to comply with the federal government's demand for more thoroughgoing desegregation. In the circumstances, I had no alternative but to withdraw my earlier acceptance and send Chancellor Taylor a letter sorrowfully declining the honorary degree.

CHAPTER 12

Jailed in Virginia

THE Works Progress Administration began to be phased out in 1939. With the prospect of graduate study in North Carolina foreclosed, I again faced the specter of unemployment, with all its humiliating implications. Those four years on work relief were seldom without anxiety, but they had made it possible for me to maintain self-respect in the face of precarious living.

Several other young women on WPA had rooms in the large apartment where I lived at 35 Mount Morris Park West, and we developed an informal community, cutting down on expenses by pooling our food money and eating cooperatively. We even managed to shrug off the uncertainties of living from paycheck to paycheck and risk small adventures. There was the summer I saved enough to buy a dilapidated Ford from a used car lot and spent my two weeks' vacation touring in New England. The car cost twenty-five dollars and an additional fifteen dollars purchased three new tires. A WPA friend went along and shared the cost of gas. Miraculously, the car carried us over two thousand miles—along the coast and out onto Cape Cod, through Massachusetts and northern Maine, and back to New York City by way of the White Mountains and Green Mountains—all without engine trouble. Upon our return, I sold the car to an auto junk dealer for eleven dollars. The scenic trip had cost me little more than a week's pay.

The urge to write was the force that sustained me during those years. The results came in dribs and drabs, sketches and lines of poetry scribbled in a notebook I carried around with me. It was undisciplined and had little focus, but it relieved frustration, and occasionally I would get a poem published in *The Crisis* or *Opportunity* magazine. In 1938 I enrolled in an evening course in poetry writing given by the distinguished poet Jean Starr Untermeyer. Most of the other students were far more advanced than I, but she took a special interest in my work and spent a great deal of time going over my awkward lines. She kept me working all term on a single poem of twelve lines called "Paradox" so that I would learn the discipline of rhyme and meter, and when the course was over she encouraged me to continue writing.

Then in 1939 I met Stephen Vincent Benét, whose *John Brown's Body* had been one of the great experiences in my college career. Benét's epic had struck a responsive chord in me because of my Grandfather Fitzgerald's Civil War military service. One of its memorable passages haunted me:

> Oh, blackskinned epic, epic with the black spear,
> I cannot sing you, having too white a heart,
> And yet, some day, a poet will rise to sing you
> And sing you with such truth and mellowness, . . .
> That you will be a match for any song
> Sung by old, populous nations in the past,
> And stand like hills against the American sky,
> And lay your black spear down by Roland's horn.

This passage was my first encounter in American literature with a white poet who acknowledged without condescension the dignity of Negroes and called upon them to make their distinctive contribution to the great saga of human experience. It gave me a sense of belonging and a burning desire to see a Negro poet respond to Benét's challenge, a poet like Langston Hughes, Sterling Brown, or Countee Cullen. Once I mentioned this dream to Countee Cullen, who said to me, "You know, I have to earn my living as a teacher. All school year I teach French to high school kids, and it takes so much out of me that when summer comes there's no energy left for sustained creative writing."

Lacking both the skill and the confidence to undertake anything as ambitious as an epic poem, nevertheless I could not shake the idea and eventually began to fill my notebook with the crude beginnings of a poem called "Dark Anger." When I discovered that Benét lived in New York City, I mustered the courage to write him about the impact his poetry had upon my own writing efforts and to request an interview. His prompt reply overwhelmed me. He apparently assumed that I was male, for he wrote that while he would be glad to see me, "if you don't mind, I would like to see some of your work first—this, because I think it's a little embarrassing to read a man's work for the first time right in front of him." He also explained that his family was moving from East Sixty-ninth Street to 215 East Sixty-eighth Street, and suggested that I send him some of my work and then call or write after a week to set up an interview. I immediately sent off to him ten poems including the manuscript of "Dark Anger," the poem that eventually became "Dark Testament."

My meeting with Stephen Vincent Benét was the beginning of a literary association, mostly through correspondence, that had a major impact on my writing career. I was as terrified as I was excited at the prospect of seeing the great poet face to face, but my initial nervousness disappeared in the warm informality of his home. He and his wife, Rosemary Benét, welcomed me like an old friend and made me feel completely at ease. Stephen Benét's study was piled everywhere with books and papers. He looked like a friendly owl behind his large round eyeglasses, and I thought he was hunchbacked when I saw him walk, because his shoulders were so bent. I did not know until years later that he suffered from severe spinal arthritis. He was easy to talk to, and I soon found myself pouring out all the yearnings and insecurities of the fledgling writer. His comments were reassuring; he told me never to become discouraged at the number of rejection slips I collected.

"Keep right on sending things out," he said. "Eventually, you may begin to get a personal note from the editor instead of the printed form, and then you'll know you're making progress."

Over the next two years, Stephen Benét acted through his letters as my patient guide and critic. Although I went to see him originally about poetry and ultimately dedicated the poem "Dark Testament" to his memory, he had an equally strong hand in the beginnings of my book *Proud Shoes*. During our interview I had talked about my family, and he was intensely interested. Afterward I sent him a prose piece I had written some years earlier. His reply was characteristic of the great care he gave to nurturing the creative impulse. He wrote:

> The sketch of your family, with the "rich Fitzgeralds" and the "poor Fitzgeralds" is perfectly fascinating material. It makes me wonder again, and not for the first time, why nobody has tried to handle this sort of subject. . . . It might take you ten years to write a real novel about it. But if you did, and did it well, that would be a book. You see we have had conventional portraits of the dear old mammy and the faithful house-servant of befo' de wa'. We have had revolt things—and very good some of those have been. We have had attempted sketches of Harlem. But nobody as far as I know, has really tried to sit down and do a "Buddenbrooks" or a "Forsyte Saga" on this particular subject . . . from the Negro point of view. And it cries to be done—and done from the inside, not the outside.

After a page of concrete suggestions on how to make the material come alive to the reader, Benét ended—as he always did—on a note of encouragement:

> It is a long road—it always is. I don't know any shortcuts—I don't know any easy way. But, if you are bound and determined to be a writer, you frequently get there. You are more fortunate than most of us in having in your own background, and your own life, a fascinating, rich mine of material. . . . all art comes out of life and out of human beings, and the richer, the more varied the life and the human beings, the greater chance for the artist. . . . Meanwhile, I shall always be interested to see anything you send me.

The sketch I sent Stephen Benét in 1939 ultimately grew into *Proud Shoes*, first published in 1956, a family memoir instead of a novel, completed twelve years after his death. But his early strong support of a book-length work on this theme and his painstaking comments on the various sketches I sent him cemented my determination to complete the project.

In the summer of 1939 I was caught up in a series of events that, over the next two years, would lead me away from creative writing and into law. In a race to get off WPA before I received the inevitable "pink slip," I took a job as acting executive secretary of the Negro People's Committee to Aid Spanish Refugees, an organization affiliated with the Spanish Refugee Relief Campaign of which Secretary of the Interior Harold L. Ickes was honorary chairman. The NPC had been set up to carry on a special fund-raising effort among Negroes in the humanitarian work of helping to resettle the half-million homeless men, women, and children who fled Franco's dictatorship after the defeat of Spanish democracy. Its letterhead read like a Who's Who of Negro notables of that period, among them Paul Robeson, who was international chairman, and Lester B. Granger, my former boss at the National Urban League, who was national chairman. (I took the job on the basis of his chairmanship.) The executive committee included Mary McLeod Bethune, A. Philip Randolph, Channing Tobias, Alain Locke, Hubert T. Delany, and Max Yergen.

The NPC job lasted only three months. Three weeks after I had gone to work on August 1, 1939, the announcement of the Nazi-Soviet pact sent instant repercussions through every liberal organization set up to fight Fascism as democratic liberals divided from Communists and their sympathizers over the issue. The political turmoil that ensued, as well as the impact of Hitler's invasion of Poland in September 1939, weakened the already precarious support of the Negro People's Committee in its fund-raising activities. By November it was clear to me that there was simply not enough interest within the Negro community to warrant a separate organization which was barely meeting administrative expenses. At a special meeting of the Committee called by Mr. Granger, I presented a report which showed that the financial returns from mass appeals and fund-raising affairs did not justify the expense of a paid official, and I tendered my resignation. A few weeks later Mr. Granger resigned as national chairman, and the Committee eventually folded up.

I was now out of a job again and dreading the prospect of having to apply for public assistance. To sit on the hard benches in the barren reception room of the Home Relief Bureau, one's identity reduced to a number on a yellow sheet, stripped one of all personal dignity. On December 6, 1939, I wrote a letter to the editor of the *New York Herald Tribune* and other local newspapers describing this experience, and having just heard Eleanor Roosevelt give a radio talk on behalf of domestic workers, I sent her a copy. Sometime later I was surprised and pleased to discover she had quoted excerpts in her column, "My Day." She wrote:

> The other day I was sent an extremely interesting letter from a woman who, after four years on WPA, with odd jobs of various kinds to fill in, finds that her family today is forced back on relief. She speaks of the humiliation which the procedure brings and the fact that the people involved lose "personal pride and self-esteem sacred to the individual." She ends her letter with the following paragraphs:
>
> "Looking at all these miserable, frustrated, unused people, we cannot help thinking that the differences between our plight and that of the European refugees is only one of degree.
>
> "We, who are the disinherited, who are forced to become public charges in spite of every effort on our part, conclude that the long-time tragedies of peace may be more devastating, if allowed to continue, than those of war. Whatever the cause of this state of being, until democratic society can find a dignified use for all the individuals who compose it, there can be no peace."

Mrs. Roosevelt added: "I don't think there is any way in which we can save people from relief registration, but I do think that letters of this kind should remind us of the necessity of continuing to solve our own economic problems. There are people who do not want steady work even when given the opportunity, but in a really successful democracy those who do want work should find work."

In the next few months, several incidents brought me into closer contact with Mrs. Roosevelt. Late that year, I was hired as executive secretary of the annual National Sharecroppers Week, an event jointly sponsored by the Southern Tenant Farmers Union and the Workers Defense League, the latter a nonpartisan civil rights organization inspired by Norman

Thomas and A. Philip Randolph, among others. David L. Clendenin was then head of the Workers Defense League and Morris Milgram, later a pioneer builder of integrated housing, was his assistant.

The purpose of National Sharecroppers Week was to focus national attention on the plight of black and white sharecroppers in the South and to raise funds for the Southern Tenant Farmers Union. Rose Shapiro, who later chaired the New York City Board of Education, ran our steering committee, and she felt that if we could secure Mrs. Roosevelt as our main speaker at a dinner we were giving in March and also get her to award a prize in an essay contest on democracy we were holding for schoolchildren, our fund-raising campaign would be a success. I was therefore directed to write to Mrs. Roosevelt, seeking an appointment for an education committee of three to present our request.

My former WPA associate Agnes Martocci (Douty) and another teacher, Layle Lane, were also on the committee, and Mrs. Roosevelt granted us an audience in her New York apartment on Eleventh Street one Monday afternoon in mid-January 1940. It was my first face-to-face meeting with her, and I discovered then what invariably happened when she met informally with a delegation. In the aura of magic that surrounded her, sober adults tended to behave like excited children, and it was virtually impossible to maintain the original size of the group appointed to see her. On this occasion she had prepared tea and cakes for three and was obviously flustered when six of us arrived! We were so excited at being in her presence, however, that the tea, set out on a low table by the fire in her sitting room, was completely forgotten. All of us were experienced teachers, but we stammered like schoolgirls. During the introductions Agnes rose and nearly stumbled, prim Layle Lane almost curtsied, and I got up and bowed so awkwardly that Mrs. Roosevelt had to suppress a smile.

As I sat on a hassock facing her low armchair, her warmth was so embracing that I soon forgot the public personage and began to feel as if I might be talking with an affectionate older relative. Whenever I was speaking to her she gave me her complete attention, as if in that moment I was the most important person in her world. I also discovered that she radiated an inner beauty I had not associated with her press photographs. I was to learn from Mrs. Roosevelt that greatness is found in simplicity, in being utterly human. We left her that day giddy with our success. She had agreed to be the guest speaker at our dinner for National Sharecroppers Week and to award the prize for the essay contest. She also contributed one hundred dollars to the campaign.

Scarcely ten days after this momentous experience, I suddenly found myself at odds with Mrs. Roosevelt over a racial incident. In 1940 she had not yet become fully aware of the extent to which all Negroes suffered almost daily humiliations and how bitterly we felt about these injustices. She was deeply compassionate, but as the President's wife she recognized political limitations on her activities, and in my impatient eyes she seemed too cautious at times. I think her gradual rise to her position as foremost champion of human rights came slowly and painfully, and that her greatness developed out of her capacity for growth through difficult experiences and from her unflinching honesty with herself and others. It was her own public disclosure of her effort to come to grips with racial segregation in Washington that moved me to challenge what seemed to me to be her ambivalence.

The incident grew out of the premiere showing of the movie *Abe Lincoln in Illinois,* with Raymond Massey in the title role. The Newspaper Women's Club was sponsoring the film as their annual benefit for the Children's Hospital in Washington and had taken over the Keith Theater on January 22, 1940, for the opening night. In those days Negroes were excluded from downtown theaters, but in this instance Negro anger was further aroused by the theater management's handling of a promotional stunt scheduled for opening night. The theater had sponsored a contest to find the man in Washington whose photograph most resembled Abraham Lincoln. Ironically, the picture selected by the judges was that of a Negro. When the management discovered this fact, it discarded the contest and canceled the ceremony it had planned for opening night. Infuriated, the Washington Civil Rights Committee organized a picket line.

When Mrs. Roosevelt reported on the movie in her column the next day, she did not mention whether or not she was aware of the contest and the canceled ceremony, but she obviously felt uneasy over having crossed the picket line. She was torn between her support of the benefit and the injustice that the picket line underscored. First she commented: "There comes a time, as Lincoln's life illustrates, when one must stand up and be counted for the things in which one believes." Then she came to the heart of the matter:

> I reached the theatre last night to find it picketed by the colored people, who are barred from all District of Columbia theatres except their own. . . . It seemed to me ironic that in the nation's capital there should be a ruling which would prevent this race from seeing this picture in the same theatre with white people.
>
> It may not have been quite fair or wise to picket this particular show, because the house had been taken over by an organization for charity and the organization had a right to sell its tickets to whomever it wished. As the evening progressed, however, I could not forget those banners outside,

partly because I have a deep-rooted dislike of crossing picket lines. Though this was not a strike where any question of unfair labor conditions was involved, still I could not help feeling that there was another question here of unjust discrimination, and it made me unhappy. This occurrence in the nation's capital was but a symbol of the fact that Lincoln's plea for equality of citizenship and for freedom has never been quite accepted in our nation.

Mrs. Roosevelt's comments touched a sore spot in me, no doubt intensified by contrast with the euphoria of my recent meeting with her. Instead of being glad she had called attention to unjust discrimination I was stung by her attempt to justify crossing the picket line. I stewed over it for a week and finally had to tell her how I felt. On January 30 I wrote to her, saying:

> I was disappointed when I read your article of January 23, in which you admitted that you crossed a picket-line against your deeper feelings. In the same article you stated, "There comes a time . . . when one must stand up and be counted for the things in which one believes. It happens sooner or later to every human being." I have not been able to reconcile these two statements in my own thinking.
>
> The continual day-to-day embarrassment of a group is greater than the momentary embarrassment of the individuals who attended the Keith Theatre performance of Abe Lincoln in Illinois. The very nature of the sponsoring organization made that picket line both fair and doubly significant. The Newspaper Women's Club represented the press, the most vital contact with public consciousness.
>
> Your article, even though it reflected some indecision, was a most effective result of that demonstration. Sympathetic editorial writers have done yeoman service in building public sentiment for the rights of labor. The rights of minority groups are equally important.
>
> There can be no compromise of the principle of equality.

Mrs. Roosevelt did not respond directly to my criticism, but her secretary, Malvina Thompson, promptly acknowledged my letter and promised to give it to her at the first opportunity. I had no way of knowing then that Mrs. Roosevelt would shortly be drawn into another racial incident, in which I was personally embroiled.

We had just completed a successful National Sharecroppers Week campaign with our dinner at the Commodore Hotel in New York, at which Mrs. Roosevelt was the guest speaker, and we had raised about ten thousand dollars for the Southern Tenant Farmers Union. Easter was approaching, and my plan was to spend the holidays with Aunt Pauline and

Aunt Sallie in Durham. Adelene McBean, one of my housemates on Mount Morris Park West, wanted to go along and see the South. I enjoyed Mac's company, but had misgivings about inviting her to come with me, because she was a peppery, self-assertive young woman of West Indian parentage who had never been confronted with segregation law and believed that southern Negroes were altogether too timid about their rights. How she would react to restrictions on her freedom of movement I could not guess. Increasingly, my own resentment against segregation was becoming difficult to control. During the previous year I had read Krishnalàl Shridharami's *War Without Violence,* a study of Gandhi's method of Satyagraha —nonviolent resistance coupled with good will—and had pondered the possibility of applying the technique to the racial struggle in the United States. Mac and I had talked about it, but our knowledge was sketchy and we had no experience in the Gandhian method. Now I was anxious to get home to see my folks without incident and felt any impulse to challenge the Jim Crow system could and should be deferred until the return journey.

We traveled by Greyhound bus, stopping off in Washington to see my sister, now Mrs. Mildred Fearing. Mildred had followed her childhood dream of becoming a nurse, like our mother, and was now a head nurse at Freedmen's Hospital. I had hoped to borrow her car so as to avoid the southern lap of the bus trip, but unfortunately the car was at a garage being repaired. So on Saturday afternoon, March 23, 1940, the day before Easter, Mildred saw us off on the bus headed for Richmond. The first leg of our journey was uneventful; there were plenty of seats in the long, luxurious bus and we rode comfortably, slightly rear of center. Our troubles began when we changed in Richmond for the Durham bus scheduled to leave at 5:30 P.M. The regular bus was already filled when we presented our tickets and we were told we would have to wait for a relief bus and transfer back to the Durham bus at some point farther south.

The relief bus was late, and when it came it was an old-style, short, broken-down vehicle. We got aboard, taking the only vacant seats in the rear, but they were directly over the wheel, which protruded into the floor space and made riding very uncomfortable. The front of the bus was not crowded; some white passengers sat singly and there were two empty seats behind the driver. The driver was trying to overtake the regular bus on the twenty-three-mile run to Petersburg, and as the old bus careened around sharp curves we were nearly thrown out of our seats and across the aisle. After this happened several times Mac complained of a stabbing pain in her side and said it became unbearable each time the bus tossed us about. Finally she proposed that we move to the two empty seats behind the driver. To her, it was the simplest and most logical solution to her problem; to me, it invited disaster. I was familiar with the rigidly enforced regulation that Negro passengers fill the bus from the rear and white passengers from the front.

Hoping to forestall a crisis, I made my way forward to the driver, explained my friend's illness, and requested that he move two white passengers sitting in the rear to the empty seats in front so that we could change to a less bumpy position. It was foolish of me to expect humane treatment within the segregation system; to make the system work fairly would threaten the entire structure of white supremacy which Jim Crow was designed to reinforce. The driver shoved me backward with an impatient elbow and told me to get out of his face and take my seat. I tried once more to explain the situation, but the driver said curtly he would not change seating arrangements until we stopped in Petersburg. Mortified, I returned to the rear and persuaded Mac to try to endure the discomfort until we reached the next stop. She went along with the suggestion, but I could see that the longer she looked at those empty front seats the angrier she became.

At Petersburg, several white passengers got off and others moved forward, leaving two rows of empty seats directly in front of us. Outside the bus, about twenty picnic-bound Negroes laden with baskets of food lined up to get aboard. The driver paid no attention to us and busied himself with tickets and baggage. We realized that if we were going to change to a more comfortable position we had better do it before the crowd got on and filled up the entire rear, so we moved one row forward. The cushion of the window seat had fallen down and we could not adjust it, so we moved forward another row. We were now in the fourth row from the back seat, still behind all the white passengers. At this point the driver, whose name was Frank W. Morris, as we learned later, looked back and saw us. He yelled from the front that we would have to move back. When I told him the seat behind us was broken, he did not bother to come and inspect it; he continued yelling from the front, ordering us to move. When we showed no inclination to comply, he threatened arrest.

Mac stood her ground. Her clear voice, which carried throughout the bus and had no trace of accent, marked her as one not easily intimidated. She told the driver she had paid her money like every other passenger and she had her rights. She said she was ill and would not ride over the wheel, nor could she ride on a broken seat. She offered to leave the bus if her money was refunded and her baggage, which had been checked on the bus ahead, was returned to her. It was clear that Morris was not listening; he was aware only that we had challenged his authority and ignored his order. He stormed off the bus, which was now electric with tension, but we could expect no support from either front or rear. The white passengers acted as if it was none of their affair and the few black passengers in the rear murmured among themselves but dared not interfere. Outside, a group of white men began to collect near the door and the picnic-bound Negroes huddled together in frightened silence.

Morris was gone nearly forty-five minutes, and while we waited my anxiety mounted. Finally, I turned to the Negro passengers and asked if anyone was going to Durham. One man volunteered that he was. I quickly scribbled our names and Aunt Pauline's name and address on a slip of paper and handed it to him. Not knowing what might happen, I asked him to get in touch with her if we were arrested and to tell her to wire Walter White of the NAACP in New York City. He promised that he would, and I was relieved. Later we learned that Morris had called his dispatcher in Raleigh for advice and instructions and apparently it had taken them a long time to decide what to do. When Morris finally returned he was accompanied by two officers from the Petersburg Police Department, both fully armed. One of them, Officer Andrews, was tall and spare, smartly dressed with a Sam Browne belt over his uniform and wearing highly polished boots. The other, Officer McGhee, was so stout his huge bulk filled the aisle and bumped against the seats as he waddled toward the rear.

I was scared, but Mac showed no sign of fear. Her face registered indignation and she exploded when police officer Andrews asked us what the trouble was. She said the police needn't think they could scare her, coming in there with their "brass buttons and shiny bullets"; she knew her rights and had told the driver several times she was ill and wasn't going to ride over the wheel or on a broken seat. She added that if she were *white* and told them she was ill they would give her every consideration, and she wanted to know why they couldn't give her the same consideration even though she was colored. The police officers were obviously embarrassed by Mac's logic and hardly knew how to cope with the situation. Her theatrical language did not fit into the ordinary pattern of disorderly conduct; nor was it apparent that we were deliberately defying Jim Crow law. Yet what Mac had done was reprehensible to them—she had openly ridiculed the official symbols of white supremacy and, in a public place, had demanded courtesy to a black woman from white men.

Temporarily stumped, the police officers withdrew to the front and called the driver outside for a lengthy conference. The waiting Negroes were put on a second bus, which pulled up, and now I could see only white faces in the crowd of men milling about near the door. After more delay the officers returned; Andrews pulled out two warrants, requested our names and addresses, and wrote in the information. When I asked to see the warrants, he refused. Still hesitant to arrest us, they returned to the front once more and held another whispered conference with driver Morris. Again Officer Andrews made his way to our seat and leaned over us, this time his voice cajoling. He said he didn't want any trouble, but he was bound to carry out Virginia law, which required that we colored folks fill the bus starting from the rear. He didn't make the law, but that was the rule and there was nothing we could do about it. He told us the police were willing to meet us halfway, if we would just move back one seat.

When I told Andrews that seat was broken, he called the driver, and for the first time Morris came back, inspected the seat, and said it wasn't broken, just out of place. He worked on it for a while and eventually reinserted the seat cushion in its frame. Had he done this an hour earlier, there would have been no dispute. I tested the seat, which seemed all right, and we got up and moved back. The police officers seemed relieved, but Mac was not through with the driver and told him she thought he ought to apologize for the discourteous manner in which he had handled the entire situation. Morris mumbled something about "wanting every-body to have a square deal" and returned to the front, followed by the policemen. As they got off, they handed the warrants to Morris, saying pointedly that he might as well hang on to them in case we gave him any more trouble.

Since we had complied with the police directive, I assumed the matter was closed. It was now nearly eight o'clock—the bus had been held up almost two hours—and we had not eaten since noon. We were as anxious as everyone else to get going. A few white passengers got on and two sat in the seat we had just vacated. Morris settled behind the wheel, swung the door shut, and turned on the ignition. Then, as an afterthought, he suddenly opened the door, letting the motor idle, jumped out, and hurried inside the bus station. He came back shortly with a packet of white cards and, moving down the aisle, distributed them among the white passen-gers, asking that they fill in their names and addresses and return the cards to him. When he reached the last white passenger he turned around and went forward, ignoring all the Negroes in the rear.

I leaned over and read the card held by the man in the seat in front of me. It was a form used in case of an accident, providing space for a brief description of what happened and for a signature indicating willingness to testify in the event of a lawsuit. Morris clearly intended that only white people would be used as witnesses. Up to this point my role in the ludi-crous affair had been relatively minor, but this final damning implication that black people were *nobodies* and did not have to be taken into account was more than I could bear. I called out to the driver and asked why he did not hand out some of the cards to the people in the rear. My question ignited the fire that had been smoldering since I first spoke to Morris. Without a word, he bounded off the bus and was back almost immediately with the two police officers, who fairly ran down the aisle. Andrews barked that we were under arrest and read a warrant to each of us in turn, charging disorderly conduct and creating a public disturbance. The charge was ridiculous, of course. Except for Mac's remark about "brass buttons and shiny bullets," our language had been restrained and we had sat quietly throughout, but we had exposed the injustice of the Jim Crow system and must be punished for our effrontery.

We offered no resistance to the arrest. I got up, hauled down my typewriter, books, and briefcase from the overhead rack and handed Mac her hatbox. As I lugged my belongings toward the front, I heard a commotion behind me. Mac had fainted and fallen across two people sitting opposite us. The two policemen half-carried, half-dragged her to the door, and when they got her outside, they sent someone for a stretcher, put her on it, and laid it on the ground to wait for the police wagon. I remember saying to the driver as I left the bus, "You haven't learned a thing in two thousand years." I could not forget that it was Easter Even.

As I stood there shivering in the chilly twilight air, worrying over what had happened to Mac, all the horrors of the South which had shaped my childhood and lurked just beneath the level of consciousness came back and left me almost rigid with fear. I had seldom felt so alone and helpless as I did now, surrounded by strange white men who looked on with bawdy amusement. Just then someone touched me on the arm and I turned to see a neatly dressed Negro man standing next to me. Under his breath he asked my name. I told him, then asked if he would wire my sister in Washington, saying he could get her address from the Washington telephone operator. He nodded that he understood and slipped back into the crowd. The man did not identify himself, but his fleeting presence reassured me that we were not alone.

In fact, my worst fears were never realized. By 1940 the Commonwealth of Virginia had become sophisticated in handling racial incidents on interstate buses. While it would tolerate no breach in its wall of segregation, it would also make sure that there was no basis for a charge of police brutality. When the police wagon arrived, we were whisked to the Petersburg City Hospital, where Mac was treated for hysteria and minor bruises and carefully examined for further injuries. The medical staff was courteous throughout, and when Mac was able to get up and walk about without assistance, we were carted off to the Petersburg City Prison.

Once there, we encountered a different attitude. We were not allowed to communicate with anyone, and when I protested, the surly deputy acting as night jailer shouted obscenities at me. "Don't you come in here trying to boss me," he said. "We're the boss now, an' if you don't shet up I'll set your ass in the dungeon. Time them rats down there get through with you, you'll wish you'd kep' your mouf shet!" An alarmed glance from Mac told me it was better to face jail together than to risk separation, so I subsided.

Since we had little cash on us, we refused bail, which meant we would have to stay in prison from Saturday night until Tuesday morning, when Recorder's Court reopened after the Easter holiday. We were stripped of our purses and luggage, but I had stuffed a small flashlight, notepaper, and pencils in the pockets of my raincoat, which I was allowed to keep. We were led upstairs, through a long corridor lined with male prisoners lying on pallets along the walls, and were thrust into a narrow cell behind a heavy door in which three other women were being held. A rust-encrusted sink and foul-smelling open toilet stood near the door. Close to the heavily barred windows at the other end of the cell were four double-decker iron beds pushed against the wall. Each bed had a grimy straw mattress, one sheet, and a grease-caked blanket. There were no towels for washing and only one bar of soap. The women were occupied in building a small smudge fire in the center of the cement floor, using scraps of paper they had saved for the purpose, to ward off the huge water bugs that crawled out of the cracks at night.

Mac and I were cold and hungry, having eaten no supper. We were afraid to go to sleep because we discovered the mattresses were alive with bedbugs, so we sat shivering on the edge of our bunks most of the night. Our three cellmates regarded us with suspicion bordering on hostility. Our speech and clothing marked us as strangers, and the reason for our incarceration did not conform to the usual offenses with which local women were charged. One woman said she had been picked up for soliciting; another claimed she was arrested for being on the street after curfew; the third told us she was there for "busting a milk bottle" over her boyfriend's head.

Next morning at eight o'clock, a Negro trusty brought in our breakfast of cold, sodden pancakes with molasses and a large pail of bitter-tasting black coffee, from which he poured a dipperful for each prisoner into a smaller pail. We drank our allotment from tin cups. At three o'clock we would get a plate of cold mashed potatoes, hunks of tough chicken, dumplings, and stewed apples. On Monday our dinner would be two slabs of soggy cornbread and white beans cooked with salt pork. Coffee was served at five o'clock each afternoon.

With the coming of Easter Sunday morning our spirits revived, and Mac and I looked about us for ways in which to keep ourselves occupied. It seemed important to continue our protest against Jim Crow even though we were behind bars. As I later wrote to a friend, describing the episode: "We did not plan our arrest intentionally. The situation developed and, having developed, we applied what we knew of *Satyagraha* on the spot." An opportunity presented itself when we read a fly-specked printed bulletin of prison regulations pasted on the wall. We penciled the following memorandum on our lined notepaper:

March 24, 1940

To: Deputy
    Petersburg Jail

We: Pauli Murray
    Adelene McBean

Request the following in accordance with
"Rules for Prisoners"—#2—"Each prisoner
shall keep his person, clothing and cell equipment
clean. Regular bath days are provided on Tuesday
and Saturday of each week." —Since we desire to
cooperate fully with the officials of this jail and
since we also desire to avoid the risk of disease
from uncleanliness, we desire:

1 sheet — Pauli Murray
1 sheet — Adelene McBean
1 Towel — Pauli Murray
1   "   — Adelene McBean
1 Bar Face Soap

We have in the office:

1 P'kg. books (held with leather carrying strap)
1 black leather zipper portfolio
1   "   typewriter case

May we have these articles?

We would appreciate your extension of the above
courtesies. We realize that you have rules which
you are *compelled* to observe and we respect them
although we may not be in agreement with them.

Thanking you very kindly for your kindness and
courtesy *thus* far.

Pauli Murray
Adelene McBean

It was not an entirely futile gesture, as we would discover later. Although inexperienced in Gandhi's method, we sensed the importance of using every opportunity to insist upon humane treatment while we ourselves were courteous in putting forth our demands. Such an approach was apparently unsettling to white officials. Hostile resentment on the part of Negroes could be dealt with by intimidation or force. Courteous behavior which nevertheless revealed a clear demand for justice sometimes pierced their outer defenses, reached their consciences, and wrung from them small concessions.

A more perplexing problem we had to deal with that weekend was our relationship to our fellow prisoners. Only our cell door separated males from females. The Negro males were crowded into the corridor because there was not enough space for them, although there were empty cells in the white prisoners' section. They relieved their boredom by focusing upon the women on the other side of the door, amusing themselves with a small mirror placed under the door and held at various angles to keep the women under constant observation. The shifting mirror robbed us of all privacy. The three other women kept up a steady flow of flippant conversation with the men outside, centered on sex and sexual gratification and laced with obscenities, all of which grew monotonous from endless repetition. When Mac and I failed to join in these conversations, the men outside began asking provocative questions about "those two New York whores in there."

Realizing it would be useless to protest against their insults, we finally decided to try the same method of approach to the Negro male prisoners we had used upon the white jailer. We composed a polite memorandum giving a brief account of our arrest and stressing the injustice of racial segregation. When we slipped it under the door the effect was surprising. The jeering remarks gradually ceased as the memorandum circulated among the men outside. During the next twenty-four hours, at least four notes were pushed under our door. Each was apologetic, expressed sympathy, and asked for help in the man's own case. One wrote: "I'm sorry you got in here and I hope you get out." Another promised to be "a little better in my behave [*sic*], as it is I am in a bad condishin and a good word from anyone will do me good in some way." A third confided: "I had some bad luck too. I am accused of shooting a cop so you can imagine how I feel and the fix I am in, but if I get over this I [will] never show my face in these parts again."

The women also became less hostile. Talking about their own problems, they gradually shed some of their defensiveness and bias against "educated Negroes," and eventually we were all agreeing on the need for solidarity in the struggle for racial emancipation.

Mac and I spent several hours that Sunday drafting a detailed Statement of Facts on our arrest and imprisonment while the incident was fresh
in our minds. We included the name of the bus driver, the names and
badge numbers of the police, and we drew a rough diagram of the bus and
its seating arrangements. Sunday evening we were surprised to receive a
visit from two local NAACP attorneys, Raymond J. Valentine and Robert
H. Cooley, Jr. They practiced as partners in Petersburg and offered to
represent us. We learned that the man who had observed our arrest and
approached me at the bus station was a member of the Petersburg
NAACP, E. C. Davis, who immediately reported the incident to H. E.
Fauntleroy, president of the local branch. Contact was made with Charles
H. Houston, in Washington, dean of the NAACP legal counsel, who in turn
telephoned Valentine and Cooley and asked them to investigate. They
complimented us on our Statement of Facts and remarked that trained
attorneys could hardly have done a better job.

The word of our arrest had gotten around, and when the police court
opened on Tuesday morning about 250 people, evenly divided between
blacks and whites, jammed the small courtroom and stood around the
walls. In court the prosecution amended the warrants to include violation
of sections of the segregation law. We were quickly convicted, Judge
Clemens of the Recorder's Court fined us five dollars and costs, and our
attorneys filed notice of appeal. The case was set down for retrial in
Hustings Court in April.

After we were released on bond and returned to jail to get our belongings, we observed that the deputy's attitude had softened considerably
since Saturday evening. He virtually apologized for his earlier conduct
and made lame remarks about "ignorant folks in both races." We took
advantage of his more friendly stance to point out the unsanitary conditions among Negro prisoners in the jail and to suggest he had a duty to
improve them. He had not bargained for this comeback and was visibly
relieved when we left the prison.

Ironically, when we caught the 2 P.M. bus out of Petersburg on Tuesday
after our trial, the driver was Frank W. Morris! This time, however, two
Greyhound guards in uniform boarded the bus at Petersburg and rode it
through to Durham. It was a new-style bus and driver Morris was the
essence of new-found courtesy. At each rest stop he called out the length
of time allotted, the location of white and colored rest rooms, and all other
information necessary for the convenience of passengers. It seemed obvious that he was under observation, and we also suspected that this was the
beginning of a change of policy toward Negro passengers.

In time, we learned that during our crisis my sister Mildred Fearing had sent an urgent telegram to Mrs. Roosevelt, who responded through her secretary about ten days later:

> Mrs. Roosevelt asked me to write you and say that she had an investigation made after receiving your telegram about your sister. She asked the Governor of Virginia about it, which was all she could do, and he says that Miss Murray was unwise not to comply with the law. As long as these laws exist, it does no one much good to violate them.

Much as I admired Mrs. Roosevelt, I was deeply troubled when I learned of her letter and was even more convinced that she had little understanding of what it meant to be a Negro in the United States at that time. Yet it was hardly surprising that she seemed to disapprove of our resistance to discrimination in the climate of 1940. Unlike the 1950s and the 1960s, when the Supreme Court had outlawed segregation, and going to jail in the civil rights struggle was commonplace, in 1940 it was somehow horrifying to "respectable" people. Isolated incidents like our arrest created only a small flurry of excitement limited to a few dedicated egalitarians.

Lewis E. Austin was one of the few who saw our arrest as a sign of coming events. In addition to a lengthy account in the April 6 issue of the *Carolina Times*, he wrote an editorial which concluded:

> Perhaps Miss Murray and Miss McBean are the beginning of a new type of leadership—a leadership that will not cringe and crawl on its belly merely because it happens to be faced with prison bars in its fight for the right.

My friend Ted Poston wrote a story for the *Pittsburgh Courier*, revealing an interesting fact brought out in the trial—namely, that Virginia segregation law did not require Negroes to fill buses from the rear; it required only that they not sit on "contiguous seats" with white people. The bus companies had adopted the more stringent regulation for their own convenience. Several friends in the Workers Defense League sent us sympathetic letters enclosing small sums to help out with travel expenses, and a sociology class from Virginia State College in Petersburg, a Negro institution, came to observe our appeal. Otherwise, the incident attracted little attention outside of Petersburg.

The NAACP, however, was on the alert to find test cases that challenged the Jim Crow system, and its legal staff decided to handle our defense in the hope of raising the issue of the constitutionality of state segregation law in interstate travel. Mac and I were invited to meet with a committee of attorneys at Howard University School of Law in Washington, to develop strategy. The group included Messrs. Valentine and Cooley from Petersburg, Oliver Hill from Richmond, Thurgood Marshall, a Washington lawyer named Henry Lincoln (Link) Johnson, Jr., and, from the law school, Judge William H. Hastie and Dr. Leon A. Ransom. It was my first exposure to a team of able civil rights lawyers in action, and I sat enthralled for several hours, listening to their spirited arguments as they constructed a theory of the case.

Andy Ransom, criminal law expert, assumed the role of devil's advocate, presenting arguments to support the position of the Commonwealth of Virginia and finding weak spots in the NAACP approach. Judge Hastie was cool and detached. He spoke seldom, but when he did, his rapier mind thrust to the core of an issue. My excitement increased as I found myself able to follow the line of argument and even to anticipate points in rebuttal. As the evening progressed I began to sense that our case was a small part of a team effort which envisioned the ultimate overthrow of all segregation law. The thought was stupefying.

But for all our careful preparation, we lost the case. Upon trial in the Hustings Court, the prosecution omitted the charge of violation of the state segregation statutes and the judge, whose name was Wilson, shrewdly avoided the constitutional issues by ruling that while we were not guilty of violating the segregation statutes, we were guilty of creating a disturbance. He rejected counsel's argument that in order to convict us of disturbing the peace the prosecution must show a threat of violence or intent of violence, and its further argument that mere hysteria or raised voices in the assertion of one's rights did not constitute a breach of the peace.

Link Johnson had anticipated this outcome and had developed the argument that the state could not evade a constitutional challenge to the segregation statute by the indirect means of punishing the defendant through the device of a disorderly conduct charge. Unfortunately, on the morning of our trial in Petersburg, he had to appear in court in Washington. Hoping to join us in time to present his argument if it was needed, he hurried through his Washington appearance and flew his small private plane down to Petersburg. During the trial we could hear his plane buzzing round and round overhead, looking for a landing field. By the time he arrived in court, the judge had already ruled in our case and was about to adjourn for lunch. Link approached the bench, explained his delay and the importance of his argument, and persuaded the judge to permit him to present it immediately after lunch. He argued so forcefully that Judge Wilson postponed his decision to give Link time to file a written brief.

On May 10 we traveled once more to Petersburg, to hear Judge Wilson's final ruling. A minute late, he rushed into court, mounted the bench, and riffled hurriedly through his papers. Without looking once in our direction, he announced, "About those two girls—there's nothing in this brief to make me change my mind—I still fine them ten dollars and costs each." For us this meant $21.70 each.

Many years later the Supreme Court upheld the point Link Johnson was trying to make, but at the time, the NAACP decided it would be inadvisable to risk an appeal, and we became one more casualty in the long, hard struggle to outlaw segregation. By that time we were so disheartened and angry that we preferred to go back to jail rather than pay the fine. Having faced the fear of southern justice on Easter weekend, I would never again regard it with the same terror.

When we arrived at the Petersburg City Prison for the second time, we got a different reception. We didn't know whether it was due to the letters we had written to the local NAACP describing the unsanitary conditions in the jail or to Mrs. Roosevelt's inquiry to the governor, but the jailer seemed anxious to create a more favorable impression. He put us in a cell by ourselves, somewhat cleaner than the other one. He let us keep our books, papers, and all other belongings except my typewriter. When we requested clean mattresses, extra sheets, a broom, soap, toilet paper, and a trash can, he said he'd do the best he could, within reason. Shortly after that a Negro trusty brought in clean mattresses for the double-decker bed, and he was followed by a crew armed with brooms, pail, mop, and disinfectant to scrub the floor and clean out the toilet. Later, another squad came with spray guns and an acetylene torch to burn out the vermin. Apparently only an acetylene torch could drive out the hordes of bedbugs concealed in the cracks of the iron beds.

Fortunately, our stay was brief. After several days Dave Clendenin and Morris Milgram of the Workers Defense League wired the money to pay our fines and we were released. Although we had lost the legal battle, the episode convinced me that creative nonviolent resistance could be a powerful weapon in the struggle for human dignity.

CHAPTER 13

A Sharecropper's Life

W<small>HEN</small> I left Petersburg in May 1940, after getting out of jail for the second time, I felt like the young man who had written "I will never show my face in these parts again." I was convinced that nothing could induce me to return to Virginia for any reason. Back in New York, I found a part-time job and tried to get on with my writing. That summer, however, I was asked to serve on the Workers Defense League administrative committee and accepted out of gratitude to the WDL friends who had supported me through the Petersburg ordeal.

At one of the weekly meetings in August, Dave Clendenin reported on the case of a young Negro named Odell Waller. Waller, who lived in Pittsylvania County in southwest Virginia, had shot his white landlord, Oscar Davis, in a dispute over their jointly owned wheat crop. Our information was sketchy, but it appeared that while Waller was away working, Davis had evicted Waller's foster mother, Annie, and his wife, Molly, from the little shack they lived in on the Davis place. When the wheat which Waller had helped to plant was harvested, Davis had taken Waller's quarter share of 208 bags and locked it in his own barn. Waller came home, went to see Davis, and they had an argument, which culminated in the shooting. Davis died two days later with four bullet wounds in him, Waller escaped to Ohio, where he was caught, and extradition proceedings were now pending.

The committee's response to Dave's report was not enthusiastic. The matter was somewhat remote and the organization had no funds for legal defense. Action was tabled until further information could be obtained. As a new member, unfamiliar with the workings of the WDL, I sat silently through these deliberations.

The Waller case was again on the agenda at the Wednesday meeting before the November election. This time Dave Clendenin reported that Francis Heisler, a veteran labor attorney associated with the WDL, had represented Waller in an unsuccessful attempt to prevent his extradition from Ohio. Once Waller was back in Virginia, Thomas H. Stone, an attorney from Richmond, had taken on Waller's case and Mr. Heisler agreed to join him as defense counsel. But on the day set for trial, Mr. Heisler had to argue a case before the United States Supreme Court. He telephoned Judge Turner Clement of the Circuit Court of Pittsylvania County, who presided at Waller's trial, explaining his predicament and asking for a one-day postponement to allow him to travel to southern Virginia. He even said he could get there by five o'clock that afternoon if necessary. The judge refused all his pleas, and Waller went to trial without representation from the WDL.

Tom Stone, Waller's attorney, had done the best he could. At the outset of the trial he moved to quash the indictment on the ground that the grand jury had been selected from a list composed exclusively of poll tax payers, in violation of Waller's constitutional rights. His motion was denied. Waller was tried before an all-white jury of ten farmers (most of whom employed sharecroppers), a businessman, and a carpenter. Virginia justice was swift; in less than two weeks Waller had been indicted, brought to trial, and convicted of first-degree murder (despite evidence to suggest self-defense), and he had been sentenced to death. Now he was being transferred to Richmond to die in the electric chair two days after Christmas.

This news shocked the WDL executive committee into action. Waller had less than six weeks to live unless we could come up with $350 in the next three weeks to file an appeal before the court's term ended, but we had no money in our defense fund. The committee felt that Richmond was the most likely place to begin a drive for financial support and decided that a WDL representative should be sent there immediately. Dave Clendenin, who as chief executive was the most logical person to undertake this crucially important assignment, was already scheduled to go on a speaking tour within the next few days and so was unavailable. Morris Milgram, his assistant, would have to stay in New York to run the office, and no other experienced member of the committee was free to go. Then someone suggested that I be asked to spend a week in Richmond, interview some of the leading townspeople on Waller's behalf, begin raising money for his defense, and organize a committee to carry on the effort after I left.

I raised objections immediately, unnerved by the very thought of returning to Virginia. Richmond was a strange southern city, where I knew almost no one; I had little experience in fund-raising and doubted my ability to persuade people to take up the cause of an unknown sharecropper. I argued that someone with more know-how should be sent. My protestations carried little weight with other committee members, who insisted that we must take the risk, that we had no alternative, and that if I did not accept the assignment Waller almost certainly would die on December 27. When it was put that way, I could hardly refuse; I could not have borne the weight of Waller's death on my conscience if I had made no effort to save his life.

Difficulties plagued the mission from beginning to end. First there was the problem of transportation. Having no car, but having vowed not to submit to Jim Crow travel again, I had no way to get to Richmond without being confronted by segregation laws on bus or train. I was being forced to choose between jeopardizing the effort to save another human being's life and compromising my personal dignity. In my dilemma, Dr. Candace Stone came to my assistance. Pan Stone was a social scientist, a vigorous member of WDL, and a passionate advocate of racial justice as well as women's rights. (She was a collateral descendent of Lucy Stone, the nineteenth-century feminist leader.) Pan offered me her most cherished possession—a ramshackle 1931 convertible coupe with an unreliable motor and a canvas top full of holes which gave little protection against bad weather. I was reluctant to take the car on a long trip alone and was just about to refuse Pan's generous offer when a mutual friend, Gene Phillips, who had driven the car and was familiar with its eccentricities, volunteered to drive down with me. Gene, who was not working at the time, was eager to help because of the strong interest in sharecropper problems she had developed as a Federal Emergency Relief Administration worker in her native Oklahoma during the Depression.

Grateful as I was for Gene's companionship, her presence on the trip presented a further difficulty. Since she was white, traveling with her below the Mason and Dixon line would generate a host of complications. We would be unable to find eating accommodations together on the road, and we would have lodging problems in Richmond. An interracial pair was then such an uncommon sight in the South that even liberals of both races might assume we were Communists and be frightened off.

Waller's impending electrocution, however, drove us to risk what otherwise would have been unthinkable. In the cold, predawn hours of the Thursday after Election Day 1940, Gene and I began our trip to Richmond with a borrowed thirty-five dollars between us, a pair of blankets, our suitcases, and some WDL literature. The car's motor was not to be hurried, and we had to drive slowly. South of Pennsylvania, we avoided restaurants and instead ate sandwiches and drank coffee from a thermos we had brought along. In Baltimore, we stopped at my sister Grace's home, and she gave us lunch. It was almost eight o'clock in the evening when we limped into Richmond, weary from driving a balky car but encouraged by the total cost of our trip, only $5.66, including $1.45 for tolls. We had one moment of panic when we were stopped by a police officer a few blocks inside the city line; apparently we had been driving without a taillight all the way from Washington. The officer told us where we could find a repair shop and, relieved, we thanked him and drove on.

Our instructions had been to go first to the office of Waller's defense attorney, Thomas Stone, who would arrange lodging for us. We had arrived so late, however, that Stone's office was closed and we could find no telephone listing for his residence. We could not afford hotel rooms, which in our case would be a double expense since Jim Crow law required that we stay in separate hotels.

Then I remembered my widowed cousin Sadie Clegg Moore, who lived with her four children in a Negro neighborhood on West Clay Street. I had not seen Cousin Sadie for a number of years and did not know how she would react to Gene's presence, but she seemed our only hope of finding a place to sleep. When we arrived, she was surprised but glad to see me, welcomed us warmly, and gave us dinner. She asked no questions about Gene's identity and we volunteered no information that night, telling her only of our mission. She insisted upon giving us her bedroom and slept with her young daughter Thelma on a narrow couch in her small front room.

The next morning, however, Cousin Sadie took me aside and asked whether my friend was white or colored. When I told her, she said it made no difference to her, but she thought I was taking an awful chance in the South. She had heard about my trouble in Petersburg and was afraid for me. She was sympathetic to our cause and willing to share whatever she had with us, but I knew we should not inconvenience her further and would have to find another place to stay.

That morning we spent several hours in Attorney Stone's office going over the court record and learning the background of Odell Waller's case. Details that we discovered later sharpened the all too familiar story of grinding poverty and exploitation and the tangled relations of black and white people within the degrading sharecropper system. The journalist Murray Kempton and I subsequently coauthored a pamphlet for the WDL which traced events from the beginning:

Odell Waller's foster parents, Willis and Annie Waller, had been a hardworking couple who farmed their own land near Gretna, Virginia, and owned a half interest in a wheat binder. During the Depression they could barely meet their mortgage payments and taxes, and Odell had to leave school at sixteen to help them in the fields. When Willis Waller died in 1938, the family lost its independence; the bank moved in to foreclose the mortgage and within two months their land was sold from under them.

Odell, nearly twenty-two at the time, wanted to give up farming and get public work, but Annie thought farming was the only way she could make a living and for her sake he stayed on, married Molly, and the three of them began farming on shares. In 1939 they took their wheat binder and two hogs and went to live in a little shack on Oscar Davis' place. They put in corn, wheat, and tobacco. Three out of every four bags of wheat they harvested and three out of every six bundles of tobacco they grew went to Oscar Davis. He also got three-fourths of the corn crop. Most of their wheat went into flour for bread, their corn was used to feed the hogs, and the cash from their share of the tobacco was barely enough to keep them out of debt.

Oscar Davis was a white tenant farmer who rented his land, and when the tobacco market fell off, he too felt the pinch of the Depression. He had tried to stave off his creditors by bootlegging liquor on the side, and he shaved his expenses by squeezing the poverty-stricken colored farmers who worked his crops. To the white people around Gretna, he was a good Christian who taught Sunday school at the Methodist Church and never spared himself or his two strapping sons in the farm work. To the colored people, however, Davis was "a mean white man" who didn't keep his promises. "He liked to dawg the colored man," we were told. "He wanted you to do all the work while he did all the ridin' 'round." His third wife was a frail, sickly woman, and his two sons hated farmwork and never failed to tell him so. They had arguments, and once when Oscar Davis had a falling out with his son Edgar, it became known that for weeks afterward he carried a gun.

When government agents assigned his tobacco allotment in 1939, Davis cut to two acres the land he rented to the Wallers and pocketed the cash benefits the government paid him for reducing his acreage. With their cash crop virtually eliminated, the Wallers faced desperate times. Odell put in the wheat and tobacco crops in the spring of 1940, then took a contract job in Maryland to earn some cash. To save his share of the wheat crop, he sent Annie Waller money from his earnings to pay a cousin, Robert Waller, to work in his place, and he instructed her to help Mr. Davis with the tobacco crop and let the Davis family use the Waller's wheat binder during the harvest of the wheat crop. While Odell was working in Maryland, however, relations between Oscar Davis and Annie Waller deteriorated. In addition to helping Mr. Davis with the tobacco crop—she said later, "when it was cold, and rainin', and so raw no 'oman oughter been outdoors, there I was workin' up to my ankles in that red mud in the rain till it was so dark I couldn't even see the rows before me" —Annie Waller did housework for Davis' wife during a period when Mrs. Davis was ill. Her pay was $2.50 a week, and Davis owed her $7.50 by the time Mrs. Davis was up and about. He kept promising to pay but never got around to it. Finally, when Annie Waller refused to help work the tobacco until the money was paid, Davis told her he wanted his house back and three days later sent the sheriff's deputy with a notice of eviction. Annie and Molly Waller had to get out, taking along their wheat binder, their hogs and chickens, and leaving behind their little garden of "greens" they had planted that spring. The local colored minister let them stay in a little cabin he owned just outside Gretna.

In spite of the eviction, Annie Waller knew she must save Odell's share of the wheat. When harvest time came, a few weeks later, she followed his instructions, let Mr. Davis use the wheat binder, and put Robert Waller in the field to help with the harvest. She put in "fifty for fifty," bringing her own food over to the Davis house to cook for the men while they worked. They threshed out the wheat and put it into two-bushel bags, then Robert Waller lined them up in two rows—three bags on one side for Oscar Davis to every one bag on the other side for Odell Waller. When Davis saw Robert Waller dividing the wheat he stopped him and said, "All that wheat's going down in my barn." The 208 bags of wheat were lumped together, carried to Davis' barn, and locked up.

When Odell came home on Sunday, July 14, he listened to Annie's story of what had happened. Next morning he borrowed a truck and got some friends to go with him to the Davis house to get his wheat. Annie Waller went along with them to dig up some vegetables from the garden she had left behind. When they arrived, Mr. Davis was standing in the yard talking to Henry Davis, an eighteen-year-old Negro youth of the same surname who worked for him. Two months later in Chatham court, Odell was to tell the story this way:

"When I walked up in the yard, I said, 'Good morning, Mr. Davis, I come here to get my wheat.'

"Mr. Davis said I won't gonna get that damn wheat away from here. I said, 'I got a truck.'

"He said, 'I told you you won't gonna carry it away from here.'

"He used some dirty words, and from one word to another, and he usually carried a gun and run his hand in his pocket like he was trying to pull out something. I had my gun and out with it. I opened my pistol and commenced to shoot at him—I don't know how many times. Mr. Davis hollered and fell. I went down by the barn in the woods and stayed down there until in the evening. . . . I left to get out of the way and keep 'em from stretching me up."

When Odell started for the woods, his last words to Annie Waller were, "Momma, get the wheat." Annie, who had been sitting in the truck and heard the first shot, told the driver, "Turn this truck 'round and le's get out of here." Oscar Davis was taken to Memorial Hospital in Lynchburg, where he died two days later. Authorities in Columbus, Ohio, picked up Odell during the first week in August. Before they caught him, white men around Gretna were out in the woods with guns and dogs, hunting Odell "like he was a rabbit." Twice someone broke into Annie Waller's little cabin, looking for photographs or letters. Molly was so frightened she refused to live in the shack any longer, and finally Annie had to move out to stay with neighbors. She was not to see Odell again until the authorities brought him back to Virginia to await trial.

At the trial, Henry Davis, the Negro eyewitness, testified that his boss was unarmed and Odell just up and shot Mr. Davis without a cross word passing between them. Two Negroes also testified that on Sunday Odell had threatened to kill Mr. Davis. Mrs. Oscar Davis testified that when she heard the shooting she ran out and led Oscar into the house and helped him get off his pants. She claimed he had nothing except his billfold in his pockets. Nineteen-year-old Frank Davis told the court his father's dying words were, "Frank, I am going to die. Odell shot me without any cause. He shot me four times, twice after I fell." It developed in cross-examination that when Frank Davis testified at the preliminary hearing several weeks earlier, he had said nothing about his father being shot twice after he fell, and it appeared that his testimony had been coached.

The only witnesses for Odell were Molly and Annie Waller, and a friend who was with him on the truck that day. None of them had seen the shooting and their testimony couldn't help Odell very much. Annie said later that Judge Clement did not let her explain many things that to her were important. "I said just a few words, and I was getting so far down to what really happened that the jedge set me down."

It hardly mattered. The jury needed little convincing by the commonwealth's attorney to reach a guilty verdict. The trial was over in two days, and Odell was sent up to Richmond to die. Ironically, after the trial the Davis boys finally brought Annie Waller her share of the wheat—fifty bags.

The whole case was disheartening. Little of the background was known to the public and it would be difficult to arouse sympathy for Waller in the face of newspaper stories that had played up the shooting as first-degree murder. Stone was looking to us to raise money for Waller's appeal, but he made no attempt to find lodging for us. We had originally planned to separate when we got to Richmond, Gene to interview white people while I approached the Negroes. We soon found, however, that Richmond was a sprawling, hilly town, cut in half by the James River and spreading into suburbs that reached more than ten miles into the countryside. The weather was cold, streetcars came at long intervals, and we had only one car. Gene was reluctant to set out alone and finally insisted that we make our rounds together.

Stone referred us to the local secretary of the Socialist party, Hilliard Bernstein, who was more familiar with living arrangements, he said, as well as fund-raising contacts. We found Bernstein huddling by his kitchen stove in a shabby house across the river in one of the poorer white sections of town. He was a wounded, unemployed veteran of the Spanish Civil War and in dire straits. His wife was in the hospital for the birth of their second child, their three-year-old was staying with his wife's mother, and he was trying to keep warm by the sparing use of seven-cent paper bags of coal whenever he could afford them. The only heat came from the kitchen stove and two open fireplaces. Apologizing for having so little to offer us, he said we could stay in a spare room in his house if we wished. I had misgivings about staying in a white neighborhood, but for want of an alternative we accepted, although I felt terribly exposed every time I entered the house.

Bernstein's pessimism about the Waller case made us even more discouraged. Although he supplied us with all the names on his contact list, he was reluctant to make any contacts for us. He told us candidly that he believed Thomas Stone's association with Waller's defense was the greatest obstacle to liberal and labor support. Stone was known as a good lawyer, but his past record as a leader of the Communist party in Richmond in the early 1930s and his continued association with the Revolutionary Workers League had alienated not only liberals but also the Socialist party. The only person he thought likely to help us was another Socialist, Mrs. C. L. Hewett, whose husband, secretary of the local Painters Union, had influence in the A.F.L. Bernstein doubted that we could get any tangible support from the Richmond area unless it came from labor unions.

Bernstein's estimate proved accurate. Mrs. Hewett, who lived in a modern bungalow eight miles out from the city, was very cordial, insisted on serving us lunch—our first decent meal in two days—and invited us back to spend the night, but beyond a small contribution, she refused to have anything to do with a case Tom Stone was involved in and thought his association with Waller's cause would hurt more than help it.

It was the same everywhere. One after another, the liberals on our list smiled nervously when they learned Attorney Stone was defense counsel, and referred us to someone else. A few pledged a dollar or two and said they would contribute more money if we succeeded in getting the support of the Negro community. The Negroes were even more cautious than the white people. Some of the leading black ministers said they would join a committee to raise funds if it was headed by a prominent white person. For several days we were shunted back and forth between the two communities, finding neither black nor white to head the committee.

The local NAACP president could offer little financial assistance because the treasury of the local branch was being drained by the NAACP campaign to equalize Negro teachers' salaries in the state; in addition, the NAACP was supporting the fight to save the lives of four young Negroes accused of raping a white woman. The man who chaired the local Committee for the Defense of Constitutional Liberties was sympathetic, and I learned that he had attended my trial in Petersburg earlier that spring, but while he was willing to contribute personally and to present the Waller matter to his executive board, he doubted if his group would take any supportive action. He arranged an appointment for us with Virginius Dabney, editor of the influential *Richmond Times-Dispatch,* and said he would be guided by Mr. Dabney's opinion in the matter.

We knew that Virginius Dabney was a key to southern opinion, and that if we could convince him Waller deserved a new trial, others would rally to us. Mr. Dabney was genial, and while we presented our case he turned to his files and pulled out two folders, one containing a sheaf of clippings on the Waller trial, the other a batch of material on the WDL. He told us it seemed to him that Waller's was no more than the usual murder case. When we stressed our belief that Waller had shot in self-defense, Mr. Dabney told us he would do nothing until he had made a further investigation of the facts as we had presented them. We left feeling our visit had accomplished little. His doubts remained throughout the early stages of the appeal, and his immediate support was not forthcoming.

After a luxurious night in Mrs. Hewett's guest room, we returned to sleep in the cold spare bedroom at Bernstein's house, bundling up at night in our coats under two thin blankets and bathing in icy water each morning. Food was also a problem. Many of the white people on our list lived in the suburbs, where I could find no place to eat, and since Gene was too loyal to eat without me, we had to go all day without a regular meal. The general response to our appeal was so lukewarm that I thought I might present a more persuasive case if I had a personal interview with Odell Waller in the penitentiary, but when I telephoned Attorney Stone and suggested it, he informed me that a man in the death house was permitted to see only his lawyer, his closest relative, and his spiritual adviser.

By the weekend we had no commitments from any of the white people in Richmond and only two openings for Negro support. One came during a telephone conversation with Professor John M. Moore of the Sociology Department at Virginia Union University. Professor Moore cordially invited me to address the student body during their chapel service on Monday morning, and promised to have the students take up a collection for Waller's cause. The Reverend Joseph T. Hill, president of the Baptist Ministers Conference, made no promises but said I might appear before the ministers' group at their regular weekly meeting Monday noon to present Waller's case.

On Sunday, we drove over to Durham for a quick visit with Aunt Pauline and Aunt Sallie. Normally it was a six-hour drive round trip, but the car developed trouble on the way to Durham and we did not get back to Richmond until shortly before nine o'clock on Monday morning. As I pulled into a parking space on the street, my rear bumper hooked into the front fender of another parked car. The owner came out to inspect his car while a policeman nearby walked over and stood looking on. I was due at Virginia Union within a few minutes and, although the damage was slight, I quickly paid the cost of a new fender, $22.50, to avoid any further encounter with the Virginia courts.

By this time I was so shaken I was hardly fit to face an audience. I had been up all night and was grimy from the long drive, but there was no time to eat breakfast or wash and change my clothes. Trembling all over and convinced the Waller case was a Jonah, I drove cautiously to the school campus and had someone direct me to Professor Moore's office. While I waited for him the bell rang and students poured out of the buildings, making their way along the paths to the chapel. When Professor Moore appeared and I introduced myself, he looked startled and somewhat alarmed. First he asked me to wait in his office, then he changed his mind and said he would meet me outside the chapel door in a few minutes. It began to rain as I stood leaning against the chapel doorway, and I felt uncomfortable under the curious eyes of students as they passed inside. I grew more anxious after the last stragglers hurried into the chapel and the monitors closed the doors.

Finally, Professor Moore came scurrying along the path. He did not offer to take me inside but stood there looking embarrassed. He apologized profusely, then confessed he had made a blunder, that he was not in charge of chapel exercises and had no authority to invite me to speak. He explained that when he told the faculty member in charge of the chapel that I was in Richmond, and asked permission for me to speak, he was informed that Monday's program was already made up and there wouldn't be time for me. He then asked about Wednesday and got the same answer. He did not believe this was the real reason; the truth was the college officials were very conservative and they did not know my organization. He had feared this would be the result when I telephoned him on Saturday, but he had thought I was *white*, and, as he put it, he didn't have the guts to tell me that a Negro school would not be interested in my cause. He had planned to let me come anyway and confront them, since he knew they would not have the courage to say that a white woman could not speak. When I arrived and it turned out that I was a Negro, he knew we didn't have a chance. He was awfully sorry, but that was the situation.

I was too taken aback by this unexpected slap in the face from my own people to say anything. The troubled professor confided that he was in a difficult position: he had tried to organize a teachers' union on campus but had failed because of the conservative atmosphere of the college. He then gave me a dollar for membership in WDL and I left with a feeling of nausea in the pit of my stomach. Fearing another rebuff, I had no heart to go on to the Baptist Ministers Conference at noon. When I got to the church, the meeting room was filled and I slipped inconspicuously into a seat in the rear. The air was close, my head was hot and feverish, my eyes burned, my temples throbbed, and I had to fight off the urge to vomit.

The ministers' meeting combined a prayer session with a community council before which representatives of various organizations appeared to plead support for their causes and to solicit funds dispensed by the ministers from the "after collections" taken up in their churches on Sunday morning. A young man from the NAACP Youth Council was present on behalf of the anti-poll-tax drive. The Community Chest was there to have its appeal circulated among Negro Baptist congregations. A local politician seeking a judgeship came to ask for black votes. The most important item on the agenda, and one in which the Negro ministers had taken the initiative, was the case of the four young Negroes charged with raping a white waitress who had hailed them for a ride after being put out on the roadside by her white male companion. Knowing that Negroes convicted of rape seldom escaped death in the electric chair, the black community was aroused and the Negro preachers had pledged themselves to see to it the four defendants received a fair trial. Their goal was to raise one thousand dollars for the legal expenses of the topflight NAACP counsel who were representing the young men.

Dr. Leon A. Ransom from Howard Law School and Thurgood Marshall from the national office of the NAACP were in town to help Attorney Oliver Hill prepare for the trial, and Dr. Ransom was present at the ministers' meeting to summarize the status of the case and stimulate the effort to raise money. Most of the meeting was given over to Dr. Ransom's moving statement, followed by reports of the after collections, as each minister came to the front and laid his cash on the table, pledging himself and his flock to see the defendants through. When they had finished counting, only ninety-five dollars had been collected and the ministers had a long way to go to meet their objective.

As I listened to Dr. Ransom's eloquent plea and watched the ministers make their offerings, the urgency of their commitment to the defense of the four youths made any additional appeal seem hopeless, and I got up to slip away by a side door. The Reverend Hill, who had asked me to come, saw me leaving and called me to the platform. Pushing me forward, he said to the assembly, "Brothers, this young lady has a problem and I want you to hear what she has to say," and sat down without any further introduction. As I faced those seamy faces and questioning eyes, all the fatigue and frustration of the past several days overcame me. When I opened my mouth to speak, my throat worked up and down but no words came out. Suddenly the tears spurted and I burst into weeping in front of the group, something I had never done before in public. "Gentlemen," I sobbed, "I haven't the strength to give you my message." Embarrassed and humiliated, I turned to the Reverend Hill, asked him to read the statement of facts I had prepared on the Waller case, and sat down to pull myself together.

The room was suddenly quiet as the Reverend Hill read haltingly the story of a boy whose mother had been put outdoors, whose landlord refused to give them their share of the wheat crop, who went in fear to ask for an accounting and shot his landlord to death when the latter cursed him and reached threateningly into his hip pocket. The young sharecropper was condemned to die in this very city unless $350 could be raised to file an appeal within the deadline, less than three weeks away. The Workers Defense League, a struggling organization without a cent in its treasury for legal costs, had entered the case on faith and was trying to raise the necessary funds from sympathetic persons and organizations.

When the Reverend Hill finished reading, I rose and faced the assembly once more. Although unaware of it at the time, I must have been praying for strength, because the words poured out as I related our struggle to come to Richmond to raise funds for Waller's appeal, how one person had sent us to another, each one too timid to be associated with our cause; how the white people had referred us to the Negroes and the Negroes had sent us back to white people; and how Virginia Union had refused to let me speak that morning, after I had been invited and had driven all night to keep the engagement. I wound up saying that almost a week had gone by without our finding any member of the community who would take responsibility for helping this unknown, friendless sharecropper, and that if men of God could not take Waller's plight into their hearts, where were we to turn for help?

Some of the ministers were wiping their eyes when I sat down. Then a thin, short, gray-haired man who had been sitting by himself on the side got up slowly and spoke in a high, squeaky voice. He told them that he knew the young man I had been speaking about. "I am his spiritual adviser in the death house," he said. He told them he believed that Waller was "a fine young feller who needs a chance," and recommended that the ministers do whatever they could to help him. He came over to me, shook my hand, and told me he was the Reverend Bowie. He said how glad he was I was trying to help Waller and that I had made a fine talk, adding that it wasn't often our young people took an interest in such things.

The Reverend Hill got up and laid a dollar on the table. "All right, brethren," he said briskly, "you've heard the problem, what are you going to do about it?" Without a word, one after another of the ministers came forward and put down a dollar bill. There were less than thirty of them, and all but two were poor men. They had pledged their burdened congregations to many causes, but this money came from their own pockets. When the last man laid down a quarter—all he had—and somebody added seventy-five cents to it, twenty-five dollars had been collected. The Waller case eventually became a cause célèbre and before it was over we raised nearly thirty thousand dollars in contributions, yet no gift was more lavish or more crucial to Waller's defense than this initial offering from a group of prayerful Negro ministers. When the meeting was over, they all came up to me, shaking my hand and telling me their prayers and blessings would follow me.

An unexpected result of the meeting was a chance conversation with Dr. Ransom later that afternoon, which pointed me toward law school. I ran into him when Gene Phillips rejoined me to have dinner at the local Negro hotel, and he and Thurgood Marshall were eating at a nearby table. He gave me a big smile and said that he was quite impressed with the appeal I had made that day. To hide my embarrassment, I told him half-jokingly that I might as well become a lawyer if I kept bumping into the law as I had been doing for the past two years. Dr. Ransom did not laugh; he said he thought it a fine idea, that I had what it takes to make a good lawyer, and why not come to Howard; they'd be glad to have me. I did not know at the time that he was chief recruiter for Howard University School of Law and scouted promising students on his field trips. I retorted that maybe I would come to Howard if they gave me a scholarship, and Dr. Ransom promised that if I sent in my application he'd see that I got one.

The remainder of our week in Richmond was not encouraging. The labor unions turned us down and Thomas Stone's association with Waller's defense continued to be a great handicap. Some people shied away from us because they confused the Workers Defense League with Stone's organization, the Revolutionary Workers League. We succeeded in arousing the interest of a business and professional women's group through E. Pauline Myers, the energetic industrial secretary of the Phyllis Wheatley Branch, YWCA, and the Unitarian Social Problems Club took up a small collection. But our week of effort produced only $37.50 in cash contributions and $25.00 in pledges, hardly enough to cover the expenses of the trip.

CHAPTER 14

A Sharecropper's Death

GENE AND I began our drive back from Richmond in an icy rainstorm with banks of fog so thick that at times we could barely see the road a few yards ahead of us. The car had no heater, the windshield wiper was broken, and chilling rain poured steadily through holes in the canvas cover. Gene, feverish with a heavy cold, huddled miserably in a blanket while I drove with my head sticking out the window to steer the car, unable to avoid the water that dripped onto my neck and rolled down my back. The dismal weather matched our despair; I was convinced the trip had been a failure.

Surprisingly, the WDL executive committee in New York, veterans at undertaking unpopular causes, were not dismayed when I made my report and in fact asked me to go to work full time for the WDL to raise funds and enlist public support for Waller's appeal. Under the circumstances I could not refuse, in spite of self-doubts, and the campaign began with a tiny staff and a few loyal volunteers. Dave Clendenin and Morris Milgram kept the phones busy seeking emergency funds for immediate expenses; Samuel H. Friedman, a veteran of the labor press, joined the staff to write news releases and handle publicity, while I immersed myself in arranging speaking dates, building contributors lists, mimeographing leaflets, and getting out mailings. Vivian Odems, a highly competent young Hunter. College graduate, ran the office and stayed long hours into the night to help me stuff envelopes and get boxes of fund appeal letters to the post office.

Annie Waller, Odell's foster mother, came to New York at the WDL's request to speak on behalf of her son before churches, labor unions, and community groups. She was a wraithlike, tiny, brown-skinned woman whose harsh life was etched indelibly in her face, making her look much older than her fifty years. Her wrinkled, discolored hands were scarred purple and were chalky between the fingers from crop blight, her thin shoulders were stooped from constant bending in the fields, and she spoke in a high, quavering voice that was almost a sob. She was a country woman who had never traveled more than a few miles from her home in Gretna, Virginia, and although the noise and bustle of the vast city bewildered her and she was obviously frightened at the prospect of speaking to groups of strangers, she had a presence and a quiet dignity which immediately won the sympathy of her listeners.

"I came to help my boy," she told them. "There was no one else to do it with my husband dead." Without bitterness, she related the stark facts of her little family's losing struggle to maintain a shred of independence and of the tragedy that finally engulfed them after her husband's death. "Oscar Davis was almost as poor as we are," she said, as if to explain why the dead landlord had gouged them out of their living and finally taken their share of the wheat. She said of Odell, "He was such a good boy. All he wanted to do was to take care of his mother and wife. He worked like a slave and didn't mind any kind of work and any hours." Of herself, she said simply, "I worked and I worked, but it was all for Mr. Davis. I didn't see nothing in the ground for Annie."

Mrs. Waller's presence gave our efforts an immediacy and authenticity no other person could have supplied. She caught the attention of several newspapers and the case began to receive publicity. When John F. Finerty, a distinguished corporation lawyer in New York and a noted civil libertarian who sat on the WDL's national board, agreed to join WDL counsel Morris Shapiro and argue the constitutional issues on appeal, the earlier wariness of liberals began to disappear and very soon responses from our mail campaign were trickling in. Many of the contributions were small sums from poor workers who had gone without lunch, carfare, or cigarettes to aid Waller's cause. A Negro sharecropper from Tennessee sent in two worn dollar bills he had been saving to pay on his grocery account. A rural minister sent a check "for one of Christ's little ones." Some who had little money themselves had collected quarters, dimes, and nickels from friends and neighbors and had sent along lists of the donors with their contribution.

By early December we had raised the initial legal expenses to file Waller's appeal and had secured a stay of execution to March 14, 1941, from Governor James H. Price of Virginia to permit application to the state's Supreme Court of Appeals for a writ of error. Murray Kempton, then a young free-lance writer, journeyed to Gretna to gather material for a human interest story, and I was asked to return to Richmond to make further investigation. Murray Kempton and I consolidated our two reports in a pamphlet entitled "All for Mr. Davis: The Story of Sharecropper Odell Waller," which was published by the WDL. It included a short preface by Dr. Frank P. Graham, president of the University of North Carolina, and received wide circulation.

During our frantic activity I passed my thirtieth birthday in late November. The only celebration of this significant milestone was a soul-searching session with myself after everyone else had left the office. I had worked hard but had little to show for the seven years since my graduation from college—a few years as a WPA teacher (not highly regarded at the time) and several short-term jobs with precariously financed "cause" organizations. I wanted desperately to write but now realized that writing would not earn my living and that without a trade or profession I would continue to live a grubby existence in rented rooms on the fringes of society.

For some time I had been thinking of studying law. The urge had first come to me when, as a WPA Workers' Education teacher, I had taken my Henry Street Settlement House class to municipal court because one of the class members had to appear in a landlord-tenant case and it had seemed an appropriate occasion to observe the administration of justice. It was an eviction proceeding and the tenant, our class member, was a poor black woman standing alone and bewildered before the court without a lawyer. Within a few minutes the landlord's attorney got a judgment and an order of eviction, and the frightened woman was out of court with no place to stay. Now the Waller case was urging me in the same direction, yet I had so little self-confidence I assumed that the study of law was beyond my ability.

It was more a tentative gesture than an act of firm decision that prompted me that night to write to Dr. Ransom of Howard University School of Law, reminding him of our recent conversation and requesting application forms for admission. When the forms came some time later, I filled them out and returned them, still without any hope of attending law school. Not even a strong recommendation from Thurgood Marshall increased my battered confidence.

The demands of the Waller case allowed me little time to worry about my future, however. The second trip to Richmond was more successful than the first, and this time I was even permitted to visit Waller in the death house. The brief interview took place in Waller's cell on death row, which faced a short corridor that ended at a door leading to the electric chair. I recall Waller as a short, stocky young man whose straightforwardness and fortitude in the face of his trouble deeply impressed me. He never denied his responsibility in the shooting but only denied his intent to kill. "I'm as sorry as I can be it all happened," he told me earnestly. "I wasn't trying to kill Mr. Davis. I was aiming to keep him from killing me."

As I listened to Waller's story in his own words, I became more convinced than ever that he was not guilty of premeditated murder, the crime for which he was sentenced to die. Manslaughter, yes, but not intentional murder. Having grown up in the South, I could fully understand the panic which had triggered the fatal action. And so could the perceptive white Southerner Jonathan Daniels, newspaper publisher in Raleigh, North Carolina, who later wrote in *The Nation:*

> It does not seem to me strange to suppose that the white man was trying to cheat the Negro. It does not seem to me difficult to believe that the young Negro went to demand his rights more in terror than in murderousness. My observation is that more scared men kill than brutal ones. I can understand the contention that poor little Waller was the product . . . of a whole system of racial oppression, racial fear.

During those few minutes spent with Waller, I glimpsed for the first time the horrible reality of capital punishment—the oppressiveness of his somber surroundings, the unrelieved gloom of barren walls and darkened cells, the desolate hours spent in waiting, and the terrifying nearness of the electric chair a few yards away. I sensed the constant dread of a condemned man who lives each hour in anticipation of the certain fate that awaits him behind that door and also knows the day and exact hour his death will occur. I never saw Waller again, but the image of that ominous door at the end of the narrow corridor was never erased from my memory. No argument in favor of capital punishment has overcome the shattering impact of that single visit to the death house.

The fate of one man facing death in a Virginia prison might have seemed of minor importance to Americans who in the spring of 1941 were anxiously following news of the German air raids over Britain as the United States moved closer to World War II, but those of us who defended Waller believed that more than a single life was at stake. As his appeal took shape, his hope for a new trial rested on a constitutional issue of far-reaching importance which had been raised but not developed at the beginning of his trial—the use of a poll tax to determine who voted and served on juries. We were convinced that a strong democracy at home was the first line of defense against the Nazi threat and that through Waller's fight we were challenging the undemocratic poll tax system, which effectively denied millions of poor black and white sharecroppers a voice in their government. This broader dimension of the case became apparent as the legal arguments emerged.

Virginia was one of eight states in the South in 1940 that required the payment of an annual poll tax in order to gain eligibility to vote. Virginia law also required that the yearly poll tax of $1.50 be paid up for three consecutive years to qualify for inclusion on the voters roll. Since jury lists were compiled largely from voters lists, the poll tax virtually barred the overwhelming majority of poor people from voting or serving on juries. Some ten million black and white citizens—more than three-quarters of the adult population—were voteless in the eight poll tax states. In Pittsylvania County, Virginia, where Odell Waller lived and where he was tried and convicted, the 1940 census showed that there were nearly thirty thousand residents of voting age. Of these, only six thousand—one-fifth—had paid the poll tax.

The WDL counsel contended that Waller had been denied his constitutional right to trial by a jury of his peers and deprived of the equal protection guaranteed by the Fourteenth Amendment because Virginia jury law was administered in such a way that those who had not paid the cumulative state poll tax were systematically excluded from jury service. The exclusion of such a large economic class, it was argued, violated the Fourteenth Amendment. If this argument prevailed, a state could no longer use the poll tax to restrict a criminal defendant's right to be tried by a representative jury. The precedent established would encourage a direct attack upon poll tax restriction on voting rights.

That spring Mrs. Waller and I traveled from coast to coast, visiting major cities of the North and West to raise funds for Waller's defense and to arouse public interest in the plight of sharecroppers. We had little money for expenses, sat up in coaches on the long overnight trips, ate sandwiches and drank coffee during transit, and stayed in private homes wherever people were kind enough to take us in. We spoke before small groups usually sponsored by local chapters of the NAACP, the WDL, or the Brotherhood of Sleeping Car Porters. A few dozen people would gather in a dreary little meeting hall or a room in a church basement to hear us. Mrs. Waller would tell her personal story, "crudely, honestly, touchingly," as one reporter put it, and I would follow with a factual presentation of conditions among sharecroppers and the evils of the poll tax system. Deeply moved by Mrs. Waller's anguish, these little groups formed a network of staunch supporters as the Odell Waller story gradually emerged into public consciousness.

Waller became a symbol of some nine million sharecroppers in the rural South condemned to a lifelong struggle against starvation and disease. As agricultural workers, they were excluded from social security and other New Deal legislation designed to protect the interests of industrial workers. Since they were isolated on separate farms, it was difficult for them to organize and take collective action in their own behalf. They were generally at the mercy of their landlords, many of whom resorted to intimidation, eviction, and even terrorism to keep sharecroppers in a state of abject dependency. Few contracts between landlord and tenant existed in writing, and when a landlord violated an agreement (written or oral), sharecroppers either lacked money to pursue remedies in court or feared that seeking judicial redress would only make matters worse. They were the chief victims of the federal government's crop reduction program during the Depression, for, as in the Waller case, many unscrupulous landlords found it profitable to evict their tenants and keep the proceeds of government subsidy checks for themselves. This practice, along with droughts, crop failures, and foreclosures, resulted in the eviction each year of thousands of sharecroppers and small tenant farmers, who then became homeless migratory workers or swelled the public relief rolls. There was little hope of improving these conditions so long as millions of sharecroppers and small tenant farmers had no political say in the affairs of their local communities or of the nation. The Waller campaign served to expose this self-perpetuating system of injustice and to strengthen the movement to abolish poll taxes.

Each stage of the court battle, however, ended in disappointment. On October 13, 1941, the Supreme Court of Appeals of the Commonwealth of Virginia affirmed Waller's conviction and death sentence, holding that nonpayers of poll tax were not specifically excluded from juries under Virginia's constitution and laws. The crucial issue of whether in fact nonpayers of poll tax were barred from jury service by the discriminatory administration of jury law was not passed upon by the court, and Waller's lawyers now sought to raise it in habeas corpus proceedings in the state and federal courts. Meanwhile, the date of Waller's execution had been postponed from March 14, 1941, to December 9, and then from one short stay of execution to another—to March, to May, to June, to July, 1942. As his final appeals moved through the judicial system, we shared both his anxiety and his desperate hope.

After the Virginia Supreme Court denied Waller's petition for habeas corpus on May 4, 1942, the Supreme Court of the United States refused to review his case. Governor Colgate W. Darden, who had succeeded Governor Price, granted him a stay of execution to June 19 to allow his attorney, John F. Finerty, to seek a rehearing of the Court's refusal, but the outlook for favorable action was dim and the WDL began to concentrate on an organized appeal to Governor Darden to commute Waller's sentence to life imprisonment. By this time Waller had become the embodiment of the anguish felt by Negroes everywhere over intractable racial injustice, and his impending fate was no longer the concern of only a handful of liberals. Editorials appeared in newspapers across the country and some seventeen thousand petitions for commutation of his death sentence poured into Governor Darden's office. Mrs. Roosevelt had become interested in Waller's plight, and I was asked to let her know if the court decision went against him. Even Virginius Dabney, editor of the *Richmond Times-Dispatch,* was won over from his skepticism of 1940. "Too much doubt surrounds the justice of the verdict that he [Waller] is guilty of murder in the first degree," he editorialized. Dabney suggested that Governor Darden commute Waller's sentence if his counsel failed to secure him a new trial from the federal courts. He called attention to the national and international implications of the case, pointing out that "the execution of this humble Negro sharecropper" might lessen the chances of the Allies to win the war. He reminded his readers of "the fact that we are in a war for survival, in which we are depending heavily on the colored races, and the significance of the Waller case becomes clear."

On June 16, twenty thousand Negroes gathered in Madison Square Garden in New York City to demonstrate their support of A. Philip Randolph's March on Washington Movement and his militant campaign against Jim Crow. Massive SAVE ODELL WALLER banners hung from the rafters, and during the course of the evening Mr. Randolph introduced Annie Waller to the wildly cheering thousands. The cheers had barely subsided, however, when Odell Waller's last hope for judicial intervention was snuffed out. Next day John F. Finerty made a final frantic effort to secure a stay of execution from Chief Justice Harlan Fiske Stone of the United States Supreme Court. As I heard the story afterward, Mr. Finerty rushed to North Carolina to intercept the Chief Justice, who was attending a meeting in that state, only to find that he had left. Then Finerty, with the aid of a police escort, traveled for several hundred miles at high speed in pursuit of the Chief Justice's automobile and finally caught up with him at a motel. The two men sat facing each other on the twin beds in the motel room and discussed the case informally. Chief Justice Stone was sympathetic but told Finerty the fatal flaw in Waller's trial record was the failure of his defense counsel to offer specific proof that nonpayers of poll tax were excluded from jury service. Thus, even if Waller's constitutional rights were violated, the issue was not properly presented in the record. The federal courts on review were powerless to go outside the record and intervene to prevent Waller's execution. Finerty's contention that a lawyer could not waive his client's rights through an inadvertent error was in vain.

The following day, Governor Darden granted Waller a final reprieve to July 2 and set Monday, June 29, for a hearing on his petition for commutation of sentence. Meanwhile several hundred prominent citizens signed a petition addressed to President Roosevelt that urged him to appoint a presidential commission of inquiry into the Waller case, as former Presidents had done in the famous cases of Joe Hill and Tom Mooney. On Monday, Governor Darden held an all-day hearing on Waller's petition. Waller was not called to tell his own story, but he was ably represented by John Finerty, assisted by Edmund N. Preston of Richmond. Testimony given by the prosecution's key eyewitness conflicted sharply with testimony he had given previously at the trial. Mrs. Waller told of the relations between Oscar Davis and her family and gave the background of the shooting. A former employer of Waller testified that he had known him since childhood, had first employed him in 1926, when Waller was about ten, and had found him to be a quiet, steady worker, honest and no troublemaker. The sheriff of Pittsylvania County testified that commutation of Waller's sentence would increase public danger, but when pressed by Waller's counsel to be specific, the sheriff offered only the belief that certain Negro elements would celebrate the victory by crowding the sidewalks.

On Tuesday night, June 30, at 10 P.M., Governor Darden announced his refusal to commute Waller's sentence, quoting with approval the opinion of the Virginia Supreme Court that Waller had had "a fair and impartial trial by an impartial jury; and has been convicted on evidence adduced by members of his own race." Darden denied that the Virginia poll tax effected any injustice and declared "the rights of the accused were not prejudiced by the class of persons from which the jury was drawn." After reading the governor's statement, I could not help but feel that his real reason for refusing to grant clemency was his resentment of the broad interest in the case, which brought Virginia's system of justice and his own role under public scrutiny. He stated at the hearing that he had received hundreds of communications asking him to set Waller free and that these requests were the result of pamphlets distributed by the Workers Defense League, which were "utterly false" and "indicted the Commonwealth of Virginia." In his statement denying commutation, the governor repeated his criticism and charged that "the widespread propaganda campaign which had been carried on without any regard to the facts in this case has resulted in grossly distorted and false public concepts of the true situation." The governor regarded such a campaign as "extremely detrimental to the public interests. The only possible effect," he wrote, "is to sow racial discord at a critical time when every loyal citizen should strive to promote unity."

Waller had less than thirty-six hours to live when Governor Darden announced his decision. A. Philip Randolph immediately proposed that a delegation of Negro leaders go to Washington next morning in an attempt to see President Roosevelt and persuade him to intervene. It was a desperate move, but as long as Waller was alive, every avenue of appeal must be exhausted. I was in New York, having finished my first year of law school at Howard, and was pressed into service to organize the delegation and act as its secretary. After working all night, we had by early morning assembled six nationally prominent men and women to serve with Mr. Randolph, president of the Brotherhood of Sleeping Car Porters. The others were Dr. Channing Tobias of the National Council, YMCA; the Reverend William Lloyd Imes, pastor of Saint James Presbyterian Church, New York City; Frank Crosswaith, director of the Harlem Labor Center and member of the New York Housing Authority; Mary McLeod Bethune, director of the Division of Negro Affairs, National Youth Administration, and founder-president of the National Council of Negro Women; Anna Arnold Hedgeman, regional director of race relations, New York Area Office of Civil Defense; and Layle Lane, vice-president of the American Federation of Teachers. In Washington the group was joined by Dr. Leon A. Ransom, NAACP National Legal Committee; Frank Reeves, Washington Bureau, NAACP; Ted Poston from the Office of War Information; Ralph Matthews, reporter for the *Afro-American* newspaper; and Albert Hamilton, who represented the Workers Defense League and was the only white member of the delegation. Our presence in Washington was underlined by a full-page ad in the July 1 issue of the *Washington Star,* reproducing the petition to President Roosevelt on Waller's behalf signed by several hundred distinguished citizens.

The day was one of unrelieved failure and humiliation. Mr. Randolph, whose threat a year earlier to lead 100,000 Negroes in a march on Washington had moved President Roosevelt to issue an executive order creating the nation's first Fair Employment Practice Committee, soon found that Negro discontent had low priority with an administration preoccupied with waging a global war. The delegation was shunted from office to office, and it became clear that the Odell Waller case was a hot coal no high official would touch. Vice-President Henry Wallace was walking toward his office building when he saw us approaching. He quickened his steps and tried to evade us, and Mrs. Bethune, who knew him well, was compelled to run after him in order to be heard. He brushed her off with the curt response, "I can do nothing, it is out of my jurisdiction." When we went to the office of an influential senator, his political secretary displayed contempt for the delegation by picking up Mrs. Bethune's cane (she suffered from arthritis) and twirling it like a drum major's baton as he talked to us.

When a rumor circulated that the delegation planned to picket the White House, we were summoned to the Office of War Information and warned by its director, Elmer Davis, of the grave national consequences of a picket line at the White House at this point in the war effort. No one at the White House would see us, and our last resort was Mrs. Roosevelt, whom Mr. Randolph had been trying to reach all day.

That night a weary, defeated delegation waited at NAACP headquarters for Mrs. Roosevelt's call to Mr. Randolph. When it finally came, around ten o'clock, ten people listened in over the five telephone extensions in the office. Mrs. Roosevelt's voice trembled and almost broke as she talked with Mr. Randolph. "I have done everything I can possibly do," she told him. "I have interrupted the President twice. He is in an important conference with Mr. Hopkins and will be displeased with me if I interrupt him again. He has said this is a matter of law and not of the heart. It is in Governor Darden's jurisdiction and the President has no legal power to intervene. I am sorry, Mr. Randolph, I can't do any more."

That Mrs. Roosevelt shared our anguish and had already pushed FDR further than we knew at the time was revealed in a White House memorandum dated July 1, 1942, written by Harry L. Hopkins and quoted in Joseph P. Lash's biography of Mrs. Roosevelt, *Eleanor and Franklin.* According to Mr. Hopkins:

> Mrs. Roosevelt called me four or five times today about the Waller case. . . . She spoke and wrote to the Governor some days ago and, indeed, the President wrote a very long letter to the Governor in effect requesting the Governor to send the man to prison for life instead of killing him.
>
> The Governor had given six different reprieves and the President felt that he could not intervene again. . . . Mrs. Roosevelt, however, would not take "No" for an answer and the President finally got on the phone himself and told Mrs. Roosevelt that under no circumstances would he intervene with the Governor and urged very strongly that she say nothing about it.

When the conversation between Mrs. Roosevelt and Mr. Randolph ended that evening, our young white friend Albert Hamilton, who had been with the delegation all day, went to the washroom and vomited. Others wept. Yet, like an animal whose head has been severed but whose body continues to make spasmodic movements, we kept trying until midnight to reach Governor Darden by telephone. Word came back that the governor had gone away and could not be reached.

Meanwhile, in the Richmond death house, Odell Waller wrote his last statement, maintaining to the end that he had not intended to kill Mr. Davis but had shot because he was frightened. He said in part:

> As my time comes near each second means I am one nearer my grave. I have asked God to forgive me and I believe that he has. . . . All you people

take this under consideration. Have you ever thought about some people are allowed a chance over and over again then there are others are allowed little chance—some no chance at all. . . . First I will say don't work for a man too poor to pay you. He will steal and take from you. . . . Mr. Davis was too poor to see me have my wheat and locked it in his store house. . . . I should have give him the wheat if I had to beg for bread and eat out of other people's garbage cans.

On Thursday morning, July 2, at 8:30 A.M., Odell Waller died in the electric chair at the state prison in Richmond. During the long sleepless hours of the previous night I kept vigil, seeing in my mind's eye the death house I had visited and the narrow corridor leading to the room in which he was electrocuted. He was buried the following Sunday after a funeral service at Fairview Baptist Church near Gretna, Virginia, where he was a member. I did not go to the funeral; I felt his death too keenly and went back to New York instead, where we held a memorial service. Morris Milgram and Layle Lane represented the WDL at Waller's last rites and were among the two thousand people who crowded around the little church near Gretna to mourn his passing. Layle Lane described the simple service in the *New York Age* of July 18, 1942, concluding her column with an epitaph:

> In the red earth of a little cemetery set in the midst of Virginia pines and oaks, Odell was laid. His death gave significance to his living which revealed more clearly than ever before the evils of poverty, of exploitation and of race prejudice. His death will not be in vain if we take renewed courage to wipe these evils completely out of our national life.

Mr. Randolph asked me to draft an open letter to President Roosevelt. Signed by the members of the delegation to Washington, it was widely publicized in the Negro press and was also picked up by one of the national news services. The letter called attention to the "complete disillusionment and embittered resentment of the Negro masses" in the United States and noted that "Negroes are beginning to express a willingness and determination to die right here in America to attain a democracy which they have never had." It also expressed the belief that Waller's execution "was a signal for the barbarous forces in this country to renew the unleashing of their hatred upon the Negro people," and pointed out that within two weeks after Waller's electrocution the press reported the lynching of Willie Vinson, a Negro youth, in Texarkana, Texas, the lynching of Private Jessie Smith, a twenty-five-year-old Negro soldier, by a posse in Flagstaff, Arizona, and the brutal beating of the noted Negro tenor Roland Hayes and his wife in Rome, Georgia, following an argument between Mrs. Hayes and a clerk in a shoe store.

Such "fascist-like brutalities," the delegation's letter continued, "are grist for the propaganda mills of the Axis powers, and undoubtedly will be used to destroy the faith of the allied nations in the honesty and integrity of the American democracy, and hasten the deterioration of the morale of the enslaved peoples of the world which hangs precariously on this faith." The letter appealed to "enlightened public opinion in America" to free the President and the country "from a poll tax southern bloc which decides the fate of American citizens it does not represent."

A. Philip Randolph was determined that protest go beyond the verbal expression of moral outrage, and he issued a call for a Silent Parade to be held on Saturday, July 25, under the auspices of the New York Division of the March on Washington Movement (MOWM). The purpose of the demonstration was to mourn Odell Waller and to protest the poll tax system as well as the recent lynchings of two Negroes and the attack upon Roland Hayes and his wife. Randolph appointed me coordinator of the event, then flew off to the NAACP convention in Los Angeles, leaving behind little organizational structure to carry out his mandate. Unfortunately, he had proposed a radical protest demonstration without having obtained in advance support from other black leaders, whose organizational and financial resources were indispensable to its success. The momentum of the New York MOWM, which had mobilized twenty thousand to come to Madison Square Garden a month earlier, had been spent. Most of its committees had disbanded, and those responsible for the success of that rally were not ready to take their protest into the streets.

Without money or organizational assistance, it was remarkable that we had any demonstration at all. With the help of two young women from labor's ranks—Maida Springer of the Dressmakers Union and Dollie Lowther from the Laundry Workers Union—from Bessie Bearden's Housewives League, and from Layle Lane, Anna Hedgeman, and a few recruits from youth groups in Harlem, we managed to mobilize the Waller Silent Parade, although it would go down in civil rights protest history as "a very minor achievement." According to the Harlem-based *People's Voice:*

> Nearly five hundred Negroes in ominous, grim silence marched to the faint throb of muffled drums with only the beat of their determined feet upon the street, in a non-violent demonstration in answer to violent mob acts of southerners.

The March on Washington Movement made its first actual march Saturday afternoon, through New York streets from 56th and Eighth Ave. to Union Square [14th Street], displaying banners denouncing lynching, jim crow and the poll tax. The most impressive of these was a large streamer reading: "We solemnly pledge that these our dead shall not have died in vain."

. . . Among the many white people who joined sympathetically was a woman with a heart ailment. She insisted on marching twenty blocks when she was forced to withdraw.

The first and perhaps the only actual march of Mr. Randolph's movement in the 1940s failed to bring thousands of protesters into the streets, but it was a beginning. Randolph's vision became a reality twenty-one years later, in 1963, when 240,000 or more people marched in Washington for jobs and freedom. A few activists in 1942 had pointed the way to the massive nonviolent protest demonstrations led by Dr. Martin Luther King, Jr., in the 1950s and 1960s. And our solemn protest did not end on a totally somber note. After the ceremony in Union Square, a truckload of marchers, including Maida Springer and me, rode back to Harlem along the parade route. This time we sang freedom songs and shouted a lively chant: "Hey, Joe, whaddye know; Ole Jim Crow has got to go!"

I heard from Annie Waller once more toward the end of the summer, a letter postmarked Kistler, West Virginia. Mrs. Waller told me: "I shall never again live in Virginia or know [sic] other state where our folks are segregated after the way they treated my foster son Odell. I am through with the southland as I can be. . . . I am now residing here in West Virginia with my sister, Dollie Harris. But we are all planning on leaving out of this old jim crow state as it is nearly as bad as down in the deep southland. Now we are planning on making our future home perhaps in Ohio state at Columbus, or maybe in New York state. . . . But you can rest assured that it will not be in the southland nowhere." After that I lost contact with Mrs. Waller and did not learn how she fared in her new life.

Twenty-four years after Odell Waller's death, the Supreme Court of the United States finally struck down the Virginia poll tax. The principle was the same one Waller's lawyers had invoked. In 1966 the Court held that "a State violates the Equal Protection Clause of the Fourteenth Amendment whenever it makes affluence of the voter or payment of any fee an electoral standard." Those who remembered Odell Waller felt that his cause had at last been vindicated.

CHAPTER 15

Writing or Law School?

WHEN I RETURNED from the Waller tour in June of 1941, law school was still a vague dream. For a few weeks that summer I enjoyed a blissful interlude devoted to writing, in an idyllic setting free from pressures. Through Lillian Bass, a young sculptor and WDL member whose uncle owned a private campsite about a hundred miles north of New York City, I was invited to give several lectures on sharecropping at the Young People's Socialist League Summer Institute, held at the camp in July. In exchange for my services, Lillian arranged with Judah Drob, director of the Institute, to let me live rent-free in one of the cabins for most of the rest of the summer.

One could not have found a more serene place to write, remote from a world at war and without radio or newspaper to intrude on one's solitude. My two-room cabin with screened porch was built into a cliff at the top of Mount Airy, some eighteen hundred feet up in the foothills of the Catskill Mountains, about five miles from Saugerties, New York. It was one of several cabins on a sixty-acre tract accessible only by a rocky, barely passable wagon track which zigzagged two miles up the mountainside from the village of Quarryville. The cabin, separated from the rest of the camp by a small hillock, sat at the edge of the cliff, its front steps giving onto a narrow ledge above a steep drop treacherously hidden beneath a heavy growth of sumac and berry bushes. From this secluded perch I could watch a miniature world below in a broad valley of tiny farms and neat squares of pastureland stretching for miles. A faint hum of motors floated up as toy cars scooted along the ribbonlike highway curving through the valley. Across the valley to the east I glimpsed the Hudson

177

River through a gap in the dark hills, and on clear days I could see the Berkshires in Massachusetts sloping down beyond the river into the Connecticut hills. When summer storms blotted out the valley below, I had the sensation of living among clouds wholly detached from earth. Often, at night, stars blazed in a clear sky above my head while a carpet of fog stretched at my feet, and the only sign of a world below the fog was an occasional eerie light flickering feebly upward through the mist.

The camp had no electricity or running water, and a kerosene lantern and two-burner oil stove provided me with light and heat for cooking. Water came from a pump up the hill and had to be used sparingly. Occasionally, when the well went dry and the pump brought up only black mud, we had to lug pails of water from a spring at the base of the mountain. Rainwater caught in a barrel served for bathing and washing clothes, and sometimes I had to wash my face in drippings from the icebox.

My main link with civilization was a wheezy jalopy nicknamed "Grandma," which I had bought in the city for twenty-five dollars and which served to transport my belongings from New York and groceries and ice from the village. My friend Mac McBean had driven up with me to take a summer job in the area, and on her days off she would come over and we would splurge on a fine meal. Sometimes Lillian Bass and Judah and Mary Drob would drop by during the evenings. Otherwise, once my lectures were delivered I spent the time alone, my steady companion a half-grown female German shepherd named Petie. My sister Grace had given Petie to me as a tiny puppy the previous November when Gene Phillips and I passed through Baltimore on our dismal return from Richmond. But my continued involvement in the Waller case had made it impossible for me to keep her, and I had turned her over to my cousin Jeff Jeffers, who lived on Long Island and had space to keep a dog. Jeff had let me borrow her back for the summer.

Most of each day I sat on the little porch working at the typewriter, naked except for a pair of shorts so I could let the mountain breezes flow over my body as I typed. When I hit a snag and words refused to come, I would explore the woods nearby, with Petie running ahead to sniff the bushes or chase a rabbit while I hunted for watercress or picked dandelion leaves for dinner. I had so little talent for cooking that to save time I usually resorted to one-pot meals of stew or ham hocks with vegetables. Often sentences would begin forming in my mind as I strode through the woods, and I would rush back to get them down on paper before the thought was lost. When the words flowed smoothly I lost all sense of time and might forget I had not eaten until I smelled burning stew or Petie reminded me that it was time for *her* dinner by pawing insistently at my arm.

Now that there were no distractions to hinder me and no excuses for not writing, I learned that a sheet of blank paper was my greatest adversary and that what seems to the reader like effortless writing is more often the result of patient drudgery than of inspired talent. Sometimes it took me an entire day of dogged effort to produce one paragraph, and next morning I might have to tear it apart and begin all over again. One of the most painful tasks in writing, I learned that summer, is the discipline required to discard those cherished phrases that clutter up a sentence or a paragraph.

Some writers are able to compose while doing other things and then produce at a single sitting a draft that needs few revisions. Others can revise as they write, simply striking out words and sentences they want to drop. I am a wastefully repetitive writer who must use and discard many sheets of paper, building sentence upon sentence and paragraph upon paragraph like someone modeling clay.

My unduly wasteful compulsion to have a draft of clean copy in the typewriter before moving on used to worry me until I learned that Stephen Vincent Benét apparently had a similar habit. His biographer, Charles A. Fenton, wrote of an incident that happened in the summer of 1925, when the young Benét spent several weeks at the MacDowell Colony in Peterborough, New Hampshire, trying to complete a historical novel. When Benét left the Colony, the writer who took over his studio arrived before it had gone through the usual cleaning process and found it exactly as Benét had left it. Benét had crumpled and tossed into a corner unfinished pages of manuscript that dissatisfied him, and the new colonist discovered a mound of Benét's discarded efforts—"enough of them to fill a bushel basket."

While nothing I wrote that summer was submitted for publication, I was learning the discipline of sustained effort. Prose sketches that started as mere exercises gradually began to develop direction and focus. Benét had urged me to write about what I knew best, so I experimented with several short stories about a little girl named Bennie, growing up in the South. More than a year had gone by since I sent Benét a few poems and a sketch of the Petersburg incident entitled "Disorderly Conduct," but his prompt response with detailed comments, suggestions for improvement, and expressions of confidence in my potential had kept my hope alive over the intervening months. He had written:

> . . . You seem to be—, well, loosening up a little is the way I'd put it— writing with more fluency and more freedom, with fewer places where the verse lets down with a bump, and with more individuality. . . . I think you are improving. Keep up the good work. As you know, none of the criticisms

I make are intended in a harsh or depreciatory spirit. They merely concern the technique of writing, that we all have to learn, that we spend our lives learning, that, even after long practice, we must still try to improve and improve—to see more clearly, hear more faithfully—if we wish to be writers at all. And you have so much to write about. You have such rich material, once you have learned to smelt it out at the core. And I think you are learning.

That a great writer like Stephen Vincent Benét, burdened with countless demands, had given my amateurish work the same painstaking care he gave to professional manuscripts was a powerful incentive for me to work hard on my writing, and encouraged by his interest, I sent him two of the Bennie stories, with a note saying: "Bennie might well be the subject of a series of stories bearing on the bewilderment and perplexity of a natural, normal American child first experiencing the frustrations of racial inequality."

Benét's response was not long in coming, and when it came I was jubilant. Written from his summer home in Stonington, Connecticut, in the now familiar elite type that crowded the margins of each page, his words created the comfortable feeling of having a chat with an old friend. As always, he combined generous praise and encouragement with specific suggestions for revision. He wrote:

> I think you really have something here, and it makes me very pleased.
> This is by far the best prose of yours I have seen. It is simple, genuine and moving. You say the stories "wrote themselves." Well, they show that. They come out without strain and real . . . you seem to be on the right track. It may seem relatively unimportant to you to present some of the days and the memories of a young Negro girl. But—when has it been done? From the inside? And with sensitiveness and truth? The field is wide, wide open.
> . . . Do some more. Think back. Remember. I am not sure, of course, but I think Bennie might be a book. But do not get gun-shy over the idea of Bennie's becoming a book. Just write some more things about her. Keep them simple. Keep them direct and telling. . . . I am not trying to tell you what to write about, what to select. But go ahead.
> Nor am I telling you either that these two sketches are works of genius, that you will get them accepted right away, or even that writing will be easy for you from now on. It won't and you will probably make several bushels of mistakes. But these sketches are genuine, they have a quality, and I think you are on the right path.

I was all set to follow up on Benét's suggestions, when in early August a letter arrived from Howard Law School, informing me that I was accepted for admission in September and was being granted a tuition scholarship. I would have been overjoyed if this letter had come a few weeks earlier, before I had begun to make steady progress in writing. Now it meant a choice between interrupting the momentum I had finally achieved and appearing utterly irresponsible to Dr. Ransom, whose recommendation had gotten me the law school scholarship. I think I might even have passed up the opportunity to study law if two racial incidents had not occurred in quick succession at the time of my return to New York City. They were more than enough to bring me back to reality after the wonderful illusion of freedom I had enjoyed on Mount Airy. Such incidents were as unpredictable as they were unavoidable, continually assaulting one's personal dignity and reopening old wounds. Whenever they happened, I felt as if the scab over a deep gash in my body had been suddenly torn off and the raw flesh underneath scraped against gravel.

The first was an encounter with the superintendent of the apartment building in Queens where my WDL friends Morris and Grace Milgram lived. They had invited me to stay in their apartment while they were away on vacation, and I had spent only one night there when the building superintendent saw me leaving the next morning. Without asking any questions, he pounced on me, shouting that I had no business in that building. He told me to "go back to Harlem where you belong," and warned me not to return. While I was out he changed the locks on the apartment door, and in order to reenter to get my clothes I was forced to call the police.

Two weeks later, during the Labor Day weekend, David L. Clendenin, the WDL's national secretary-treasurer and one of its founders, was killed in an automobile accident while driving back to New York from Nevada. Dave had been the guiding force of the WDL as well as its chief executive. The son of a wealthy mining magnate, he had graduated from Yale in 1928 and was working full time as a dollar-a-year man, spending his inheritance fighting for the rights of the underdog—poor miners, striking seamen, and southern sharecroppers. His death was a great shock to all of us who had worked closely with him on the WDL staff, and on the day of his funeral Vivian Odems and I went to the home of his sister, Mrs. Stanley Bailey, on East Seventy-fifth Street, where the service was being held. When we got to the building the doorman stopped us, insisting that we go to the service entrance. It was not until we called the management and threatened to create a scene that we were permitted to ride up in the front elevator.

These infuriating reminders that one could not escape Jim Crow even in cosmopolitan New York City erased any lingering doubts I had about suppressing my urge to write in favor of becoming a civil rights lawyer.

Three days after Dave's funeral, I heard Odell Waller's appeal before Virginia's highest court and then went on to Washington to enter law school, with the single-minded intention of destroying Jim Crow.

Ironically, the three years I spent at Howard thrust me into the rigidly segregated environment of wartime Washington. After the comparative freedom of New York, I found the racial segregation of the nation's capital so repugnant that I would have spent all my free time in the law library if I had been able to. Such luxury was impossible, of course. When I entered school I had only my tuition scholarship and enough money to pay two weeks' rent on a small room, and so throughout my three years I had to find part-time work to earn my living expenses. I was lucky, however, to have financial help from a friend in California, Jessie Overholt. A WDL supporter who contributed heavily to Odell Waller's defense, Mrs. Overholt had become interested in my desire to study law and sent periodic checks to supplement my earnings.

Howard Law School provided excellent training for anyone devoted to the struggle to enforce civil rights. We had a small student body, and students and faculty shared a camaraderie born of our mutual commitment to the battle against racial discrimination. Our faculty included prominent lawyers who won brilliant Supreme Court victories in the 1940s and 1950s—William H. Hastie, Leon A. Ransom, George E. C. Hayes, George M. Johnson, William Robert Ming, James N. Nabrit, and, among the younger, recent graduates, James A. Washington, Spottswood W. Robinson III, and Louis Berry. Many of the briefs in key cases before the Supreme Court were prepared in our law library, and exceptionally able students were rewarded for excellence by being permitted to do research on a brief under the supervision of a professor. When a major case was to be presented to the Supreme Court, the entire school assembled to hear dress rehearsal arguments. Faculty members and alert students subjected the NAACP attorneys who argued these cases to searching questions, and by the time the attorneys appeared before the nine justices they were thoroughly prepared to defend their positions.

Our training included not only learning the law and how to think on our feet but also how to conduct ourselves in hostile situations. Many of the students planned to practice in the South, where it was still rare to see a Negro attorney in a courtroom. One of our best teachers was Dr. Ransom, professor of both criminal law and constitutional law. He had great skill in forcing students to develop their arguments while remaining calm under harassment. Genial and kindly outside class hours, he could be ruthless in the classroom. He would pose a question and goad a student unmercifully, demolishing every argument with a counterattack. Dr. Ransom had once been knocked down on the courthouse steps by a white racist in a southern state where he had gone to argue a civil rights case, and he knew that Negro lawyers must be able to endure public humiliation, even physical danger, when challenging deeply entrenched racial customs. He was determined that his students would be tough enough to survive in no-holds-barred legal combat.

Ironically, if Howard Law School equipped me for effective struggle against Jim Crow, it was also the place where I first became conscious of the twin evil of discriminatory sex bias, which I quickly labeled Jane Crow. In my preoccupation with the brutalities of racism, I had failed until now to recognize the subtler, more ambiguous expressions of sexism. In the all-female setting of Hunter College, women were prominent in professional and leadership positions. My awareness of the additional burden of sex discrimination had been further delayed by my WPA experience. Hilda Smith, national director of the WPA Workers' Education Project, was a woman, my local project director and my immediate supervisor were both women, and it had not occurred to me that women as a group received unequal treatment. Now, however, the racial factor was removed in the intimate environment of a Negro law school dominated by men, and the factor of gender was fully exposed.

During my first year at Howard there were only two women in the law school student body, both of us in the first-year class. When the other woman dropped out before the end of the first term, I was left as the only female for the rest of that year, and I remained the only woman in my class for the entire three-year course. While I was there, not more than two or three women enrolled in the lower classes of the law school. We had no women on the faculty, and the only woman professional on staff was Ollie M. Cooper, the registrar, who had graduated from the law school many years earlier.

The men were not openly hostile; in fact, they were friendly. But I soon learned that women were often the objects of ridicule disguised as a joke. I was shocked on the first day of class when one of our professors said in his opening remarks that he really didn't know why women came to law school, but that since we were there the men would have to put up with us. His banter brought forth loud laughter from the male students. I was too humiliated to respond, but though the professor did not know it, he had just guaranteed that I would become the top student in his class. Later I began to notice that no matter how well prepared I was or how often I raised my hand, I seldom got to recite. It was not that professors deliberately ignored me but that their freewheeling classroom style of informal discussion allowed the men's deeper voices to obliterate my lighter voice, and my classmates seemed to take it for granted that I had nothing to contribute. For much of that first year I was condemned to silence unless the male students exhausted their arguments or were completely stumped by a professor's question.

My real awakening came several months after school began, when I saw a notice on the official bulletin board inviting "all male students of the First Year Class" to a smoker at the residence of Professor Leon A. Ransom. The exclusion of women from the invitation was so pointed that I went to Dr. Ransom's office to seek an explanation. He told me blandly that Sigma Delta Tau, a legal fraternity limited to male students and members of the legal profession, had established a chapter at the law school and that the purpose of the smoker was to look over first-year men for likely prospects. Through their association with experienced lawyers these young men would enhance their professional development. I had not yet become aware of the sexist bias of the English language, and recalling that the national professional English "fraternity" to which I had been elected while in college included both sexes, I asked Dr. Ransom, "What about us women?"

To my surprise, Dr. Ransom merely chuckled and said that if we women wanted an organization we could set up a legal sorority. Angrily, I said it was ridiculous to speak of a legal sorority for two women, but he did not seem concerned about our plight. I left Dr. Ransom's office feeling both bewildered and betrayed, especially because he was one of the most liberal professors on the university campus and had always treated me as a person. He had encouraged me to come to law school and used his influence to have me awarded a scholarship. Yet he did not seem to appreciate fully that barring women from an organization purporting to promote professional growth had the same degrading effect upon women as compelling us as Negroes to sit in the back of a bus or refusing to admit black lawyers to white bar associations. The discovery that Ransom and other men I deeply admired because of their dedication to civil rights, men who themselves had suffered racial indignities, could countenance exclusion of women from their professional association aroused an incipient feminism in me long before I knew the meaning of the term "feminism."

Despite the realization that I was not recognized as a member of the fraternity of lawyers who would make civil rights history, civil rights continued to be my primary concern. At the NAACP Annual Student Conference held at Hampton Institute in November, I was elected to chair the national student organization for the coming year. The conference was an enthusiastic gathering full of brave speeches, but in 1941 the student civil rights movement was impotent. We had no funds and little influence, and we were unable to do much more than adopt strong resolutions. A few weeks later, the formal entry of the United States into World War II only intensified my internal conflict over demands for patriotism, coupled as they were with blatant denials of citizenship rights. I felt this conflict most keenly when I listened to my schoolmates anxiously discussing the likelihood of being drafted into a segregated army, a prospect they found abhorrent. My own immunity from this ordeal because I was a woman made me feel an extra responsibility to carry on the battle for democracy at home while my colleagues were being ordered into uniform to fight for the United States abroad.

One of the young people in Washington who shared my intense frustration was my friend Pauline Redmond, whose strategic position on the staff of the National Youth Administration made her aware of the conditions throughout the country that were provoking rumblings of protest among young Negroes. An opportunity to publicize this angry mood arose when Pauline was asked to do an article for the national student magazine *Threshold*, official organ of the United States Committee of International Student Service, an organization that included among its purposes the determination "to help students toward a fuller comprehension of the origins and meaning of American democracy" and "to encourage active participation in the problems of democracy." Pauline was a friend of Eleanor Roosevelt, and we felt a hard-hitting piece would come to the First Lady's attention since she actively supported the International Student Service. The two of us collaborated on the article, entitled "Negro Youth's Dilemma," but because of Pauline's vulnerable position as a federal employee, it appeared under my name only in the April issue of *Threshold*.

Written in the first person, the article was an impassioned outcry against pervasive wrongs which sapped the loyalty of Negro people and impelled them to ask, "What are we fighting for? If this is a war for democracy, where do we fit in?" Quoting Congressman Clifton I. Faddis, who had said on the floor of the House that the war in the Philippines is "to preserve the fate of the white race in the Orient," we pointed out that Negroes "frankly ask ourselves why we should fight a white man's war." Citing a recent lynching in Sikeston, Missouri, we compared that evil to Hitlerism and bluntly declared that potential victims of mob violence "cannot be expected to distinguish between brutalities. It is difficult to find personal security in the fact that the lynch curve has gone down. That one man has been lynched in 1942 means that I and my brothers cannot walk the streets of our native land without fear." Despite racial rebuffs, we went on, the Negro people "clamor for the opportunity to participate fully and equally in this struggle because we need so desperately to believe that we do have a place in this country—not a place arbitrarily assigned, but one we know we have earned."

"What has been America's response?" we asked. In answer we reminded *Threshold* readers that defense industries had to be threatened with the loss of profitable government contracts before they would employ Negro workers. Even then, those workers were often assigned to menial jobs as cleaners and sweepers. Black workers who did attain production-line jobs sometimes found white employees refusing to work beside them. In some areas defense plants recruited entire white families from other parts of the country rather then employ local Negro workers. The federal government displayed similar bias. Negro women who had passed civil service examinations and had received telegrams to report for work in the nation's capital came to Washington at their own expense only to be told there must have been some mistake because no vacancies existed; or Negroes were hidden away in some corner of a defense agency under a government official who was "not too particular." Negro workers in Washington were refused taxi service, and they could not eat in restaurants or buy theater tickets.

The most galling insult was the government's policy of segregating blood plasma, a humiliation we underscored when we wrote:

If I am a soldier my blood may be spilled freely in the battles of democracy, but as a private citizen it cannot go into a [common] blood bank to save human life. Does a dying man question the source of new life? Is America willing to sacrifice life itself for her prejudices?

Bigotry in the regimented life of the military was a harrowing ordeal for young Negro men:

As a soldier in the United States armed forces, I have been cursed, beaten, and shot—my uniform and the flag for which it stands made a mockery. . . . Huddled away in a corner of the camp, isolated from other soldiers, I soon learn there is never separation with equality. . . . I see white soldiers enjoying elaborate recreational facilities while I must walk a mile or more for a postage stamp. . . . If I stray to another section of the post, I am shunned at the exchange, shooed up to the "buzzard's roost" at camp movies, and ignored at the soda fountain. If I seek to advance my position as would any other normal youth by seeking entrance into an officer's training school, my superior officer squelches my enthusiasm and conveniently forgets to notify me when applications are due or I am disqualified on trumped up physical defects. . . . [In southern states] I am herded to the rear of busses, shoved about on the streets, and made a ridiculous pawn in the hands of military police and town officers. I read of increasing "incidents" where a khaki uniform and a brown face are open invitations to cold-blooded murder, and I leave my post wondering if my role in the defense of my country will be to stop a bullet discharged by the blind racial hatred of my own countrymen.

We pointed out that a Negro man who volunteered to serve in a division for which he had special training was often told there was no room for him; then he would be drafted a few months later and assigned to a post without regard to his qualifications. "Hundreds of brown youths who volunteer for the air corps are delayed or deferred because a jimcrow squadron is not equipped to give the varied types of training necessary," we wrote. While the radio blasted forth daily appeals to join the navy, and the Secretary of the Navy, Frank Knox, announced that Navy enlistments had fallen off 15 percent,

> The Navy . . . prefers to take workers from defense industries rather than use eager black men. The Navy excludes me as a seaman, gunner, marine or aviator. I may serve only as a messman. . . . Under these circumstances am I to be blamed for the bitterness and skepticism that well within me? . . . Am I to maintain my devotion for a country which, while exacting from me the same sacrifices demanded of all American youth, still robs me of my last chance to be free, relegating me, even in death, to an inferior position?

Observing that "the enemies of the United States quickly seize upon her internal paradoxes to alienate her foreign friends," the article noted that within twenty-four hours of the beating and shooting of twenty-eight Negro soldiers in Alexandria, Louisiana, the Japanese propaganda agency had broadcast news of the incident, "warning the colored peoples of the world that this would be their fate if Great Britain and the United States won the war. When it is realized that more than one-half of the population of the New World is non-white, the sinister effect of this propaganda becomes apparent." The piece concluded:

> I know in my heart that this is not the total picture. Valiant efforts are being made by some to extend democracy to the Negro, but to us down in the ranks these efforts seem faint and far away. The simple facts of oppression are much more real. Will America pamper this gangrenous infection in her body politic, or has she the good sense to amputate before it reaches the vital organs? Until she does, it is difficult for the Negro to locate the battlefield. Is it Java or Sikeston [Missouri]—Luzon or Alexandria, Louisiana?

Whatever impact the published article may have had on its wider readership, for me at least it was the beginning of my student activism at Howard University, and because I had voiced in print the pressing issues which plagued my colleagues, it improved my status at the law school. I had scored highest in every course I had taken, and I was beginning to win the respect of the male students and to break down their traditional resistance to women as peers. During the next year, as the ranking student in my class, I felt less an outsider and was even elected to be one of two representatives from our class to the Court of Peers, executive body of the Law Students' Guild and a quasi-honor group the students had organized in the absence of a law journal.

CHAPTER 16

Getting to Know Mrs. Roosevelt

THE SUMMER OF 1942 marked the beginning of a closer relationship with Mrs. Roosevelt which grew, oddly enough, out of spirited correspondence that bristled with strong feelings on both sides. Although Mrs. Roosevelt's efforts on behalf of Odell Waller just before his electrocution had overcome my lingering doubts about her sincerity on racial matters, I still seethed with anger at FDR's seeming lack of moral outrage over the continued brutal treatment of Negroes in the South, and I addressed an ill-conceived letter to him, which I sent to Mrs. Roosevelt to make sure he would receive it. The unintended consequence was a bruising dialogue by mail and a face-to-face encounter with the First Lady.

My letter to the President, which obviously angered Mrs. Roosevelt, contained references to the highly sensitive issue of the forced removal of Japanese-Americans from their homes on the West Coast and to Wendell Willkie, Republican standard bearer in the last presidential election. A friend from Oregon, apparently accepting the propaganda being circulated to justify the Japanese removal, had written me that she was "glad for the protection of the Japanese-Americans [that] they have been evacuated." Such a cynical rationalization of a racially motivated government policy prompted me to write President Roosevelt, calling attention to his almost unlimited wartime powers and the parallels he had drawn with Lincoln's administration. In a confused attempt to suggest that the President could use these powers to curb violence against Negroes, I stated: "If Japanese-Americans can be evacuated to prevent violence being perpetrated upon them . . . then certainly you have the power to evacuate Negro

189

citizens from 'lynching' areas in the South, and particularly the poll tax states."

Pointing to the disappointment of Negroes whose votes had helped elect President Roosevelt but who "feel you have never come out openly on the question of the Negro," I said: "They watch Mr. Willkie's present campaigning on the race question with interest, knowing full well that both the Democratic and Republican parties have an eye on the Negro vote in 1944," and closed with the hope that Mr. Roosevelt would take "a more forthright stand on this whole problem of color."

I was astonished to receive a stinging reply over Mrs. Roosevelt's own signature instead of the customary acknowledgment from her secretary. She told me she was giving my letter to the President, "but on my own I want to answer some of the things which you say and which you imply." Sidestepping the issue of preventing violence, she seemed horrified at the parallel I had drawn between Negroes and Japanese-Americans. "How many of our colored people in the South would like to be evacuated and treated as though they were not as rightfully here as any other people?" Although "deeply concerned that we had to do that to the Japanese who are American citizens," she justified the action on the ground that "we are at war with Japan and they have only been citizens for a very short time. We would feel a resentment if we had to do this for citizens who have been here as long as most of the white people have."

Mrs. Roosevelt seemed exasperated by "what you say about the President's not having been forthright and the interest with which you are watching Mr. Willkie." She wondered if it had ever occurred to me "that Mr. Willkie has no responsibility whatsoever? He can say whatever he likes and do whatever he likes, and nothing very serious will happen." If he were to be elected President, however, "on that day he would have to begin not to just plan a program to meet the conditions in the country which he would like to see changed, but he would have to take into consideration the people who are the heads of important committees in Congress, none of whom he has chosen but with whom he must work, and who are the people on whom he must depend to pass vital legislation for the nation as a whole." The only thing Willkie could do would be to initiate legislation "and of course they could refuse to pass it."

"For one who must really have a knowledge of the workings of our government," Mrs. Roosevelt continued, "your letter seems to me one of the most thoughtless I have ever read." Explaining her own position in the White House, she said:

> Of course I can say just how I feel, but I could not say it with much sense of security unless the President were willing for me to do so. I have no

responsibility; I am not elected and not running for office; I am responsible only to myself for what I do; I do not have the same responsibility to the people as a whole. It is very easy for us as individuals to think of what we would do if we were in office, but we forget that with the election to the office of President go at the same time infinite restrictions and the kind of responsibility which is never ours as private citizens.

Mrs. Roosevelt declared that the creation of the Fair Employment Practice Committee "in itself indicates where the President stands," and while FEPC might not achieve everything we would like it to achieve, "that only means that we have to face realities and that we cannot move faster than the people wish to move."

The shock of having provoked Mrs. Roosevelt to use such strong language made me realize that at least I had her ear. Her response gave me an opening to make her more fully aware of the mood of bitterness among Negroes, a bitterness that would explode into riots the following summer. Instead of backing down, my reply was an equally frank statement of the situation as I saw it:

I do not deny that my letter to President Roosevelt seems thoughtless, even reckless. Certainly, it was not intended to offer any fundamental solution to a major problem. It was written from a depth of desperation and disgust, such as every thinking Negro often experiences. Desperation —in that there must be some way of bringing home to the American people our utterly untenable position of fighting in democracy's name for supremacy over the Axis powers, while 13,000,000 of our own citizens are victims of a racial theory as vicious as Hitler's. Disgust—because our President has the power and the prestige to set in motion the wheels of public opinion for the support of legislation and other measures which are necessary to eliminate some of the very evils of which you . . . speak, and some of us cannot understand why he does not use this power more vigorously.

Someone had to make clear to the entire country that continued pursuit of Fascist-like policies of racial supremacy was suicidal, I said, and no one could do so more effectively than President Roosevelt.

The very nature of democracy demands that the President go often to the people with a report on the State of the Nation. If his report is sound, if his policies are in the interests of all the people, including Negroes, then can he not count on the support of the people, even in the face of opposition from Congress? This view was really the crux of my letter. . . . All I am pleading for is that he take the initiative in these matters, and point out we cannot come into the world struggle for democracy with dirty hands.

On the point of Mr. Willkie, surely Mrs. Roosevelt did not think me "so politically immature as to be taken in by any statement or promise from the Republican Party," but I wanted her to know that I had raised the question since "many Negroes do not share my lack of faith" in Republicans. "Neither the Republican Party nor the Democratic Party holds any promise for Negro Americans as I see it. Mr. Roosevelt's party has in it a southern bloc which is perpetuated by the southern poll tax and the Northern Democrats and which is pledged to the Hitler theory of racial supremacy, whether we like to admit it or not." As to the FEPC, I reminded Mrs. Roosevelt that while it was a step in the right direction, it was created "mainly because the Government was faced with a march on Washington by Negroes throughout the country. If anything, it seems to indicate that the President will remain aloof from the Negro question until there is such organized resentment and pressure as to make it a national embarrassment if he does not act." The President "must search out scathingly the denials of democracy to Negroes, Asiatics, Jews and other minorities at home, and abroad, as a war measure. . . ."

I tried to make clear that some of us could no longer compromise with the notion of race supremacy, "for to do so would be to give up the last shred of integrity we have left." We were compelled to speak out, "appealingly, caustically, bitterly, as long as we are able, that Americans may not forget for one moment this race problem is a war issue, and that fundamental approaches must be made to eliminate it, now, not after the war is over." Pointing to the international implications of this issue, I asserted that "American Negroes cannot separate their struggle for equality from the [East] Indians' struggle for independence, and the silence of our government on this crucial question will be construed to mean that we too can hope for no real stakes in the war or the peace to follow the war." My letter ended on a deeply pessimistic note:

> Viewing these stupidities, I wonder whether the white man has the courage or the imagination to save himself or civilization from utter ruin. Three hundred years of oppression have given us patience to bear hardship, but I doubt whether it has given us patience to bear with the instruments of hardship. Though the issue may be freedom and not race, as you say, nevertheless Hitler is taking advantage of our inability to handle our minority question intelligently and still counts up victories while we "muddle along."

While such outspoken views gave me a reputation of being hotheaded and Mrs. Roosevelt later referred to me as a "firebrand," they also earned her respect. As I grew to know her better, it seemed to me that the measure of her greatness was her capacity for growth, her ruthless honesty with herself, and the generosity with which she responded to criticisms of this kind. Her spirit was attuned to the cries of the disinherited and her response was immediate. She might have passed over my outburst with a polite acknowledgment. Instead, her secretary, Malvina Thompson, wrote promptly that Mrs. Roosevelt would be glad to have me come to see her in her New York apartment on Washington Square West on the afternoon of August 27. "She feels it is much easier to talk these things over than it is to discuss them through correspondence," Miss Thompson added.

I was more shaken by Mrs. Roosevelt's invitation to visit than I had been by her earlier rebuke. Recognizing it as a "command performance" and aware of the tremendous power of her presence, I did not dare face her alone for fear that once within what I always thought of as her magnetic field I would be mesmerized. I called an older friend, Anna Arnold Hedgeman, whom I had first met when she was membership secretary of the 137th Street Y. By now she had become skilled in political and civil rights matters and only a short time earlier had been a member of the delegation to Washington on behalf of Odell Waller. When I asked her to go with me she agreed, and then I got Mrs. Roosevelt's permission to bring her along.

Characteristically, Mrs. Roosevelt met us at the door herself and disarmed me completely by throwing her arms about me and giving me an affectionate hug. Referring to Odell Waller's execution the preceding month, she said with great feeling, "Oh, that was a terrible night, wasn't it?" Although Mrs. Roosevelt spent over an hour with us, I was too bemused to remember more than a few details of the meeting, but after we left Anna Hedgeman told me laughingly, "Pauli, you threw the dynamite while I threw the sand!" However militant I may have sounded during our visit, at some point my wariness of Mrs. Roosevelt had begun to dissolve and be replaced by unreserved affection.

She had been deeply moved by the troubling picture I had presented in my letter and, although I cannot remember her words, must have voiced her feeling that somehow her generation had failed us, for the next day I wrote her a note saying: "I cannot tell you how much personal reassurance I found in the interview yesterday. There is no need for any apology to our generation. I only hope we can keep alive the flame of human compassion and freedom as you are doing."

Yet barely two weeks later I was again sparring with Mrs. Roosevelt, this time on an international issue. In early September 1942, the International Student Assembly convened in Washington under White House sponsorship, or at least with White House blessings. I was a delegate from Howard University Law School and participated in the caucus of the

American delegation, led by Lou Harris, the future pollster. The presence of two Soviet delegates—a man and a woman, both in military uniform—generated considerable excitement. Along with the British, the Russians were chiefly concerned about the opening of the second front in Europe by the Allied forces. As our principal allies, both delegations were treated with great deference.

Some members of the American delegation, however, were deeply concerned with issues of human rights—British colonialism under which Gandhi, Nehru, and other Indian nationalist leaders were imprisoned, and Soviet imperialism in the Baltic states. Along with Lou Harris, Mary Lou Roberts, Bill Goldsmith, and several other American students, I was involved in an effort to get the Assembly to adopt resolutions calling for the release of the Indian leaders and condemning Russian occupation of Lithuania. In addition, the Negro members of the United States delegation drafted and circulated a statement calling for the destruction of the doctrine of race supremacy and urging the United States to demonstrate its moral leadership by taking the initiative toward the complete elimination of discriminatory racial distinctions in the democratic nations.

The White House was especially anxious to maintain harmony among students representing the Allied powers and fearful of any activities that threatened to create dissension at the conference. Mrs. Roosevelt, who served on the executive committee of International Student Service, a leading force in the Assembly, monitored the proceedings. She was aware of our efforts and focused on me both as a ringleader of the radical students and as someone who was less easy to control than some of the others. She was prepared to use her tremendous prestige to keep me in line.

A picnic for the Assembly was held on the White House lawn, and as I passed through the formal receiving line, Mrs. Roosevelt caught my hand, fixed her searching blue eyes upon me, and said, "Pauli, I want to talk to you later." I had an inkling of what she wanted to talk to me about and, not trusting my ability to withstand her, attempted to avoid her for the rest of the picnic. But one simply did not evade Mrs. Roosevelt when she had a concern. She found me in a far corner of the lawn, where I had retreated, and took me aside. She wanted to persuade me and my cohorts not to push for the two resolutions on India and Lithuania because there was grave danger, if we did, that the Russians and British would walk out and leave the Assembly in disarray. She carefully explained that the objective of the conference was to express unity of purpose and mutual confidence among the countries allied to combat the Axis powers, an alliance then becoming known as the United Nations. This purpose would be frustrated if our strongest allies walked out. Since they were clamoring for the second front, we could not afford to offend them.

Mrs. Roosevelt could be stern at times, even when she spoke kindly, and this was one of the times. I listened to her in silence, deeply torn over what to do. It was difficult to refuse Mrs. Roosevelt any request—she was always so generous in responding to the needs of others—but as I wrestled with a decision, I felt more and more the need to draw a line between official United States policy and the voice of independent private citizens speaking out on behalf of human rights. Eventually I went back into the afternoon session and fought for the two resolutions our caucus supported. We lost on Lithuania but managed to get a compromise resolution adopted on India. The draft of the final statement issued by the Assembly declared: "On the basis of a national coalition government in India, we urge that negotiations be reopened at once between Great Britain and the Indian people toward the granting of political freedom to mobilize the Indian people for an all-out war effort along side of the United Nations." The statement condemned the doctrine of racial supremacy, renounced imperialism and all its evils, and called for the recognition of "the principle of independence for colonials and equal rights and opportunities for national, religious and racial minorities." It also called for "the abolition of all limitations on the participation of peoples in their governments" and "the abolition of all discriminations based solely on race, color, creed, or national origin." There was no mention of discrimination because of sex, and it would be another six years before the concept of rights and freedoms without distinction because of sex was included in the Universal Declaration of Human Rights. While some of us might have wished for stronger and more explicit language in our student statement of 1942, we were pleased that we had not given away too much, nor had we split the Assembly, as Mrs. Roosevelt feared. The principles we set forth in embryonic form were elaborated upon and incorporated under Eleanor Roosevelt's leadership in the Universal Declaration of 1948, which became the standard for human rights around the world.

Not all my contacts with Mrs. Roosevelt during her White House years were intensely political. There were brief visits to the White House for tea when group tensions and political crises were not on the agenda. On such relaxed occasions I basked in the maternal warmth Mrs. Roosevelt radiated, feeling like a member of her family. She could be great fun, regaling her friends with tales that revealed her delightful sense of humor and her ability to laugh at herself.

My first visit to the White House for tea was such an occasion. It was in late May 1943 and Mrs. Roosevelt had issued the invitation jointly to me and my National Youth Administration friend Pauline Redmond (who had recently become the bride of Tee Coggs, a young soldier who had gone off to military camp as soon as they were married). Pauline was thrilled;

I was ecstatic. We both knew how privileged we were to be having a social visit with Mrs. Roosevelt in the White House during wartime. Strict security measures were in force; White House schedules were very tight. Giving us a half hour of her time meant careful planning on Mrs. Roosevelt's part and punctuality on ours. We were sent the necessary admission cards and were instructed to arrive promptly at five.

The news of my invitation to tea at the White House created excitement on the Howard University campus, especially among the women undergraduates. That afternoon several of them picked a bouquet of flowers, insisting that I present them to Mrs. Roosevelt on their behalf. It was an innocuous request which I did not mind carrying out, but as the hour of our appointment neared, serious complications arose that threatened to torpedo our visit. About three o'clock, Tee Coggs flew in unexpectedly from camp on a short weekend pass. He had just been commissioned a lieutenant and hurried home proudly wearing his bars to celebrate with his bride. Pauline, who had not seen her husband since their marriage several months earlier, immediately lost interest in everything except their chance to have a few hours together. She telephoned me to say that she was not going to the White House because she wanted to spend all her time with Tee.

I was stunned. Not being a war bride I simply could not comprehend anyone turning down an opportunity to have tea with Mrs. Roosevelt in the White House, and yet it never occurred to me to go on alone. As far as I could see, Mrs. Roosevelt had invited both of us and expected us to come together. I begged and wheedled Pauline over the telephone and finally got her to promise that she would keep the engagement if I secured Mrs. Roosevelt's permission to bring Tee along.

This change of plan was more complicated than it seemed. I had never before telephoned the White House, and the thought of it seemed awesome. Then I had to negotiate the busy switchboard and hang on through numerous transfers and delays until I reached Miss Thompson and explained my predicament. She consulted with Mrs. Roosevelt and got back to me, saying it was all right to bring Tee Coggs with us. Triumphantly, I rushed over to Pauline's apartment near the Howard campus with the news. It was now four-thirty and time for us to leave. At that point, however, another unforeseen obstacle materialized. When Tee realized that *he* was also being invited, he became as embarrassed as a schoolboy. He had rushed off from camp bringing only the uniform he was wearing, now badly wrinkled from a long plane trip. He refused point-blank to appear at the White House in his rumpled state, and insisted upon having his pants pressed.

This meant I had to get back on the telephone and fight my way through the White House switchboard to Miss Thompson again. I was utterly ashamed to tell her the real reason for my call, so I spluttered something like, "There's been a slight delay and we'll be late. May we still come?" Miss Thompson wanted to know how late we would be and I hazarded that we could get there by five-thirty. She conferred again and then said briskly, "All right, but hurry up."

It was twenty minutes past five when we scrambled into Pauline's car and tempted fate in the high-speed run necessary to get to the White House in ten minutes. When we were stopped at the Pennsylvania Avenue gate for our admission cards, Pauline, who had been carrying our documents, suddenly realized that she had changed handbags for the occasion and had left all our identifications at home in her other bag. After more delays and checking through, we finally got inside, me incongruously clutching a small bunch of wilted roses in a room filled with vases of freshly cut flowers. Mrs. Roosevelt accepted them graciously, however, and seemed touched by the spirit behind the humble gift.

The newlyweds sat there transported; sharing their wartime honeymoon in Mrs. Roosevelt's presence was a special benediction they had not anticipated. She had worked with Pauline on many youth projects and was particularly fond of her, so it seemed highly appropriate that Pauline and Tee have a mini-reception at the White House. As I sat with them on the south portico overlooking the White House lawn, I glanced at Mrs. Roosevelt's sensible Red Cross shoes and decided she would enjoy the story of why we were late, so I told her. Her spontaneous laughter was sufficient reward for the harried trials of the afternoon.

She would have been even more amused had she known of my own foolish caper at the White House. Some of my Howard University cronies had asked me to bring back a souvenir of my visit. Since taking a concrete object of any value was unthinkable, I was about to leave empty-handed when I spied a shiny, bronze-colored paper clip just as we passed through the front door. I picked it up and saved it carefully in my purse, only to discover its exact government-issued duplicates everywhere in evidence when I got back to the Howard campus!

CHAPTER 17

Jim Crow in the Nation's Capital

DURING my second year in law school I met the social historian Caroline
F. Ware and her economist husband, Gardiner C. Means, distinguished
scholars from New England who came to Washington to work for the
government in the early days of the New Deal and settled on a seventy-
acre farm in Vienna, Virginia, about twelve miles from the city. Dr. Ware
had joined the Howard faculty, and the stimulating intellectual association
that began when I audited her undergraduate course on constitutional
history in the fall of 1942 developed into a community of interests span-
ning more than four decades.

For half a century the Ware-Means home, known to friends as The
Farm, has been a sanctuary for city-weary students and government workers, intercontinental travelers on diplomatic missions, writers, professionals, and leaders of various humanitarian causes—as well as to flocks of
migratory birds. The Farm provided the proper blending of lively discourse and idyllic rural life. Gardiner and Lina (always "Skipper" to me)
lived simply in a white clapboard house overlooking rolling fields and
forest land, once surrounded by dairy farms but today encircled by building developments and close to the Dulles Airport highway. The center of
their house, a community living room, was built as a log cabin in the 1760s,
and its original beams survived. A wall of books and a huge stone fireplace
where Lina broiled steaks over hot coals for Saturday night dinners were
the room's dominating features.

Gardiner and Lina combined their intellectual pursuits with rugged
outdoor life. At one time they raised sheep, and during the winter a
weekend visitor might be pressed into service rescuing newborn lambs

from the snow and nursing them back to life in the warmth of the kitchen. Later Gardiner raised a few head of cattle for beef, and still later, in partnership with a friend, he put in acres of zoysia grass and developed a profitable business from it. Skipper raised a vegetable garden each year, while Gardiner specialized in growing magnificent specimens of iris and peonies. A visitor was free to disappear with a book in one of the numerous nooks about the house or to join in the physical chores as a FIBUL (Skipper's acronym for "Free Intelligent But Unskilled Labor"), painting the barn, cutting and stacking wood, pulling up weeds in the garden, raking and bagging leaves, or just walking along a wooded lane accompanied by one or more of the five Ware-Means Shetland sheep dogs, successive generations of which have inhabited The Farm. Skipper called them her "staff of psychiatric dogs," each sufficiently distinctive in personality to match the moods of various visitors and to create an engaging diversion from weighty matters.

During my law school days, The Farm was an extension of Dr. Ware's classroom, for Howard University students were welcomed there when they wanted to escape the crowded campus and enjoy the bracing atmosphere of the country. Spontaneous seminars developed as we sat around the fireplace, horizons were widened, and learning was as effortless as eating after-dinner cookies. Dr. Ware had taught at Vassar (then a college for women) before coming to Washington, and she was struck by a similarity she observed at that time between a women's college and a Negro college. She noticed that in each case faculty and students showed a self-conscious tendency to measure their school against prestigious white or male-dominated colleges and to adopt a slightly defensive "we're as good as they are" stance instead of emphasizing the uniqueness of their own particular institution. Out of our many conversations I began to develop a broader perspective on my minority status and to see parallels between racism and sexism. Through Dr. Ware I became increasingly conscious of the damage racial discrimination inflicted upon white as well as black people. Once I was surprised to hear her say that white people were being deprived of a vastly enriching experience by racial segregation. "*My* constitutional rights are being violated," she told me, "when I am prohibited by segregation laws from associating with my friend and am compelled to sit in a separate car!"

When these conversations took place in the living room, Gardiner sat silently in his chair on one side of the fireplace with his clipboard on his knee, seemingly engrossed in mathematical calculations or in writing. Suddenly he would inject a cogent observation and one realized he had been listening intently all the while.

The quiet but firm commitment to equality demonstrated by individuals like Caroline Ware and Gardiner Means was part of the leaven working in wartime Washington to change the racial atmosphere and provide a basis for more frontal attacks on Jim Crow. Two such attacks were staged in April 1943 and April 1944, when Howard University students carried out sit-in demonstrations in segregated Washington restaurants. The sit-ins were experimental and fleeting, launched by a transient group at the end of the school year, but although they could not be sustained, they were carefully planned, the successful forerunners of the more widespread sit-ins by Negro college students in southern and border states during the early 1960s. That this method of protest had surfaced in Washington seventeen years earlier was due to several factors.

Washington was seen by many as the symbolic capital of the nations allied against the Axis, and its advocacy of war aims such as the Four Freedoms made it the logical place for Negro activists to press their claims for equality. At the same time, the city epitomized the great gap between official United States war propaganda and racial practices within our own borders. Segregation in the nation's capital was an especially galling indignity. Aside from some government cafeterias and the YWCA cafeteria at Seventeenth and K streets, N.W., Union Station was the only place in downtown Washington where a Negro could get a meal or use rest room facilities. Although the city had no segregation ordinance requiring separation of the races, Negroes were systematically barred from hotels, restaurants, theaters, movie houses, and other places of public accommodation. Ironically, streetcars and buses were not segregated.

In contrast to this rigid pattern of separation, the faculty of Howard University was integrated, and its graduate and professional schools had a sprinkling of white students. Under the leadership of Dr. Mordecai W. Johnson, the university's first Negro president, Howard had assembled a teaching corps of extraordinary diversity and talent, drawing together distinguished black and white American scholars and a number of refugee professors from European universities. In addition to a brilliant law school faculty, the rosters of its other schools sparkled with the names of outstanding professors in their respective fields—Alain Locke, Ralph Bunche, Rayford Logan, E. Franklin Frazier, Martin Jenkins, Howard Thurman, Caroline F. Ware, Charles Drew, Sterling Brown, and many others. The concentration and accessibility of these scholars on a small campus was both intellectually stimulating and a powerful affirmation of human dignity and equality, which communicated itself to the student body.

In 1942 some two thousand students from forty-five states and twenty-four foreign countries were enrolled at the university, young people who for the most part came from middle-class Negro homes and achieving families. Over half were from northern and border states or midwestern and western communities, and many had never before been exposed to segregation in public facilities. Unaccustomed to southern patterns of racial etiquette, these students were unprepared for the insults and humiliations that descended upon them when they left campus and went downtown to see a movie or stopped at a soda fountain while shopping. Conscious of wartime appeals for sacrifice on behalf of freedom, they were unwilling to accept Jim Crow as an unalterable way of life.

The tensions produced by segregation in Washington were aggravated by steadily mounting evidence of the ill treatment Negroes were receiving in the armed forces. In January 1943, William H. Hastie, who had been on leave from his post as dean of the law school, resigned as civilian aide to Secretary of War Henry L. Stimson to protest official failure to outlaw discrimination in the military. My fellow students in law school, most of whom were subject to the draft, became increasingly bitter and desperate. I remember that one of my classmates, in a pathetic effort to avoid induction, drank a large bottle of honey the night before he had to report for his physical examination, hoping that enough sugar would show up in his urine to disqualify him on health grounds. When another student, Lewis Jones, refused to be inducted into a Jim Crow army in the fall of 1942, forty Howard University students signed a letter to the editor of *PM,* a liberal New York City daily newspaper, supporting the spirit that led Jones to take such action.

Ideas about the use of nonviolent resistance to racial injustice, modeled on Gandhi's movement in India, were in the air. A. Philip Randolph announced publicly in late December 1942 that the March on Washington Movement was considering a campaign of civil disobedience and noncooperation. Although Mr. Randolph stood virtually alone among established Negro leaders in advocating this form of protest (the influential Negro weekly *Pittsburgh Courier* denounced his action, declaring editorially, "Randolph is guilty of the most dangerous demagoguery on record"), several young Negroes were eager to adapt Gandhian techniques to our own struggle, and I was among them. Bayard Rustin and James Farmer, staff members of the pacifist organization Fellowship of Reconciliation (FOR), were already experimenting with the technique in small groups, and both were active in founding the Congress of Racial Equality (CORE) in the spring of 1942. I was a contributing member of FOR and had studied its literature on nonviolent direct action. Although I was aware of the philosophical and religious principles upon which nonviolent protest was based in Gandhi's movement—and had even tried to apply them two years earlier in the Petersburg jail—I also felt that the most effective way to use nonviolence in our racial struggle was to combine it with American techniques of showmanship.

A change in my housing situation at the beginning of that second year exposed me to the tensions building up among the undergraduates caused by off-campus racial incidents. Unable to find an available room near campus, I appealed to the dean of women, Susie Elliott, for help. This was the same Susie Elliott, my cousin, who thirteen years earlier had found me a job at the 137th Street Y in Harlem, and it was my good fortune that she was now a member of the administration at Howard. Although no provision was made for housing women graduate students on campus, Dean Elliott was sympathetic to my problem, which involved having to lug heavy lawbooks over long distances, and she finally hit upon a practical if unorthodox solution. She consented to let me occupy the "powder room" on the first floor of Sojourner Truth Hall, the freshmen women's dormitory. Isolated at the end of a corridor beyond the stairs, the powder room was a narrow, self-contained unit with a basin and toilet concealed behind a swinging door. It was just big enough to accommodate a cot, a bookshelf, a small study table, and my trunk. Since there were no living quarters on that floor, and the large sitting room designed for socials and dances was seldom used, it was an ideal place for concentrated study, at least until some of the freshmen and sophomores, intrigued by the presence of a woman law student close by, began to make shy visits, bombarding me with questions on law and particularly on civil rights. Gradually my room became an informal meeting place for undergraduate women interested in civil rights, including one quiet, soulful-eyed first-year student from Chicago, Patricia Roberts (Harris), the future Secretary of Housing and Urban Development, and later of Health and Human Services, in President Carter's cabinet.

The spark that ignited campus civil rights activity was the arrest in January 1943 of three sophomore women who had been overcharged for hot chocolate in a United Cigar store on Pennsylvania Avenue. Ruth Powell from Massachusetts and Marianne Musgrave and Juanita Morrow from Ohio had sat down at the counter and ordered the hot drinks. When they were refused, they asked for the manager and were told he was out. They said they would wait for him, still maintaining their seats at the counter. Two policemen were summoned, who, after questioning the students, told the waitress to serve them. When she brought their checks they discovered they had been charged twenty-five cents for each cup of chocolate instead of the usual ten cents. The young women placed thirty-five cents on the counter and started to leave, whereupon they were arrested, held until the arrival of a police wagon, carted off to jail, searched, and thrown into a cell with prostitutes and other criminal suspects. "The policeman who arrested us," Ruth reported later, "told us we were being taken in for investigation because he had no proof that we weren't *'subversive agents'!"*

After several hours Dean Elliott was notified and the young women were discharged in her custody. No charge was lodged against them, the purpose of their arrest having been intimidation, but the incident unleashed a torrent of resentment within the student body. Admonished by cautious Howard administrators not to stage individual demonstrations against Jim Crow but instead to work through established civil rights organizations, the students promptly took their case to the Howard University Chapter of the NAACP, then headed by second-year law student James T. Wright.

Many of us in the law school had already been discussing legal and extralegal methods of attacking segregation. Another of my classmates, William C. Raines from North Carolina, had agitated for several months to get support for what he called "the stool-sitting technique." His reasoning was that if white people wanted to deny us service, they should be made to pay for it. Since no lunchroom open to the public could keep us out, Raines argued, "Let's go downtown some lunch hour when they're crowded, and if they don't serve us, we'll just sit there and read our books. They'll lose trade while that seat is out of circulation. If enough people occupy seats, they'll lose so much trade, they'll start thinking."

Although Raines was not around to see his idea take shape (he left law school shortly afterward to enter the flight instruction program at Tuskegee Institute), his discussions deeply impressed me. Considered in the light of the Negro student rebellion against segregation in the 1960s, the proposal may not seem very original or startling, but in 1942 it was spine-tingling merely to entertain such an idea, especially in Washington. Even in the absence of a segregation law, such bold defiance of entrenched custom could be construed as a disruptive attempt to embarrass the government and impede the war effort, an act of disloyalty. Furthermore, Washington was a southern city whose predominantly white police force, we believed, would not hesitate to use force to protect the southern way of life. Nor did we have reason to believe we could rely upon the active support of the black community. In early 1943 the *Pittsburgh Courier* published the results of a poll taken among Negroes which indicated that 70.6 percent opposed a "non-violent disobedience campaign" as not likely to help Negroes, 25.3 percent approved, and 4.1 percent were uncertain. Then, too, many parents of Howard University students, particularly the parents of teenage girls, adhered to middle-class standards of respectability and would be horrified at the thought of their daughters tangling with the police, being arrested and thrown into jail. College administrators,

conscious in those days of their role *in loco parentis,* were acutely sensitive
to parental pressures, and breaking the code of respectability enforced by
parents was as formidable a psychological barrier to action as the prospect
of police brutality.

What we now discovered to our amazement was that for more than a
year one of the three young women arrested in the hot-chocolate incident
had already been quietly carrying on a one-person campaign along the
very lines Bill Raines was proposing, wholly unaware that her action would
become a model for group protest. Ruth Powell was the essence of respectability, a proper New Englander who had lived all her life in the
small town of Milton, Massachusetts, a Boston suburb, insulated from the
cruder expressions of racial discrimination. "I was a Negro, but in name
only," she told me later. "I knew nothing about Negroes as a *race* and even
less about the problems existing among them. And so I came to Washington, thrilled not only because I had chosen the finest Negro college in the
world but because I was coming to the nation's capital, the center of
democracy and everything that meant Americanism."

Ruth's first encounter with Jim Crow had been devastating. When she
entered a downtown drugstore and ordered a sandwich at the soda fountain, she was ignored. As she waited, she noticed the waitresses whispering
among themselves and looking in her direction and people on either side
staring at her. "But I vainly attributed it to the school button I wore and
to the evident newness of my Howard school cap with the letters '45 on
it. Well, I sat there for about ten minutes watching the waitresses whizzing
back and forth in front of me, when suddenly the awful truth dawned and
I realized what was happening. I had been informed back at school that
I couldn't eat downtown, but somehow I had never applied that to public
drugstores, where they sell you other things. I sat there undecided as to
what to do and mostly trying to hold back the tears of embarrassment and
hurt, when the manager of the store came over and said, 'I'm sorry, but
we don't serve Negroes here.' I managed to gasp a feeble 'But why?' just
to preserve my pride, and dashed from the store. It was a long time before
I left the campus again."

When Ruth discussed the situation with some of the other students,
especially those from the South, she was puzzled by their attitude of
resignation. They attempted to laugh it off, but when she tried to pin them
down, their fear surfaced. "People have been lynched for less than that!"
she was told, and "What can you do when the government's on their side?"

"Then came the war," she recalled, bringing appeals for loyalty and
patriotism on the one hand but no material improvements in civil rights
or labor laws on the other—only the added disgrace of increased discriminatory practices in war industries and the army. "I knew that I, alone,

couldn't do anything concrete to revolutionize conditions," Ruth said, "but I also knew that I had to do something to preserve what remained of my self-respect."

That "something" evolved into a one-woman campaign in the downtown drugstores and restaurants. Ruth would go in, ask politely for service, and when she was refused, would sit quietly, sometimes for hours at a time. During those "sittings" she would pick out a waiter and just stare at him with a perfectly blank expression on her face. Waiters found it very confusing and nerve-racking to be singled out and simply stared at for perhaps an hour or more. She answered anyone who felt disposed to argue for segregation with a quiet, impregnable wall of questions: "Why?" or "Just give me one good reason why," or "Will you state the law that says I can't be served?" always couched in a low, steady voice with no outward sign of nervousness or emotion.

Once a soda fountain clerk became so provoked when two unmistakably southern white soldiers walked out, saying, "If she can't be served, neither can we!" that he came around to Ruth's side of the counter, unscrewed and removed the stools on either side of her, and placed a card on the counter reading COUNTER CLOSED AT THIS END.

"Whether I was finally served was unimportant," Ruth explained. "What I believed was that all these little bits of agitation would go toward that vital and I hope not too distant awakening process."

Ruth's last invasion of forbidden territory was when she and her two classmates were arrested. As in the case of Rosa Parks and the Montgomery Boycott a dozen years later, one determined individual succeeded in arousing others to mount a collective assault on segregation.

The fact that an accident of gender exempted me from military service and left me free to pursue my career without interruption made me feel an extra responsibility to carry on the integration battle. Many other Howard University women were feeling a similar responsibility, which was heightened by the dramatic leave-taking of sixty-five Howard men, who marched off campus in a body to report for military duty. We women reasoned that it was our job to help make the country for which our black brothers were fighting a freer place in which to live when they returned from wartime service.

From the nightly bull sessions in Truth Hall a plan of action emerged, modeled on Ruth Powell's experience. It was designed to attract the widest possible support from all segments of the university community, with direct action reserved for the last of a series of steps. My role as student "legal adviser" was to make sure that our proposed actions were within the framework of legality so as not to arouse the official disapproval of the university administration. The undergraduates formed a temporary

Student Committee on Campus Opinion, and drafted and distributed a questionnaire to test potential support for an active campaign against segregation in the District of Columbia. Of the 292 people who responded, 284, or 97.3 percent, said they did not believe Negroes should suspend the struggle for equal rights until the end of the war. Of those answering the question on student involvement, 262, or 96 percent, stated that Negro students should actively participate in the struggle for equality during wartime. On the crucial question of a campaign against segregation in the District of Columbia, 218 said they would actively join such an effort, 38 said they would not participate themselves but would support others who did, and only 6 disapproved of the idea.

Based upon this expression of support, a Civil Rights Committee was formed under the sponsorship of the Howard Chapter of the NAACP to bring about equal accommodations in the city of Washington. A survey of local laws unearthed a civil rights bill for the District of Columbia (H.R. 1995) recently introduced into the House of Representatives by Congressman William A. Rowan from Illinois, and a companion bill (S. 442) introduced into the Senate by Senator Warren Barbour from New Jersey. One of our activities was to educate the campus community on the existence of this pending legislation so that students could lobby their home-state representatives through visits and letters urging support of the bills.

The major excitement, however, centered on the work of the Direct Action subcommittee, chaired by Ruth Powell. Its purpose was "to enroll students who will participate in small carefully planned demonstrations for equal rights in the District of Columbia," such as "weekly visits to certain downtown restaurants, sitting quietly, requesting service." Although we were engaged in serious business, our planning sessions were fun and challenged our powers of imagination. The fact that we were doing something creative about our racial plight was exhilarating and increased our self-esteem. The Direct Action subcommittee attracted some of the leading students on campus, for it was important that those undertaking unorthodox activities maintain academic excellence. Also, we proceeded cautiously, aware that a misstep would compromise our goal. Instead of rushing precipitously into "hostile" territory, a group of students surveyed public eating places in the neighboring, mostly Negro community on Northwest U Street that still catered to the "White Trade Only." One of the most notorious of these lily-white establishments was the Little Palace Cafeteria, located at the busy intersection of Fourteenth and U streets, N.W., and run by a Mr. Chaconas. Because of its strategic location, the Little Palace had long been a source of mortification for countless unsuspecting Negroes, who entered it assuming that at least they would be served in the heart of the Negro section of the city.

The Little Palace Cafeteria was selected as our first target. For a week prior to our move against the cafeteria we held campus pep rallies and drummed up support for our effort through noon-hour broadcasts from the tower of Founder's Library. We decorated hot-chocolate cups and used them around campus as collection cans to solicit the funds we needed for paper, postage, and picket signs. We held a midweek Town Hall meeting and brought in experienced political leaders—Thomasina Johnson, legislative representative of Alpha Kappa Alpha Sorority, and Albert B. Herman, political aide to Senator Barbour—to lead a forum on civil rights legislation and methods of achieving it. We conducted classes on the legal aspects of picketing and disorderly conduct in the District of Columbia, spent hours in small groups discussing public decorum, anticipating and preparing for the reactions of the black public, the white public, white customers, and white management respectively. We stressed the importance of a dignified appearance, and the subcommittee directed that all participants dress well for the occasion. We also pledged ourselves to exemplary nonviolent conduct, however great the provocation.

Finally, on April 17, a rainy Saturday afternoon, we assembled on campus and began to leave the Howard University grounds in groups of four, about five minutes apart, to make the ten-minute walk to the Little Palace Cafeteria. The demonstration was limited to a carefully selected group of volunteers—less than twenty students—who felt confident they could maintain self-restraint under pressure. As each group arrived, three entered the cafeteria while the fourth remained outside as an "observer." Inside, we took our trays to the steam table and as soon as we were refused service carried our empty trays to a vacant seat at one of the tables, took out magazines, books of poetry or textbooks, notebooks and pencils, and assumed an attitude of concentrated study. Strict silence was maintained. Minutes later the next group arrived and repeated the process. Outside, the observers began to form a picket line with colorful signs reading "Our Boys, our Bonds, our Brothers are Fighting for YOU! Why Can't We Eat Here?"; "We Die Together—Why Can't We Eat Together?"; "There's No Segregation Law in D.C. What's Your Story, Little Palace?" Two pickets carried posters (prepared for the War Manpower Commission by the Office of War Information) depicting two workers—one black and the other white—working together as riveters on a steel plate. The inscription on the poster read "UNITED WE WIN!"

My heart thumped furiously as I sat at a table awaiting developments. The management was stunned at first, then after trying unsuccessfully to persuade us to leave, called the police. Almost immediately a half-dozen uniformed officers appeared. When they approached us we said simply,

"We're waiting for service," and since we did not appear to be violating any law, they made no move to arrest us.

After forty-five minutes had passed and twelve Negro students were occupying most of the tables of the small cafeteria, Chaconas gave up and closed his restaurant eight hours earlier than his normal closing time. Those of us who were inside joined the picket line and kept it going for the rest of the afternoon. Chaconas told reporter Harry McAlpin, who covered the demonstration for the *Chicago Defender:* "I'll lose money, but I'd rather close up than practice democracy this way. The time is not ripe." When Juanita Morrow, a journalism student, interviewed Chaconas several days later, he admitted that he had lost about $180 that Saturday afternoon and evening, a considerable sum for a small business.

Actually, the incident did not arouse the furor we had feared but revealed the possibilities for change. When told why the place was closed and being picketed, a white customer named Raymond Starnes, who came from Charlotte, North Carolina, said, "I eat here regularly, and I don't care who eats here. All I want is to eat. I want the place to stay open. After all, we are all human." Another white bystander, asked what he thought of the students' action, replied, "I think it's reasonable. Negroes are fighting to win this war for democracy just like whites. If it came to a vote, it would get my vote."

When Chaconas opened his place on Monday morning, our picket line was there to greet him, and it continued all day. Within forty-eight hours he capitulated and began to serve Negro customers. We were jubilant. Our conquest of a small "greasy spoon" eating place was a relatively minor skirmish in the long battle to end segregation in the nation's capital—a battle that was ended by a Supreme Court decision ten years later—but it loomed large in our eyes. We had proved that intelligent, imaginative action could bring positive results and, fortunately, we had won our first victory without an embarrassing incident. (One other small restaurant in the area was desegregated that spring before final examinations and summer vacation interrupted our campaign.)

Significantly, the prominent role of women in the leadership and planning of our protest was a by-product of the wartime thinning of the ranks of male students. Twelve of the nineteen Howard University demonstrators at the Little Palace on April 17 were female. (The twentieth demonstrator was Natalie Moorman, a red-haired, six-foot-tall woman from Arlington, Virginia, and a legendary figure in the struggle to desegregate the Washington area. Armed with an umbrella and a commanding voice, she regularly rode the bus from the District to its Arlington suburb and challenged bus drivers to try to enforce segregation under Virginia law once the bus reached the midpoint of the Fourteenth Street Bridge.)

Many of those young women who had joined together to defy tradition would continue to make breakthroughs in their respective fields after their college days. Ruth Powell went into mental health and became a chief of service at the Bronx Psychiatric Center in New York City. Marianne Musgrave chose the academic route and became a professor of English at Miami University in Oxford, Ohio. The youngest member of that little band of demonstrators, Patricia Roberts, carried the impact of her civil rights experiences from Howard University to the cabinet level of the federal government. Of the three pioneers whose arrest sparked the student protest, only Juanita Morrow followed nonviolent direct action as a way of life. With her pacifist husband, Wallace Nelson, she was an active leader of CORE sit-ins and other civil disobedience campaigns for many years.

CHAPTER 18

National Despair, Personal Vindication

I LEFT Washington for summer vacation especially proud of our student exploit, but the glow of success in striking a tiny blow against segregation was quickly overshadowed by the racial violence that exploded during the summer of 1943. Outbreaks like the ones in Beaumont, Texas, and Los Angeles, California, signaled more widespread disorders to come. An oppressive cloud of tension and fear hung over us like an approaching storm.

When I arrived home in Durham to visit Aunt Pauline and Aunt Sallie, the normally peaceful town was in an uproar over a local bus incident. A sixteen-year-old Negro schoolgirl, Doris Lyon, was reportedly struck by a white plainclothes police officer when she refused to surrender her seat just past the rear exit door of a crowded bus to a white passenger. She was charged with disorderly conduct and violation of the state segregation law covering public transportation, and the white detective was named defendant in a countercharge of assault. My aunts were visibly terrified and begged me not to do or say anything that would aggravate an already inflamed situation.

While in Durham I went to our family physician, Dr. John Cordice, for a medical checkup. Although widely respected, Dr. Cordice was not permitted to practice at Duke University Hospital because he was a Negro. In order to get certain tests he wanted, he had to refer me to a white physician, a Dr. Ruffin, with whom he had made an appointment for me at the university clinic. At the time of the appointment the clinic's reception procedure seemed to be routine and I was sent to an examining room. But when Dr. Ruffin came in and began to ask me questions I noticed he seemed increasingly ill at ease. Suddenly he announced that he was not going to examine me and told me to put on my clothes and leave. Flabbergasted, I asked him why.

"I'm not going to have anything to do with Eleanor Roosevelt movements!" Dr. Ruffin shouted as he stormed out of the examining room.

It gradually dawned on me that I was the luckless victim of a suspicion born of hatred and fear. Mrs. Roosevelt had become the target of vicious attacks, especially in the South, for her espousal of racial justice. Persistent, false rumors had spread among the white population of the southern states that Negroes, inspired by Mrs. Roosevelt, were organizing "Eleanor Clubs" in North Carolina and elsewhere with the objectives of forcing all black women out of domestic service, obtaining "social equality," and bringing about an uprising against white people. The rumor apparently originated in the fact that numbers of Negro women were leaving domestic service for better-paying jobs in wartime industries. As ridiculous as this rumor seemed to colored people, it had taken such hold on white people of all classes that my good friend Lewis E. Austin felt compelled to write a full-page editorial in the *Carolina Times* which he titled " 'Eleanor Clubs' and the Negro." Because my bearing was completely at variance with the southern racial stereotype, Dr. Ruffin apparently jumped to the conclusion that I was an organizer of this nonexistent "movement."

I was so outraged that when I got home I told Aunt Pauline I was finished with the South, that I would come back to Durham to bury her when she died, but not for any other reason.

Few Negroes were surprised when the Detroit riot broke out on June 16, for the racial tensions that produced it had been building steadily throughout the war. By the time President Roosevelt proclaimed a state of emergency and sent in six thousand soldiers to patrol the city, more than thirty hours of carnage had brought death to twenty-five Negroes and nine white persons, six hundred or more people had been injured, and property loss and damage was estimated at two million dollars. Like others, I wrote letters to editors and to government officials—futilely, it seemed—protesting the situation. A letter I wrote to President Roosevelt's aide, Marvin McIntyre, two days after the riot, proposed that "a National Commission be set up by executive order to make a thorough and complete study of the racial situation, with a view toward marshalling the pertinent facts and toward drawing up a national legislative program." I do not recall hearing from Mr. McIntyre, but Virginius Dabney, editor of the *Richmond Times-Dispatch,* responded to a similar letter, saying: "I think the question whether a Federal commission to investigate the race question would be good or bad would depend largely on the identities and attitudes of those composing it. It would have to be very carefully and diplomatically handled in order to help, rather than hurt." (Three years later President

Truman created the President's Committee on Civil Rights by Executive Order 9808.)

President Roosevelt was strangely silent about the worst racial outbreak to occur in the nation since 1919. His comment came more than a month later and was then only in response to an inquiry from New York Congressman Vito Marcantonio. The President stated: "I share your feeling that the recent outbreaks of violence in widely scattered parts of the country endanger our national unity and comfort our enemies. I am sure that every true American regrets this."

My reaction to the President's statement was fairly typical of Negro feeling at the time. It seemed so mealy-mouthed that I sat down immediately and wrote an angry poem, "Mr. Roosevelt Regrets":

> What'd you get, black boy,
> When they knocked you down in the gutter,
> And they kicked your teeth out,
> And they broke your skull with clubs
> And they bashed your stomach in?
> What'd you get when the police shot you in the back,
> And they chained you to the beds
> While they wiped the blood off?
> What'd you get when you cried out to the Top Man?
> When you called on the man next to God, so you thought,
> And you asked him to speak out to save you?
> What'd the Top Man say, black boy?
> "Mr. Roosevelt regrets . . ."

The poem was accepted by Roy Wilkins and published in the August 1943 issue of NAACP's official organ, *The Crisis.* I also sent a copy to Mrs. Roosevelt, whose response was prompt and to the point. "I have your poem dated July 21. I am sorry but I understand."

By this time I was back in New York working as a breakfast and luncheon waitress at the Allerton House for Women in midtown Manhattan. I had rented a tiny room from my friend Vivian Odems Lemon, who had an apartment in the lower Bronx, and I spent my afternoons and evenings working on the long poem "Dark Testament," which Stephen Vincent Benét had encouraged me to write. His sudden death in March 1943 was spurring me on to complete it in his memory. As the poem took shape I experimented with different patterns of Negro speech and sometimes tramped the streets at night, beating out the rhythms in my head.

I also wrote an article predicting further riots, which proved to be prophetic. It was titled "Negroes Are Fed Up," and no sooner had it appeared in the August issue of *Common Sense,* a liberal magazine edited

Pauli Murray at her graduation from Richmond Hill High School,
New York City (June, 1927).

CLASS of 1944
SCHOOL of LAW
HOWARD UNIVERSITY

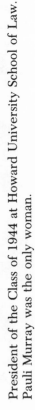

President of the Class of 1944 at Howard University School of Law. Pauli Murray was the only woman.

PAULI MURRAY

for CITY COUNCIL

10th Senatorial District

FORMER DEPUTY ATTORNEY GENERAL

Citizen's Union says: A lawyer with an unusually keen intellect, broad social vision, and a wealth of experience in public affairs.

Education
Hunter College B.A., 1933
Brookwood Labor College, 1936-7
Howard University, L.L.B., *Cum Laude*, 1944
University of California, L.L.M., 1945

Background
Lawyer
Formerly staff member, Workers Defense League; American Jewish Congress; National Urban League
Deputy Attorney General, State of California

Member:
N. A. A. C. P.
National Council of Negro Women
Citizens Committee of Children
N. Y. County Lawyers Association
Liberal Party, Civil Liberties Committee

Indorsed by Americans for Democratic Action.

TENANTS — IF YOU HAVE LANDLORD TROUBLES CONSULT YOUR LOCAL LIBERAL PARTY CLUB FOR FREE SERVICE

Issued by the LIBERAL PARTY, Kings County
66 Court Street • TR. 5-8026

A campaign poster for Pauli Murray's first venture into city politics in New York.

Aunt Pauline in Brooklyn, New York, 75 years old.

Thelma Stevens and Pauli Murray with the latter's first book,
States' Laws on Race and Color (1949).

Maida Springer (1951)

Mildred Fearing

Pauli Murray and Mrs. Eleanor Roosevelt at Valkill Cottage, Hyde Park,
New York (July 14, 1962). *Photograph by Raymond Murray.*

Pauli Murray in Eucharistic vestments, Holy Nativity Church,
Baltimore, Maryland (February, 1981). *Photograph
by Susan Mullally Weil.*

by Alfred Bingham, than the Harlem riot erupted on Sunday night, August 1. Six persons were killed, several hundred were injured, and property damage was in the hundreds of thousands of dollars after two days of burning and looting. The riot had been triggered by a rumor (which turned out to be false) that a white police officer had killed a Negro soldier in an altercation over the arrest of a Negro woman.

Monday afternoon following Sunday night's outbreak, I walked through the riot area along 125th Street and up and down Lenox, Seventh, and Eighth avenues. That part of Harlem was like a bombed-out war target; it was difficult to believe that human beings could have accomplished such utter destruction so swiftly and ruthlessly. Steel gratings on doors and windows were ripped away; buildings were gutted by fire; shards of smashed plate glass and other debris covered the sidewalks. Looters darted in and out of stores in open defiance of the police. I watched a woman carry a leg of meat from a butcher shop, followed by a man hugging a ham under his arm, while a nearby police officer turned his back. By Monday night the area looked like territory under an army of occupation as eight thousand helmeted police and civilian guards patrolled the Harlem streets.

The mob had lashed out blindly in frenzied release, and yet it had been selective in its terrible revenge. Businesses known to be owned by Negroes had been left intact. I tried to express the mood of Harlem in an eyewitness account of the riot scene which appeared in the Socialist *Call:*

> Call them "hoodlums" if you will. But what the "hoodlums" had wrought the mass mind had thought. Though responsible housewives and breadwinners walked in the streets and mumbled, "Isn't it terrible? They ought to put every one of them in jail," yet the undercurrent everywhere and from every lip was *"These riots had to come."*
>
> And the mob, made up of a collection of little individuals, each of whom carried in the back of his mind the burning image of some injustice the "white man" had done to him, or to his mother, or his sister, or his brother in the armed forces, instinctively moved to a different level from the Detroit riot. There was little violence against individual whites. For this mob argued, "What'll it matter if we shoot up or cut up a few cops, or get a piece of white meat? That ain't doing much—but if we smash up everything and cut off the white man's income, that'll get him where it hurts the most.
>
> "But what *good* has it done?" I asked.
>
> "Oh, it's done some good all right! The white man'll see that the colored man just ain't gonna take no stuff no more. This'll show him."

And what could anyone say to that? Those of us who had literally screamed at the white race for its failure to disclose the seriousness of the race problem in this country could not get to first base. Yet the "hoodlums," the fellows who said they would not have been loyal to Harlem if they hadn't taken some "souvenirs" on Sunday night, had in a few hours blasted open the front pages of every metropolitan newspaper the country over with the products of segregation and discrimination and home-grown fascism.

It was quiet Monday night. . . . The mob had done its deadly work with the swiftness of a Nat Turner. It had turned its fury against the symbol of property ownership which combined with prejudice to keep it submerged below the human level. For the moment it was satisfied and could sleep. But the fires still smoulder in the hearts of every Negro who lives in America. What must we do to extinguish them; or better still, to turn them, purified, into the useful flames of co-operation and constructive brotherhood?

In my anguish over what I had seen in Harlem, I realized that I felt the same intensely violent urge to strike back against the accumulated hurts, insults, and humiliations as did the rioters (one of my cousins among them) who had reduced the area to smoking rubble. My despair was expressed in a poem called "Harlem Riot, 1943":

> Not by hammering the furious word,
> Nor bread stamped in the streets,
> Nor milk emptied in gutter,
> Shall we gain the gates of the city.
>
> But I am a prophet without eyes to see;
> I do not know how we shall gain the gates of the city.

For the rest of August I wrote as one possessed, pouring all my pain and bitterness into "Dark Testament." When the poem was completed, I felt as if a demon had been exorcised and a terrible fever inside me had been broken. Earlier I had doubts about continuing to study law—it seemed so hopeless—but now a calmer mood prevailed and I was ready to go back and finish my senior year.

It was about this time that my education in feminism took an important step forward. My discovery of the historical links between the struggles for the abolition of slavery and the rights of women gave me a new perspective that helped me balance the tensions created by the double burden of race and sex. Until now my haphazard awareness of discrimination because of gender had been submerged in an all-consuming preoccupation with racial injustice, and I tended to treat my first conscious exposure to sexism as an individual problem rather than one shared with other women. I was dismally ignorant of the history of the women's movement. When I cast my first vote at the age of twenty-one, I did not appreciate that women had won suffrage only twelve years earlier. Nor did I fully grasp the significance of my Grandfather Fitzgerald's proud recollection that in his youth he once had the honor of sitting on the same platform with Susan B. Anthony.

Now what was to become for me an abiding interest in feminist tradition was ignited by a new friend, Betsy Graves Reyneau, a veteran of the final struggle for woman suffrage. An accomplished portrait painter, she was staying on the Howard campus to complete an oil portrait of the university's president, Mordecai Johnson, when I returned to find new lodgings for my senior year. In our first conversation Betsy and I established an immediate rapport; it was the beginning of a warm friendship which continued until her death some twenty years later.

Betsy Graves Reyneau was a fragile toothpick of a woman, in her fifties at the time, whose bodily frailness belied her fiery spirit and passion for social justice. Afflicted with a digestive ailment that required several operations, including the removal of her stomach, she existed on a rigorous diet but refused to let her physical limitations deter her in her single-minded dedication to justice. Betsy was an engaging conversationalist with an encyclopedic knowledge of world affairs, and her reminiscences, sprinkled with caustic comments, were the stuff of oral history.

We discovered common ground in our abolitionist heritage. My Grandfather Fitzgerald had fought for freedom in the Civil War and his boyhood memories of the Underground Railroad in Pennsylvania were part of my family tradition. Betsy had grown up in Michigan, where her paternal grandparents had also been immersed in the slavery controversy. Grandfather Graves was chief justice of the Michigan Supreme Court during the late antebellum period. Although personally opposed to slavery, he was sworn as a judge to uphold the laws of the United States, including the Fugitive Slave Law of 1850, and his problem was aggravated by the activities of his determined wife. Grandmother Graves, a close friend of Sojourner Truth, the former slave who was an abolitionist and an advocate of women's rights, was operating a station of the Underground Railroad right in the Graves home.

Betsy laughed as she told me of her grandfather's dilemma and how one day Chief Justice Graves confronted his wife, asking:

"What am I going to do? *You* know I must enforce the new law and *I* know what *you* are doing."

"Just walk right out of the front door and never look back to see what's going on," Grandmother Graves retorted.

Betsy had inherited her grandmother's penchant for social activism. As a young married woman during World War I, she was in the thick of the movements for peace, birth control, and woman suffrage. She handed out leaflets on New York's Fifth Avenue as a part of Margaret Sanger's campaign for birth control and became an active member of the National Women's Party, the militant wing of the women's movement led by Alice Paul in the closing stages of the struggle for women's right to vote. Mrs. Paul Reyneau (as Betsy is referred to in Inez Haynes Irwin's *The Story of Alice Paul and the National Women's Party*) was one of the sixteen women arrested in Washington on Bastille Day, 1917, for picketing the White House with banners reading "Liberty, Equality and Fraternity." They were subsequently convicted on a charge of "obstructing traffic" and sentenced to sixty days in the Occoquan Workhouse. Among other indignities they suffered in prison, the women reported finding worms in their cereal, in their cornbread, and sometimes floating on top of the soup. When they refused to eat, they were forcibly fed. After their release the women commemorated their experience by having sixteen silver pins made up, each a replica of a prison door with a tiny chain and small peephole representing an opening through which food was passed. This symbol of the struggle for women's rights had the same effect on me as my Grandfather Fitzgerald's Civil War saber and pistol that Grandmother always kept under her bed during my early childhood. When, after Betsy's death, her daughter Marie gave the pin to me as a memento, it became one of my most cherished possessions.

Before the outbreak of World War II, Betsy had lived in Europe for more than twelve years. She had painted such literary figures as H. G. Wells, William Butler Yeats, and George Santayana and had watched the growth of Fascism, fighting against it with characteristic intensity. When the war engulfed Europe she returned to the United States, convinced she would never paint again because she felt that portrait painting had become irrelevant in a world being swallowed by dictatorships. She changed her mind during a visit to Coconut Grove, Florida, when she saw benches in the park marked "For Whites Only." The reporter Dorothy Dunbar Bromley, who interviewed Betsy several years later, wrote of this incident: "That she should come home and find Fascism was a bitter experience for the artist who refused to paint Mussolini in 1929. . . . She had naively supposed, Mrs. Reyneau told a tea party in Florida, that she had left racism behind her in Europe. The ladies could not see why she was so shocked."

The incident launched Betsy on a career she was to pursue passionately for the remainder of her life: she decided she would use her art to combat racism in the United States. She was convinced that American Negro leaders who were trying to overturn a system of *apartheid* in a country where it was generally taken for granted were the true American revolutionaries of the 1940s. As an artist she also saw the rich variety of color among Negroes—from blond, blue-eyed Walter White of the NAACP to dark, mahogany-hued Mary McLeod Bethune—a treasure trove for a painter in oils. She was determined to capture these public figures on canvas before they passed from the scene. Her painting of George Washington Carver at Tuskegee Institute, completed a few months before his death, became the first portrait of a Negro to be accepted by the Smithsonian Institution. When I met Betsy Reyneau she was in Washington to paint portraits of Mrs. Bethune, Dean William H. Hastie, Charles Houston, Dr. Charles Drew, and Mary Church Terrell, in addition to Dr. Johnson. Within the next few years she had a collection of more than twenty-five portraits of leading Negroes, which also included Thurgood Marshall, A. Philip Randolph, Judge Jane M. Bolin, Anna Arnold Hedgeman, and Martin Luther King, Jr. She joined forces with the painter Laura Wheeler Waring, a Negro, and the interracial team traveled about the country under the auspices of the Harmon Foundation, taking their exhibit, "Portraits of Outstanding Americans of Negro Origin," to various cities. When Mrs. Waring died in 1947, Betsy continued the traveling exhibit alone and discovered that everywhere the collection was shown it served not only as an artistic antidote to racial stereotypes but also to stimulate spontaneous demonstrations and sit-ins against racial discrimination.

Betsy Reyneau's presence on campus for several months and her iconoclastic temperament nourished my budding feminism. She was a living link with an earlier phase of a struggle that had faded into obscurity by the time I grew up and became aware of social movements. I now realized there was a history of women's efforts to achieve equality, that I was not alone, and that I was not especially excessive in the ways I went about working for change.

By the time I was a senior, two more women—Helene Southern and Grace C. Rowe—had entered the law school, and while their presence made me less of an oddity, my status remained ambiguous. Traditionally, the top-ranking second-year student at Howard was elected by the Law Students Guild at the end of the school year to serve as Chief Justice of the Court of Peers (the Guild's executive committee) during that student's senior year. At that time, becoming Chief Justice of the Court of Peers was the highest honor bestowed upon a member of the law student body—it was Howard Law School's equivalent of editor in chief of the law review in more prestigious law schools—and the title carried luster and immense prestige on campus. Although I led my class in academic standing and had been elected an associate justice in my second year, no woman had ever been made Chief Justice of the student organization. Since my classmates were not prepared to recognize a woman as the acknowledged leader of the student body, no election was held, the office of Chief Justice remained vacant, and for the first half of my senior year the Court of Peers was defunct. The obvious slight wounded both my vanity and my sense of simple justice, but I had too much pride to admit it and chose instead to endure my hurt in silence.

Then an unforeseen event changed everything. Because the military draft had decimated our ranks, the second- and third-year classes were combined for a course called Bills and Notes, which dealt with commercial paper. It was a heavy course requiring us to learn a mass of technical rules governing checks, promissory notes, drafts, bills of lading, and other commercial documents in the various jurisdictions. In addition to the daily assignment of cases and materials, which took many hours to prepare, we were responsible for the detailed lectures of our instructor, Spottswood W. Robinson III (who later became dean of the law school and ultimately chief judge of the U.S. Court of Appeals for the District of Columbia). "Spots," as we called him, was known as a "tough man," whose final examinations were terrifying even to the best students. Since he had failed nine of the fifteen who took Bills and Notes the previous year, we were all understandably apprehensive. We had no tape recorders or Xerox machines in those days to aid us in reproducing materials, and if we missed a lecture or fell behind in briefing our daily quota of cases, it was virtually impossible to catch up.

Difficult as it was for those of us who attended every class session and took copious notes, Billy Jones, a slight, likable second-year student with a good mind but a serious visual ailment, was in a desperate position. Billy had begun law school in my class and had done well, but at the beginning of our second year he was stricken with a disease that caused periods of blindness, and he lost a year in school. He had come back to make another try, when the blindness recurred, and he spent two more months in the hospital. By the time Billy could return to class the semester was almost over, and while we admired his gutsy determination to pass Bills and Notes, all of us felt his attempt to make up for lost time was hopeless. When groups began to form to review for the final examination, no one wanted the extra burden of a member who had not attended classes regularly and had no notes to contribute to the discussions. Each group found some excuse to exclude Billy Jones.

From previous experiences with my classmates I had learned that to avoid time-consuming arguments it was sometimes better to study for finals alone. Just as I was preparing to shut myself off in order to memorize the mass of materials in Bills and Notes, Billy came to me in despair. Fearful as I was about the outcome of Spots' exam, it was difficult for me to refuse Billy's appeal because I remembered my Grandfather Fitzgerald's blindness when I was a small child, and reluctantly I agreed to study with him.

To save Billy from eyestrain, we had to adopt unorthodox methods of review. We trained like athletes, using every spare moment of each day to study, doing most of our work outdoors. In advance of our sessions I wrote summaries of the principal rules to be memorized, then I read them aloud to Billy as we walked back and forth across campus to lunch or hiked along the city streets oblivious of everything but our subject matter. On these long walks I would drill Billy on the materials covered. We closed our books early on the afternoon before the exam, splurged on a good meal off campus, relaxed at a movie, and wished one another good luck as we parted to get a full night's rest before our ordeal, scheduled for eight o'clock next morning.

When the exam results were posted on the bulletin board some days later, the Bills and Notes grades became the talk of the entire law school. I was astounded to discover that my grade was 95, Billy Jones was second, with a mark of 85, and everyone else in the course had received 70 or below. I had been so absorbed in the process of getting the material across to Billy that, without realizing it, I had applied the educational principle that the best way to master a subject is to try to teach it to someone else.

The reaction of my fellow law students was even more astounding. The men did a sudden flip-flop, behaving like people who have experienced a dramatic religious conversion. The Law Students Guild called a meeting and quickly elected me Chief Justice of the Court of Peers. Not satisfied, my own classmates chose me president of the senior class. For the first time I began to hear heated discussions about the exclusion of women from the legal fraternity. Opinion was divided between those who proposed to resign their membership in protest and those who favored remaining inside the fraternity and fighting to remove the exclusionary clause from its constitution.

Billy Jones's courage and tenacity also made him a hero among his fellows. He succeeded me as Chief Justice in his senior year and went on to become a successful lawyer and later a judge in East Saint Louis, Missouri, his hometown.

CHAPTER 19

Perfecting Our Strategy

My last semester in law school was dizzying, because everything seemed to happen at once. In addition to carrying a heavy course load, as graduation approached I found myself battling simultaneously on three fronts which required constant shifting of intellectual and emotional gears. I was at once a minority voice within the law school in an ongoing debate over civil rights legal strategy, a student leader in the renewed direct action assault upon Washington's segregated restaurants, and a solitary challenger of Harvard Law School's traditional exclusion of women students.

In the early 1940s Howard Law School stood virtually alone in its strong emphasis upon civil rights. Our senior Civil Rights Seminar was easily the most popular course in the curriculum. Presided over by my early supporter, jovial Leon A. Ransom, whose brilliant Supreme Court victories included reversal of the death sentence of one of the famous Scottsboro defendants, the seminar was a forum in which eager students tested their abilities against experienced civil rights lawyers and vied with one another to present the most persuasive arguments for the overthrow of Jim Crow.

Bound together by an overriding passion, we were a tiny band of fighters trying to establish defensible positions from which to launch a massive attack upon the entire system of legally enforced segregation, reinforced as it was by decades of court decisions. We sifted through hundreds of judicial opinions in search of fragments of language to bolster our moral convictions, and although the same ground had been covered many times over, any fresh idea that emerged in the heat of our forensic struggles would be refined through research and developed into a seminar paper. These student efforts added to the law school's reservoir of constitutional theory. In the absence of a law review, our papers remained unpublished, but some of our ideas eventually found their way into briefs presented to the Supreme Court, and in later years we could look back with pride on our performance as anonymous foot soldiers in the early waves of the struggle leading to the great civil rights legal victories of the forties, fifties, and sixties.

Two great roadblocks in our advance toward equality under the law were the Supreme Court's landmark decisions in the *Civil Rights Cases* of 1883 and *Plessy* v. *Ferguson* in 1896. In the 1883 decision, the Court struck down sections of the Civil Rights Act of 1875, which had prohibited denial of equal accommodations in hotels, in theaters, and on railroads and other public conveyances, thus leaving Negroes unprotected against discrimination by private establishments. This decision set the stage for the more far-reaching doctrine of "separate but equal" treatment laid down in the later *Plessy* case, which held that states had the power to enforce separation by race so long as the separate facilities were equal. These two cases, generally presumed to be settled law, locked us into a permanent and visibly inferior status. We needed no sociological data to tell us the decisions were morally wrong and judicially biased—our personal experience contradicted their validity—but our problem was how to overcome an almost impregnable wall of judicial precedent.

One day during class discussion, in a flash of poetic insight, I advanced a radical approach that few legal scholars considered viable in 1944—namely, that the time had come to make a frontal assault on the constitutionality of segregation per se instead of continuing to acquiesce in the *Plessy* doctrine while nibbling away at its underpinnings on a case-by-case basis and having to show in each case that the facility in question was in fact *unequal.* In essence I was challenging the traditional NAACP tactic of concentrating on the *equal* side of the *Plessy* equation.

One would have thought I had proposed that we attempt to tear down the Washington Monument or the Statue of Liberty. First astonishment, then hoots of derisive laughter, greeted what seemed to me to be an obvious solution. My approach was considered too visionary, one likely to precipitate an unfavorable decision of the Supreme Court, thus strengthening rather than destroying the force of the *Plessy* case. Spottswood Robinson, the young Bills and Notes professor, who had graduated several years earlier with the highest academic record in the history of the law school and whose encyclopedic knowledge of case law inspired awe among students, not only pooh-poohed my idea but good-naturedly accepted my wager of ten dollars that *Plessy* would be overruled within twenty-five years. None of us dreamed that the Supreme Court would deliver a death blow to the *Plessy* doctrine, in *Brown* v. *Board of Education,* not twenty-five but only ten years later.

Opposition to an idea I cared deeply about always aroused my latent mule-headedness, and I chose for my seminar paper the ambitious topic "Should the *Civil Rights Cases* and *Plessy* v. *Ferguson* Be Overruled?" An inexperienced third-year law student was hardly equipped to deal adequately with an enormously complex constitutional problem which would later tax the best efforts of scores of legal scholars, but Andy Ransom, delighting in what he must have thought of as my naive audacity, egged me on and even extended the deadline for my paper to the end of the summer following graduation.

As I wrestled with the legal aspects of segregation that spring, the Howard Chapter of the NAACP, again sparked by Ruth Powell, decided to renew its "non-violent direct action" campaign against Jim Crow, this time at downtown Washington restaurants. Local groups like the NAACP, the Minorities Workshop, and the Institute of Race Relations had lobbied for the District of Columbia civil rights bill during the fall and winter, with discouraging results. The House bill was bottled up in committee and only fifteen signatures had been obtained on a discharge petition. The Senate version was virtually certain to die in the District of Columbia Committee, chaired by Senator Theodore G. Bilbo of Mississippi, the most rabid anti-Negro voice in Congress. The student activists, having tasted victory the previous spring, were impatient with delays, and warm weather brought another upsurge of restless energy. They were determined to dramatize the issue by demonstrating the technique that had worked at the Little Palace.

This time the campaign was directed against one of the three local cafeterias in the John R. Thompson Company chain, specifically the one located at Eleventh Street and Pennsylvania Avenue, N.W. Thompson's was selected because of its convenient location, its moderately priced food, and the fact that service was maintained on a twenty-four-hour basis. If Thompson's Jim Crow policy could be broken down, it would be of special benefit to thousands of Negro government workers during the hours when government cafeterias were closed.

Once again I was asked to serve as student adviser. Our preparation was more rigorous than it had been the previous year, because now we were entering "foreign territory," outside a Negro neighborhood, and we did not know what hostilities we might encounter. In our literature we stressed that "intelligent showmanship and an attitude of good will on the part of the demonstrators is calculated to minimize antagonism and to 'swing the crowd on our side.' " Student participants not only were instructed in picketing and public decorum but also were required to sign a written pledge accepting the philosophy and discipline of the Civil Rights Committee. Volunteers who felt they might not be able to maintain self-control under provocation were assigned to tasks, such as making signs and posters, that would not expose them to confrontations with the police or the public. The pledge declared in part:

(1) . . . I oppose . . . discrimination . . . particularly where such exclusion is not sanctioned by laws, as contrary to the principles for which the present World War is being fought. . . .

(2) I conceive the effort to eliminate discrimination against any person because of race or color to be a patriotic duty and an act of faith in the American boys who are fighting for the Four Freedoms in foreign lands, and who have every right to expect a fuller share of these freedoms when they return home. . . .

(4) I understand the aims of the Civil Rights campaign to be the opening up of places to Negroes through the art of persuasion and good will, and the developing of public opinion to extend the privilege of service to all members of the population. I understand further that there is no law enforcing segregation in Washington, D.C., and that I may enter any public place and remain there so long as I conduct myself in a lawful and proper manner.

(5) I therefore pledge . . . to serve in whatever capacity I am best fitted —whether picketing, "sitting in" restaurants, making posters and signs, handing out leaflets, or speaking.

(6) I further pledge to abide by the rules and regulations of the Civil Rights Committee in carrying out this campaign; to do nothing to antagonize members of the public or the management of public places; to look my best wherever I act as a representative of the Committee; to use dignity and restraint at all times; to refrain from boisterous or offensive language or conduct no matter what the provocation; and to do or say *nothing* which will embarrass the Committee or the University.

The demonstration began at 4 P.M. on Saturday afternoon, April 22, 1944. Following the pattern of the previous year, we began to stroll into Thompson's in twos and threes, separated by ten-minute intervals. When we were refused service, we carried our empty trays to vacant tables, maintaining strict silence; students had been instructed not to be drawn into verbal harangues and all questions were referred to a designated representative. Three white participants polled the customers inside the cafeteria and found that of ten people questioned, seven favored serving Negroes and only three objected. Outside, we set up a picket line, walking in single file far enough apart not to block the sidewalk and carrying signs, one of which read: "Are You for HITLER'S Way (Race Supremacy) or the AMERICAN Way (Equality)? Make Up Your Mind!"

Our picket line quickly attracted a large crowd, heavily sprinkled with men and women in uniform. Most of the onlookers were white. Although some of the soldiers yelled catcalls and one woman spat as the pickets passed, others, including some Wacs and Waves, cheered and called out words of sympathy. Neither jeers nor cheers brought any outward response from our pickets. Several police officers stood by, watchful but not openly hostile.

A dramatic moment occurred when six unidentified Negro soldiers, smartly dressed and wearing corporals' and sergeants' stripes, filed into the restaurant, requested service, were refused, took seats at empty tables, pulled out *PM* newspapers, and began to read. At nearby tables a dozen or more white soldiers and sailors were eating. The Negro soldiers had no connection with our student group, but their act of solidarity was the high point of our demonstration, underscoring the message of one of our signs outside: "We Die Together. Why Can't We Eat Together?"

Within an hour, fifty-six demonstrators, including the six Negro soldiers, were occupying tables. From time to time the manager approached members of the group, pleading with them to leave. The student representatives were polite but firm in their refusal to go without being served. Later the district supervisor of the Thompson chain arrived, but his bluster was equally unsuccessful. Then two white MP's entered the restaurant and asked the Negro soldiers to leave. The soldiers replied that they were waiting for service. When the MP's were unable to dislodge the Negro GI's, they left and returned shortly with a white lieutenant wearing an MP armband, who apologetically asked the Negro soldiers to leave "as a personal favor so the Army won't be embarrassed in case of an incident." As the designated representative of the demonstrators, I pointed out to the lieutenant that if the Army was afraid of being embarrassed, it should request *all* military personnel to leave. We won a small victory when the MP's cleared the restaurant of all men in uniform.

Within four hours Thompson's trade had dropped 50 percent. The management put in frantic calls to its main office in Chicago and finally, at 8:30 P.M., was ordered to serve us. They were so anxious to be relieved of our presence that when two waitresses balked, the manager and district supervisor quickly took their places.

It is difficult to describe the exhilaration of that brief moment of victory. So far as we knew, nothing like it had happened before in the city of Washington. As a Civil Rights Committee representative declared: "With this technique we hope to tear down some of the stereotyped impressions in the minds of our white fellow citizens and to evoke their respect. We want to demonstrate our good will, but at the same time we are equally determined to secure our rights."

The most abiding gain, however, was in our own self-respect; unfortunately, our weeks of planning and tremendous effort created scarcely a ripple beyond Eleventh Street and Pennsylvania Avenue. For all the excitement of that Saturday afternoon in the heart of downtown Washington, a few blocks from the White House, the local metropolitan press ignored our exploit. The only mention I saw of the incident in a white newspaper was in I. F. Stone's *PM* column a week later.

Notwithstanding the silence of the press, members of Congress who were determined to maintain segregation got the message and moved swiftly, if indirectly, to snuff out a brushfire that might spread if aired in public. Our success was short-lived and our momentum broken by the unanticipated intervention of our own university administration. For two days after the Saturday demonstration, student scouts were served in Thompson's without difficulty, but then a student was refused. Before the Civil Rights Committee could negotiate with the restaurant's management, a directive from President Mordecai Johnson's office requested that our activities be suspended pending a clarification of administration policy toward the civil rights activities of the NAACP student chapter. An emergency meeting of the deans and administrators held on May 1 resulted in a letter from Dr. Johnson addressed to Professor Leon A. Ransom, faculty adviser to the Howard Chapter of the NAACP, which effectively forced the branch "to desist from its program of direct action in the City of Washington." The letter included notification of the right of appeal to the board of trustees.

We students were stunned by what seemed to us a high-handed and even hypocritical action on the part of the university administration. There had been no previous indication of disapproval of our activities. We had acted with the knowledge of our faculty adviser and in accordance with what Dr. Johnson had been preaching to Negro groups around the country. The administration's directive deflected our energies from our central objective and involved us in an angry confrontation with the school authorities, which was aggravated by the approach of final exams and preparations for commencement. A university-wide meeting of student leaders was held, and a letter to Dr. Johnson signed by the heads of sixteen of Howard's student organizations requested a conference of student and faculty-administration representatives. The letter affirmed our belief in "the principle of freedom of action for student groups within the democratic framework of this institution, so long as such action is taken in a lawful, proper and dignified manner," and set forth a list of questions as a basis for the discussion. In view of President Johnson's militant and widely publicized speeches on the rights of minorities and the lines of action he had suggested, why, we asked, "is it surprising or unwise that his own students should be the most inspired to put into practice . . . some of the philosophies he has outlined in pulpit, platform, and over the radio?" We also pointed out that President Johnson's speeches were no less identified with Howard than actions taken by Howard students.

In the next few days we were to learn that self-inflicted wounds within a group deeply committed to the same objective are often more painful and difficult to bear than hurts imposed by enemies, because they have the effect of dividing one against oneself in ways seldom achieved by an outsider. An off-the-record report of the May 1 University Council meeting, attended by the deans of the nine schools on campus, various top administrators, and faculty representatives from each school, revealed that Dean Hastie and Professors Ransom and James N. Nabrit were present, as well as Howard Thurman from the School of Religion and other stalwarts sympathetic to our confrontational approach. Yet the University Council's decision to forbid "direct action" activities by organized groups of students identified with Howard had been unanimous. Were we to conclude that our idols, Hastie and Ransom, had betrayed us?

We learned that the University Council's main fear was retaliation by the institution's enemies in Congress, who might threaten to cut off the school's appropriations. We discovered that 60 percent of the university's income came from the federal government; only 22 percent came from student fees, while income from endowments amounted to 2 percent. Since university appropriations had to be approved by the Senate District Committee, headed by the passionately racist Senator Bilbo, the school's principal source of financial support was in jeopardy.

The Council also feared that the university's public relations would be impaired through identification of the student actions with "abortive" or "crackpot" movements. The university saw itself as having parental responsibility for student activities originating on the campus. True, questions arose as to whether the institution should concern itself with "dynamic education"—education in practice—or only with "static education," but the consensus seemed to be that the university must weigh the greater good against possible gains to be achieved by organized student action. The resulting decision was that students should associate themselves with outside groups only as individuals if they wished to carry on direct action for civil rights.

The administration's ban on our sit-in activities produced a flurry of news stories and comments in the Negro press, which reported a sharp division of opinion among teaching and administrative personnel and indicated that a number of Howard University staff members were known to be opposed to Dr. Johnson's position on the issue. The New York *People's Voice*, a militant newspaper, editorialized under the caption "WE AIN'T READY Dept.":

> President Mordecai Johnson is apparently completely out of tune with the temper of the New Negro. . . . There is no other way to interpret his official stand in the matter of the proposal of the campus chapter of the NAACP at Howard to take "direct action" against food establishments which deny service on the basis of race. . . . No doubt, the good prexy wants the students to endure indignities and discrimination until some millennium date when those perpetrating the disgraceful indignities against the people decide in their own good time to discontinue the practices. Meanwhile, what does President Johnson expect the offended people to do, sit idly by and twiddle their thumbs? . . . Well, the New Negro doesn't think (OR ACT) that way. . . . Not in the midst of a war against fascistic practices, anyway.

And while normally a student election held little interest beyond campus, the press also reported the results of the student council election held shortly after the ban. The choice of Ruth Powell, who chaired the Direct Action Committee of the NAACP chapter, as president of the student council for the 1944–45 school year was widely construed as a direct endorsement of our sit-in activities by the students themselves.

We activists found ourselves in a cruel dilemma. As a disciplined group, our Civil Rights Committee was not prepared to defy the administration on an issue as vital to the university's existence as its major source of income. On the other hand, we were equally loath to give up an effort into which we had poured so much thought, time, and energy, a technique that went to the heart of the struggle for personal dignity and had clearly demonstrated its effectiveness as a powerful weapon against racial discrimination.

The Howard Chapter of the NAACP decided unanimously at a full membership meeting that "we are unwilling to discontinue our campaign as it is now outlined." The Law Students Guild met in special session, voted unanimously to support the activities of the Civil Rights Committee, and authorized its executive body, the Court of Peers (which I headed), to issue a statement, which declared in part:

> It is our considered judgment that it is the fundamental purpose of the University to train students to become functional units of the American democracy. . . . We consider any tendency on the part of the Administration of Howard University to compromise or mitigate its previous policy of freedom of student action . . . to be a retrogression which we cannot and will not condone. The tradition of Howard University is one of positive

progress. We feel, therefore, any departure therefrom is a retreat in the fight for freedom.

Other student organizations took similar action, and Professor Ransom was notified of the intention of the NAACP student chaptèr to appeal the administration ruling to the board of trustees, which would meet in June. But our brave words were more an obituary notice than a call to action. Our student campaign was dead. It had been a brief act of imaginative defiance, a commando raid against entrenched racism using an alternative weapon to violent rebellion, which, if expanded, could have brought new hope to millions of black Americans. But it had been aborted by our own black administrators, held hostage themselves to the forces of bigotry in government. As Dr. Howard Thurman reflected when I went to him for spiritual guidance in the midst of the campus crisis, "A characteristic of evil is that we never fully destroy it. When we beat it down in one place, it pops up in another."

For me, personally, it was one more bitter defeat and one that included the sacrifice of the scholastic goal I had set for myself as a member of the female minority in the law school. In the turmoil of events my dream of equaling Spottswood Robinson's student record went down the drain. The controversy with the administration developed just before final exams, when, as one of the leaders in the civil rights campaign, I was engulfed in time-consuming responsibilities that completely disrupted my study schedule. In addition, I was by then fighting a private battle on another front—this one against Harvard Law School—and the cumulative pressures were just too much. I risked disaster by going into finals without adequate preparation. Predictably, my grades dropped about ten points below my normal standard in several courses and my grade point average fell a fraction below the level needed to graduate magna cum laude.

Sixteen years passed before the ashes of our dreams at Howard University glowed again and Negro college students in North Carolina touched off the massive sit-ins of 1960. I was on my way to Africa at the time and did not learn of this spontaneous uprising until our boat docked at Monrovia, Liberia, but I like to think there was continuity in our struggle. Ruth Harvey (Charity), an undergraduate who chaired the Howard University Chapter of the NAACP in 1944, went on to the law school and in 1960 was practicing law in Danville, Virginia, where she represented Negro defendants arrested for demonstrating against segregation. Elsewhere in the South, lawyers who attended Howard in the 1940s were legal counsel for civil rights demonstrators in the 1960s. The wartime student body produced other effective civil rights advocates, among them Aileen C. Hernandez, the first woman to serve as a commissioner of the federal Equal

Employment Opportunity Commission (EEOC), and Gloria Richardson, who led demonstrations against Jim Crow in Cambridge, Maryland.

It remained for historians to place our wartime effort in proper perspective. Eleanor Holmes (Norton), a student activist of the early 1960s, who graduated from the Yale Law School in 1964 with a simultaneously awarded graduate degree in American Studies (and who later chaired the EEOC in the Carter administration), chose for her history honors paper the topic "World War II and the Beginnings of Non-Violent Action in Civil Rights." I was working on my doctorate at the Yale Law School at the time and gave her access to my files. After analyzing the records of the 1943–44 Howard University sit-ins, she wrote: "They had achieved a nearly perfect demonstration based on Gandhi's methods. . . . After the coordination and mastery their effort revealed, non-violent resistance awaited only a mass following." Her conclusion affirmed my own feeling about the continuity of social movements, even when interrupted for a period of time:

> Non-violent resistance to gain civil rights did not begin with the bus boycott in Montgomery, Alabama in 1956. It began with bus incidents in 1940 and was perfected as a technique before 1945. The Negro movement for integration today [1963], like mass movements before it, had its dedicated *avant-garde.*
>
> Economic distress, armed forces segregation, and war slogans denouncing racism produced bitterness that ran through all classes of Negroes in the early forties. Out of their anger came interracial conflict in countless incidents. But out of it also came the search for a new, dignified, and more direct way to protest. . . .
>
> Perhaps the greatest gain from the war years is that they inspired the use of a tactic that would be consistent with militancy and peaceful protest. The non-violent experiments reduced tension and encouraged hope among Negroes. And they pointed the way toward a movement for integration that would for the first time reach the Negro masses and bring daring campaigns to the very heart of racism.

A more immediate consequence of our 1944 campaign was the discovery that ultimate victory over Jim Crow in the city of Washington did not require the enactment of civil rights legislation by Congress. Professor A. Mercer Daniel, our law librarian and the oldest member of the law school faculty, recalled talk among older Washingtonians of an earlier civil rights law in the District of Columbia. If such a law had existed, no one seemed to know what happened to it.

"Poppa" Daniel, as we students affectionately called him behind his back, did not pretend to be a brilliant legal theoretician, but he possessed a plodding patience necessary to sustained legal research. He conscientiously rummaged through forgotten dusty volumes in the library stacks and, one day toward the end of the school term, gleefully showed me what he had unearthed in a book entitled *Compiled Statutes in force in the District of Columbia in 1894.*

The volume included an act passed in 1872 by the Second Legislative Assembly of the District of Columbia (a local body to which Congress had delegated legislative authority during the years 1870–74), which made it a misdemeanor, punishable by a fine of $100 and forfeiture of license for a period of one year, for proprietors of restaurants, ice cream saloons, soda fountains, hotels, barbershops, and bathing houses to refuse to serve "any respectable, well-behaved person without regard to race, color or previous condition of servitude . . . in the same room, and at the same prices as other well-behaved and respectable persons are served." (An act of 1873, discovered later, strengthened and extended the coverage in the 1872 law.)

With the galling Thompson's cafeteria fiasco fresh in my mind, I could hardly contain myself when I read those words, and I set out to discover why this law had fallen into disuse. Preliminary research showed that it did not appear in any code of laws for the District of Columbia after 1894; yet I could not find an express repeal of the statute. Nor could I find any citation that it had been declared invalid by judicial decision.

The D.C. Code of 1901 omitted the civil rights ordinance but contained an enabling clause which declared that all laws hereinbefore enacted but not expressly repealed were held to be in full force and effect. I concluded that the omission was deliberate on the part of the compilers of the 1901 code. The law had fallen victim to the general disregard of civil rights following the Supreme Court's invalidation of the federal Civil Rights Act of 1875 in the *Civil Rights Cases* decision of 1883. By the early 1900s, and particularly during the administration of President Woodrow Wilson, a rigid pattern of segregation by custom had been imposed, which escaped legal challenge by a later generation of lawyers who were unaware of the existence of the earlier local law.

Elated over these preliminary findings, I went around the law school waving the statute and arguing that the old civil rights legislation was still in force. We should bring a test case to get the issue of segregation in the District of Columbia before the courts, I maintained. Although our direct action campaign had been stifled, a successful court test would vindicate our initial efforts. I have wondered since then whether my theory would have been acted upon more promptly if discovery of the statute had come earlier in the school year, giving me time to incorporate my proposal into a formal legal memorandum. And I have also wondered whether it would have made any difference if the suggestion had come not from a woman but from a man, whether a residue of skepticism remained about a woman's capacity to advance bold new ideas. Perhaps costly experimental litigation was too risky at the time or perhaps law professors' agendas were overburdened with more pressing matters. Whatever the reasons, my suggestion was not taken seriously in 1944, although after graduation, and far from the Washington scene, I continued to peddle it in civil rights circles. Five years later, seven other lawyers, including the NAACP's Charles H. Houston, presented the same theory in a written opinion, and the idea of a test case became a reality.

One determined individual had not forgotten the existence of the old District of Columbia civil rights law. Mary Church Terrell, militant civil rights activist and longtime feminist who had fought for woman suffrage, completed the struggle we Howard University students had begun. A patrician born in the year of the Emancipation Proclamation, and the essence of Victorian respectability, Mrs. Terrell led picket lines against downtown eating places and ultimately chaired the Coordinating Committee for the Enforcement of the D.C. Anti-Discrimination Laws.

Appropriately, when a test case finally materialized in 1950, our old adversary, Thompson's cafeteria, was the defendant in a prosecution under the 1872 and 1873 laws. The management's refusal to serve Mrs. Terrell and her interracial parties on several occasions culminated in a bitterly fought contest in the local municipal and federal courts. The case of *District of Columbia* v. *John R. Thompson Co., Inc.* reached the Supreme Court of the United States in the spring of 1953, and in June of that year the high court ruled that the acts of 1872 and 1873 had not been repealed by subsequent legislation and that failure to enforce a law does not operate to repeal it. The decision came down nine years after our sit-in at Thompson's cafeteria and three months before Mrs. Terrell's ninetieth birthday, and it spelled the end of racial segregation in public places in the nation's capital. Mrs. Terrell died the following year.

CHAPTER 20

"Don't Get Mad, Get Smart"

THE EVENTS of my final days as a student in Washington climaxed six years of intense personal involvement in the struggle against segregation that had begun in 1938 with my application for admission to the University of North Carolina. If there were moments of deep despair in those years, there was also the sustaining knowledge that the quest for human dignity is part of a continuous movement through time and history linked to a higher force. Years later Dr. Martin Luther King, Jr., expressed the same concept when he said that in the struggle for justice one has "cosmic companionship." Pitting my intelligence against the ludicrous authorities who enforced an irrational set of arrangements and, above all, learning to harness my emotions to an innovative power instead of exploding in a fury of destructive waste were challenges I could respond to. Somewhere along the way I adopted the slogan "Don't get mad, get smart."

The tension between my urge toward kamikaze defiance of Jim Crow and the more demanding discipline of plodding research—which often seemed to lead nowhere—kept me striving continually to achieve some kind of balance. In the process I discovered that joining others in the effort to overturn an entrenched system of injustice is often like running a relay. There were times when I didn't even know the outcome of the race, other times when it was my privilege to break the ribbon at the finish line, and still others when I shared an overwhelming sense of accomplishment and exhilaration even though my contribution had been made early in the contest, not at its culmination. It was this last kind of triumph that I experienced when the Supreme Court, in a case known as *Morgan* v. *Virginia*, finally invalidated segregated travel across state lines.

Today, in a time of unrestricted movement in the United States, it is difficult to convey to anyone who did not live through them the intolerable irritations of Jim Crow travel during World War II. Bad as the system had been in the past, wartime restrictions on the use of automobiles, which grew out of gas rationing, and the large number of civilians and military personnel constantly moving in and out of Washington, overburdened public transportation and aggravated the already flammable situation. Commuting between the city of Washington and its northern Virginia suburbs was especially explosive. Harassed white drivers (there were no Negro bus drivers in the Washington area in those days) on Virginia-bound buses often attempted to segregate Negroes within the city limits so as to avoid confrontations later on when the bus reached the midpoint of the Potomac River and Negro passengers were required to move to the rear. Negroes, equally determined to maintain their right to sit where they pleased as long as it was lawful to do so, often insisted on postponing the move to the back of the bus until it actually reached the Virginia line. Shouting matches, threats of arrest, and the intervention of Virginia police became increasingly commonplace, and Negroes who refused to be intimidated usually ended up with a conviction and fine for disorderly conduct—an outcome that left the segregation laws intact.

It had become the custom for Dr. Caroline Ware to hold a spring picnic at The Farm not long before the Howard University commencement. In 1944 the picnic was scheduled for Sunday, May 14, and I was spending the weekend there with another guest, Anne Ramsay, a Vassar graduate and an early organizer for the CIO. To avoid embarrassing travel situations, Dr. Ware usually either transported her Negro guests in her own car or made sure they drove out with someone else. (It was my experience driving in her convertible, as she whizzed around blind corners and up and down narrow roller-coaster roads, that led me to nickname her "Skipper.") When she issued an invitation to the picnic to her first-year social science class, however, the number of those accepting was indefinite and so she had left the matter of transportation up to each individual.

For students confined on a small campus, a visit to the Ware-Means farm was a special event. Dr. Ware was one of the most loyal faculty supporters of our civil rights campaigns, and she had picketed the Little Palace Cafeteria with us the previous year. It was not surprising, therefore, when eight undergraduate women arrived Sunday morning. All were friends or acquaintances of mine, fellow participants in the endless bull sessions in which we discussed ways to fight Jim Crow. Four were first-year students, and three out of the other four, including Ruth Powell, had been active in the Thompson's cafeteria sit-in. What was surprising was not that they had come, but that they arrived on foot.

When Dr. Ware asked about their transportation, they explained with great aplomb that they had taken a bus and then hitchhiked. Overcome with glee, they told us how they had sat where they pleased on boarding the bus in Washington and how, when the driver told them the bus was going to Virginia and they would have to move back, they had simply replied, "We're not in Virginia yet." Unaccountably, the bus driver did not press the issue when they crossed the Potomac but let them ride peacefully to their stop at Beulah Road in Vienna. From there they hitchhiked the last three miles along Beulah Road to the lane leading to the Ware-Means farm. They were obviously pleased with themselves for having circumvented Jim Crow without incident.

Nothing more was said about transportation, and the picnic was a relaxed interlude between the pressure-cooker events of final exams and graduation. When it came time for the students to leave, they were loaded into cars and dropped off at the bus stop. As Dr. Ware drove away, she heard one of the seniors say to the others, "What are we going to do when the bus comes?" but she did not hear the answer, for the bus arrived suddenly and the women clambered aboard.

The telephone at the farm rang about an hour later and in an excited voice, one of the young women asked for Dr. Ware.

"Where are you?" Skipper wanted to know.

"We're in the Fairfax County jail," came the not unhappy answer.

As we got the story later, the students had not planned to challenge Jim Crow. Angela Jones, a senior, had boarded the bus first and started toward the rear, but the second student, sixteen-year-old Ruby O'Hara, a freshman from Beaufort, South Carolina, had flopped down on a front seat and the others spontaneously followed suit. When Angela Jones turned around and saw what had happened she quickly joined the group.

"Here it comes," Ruth Powell remembered saying to herself as she sat down. About fourteen white people were scattered through the center of the bus and five Negroes were sitting in the back. The stage was now set for an all too familiar script—to the thoughtful observer, a ridiculous farce; to the participants, a high-stakes game played with deadly seriousness.

Without prior rehearsal, the young women gave a flawless performance. As the driver, Mitchell B. Lee, Badge No. 72, started the bus, he told the young women they would have to move back. Ruth Powell, taking the initiative, responded quietly that under the Interstate Commerce Law they were not required to move. The driver pointed to the sign at the front of the bus near the entrance, stating Virginia law with reference to the segregation of passengers on public carriers. The women ignored his gesture and sat silently, reading. The driver pulled the bus to the side of the road and stopped.

"We'll just sit here until you move back," he announced.

No response.

Then Lee asked the white people to move up and occupy the seats taken by the Negro students. Only one responded, and he sat down beside another white passenger near the front. Finally, Lee threatened to call the police. Again no response. When a white man asked the driver why he did not force the women to move back, Lee replied that he would handle it in his own way, and got off the bus.

While he was gone, the young women consulted quietly among themselves. The four upperclasswomen—Ruth Powell, Marianne Musgrave, Angela Jones, and Erma McLemore—sent the four first-year students— Cynthia Kennedy, Doris King, Ruby O'Hara, and Ruth Ann Robinson— to the rear to prevent them from being involved in an arrest. They also instructed them to ride the bus to Washington, notify the dormitory directors of what had happened, and telephone Dean Hastie. The four students who remained in the front were all NAACP members.

Driver Lee returned shortly and sat waiting for the police. By this time a second bus had come along and pulled up in front of the first bus. After some palaver, all the Negroes who had been sitting in the rear and about nine of the white people were allowed to board the second bus and it went on its way.

Two white policemen appeared. One, swinging his club as he got on, ordered the women to move back. No one moved or spoke. Then he said, "If you don't move, we'll take you in."

Angela Jones asked if he had a warrant, and the police officer said he would get one at the station.

The four women sat motionless.

"Come on," said the first policeman, grasping Marianne Musgrave firmly by the arm and urging her toward the door. She gave no resistance, and Angela Jones, who was sitting beside her, got up and followed her out. The second policeman tapped Erma McLemore on the arm and asked her to leave the bus. She said, "All right," and got off. Ruth Powell, the last of the four, made no move to leave, but sat staring into the policeman's eyes, as inscrutable of face as she was firm of resolve.

When he again ordered her to leave, she announced quietly, in her crisp New England accent, "We are operating under the Interstate Commerce Law."

The policeman blinked, then stammered, "But this is Virginia law."

"But the Interstate Commerce Law is the federal law," Ruth declared as she left the bus. Only a dullard would have failed to recognize that a classic test case was in the making.

The young women were then driven in a squad car to the Fairfax

County Prison, where the bus driver had already arrived. The name, address, age, weight, and sex of each was recorded. No warrants were sworn or read to them. When they asked the police what the charges were, they were told, "Violation of the Jim Crow law in Virginia." When Angela Jones asked the police sergeant to state the particular statute, he snapped, "You can look it up."

The police sergeant asked the bailiff what bail he was setting. The bailiff said something to the effect that if the case was going to become an issue, they might as well make it good: one hundred dollars each. When the young women told him they did not have the money with them, they were allowed to call Dr. Ware, after which they were placed in a cell.

Back at The Farm, we were all jubilant when we learned that the students had been charged with violation of the Jim Crow law. We all knew what that meant: *they had successfully avoided a charge of disorderly conduct,* the Commonwealth of Virginia's chief weapon against those who challenged the state's segregation laws. This might be just the test case civil rights lawyers were looking for. The ebullient students knew it too, of course, which accounted for the suppressed excitement Dr. Ware detected in the guarded telephone conversation.

After consulting with Attorney Charles Houston of the NAACP by phone, Dr. Ware set about trying to scare up four hundred dollars bail money—not an easy task on a Sunday evening—while Anne Ramsay and I made sandwiches for the prisoners. Remembering our own jail experiences, we had both said aloud and in unison, "They'll be hungry!" As Anne handed the paper bag to Dr. Ware, she spoke almost wistfully of going to jail in the thirties as a union organizer. I had no such nostalgia. Petersburg had been a humiliating experience.

After some more telephoning, Dr. Ware learned she would not have to raise cash; as a property owner in Fairfax County, she could "go bail" using her real property as collateral. This simplified matters and off she went to rescue the "jailbirds." She found them in high spirits. Not anticipating her ability to raise bail before Monday morning, they had prepared themselves to spend the night as comfortably as possible. And they had managed to contrive just the right behavior to needle as well as amuse their jailers. They asked for towels and soap. One girl had a sore foot and requested medication. They made up a song about "the ole Fairfax County jai-ai-ail" to the tune of Leadbelly's "Boll Weevil" song, and sang it lustily, to the entertainment of inmates and prison guards alike.

They were released at 9:30 P.M.—three hours after they had boarded the bus—and when Dr. Ware got them into her car she asked them why they had done it.

"We did just what Dr. Johnson said we should do," she was told. "We acted as individuals, not as representatives of the college or any organization of the university."

When the case was tried before the Fairfax County municipal court, it was handled by NAACP attorneys. The crucial point was that there had been no hint of disorderly conduct; the only issue was violation of the segregation statute. Although judgment against the defendants was automatic, defense lawyers laid the groundwork for appeal on the basis of interstate commerce. Riding in Dr. Ware's car on the way back from the trial, the group circled the Lincoln Memorial, paused in front of the steps to wave at the statue of Abraham Lincoln, and someone called out, "Abe, here we are, still at it!"

The case was appealed to the Virginia Court of Appeals and a date was set, but before the time came for argument, the attorney general of Virginia confessed error, withdrew the charge, and the case was dropped. The young women had done their job too well; clearly the commonwealth dared not risk the likelihood of losing on constitutional grounds.

By sidestepping the issue just as it had done in my case, the commonwealth merely delayed the inevitable challenge, for within a few weeks another case, involving identical circumstances, came up on appeal. On July 16, 1944—nine weeks after the Fairfax County incident—twenty-eight-year-old Irene Morgan, recovering from an operation and traveling on a Greyhound bus from Gloucester, Virginia, to Baltimore for further medical treatment, was arrested at Saluda, Virginia, for refusing to give up her seat so that a white passenger who had just boarded might sit down. She was convicted and fined in the circuit court on two charges: one hundred dollars for resisting an officer and ten dollars for violating the state Jim Crow law. She paid the hundred-dollar fine and appealed the second conviction. This time the commonwealth decided the question could no longer be postponed, and the appeal was argued. The Virginia Supreme Court of errors upheld the conviction on the ground that the Virginia segregation statute was constitutional and applied to interstate as well as local passengers.

The test case we had all been waiting for was finally on its way to the Supreme Court. When it was scheduled for argument in the spring of 1946, I wrote to NAACP Special Counsel Thurgood Marshall; his reply was reassurance that our efforts, though unsuccessful, had been worthwhile. He wrote:

> ... I am sending you ... our brief and the record in the [*Morgan*] case for your personal files because of your interest in the case and the ground work that you and Miss McBean performed. I think we all agreed that we would have preferred that your case could have been carried up. Unfortu-

nately, the boys outsmarted us in refusing to convict you of violating the Jim Crow statute. Their mistake in the Morgan case, we hope will bring about the result we all wish for.

Vindication came six years after Mac McBean and I had been convicted in Petersburg and two years after the Fairfax County incident, for in *Morgan* v. *Virginia* the Supreme Court held that the validity of the Virginia statute must be decided "as a matter of balance between the exercise of the local police power and the need for national uniformity in the regulations for interstate travel. It seems clear to us that seating arrangements for the different races in interstate motor travel require a single, uniform rule to promote and protect national travel. Consequently, we hold the Virginia statute in controversy invalid."

Although the decision did not wholly settle the matter, and bus companies operating in the South continued for some time to enforce segregation through company regulations with the aid of the state courts, the *Morgan* decision signaled the beginning of the end of segregated travel within states as well as across state lines.

I had entered law school preoccupied with the racial struggle and single-mindedly bent upon becoming a civil rights attorney, but I graduated an unabashed feminist as well. Ironically, my effort to become a more proficient advocate in the first struggle led directly into the second through an unanticipated chain of events which began in the late fall of my senior year.

One day Dean Hastie called me into his office to discuss what I planned to do after graduation. To my utter surprise, he spoke of the possibility of my returning to teach at the law school after a year of graduate study, and with that possibility in mind he recommended that I apply for a Rosenwald fellowship. For a number of reasons, "graduate study" meant to me "graduate study at Harvard University." At least half of the Howard Law School faculty had studied at Harvard, both Hastie and Ransom held doctorates from its law school, and it had become a tradition at Howard to groom an exceptionally promising law graduate for a future faculty position by sending him to Harvard "to put on the gloss" of a prestigous graduate degree in law. My greatest rival in the preceding class, Francisco Carniero, who had graduated with top honors and as Chief Justice of the Court of Peers, was now completing his year of graduate law there. We had run neck and neck in courses we took together, he topping me by a couple of points in one and I topping him in another.

Naively unaware of Harvard's policy toward women, I was stunned when my schoolmates began kidding me. "Murray," someone said, "don't you know they're not going to let you into Harvard?" Harvard, it became clear, did not admit women to its law school.

Then my hopes were raised by a rumor which circulated around campus that Harvard was opening up to women students. Accordingly, when filling out my application to the Rosenwald Fund, I wrote in the space provided for choice of law school: "I should like to obtain my Master's degree at Harvard University, in the event they have removed their bar against women students. If not, then I should like to work at Yale University or at any other University which has advanced study in the field of labor law." I also wrote to the secretary of Harvard Law School, requesting confirmation or denial of the rumor I had heard. The answer was prompt. On January 5, 1944, the secretary's office wrote back: "Harvard Law School . . . is not open to women for registration."

This verdict was disappointing, of course, but with all the other preoccupations of my senior year, the matter probably would have rested there if I had not won the Rosenwald fellowship or at least if the names of the award winners had not been published nationwide. The announcement, made in late spring, listed me among fifteen white Southerners and twenty-two Negroes (including such notables as E. Franklin Frazier, Adelaide Cromwell Hill, Chester Himes, Rayford W. Logan, Dorothy Porter, and Margaret Walker) who received awards "for creative talent or distinguished scholarship." Mine was the only award in the field of law, and all the news stories reported that I was to do graduate study in labor law at Harvard University.

I was embarrassed to receive congratulatory messages from a number of people who were either unaware of Harvard's restrictive policy or assumed I had broken the barrier. At the same time, some of the men at Howard stepped up their banter, not without a touch of malicious glee. Until then I had been able to lick my wounds in private, but the public disclosure of my dilemma mortified me and presented a challenge I could not pass over lightly. If my schoolmates expected me to dissolve into tears under their stinging gibes, they were disappointed. I simply sat down and wrote a letter of application to Harvard Law School, which was duly processed, and I received a written request for my college transcript and a photograph.

In due course there came from Professor T. R. Powell, who chaired Harvard Law School's Committee on Graduate Studies, a letter that must have been dictated with an impish smirk. As nearly as I can recall, it ran: "Your picture and the salutation on your college transcript indicate that you are not of the sex entitled to be admitted to Harvard Law School." To appreciate the impact of this letter upon me, it is only necessary to remember the similar letter of rejection I had received in 1938 from the dean of the graduate school of the University of North Carolina in Chapel Hill: "Under the laws of North Carolina and under the resolutions of the Board of Trustees of the University of North Carolina, members of your race are not admitted to the University."

The personal hurt I felt now was no different from the personal hurt I had felt then. The niceties of distinction that in one case rejection was based upon custom and involved my sex and in the other was grounded in law and involved my race were wholly irrelevant to me. Both were equally unjust, stigmatizing me for a biological characteristic over which I had no control. But at least in the case of racial rebuffs long experience had taught me some coping mechanisms and I did not feel alone in that struggle. The fact that Harvard's rejection was a source of mild amusement rather than outrage to many of my male colleagues who were ardent civil rights advocates made it all the more bitter to swallow.

The harsh reality was that I was a minority within a minority, with all the built-in disadvantages such status entailed. Because of the considerable snobbery that—even apart from race and sex—existed in the highly competitive field of law, one's initial entry into the profession was profoundly affected by the law school one attended. This was particularly true for anyone who had ambitions to teach law. Since in my case the most common hurdles—lack of funds and a poor scholastic record—did not apply, I felt the injustice of the rejection even more strongly. I knew that however brilliant a record I had made at Howard, among my teaching colleagues I would never be considered on equal academic footing with someone who could boast of Harvard training. I also knew that the school of my second choice, Yale, had suspended its graduate program in law during the wartime emergency. Hastie and Ransom, my law school mentors, understood my academic dilemma and were quietly supportive of my decision to pursue the Harvard matter further. Dr. Ware, whose great-great-grandfather Henry Ware had been the first dean of Harvard Divinity School and who grew up surrounded by the Harvard tradition, identified with me wholly in my fight. The only one of five generations of Phi Beta Kappas in her family not to take a Harvard degree, she held a Ph.D. from Radcliffe.

Then began the disheartening effort to budge a sluggishly corpulent bureaucracy on which my protests and appeals made about as much impression as a gnat on an elephant's hide. Harvard, being a private institution, was immune from legal attack and thus I had only the force of reason and logic with which to plead my case. A letter to Professor Powell asking what procedure to follow in appealing the law school's policy brought the information that the law school was bound by the rule of the Harvard Corporation not to admit women, and any appeal from that ruling would have to be submitted to the Corporation through its secretary, A. Calvert Smith.

Since my exclusion from Harvard was based solely on gender, my appeal necessarily was strongly feminist in tone:

> I have met a number of women and have heard of many more who wished to attend Harvard and yet were refused. This fight is not mine, but that of women who feel they should have free access to the very best of legal education. . . .
>
> Women are practicing before the Supreme Court, they have become judges and good lawyers, they are represented on the President's Cabinet and greater demand is being made for women lawyers in administrative positions as the men move into the armed forces. They are proving themselves worthy of the confidence and trust placed in them. . . . They are taking an intelligent view toward the political events at home and abroad, and statistics show they are in the majority of the voting population this year. A spot-check on memory would indicate there are only four important places they are not now holding—(1) As graduates of Harvard University, (2) as President of the United States, (3) as a member of the United States Supreme Court, and (4) as workers in the mines. Although [by admitting women] Harvard might lose in the sense of a loss of tradition, it might gain in the quality of the law school student personnel.

Meanwhile, two influential (if wholly unanticipated) male supporters sympathetic to the rights of women materialized. One was President Franklin D. Roosevelt! I had sent copies of the correspondence with Harvard to Mrs. Roosevelt, suggesting that the President might be amused at this attempt to storm the walls of his alma mater, never dreaming it would evoke more than a chuckle on his part. FDR was not merely amused; he actually wrote a letter on my behalf to President James B. Conant of Harvard University.

It would take more than one of that institution's most illustrious graduates to overturn a three-hundred-year tradition of male exclusiveness, however. President Conant's reply, sent on to me by FDR's secretary, only confused the issue. The letter assured President Roosevelt that I was free to do graduate work at Radcliffe, and even sent along a Radcliffe catalogue —never mind the obvious fact that Radcliffe did not offer graduate courses in law. I was flattered that the President of the United States had intervened on my behalf, but I was no nearer my goal. Mrs. Roosevelt was unequivocally in my corner, and wrote me a note saying: "I loved your Harvard appeal."

Lloyd K. Garrison, who was to become a lifelong friend and sponsor, was my second unexpected supporter. Mr. Garrison, former dean of the

University of Wisconsin School of Law, was then a member of the National War Labor Board, which he later chaired. He was also a member of the Harvard Board of Overseers. I first met him through an ambitious undertaking of our student organization, the First Annual Court of Peers Dinner, jointly sponsored by the faculty and the Student Guild of Howard University School of Law. Mr. Garrison was our guest speaker, and as chief officer of the Student Guild it was my function to preside over the dinner and sit next to him at the speakers' table.

The great-grandson of abolitionist William Lloyd Garrison, Lloyd K. Garrison bore a striking resemblance to his famous ancestor and had inherited his commitment to human freedom. Unlike the fiery nineteenth-century Garrison, however, Lloyd K. Garrison combined a gentleness of disposition with a tough-minded pragmatism. Over the years, I learned to trust his candor, although it often had the effect of an ice-cold shower upon my hopes and expectations. He was intensely interested in my effort to get into Harvard but warned me that I did not have a chance against the archconservative Harvard Corporation. Under the circumstances he encouraged me to follow an alternative plan for graduate study elsewhere, in the meantime pressing my appeal.

A. Calvert Smith informed me that the Harvard Corporation would review my appeal on July 10, by which time I had already applied to Boalt Hall of Law, University of California at Berkeley, one of the few schools in the country whose wartime faculty of distinguished scholars remained relatively intact. On July 12, Mr. Smith wrote me to say that since I was asking, in effect, for a change in the long-established practice of the law school not to admit women, and since the conditions of admission to any department were in general set up by the faculty governing that department, "Whether or not women should be admitted to the Law School is . . . a decision for the Faculty of the Law School." Mr. Smith indicated that since no recommendation from the faculty of the law school was then before the Corporation, "it does not feel itself in a position to take any action on your application."

By sidestepping my appeal, the Harvard Corporation had rid itself temporarily of an annoying question, but it had also called into play a theory about the significance of individual action I had once announced half-seriously to Dr. Ware: "One person plus one typewriter constitutes a movement." If I could not compel admission to Harvard, at least I could raise the issue in such a way that its law school would be unable to avoid it. I was also learning the process of patiently following whatever administrative procedure was available even when there was every reason to believe the result would be futile.

My next letter was addressed to the Faculty of the Harvard Law

School, summarizing the correspondence to date and requesting a meeting of the faculty "to reconsider my application and to decide whether it will recommend a change of the policy now in practice." I included a copy of my appeal to the Harvard Corporation and closed on a humorous note:

> [G]entlemen, I would gladly change my sex to meet your requirements but since the way to such change has not been revealed to me, I have no recourse but to appeal to you to change your minds on this subject. Are you to tell me that one is as difficult as the other?

As I had learned in the case of the University of North Carolina, correspondence could accomplish little more than stir up interest among a few key individuals and keep the issue flickering feebly. At the suggestion of Dr. Ware, I wrote to Judge Sarah T. Hughes of the United States District Court of Texas, who also chaired the Committee on Economic and Legal Status of Women. She replied that this was not a matter her committee had considered, but she said, "I shall be glad to discuss the problem at the next meeting which is in September," and asked that I keep her informed. After I left Washington, Dean Hastie wrote: "My best information on the Harvard situation is that the faculty is sharply divided on the matter of admitting women and will probably take the position that no action should be taken while a majority of the permanent faculty are on leave for war work." Lloyd K. Garrison's analysis prepared me for the inevitable. He wrote:

> From what I could pick up in Cambridge, my guesses are:
>
> (1) That the corporation will do nothing unless the Law School takes the initiative in asking that the rules be changed to admit women.
>
> (2) That the Law School will do nothing . . . , certainly not until Dean Landis gets back next fall and probably not then.
>
> (3) That this is due to a combination of long tradition, an excessively high enrollment which has become an increasing headache [and]
>
> (4) A touch of some undefinable male egoism, which is, I think, rather particularly strong in and around Boston as compared let us say with the middle west where we take our co-education for granted.
>
> At my last meeting on the Board of Overseers [at Harvard] there was a great debate as to whether women should be admitted to the Medical School and, so I was told (I had to leave the meeting early), the proposal mustered only two votes out of a dozen. . . .

I was in California when the faculty of the Harvard School of Law met on August 7, 1944, and took action on my petition for review. A few days later, Acting Dean E. M. Morgan informed me of their decision. His letter said in part:

In October, 1942, the Faculty thoroughly considered a proposal to request the University authorities to change the general rule. The first proposition was to admit women only during the emergency. This was almost immediately and unanimously rejected. The second proposal was for a permanent policy admitting women on exactly the same basis as men. This was debated by the Faculty at intervals for about three months, and the views of all members fully considered. There was much difference of opinion, but it was finally unanimously voted that no action looking to a change in the present practice be taken until after the emergency and after the School has returned to normal conditions with its full Faculty in residence. At that time the question will be debated anew. Accordingly it has been necessary to deny all applications for admission by women.

At its meeting on August 7, the Faculty determined to abide by its previous decision.

Having lost my first battle against "Jane Crow," I was somewhat comforted to learn indirectly that the effort was not entirely wasted. That fall when I registered at the University of California's Boalt Hall of Law, I was surprised to discover that news of the Harvard affair had traveled across country, and I was greeted with the remark, "So you're the woman who caused the Harvard Law School faculty to split 7–7 on your application." I also learned later of Harvard's announcement that women would be admitted to its medical school in 1945.

Fortunately, my controversy with Harvard was unresolved when I graduated from Howard in June, and it did not affect the high excitement of the ceremonies. Aunt Pauline came from Durham and Uncle Lewis Murray from Baltimore, each filled with proprietary pride and vying to share the honor of a niece who had "turned out so well." The high point of Aunt Pauline's visit was having tea at the White House with Mrs. Roosevelt. Then on Commencement Day an unexpected recognition electrified the huge outdoor gathering. Harry McAlpin, reporter for the *Pittsburgh Courier*, captured the mood of the occasion in a story headlined "Flowers from the First Lady." He wrote:

> Flowers—a huge bouquet of them—delivered near the close of the Howard University commencement exercises last Friday, overshadowed all the previous proceedings of the impressive occasion. They were from Mrs. Roosevelt, wife of the President of the United States. They were for brilliant, active, strong-willed Pauli Murray, graduate cum laude of the Howard Law School.

According to McAlpin—no stranger to hyperbole—the arrival of the flowers overshadowed the commencement address delivered by the Right

Reverend Angus Dun, bishop of the Diocese of Washington, the conferring of an honorary degree on Dr. Charlotte Hawkins Brown, and the disappointment caused by the absence of Philip Murray, the labor leader, who was to have been present to receive an honorary degree.

Actually, the flowers had been delivered to the law school a half hour before the ceremonies began. When I came in to get my cap and gown, I glanced at them admiringly and mistakenly thought they were for Philip Murray, whose citation Dean Hastie had been preparing earlier that day. When someone finally made me realize it was *my* name on the card, I removed it, suggesting the flowers be placed on the platform for all the graduates to share. A few minutes later, the sight of University Secretary James N. Nabrit parading across campus with the spectacularly beautiful display only moments before the academic procession began created an extra touch of excitement and added a special luster to the pageantry of the event.

On Sunday morning Aunt Pauline and I attended Holy Communion at the Church of the Atonement, where our former vicar at Saint Titus in Durham, the Reverend Eugene L. Henderson, was the celebrant. Mrs. Roosevelt's flowers graced the altar and later were taken to hospitals to cheer the sick. No one could have conceived that morning that thirty-five years later I would be serving in the same church as an Episcopal priest.

CHAPTER 21

Further Adversities

Commencement was over, but the dilemma of graduate study was not. Boalt Hall of Law seemed my best bet, but moving to Berkeley would mean living at a great distance from Aunt Pauline and Aunt Sallie, both of whom were becoming more dependent upon me as they grew older. Their letters revealed their loneliness and growing insecurity, and they wanted me nearer home. Aunt Sallie did the housekeeping but was restless and anxious to leave the old homeplace behind the cemetery, while Aunt Pauline, at seventy-four, continued to teach. She had been invited back by the Durham school board each year since reaching sixty-five, and she accepted partly because she was devoted to her classroom and partly to increase her modest retirement benefits. North Carolina had only recently instituted a pension plan and now, belatedly, was announcing the equalization of Negro teachers' salaries. Because of her late start and low pay, Aunt Pauline feared her pension would be little more than twenty-five dollars a month. Only a plodding determination kept her going through the school year.

In addition to my family concerns, I had ambivalent feelings about leaving the South in spite of my resolve not to live there. On the Sunday before commencement this inner conflict was stirred up again by Dr. Mordecai Johnson's impassioned appeal to the graduating class in his baccalaureate address. One of the great spellbinders of his time, he had the capacity to sway even the most skeptical of his listeners. That Sunday he was at his best as he urged the graduating seniors of Howard's professional schools to go south, placing their knowledge and skills at the service of southern Negroes. "Why don't you put your degree in your back pocket or hand it to your mother," Dr. Johnson asked us, "and go down to 'Brassos Bottom' in Mississippi where you are needed most?" He reminded us that more than three-fourths of the nation's Negro population lived in the southern states, while two-thirds of the twelve hundred Negro lawyers in the country lived outside the South. "If men like Bilbo and Rankin refuse to see the needs of our beloved Southland because of their blind spot on race," he said, "why don't you go down there and become the true spokesmen for those people?"

The baccalaureate address made such an impression on me that I felt impelled to address an "Open Letter to the Graduating Class of 1944," in which I asked my fellow students who were about to receive their law degrees, as well as those who were graduating in medicine, religion, social work, and other fields: "Have we the courage of our convictions? . . . Shall we move to the relatively freer areas where we may also have a little breathing space for ourselves and our children, or shall we go back down to 'Egypt' . . . and rescue our people . . . [winning the land of our grandparents] for democracy inch by inch, with books and ballots, and tolerance and understanding, and love and generosity in place of bullets and the instruments of violent conflict? Can we attract young white graduates of the great universities to come down and join with us?"

The ephemeral idea of interracial college-trained youth invading the Deep South in large numbers attracted little notice in 1944. The newspaper *PM* published portions of my letter on June 14, but the *Afro-American* reacted to Dr. Johnson's proposal with an editorial entitled "Go South— Commit Suicide." After that the notion sank into obscurity. It would emerge in a different form twenty years later when the Student Nonviolent Coordinating Committee (SNCC) spearheaded the Summer Project of 1964, involving hundreds of young black and white Northerners in voter registration campaigns and other civil rights activities in rural Mississippi, Georgia, and Alabama.

It is just as well that my fleeting impulse to go south as a civil rights crusader got no encouragement. Widespread resistance to segregation was still decades away, and individual challengers to the system at that time would have been isolated and neutralized. In any event, my decision to go west was helped along by my sister Mildred, who, wanting a change from her job at Freedmen's Hospital, accepted a position as nurse in a Los Angeles hospital. We decided to drive to California together in her car. I would be unable to register at Berkeley until the fall term began in October, but I had an arrangement to work as a special correspondent for *PM*, earning money for stories accepted, and I hoped to find a summer job in Los Angeles to carry me until fall. We shipped our clothing and books by freight and set out from Washington in late June.

Had we foreseen the difficulties of relocation under wartime conditions, we probably would not have attempted the trip. Rationing was in full force and our limited funds allowed little margin for emergencies. Nor had we anticipated the strain on tires and synthetic inner tubes of steady travel on roads in various stages of completion. On the first day we drove four hundred miles, had two flat tires and a cracked water pump. Having to change tires twice in a temperature of 102 degrees was not my idea of pleasure.

By the time we reached Pittsfield, Illinois, near Missouri, our front tires had worn down to the fiber, our money was low, and I was near exhaustion, having stayed up almost the entire night before in order to write a story for *PM*, which I sent off by air special. Tires were an extra expense we had not counted on, so I wired *PM* for a fifty-dollar advance on the story or a personal loan to be sent to Denver. As if we did not have enough complications, a man flagged us down near Pittsfield and asked if we would take on board two boys who were trying to get to Denver. One, in uniform, was in the Civilian Air Patrol; the other was anxious to reach an air base near Denver before his brother, who was stationed there, shipped out.

Finding space for two extra passengers in that tiny car was almost an impossibility. Mildred had packed it with enough equipment for a full-sized trailer: an ironing board and iron, blankets and bed linens, a radio and turntable, cartons of canned goods, picnic icebox, coffeepot and electric hot plate, frying pan, cooking utensils, lamps and extension cords, in addition to our suitcases and my typewriter. The man was so appealing on behalf of the boys (who were about seventeen) that Mildred finally said we would take them if we could get new tires. He put them out on the village green, where they sat waiting for us while we went to find a bureau of the Office of Price Administration.

It was Saturday morning, and the OPA office, which issued certifications for rationed items, was closed, so we could not get tires. With most of the weekend ahead, our only course seemed to be to start for Denver, eight hundred miles away. Having raised the boys' hopes, we felt we could not leave them stranded, so we repacked the car, wedged one of them into a cramped corner in the back seat, and let the other one squeeze in with us.

For two days all four of us rode cramped together in the little car through the nearly unbearable heat of flat country in Missouri, Kansas, and eastern Colorado. Much of the highway was sandy gravel, which threw up great clouds of blinding, choking dust whenever we met another car.

We drove in three shifts of fifty miles each, one of the boys taking the third shift. Once a shift was over, the driver would fall into exhausted sleep. That Saturday night when we were too weary to drive farther, we pulled into a trailer camp in the small town of Hiawatha, Kansas, and asked for two separate cabins. The woman in charge showed us one cabin and the two boys, who were white, took it. She was leading us to the second cabin when she stopped suddenly, looked at me closely in the half-light, and asked, "Aren't some of you people colored?"

It was our only experience with Jim Crow on our journey, but it came when none of us was fit to drive on and the next town was forty-one miles away. The woman refused to rent us a cabin, saying the other people in the camp would not stand for it. I argued with her that no one who had been driving all day would bother to come peering in our windows to see what color we were, but after hemming and hawing she stuck to her refusal. When we left, the boys, who had been listening to the argument, followed us out silently and got into the car.

I drove eleven miles farther, barely holding the car on the dusty road, and stopped for gas at a lonely crossroads store. When I asked the proprietor how far the next cabins were, he surprised me by saying, "We've got some right here." The proprietor and his wife were very kind, but they were also very poor. Their ancient cabins resembled spruced-up outhouses, full of crawling insects. The sheets were dingy and the blankets were grimy.

Mil and I first selected a cabin with a gas range in it, but she then decided she wanted one with a shower and persuaded the boys to switch. It was lucky we did. The little crossroads store was the gathering spot for farmers and laborers, who came in on Saturday nights to drink and carouse. We dared not change into our pajamas, and lay silent in the darkness, our hands on our flashlights, afraid to go to sleep. During the night three tramps wandered into the boys' cabin, tried to get in bed with them, and asked where they kept their money. Had Mildred and I not switched cabins, the tramps would have found us there and we might have had considerably more trouble than the boys in getting rid of them.

Weary as we were, we left at 3:30 A.M., determined to get to Denver by nightfall. By Sunday, however, our money was lower, the day hotter, the tires thinner, and the roads more bumpy, finally trailing off into endless miles of thick yellow dust. Houses disappeared. We passed through a stretch of oil country and several ghost towns. Filling stations were farther apart, and they were either closed or were not carrying standard gas. We had left the wheat country and were entering the cattle range, where there were no more towns, only ranches many miles apart. The land had become desolate, and cars came along only at great intervals. In spite of our Polaroid sunglasses, the blazing glare of the sun made us dizzy and our eyelids heavy.

By midafternoon, lack of sleep and the strain of driving made us short-tempered and triggered a quarrel which almost brought me to grief. Driving along in a haze about a hundred miles from Denver, I did not notice that the speedometer had climbed past sixty. We had no spare, and since Mil was justifiably worried about the tires, she sailed into me, complaining loudly that I was tearing her car to pieces. She kept watching the speedometer and singing out whenever it slipped past fifty, until finally, losing patience, I slammed on the brakes. The tires whined and the car lurched to a stop.

"O.K. Drive your little old car to California yourself," I stormed. I got out and walked over to the side of the road to cool off, so angry I did not hear Mil ask me if I planned to go on. I suddenly realized that my sister —who was as hot-tempered as I—was driving off toward Denver, leaving me standing empty-handed in the middle of nowhere, with only two dollars in my pocket.

My rashness had placed me in a sorry predicament. I was utterly alone, hot, thirsty, and not a little frightened. At first I started east, then I turned around and began plodding west. A half hour passed and only two cars came along, whizzing by without stopping. I became more frightened when a heavy black cloud with a long tail appeared in the west. I looked about for shelter but saw no houses or barns, only a haystack in a distant field, which I could crawl under for safety if the storm reached me; otherwise I would have to lie down in a ditch at the roadside until it passed.

Just as I was about to abandon the road for the haystack the tornado changed course, and soon a westbound car with a New York license plate came along, slowed down, and stopped. The people were from Long Island, en route to California, and kindly gave me a ride. We had gone only a short distance when up ahead I saw a little white car traveling slowly in our direction. When it got closer I recognized Mildred's Chevrolet; she was coming back to meet me and was driving alone. We were so glad to see one another we said nothing about our blowup until much later, when we were able to laugh about it. The hitchhikers had left the car at the next filling station when my sister told them she was going to go back for me. Since they were now only ninety-four miles from Denver, they thought another hitch would be easy. They soon discovered how lucky they had been with us. No one who pulled in for gas would give them a ride. They were still waiting when we came by, and sheepishly climbed in when Mildred opened the car door. We dropped them off just outside Denver, where they could go on to the air base.

In Denver our travel problems worsened. *PM* had wired me fifty dollars, which would cover the cost of tires, and we were able to stop over with friends, but meanwhile Mil had lost her gas rationing book and we were stuck for four days while we sent frantic wires to the OPA in Washington trying to get authorization for a replacement. As for tires, we found ourselves in a veritable no-man's-land. We learned that since we were not in Washington, no permits for tires could be issued to us from the Washington quota. Not being residents of Denver, we could not be certified from the Denver quota. And not having arrived and taken up residence in California, we could not get permits from any quota in that state. We finally wangled permits for grade-three tires and upon local advice took them to a store where we were able to buy government-rejected but new irregulars, which were superior to recapped or secondhand tires. However, when we had spent fifty-five dollars for the tires, some repairs, and tools, we left Denver with barely enough money to cover food and gas for the rest of the trip.

Further adversity greeted us in California. When Mildred reported for duty at the hospital, she learned she would not receive a paycheck until after she had worked a month. We survived the first few weeks on money I earned from *PM*. Later I got a job for the summer as a reporter for the *Sentinel,* an enterprising Negro weekly published in Los Angeles by Leon H. Washington and his cousin, civil rights attorney Loren Miller.

Our most serious problem was finding a place to live. The Negro population in Los Angeles had tripled between 1940 and 1944, increasing from 49,000 to 150,000. During the same period about 500,000 white people had moved into the area, and housing had become a battleground as the congested black ghetto expanded and white neighborhoods resisted. A few Negroes had been able to buy or rent well-kept homes vacated by Japanese-American families when they were sent to relocation centers in 1942, but most of the newcomers, like us, had to take whatever shelter they could find. We were ready to try anything, even living in an isolated unfurnished cabin miles from the city.

For a few days after our arrival we roomed with an acquaintance, but she could not let us stay longer because her husband was returning from military service and she needed the space. Hearing of our distress, a friend of hers who was a real estate agent offered a stopgap. In a deal with a bank, he had just bought an old wooden four-family dwelling on South Crocker Street a half block from Clauson Avenue, an industrial area lined with warehouses, lumberyards, and freight depots. The barnlike structure looked ready for demolition and was an eyesore in an otherwise neat neighborhood, but people still lived in it and one unit was vacant—a cold-water railroad flat on the ground floor. The Negro real estate man had apparently bought the place on speculation but told us if we were game enough to live in such a building he would let us move in and would wait for his first month's rent.

Having little choice, we set up housekeeping with a single piece of furniture—one narrow bed. I slept on the mattress on the floor and Mil slept on the frame and box springs. We ate out of cans, cooking our meals on a small electric hot plate and using our upended suitcases as chairs. Eventually, with some wooden crates and a few pieces of unpainted furniture, we managed to make the place livable.

We were soon reminded that Jim Crow had pursued us relentlessly to the West Coast. On our first visit to a movie, we were approached by a local Red Cross representative to give blood for incoming casualties from the South Pacific war zone. Although willing to do our part, we were unwilling to cooperate with the policy of racially segregating blood, which we knew prevailed in Washington. A face-to-face appeal was difficult to refuse, so we said we would be happy to give blood as long as it was not segregated. When assured there was no such policy in Los Angeles, we signed up and made tentative appointments, only to be told when I called to verify the date that the local blood bank, on instructions from the office of the surgeon general in Washington, did indeed enforce a policy of blood segregation.

This was for me a peculiarly maddening form of bigotry. The rejection of one's life blood, offered to relieve human suffering, seemed the final racial insult short of death itself. However futile individual protest might appear, to accept this indignity in silence would be reprehensible. In a letter to the director of the local Red Cross Blood Bank stating why my sister and I felt it necessary to withhold our blood, I expressed the conviction that "it is criminal negligence on the part of any public official . . . to let men die because of a policy which rivals that of Hitler for its official approval of 'racial supremacy.' " I also pointed out that Dr. Charles R. Drew, one of the country's outstanding authorities on blood plasma, who helped set up the Blood Bank Plan, was a Negro. I sent similar letters of protest to the Washington headquarters of the American Red Cross and the Surgeon General's Office.

The replies were disheartening. The national director of the Red Cross Blood Donor Service, G. Canby Robinson, M.D., wrote that he had read my letter with interest and appreciation. "No statement has ever been made by a responsible official connected with this project that there is any evidence that the blood of Negroes differs in any respect from that of white persons," he said, adding, however, that since the policy had been approved by the secretaries of War and Navy, it was not likely to change. Dr. Robinson's letter ended apologetically: "I might say that Doctor Charles R. Drew has the highest respect and regards of all of us in the Blood Donor Service."

Major F. N. Schwartz of the Blood Plasma Section, Surgery Division, Surgeon General's Office, U.S. Army, was equally candid. He wrote:

> Your statement that there is no scientific basis for the practice of plasma segregation is entirely in accord with the thought of this office.
>
> Unfortunately, there is a disinclination on the part of many whites, which you of course recognize, to have Negro blood injected in their veins. Whether that disinclination is the result of prejudice or ignorance, it nevertheless exists, and is a factor with which this office must reckon in carrying out the plasma program for the Army. It is the conviction of this office that disregard of that feeling would greatly mitigate [*sic*] against the successful conclusion of the program for collecting blood plasma for the armed forces.

Wearily, I sent copies of the correspondence to Roy Wilkins at the national office of the NAACP with the comment: "Jimcro is like the itch. It almost drives you mad while you're treating the darned stuff."

Only days later we were made aware that our physical presence was unacceptable to the white people in the South Crocker Street area. Though our barnlike building was less than six blocks from Central Avenue, the heart of the Negro district, unwittingly we had moved a half block south of Clauson Avenue, the line where white people had decided to take their stand to prevent Negro penetration.

We had been there about two weeks when I came home one day and found in our mailbox an unsigned typewritten letter with no return address, purporting to be from the South Crocker Street Property Owners' Association and addressed to Mrs. Mildred Fearing and Pauli Murray. The letter stated:

> We the property owners of Crocker Street wish to inform you the flat you now occupy . . . is restricted to the white or Caucasian race only. We are quite sure you did not know of this restriction or you would not have rented the flat. We intend to uphold these restrictions, therefore we ask that you vacate the above mentioned flat, at the above address, within seven days or we will turn the matter over to our attorney for action. Thank you.

This anonymous threat temporarily shattered our security. We were strangers in an isolated area and our ground-floor flat was vulnerable to acts of intimidation and even outright violence. Our landlord was in Mexico for three weeks and we could not seek his advice. I was especially frightened because Mildred was working a late shift at Veterans Hospital, Bonsall, West Los Angeles, and most evenings I was alone until well after midnight.

Fortunately, the *Sentinel* was a crusading paper with growing influence in the community, and as an attorney, its copublisher, Loren Miller, was familiar with restrictive covenant cases. We immediately sought police protection; soon squad cars began to patrol our neighborhood at night, and the FBI was asked to investigate the matter. Our greatest protection, however, was public exposure. I was assigned by the *Sentinel* to dig up the facts and write a story, and I quickly learned that ours was not an isolated case but one of many restrictive covenant battles. A neighborhood news sheet announced the formation of the Southside Property Owners' Protective League, which reputedly had organized a thousand white property owners to keep Negroes out of "white areas." At their first meeting, attended by two hundred people, they resolved to enforce restrictions against "two non-caucasian families" living in the allegedly restrictive area. My sister and I happened to be one of the two families targeted for removal.

Within the next few days two white property owners, relying upon racially restrictive covenants placed upon the land in 1927, filed suits against twelve different sets of Negro property owners and named forty additional defendants as "John Does" until their true names could be ascertained. The Negro property owners organized to fight back, petitioning the City Council to declare a moratorium on the alleged restrictions. Meanwhile we stayed on at the Crocker Street address, and while we remained anxious, we encountered no further difficulties.

This embattled introduction to living in California fueled my determination to find the key to a successful legal attack upon racial segregation. I turned back to the civil rights paper I had yet to complete for Dr. Ransom's seminar, and spent every spare moment in the Los Angeles County Law Library, researching and revising it. Instead of discussing the inequalities of separate facilities, I made a frontal attack. My approach was to enumerate the rights that affect the individual's personal status in the community, one of which is "the right not to be set aside or marked with a badge of inferiority." In developing the argument to overrule the "separate but equal doctrine" of *Plessy* v. *Ferguson,* I asserted that the effect of this doctrine "is to place the Negro in an inferior social and legal position" and "to do violence to the personality of the individual affected, whether he is white or black." Having no legal precedents to rely on, I cited references to psychological and sociological data supporting my assertion. Before sending the finished paper to Dr. Ransom I showed it to Loren Miller and also to Carey McWilliams, who later left law practice to become editor of *The Nation.* Their comments were encouraging; they both thought I was on the right track.

Vindication of this approach came ten years later when the Supreme

Court concluded unanimously in *Brown* v. *Board of Education* that "in the field of public education the doctrine of 'separate but equal' has no place." Speaking of children in grade and high schools, Chief Justice Earl Warren's opinion declared: "To separate them from others of similar age and qualifications solely because of their race generates a feeling of inferiority as to their status in the community that may affect their hearts and minds in a way unlikely ever to be undone."

From childhood experiences in the South reinforced by fresh hurts suffered during those first few weeks in California had come the germ of an idea which anticipated the reasoning of the Supreme Court. In 1944 I typed up my paper without making a carbon and mailed it off to Dr. Ransom. Although I heard it caused much comment around Howard Law School, nineteen years passed before I discovered that its affinity with the Supreme Court's pronouncement was not entirely accidental. In 1963 I visited Howard Law School and asked Spottswood Robinson, who was then dean, if he knew what had happened to my paper. (I also collected the bet I had made with him many years earlier.) To my surprise, he promptly produced it from his files and had a copy made for me. While waiting for the paper to be reproduced, he casually mentioned that when he had left the law school to go into private practice, he had taken my paper with him. He had not thought much of it when he first read it, he told me, but in 1953 when the NAACP legal team was preparing arguments for *Brown* v. *Board of Education,* he took another look at it and thought it better. "In fact," he went on, "it was helpful to us. We were able to use your paper in the *Brown* briefs just as my student paper on real property was used in the restrictive covenant cases in 1948."

Thinking of all the years that had passed without my knowing that my work had not been wasted effort, all I could say was, "Spots, why on earth didn't you tell me?"

That summer in California was productive in another way. I was learning that creative expression is an integral part of the equipment needed in the service of a compelling cause; it is another form of activism. Words poured from my typewriter and several of my articles were published. One, "An American Credo," appeared in *Common Ground* magazine and brought an enthusiastic response from a Negro soldier "somewhere in the Marianas Islands." Another, called "Footnote for Minority Americans," which appeared as a full-page spread in *PM,* outlined a philosophy and "code of conduct" for Negroes trying to live with dignity in the United States while struggling as individuals against racial discrimination. Urging Negroes to act upon a positive self-image, I wrote: "Believe in your dreams —that some day you or your posterity will be President of the United

States, a justice of the Supreme Court, an ambassador to China or India or England, a member of the Cabinet. . . . Then do not wait for the opportunity to open. Equip yourself for the position and open the door."

How far this "code" traveled and what impact it made on at least one reader was reflected in a letter I received from Private Charles F. Thomas, Jr. Written "somewhere in France" and dated October 22, 1944, it read:

> I am writing this letter in a French field, it is very muddy here, and I'm very dirty and need a shave, and my pup tent has sprung a leak, another thing before I go into details, I'll ask you to forgive my spelling and handwriting as I'm writing by a dim flashlight. I don't have much time so I'll get to the point:
>
> Miss Murray a few days ago I found an old PM newspaper on the hiway dated August 20 with your article facing me, so I read it. You are really on the ball, it is one of the best articles in [the] world for a Negro to read, you are right as can be in everything you say. . . . I'm in France, trying like everything to get back to the states, and I want to feel as an American, and [be] treated like one, and it takes people like you, to see that it [is] done, if you only knew how much your article has built up my morale, it's 100% now (smile). . . .
>
> Just a soldier named Chuck.
>
> P.S. Miss or Mrs.?

A great boost to my literary fortune came when Lillian Smith, whose best-selling novel *Strange Fruit* was published that year, accepted my long poem "Dark Testament" for publication in the winter issue of *South Today,* a magazine that she coedited with Paula Snelling in Clayton, Georgia. I was overjoyed not only because the magazine was highly regarded for its literary quality and its emphasis on racial justice in the South but also because she paid me the handsome sum of one hundred dollars —the first money my poetry had ever earned!

My last assignment for the *Sentinel* before I entered school at Berkeley was to cover the final day of court-martial proceedings against fifty Negro seamen charged with mutiny and conspiracy for refusal to load ammunition on a South Pacific–bound transport. The trial, held on Yerba Buena Island in San Francisco Bay, lasted thirty-three days and was said to be the longest and largest mass trial in naval history and the first since the Civil War.

The prosecution maintained that the defendants, when ordered to load ammunition on August 9 and 11, had shown "defiance and a persistent and deliberate refusal to do military duty." Further, it characterized some of the men as "insolent" and "smart." The evidence showed that the men on trial were survivors of a tragic explosion at nearby Port Chicago on July 17, in which two naval ammunition ships blew up, killing 323 men, the majority of whom were Negroes. Twelve of the defendants had been hospitalized and several others treated for shock, burns, and bruises. Some of the defendants had been detailed to clear up the debris after the explosion and, using baskets, had gathered up pieces of their comrades—an arm, a leg, a torso.

Testimony showed that of the 328 men ordered to muster for duty on August 9, 258 fell out and indicated their fear and unwillingness to load ammunition. Of that number, only fifty were placed under general court-martial. The defense argued that the men were still suffering from shock and had a "normal reaction of deep and terrifying fear" after their ordeal of July 17. The defense also showed that seamen who were detailed on mess duty at the time of the alleged mutiny were nevertheless questioned as to whether they would load ammunition and were court-martialed when they expressed unwillingness to do so.

Some observers at the trial who had served with the defendants or were at the scene of disaster at Port Chicago called my attention to a fact generally suppressed at the trial: these men deeply resented the Navy's policy of placing large, segregated units of Negro men in details to load ammunition while ignoring their appeals for assignment to sea duty.

One of the most attentive observers at the summation that day was an attractive Negro woman who sat alone. I learned she was Edna Seixas, a member of the Berkeley Interracial Committee and the mother of a soldier killed in the Italian campaign. She had attended every session and while she could not speak to the defendants, her silent presence and kindly gaze signaled sympathy and support. She told me that the men smiled gratefully whenever they looked in her direction.

When the men were found guilty and sentenced to fifteen years each, Mrs. Seixas was so disturbed she wrote a letter giving her impressions of the trial. I forwarded it to Mrs. Roosevelt, who wrote: "I read Mrs. Seixas' letter with extreme interest and I am passing it on because it is such a fine one." Later, upon review, forty of the defendants received reduced sentences ranging from eight to twelve years, and eventually, as I recall, the sentences were commuted.

CHAPTER 22

Boalt Hall and
International House

M̲Y YEAR of graduate study in Berkeley provided some respite from the hectic scramble for existence. I lived at International House, near the campus at the foot of the Berkeley hills; that eased most racial problems, and the physical setting was idyllic. Climbing the hills, one could look down on seven cities and across the great bay to the coastal mountain range. One could watch spectacular sunsets over the Golden Gate Bridge and sometimes see the bridge itself swallowed up by great rolling clouds of tule fog. Although I missed the seasons, the bay area's mild climate was a pleasant change from the sharp edges of winter back east; on the coldest day the temperature stayed above freezing.

International House, an embryonic United Nations, was the high point of my California experience, and it swept me into broad currents of global diversity. More than 150 students of all colors and some thirty nationalities lived there in close contact under wartime conditions—Chinese, Icelanders, Panamanians, Poles, Mexicans, Arabs, Palestinian Jews, British, Indians, Latin Americans of many complexions and political hues, as well as white and Negro North Americans from the United States and Canada. The regular International House residence having been leased to the Navy during the war, we were housed in four large fraternity residences nearby. Forty-four women shared my house, three or four to each room. We studied and dressed there but slept in double-decker bunks on communal, unlighted porches open to wind, stars, and frequent Berkeley fogs.

A dozen or more languages struggled for dominance in the small dining halls where we ate family style and where at the student level we fought out issues of the international conflict. Arab students, for example, bitterly denounced the house policy of having a Jew represent Palestine at the annual Candle Light ceremony. We debated the relative merits of minority and majority strategies on national and global fronts. Discussions of postwar plans, the internal situation in China, Britain's policy toward India, the Dumbarton Oaks proposals, the Bretton Woods formula, the Pan American Conference, and the upcoming United Nations Conference in San Francisco made the place hum like a beehive.

Over coffee and cigarettes I listened to heated conversations on the rights of small countries and the responsibilities of large ones and to frequent expressions of resentment over the "superman complex" of the United States. There were laments over "forgotten Africa" and proddings from Zionists on the right of Palestinian Jews to a homeland. American missionary students toiled over Chinese characters to learn the language and bring the "Christian Message" to the Chinese, while sadly admitting that all too many of their own people were deaf to their message. Chinese students regarded their ardor with considerable skepticism and wondered aloud if China did not need technicians more than soul-savers.

There were deeper and more personal levels of communication in individual encounters when we removed our public masks and revealed our vulnerability to pain. There was the bitterness of Doug Greer, a native Californian who had just returned from military service in the segregated air force unit reserved for Negroes at Tuskegee, Alabama. Doug's first, sudden exposure to the Jim Crow system was so shattering he was now consumed with hostility toward all white people. He told me, "When I was down there, I felt like I had ground glass churning in my chest all day and all night." He said he had reached the point where he did not want anything white to touch him. "I don't even want to sleep on a white sheet or pillowcase," he said. Listening to Doug, I reflected upon my growing friendship with Sarah Webb, a white student from Georgia who lived in my house, and upon the irony of our discovering an affinity based on our regional heritage which neither of us shared with our racial counterparts from the West.

There were other vulnerabilities—for example, the glancing blows of insensitive remarks. Bertilda, born in Panama, was exasperated when asked how long she had been in America. As far as she was concerned, she had been in America—Central America—all her life. The Panamanians recoiled as a group when one of their number was described as "that Chinese boy who speaks Spanish," for to them Julio Wong was a Panamanian, period.

Then there were those of us who found a bond of kinship in the realities of our minority status. Each in her own way had suffered from exclusion and rejection because she belonged to an unpopular or despised group, and each was surprised to find how similar her experiences were to those of other minorities. Sharing with these women gave me new perspectives on my own racial problem.

My broader education began in bull sessions at night with my two roommates—Mijeyko Takita and Eva Schiff. Mijeyko, a Nisei, had just returned from three years' internment in the Japanese relocation center at Topaz, Arizona. She was one of approximately 120,000 Japanese-Americans, some 70,000 of them native-born citizens, uprooted almost overnight from their homes on the West Coast and confined to makeshift camps in the interior. Like other young people in the camps, she had sustained the total disruption of her life and education, but she carried the scar of that experience with quiet dignity and showed no sign of bitterness. She once betrayed her deep anxiety over anti-Japanese attitudes on the West Coast when she confessed that it might be better to let people think she was Chinese in order to escape the onus of an ancestry that frequently provoked insults and even violence. A native-born American and loyal to the nation, Mijeyko nevertheless suffered the terrible paradox of World War II in ways I could only imagine. I would never forget the anguish concealed in her single comment at the news that a second atomic bomb had been dropped on Japan. She said quietly, "My grandparents live in Nagasaki," and turned her face away.

Eva, on the other hand, came from Cologne, Germany, by way of Switzerland and Holland. Her memories of her early childhood were filled with the horror of small children being stoned and human beings branded during the first Nazi pogroms. Although her immediate family of four left Germany shortly after Hitler came to power, in 1945 the fate of relatives in Germany, France, and Holland was uncertain. (She learned after the war that most of them had died in the Nazi holocaust.) Eva had embraced the United States with the ardor of a new American who had found a haven where she would no longer be tormented by nights of terror. Yet echoes of that terrifying past were reawakened when she was refused admittance to membership in a sorority at UCLA after someone discovered she was a Jew. She had also seen her young brother grow depressed and his schoolwork suffer after he was refused a room near his polytechnical school because he was "not a Gentile." Finally, when she read a book about the Deep South for an assignment in a course in social welfare, she burst out, "My God, Pauli, this is just what happened in Germany!"

Three others often joined our discussions. Jane Garcia, whose ancestors had come from Mexico but whose family, after five generations in the United States, was as American as, in her words, "the Saturday night movie," continually carried a burden of proof as to her race and nationality because of her swarthy complexion. When she won the distinction of representing her high school at an American Legion patriotic ceremony, she was told by a cruel teacher that she could not accept the honor because she was "not an American." Recently, she had been evicted from her coed boardinghouse two blocks from the Berkeley campus because a young Negro high school classmate had stopped by to say farewell before going overseas.

Lillian Li, born in China, where she had been part of a dominant culture and accepted as an individual, had spent more than half her life in the United States and loved her new country, but she could never become accustomed to being treated as a peculiar foreign specimen. She could not understand, she said wryly, why she was expected to know every Chinese laundryman between the Atlantic and Pacific coasts. When the lurch of a crowded trolley threw her against a white American one day, she was stunned to hear the woman yell at her, "Why don't you look where you're going, you drunken Chink?" In Lillian's family tradition, no inebriated Chinese would dare appear in public, and drunkenness was almost unheard of in interior China. Genevieve Tutell, Lillian's friend, was a Caucasian born in China of American missionary parents. She was drawn to our discussions because of her childhood experiences in China; she still remembered how it felt to be surrounded by children who saw her only as a "foreign devil."

Our sessions became so exciting that we wanted to share our insights with others. The six of us formed a panel and appeared before several interested groups in the area, showing the interrelatedness of minority problems and presenting facts and figures as part of our informal dialogue. The panel was a great success with our audiences; it was a form of consciousness raising, although we did not know the term in those days. It was also a significant step in my own growth; I was learning to see the civil rights struggle within the wider context of all human rights.

Meanwhile, at Boalt Hall of Law, where I was the only enrolled graduate student, I was looked upon as an oddity. I was an outsider, trained elsewhere, in a school jealous of its local reputation. My professors reminded me that if I took the California bar examination and flunked, my failure would be a bad mark against Howard Law School, not Boalt Hall of Law. I missed the cameraderie of students and professors bound together in a compelling cause. I was learning the loneliness of independent research and the frustration of months of drudgery in the library that yielded meager returns.

Continuing the research begun at Howard, I hoped to find a firm basis for overturning the "separate but equal" doctrine by studying the history of the adoption of the Thirteenth and Fourteenth amendments to the Constitution. To determine the intentions of the framers as to the scope of these amendments required a thorough examination of the debates in Congress when the amendments were being considered. When I submitted my summary and analysis of the debates, Professor D. O. McGovney, under whom I carried out the research project and who was sympathetic, found the results inconclusive but gave me an A for the course. The grade was insufficient consolation for what seemed to be months of wasted effort. I had no way of knowing then that teams of lawyers with the same objective would cover the same ground in later years and that even though the Supreme Court would pronounce their findings inconclusive, it would still arrive at the decision they sought. Mr. McGovney, who was a law school classmate of FDR and a personal friend of Chief Justice Harlan F. Stone, told me wryly, "Fishermen go out to fish, but catch few fish."

My master's thesis, "The Right to Equal Opportunity in Employment," was more successful, but it was produced at great emotional cost. To earn the degree I was required to write a publishable thesis, and I was greatly handicapped by having had no law review experience. I did the work under the supervision of Barbara N. Armstrong, who in those days stood almost alone among women as a member of a law school faculty. An expert in labor law who had been called to Washington to work on a plan for old-age insurance when the Social Security Act was being drafted, Mrs. Armstrong was hard-driving, had strong opinions, and was merciless in her criticisms. She also had a disconcerting candor, which pulverized my self-confidence. Draft after draft of my thesis was rejected, and once she told me, "We may be trying to make a second-rate lawyer out of a first-rate writer." (I had shown her the poem I had written after FDR's death that spring; it was later published in *Common Ground*.)

Every conference with Mrs. Armstrong became an ordeal, and my anxiety increased as the work dragged on. At the end of the spring term she announced I would have to stay through the summer to complete the thesis to her satisfaction, a delay that added to my worries. My Rosenwald funds were exhausted and I had to apply for an extension of the grant. The fact that I had not yet taken a state bar examination was a serious handicap for future job prospects. Many lawyers felt that the longer one waited after graduating from law school, the more difficult it was to pass a bar exam, and the earliest examination to be given in California was scheduled for the first week in October. I decided to sit for the exam then and planned to enroll in an evening bar review course to overcome the disadvantage of not having been trained in California law.

When Mrs. Armstrong got wind of my plan she was furious. She called me into her office and told me bluntly she did not think I had the mental or physical capacity to both complete my paper and pass the bar examination. She went further and threatened to withhold approval of the thesis unless I canceled the course. With my degree at stake, I was forced to accept her ultimatum, but her stinging remark was the challenge I needed. Grim determination replaced despair, and somehow I found the strength to complete the thesis and get her formal approval in time for it to be published as a leading article in the September issue of the *California Law Review.* I then astonished Mrs. Armstrong (and myself) by taking the three-day October bar exam and passing it!

When the exam results were published, Mrs. Armstrong was so impressed with my performance that she voluntarily wrote a strong letter of recommendation on my behalf. "I regard Miss Murray as a young woman of exceptional competence," she said. "She has, in addition to a very keen and quick mind, the capacity for hard work and an exceptionally pleasing personality. . . . I may add that Miss Murray had exactly three weeks in which to prepare for our recent bar examinations and that she passed these examinations when some of the graduates of our School who studied all summer were unable to do so."

I now had a master's degree and a published law review article to my credit and had passed a tough bar examination, but in my case scholastic achievements would not automatically translate into job opportunities. Ahead were the formidable barriers of race and sex, which would rise even higher now that the war was over and large numbers of war veterans were returning to the legal profession. Several of my Howard Law School classmates were already working as government attorneys in Washington, but my applications met with no success. My hope to work in the Legal Department of the NAACP disappeared when Thurgood Marshall wrote me there was no possibility of increasing the staff beyond the three lawyers and one part-time clerk presently employed. I seriously considered settling in California and tried to entice Aunt Pauline to come out for a visit. She replied that she was too feeble to make the trip. Although her letters continued to be filled with hints of declining health, she had begun her thirty-ninth year in the Durham public school system. My sister Mildred had returned to her old job at Freedmen's Hospital after six months in Los Angeles, and Aunt Pauline fully expected me to come east as soon as my studies were completed. From childhood she had supported my decisions, and she had an uncanny awareness of my troubles even when I was far away and did not write. I fully believed her prayers had carried me through the bar examination. All this made me feel a greater sense of obligation to her than if she made constant demands upon me.

After passing the bar exam, I delayed my departure from the West Coast in order to be admitted to practice on December 8, 1945. My things were packed ready for shipment and I had my railroad reservations for the day of the swearing-in ceremony. Then a surprising turn of events changed my plans. I was among a hundred or more lawyers who were being sworn in by California's attorney general, Robert W. Kenny, a jovial, immensely popular politician. The only Democrat to hold a big job in a state that had elected Republican Earl Warren as governor, Bob Kenny was known as a maverick liberal. At the time, he was president of the National Lawyers Guild and honorary chairman of a statewide committee organized to push for fair employment practice legislation in California. He also had his eye on the governorship.

After the ceremony I was introduced to Mr. Kenny, and when he learned I was the author of the law review article on equal employment opportunity which he had just read he told me he would like to have me on his staff of deputies. He could not offer me a regular appointment, he said, since the position of deputy attorney general was controlled by civil service regulations, but he had one or two vacancies he could fill on a temporary basis subject to the return of staff members who were on leave for military duty and also subject to the establishment of new civil service lists, for which an examination would soon be announced. He encouraged me to gamble on the temporary position in the hope I might pass the exam and get on the new list, and he proceeded to dictate a memorandum to his supervising deputy in Sacramento, arranging the details. I had grave misgivings about changing my plans on short notice and taking a job in California under such tenuous conditions, but Mr. Kenny was very persuasive and in the end I accepted a temporary post, canceled my reservations, and agreed to report to work on January 2, 1946.

My misgivings proved to be justified. On the way to Los Angeles to spend the Christmas holidays with Eva Schiff and her family before starting the new job, I had an attack of nausea accompanied by dull pains in my right side. Two months earlier during the bar examination I had suffered similar attacks but attributed them to exam jitters. Now they were worse, and I had to spend Christmas in bed. Eva's parents were both physicians, he an internist and she a pediatrician. Dr. Hans Schiff took me in hand and put me through a series of laboratory tests, which confirmed his diagnosis of chronic subacute appendicitis aggravated by the strain of completing my graduate work and passing the bar. He recommended five or six weeks' rest and eventual surgery.

This was disastrous news. I had no health insurance and no money for hospitalization and surgical fees. In addition, I had learned I would be the first Negro deputy in the attorney general's office and the opportunity represented an important breakthrough. The Schiff family understood my dilemma and tried to help me resolve it. Dr. Hans thought that if I was careful with my diet, surgery could be postponed for a while, and he suggested that I report to work as planned, become familiar with my new duties, and then take time off for an operation.

The odds were against me. I had been on the job barely two months —half sick most of the time—when I got ominous news from home. Aunt Pauline had been ill since January, first with bronchial pneumonia, then from attacks of weakness and drowsiness. Her physician had been unable to determine the nature of her ailment, and it was doubtful that she would finish her school year. Aunt Sallie felt she was getting worse and that my presence was needed immediately. I then learned to my dismay that in a temporary appointment there was no provision for sick leave or for a leave of absence without pay. The deputy director saw the problem as a mere technicality, however, and suggested that if I left, I would be reappointed to the job upon my return to California. It did not work out that way. Shortly after my departure for the East, the civil service examination for the position I held was given on two weeks' notice, my request to take it in absentia was turned down by the California Personnel Board, new civil service lists were established, and several veterans returned from military duty, foreclosing the possibility of my reappointment. The entire episode was embarrassing because the publicity given to my appointment as a "first" had failed to note that it was temporary in nature and subject to civil service regulations.

Meanwhile, unaware that circumstances would bar a return to the job, I flew to Washington on my way to Durham. Just before I left California, a letter had come from Mary McLeod Bethune informing me that I had been nominated by the National Council of Negro Women as one of the twelve outstanding women in American life for the year 1945, "because of the selfless devotion and contribution you have made to the humanities and to the creation of a better life for all people." I stopped off in Washington long enough to attend the awards ceremony and was overjoyed to find that another of the recipients was Maida Springer, whom I had not seen since we marched together in the Odell Waller Silent Parade in 1942.

When I got home next day, Aunt Pauline's condition was alarming enough for me to arrange—at Mildred's suggestion—for her to be brought to Washington and admitted to Freedmen's Hospital. It developed that she had been suffering from diabetes, a condition her local physician inexplicably failed to detect, and that she had barely escaped slipping into a diabetic coma. Her health was so precarious that she remained in the hospital nearly two months before it improved enough for her to return to Durham.

Aunt Pauline's hospitalization brought me to Washington at a turning point in the history of Howard Law School. President Harry S. Truman had nominated William H. Hastie to be governor of the Virgin Islands, and the school was agog. Dean Hastie's departure meant changes on the school's faculty, and Dr. Leon A. Ransom was seen as his likely successor. Both of them welcomed me back warmly and talked enthusiastically of my joining the faculty in the fall. I was ecstatic over the possibility, especially as it had been the reason for my year of graduate work.

No decisions could be made, however, until Dean Hastie's nomination was confirmed. Southern Senators James O. Eastland and Allen J. El-lender, opposed to the selection of a Negro, had created a public furor and demanded public confirmation hearings by the Senate Committee on Territories and Insular Affairs. Eastland and Ellender sat on the subcom-mittee appointed to hear testimony, and the hearing began shortly after my arrival in the city.

At the hearing, one Leslie F. Hunt, an accountant and former vice-president of the Virgin Islands Company, filed a memorandum and tes-tified against Dean Hastie's confirmation on the alleged ground of "his sympathies with Communistic ideology and Communistic organizations." Hunt charged that Dean Hastie had been affiliated with five "Communist front" organizations, naming the National Lawyers Guild, Southern Con-ference on Human Welfare, Washington Committee for Democratic Ac-tion, National Negro Congress, and the Abolish Peonage Committee, and he asserted, "I and many others informed on the Islands' problems are fearful that the Virgin Islands are not the place for a Communist to hold such an important post as Governor."

To everyone who knew Bill Hastie, Hunt's charge was ridiculous, but Senator Eastland was making the most of it and it could not go unan-swered. Dr. Ransom acted as Hastie's counsel in the hearings, and the entire law school—faculty, students, and alumni—mobilized an all-out effort to support the nomination. A number of Hastie's former students got together and drafted a strong statement on his behalf. The group selected me as its representative to testify before the subcommittee, and I joined a parade of witnesses which included such prominent non-Communist figures as Lloyd K. Garrison, Secretary of the Interior J. A. Krug, and Socialist leader Norman Thomas. When called to testify, I was amused to hear the clerk announce, "Mr. Pauli Murray, Deputy Attorney General of California," obviously not expecting a woman to hold such a title.

In line with our prepared statement, I called attention to the achieve-ments in public office and community life of many of Dean Hastie's former students. As products of his leadership at Howard University School of Law, I announced, "we wish to deposit with this Committee our personal achievement records to the credit of Dean Hastie." I had the satisfaction of looking Senator Eastland straight in the eye and testifying that one of my former schoolmates had recently won the Bronze Star "for meritorious service against the enemy." On the issue of communism, our position was clear:

> Dean Hastie is a man of independent thought and action in our opinion; a man of principle and not of "party line." . . . We know that a man of Dean Hastie's breadth and high calibre has evolved out of the highest and best traditions of our native American heritage. We object to any implication that he can be contained within the narrow framework of the American Communist Party. We do not want this political group to receive any credit, even by implication, for his achievements, his public acts or his associations.

The charge of "Communist tendencies" against Hastie fell flat. Under questioning, Hunt admitted he knew nothing of the truth of his allegations and that his "evidence" had been collected and given to him by an investigator for the House Un-American Activities Committee. His testimony was ruled out for failure to offer substantiation of his charges. Senator Eastland's grilling of Dean Hastie was embarrassing only to the senator as Hastie firmly answered "Yes" or "No" and made no effort to deny principled stands he had taken. At one point, when Eastland asked if he had taken part in a demonstration against the blood bank, Hastie replied forcefully, "I most certainly did." The demonstration against the American Red Cross segregated blood bank had been held under the auspices of the local branch of the NAACP. Other questions intended to discredit Dean Hastie gave him further opportunities to demonstrate his fitness for the post. The Senate promptly confirmed his nomination, with only Eastland and Ellender voting "No."

Jubilant over the Hastie victory, the law school now faced the problem of finding a new dean. Andy Ransom, the third of the Houston, Hastie, and Ransom team which had built the school's reputation, seemed the logical choice. In addition to being a remarkable lawyer and a brilliant teacher, he was universally loved by students and many graduates because of his selfless devotion to the school and its student body. He had served as acting dean on two previous occasions—once during Houston's absence and once while Hastie was on leave as civilian aide to the secretary of war. During the critical wartime period he had held the school together. He had been the school's chief recruiter of promising students and had seen many students without funds through to graduation by digging up scholarships, finding jobs, helping them with personal adjustments, and encouraging them in other ways. Six of us who were graduates submitted a statement to the board of trustees describing Dr. Ransom's qualities and our estimate of his leadership. We were optimistic about his chances and I think Ransom himself fully expected to get the job.

In our concern for the continuity of tradition, we had overlooked the fact that the deanship of Howard Law School had become a visible post in the capital city, a stepping-stone to high public office, and that Andy Ransom had strong competitors working quietly behind the scenes. We were sadly disappointed when the board of trustees passed over him and named Dr. George M. Johnson, who had returned recently to the faculty from several years with the Fair Employment Practice Committee. The announcement was such a devastating blow to Ransom that he resigned immediately. Another faculty member who had been an unsuccessful candidate also resigned.

The bitterness surrounding these resignations not only left the law school faculty in disarray but also created an untenable situation for me. My hope of becoming part of a vital center of the legal campaign for civil rights perished with Ransom's departure. Although my loyalty to him made it unthinkable for me to take a job at the law school under the circumstances, nevertheless it was a heartbreaking decision to make. When I learned shortly afterward that there was no possibility of my returning to the job in California, my fortunes seemed at their lowest point. There was nothing left to do but go back to New York and start afresh.

The one bright spot in that gloomy picture was Aunt Pauline's recovery and her determination to end her school year on her feet and in harness. In June she wrote me triumphantly that school was over "and so is my work in the Durham City Schools." She had been able to finish the last thirteen days and give all her examinations, correct all her papers, and do all the other necessary paperwork. Both a sixth-grade class and a student patrol had presented her with gifts of money—five dollars each—and the Parent-Teacher Association, together with a group of mothers, the principal, and a number of teachers and students, had given her a fifty-dollar War Bond. Some fifteen hundred people were at the graduation exercises, including more than one hundred of her boys and girls, and officials of both the white and colored schools. When the superintendent of schools made his speech, she reported,

> I was sitting in the balcony 100 feet from the stage but exactly in front of it. He said, "I could not fail to speak of one of our teachers who is retiring this year, she has had a rich heritage from the wonderful work she has done with the boys and girls who have come under her care. I must commend her for her long and faithful service. If she is in the house I wish her to

stand. She is Mrs. Pauline F. Dame. Yes, there she is, Mrs. Dame, high up, Mrs. Dame always stands high, will Mrs. Dame please stand?" Every eye was turned to the balcony and me. So you see he and the Board of Education did show some appreciation for my work.

For Aunt Pauline, at seventy-five, it was the close of a long and honorable career. For me, her retirement coincided with the beginning of the struggle to find my place in a new and demanding profession in ways I had not contemplated upon entering law school five years earlier. I had been interested primarily in civil rights, and the private practice of law had not been my objective, yet for the next fifteen years private practice would shape much of my life.

CHAPTER 23

Inching Along

NEW YORK CITY in 1946 was hardly the place to establish a successful law career unless one had high marks from a top school, solid legal experience, influential contacts, or a financial cushion. Trying to enter a highly competitive field without one or more of those assets was tough for anyone; for me, the odds were tripled. Yet I was determined to pursue my profession, and at least New York was familiar ground where I had survived many hardships in the past.

Fortunately, I got a job almost immediately with the Commission on Law and Social Action, an agency of the American Jewish Congress comparable to the legal staff of the NAACP. Although the CLSA dealt with civil rights issues, it did not provide the experience in legal practice I needed, so after nine months I left, entered the hospital for surgery to remove the appendix which had long plagued me, and then set about preparing for the New York bar examinations. For a short while I stayed at International House, earning my meals by working the morning shift in the cafeteria and spending my free time looking for a job in a law office.

It was a grueling business, filled with constant dread of rejection. I had no practical legal experience and was not yet admitted to practice in New York State. In addition to the hurdles presented by my color and sex, my appearance was just short of being seedy. I had only one dress to wear for job interviews—it was black with white polka dots—and each night I washed it and hung it up to dry for the next day's ordeal.

Everything counted in the relentless process of selecting applicants— the reputation of the law school one attended, one's class rank, whether one had served on a law review, or had clerked for a Supreme Court justice, a judge of a federal appellate or federal district court, or a state court judge, in that order. Graduates from the law schools of Harvard, Yale, or Columbia who had one or more of the other credentials were hired by the big law firms. Others, like me, had to follow whatever leads we had, tramping from one small office to the next. I would be interviewed, told that my background did not fit the needs of the particular firm, and then, if I was lucky, the interviewing lawyer might refer me to another firm, where he had a contact and thought a job might be available. These referrals, doggedly repeated in an endless round of interviews, were usually fruitless.

Since I had only one of the credentials required by the large firms— class rank—I had to seek out offices with links to liberal causes in the hope they would be willing to hire a Negro, a woman, or, as in my case, both. Most of these firms felt too vulnerable to risk having a visible minority on the staff. The usual explanation was that some of their clients would object. Once when I succeeded in getting past the racial barrier, the sex factor was the stumbling block. Four partners needed a managing clerk; two of them were labor lawyers who had handled cases for the Workers Defense League, knew me personally, and were enthusiastic about having me come to work for their firm. The other two partners, however, vetoed the idea without bothering to interview me, for the reason that the firm had hired a woman attorney the previous year, "who didn't work out." I had no better luck with the few Negro law firms I approached; most of them were struggling simply to keep afloat.

About this time I was referred to former Municipal Court Judge Dorothy Kenyon, then in private practice, who was known for her liberal views and her active association with the American Civil Liberties Union. Judge Kenyon was an energetic, youthful-looking woman of about sixty, with a barbed wit and a penchant for wearing large floppy hats and colorful dresses. She interviewed me in her cramped little office on lower Broadway, and while it was obvious she had no job to offer me, her identification with my struggle boosted my sagging morale. She told me:

"The legal profession is a long, hard battle for a woman. We are still only barely tolerated, and you're facing the same problem now that my generation of women lawyers had to contend with after World War I. A few of us got a foot in the door during the war, but when it was over the men began pushing us out again. All I can tell you is what I've observed over the years, that if a woman has the guts to stick it out she somehow survives."

Dorothy Kenyon reassured me that much of my difficulty in finding placement had little to do with personal qualifications but much to do with an entrenched bias against women in the legal profession. Few women had achieved partnership status in the large law firms and many were practicing on their own. When the racial factor was added, the prospect was even bleaker. I knew several Negro women who had studied law but who ultimately had to take jobs in other fields, often finding themselves overqualified for the positions they held and oppressed by a gnawing sense of personal failure. Some worked for Negro male attorneys as glorified clerks, doing legal drudgery and seeing little chance for advancement. A few courageous enough to strike out for themselves carried on their practice in a cubbyhole of another lawyer's suite or conducted it from home to save overhead. And I knew of one woman with a criminal-law practice who interviewed most of her clients on the courthouse steps.

I wound up with a job as law clerk earning twenty-five dollars a week, barely enough even in those days to cover food and shelter. In fact, while I was on that job I ate so many cheap hamburgers to save money on lunch that I developed a tapeworm. At least the job had one initial advantage; my employer, Charles L. Kellar, an aggressive, enterprising lawyer with a busy neighborhood practice on Fulton Street in the Bedford-Stuyvesant section of Brooklyn, also had a profitable business in buying and selling real estate. To induce me to work and live in Brooklyn, he offered to rent me an apartment in a house he had just purchased for resale. I had been living in a succession of rented rooms in Manhattan and wanted a place of my own. The rent of forty-five dollars was as reasonable as I could hope to find, and in addition, for another sixty dollars Mr. Kellar let me buy used furniture and household wares from another house he was selling.

Shortly after I moved in and got the place fixed up, Aunt Pauline came for Christmas and spent a month. The apartment was on the top floor of a small row house on Chauncey Street near the corner of Saratoga Avenue, across from a public school. An Italian family lived on the floor below and the new owners moved into the ground floor. It was a very humble place, but Aunt Pauline enjoyed it because there was steam heat, plenty of sunshine, everything was on one floor, and she could sit at the front room window and watch the children in the schoolyard across the street playing games under the supervision of their teachers. She would look at the teachers' gestures and tell you what they were saying to their classes.

Actually, the apartment was a railroad flat, with no privacy. All the rooms opened into one another and there were no doors, only doorways. Despite this inconvenience, six months after she returned to Durham, Aunt Pauline put the old family homeplace up for sale and she and Aunt Sallie arrived in Brooklyn to stay. Cramped as it was, at least I had my family problems under one roof and my two aunts would spend their last years with me.

Meanwhile I was breaking into legal practice the hard way. In the hierarchy of relationships in the court system, a law clerk not admitted to practice occupied the most menial position. I had no authority, no standing, and was a mere errand girl for my employer, running from court to court to file papers or answer calendars. When my employer was late, the judge bawled me out; when there was some minor irregularity in court papers, clerks would reject them and I was not permitted to make the corrections myself. I would have to take them back to the office and make an extra trip downtown. My waiting period for admission to practice was prolonged because I had moved to Brooklyn. I received notice of having passed the October bar examination around Christmas 1947, but I was required to reside in my new judicial department at least six months before presenting my papers to be processed. On the strength of having passed the bar I did manage to get another job, earning forty dollars a week as a law clerk to an attorney in lower Manhattan, but it made little difference in the lowliness of my position.

When finally sworn in and qualified to practice, I was again without a job, heavily in debt, and without a single client. My employer had nothing to offer me beyond a clerkship, and to continue working as a typist–errand girl had become an intolerable option. Then an opportunity developed which seemed ideal at the time. An attorney (whom I shall call Leighton Johns) practicing in lower Manhattan needed an associate to handle an overload of cases which came to him through his activity as coleader of a political club in Harlem. We worked out a fee-sharing arrangement which would allow me to build my own practice while working on matters he assigned me. I agreed to pay him a percentage of my fees toward office expenses, and he agreed to have my name added to his office door as a practicing attorney. I could hardly wait to get my own letterhead and printed announcements, and I christened my new legal stationery with a letter to Aunt Pauline (who had not yet left Durham), describing my first week of practice:

> Yesterday I presented my first case in court—lost it, but collected $25 from the client. We had a bad judge and our case was not too strong, so I didn't feel badly. I spent all Saturday tearing around, trying to keep a woman from being put out on the street and having her little place of business, her only means of livelihood, put out on the street by the Marshal. We succeeded and collected $75.00 for our pains. . . . Mr. Johns is having me handle criminal matters, and I have already appeared for two women charged with prostitution and a man charged with possession of numbers' slips. So you can see I am as busy as I can be even though my own business has not started. Mr. Johns has indicated he would like us to develop a partnership.

My letter did not mention that I had been embarrassed and angered during my first appearance in magistrate's court on behalf of the two women from Spanish Harlem arrested as prostitutes. The whole process was insulting to women—all women. Only the females were charged with an offense; their male customers were coerced into cooperating with the government as witnesses for the prosecution. At the end of the hearing the women were penalized, while the men went free. As if to underscore a general contempt for women implied in such prosecutions, the first witness, a white man from New Jersey, testified on the details of the sexual transaction and his payment of money. When asked to identify the woman with whom he had engaged in sexual intercourse, he unhesitatingly pointed directly at me, seated beside my two clients at the defense table! My face flamed, the court clerks took it as a huge joke and tittered audibly, the flustered prosecutor hastily tried to rehabilitate the witness' testimony, the judge denied my motion to dismiss the charge for failure to identify the defendant, and the unfortunate woman went to jail. My impassioned argument that the law was unfair to punish the woman while leaving her equally guilty partner free to continue his unsavory conduct had no effect upon the presiding judge.

About six months later I had a case that taught me the crucial importance of maintaining high professional standards. It showed how easily a hard-pressed lawyer, someone much like me, struggling alone, could fall into sloppy habits of practice which had serious ethical consequences. I was asked as a professional courtesy to represent another attorney, whom I did not know (and whom I shall call Judith Hinson), before the grievance committee of the bar association on a charge of professional misconduct. As a recently admitted lawyer who had just undergone intensive scrutiny by the Committee on Character and Fitness, I was deeply alarmed by the implications of such a charge. I doubted my competence to handle the case but could hardly refuse another member of my profession.

The facts were simple enough. A woman appearing as Mrs. Hinson's client complained that the attorney had borrowed several hundred dollars from her and given her a worthless check to cover the loan. When Mrs. Hinson failed to make good on the check, the complainant hired another attorney and brought suit. Mrs. Hinson entered a general denial of liability in the court action although she had no defense. She then failed to appear for trial, and the complainant got a judgment by default against her. When efforts to collect the judgment were unsuccessful, the complainant brought her grievance to the bar association. Ordinarily it would have been a simple matter of an uncollected debt, but the fact that an attorney was involved gave the case more serious implications. If the grievance committee found that Mrs. Hinson had attempted to defraud a client, she faced possible disbarment or suspension of her license to practice law.

In my first interview with Judith Hinson to prepare for her defense, I saw a middle-aged, almost threadbare, thoroughly frightened Negro woman and heard an all too familiar litany of a harsh struggle of someone at the bottom of the professional ladder, constantly threatened with defeat. As we talked, a picture emerged of a vulnerable woman in precarious circumstances scrabbling to make a living from a practice of small and uncertain fees. She was trapped in a web of restrictions which made a travesty of her high aspirations. Mrs. Hinson had grown up in the South, the daughter of a mother who taught school before her marriage and a father who was a professor and administrator at a small Negro college. After graduating from college, she taught there several years, then married and came to New York in the early 1930s. Caught in the Depression, she finally got a job teaching English on the WPA Adult Education Project. Her marriage ended in separation, "because I got tired of supporting my husband after seven years." When the teaching project was discontinued in 1940, Mrs. Hinson put herself through law school by working as a waitress, hotel maid, and household employee. She was thirty-six years old when admitted to practice law; she was now forty-one.

Isolated from the mainstream of her profession by her race and sex, she set up practice in a storefront office in Harlem and lived in a rented room. Her cases were mostly small matters in the lower courts, and her records showed that her earnings averaged about two thousand dollars a year. During some months her gross income was barely one hundred dollars.

At the hearing, Mrs. Hinson testified that the complainant was not her client but an acquaintance with whom she had developed a friendly relationship and whom she had represented in court without charge on six or seven occasions in a long-standing dispute between the complainant and her landlord. In the spring of 1948 a family emergency had arisen, and to save a relative from criminal prosecution Mrs. Hinson had borrowed over three hundred dollars from the complainant and given her a postdated check for the amount, with the understanding that the check would not be deposited without Mrs. Hinson's knowledge. She stated that she had offered a check instead of a promissory note to show her good faith and also in expectation of receiving a substantial fee for handling the sale of a building. Negotiations for the sale had not been completed on the due date of the check, which the complainant deposited without notifying Mrs. Hinson and which was returned for insufficient funds. The court proceedings followed.

My problem was to interpret the facts of this case in such a way that the affluent members of an all-white, all-male grievance committee, who were far removed from conditions in Harlem, could appreciate the difficulties of a marginal practice in an impoverished community where most of one's clients could not even afford to pay the barest expenses of their cases. An attorney dependent upon such a clientele would be as poor as the people she served and would find herself in such desperate straits, living from case to case and trying to juggle her finances, that she might well be unable to meet a particular financial obligation. I described the nature of Mrs. Hinson's practice, gave a graphic picture of the conditions under which she worked in a poor neighborhood, and pointed out that she had no clerical help and had to type all her own court papers and documents. Analyzing her income and expenses over the five years of her practice, I pointed out that Mrs. Hinson, like many lawyers in Harlem, was trying to gain a foothold on the slippery ascent of her profession, with none of the supportive structure to which downtown lawyers were accustomed. While she was expected to maintain the same standards of excellence, she and they in fact lived in different worlds. On the question of professional misconduct, I argued that the evidence at most indicated poor judgment and imprecise practice but not a willful intent to defraud. When beset by her own troubles, Mrs. Hinson had acted like a layperson. Her failure, I contended, was not one of evil intent but the inevitable outcome of her straitened circumstances.

The grievance committee was sufficiently persuaded to recommend no harsher discipline than a strong censure of Mrs. Hinson's conduct. When the hearing was over, the committee members called me in to commend me on my presentation. I was told it was the first time they had been made aware of the appalling conditions under which many Negro attorneys struggled against poverty and discrimination. Mrs. Hinson was vastly relieved, of course, to have escaped the humiliation of suspension or disbarment. I do not recall that our paths ever crossed again, but unknowingly she had rendered me a great service by making me realize the pitfalls of trying to practice law on the edge of insolvency. At the time, my own debts were more than twice the amount that had brought her to grief, and they would increase as my practice continued. Her case made such a strong impression on me that throughout my practice I kept on my desk an index card file of the individuals to whom I owed money and the amount of each debt. Whenever I could squeeze a payment on account, I entered the date, amount, and balance due on the card. Some of the installments were as little as five or ten dollars, and it took me more than twelve years to pay off my last obligation.

It was well that this lesson came early in my career, because I was never to have a financially thriving practice on my own. During the four years I had my own office, I was busy most of the time but operated what amounted to a one-woman "office of legal services," charging fees based more on a client's ability to pay than on the amount and quality of service rendered. Looking back on that period in later years, I would laugh and say, "My clients were poor but they were satisfied clients, and they referred to me their friends who were also poor, so we all starved together!"

After nine months of association with Leighton Johns, I still did not have my name on the office door as he had promised and he owed me more than four hundred dollars as my share of the fees he had collected on cases I had handled for him. Self-respect as well as economic necessity demanded that I strike out independently rather than continue to have my professional recognition and income dependent upon the whims of another. Clearly my sex made me an easy target for that kind of exploitation.

About this time, I was fortunate enough to develop a professional relationship with Ruth Whitehead Whaley, a native North Carolinian who had been admitted to practice law in New York State around 1925, the first Negro woman so qualified. She was winding up her private practice at 277 Broadway and moving toward public office, where she would end her career as secretary to the powerful New York City Board of Estimate, and she began referring me cases to handle for her. Mrs. Whaley was a short, dark woman barely five feet tall, whose quiet, deliberate speech and inner strength belied her small stature. She had a deeply religious faith and sprinkled our conversations with apt quotations from the Bible as often as she cited legal decisions. Listening to her, I felt she might easily have been an ordained minister instead of a lawyer. I greatly admired the qualities that had enabled her to pioneer for more than twenty years—part of that time as a widow bringing up her two children—in a field in which it was extremely difficult for a black woman to make headway. Our relationship of mutual trust deepened and continued until her death, nearly three decades later.

The difficulties of trying to establish a practice had their counterpart in pressures resulting from my changed living arrangements. Sharing the cramped Brooklyn apartment with Aunt Pauline and Aunt Sallie was not an easy adjustment for me after many years of being on my own. I also felt a heavy emotional responsibility for my aging aunts. They had uprooted themselves from the homeplace, where they had spent most of their lives and were accustomed to flower gardens, shade, fruit trees, and space to move about, to come to a strange city and be confined to three boxlike rooms. I worried over their separation from old friends and relatives. I worried even more about their growing frailties and the danger of costly illnesses that would wipe out our slender resources. By moving to Brooklyn they were at least closer to Aunt Marie Jeffers, their sister, who had been living in Manhattan for many years, but her precarious situation aggravated our anxieties. She was living alone, isolated without a telephone, in a run-down apartment house on Second Avenue near 125th Street, an unsafe neighborhood for an aged, decrepit person. Our constant fear was that she might be mugged or robbed on the street or in the dark hallways of her building. Every time I made a visit to check on her I was apprehensive, and it was a great relief to all of us when her son Jeff (Gerald), who lived on Long Island, persuaded her to move to Riverhead. There she lived in a little cottage with a telephone, and he was able to make daily visits.

Back at Chauncey Street, we scraped along on the edge of poverty, barely making ends meet. My earnings were sporadic, my aunts' pensions were meager, and there were times when our combined household income was less than the allowance for a family of three on public welfare. My aunts were sturdy souls, however, and continually amazed me by their capacity to get along on so little and their sense of ongoingness. For all their ailments, they had a tenacious grasp on life. Aunt Pauline's arthritis made it increasingly difficult for her to get about, but she busied herself at home writing poetry and almost every Sunday she managed to attend Saint Philip's Church on Macdonough Street, even when it meant walking long blocks to the bus stop in bad weather. Aunt Sallie spent most of her time making tailored clothes, when she was not immersed in a correspondence course on short story writing. We could not do much entertaining in our crowded quarters, but Aunt Pauline always managed to have ice cream and cake on hand when my brother Raymond (who had settled in Brooklyn with his wife and children) brought his family by for a visit, or Cousin Maude came over from Richmond Hill.

My great diversion in those days was an engaging tricolored Shetland sheep dog whose black-brown-and-white markings prompted me to name him Smokey. He was company for my aunts, and a succession of small boys from the neighborhood, whom I engaged to take Smokey out when I was away at work, also helped to keep them entertained.

At home, whenever I felt too confined or bottled up inside, a walk with Smokey eased the tension. Our favorite stop on those strolls about the neighborhood was the home on Macon Street of my old friend Maida Springer. I loved the bubbling exuberance and international flavor of the Springer household. Maida, who was my age, was born in Panama and had been brought to the United States when she was a small child. Her husband, Owen, had West Indian parentage, and they lived with their son Eric, then a student at Rutgers University, and Maida's vivacious mother, Adina Stewart. Their roomy four-story brownstone house served over the years as unofficial headquarters for people as diverse as trade union activists, visiting diplomats, newly arrived immigrants from Panama seeking jobs and sometimes emergency shelter, and African nationalist leaders who were in the United States to petition the United Nations and were grateful for a few hours of family warmth in a strange country.

"Moms" Stewart was a woman of such mischievous sparkle and infectious gaiety that everyone who entered the house immediately fell under her spell. As generous as she was effervescent, she had a talent for gathering in people from all walks of life, and she loved nothing better than to spread a feast for a small army of hungry guests. An elite chef when she first came to the United States from Panama, she seemed incapable of limiting her meals to her family of four. My fondest memories of the house on Macon Street are the odors of garlic and delicate spices, and of sitting at the kitchen table stuffing myself on Moms Stewart's huge, flaky biscuits, piles of steaming yellow rice cooked pilaf style with chicken, ham, and shrimps, crispy brown porgies, fried plantains, pickled salt mackerel, boiled codfish, and peas and other exotic Caribbean dishes.

As vibrant as her mother, Maida had a quiet grace that sheathed her passionate devotion to social justice, particularly for industrial workers. She had entered the garment trades as a young woman during the Depression years. A veteran of bitter picket line struggles when the industry was being organized in the 1930s, she was now business agent of the Dressmakers Union, Local 22, ILGWU, adjusting the daily grievances of some two thousand workers spread over the sixty shops of her territory in Manhattan's busy garment center. Trying to settle petty disputes between workers and employers who screamed at one another over the noise of throbbing machines was a contentious job, but Maida's gracious manner and sense of proportion made her a remarkably effective union representative.

During the twelve years I lived in Brooklyn, Maida and I were closely associated in various liberal causes. We were both members of the Liberal party of New York State, rang doorbells for Franklin D. Roosevelt, Jr., and for Jack Javits when the Liberals supported them in their elections to Congress, and campaigned vigorously in Brooklyn for Harry Truman on the Liberal party line in the presidential election of 1948. We were among the few Truman supporters in our district who believed he had a chance to beat Thomas E. Dewey, and I recall that on Election Night, even after Truman lost New York State, we refused to give up and stayed by the radio, keeping track of returns in other states until his victory was assured the next morning.

Our most ambitious political project, however, was my first—and only —bid for public office. I had never thought of running for anything until officials of the Liberal party approached me in 1949 and asked me to be the party's candidate for the City Council seat from Brooklyn's Tenth

Senatorial District, in which Maida and I both lived. I was flattered by the recognition. It was still rare in those days for women to be considered serious political contenders for any office, and they were all but ignored by both major parties. Of the more than sixty-five seats at stake in the city election that year, the Republicans and Democrats each named women for only two contests. The slightly more frequent appearance of women on minor party tickets was largely symbolic, since they had no chance of winning.

My first inclination was to refuse the designation because I did not relish a no-win contest on a third-party ballot. It would be an impossible situation; without financial resources, I was expected to cover an area which had the same boundaries as a congressional district and more than 100,000 voters. It included three assembly districts—Bedford-Stuyvesant, in which I lived, and the Bushwick and East New York sections of Brooklyn. The mainly white working-class residents of the last two districts were not likely to give many votes to an unknown Negro. I would also be running in a four-way contest against an organization Democrat, a Republican, and an American Labor party nominee in a traditionally Democratic stronghold. The Democrats had piled up 51 percent of the votes cast in that district in 1948, while the Liberals had trailed the other three parties, polling only 7 percent. (The party bigwigs didn't expect me to win, of course. They wanted a candidate at the bottom of the slate to help campaign for the top offices.)

On the other hand, as a budding feminist I recognized the importance of women actively seeking public office, whatever the immediate outcome, especially Negro women, who were then virtually invisible in politics. I had read with admiration of Maida's campaign for a seat in the New York State Assembly several years earlier under Labor-Liberal auspices, and although she did not win, she had given visibility to minority women in politics, and keeping alive that tradition was a worthy objective. A further nudge came from my mentor, Dr. Caroline Ware, when I telephoned her for advice. (Skipper's enigmatic response was, "If you're certain that you *won't* win, I think it's a capital idea!" I wondered how I could carry on an effective campaign unless I ran to win and believed there was an outside chance of victory.) Finally, Maida agreed to be my campaign manager. Her organizational experience and realistic grasp of Brooklyn politics were decisive factors in my decision to run.

As I look back on that campaign, I am still amazed at our chutzpah. We started from scratch, with no money and no organization. On sheer faith we rented the second floor of a creaking old building on Fulton Street, got together a little band of volunteers who had more enthusiasm than political savvy—except for Henry Pope, a friend and neighbor from the Urban

League, who chaired our committee—and operated on a budget of less than eight hundred dollars, which we raised in contributions, including twenty-five dollars that Mrs. Roosevelt sent me. We had no money for radio time, very little for paid advertisements or posters, and we could afford to use a sound truck only on the last few nights before election. Our forces were too thin to cover the district in house-to-house canvassing, so we had to reach the voters mainly at busy intersections in widely scattered neighborhoods. Night after night we stood on street ladders, shivering in the brisk October air, shouting ourselves hoarse and passing out little blue-and-white fliers containing my photograph, qualifications, and platform. We made enough noise to worry my Democratic opponent. He got hold of a flier, which listed my industrial work experience as well as my professional legal training, and since I had no political record he could attack, he charged that I was not qualified for public office because I was only a waitress. (He was in the hat business.)

Unlike my three opponents, who ran on straight party tickets, I had to campaign for the Liberal party's checkerboard slate, and that required some political dexterity. At the top of the ticket we supported former governor Herbert H. Lehman, a Democrat, running against Republican John Foster Dulles for the United States Senate. For mayor, the Liberals endorsed Republican-Fusion candidate Newbold Morris against the Democratic incumbent, William O'Dwyer, and the American Labor Party nominee, Congressman Vito Marcantonio. We had to explain to voters why Liberals supported a Democrat for a seat in the U.S. Senate while simultaneously fighting control of City Hall by the Democratic party's Tammany machine. In the councilmanic race at the bottom of the ticket, we stressed neighborhood concerns. Under the slogan "Good Government Is Good Housekeeping," our platform called for more traffic lights to protect the lives of children, cleaner streets and more frequent collection of garbage, keeping libraries open daily, more schools and playgrounds, and adequate housing for the aged and middle-income residents.

It boosted our morale when my candidacy received the endorsements of the *New York Post,* Americans for Democratic Action, and the Citizens Union, the last a prestigious nonpartisan body which issued a Voters Directory rating the various contestants. CU described me as "a lawyer with an exceptionally keen intellect, broad social vision and a wealth of experience in public affairs." The most touching endorsement, however, came from Aunt Pauline, who attended our final rally, held in a church basement on the Sunday before the election. When asked to say a few words, she made a motherly little speech about me, remarking, "My little girl is just like a little inchworm; in everything she does she just keeps inching along."

My predictable defeat on Election Night was overshadowed by the dismal failure of coalition politics for the top candidates in the city election. The Democrats won handily over their Republican-Fusion-Liberal party opponents. Newbold Morris, the reform candidate for mayor, lost to incumbent O'Dwyer by more than 300,000 votes. In the councilmanic race, my Democratic opponent, Sam Curtis, was swept into office with over 44,000 votes to my 14,145. Yet I had done far better than anyone expected, forging ahead of the Republican and ALP candidates to come in second, doubling the Liberal party vote of 1948, and polling 17 percent of the votes for the City Council seat from my district. I was surprised to receive letters of congratulation from friends who were active Democrats, telling me I had done an amazing job and that a political unknown who rolled up more than fourteen thousand votes was a potential vote-getter and had a future in politics. Although I had no desire to run for political office again, I thought of that campaign as a harbinger of things to come when, nineteen years later, Shirley Chisholm ran as a Democrat in the same general area of Brooklyn and was elected as the first Negro woman in Congress.

CHAPTER 24

States' Laws *and Visits with Mrs. R*

MY CAREER as a political candidate, brief as it was, would not have been possible if I had not managed to become my own boss. I had begun work on a preliminary study of racial segregation in the various states of the United States at the request of the Women's Division of Christian Service, Board of Missions of the Methodist Church, and it was on the strength of their small retainer fee that I opened a law office on April 1, 1949.

It was a big gamble, but for better or worse I was at least my own woman. After paying the first month's rent to sublet an office from Curtis F. McClane in a suite at 6 Maiden Lane, I had only two dollars left and the promise of a further retainer, which would carry me several months. The Maiden Lane suite was off Broadway about two blocks north of Wall Street and within walking distance of the law library and the courts. I now shared office space with three young lawyers—McClane, Vertner C. Tandy, and, occasionally, David Jones. We practiced separately and called ourselves The Wall Street Independents. We got along well together because we had two characteristics in common—very few clients and a fierce determination to practice law by the same standards as more affluent downtown lawyers. Most of the time we had to do our own clerical work, and so we considered we had made great progress when McClane, Tandy, and I were finally able to share a part-time typist–law clerk, an efficient young law student named Lydia P. Wilson, whom we each paid five dollars a week. Our work was competent, but we simply could not bring ourselves to "hustle up" clients in ways customarily recommended to newly practicing lawyers—joining a local political club, becoming active in many community organizations, or hanging around courthouses waiting to be assigned criminal cases. Our fastidiousness left us on the edge of insolvency a great deal of the time.

For two years after hanging out my shingle at 6 Maiden Lane, the research project for the Women's Division of the Methodist Church absorbed much of my energies. The unusual sponsorship of a massive legal study of laws on race and color by a churchwomen's group was the result of a leaven at work over many years among certain Methodist women. They had campaigned throughout the South for antilynching legislation in the 1920s and 1930s. Since 1941 they had issued pronouncements condemning racial discrimination and calling for a review of racial policies within their own denomination in order to bring their practices into harmony with their religious creed. A prominent member of the Women's Division, Dorothy Tilly, known for her courage in standing up to a lynch mob, served on President Truman's Committee on Civil Rights in 1946–47. The Committee, which issued a report unequivocally condemning the "separate but equal" doctrine, recommended "the elimination of segregation, based on race, color, creed, or national origin, from American life." Spurred by Mrs. Tilly's presentation of the Committee's findings, the Women's Division saw the report as a call to action.

The idea of a study originated with two staff members, Thelma Stevens, a native of Mississippi, and Dorothy Weber, a native of Louisiana. What they wanted was a memorandum from legal counsel advising them what they could or could not do under the law with respect to segregation in the thirty-one American states where they operated various church institutions.

When Thelma Stevens consulted the NAACP and the American Civil Liberties Union, she was dismayed to find they could offer little guidance. These groups examined the laws of a particular state when a case arose in it, but they knew of no available source that presented a comprehensive view of racial laws throughout the country. In fact, none existed. ACLU staff counsel Clifford Forster, recalling my law review article on fair employment practice legislation, thought I might be able to assist Miss Stevens and referred her to me. In a one-page memorandum addressed to me, she wrote:

> The point where we need your counsel most is in relation to a possible study of state laws that may or may not determine *practices,* in order to discover whether or not our policies are based on *custom* or *law.* We need to stem our action from that knowledge.
>
> Note the following illustrations: In Jacksonville, Florida, we have Brewster Hospital for Negroes, where segregation is practiced, *for exam-*

ple, in dining room service. Is this *law* or *custom?* What are the possible directions in which we can move?

In Tennessee, we have Scarritt College, a training school for missionaries and other Christian workers. All races *except* the Negro are full fledged students at Scarritt. How does the law relate to this practice in the light of the recent Supreme Court ruling? What are the possible directions in which we might move in order to admit Negroes to Scarritt College, the only graduate school of its type in the Methodist Church?

Citing examples of settlement houses, community centers, and other institutions run by the Women's Division in various southern states, Miss Stevens wanted to know whether these facilities could be opened to all groups without discrimination, and asked: "Do you think it advisable to have a study made of state laws as they relate to such problems as the above? If so, what procedures would you advise?"

At first I resisted the assignment because it would take time from my private law practice, but the seed for such a study had already been planted in my mind during student days at Howard University Law School. In our Civil Rights Seminar, Dr. Ransom had insisted that each student digest the segregation laws of the particular southern state in which he or she intended to practice. The result had been startling. Until then, we had concentrated our resentment upon the bus driver who ordered us to the rear of the bus or the conductor who ejected us from a train when we refused to sit in the Jim Crow car. Now we learned that the bus driver, under pain of criminal penalty, was required by law to segregate Negro and white passengers and was given the powers of a peace officer to enforce this policy. What we needed to do was to attack the legality of the laws under the authority of which local officials acted. And we needed to make the public aware of the existence of these laws. Miss Stevens' request coincided with this desire on my part.

In November 1948, however, neither Thelma Stevens nor I dreamed that her one-page inquiry would generate a printed volume of 746 pages! Had I known where it would lead, I would not have attempted such a prodigious task, and the Women's Division certainly would not have approved such an expensive venture. We were all blessedly ignorant of the scope of the study, and fortunately it could develop by stages.

In the process of answering Miss Stevens' inquiry, I found that southern states had such detailed racial codes that the restrictions they imposed affected the internal policies of private institutions not specifically covered by the statutes. On the other hand, a number of states outside the South had moved in the opposite direction and enacted numerous laws to protect civil rights. Given the large number of states in which the Women's Division was operating and the wide variation of laws from state to state, I recommended in my memorandum to Miss Stevens a presentation of *all* state legislation relating to race or color, whether to enforce racial separation or to prohibit racial discrimination.

Thelma Stevens, a stalwart, dedicated Christian then in her mid-forties, defied my racial stereotype of a white Mississippian. Her commitment to the demise of racial segregation was as unswerving as my own. A graduate of Scarritt College, who had devoted her entire career to church work, much of it in the South, she saw immediately the tremendous educational value of exposing churchwomen of conscience to the actual texts of segregation statutes and allowing them to compare this legislation with civil rights laws. With characteristic forthrightness she was able to lead her organization step by step along an uncharted path. First she persuaded the Methodist women to accept my recommendation on faith, then she went back again and again for additional funds to complete a study, which eventually came to seem endless. One of her strongest allies was Susie E. Jones, a prominent Negro woman from Greensboro, North Carolina, wife of the then president of Bennett College, who worked ceaselessly in the policy-making committee to keep the project alive and bring it to a successful conclusion.

This opportunity to serve the cause of civil rights, which had come from a wholly unexpected source, challenged my skills and imagination in ways I had never anticipated while in law school. The work had none of the drama and excitement of arguing a test case before the Supreme Court, which most lawyers dream about. It lacked the intellectual stimulation of developing legal theories persuasive to lawyers and judges. There was only the drudgery of ferreting out and presenting the texts of laws which I hoped would carry an intrinsic argument against Jim Crow, and it was this hope that kept me doggedly at the task. I spent every spare moment at the New York County Law Library, including evenings, weekends, and holidays, laboriously copying voluminous statutes in longhand, followed by endless hours in the office typing out what I had copied. (There were no photocopying machines in those days and making photostats was too expensive.)

Between the copying and the typing I developed a ritual that seemed as important to the study as the work itself. To get to the law library from Maiden Lane, I walked up Broadway and cut through the churchyard of Saint Paul's Chapel to the gate that brought me out on Vesey Street, near the library entrance. Whenever I passed through the churchyard at noon I stopped in Saint Paul's for the noonday service. At other times I would slip inside whenever the doors were open and sit in the rear of the empty chapel for a few minutes before heading for the library stacks. The fact that I was authorized by a church organization to work in an area of human relations claiming my deepest loyalties had profound significance for me.

Although the study was entitled *States' Laws on Race and Color,* I added a set of appendixes which included a number of local ordinances, relevant provisions of the federal Constitution, acts of Congress, executive orders, departmental regulations, the texts of the Universal Declaration of Human Rights and related United Nations documents, as well as three recent Supreme Court decisions that had struck down segregation on railway dining cars and in two state universities.

The piled-up pages of the final manuscript were more than a foot high. When I put it in outsized three-ring binders and lugged it up to Thelma Stevens's office, we spread the binders on a table and gazed at our mutual project with unbelieving eyes. The Women's Division had originally envisioned a mimeographed booklet; they were now confronted with an unwieldy document which would be of limited use in its present form. Thelma Stevens had to go back to her committee, which, confronted with the sheer bulk of the manuscript, took the final step and authorized its publication in book form. Months of patient forbearance followed as the editorial and publications department of the Methodist women wrestled with my many drafts, revisions, and corrections, and I agonized over changes in the laws that occurred before the book was in print.

Monday morning, March 5, 1951, began as any other day in my law office, until the telephone rang and I recognized Thelma Stevens' voice at the other end.

"This is the day which the Lord has made!" she almost shouted over the wire. Her triumphant announcement needed no translation. My first published book, *States' Laws on Race and Color,* was off the press!

Miss Stevens had called from her home, where she was in bed with pneumonia, but she told me that five copies would be delivered to my office within the next hour. I was so excited I told her not to bother sending the books; I would pick them up in person. I bolted from the office to the nearest subway and arrived at the Methodist building as though propelled. Dorothy McConnell, editor of the Methodist publication *World Outlook and Literature,* had left the package at the reception desk for me, with a note saying, "Miss Murray, Here is the baby. . . ."

I dared not open the package. It was a moment I could not endure alone, so I called Maida Springer at the Dressmakers Union and shortly thereafter arrived at a small cafeteria in the West Thirties, the heart of New York City's tumultuous garment center, lugging a heavy briefcase in one hand and my precious package in the other. Maida met me there, and after much fumbling I got the wrappers off. I sat in a daze, staring at the bright-yellow dust jacket with the title and my name in bold green letters on the front cover, wholly oblivious of the usual lunch hour clatter and confusion. From far away across the table I heard Maida's voice reflecting my own awe.

"Pauli, this is it! It's really happened! It's beautiful!"

A few weeks later, the Women's Division of Christian Service released the book with appropriate fanfare. Their executive committee, presided over by Mrs. Frank Brooks of Mount Vernon, Iowa, held a ceremony at their headquarters to present "first copies" of *States' Laws on Race and Color* to distinguished representatives of the United Nations, the clergy, the law, and American libraries—Ben Frederick Carruthers from the U.N. Commission on Human Rights, retired Bishop Francis J. McConnell for the clergy, Judge Dorothy Kenyon for the law, and Paul Rice North, chief of the Reference Department of the New York Public Library, for library organizations.

I was not present, having landed in the hospital with a misbehaving thyroid, but Maida took Aunt Pauline and Aunt Sallie to the ceremony. They were all as proud as peacocks, but Aunt Pauline, as my representative, received special attention. Wearing her best broadcloth tan suit and a flowered hat, she relished all the congratulations, the large bouquet of orchids presented to her, and the picture-taking with the dignitaries, each holding a "first copy."

Although the Methodist women had published the book for distribution within their own organization, they accomplished more than they had anticipated. Carol K. Simon, a member of the New York State Commission Against Discrimination, reviewing the book in the New York County Lawyers' Association *Bar Bulletin,* wrote that it "constitutes an important addition to the growing body of literature concerned with human relations" and "will serve as a primary source useful to public and private agencies charged with the responsibility of building better inter-group relations." Noting its sponsorship by the women of the Methodist Church and that it was intended to answer the recurring question of whether that church's own racial policies were based on "law," "custom," or "tradition," Commissioner Simon observed: "A study of this comprehensive book will be helpful not only for answering that question but to aid lawyers in giving sound advice to those clients who seek their opinions in this field." The reviewer predicted that the study's "usefulness will be far beyond the original scope as outlined by the Women's Division of the Methodist Church."

The book had a short but strategic career. The American Civil Liberties Union secured a grant from the Field Foundation to purchase and distribute nearly a thousand copies to all state law libraries, Negro colleges, selected law schools, human rights agencies, and key individuals around the country concerned with human rights. I was told that Thurgood Marshall kept enough copies on hand to supply each member of the NAACP staff and that he called *States' Laws on Race and Color* the "bible" during the final stages of the legal attack upon the "separate but equal" doctrine. Three years after the book came out, the Supreme Court struck the fatal blow to "separate but equal" by its ruling in the historic school desegregation case *Brown* v. *Board of Education*. Although a 1955 supplement of *States' Laws* was prepared with the assistance of a young attorney, Verge Lake, and published by the Women's Division, the laws changed so rapidly after *Brown* that the book was soon out of date and within a few years had become a historical document. During its brief existence, however, it had helped to further the developments that made it obsolete.

At the time I was beginning to research racial segregation in the United States, Eleanor Roosevelt was completing her monumental achievement as a delegate to the United Nations—the creation of the Universal Declaration of Human Rights, adopted by the U.N. General Assembly on December 10, 1948. I had followed her public activities closely after she left the White House and felt an almost personal pride in her emergence as a world leader. From time to time I would send her one of my published articles or a poem I thought she might like, and our friendship continued to grow.

During that period, in spite of her crowded schedule, Mrs. Roosevelt found time to invite me to her New York apartment for tea or dinner once or twice a year, or for an occasional weekend at Val-Kill Cottage in Hyde Park, New York. She liked having young friends around, and I think she admired and trusted my habit of not letting her high position prevent me from speaking out on a political issue when I disagreed with her. For me, these visits were like pilgrimages for renewal of the spirit. I sensed an unspoken spiritual bond between us, and I treasured them so much I could not bear to keep them all to myself. With her amused indulgence, I usually contrived to bring along a family member or close friend to share the magic of her presence. The excitement these social calls generated was a blend of awe and delight in about equal measure, and I enjoyed watching each person who met Mrs. Roosevelt face to face discover, as I had done, that the First Lady of the World was as comfortable to be with as one's own favorite aunt.

My greatest thrill was taking Aunt Pauline and Aunt Sallie to Hyde Park in mid-August 1952 to have lunch with Mrs. Roosevelt at her cottage and to tour the Roosevelt Memorial Library. I borrowed a car for the day and drove "my ladies" up in grand style. Characteristically, Mrs. Roosevelt treated them like royal guests in an informal family setting which made them feel right at home—a picnic luncheon on the lawn with just ourselves, her personal secretary, Malvina (Tommy) Thompson, several small grandchildren, and a few in-laws. Mrs. Roosevelt herself, with Tommy's help, served the tables.

It was a historic occasion for my aunts, and Aunt Pauline, in what was probably the longest letter she had written in her eighty-two years, sent a round-robin account to all of our relatives and friends in Durham, savoring every detail of our day-long trip. She told them, for example:

. . . We got lost and went about 5 miles too far because we missed the two stone gateposts that lead to Mrs. Roosevelt's home, Val-Kill Cottage. . . . It was all right because Mrs. Roosevelt had forgotten to order the fish and so lunch was delayed anyway.

. . . When we got to the house, Mrs. Roosevelt came right out to greet us just like Aunt Mary would have done. . . .

[At lunch, everybody] was engaged in conversation. Pauli and Mrs. Roosevelt talked politics, Miss Thompson and I on teaching, Sallie and Mrs. John Roosevelt on the raising and training of children. The young Mrs. Roosevelt [wife of Curtis Roosevelt] just listened. I peeped into the kitchen and saw this lovely looking cook and handsome butler and wondered if she were Rosebud's girl [daughter of a neighbor in Durham].

. . . Before we left, Pauli took pictures of Mrs. Roosevelt standing between Sallie and me.

Mrs. Roosevelt had driven us through the woods to the Roosevelt Library and had then seen to it that we had a personally conducted tour of FDR's boyhood home: "Thirty-five rooms and nine baths," Aunt Pauline reported in awe, ending her letter: "It was a wonderful day that I'll never forget. We will all remember it."

Because of her heavy schedule, "Mrs. R," as close friends referred to Mrs. Roosevelt, often squeezed in a purely social visit with me while she pursued more weighty matters of international importance. One weekend at Hyde Park, I found myself staring across the luncheon table at the Soviet delegate to the United Nations, Andrei Gromyko, and his wife. (I suspect they were as startled to see my brown face as I was to see them, but it was Mrs. Roosevelt's way of getting to know Mr. Gromyko and telling him "a few things I feel," as her biographer Joseph Lash later wrote.) Another time, some years later, I arrived for tea at her New York apartment, to discover that Mrs. Roosevelt had gathered a small group of Protestant religious leaders for an informal discussion of the Israeli-Egyptian crisis with Golda Meir, then Israel's U.N. representative, and Judge

Justine Wise Polier, whom I greatly admired. Such encounters gave me the heady experience of being a spectator of world history in the making. At other times I got intimate glimpses of the private person—Mrs. Roosevelt at her breakfast table in Val-Kill Cottage, gaily feeding her Scottie dog bacon scraps from her plate and saying with a guilty chuckle, "I don't dare do this when my son John is around. He always chides me for it." Or watching Mrs. Roosevelt quietly putting money in her pledge envelope for Saint James Episcopal Church in Hyde Park while we talked about politics.

Of course, tales of Mrs. Roosevelt's enormous resourcefulness in coping with sudden emergencies are legion. My fondest recollection of her is her refusal to let a major hurricane disrupt her schedule of commitments. My twenty-one-year-old niece, Bonnie, and I were invited to spend a quiet weekend at Val-Kill Cottage in October of 1954. Bonnie's dream was to meet Mrs. Roosevelt in person. A true child of the Roosevelts' White House years, she had been born in Washington the month Mrs. R became First Lady. As a precocious eleven-year-old, she had avidly supported my sit-in activities when I was a student at Howard Law School, and she was heartbroken over being left at home when her mother, Mildred, went with Aunt Pauline and me to have tea at the White House in 1944. I promised her then that I would make amends, and now, ten years later, the Hyde Park weekend was in honor of her recent graduation from Catholic University.

I could not have conceived a more spectacular graduation present. According to plan, Bonnie and I arrived at Mrs. Roosevelt's apartment promptly at five o'clock on Friday afternoon, the fifteenth, to drive with her to Hyde Park. Just as we were leaving the city, Hurricane Hazel roared into New York. We sped along the parkways, trying to outrun the storm, Mrs. Roosevelt on the front seat, her chauffeur, William White (brother of the singer Josh White), at the wheel, Bonnie and I huddling in the back, the wind and rain raging in violent gusts about us, snapping off branches of trees and scattering debris in our path. As the storm increased in fury, Bonnie and I became more and more frightened, but Mrs. Roosevelt merely relaxed and took a nap, as she often did to rest between engagements.

We arrived at Val-Kill Cottage barely ahead of Hazel's full force and greatly relieved to have reached shelter, only to find that the storm had knocked out the electric plant. The house was in total darkness and without water. Unperturbed, Mrs. Roosevelt lighted a candle and led the way upstairs, as we followed with our bags. Then came her astounding announcement: "Hurry up, girls, and put your things down. We have an engagement at Bard College and we don't want to keep them waiting."

Mrs. Roosevelt had promised to read selections from *Winnie-the-Pooh,*
T. S. Eliot, and James Stephens to a group of students at the college, in
Annandale-on-Hudson, and her schedule included having dinner with
President James H. Case and his wife before her reading began. The school
was more than an hour's drive away in good weather, and I doubt that
anyone else would have braved Hurricane Hazel to keep the appointment, but of course Mrs. Roosevelt was *not* just anyone else. She had made
a commitment and did not want the students to be disappointed.

She bustled us out into the storm again without giving us time to
change our clothes. We skittered along the utterly deserted road littered
with fallen tree limbs, at times plowing through swirling rivulets up to our
hub caps, while the wind screamed and rain smashed against the windshield, blocking our vision beyond a few feet. If Mrs. Roosevelt worried
about our safety, she said nothing; her main concern seemed to be
whether we would get to Bard College in time for the reading. She lightly
dismissed the fact that none of us was dressed for dinner.

We succeeded in getting within walking distance of the school before
an uprooted tree lying across the road stopped us. Abandoning the car, we
stumbled on foot the rest of the way, arriving bedraggled and hungry well
after the dinner hour, to be greeted by astonished students who had long
since given up hope that anyone would venture abroad on such a night.
Mrs. Roosevelt's presence had an electrifying effect. Vigorous as ever, she
proceeded immediately to the business at hand, and we all sat on the floor
in front of the blazing fireplace of a big common room, enthralled as we
listened to the cadences of her lovely reading voice. Mrs. Roosevelt had
a gift for dramatic reading I had not known about, and her sparkling
performance that evening was well worth all the trouble we had in getting
to Bard. We finally got something to eat, but only after the students (who
insisted upon encores) let her go; Mrs. Case fixed us sandwiches and coffee
before we started back to Hyde Park.

Luckily, by the time we were ready to leave, Hurricane Hazel had
blown northward, leaving only a steady downpour behind, which battered
the car as we drove slowly back to Val-Kill. The power plant was still out
when we arrived, and we found our way about the house with candles.

"Breakfast at nine, girls," Mrs. Roosevelt told us cheerfully as she
showed us to bed.

Hazel's aftermath had its comic side. Next morning I woke at eight
o'clock and tested the light above my bed. Since the electricity was still
off, my one worry was whether there would be any water for coffee. I was
startled by a knock on the door, followed by the appearance of a tall
apparition in the doorway, clothed in a white terry-cloth robe, a towel
turbaned about the head, a barely visible face freshly scrubbed and strawberry pink. The apparition was Mrs. Roosevelt.

"I'll tell you girls what you can do this morning, since there's no water for a bath," she sang out, her mind on cleanliness. "There's a swimming pool around by John's house and nobody uses it this time of year. I just came back. I took my soap and towel down with me, rubbed myself all over with soap, looked up and down the road to see that nobody was coming, and I just went right down in the pool and took my bath. If you hurry, you can do the same. Just be sure nobody's looking," she finished, and went off down the hall to dress.

Bonnie and I exchanged dubious glances over this Spartan proposal. Reluctant to take a bath outdoors in an exposed area in mid-October, we were equally ashamed to admit we were less sturdy than Mrs. Roosevelt, who was then seventy years old. Putting on our bathrobes, we got soap and towels and made our way out into the crisp morning air, walking self-consciously across the lawn in hope that no one in the John Roosevelt house would see us. Just as we were sneaking past the back door, Anne Roosevelt, John's wife, came out and stared at us in utter bewilderment. Sheepishly, we told her we were looking for the pool.

"Oh, but you *can't* take a swim in the pool this time of the year," she told us.

When we explained that Mrs. Roosevelt had suggested we take our baths in it, she politely showed us the pool, which was in plain view of the long road leading into the Val-Kill Cottage grounds. As we approached, we saw a truck coming along the road, carrying several large milk cans. (Mrs. Roosevelt had sent her handyman to fetch an emergency supply of water.) As if the oncoming truck were not enough to shatter any thought of privacy, the John Roosevelt family's huge dog—part St. Bernard and part shepherd—ambled down to the pool and leisurely began lapping water. We gingerly stuck our toes into the pool, made a stab at washing, and hurried back to the cottage, to find that the power plant had come on and we could take our baths in normal fashion.

Our embarrassing escape was not allowed to pass in silence. Over in the John Roosevelt house, little seven-year-old Sally Roosevelt was excitedly describing to her mother how she had looked out the window earlier and watched "Grandmere" take off her robe and march down the steps into the pool. Anne Roosevelt, thinking the whole incident funny, made it the conversation piece of the day. At luncheon she told of finding two bemused strangers near her back door that chilly morning, searching for the swimming pool. Mrs. Roosevelt had a wonderful sense of humor and laughed heartily at the tale. Underneath all the merriment, however, I saw an example that weekend of the indomitable courage—"lighting a candle in the darkness" became Mrs. Roosevelt's epitaph—which shone as a great beacon light to women like me in the years ahead.

CHAPTER 25

"Past Associations"

IN THE EARLY 1950s, few people active in public affairs escaped un-
harmed from the growing fear of communism and the resulting suspicion
of disloyalty among American citizens which had been building since the
end of World War II. U.S. Senator Joseph R. McCarthy seized upon the
issue of "Communists in government," or in other positions of influence,
and fanned the flames of suspicion into a national hysteria. My own encounter with McCarthyism in 1952 delivered a shattering blow to my
self-esteem and changed the course of my career for a time.

Under the Internal Security Act of 1950, which Congress passed over
President Truman's veto, millions of Americans in and out of government
were subjected to loyalty clearance programs, which included intensive
investigations into their lives reaching back to childhood. Mere membership at some time in the past in an organization listed by the attorney
general as a "Communist front" was sufficient to cause one to be discharged from government service as a "bad security risk." Reputations
were destroyed overnight, and professional people were blacklisted on the
basis of rumor, gossip, and other unsupported charges of subversive activities.

The legal profession reflected the sharp change in the political climate
by altering its admission procedures. In 1945 I was admitted to the California bar on a simple affidavit. By 1948, when I applied to practice in New
York State, the regulations of the Committee on Character and Fitness of
the Appellate Division, Supreme Court of New York, Second Judicial
Department, which passed on my application, required each candidate to
answer a detailed questionnaire designed to test the issue of loyalty to the

United States and its institutions. I was obliged to list every organization to which I had belonged, with dates of membership, every article I had published, with date of publication and name of periodical, and I had to be prepared to submit copies of the articles upon request. Every address where I had resided from birth on was to be listed in chronological order, supported by sworn affidavits from two persons not members of my family who had visited me at that particular address and could describe the character of my surroundings and associates. All documentation was scrutinized by a member of the Committee, who then examined me orally and called for additional material if any questions remained. When I was finally approved at the end of this formidable process, I told my friends that I had just experienced the earthly version of the Final Judgment!

In my relief over having been cleared to practice law, I did not foresee that in the atmosphere of McCarthyism the issue of one's loyalty was never finally resolved. It resurfaced in new situations, to be tested by differing standards, so that trying to prove one's loyalty was like searching for firm ground in an area of treacherous quicksand. In early 1952 I applied for a position which perfectly matched the technical skills I had gained in compiling *States' Laws on Race and Color.* The job was that of research assistant to the Director of Codification of Laws of Liberia, one of many projects developed under Point Four, the program President Truman initiated to provide technical assistance to underdeveloped nations. By an agreement between the U.S. Department of State and the Republic of Liberia, the three-year project would be conducted under the auspices of the New York State School of Industrial and Labor Relations at Cornell University. Dr. Milton R. Konvitz, a professor of that school and a specialist in constitutional and labor law, would direct the project and under his supervision the assistant would carry the main responsibility for technical research, working in close cooperation with the New York State Law Revision Commission, also located at Cornell.

The scarcity of Negroes in international jobs was a matter of concern among civil rights advocates, and the opening presented an opportunity for a significant breakthrough in this field. My qualifications boosted me over the hazards of race and gender, so that I was easily the leading candidate for the position. However, in my job interview at Cornell with project director Konvitz and M. P. Catherwood, dean of the School of Industrial and Labor Relations, who had the power to make the appointment, I discovered that the latter was an extremely cautious man, whose main concern seemed to be the issue of loyalty. He said he did not know whether the State Department would set up loyalty requirements comparable to those for federal employees, even though the work would be done under contract with a nongovernmental institution, but anticipating that this *might* be the case, he wanted to know if there was anything in my background that might raise questions in this area. I summarized my political and organizational background, and having no reason to suppose that the inquiry made by the Committee on Character and Fitness would not satisfy Cornell, I offered to submit the same documentation, which I did.

I underestimated the degree to which academics had become captives of McCarthy's scare tactics. A warning of trouble came some days later when Dr. Konvitz called to say that while my references had made laudatory statements about my character and qualifications, they had said very little about my loyalty to the United States. In addition, he said, Dean Catherwood felt that a recommendation from someone of more conservative reputation than the references I had supplied would be extremely helpful to my candidacy. It seemed that the Cornell hierarchy wanted to be "covered" in the event a conservative member of their board of governors raised a question about my activist background, and they felt it imperative that my personnel record show an exhaustive examination had been conducted and that the university had satisfied itself I was a loyal citizen. I was dumbfounded. In my view, the people who had written letters of recommendation on my behalf had unimpeachable credentials; they were nationally known leaders who held positions of public trust and whose integrity was beyond question, including Mrs. Franklin D. Roosevelt; my friend and sponsor for admission to the New York bar, Lloyd K. Garrison; William H. Hastie, then serving on the United States Court of Appeals for the Third Circuit; the future Supreme Court Justice Thurgood Marshall; and the nationally known non-Communist labor leader A. Philip Randolph. I had to tell Dr. Konvitz I simply did not know anyone of more "conservative" persuasion who was well enough acquainted with me to give an informed opinion. The people who had recommended me had worked with me over the years in various settings and could speak authoritatively about my political outlook. If *their* judgment was questionable, then there was no one who could vouch for my loyalty. I did get in touch with my sponsors, however, to tell them about the problem and request them to send in supplementary statements. I also suggested to Dr. Konvitz that he have me subjected to the same loyalty clearance required of federal employees for overseas assignments so that the issue could be resolved by standardized procedures. Dr. Konvitz, who genuinely wanted me on the project, immediately consulted the State Department, which informed him such clearance would take too long—at least five months— and besides, the State Department used the practice of having projects carried out under contract with academic institutions for the very reason that it wanted to be relieved of protracted investigations of prospective personnel. It left the resolution of the loyalty issue entirely with Cornell University.

A letter from Dean Catherwood informed me that Cornell found it expedient to reject my application. He wrote:

> As indicated in interview and discussions we think well of your qualifications ... however, there were some questions concerning your past associations which I felt might place the University in a difficult situation. . . . Without any prejudice to or against you, under conditions where it is difficult, if not impossible, years after the event to resolve such questions completely, it has seemed to me that we should not consider further the possibility of your appointment to the position in question.

Dr. Konvitz, the unhappy go-between, had already telephoned to explain the rationale of the Cornell University administration. He said there was absolutely no question in their minds as to my high character, integrity, and personal honesty, or my qualifications for the job. However, they thought they ought to give "one hundred percent protection" to the university in the area of "public relations"; that in view of "the troublous times in which we live," they felt they ought to be extraordinarily cautious in the matter of employment; that "being well," they "ought not to invite a sick bed"; in short, they ought not to take any chances by inviting criticism that *might* arise out of the employment of a person with a background like mine, when they might be able to find a person equally qualified who did not have such a background.

What infuriated me was that I was being rejected on the basis of innuendo, a vague and shadowy inference more difficult to confront than a specific charge of disloyal conduct. "Past associations," a catchall term hinting disgrace, raised and left dangling the vital question of my relationship to my country, yet foreclosed any opportunity for me to clear my name, since Cornell had taken the position it owed no obligation to anyone not already employed by the university. I could take no appeal from a judgment that cast a shadow on my future career. Influential liberal friends counseled that I do nothing, apprehensive that any attempt to challenge the decision would expose my reputation to public damage. I was locked into an intolerable situation with no way to fight back.

Aunt Pauline and Aunt Sallie indirectly pointed out the answer to my dilemma. They did not attempt to deal with the political complexities of my situation but spoke from the wisdom of years of human experience. Aunt Pauline saw it as just one more test of my character and told me I would overcome this trial as I had overcome others in the past if I just trusted in the Lord and did not lose faith in myself. Aunt Sallie quoted an old saying that when one door in life is closed against us, God opens another to a greater opportunity than we ourselves could have planned. At the time I was too bruised and rebellious to share fully my aunts' serene faith. I was undergoing a crisis of my own faith, screaming against the unfairness of life and asking myself whether my years of struggle to prepare myself had been worth it if I was to be chopped down at the very moment I reached for my greatest opportunity. I was standing at a crossroads in my career, not knowing which way to turn.

For a time I was caught up in a tension between two warring values —the familiar words of faith and hope that were the essence of my family tradition and the fear and suspicion that ruthlessly stripped me of individuality and discarded me like unwanted refuse. Then, in one of those inexplicable flashes of insight, the phrase that had tormented me suddenly took on new meaning. The Fitzgeralds, my mother's family, with whom I had grown up, were actually my earliest and most enduring "past associations." They had instilled in me a pride in my American heritage and a rebellion against injustice. Those proud, independent forebears who stubbornly held their ground and refused to be cowed by adversity had peopled my childhood. The example of courage they set had fueled my own political activism. My best answer to Cornell in defense of "past associations" would be to turn the phrase on its head and present the doughty Fitzgeralds as my first exhibit.

The thought grew so compelling that I rolled a sheet of paper into the typewriter and began to write:

> If Grandfather Robert George Fitzgerald had not volunteered for the Union forces in 1863, and come South three years later as a missionary among the Negro freedmen, our family might not have walked in such proud shoes and felt so assured of its official place in American history. We might have fought our battles with poverty and color troubles, thinking of ourselves as nobodies or not thinking of ourselves at all, and died out with nothing to remember about us except a few census figures. Grandfather's struggle made all the difference, although Grandmother Cornelia supplied her share of pride. He was our beacon light. This unknown Civil War landsman and private who served only six months in the Union Navy and less than ten months in the Union Army, who fought in only one battle and was twice discharged as physically unfit, nevertheless gave us a sense of belonging, to which we clung no matter how often it was snatched from us.

In the depths of frustration, a door had opened unexpectedly. It was the beginning of my journey back in time to rediscover the strength of my roots and to reaffirm my identity. The idea of writing a family story "from the inside," as Stephen Vincent Benét once urged me to do, had been on my mind for many years. I had done some preliminary research and even scribbled some sketches, but had never found time for a sustained effort. Now, without my planning it, *Proud Shoes* presented itself, demanding to be written.

I had no idea at the time that I was embarking on a project so absorbing that it would cause me to suspend my law practice and would take four years to complete. Fortunately, I had a good friend in the publishing field who had faith in me. Marie F. Rodell, a literary agent, who had been trying to sell my poetry manuscript, had also been prodding me to write a book. I sent her a draft of the first chapter of *Proud Shoes,* with a note saying: "If you think this is a good piece of writing, then you can thank Cornell for it. . . . Anyway, this writing madness is causing me to neglect what little practice I do have."

Marie Rodell was more than a competent author's representative with a command of the literary market. She was a warm, sympathetic human being who understood the peculiar problems of writers. Herself a former author and editor of mystery fiction, she knew how vulnerable many writers are to editorial rejections, writing blocks, chronic lack of funds, and other impediments to steady creative production, and she worked as hard to ease her authors over these difficulties as she did to sell their manuscripts. Without her continual support, I doubt whether *Proud Shoes* would have reached publication. I was a skittish author, easily discouraged by editorial criticism and constantly needing to be rescued from financial difficulties which slowed the progress of the book. When I panicked and lost confidence in myself, Marie wheedled and coaxed me back to the typewriter. When funds were low she steered me toward resources that kept me going. At her suggestion I applied for and got a grant from the Eugene F. Saxton Memorial Trust, established by Harper & Brothers (now Harper & Row) to encourage distinguished writing and assist creative writers. To accept the $2,500 grant and devote full time to the book, I first had to pay off some debts, so I closed my law office to save expenses and took a job for six months as a social investigator in the Department of Welfare.

By the fall of 1953 I had written an outline and several chapters, which Marie submitted to Elizabeth Lawrence (Kalashnikoff), a senior editor at Harper & Brothers. Elizabeth, a woman with a keen appreciation for the many cultural strains in American life, thought my story was an important one which should be told, and she and Marie together shepherded the book to completion. Harper & Brothers gave me a contract with a modest advance, and upon Elizabeth's recommendation I was accepted for several weeks' residence at the famous MacDowell Colony for artists in Peterborough, New Hampshire, where I could write in privacy without interruptions. (It is a commentary on the times that James Baldwin and I were the first Negro writers to be admitted to the Colony, both in the summer of 1954.) Toward the end, when my funds ran out, Marie enabled me to support myself by transcribing dictation belts and typing final manuscripts for some of her authors who needed clerical assistance.

At first my three aunts, who were the oldest surviving Fitzgeralds and whose memories were vital to the story I was writing, were nervous about the undertaking, apprehensive that it might expose embarrassing details of family history. Once they got over their initial fears, the project became a family enterprise. They developed a proprietary interest in the saga that was unfolding and supplied me with numerous anecdotes and valuable clues to the past. When I worked at home, Aunt Pauline and Aunt Sallie would hover over my desk, each vying with the other to give her version of an incident as she remembered it. When I visited Aunt Marie to get her account, I would sometimes have to choose among three variations of the same episode. They listened avidly to my reports of field trips in which I traced the movements of the older Fitzgeralds, and their eyes glowed with satisfaction when they learned that their ancestors had left the mark of their existence in local census, property, and tax records which confirmed the legends my aunts had heard in childhood.

My own exhilaration over successfully tracking down clues to the past sometimes bordered on a mild sort of lunacy, a common affliction of genealogical buffs. I saw it erupt once in a woman bent over a pile of old records at the National Archives in Washington, who suddenly jumped up and raced down the corridor, screaming at startled researchers, "I've found it! I've found it!" She wanted everybody around to know that she had finally confirmed a family legend she had been pursuing for years— that an ancestor, a blacksmith, was commissioned to shoe horses for soldiers in Washington's army during the American Revolution. The same intoxication with discovery came over me when I found the location of my Great-grandfather Thomas Fitzgerald's farm in Pennsylvania and saw his signature in a court record. The farm was in Chester County, close to the borders of Maryland and Delaware, both slave states when my Fitzgerald ancestors settled there in 1855. A county map dated 1860 showed the name Thos. Fitzgerald next to a dot representing the farm, and with the aid of old deed descriptions I was able to stand at the very spot, a short distance from the present entrance to Lincoln University. The university's president, Dr. Horace Mann Bond, shared the excitement of my search for the records of a free Negro family whose residency coincided with the beginnings of the pre–Civil War Negro school that was to become Lincoln.

Deep in the dusty-musty vaults of the County Court House—where the clerk permitted me to poke about to my heart's content among records piled in disarray on the floor, in boxes, on the tops of cabinets—I came upon the actual papers filed in a lawsuit involving my great-grandfather and a neighbor who owed him money. Amid pleas, bills, and testimony written by hand on all sizes of nondescript scratch paper (court records that looked more like a stack of fifth-grade themes than official documents) was a bill of costs bearing the original signature of Thomas Fitzgerald.

A local historian and genealogist, L. C. Ficcio, provided me with yellowed newspaper clippings that brought to life local events affecting my family and their neighbors a century ago. Mr. Ficcio, who was also the local postman, drove me many miles over the bumpy back roads of Chester County and tramped with me through the woods, following branches of the Underground Railway and retracing the movements of slave catchers and kidnappers. After one such day I returned to my room at Lincoln University's guesthouse, exhausted but so drenched with local and family history that I poured out my impressions in a letter to Maida Springer:

> ... I have seen the snaky Octorora Creek and watched the sky peppered with blackbirds. ... [We] followed the state line—saw barns, half of which were in Maryland, the other half in Pa., saw the old boundary stones which, if a fugitive slave had taken to the woods and stumbled upon, told him he was on free soil at last; went to the scene of the Christiana Riot—the very spot on which the house stood, the lane where the battle took place, the woods through which the posse turned tail and fled. ... [I] was treated to glimpses of old grist mills, dams, stone houses with tunnels under trap doors where fugitive slaves were hidden, the hilltop where the informer came down the creek and looked for his blood money under a stone where it had been laid for him, the old Pine Grove school site where we think the Fitzgerald children attended, the old Brick Meeting House in Homeville ... where some historians say the first Anti-Slavery meeting in Pennsylvania was held, the Hambleton's place—an Underground Railroad station within 1 mile of the Fitzgerald place, an old covered bridge and the bumpy, lumpy, almost impassable roads reminiscent of the 1850's. ...

As I pursued the family story, the past merged into the present in a continual drama of ordinary people who, although not found in textbooks, nevertheless illuminated the history of an era. With dignity and quiet courage, they made their way through national turmoil, civil war, and its aftermath of Ku Klux Klan killings and burnings in the South, never surrendering their will to survive, and passing on their strength to the next generation. The bright thread of this unrecorded history became more and more vivid to me in the spring of 1954 as I lived simultaneously in two periods of time. (So much so that I found myself dating correspondence 1854 instead of 1954!)

Guided by my Grandfather Fitzgerald's diary, I traveled to Virginia and North Carolina, reliving his struggles to set up the first schools for Negro freedmen with no public support and often in the face of open hostility from local white people. The reality of this early mission was embodied in an old man I met in Amelia County, Virginia. He lived to be one hundred years old and was the lone survivor of the school my grandfather established there in 1866.

On May 17, a few weeks after I returned to New York aglow with a new appreciation for the work of those pioneers of Negro education in the post–Civil War South, the United States Supreme Court announced its momentous decision outlawing racial segregation in the public schools. The congruence of the Court's decision with my journey into history and my family's involvement in public school education over several generations made the event intensely personal, as if I had been one of the victorious plaintiffs. I was witnessing a climax of the long steep climb out of black slavery—when teaching a slave to read and write was a crime—toward an unequivocal declaration of the constitutional right to equal educational opportunity, a struggle that defined my family's role in the history of their times. My grandfather had begun the ascent as a young teacher when freedom was gloriously new and hopes for equal treatment were high. His daughters had followed their father's tradition and were themselves young teachers when reaction set in and the degrading "separate but equal" rule fastened upon the South. My aunts had borne the brunt of enforced segregation in impoverished Negro schools for more than half a century, enduring humiliations from their white superiors while striving to overcome the stigma of inferiority and give incentives to Negro children during the darkest days of racial *apartheid*. Now, coming at the close of their lives, the Court's ruling seemed almost like a benediction.

Within the next two years, all three of my aunts passed from the scene, not one living long enough to see the story of their struggle in print. Aunt Pauline's death in 1955 was more than the loss of the only mother I had ever known. It was the passing of the oldest member of our family, our sturdy oak whose strength and wisdom we sought in times of trouble. It was also a life-changing experience for me, although I was too baffled at the time to recognize its significance. In my first confrontation as an adult with the ultimate crisis of human existence, I was thrust into a role of such awesome spiritual depth that eighteen years later I looked back upon it as a sign clearly pointing me toward the ordained ministry.

It had been a time of illness and death. In June 1954 I was hospitalized to have a growth removed from my thyroid gland, and while I was there Aunt Marie became ill, was rushed to a local hospital and died shortly after surgery for an intestinal obstruction. A few months later, Uncle Lewis Murray, who had recently retired after teaching fifty-two years in the Baltimore schools, died of a heart attack. Aunt Pauline carried on in her usual stoical manner, but I noticed her growing fragility and sensed her unspoken dread of becoming helpless and having to go to a nursing home, a decision I prayed I would never have to make. After my own operation I had spent two months at the MacDowell Colony, making great progress on the book, and I was now racing with time to finish it and get a stable job.

On September 25 we celebrated Aunt Pauline's eighty-fifth birthday, and I remember how pleased she was to have achieved the same number of years as Great-aunt Mary Jane Fitzgerald, who, at her death, had lived longer than any other member of the Fitzgerald family. My application for another stay at the MacDowell Colony having been approved, I left Aunt Pauline in good spirits and went off to tackle the final chapters of the manuscript. A few weeks later she wrote that she was having trouble with her eyes and was afraid she was going blind. Her letter distressed me so much that I dropped my writing and came home for a week to take her to her doctor for a thorough checkup. She must have had a premonition of her death, for the night I arrived home she had gone to the trouble of preparing my favorite meal, adding the luxury (for us) of ice cream and cake. She explained, "Since you won't be home on your birthday next month, I wanted to share it with you now."

It was our last ceremonial meal together. In the predawn hours of October 26—the day scheduled for her medical appointment—Aunt Pauline was stricken with what I later learned was a massive heart attack. It was the worst possible hour to get medical aid, but we did reach a doctor who covered her physician's night calls and was willing to make a house visit. He gave her some medication, which relieved her temporarily, and advised me to get her into the hospital as soon as possible, saying guardedly that she might be having a gall bladder upset or it might be her heart.

In an abrupt reversal of roles, I had to assume the place of a parent and make the crucial decisions. Yet every effort I made to stave off the inevitable was doomed to failure. Saint John's Hospital, where she had once been a patient, refused to accept her until her physician authorized her admission; it was midmorning before he came and made the necessary arrangements. Then, unaccountably, and despite frantic calls and appeals, ambulance service was delayed for several hours. During the interminable wait, Aunt Pauline said matter-of-factly, "I don't think I'll live to get to the hospital. I've got death rattles in my throat."

The nakedness of that statement wrenched me from the thin hope to which I clung and brought me face to face with the awesome reality of approaching death, although I dared not acknowledge it to myself. I knew that Aunt Pauline's devotion to her church was central to her existence, and the thought that she might die without a priest to administer Holy Communion was terrifying to me. I tried desperately to reach the Reverend Coleman or the Reverend Sedgewick at Saint Philip's Church, but here again I was frustrated; both priests were out and no one knew where to reach them. It seemed like the ultimate calamity.

As the minutes passed and I watched Aunt Pauline's breath coming in short gasps, I asked her if she would like me to read the Order for the Visitation of the Sick from the Book of Common Prayer while we were waiting. She nodded her head. I was conscious at that moment that in all our family devotions I had never been asked to lead in prayer. It was a special privilege reserved to an older member of the family and it would have been presumptuous of me to take the initiative. Now that the responsibility was thrust upon me, I was agonizingly aware of my inadequacy, for as a lay person, I felt I had no authority to give a blessing. Nevertheless, I read aloud the psalms and all the prayers, with their familiar, comforting phrases:

> . . . defend her in all danger,
>   and keep her in perpetual peace and safety . . .
> . . . bestow upon her the help of thy merciful consolation . . .
> . . . grant her an abiding sense of thy loving-kindness . . .
> Unto God's gracious mercy and protection we commit thee. . . .

It was the best I could do. I did not know then that I was engaged in a ministry to the dying or that those prayers would be the only rite Aunt Pauline would receive before her death. That night, at the hospital, she slipped away peacefully in her sleep after telling me she was all right and that I should go home and get some rest. She was prepared for that moment; earlier, as she was being carried out to the ambulance, she pointed to her hatbox in a corner of her room. I opened it later and found the burial undergarments she had put aside. Yet for a long time after her death I felt an incompleteness, as if I had somehow failed her, and I kept asking myself why, in the ultimate crisis of a devout Christian life, I was called upon to render the service that I then believed was authentic only when performed by an ordained member of the clergy. I would wrestle with that question over and over before finding an answer.

Aunt Sallie never recovered from the shock of Aunt Pauline's death. After years of dependency upon her older sister, the sudden separation sapped her will to live. She lost her appetite and was so forlorn I became anxious and called in a doctor over her protest—she had not consulted a physician in thirty-seven years. When he examined her he found a mass in the abdominal area and recommended hospitalization for further tests. The diagnosis was cancer of the liver. Over the next seven weeks I made daily trips to the hospital, watching her grow weaker and more wasted. For the second time in a few months there was the tremendous emotional exertion of just *being* with a dying person, watching a life slip away, helpless to offer more than the comfort of one's presence. Mercifully, the demands of the manuscript kept me going in those anxious weeks; I would come home from the hospital at night drained of all feeling but driven to the typewriter to finish the revisions required for publication. Aunt Sallie clung to life until the job was done, and died in May 1956, just a few days after *Proud Shoes* went to press.

It had been less than seven months since I buried Aunt Pauline. When it was all over, there was a great void in my life. The manuscript was out of my hands and there was no cushion for my loss. Aunt Sallie was the last of the older generation, and with her passing I was cut adrift, no longer anchored to the ties of my childhood and to those I had always revered as my elders. At the same time, having watched over my aunts for eight years and seen them through to the end, I felt as if I had lost my children. I had now to begin a new life without their faith to lean upon and with only the presence of my little dog Smokey to break the unaccustomed stillness of an empty apartment.

CHAPTER 26

Neither "My Girl" nor "One of the Boys"

By a coincidence, Adlai Stevenson's two unsuccessful campaigns to win the presidency bracketed my four-year effort to write *Proud Shoes* and marked both the beginning of the manuscript and the publication of the book. In 1952 I was so impressed by Stevenson's integrity, eloquence, wit, and liberal civil rights record as governor of Illinois that I took time off from the manuscript long enough to work for his election. As a Volunteer for Stevenson, I was part of a team headed by Lloyd K. Garrison to bring out the Negro vote in New York City. The Stevenson magic was contagious, the campaign exciting, and in the 1952 election he captured an estimated 79 percent of the nationwide black vote. Our efforts in Harlem, where Stevenson appeared at a rally, produced 83 percent in his favor.

Except for final revisions, I had finished my work on *Proud Shoes* by the time Stevenson began making his second bid for the Democratic nomination. He had the strong backing of Eleanor Roosevelt, and I enthusiastically accepted an invitation to join the Stevenson for President Committee. From the beginning, however, and notwithstanding my preference for Stevenson over the other early contenders, Averell Harriman and Estes Kefauver, I was disturbed by his approach to the explosive civil rights crisis, which then dominated the front pages of the *New York Times*. The racial climate had changed drastically since 1952. In the wake of the 1954 Supreme Court decision on school desegregation, Negroes were making a determined assault on the Jim Crow system in the South. In the Montgomery Boycott, which began in December 1955, nonviolent direct action was being used successfully to combat segregation on local buses—

the campaign that brought Dr. Martin Luther King, Jr., to national prominence. At the same time, southern Democratic politicians were leading
campaigns of "Massive Resistance" to the Court's ruling, maintaining that
states could interpose their sovereignty between the people and the federal government to nullify actions the states held to be in violation of the
federal Constitution. This instigation to defy federal authority encouraged
increasing acts of intimidation and violence intended to suppress civil
rights activities in the South. As historian-journalist Thomas R. Brooks
summed up that period: "blacks, particularly in the South, were caught in
a cruel dilemma. On the one hand, there were the decisions of the Supreme Court against segregation and the encouraging—indeed exhilarating—victory of the Montgomery bus boycott; on the other hand, there was
a growing—and partially successful—white reaction and repression, especially against school desegregation."

Stevenson, in his preoccupation with mending fences in a party badly
split on the question of compliance, seemed bent upon placating southern
Democrats at the expense of reaffirming the moral principles at stake in
the gravest issue facing the nation in 1956. As one of his earliest supporters, I wrote him in January of my concern that he had not publicly expressed his views on two critical issues: (1) continued economic reprisals
and violence against Negro citizens in southern states who had evidenced
leadership in the NAACP, and (2) the recent vote in Virginia to call a
constitutional convention for the express purpose of evading the Supreme
Court mandate on integration of the public schools. "I am acutely aware
of your silence and the news stories surrounding your silence," I wrote,
adding: "I strongly urge you to clarify your position on the issues posed in
this letter. Unless and until you do, it will be difficult for independents and
liberal Democrats in New York to withstand the pressures that will take
advantage of your silence to swing opinion in favor of some other candidate." Knowing her desire to maintain support among Negroes for Stevenson's candidacy, I sent a copy of my letter to Mrs. Roosevelt.

The burning question to Negroes was what firm measures the federal
government, when confronted with southern defiance, would take to enforce the Supreme Court's decision outlawing segregation in public
schools. Forced to address himself to this question in early February when
speaking to a group of Negroes in Los Angeles, Stevenson angered the
embattled civil rights leadership by dismissing Congressman Adam Clayton Powell's proposed amendment to a federal school construction bill. Of
the Powell proposal, which would bar funds to segregated schools, Stevenson declared: "I hardly think such an amendment is necessary." When
asked whether, as President, he would use the army or navy, if necessary,
to enforce school desegregation, he replied, according to *New York Times*

reporter W. H. Lawrence: "I think that would be a great mistake. That is exactly what brought on the Civil War. It can't be done by troops, or bayonets. We must proceed gradually, not upsetting habits or traditions that are older than the Republic." Several days later Stevenson urged that all candidates ban the integration issue from the presidential campaign, as if a conflict people openly spoke of as impending civil war could be resolved by silence on the part of anyone aspiring to become President of the United States.

The questions put to Stevenson were realistic ones for Negroes, who knew that ultimately only the superior authority of the federal government would prevent the violent suppression of rights so painfully won and finally reaffirmed under the Constitution. They anticipated the 1957 crisis in Little Rock, Arkansas, some eighteen months later, when President Eisenhower (who also thought the use of armed force inconceivable) had to send in federal troops to carry out a federal court order to desegregate the schools.

Stevenson's rejection of specific measures without offering alternatives, together with his emphasis upon gradualism, touched off a bruising controversy within liberal ranks. A mark of the deepening crisis was the intense Negro reaction against white liberal supporters who called for moderation and conciliation in the struggle while passing over in silence the recalcitrance of southern segregationists. To victims of the Jim Crow system, this posture was a retreat from principle, abandoning Negroes to the unrestrained violence of white racism. My own strong reaction to Mr. Stevenson's various statements boiled over in correspondence with syndicated columnist Doris Fleeson, a Stevenson enthusiast who saw him as a leader steeped in the lore of Abraham Lincoln, someone who reflected the moderation and conciliation of Lincoln in his determination to avert a second Civil War. On February 11, I wrote to her that I believed "as of *now* Mr. Stevenson has lost the Negro vote." I also said:

> It is all very well for Mr. Stevenson to be preoccupied with conciliation and with the dangers involved in upsetting the "traditions of centuries," but unless he understands how passionately determined the Negro is that once and for *all* we will be brought up to par, or die in the attempt, he will underestimate the new situation we are facing in the United States today. . . . Civil rights cannot be dealt with with moderate feelings. It involves a passion for justice and for human decency, and if Mr. Stevenson has not felt this passion, then he does not belong in the White House.

To me, the most distressing aspect of this phase of the campaign was that not even Mrs. Roosevelt seemed to appreciate fully the depth of our feeling that the subordination of the moral imperatives of our struggle to political expediencies was little short of betrayal by our friends, hence our outrage. Although she sat on the NAACP board and was abreast of developments, she angrily defended Stevenson from NAACP executive director Roy Wilkins' sharp criticism of his emphasis upon gradualism. In dismay, I wrote her that the apparent cleavage between her point of view and that of the Negro leaders she had known and worked with over many years "may be more fundamental than you realize. If so, it would be tragic for all of us." Because she had spoken of her perplexity over the confusion and misunderstanding Mr. Stevenson's statement caused, and because I feared further misunderstandings, I urged her "to counsel informally with leaders in this field whose opinions you respect and in whom you have trust and confidence." After suggesting a meeting with Ralph Bunche and several others, I added: "I think such an informal exchange of views might clarify the issues and help all of us to formulate a sound approach to the present crisis."

It may have been one of those times when Mrs. Roosevelt wanted no qualms of conscience to interfere with her course of political action, but she was sufficiently affected by my disturbed view to have a long talk with Ralph Bunche, which she reported on in her reply. Although affectionate as always, her letter possessed a tone of defensiveness. She did not think there was any "fundamental cleavage" between the point of view she shared with Stevenson and that "of the really wise Negro leaders."

> I did not like Roy Wilkins' hot-headed statement which I thought poorly thought out, nor did I like the garbled reporting of what Mr. Stevenson said in Los Angeles. Unwittingly Mr. Stevenson used the word "gradual" and this means one thing to the Negroes but to him it is entirely different.

Mrs. Roosevelt did not attempt to explain what Mr. Stevenson really meant, but declared that his "record remains remarkably good and he certainly was courageous in the statements he made in the last campaign." She considered it "a mistake for the Negro leaders to be tearing down Stevenson who is after all the only real hope they have," since President Eisenhower had indicated "that he would make no statement on whether the Executive would refrain from allocating funds where schools were segregated. Yet the papers and the Negro leaders have not attacked the President. Why this discrimination?"

Unhappily, Mrs. Roosevelt and I were separated by differences in our perception of the racial experience as well as by the intensity of feeling I shared with other Negroes against segregationist efforts to snatch away a hard-won victory almost within our grasp. She perceived the civil rights issue as secondary to winning the White House for Adlai Stevenson. At the Democratic convention in August, her concern for party unity led her to support a civil rights plank that omitted endorsement of the Supreme Court decision on desegregation of the public schools. "You can't move so fast that you try to change the mores faster than people can accept it," she advised Negro and other civil rights leaders who fought for a stronger statement. "That doesn't mean that you do nothing, but it means that you do the things that need to be done according to priority." Her pragmatism, directed toward holding southern Democrats within the party, ignored another reality—the increasing momentum of the civil rights movement and the growing militancy of Negroes who found that with each advance toward the goal of equality, remaining barriers to its fulfillment became all the more intolerable. Cautioning us against moving too fast while watering down the civil rights plank of the Democratic party platform blunted the moral force of the Supreme Court decision. It had the same jarring impact as reminding us "how far you have come" when our privations were so many that our primary focus was on "how far we still have to go."

For all the affection and esteem Mrs. Roosevelt enjoyed among Negroes, she was unable to bridge this gap in perception and feeling. At best, Negroes looked upon the 1956 campaign as an uneasy alliance, and Stevenson could not recapture the high enthusiasm they had felt for his candidacy four years earlier. In spite of my own reservations, Lloyd K. Garrison persuaded me to work with him again that fall, along with Sylvia Ravitch and Frank Horne, to mobilize the Negro vote in New York City. It was a disheartening effort, the sparkle was gone, and days before the election we felt the gloom of Stevenson's impending defeat. When the returns were in, they showed not only that Stevenson had lost to Eisenhower by a wider margin than in 1952, but also that Negroes had defected in large numbers, their percentage of votes for Stevenson dropping from 79 percent to 61 percent. Negroes in southern cities, who voted overwhelmingly for Stevenson in 1952, rolled up substantial majorities for Eisenhower, and Stevenson lost strength in the black districts of urban centers in the North and West as well. His equivocation on civil rights, rather than aiding his cause, had increased the black vote for the Republican party for the first time in twenty years.

My disappointment over Mr. Stevenson's second failure to win was softened considerably by a happy event that took place about three weeks before the end of the campaign. *Proud Shoes* was published on October 17, and it was greeted with glowing reviews. The one note of sadness tempering my elation was that Aunt Pauline and Aunt Sallie had not lived long enough to share the warm reception of their family story.

Saunders Redding gave *Proud Shoes* a big send-off in the book review section of the New York *Herald Tribune,* writing that it "is a book with such variety of incident and such depths and changes of tone as to astonish one who mistakes it simply for a family chronicle. It is that, surely, but it is something more. It is a personal memoir, it is history, it is biography, and it is also a story that, at its best, is dramatic enough to satisfy the demands of fiction. It is written in anger, but without hatred; in affection, but without pathos and tears; and in humor that never becomes extravagant." In the *New York Times,* Henrietta Buckmaster called it "a gallant book . . . unique in the saga of the American Negro, the biography of a family in an uncommon sense." Ted Poston told *New York Post* readers that it was a "magnificent book. . . . Today's dark picture on the school integration and other civil rights fronts gives an especial pertinency to this volume." And in her column, "My Day," Mrs. Roosevelt said it was "American history which all American citizens should read. It will bring pride to our Negro citizens and greater understanding to all of us."

Judged by its reviews, *Proud Shoes* was a literary success. It attracted a limited audience, but it made enough of an impact to break even financially, considered no mean achievement for an unknown author. (The book earned exactly forty-five cents in excess of the publisher's thirteen-hundred-dollar advance.) More significantly, it was a forerunner of family stories growing out of the complex racial history of the United States, and twenty years later one of those family chronicles was to achieve international fame. A sentence in *Proud Shoes* anticipated the title of Alex Haley's major work, published in 1976: *"It had taken me almost a lifetime to discover that true emancipation lies in the acceptance of the whole past, in deriving strength from all my roots, in facing up to the degradation as well as the dignity of my ancestors."*

Proud Shoes was barely off the press when the professional opportunity that had eluded me in the past opened so unexpectedly that I felt like a sandlot player catapulted overnight into major league baseball. Shortly after the election, Lloyd Garrison called with the startling news that his firm, Paul, Weiss, Rifkind, Wharton & Garrison, needed extra help in their litigation department and he had recommended me for a job. Recalling his candid observation ten years earlier that the big New York law firms would not even consider an applicant from a law school with no national reputation, I was even more surprised when his firm actually hired me as an associate attorney.

This amazing good fortune, coming after years of scrabbling to earn a living, nevertheless filled me with anxiety. I was now a middle-aged woman reentering a highly competitive profession after several years' absence. Not only was I rusty from lack of continuous practice; my major interest in law was civil rights, and I was woefully deficient in knowledge of commercial practice on a large scale. There were as well the subjective factors of age, sex, and race. My status was that of a triple minority. Fifteen to twenty years older than the others at my entry level, I was painfully aware that I had few of the prestigious credentials of these bright, energetic young men with whom I would work. And of the sixty-five or more attorneys then working in the firm's New York office, I was one of three women and the only Negro.

The magnitude of the firm's operations and the size of its offices, which covered several floors, were dazzling to one accustomed to working alone with responsibility for every aspect of a particular case. Practice in a big law firm was an assembly-line process; associates at my level seldom saw a client or a courtroom but were kept busy drafting court pleadings, handling the technical details of litigation, doing research, and preparing legal memoranda and briefs. The pace was rapid and the ceaseless pressure frequently kept skeleton crews working around the clock to meet court deadlines.

My apprehensiveness in the new job was aggravated by the feeling that I was on trial on several counts, and a persistent fear of failure dogged my first weeks at the firm. I had to research and submit memoranda on questions foreign to my experience—corporate mergers, bankruptcies, mechanics' liens, and the like—and I was so panic-stricken that my work bordered on disaster. The partner to whom I was assigned returned my laboriously written memoranda with comments that my arguments were wavering and my conclusions timid and uncertain. After several unsatisfactory efforts I was ready to quit the job in despair and might have done so if Lloyd Garrison had not rescued me with some sound advice.

He took me out to lunch one day and let me pour out all my self-doubts, then said reassuringly that of course I was having difficulties and that it would be most strange if I were not. He told me the story of his own return to private practice in 1946, after teaching law for ten years and spending another four years at the War Labor Board. In his absence the whole structure of tax law had changed, and so he found himself completely at sea in the very area he had claimed as his field of expertise. It had taken him five or six years of hard work before he began to feel at home again in that branch of the law. He assured me that because litigation is so diverse and touches so many areas of substantive law, no one can possibly master it overnight. "The criticisms do not mean you have failed," he said. "They should be used as a grindstone to sharpen your tools." As a result of that conversation with Mr. Garrison, I attacked my work with more confidence and eventually survived the initial test of job performance, although I never felt entirely comfortable with large-scale commercial law practice.

After my two women colleagues left the firm for other jobs, I was the solitary female on the legal staff in the New York office. (Carolyn Agger, the firm's only woman partner, had her office in the Washington, D.C., branch.) The differences that set me apart prevented me from having the kind of buddy relationships my younger male associates enjoyed, and office protocol dictated formal reserve in my dealings with the partners, who were addressed as "Mr." and given great deference. Indeed, a woman associate in a hierarchy of male attorneys had an ambiguous status. She was neither "my girl"—a condescending reference to a female secretary —nor fully accepted as "one of the boys." Her indeterminate position sometimes created an awkwardness in office relations.

An amusing example of this ambiguity involved one of the partners, Martin Kleinbard, not long after I joined the staff. In the course of working together on a complicated case, we developed a professional rapport which relaxed some of our initial stiffness. We had just returned from a hearing late one afternoon, jubilant over the success of our efforts. Mr. Kleinbard was hurrying to keep a dinner engagement but wanted to go over some details of the case before dashing off. As I sat in his office, briefing him on what remained to be done, he glanced at his watch and said, "I'm late, but you keep right on talking while I tidy up."

With that, he loosened his tie, unbuttoned his shirt collar, reached in a drawer for his electric razor, and began shaving. He was almost finished when he suddenly looked at me aghast, his face aflame, and blurted out, "Oh, I'm sorry. I completely forgot about you—"

"It's quite all right," I assured him, secretly pleased that, however embarrassing that moment was for him, his act unconsciously signaled his acceptance of me as a person and a colleague.

I also had trouble trying to figure out proper decorum, and on one occasion got caught in a conflict between office customs and gender roles which placed me in a comical predicament. As a new staff member anxious to fit in, I followed the example of other associates in their deference to partners, especially Simon H. Rifkind, a senior partner and former federal judge, who headed our litigation department. Judge Rifkind's prestige as a brilliant trial lawyer and the judicial tenor of his presence in the office inspired awe among otherwise cocksure young associates. I absorbed their reverent attitude so fully that one evening on leaving the office and finding myself standing near Judge Rifkind at the elevator, it seemed natural for me to recognize his rank and step back to allow him to board the car when the door opened. Meanwhile Judge Rifkind, who was rumored not to think too highly of women lawyers but was the essence of courtesy toward "a lady," had stepped aside for me to get on first. Intent upon our respective code of behavior, both of us stood there while other passengers piled in, the door closed, and the elevator continued downward, leaving us staring foolishly at one another.

The awkwardness of my position gradually disappeared as my work as a lawyer improved and was accepted. Later I looked back on the job at Paul, Weiss, Rifkind, Wharton & Garrison as decisive for my future growth. When I left the firm after three years, I carried with me the assurance of having been tested by the most exacting standards of the legal profession, an experience that enabled me to face new challenges with greater self-confidence. Indeed, the crucial gain of that period was psychic. Like many others restricted to the backwaters of minority existence, I found that moving into the mainstream was not an automatic liberation from my past. For months I had to struggle with phantoms lurking in the background, secret fears that gaps in my knowledge or inadequacies in performance would be attributed to my race or sex. Only as I learned through dogged effort to handle day-to-day assignments with reasonable competence were those nagging fears laid to rest.

My most persistent problem during that time was handling the loneliness of the woman professional isolated in a large commercial or legal institution. I seldom met a female counterpart when dealing with other firms, and in those days there were no informal networks of women to provide the camaraderie of equals or to bolster morale and self-esteem. Fortunately, I was not entirely alone. Irene Barlow, the office manager–personnel director and one of the few women to hold that position in a large law office at the time, was the one other person in the firm who shared my token status in a predominantly male domain, and we gravitated toward one another for mutual support. Although we would not have dared to think of ourselves as feminists in 1957, in fact we were part of an "unconscious underground," as Betty Friedan put it, an embryonic sisterhood from which the feminist movement emerged in the 1960s.

Irene Barlow was one of those remarkable women who foreshadowed the strength and competence of the movement that followed. In her early forties when I first met her, Renee (pronounced to rhyme with Jeannie) was tall and slender, and she carried herself with an air of quiet self-assurance. Her strong, attractive face and blue-green eyes radiated generosity and kindness. Even-tempered, witty, and an able administrator, she made her nerve-racking job look easy, handling a volatile mix of personalities with such skill that she was often referred to by the staff as "the managing partner." Her job kept her on the go, moving unobtrusively through the corridors, untangling snafus which interrupted the flow of paperwork, hustling messengers on their rounds, putting out brushfires of revolt in the stenographers' pool, mediating between lawyers and secretaries, solving problems of space, or, on occasion, offering a kind word to an associate who had just been humiliated by an irate partner. Years later, Lloyd Garrison, who had recruited Renee for her job with the firm, said that the true work of her life was helping people with their problems and personal difficulties, and indeed she was a humanizing influence in a small segment of the commercial world. She reached out and gathered in countless folk who needed a friendly shoulder, people who later called her "my best friend."

As I came to know Renee, our association lifted me beyond my narrow parochial concerns to a broader understanding of the human condition. Beset with problems of race and color all my life, I had no idea until I heard her story that a white Anglo-Saxon Protestant child might grow up in the United States feeling an "outsider." (I looked upon WASPs as America's most favored people.) Renee was English-born, the youngest of five Yorkshire sisters whose father deserted the family because there were too many mouths to feed. Renee was a child of six when her mother, plucky Mary Jane Barlow, who had earned a living as a greengrocer, scraped together enough money for passage and brought her brood to the United States. Virtually penniless, they were confined on Ellis Island for weeks, fighting deportation and existing on a meager ration of bread, tea, and apples until a relative could be found to vouch for their entrance into the country.

Renee's childhood in New England was one of continual struggle against poverty. The family moved often, either to find jobs for the older girls in the mill towns of Massachusetts and Rhode Island or because they were frequently evicted when they could not pay their rent. Renee felt set apart from other children, conscious of her threadbare hand-me-down clothing and laughed at because of her strange English accent. Her sisters worked in the mills until they got married, and Renee and her mother took hotel or sleep-in jobs, doing heavy housework. Renee had struggled out of her impoverished background through grit and determined effort, working her way through high school and two years of college before she had to stop her education to earn a living for herself and her mother. She moved from YWCA work into industry during World War II, bringing with her a sensitivity to people as individuals and an orientation to service which she never surrendered to the sometimes brutal jostling of the marketplace. After she came to work for the law firm, she went back to school and attended evening classes to complete requirements for her undergraduate degree. Her mother, a wiry woman in her late seventies, lived with her in their modest midtown Manhattan apartment.

Renee's strong identification with "those who are shut out," as she put it, was rooted in her childhood experience. Although not a visible crusader, she worked quietly and effectively for civil rights, including women's rights. Known among her colleagues in the personnel field as one who could be counted on to offer a job to a qualified worker rejected by other offices because of a concealed bias (New York had a fair employment practices law), Renee applied principles of affirmative action long before the term came into common usage. She had a standing order with a friend at the National Urban League to send promising Negro applicants for an interview, even when she had no opening at the time, so that she would have their names on file when a vacancy occurred. She also used other sources of recruitment outside conventional employment offices, with the result that the clerical staff at Paul, Weiss, Rifkind, Wharton & Garrison was a sparkling showcase of equal opportunity, a diverse blending of Negroes, Hispanics, Asian-Americans, and other ethnic minorities as well as Catholics, Protestants, and Jews, a mix still rare in New York business offices in the 1950s.

In an office of constant pressures, Renee's gift of spontaneous humor was a delight to those who worked with her. She could defuse an explosive situation with some quaint expression from her English background. "Now don't get up in the boughs," her calm rejoinder to an angry outburst, was so unexpected that it deflected attack. When so taken aback that she had no words, she would respond, as if closing a letter, "I remain." Her invective "Oh, blast!" on those rare occasions when she gave vent to frustration, had the unintended effect of sending a listener into spasms of laughter, thus breaking the tension.

Although Renee and I were very different in background and personality, in our approach to situations, and in many of our interests, the chemistry of our friendship produced sparks of sheer joy. Our common search for truth and knowledge often ended in hilarity or in spirited discourse, often in the discomfiture of mutual growth. An underlying spiritual dimension which had been present from the outset gave our relationship a special quality I had not found in other friends of my own age. In our first conversation outside the office we recognized in each other a religious commitment which a natural reserve prevented us from revealing to other business associates.

Some weeks after I came to work for the firm, Renee invited me to lunch as a courteous gesture to a new employee. Our conversation was tentative and formal until she unconsciously used the phrase "the blessed company of all faithful people," which I immediately recognized as coming from the Book of Common Prayer. Our discovery that we were both worshiping Episcopalians was the beginning of a spiritual bond which found its first expression during Lent that spring, when we used our lunch hours to attend the Wednesday services at Saint Bartholomew's Church on Park Avenue a few blocks from our office. The bond deepened over the sixteen years I knew and worked with Renee within the Episcopal Church. It helped to reinforce our faith as we struggled in the 1960s to express the full personhood of women in our religious communion and felt the pain, and often the rage, of rejection at the deepest levels of our being.

CHAPTER 27

A Question of Identity

Early in 1959, Maida Springer, who had just returned from a conference in Ghana, gave me a clipping from the *London Times* advertising faculty openings in the newly established Ghana Law School in Accra. I answered it immediately. The New York law firm had been a great training ground and it had given me financial security, but I was restless and could not see myself settling into the career of a desk lawyer in an assembly-line practice. For some time my growing interest in the emerging movements for African independence had been spurred by Maida's enthusiastic reports of her trips to Africa as an American trade union representative and by challenging conversations with the young nationalist leaders Tom Mboya and Julius Nyerere, among others, whom I had met in her home. Teaching law in a West African country which had gained its independence only two years before would be a pioneering experience. It would also allow me to satisfy a nagging curiosity about the African component of my ancestry.

After months of correspondence and negotiation, I received a formal offer from the Ghana Board of Legal Education to teach as a senior lecturer (the equivalent of a full professorship) at the Ghana School of Law. On February 3, 1960, I left New York bound for Ghana aboard a Norwegian cargo ship, S.S. *Tatra*, carrying my worldly belongings, my dog Smokey, several boxes of lawbooks donated by my colleagues at the firm, two huge baskets of fruit given to me at a farewell party, and a case of twenty-four one-pound cans of Savarin coffee, a send-off present from the women in the firm's mailroom.

For the next twenty days I lived in the tiny, self-contained world of a seagoing freighter, learning to endure its ceaseless groaning and creaking, heaving up and down and sideways on an awesome ocean which seemed to stretch to infinity. Commanded by Captain J. B. Bye, who came from a town near Oslo, the boat carried a foreign crew of forty, eight American passengers, and a cargo of six thousand tons of rice, potatoes, tractors, and other heavy machinery consigned to West African ports. From New York we sailed north two days to take on four hundred tons of Canadian flour at Halifax, Nova Scotia, but since we arrived in the wake of a blizzard that had blocked all railroad shipments to the coast, we had to wait three days for the tracks to be cleared. The delay was a respite for Smokey, who was having a hard time adjusting to life aboard ship.

As a neophyte, who had never traveled outside the United States, I could hardly have found more experienced and reassuring companionship to prepare me for my new venture. Six of the other seven passengers (five women and two men) were veteran travelers to Africa, and they took delight in briefing me on what to expect. Three were employees of the Firestone Plantation Company, returning to Liberia from home leave. One young woman, Judy Lineberger, a nurse and medical missionary in the Methodist Church, was making her first trip overseas and would put ashore in Monrovia for her upcountry station. There were also two women from Seattle, missionaries for the Assembly of God Church, who had served nearly fifteen years in Africa and were headed for their post in Upper Volta, 850 miles inland in the heart of lion country.

Another veteran, Warren Buck, was a genial animal trader on his twenty-seventh trip to Africa to bring back live animals for zoos in the United States. He kept us laughing with a running account of his adventures. It might be about a skittish lion that broke loose from its crate in a boxcar also carrying monkeys, puppies, and boxes of restless bees—and of the uproar that followed. Or it might be about a shipment of poisonous horned vipers unexpectedly giving birth to hundreds of offspring, which slithered all over the floor of the ship's hold and had to be scooped up in buckets before they created panic in the rest of the ship. However terrifying the story, Mr. Buck had a knack of turning it into hilarious comedy.

Captain Bye, a veteran seaman of World War II, who had transported Allied soldiers and materials to the South Pacific and been part of the invasion of Italy, was unsparing in his efforts to make the voyage pleasant for his passengers. When he discovered I had a lively interest in the workings of the vessel, he gave me the run of the ship, took me up to the wheel room, where I could watch the helmsman, and into the chart room, where he showed me how to read sailing charts. Before a week had passed, Warren Buck and I had inspected the entire ship except the engine room. We had been up on the boat deck and peeped under the covers of the lifeboats to see if they were equipped with the required food, water, and gear. Captain Bye, watching all this, told Judy Lineberger with a chuckle, "Miss Murray knows more about this boat right now than I do. If something happens to me, you don't have to worry; she can take over and run the ship." The captain's liberal attitude toward women was influenced, I think, by the fact that many Norwegian women worked as ship's personnel. He told me that 40 percent of the radio operators in his shipping company, the Barber West African Lines, were female, that on one of his ships the engineer was a woman, who worked in dungarees down in the engine room with her male subordinates, and that once he had encountered a female first mate on a Russian ship. Not surprisingly, before the voyage ended I had been dubbed "fifth mate."

The missionaries made the deepest impression on me, perhaps because they quietly shattered my secular stereotypes of people who followed their calling. I learned that they had not come to Africa to change the culture or the politics of the people among whom they lived, as some critics charged, but to carry out more fully their commitment to service while sharing a religious experience they believed the Africans could adapt to their own uses. Wasn't this pretty much how I viewed my own coming to Africa with my legal experience? I learned that each of these women had undergone rigorous training for her mission and was equipped with professional skills—nursing and teaching—so that she could give practical assistance to the people in their daily lives. (Later I recalled how many African political leaders had received their basic education in missionary schools.)

Most of all, I was moved by their remarkable bravery in facing the physical hazards of the rugged life they had chosen, and listened transfixed as Marie Johnsrud and Eva Radanovsky, the Assembly of God missionaries, talked of their work among the Mossi tribe in Upper Volta. Marie was robust and inured to heavy, outside chores, but Eva was a tiny wisp of a person, so fragile that her physician in the United States had almost refused to give her medical clearance to return to Africa. An ordained minister who had also studied nursing, she not only taught at the mission seminary but in the days before the government had established a health station in the area, she had run a dispensary as well. The needs were so great that sometimes she had more than two hundred medical cases a week.

Physical survival in the formidable environment where the Mossi people lived depended upon constant awareness of danger. Eva had once opened her dresser drawer and found a poisonous snake curled up in a corner. Lions were a continual worry. The Mossi had built a lion pit just outside their compound and in recent years had trapped at least thirty-six lions. Eva said she never went out on an emergency call after dark without being alert to the tiniest movement in the bush. One night, returning from a call, she had barely closed the door when a pig squealed, its cry of terror cut off in the middle. Everyone knew what had happened; someone had forgotten to bring the pig inside the compound and a lion had made its kill. Eva might have suffered the pig's fate had she come along the path a few seconds later.

The spirit of these stouthearted women would help me later in my adjustments to African life, although I lived in the comparative comfort of a coastal city, would never see a lion, and experienced nothing more unsettling than a harmless lizard clinging to my ceiling. They were perceptive and had anticipated many of my anxieties, helping to cushion the shock of my first exposure to privation and suffering on a mass scale. Eva told me wisely that Africa would compel me to use every talent I possessed and resources I did not even know I had; that there would be times when even though I thought it impossible to give more, I would have to find the strength to do so. She felt that although book knowledge would give me some perspective, I would survive only by calling on inner resources not found in books. I would succeed in Africa, she predicted, because I had a "compassionate heart" capable of penetrating beyond language barriers. Africans would love me, she said, because they responded quickly to anyone who showed a personal interest in them.

When the *Tatra* docked for two days in Monrovia, Liberia, to unload and take on cargo as well as an African crew to make the coastal trip, I got my first glimpse of humanity on African soil. Borrowing a car, I drove about the city and into the near countryside. Nothing I had read or heard prepared me for the contrast between the opulence of a wealthy nation like the United States and the overwhelming poverty of the masses of people I saw everywhere in this African city—the mildewed dilapidation of the few stores on the main street; the flies and insects swarming over the smoked fish sold on the ground in the native markets; the naked children with protruding stomachs wading through cesspools of muck; a child with large tumors growing out of his neck begging in the street; the furnitureless mud shacks with dirt floors and roofs of straw pieced together with old tarpaulins or discarded fragments of rusty tin; the mangy, half-starved dogs creeping along the gutters; the ragged dockworkers in westernized shirts and trousers, their bodies glistening through their tatters; and the half-comatose, scurvy-ridden old people dozing in the sun and looking like breathing corpses.

The presence all over the city of skeletons of cinder-block houses, all in the same state of incompletion, was a symbol of the people's strangled aspirations. The outside walls were there, but partitions, floors, and roofs were not. I learned later that this was a fairly common sight in Africa. Many Africans had a dream of building their own homes; they had managed to get the walls up, but often their money ran out before they could get the roofs on and they had to abandon their half-built structures to the weeds. Ghana had started a roof development plan through which money for the roof was lent to a builder once the walls were erected.

My voyage ended on February 23 at Takoradi, Ghana's western seaport, 180 miles from Accra. It took a fair-sized gang of dockworkers to get my baggage assembled on the dock and much "palaver" to get me through customs with clearance for Smokey and without paying more than thirteen shillings duty (about $1.50) for my Savarin coffee and what was left of the fruit. Fortunately, Jean Lang, the wife of John Lang, director of the law school under whom I would work, drove down from Accra to meet me. After my trip at sea, all I can recall during the long ride to Accra was how reassuring it was to be on land again and how much of the countryside along Ghana's coast resembled parts of the rural United States I knew. I had naively expected *everything*—even the earth—to be strange.

My arrival in Ghana coincided with the completion of the beautiful new law school building, located in downtown Accra between Parliament House and the Supreme Court building, and I was overjoyed to learn that I would have an air-conditioned office. I also arrived in time for the opening of the National Assembly and the debates on the proposed constitution and plebiscite, the latter held in April 1960, when the people voted to make Ghana a republic and elected Kwame Nkrumah its first president. These events had special significance for me because I learned that I had been assigned to teach the first course on constitutional and administrative law to be given at the law school.

The most momentous news for me, however, was from the United States. While I had been at sea and the only news of the outside world passed along by the ship's radio operator had been the birth of England's Prince Andrew, a spontaneous uprising against racial segregation had begun in southern states. Negro college students were conducting sit-ins at lunch counters in cities and towns across the South, and they were using the same nonviolent direct action techniques we Howard University students had used in the 1940s. Reading the glorious news of the widespread onslaught that had finally been mounted against Jim Crow left me simultaneously exhilarated and frustrated because the moment of action had come when I was thousands of miles from home and able to follow events only through fragmentary reports.

My first few months in Ghana were absorbed in settling into my new surroundings, learning my way about, listening to the debates in Parliament, observing procedures in the courts, and preparing materials for my course work. After three months I wrote home:

> I still find it difficult to sort out my impressions [of Ghana]. It is at once exciting, stimulating, frustrating, exasperating, and challenging. . . .
>
> One is immediately drawn into the turmoil and confusion of a country trying in one generation to leap over several centuries of painfully evolved human development. One also has the feeling at times of looking at the entire range of problems encountered in human history from the beginnings of the human race to the mid-twentieth century. I marvel at any observer who can speak with assurance about what goes on in Africa.
>
> There are levels of understanding, of course. Accra is like any bustling Western city, feverish with trading and with building operations and road construction. There is an informality and friendliness which helps to ease the discomfort of the climate and the lack of know-how which makes mere living sometimes tedious. But the stranger is at great disadvantage in wanting to know what the people really think and feel. One lives on an island of English surrounded by an ocean of indigenous languages. Out of courtesy and for business purposes, Ghanaians speak to one in varying degrees of English. Among themselves they speak their own tongues and are able to communicate even though they come from different tribes and have different tribal languages. Once one leaves the intellectuals, civil servants and clerks, one has to communicate in simple basic English without elaboration, or one is apt to experience the strangest consequences. In these circumstances, conversational English is virtually impossible.

Those first months of "settling in" taxed my good temper and physical stamina. Fresh from the brisk pace of New York, I found it hard to adjust to the infinitely slow tempo of people who live in tropical climates. I found the heat intolerable, and though I showered and changed my clothes as many as three times a day, it kept me in a state of irritability. I had to grow accustomed to driving on the left side of public thoroughfares, but since most people tended to drive in the middle of the narrow streets, and deep, open drain ditches lined each side, I was in continual danger of avoiding a head-on collision by driving into a ditch and breaking an axle. I also had to restrain my impatience at the unavailability of all sorts of necessary (to me, at least) store-bought items. Since most manufactured goods were brought in by ships arriving at long intervals, a common screw might be out of stock for months. Store clerks would simply dismiss me with a terse "Finished!" and give no further information.

These were petty inconveniences; the more serious problem was health. While waiting for the house assigned me to be built in a new

development called the Ringway Estates, I was lodged in a former government rest house which had seen better days and no longer had effective
screening. At night I slept under mosquito netting, but this device merely
trapped the insects *inside* the netting. My once-a-week anti-malaria pills
proved inadequate, and within a short time I had my first violent attack
of malaria, a condition that plagued me throughout my stay in Ghana. I
was so ill that Constance E. Stone, an American from Vermont who directed United States Information Service libraries in West Africa and
whom I had met at the library in Accra, carted me off to her home and
took care of me until I was able to creep about again. We developed a
staunch friendship, and Connie's professional help was crucial to my work
at the law school.

Perhaps my greatest initial adjustment was getting used to the custom
of hiring a young male African as cook-steward to do my housework and
marketing. It was expected of foreign professionals, an important part of
the local employment market, and all those with whom I talked insisted
that a steward was indispensable to my home life, especially since I was
a woman living alone. I resisted the idea because I had never employed
a houseworker, was sensitive to the low status and exploitation of Negro
domestic workers in the United States, and had already reacted strongly
against the Europeans' habit of describing their employees as "head boy,"
"small boy," or "garden boy." I also resented the subservience I had seen
in employees who addressed their employers as "Master" or "Mistress,"
evoking in my mind images of master-slave relationships in the antebellum United States.

My squeamishness, however, was a poor shield against entrenched
custom. As soon as a newcomer was known to be in a neighborhood, a
steady stream of prospective stewards, gardeners, laundrymen, and
"watchnights" appeared at the door asking for jobs. With my English
hostess Jean Lang at my elbow, urging, coaching, and censoring, I interviewed and finally hired Yaro, a tall, fine-looking, twenty-eight-year-old
man whose dignity and lack of obsequiousness impressed me. Yaro was a
member of the Fra Fra tribe, from the Northern Region of Ghana, close
to the Upper Volta border. Barefoot, he wore a clean shirt and old cordu-
roy trousers. He spoke Hausa and his tribal vernacular, but managed to
communicate with me in pidgin English. Like all licensed household
workers in Ghana, Yaro carried his registration, a long document showing
his picture, age, and other identification and including his employment
record signed by previous employers. He had worked as a steward for ten
years and his last job had ended five months before our interview. Various
employers had commented "punctual," "honest," or "very honest" in
their remarks.

I had been warned that many stewards were lazy and thievish, that I would have to watch mine constantly and lock up supplies. I told Yaro that he would have the heavy responsibility of doing his work without my watching him, because I did not believe in locking things up and would have to trust him completely. Afterward, Jean Lang insisted that Yaro had understood very little of what I had said, for she had asked him, "Did you hear [understand] Madame?" and he had replied, "No, I no hear Madame." But he had comprehended the gist of my remarks and told me, "If you no trust me, I no trust you." And this was enough to seal our bargain.

In spite of the language barrier, which limited conversations, ours was a happy relationship of mutual trust. Yaro was my introduction to tribal customs in Ghana. His tribal scar, an angry-looking gash on his left cheek, which resembled the healed wound of a razor slash, distinguished him from other Ghanaians as my color distinguished me from white people in the United States, and sometimes it served a similar purpose. The Fra Fras of the Northern Region came from the most impoverished and educationally deprived area of Ghana and were considered by many coastal peoples to be "bushmen" and of a low order. The Gas, who inhabited the coastal towns, were usually traders, but the Fra Fras who came south did menial labor. Their status was not unlike that of a racial minority and they were victims of sporadic discrimination in stores and other public places. Although tribal scars were discouraged by the Ghana government and were disappearing in the coastal areas, they were still prevalent in the interior.

I learned that tribal marks were the continuation of a custom growing out of practical needs in the past. According to legend, they originated during the slave trade, when weaker tribal groups tried to protect their young from slave-catchers. When a child was a few months old, its cheek was cut with a knife, the skin laid back and the wound packed with a mixture to prevent the gash from closing. Since slave traders wanted healthy, unmarked young blacks, a prominent facial disfigurement gave an African youth in the bush a fair chance of being rejected when captured. Later the mark served to identify members of the same tribe and enabled them to recognize one another. When they traveled to strange places they looked for others with similar markings, whom they considered "brothers" and who, according to tribal custom, were bound to take them in and support them until they could find work and support themselves. Yaro had brothers and sisters whom he distinguished from his tribal "brothers" by describing them as "same father–same mother."

Employers were expected to supply stewards with uniforms, but I could not live with the custom, lingering from colonial days, that required a servant to wear stuffy white long-sleeved uniforms and serve formal meals. I opted for comfort and informality, taking Yaro with me to select the cloth and having a tailor make him two white and two khaki sets of informal shirts and shorts. He was so pleased with his new clothes that on his second payday he bought himself a pair of sandals for work and two pairs of shoes, symbols of his changing status.

In a very short time he dropped the formal "Madame" and began addressing me as "Ma," a signal that he had adopted me and looked upon me as a mother. Indeed, he became my "family" in Ghana. One by one he brought around his "brothers" and their wives to introduce to me. I learned that he had left his wife and two children in the north and was trying to earn enough money to pay off the "bride price" he still owed his father-in-law. The bride price of three cows, or roughly $112, had to be paid before Yaro's family could rejoin him. Since he had never earned over $28 per month, he had managed to pay only the price of one cow when he began working for me.

Yaro could not read or write, which pained me, coming as I did from a teaching tradition, and as an incentive I told him I would raise his pay if he went to school and learned. I then rearranged his working hours so that he could attend a late afternoon mass education class. His response to my interest was an increasingly protective attitude. He insisted that I not shop alone for foodstuffs in the markets run by "mammy traders" because they would "cheat white man" and make their prices "too deah." When we moved to my permanent residence—a two-story house with a one-room cottage attached in the rear for the steward's quarters—he also insisted that I hire a "watchnight" to prevent thieves from breaking in while we slept. "Watchnights" were notorious for sleeping more than they watched, but their presence was a form of paid protection. They were said to be in with the thieves, who usually bypassed a house where one of their friends was employed.

After some weeks I received my first reward from Yaro's efforts in school. He was intensely security-conscious, and whenever we were both away from the house he would lock the doors of every room and hide the keys. One evening I came home while he was out and could not find the keys in their customary hiding place. In looking about, I happened to see a scrap of paper on top of a covered dish in the living room. Yaro had printed neatly the words "IS IN" and left the keys inside the dish. Later, when he could write his name, he proudly brought his notebook to show me his achievement. Only then did I discover that "Mr. Yaredi Akare," and not the casual "Yaro Fra Fra," which was on his license and which he had used in the census, was his true name. I learned it was a high compliment when a Fra Fra man trusted one enough to reveal his real name.

Behind Yaro's halting English was a keen intelligence and ambition.

His hobby was photography, and he had acquired an old camera and learned to take pretty good pictures. Then he wanted to get a bicycle for his long daily trips to market. To facilitate this transaction, I made the initial outlay, allowing him to repay a monthly sum from his wages. He bought accessories and fixed up the bicycle to his liking, and then I noticed he was not riding it. The hitch was that it had no license. When we went down to the Municipal Council to get the license, Yaro was told it would not be issued until he paid his head tax, which was cumulative for the previous seven years. Yaro balked at paying the tax; like many of the poor people in Ghana, he did not see why the government should take his money and give him nothing concrete in return. I had to explain that the government used the tax money for everyone, building schools, roads, and hospitals. He was finally convinced, and when he got the license I had the pleasure of seeing him sign his own name officially for the first time in his life.

This mark of responsible citizenship was an important step in Yaro's development. In time, he began writing his own grocery lists, and he asked me for the magazines I was about to discard so that he could pick out words he had learned. The test of our relationship of trust came unexpectedly, when he got word from the north that his father-in-law was taking back his wife because of the unpaid bride price. He needed a sum representing the cost of two cows and had not worked for me long enough to save anywhere near that amount. The sum in question was thirty pounds (eighty-four dollars), or more than two months' wages, but he thought he could bargain with his father-in-law and redeem his family for twenty-five pounds. I considered his predicament and decided to advance him thirty pounds and give him two weeks off to go north and settle his debt. It was understood that I would deduct five pounds a month from his pay until I had been repaid. Yaro went off, leaving one of his "brothers" to work in his place until he returned.

My skeptical friends thought I was foolish to entrust such a large amount of money to a steward I had known only a few months, and warned me that I might never see Yaro again. Indeed, when the two weeks passed and he had not come back, I began to think my critics were right. That evening at dusk I looked out and saw a small caravan coming slowly along the roadway on foot. Yaro led the procession, carrying a bundle of firewood on his head. His hair had been shaved off and I hardly recognized him. Behind him filed a small woman with a child on her back, a little girl clinging to her hand, and, bringing up the rear, a young boy about ten years old, leading a goat. I learned that Yaro's brother had died in the north, and Yaro had shaved his head in mourning. He had taken custody of his fatherless nephew and, according to custom, had brought back the firewood and goat to make a religious sacrifice. (Fortunately for me, he performed this ritual elsewhere.) I had now inherited a family of five—Yaro's wife, their two children, and Yaro's nephew in addition to Yaro himself—who lived unobtrusively in the tiny one-room cottage at the rear of my house for the remainder of my stay in Ghana.

Coming to grips with my African background was a complex experience which I tried to put into words in a piece entitled "What Is Africa to Me?—A Question of Identity." The following is abstracted from this unpublished essay:

> Accra, Ghana
> December, 1960

I came to Africa, among other reasons, to see for myself black people in their own homeland and come to grips with the pervasive myth of innate racial inferiority that stigmatizes all people of discernible African descent in the United States. Although now widely discredited, this powerful myth shaped my growing years and gave me ambivalent feelings about myself. A remote African ancestry about which I knew little, linked with a heritage of slavery and continued inferior status in America, has been the source of a hidden shame. I need to confront the vestiges of shame embedded in my identity by making an on-the-spot assessment of my African background and my relationship to it.

Since coming to Ghana I have traveled a bit in West Africa, immersed myself in its history, and observed the life of its peoples. After living and working here for almost a year, I find that my peculiar racial history has made me irrevocably an American, a product of the New World. The romantic notion of "coming back to Mother Africa to see my people" voiced by some Negro visitors from the United States cannot change this stubborn fact. America is "home" to me, however alienated or disinherited I have felt at times.

When I ask myself "What is Africa to me?" I discover that without knowledge of personal antecedents the African past exists in a great vacuum. I haven't the slightest notion who my particular African ancestors were, what region or tribe they came from, whether they were traders, fisherfolk, herdspeople, or farmers, what their customs were or what language they spoke. There is no African village to which I can make a sentimental journey. My genetic heritage over several centuries has been too diverse to preserve physical characteristics identifying me with any tribal group. Facing a vast continent of varied peoples whose appearance, language, and customs differ from my own, I am unable to conjure up some vicarious identity and can do little more than relate to the people I meet on the basis of our common humanity. More and more I am convinced that feelings of kinship grow out of shared experience.

My foreignness is evident in my physical appearance and in my bearing, betraying my American origins. As has happened throughout human history when peoples of different cultures have come together in close contact, I am the result of considerable biological intermixture as well as cultural cross-fertilization. Some anthropologists estimate that from 70 to 80 percent of all people of color in the United States are of mixed ancestry, having European, American Indian, and Oriental as well as African forebears in varied proportions. Ashley Montagu has theorized that in the American Negro, "we are developing a distinctively new ethnic type," and suggests that the physical stamina and adaptive qualities of this type are due to "hybrid vigor." In any event, many Africans (and some Europeans living in West Africa) are puzzled by the appearance of Negroes from America. They know vaguely of their "brothers who went across the sea," but their image of these "brothers" is that of black people like themselves. Unsophisticated Africans will describe a male or female Negro from the United States as "brown man," "copper man," or sometimes "American man"—seldom "black man," as they describe themselves.

Even if my tawny color did not make me stand out from the masses of black Africans, my unconscious movements reveal my origins. On my second day in Ghana, a young workman at the law school confronted me with the question, "Tell me, Madame, are you English lady or American lady?" "What do you think?" I responded. "I think you are American lady," he said. Curious, I asked him, "How do you know?" thinking that my complexion and accent had given him the clue. Instead, he replied, "I tell by your walk; American people walk different from English people." An Israeli diplomat later confirmed this observation, assuring me that he could pick out an American walking along the street from a distinctive relaxed hip movement. I have also watched a mahogany-colored young man from the United States decked out in gorgeous Nigerian robes and headdress, only to have the local Africans laugh at him as he strolled along the street. His coloring blended with his human surroundings but he could not conceal his American gait.

Understandably, people from the United States who have suffered so many indignities because of their color hope to find an acceptable identity here, but the poignant reality is that a dark skin does not automatically qualify one to fit into the African environment. I have seen a few American Negroes exerting great effort to merge with the local population of Ghana. They have worn the *Kente* (the Ghanaian national cloth, a brilliantly colored woven fabric), eaten the local "chop," and attempted to associate only with Ghanaians. In time, they have quietly discontinued the local dress and little by little returned to American-sponsored functions. They have also wound up with digestive disorders and related ailments. On the other hand, I have met a white American born and reared near the swamps of

Georgia who tells me he is able to eat local food, drink local water, and fare better against health hazards than his Negro friends from the northern United States because he built up an immunity to malaria and hookworm during his Georgia youth.

Particularly because African ancestry is associated with cruel rejections in America, finding themselves aliens in Africa is a severe jolt to those who come expecting instant acceptance from their "African brothers." They are shut off from the masses of people by barriers of language and custom and feel like outsiders in a way they never felt in the United States. They must make themselves understood by resorting to pidgin English, which offends their sensibilities. They experience all the irritations of those who come from highly industrialized countries. They have a different tempo from that of the local people and discover that their humor is not the same as African humor and their spontaneous laughter serves different functions. By contrast, white and colored Americans living and working in West Africa discover their kinship, feel outsiders together, and often find themselves seeking out one another in preference to their European or African counterparts. They speak the same language—"American"—understand the same nuances of humor, react alike to local conditions, and have a similar political outlook. Both groups recognize that their common identity sets them apart from Africans and Europeans.

Traveling about the countryside, I have not only seen piercing reminders of a radical break with the African past but have also realized how subsequent distortions of this past to justify chattel slavery in the United States contributed to a legacy of shame. When I go to villages in the interior of Ghana, where the people continue to follow many of their ancient customs, I am struck by their innate dignity, their ceremonial courtesy, and their strong sense of community cooperation in building a house or road. Although they are nonliterate and have few belongings or creature comforts, they are rooted in their own land and have a strong sense of self. An African man may house his family in a mud hut, sleep on the ground, barely make a living scrabbling in parched earth, and have only one ceremonial cloth of cheap fabric. Yet when he drapes his toga about his shoulder and comes to greet a stranger, he walks with such self-assurance that I cannot help thinking how his proud bearing contrasts with the bearing of his sharecropper counterparts I have seen in rural America. I find myself pondering the great violence done to the human spirit through American slavery and its aftermath, originally in the name of "Christianizing black savages."

The contrast is even more sharply drawn when I visit a local chief seated on a raised platform in his inner courtyard, dressed in colorful robes and surrounded by his toga-clad council of village elders. An umbrella is held over his head and his linguist stands by to communicate his greetings and responses, although the chief understands and speaks fluent English. He receives visitors according to a formal ritual marked by gravity, which includes an exchange of gifts and the pouring of a libation from the visitors' gift of costly gin drop by drop upon the ground, accompanied by solemn incantations. Here again I saw the self-possession of black people whose spirits have not been crippled by generations of repression.

I saw evidence of the break with the past and the beginnings of a new and sorrowful history in the monuments to the slave trade along the West African coast. To relive these beginnings I had to stand on the shores of the South Atlantic, in the shadow of Elmina Castle, now one of Ghana's popular tourist attractions. This great slave-trading fort on the Gulf of Guinea was built originally by the Portuguese in 1481, was captured by the Dutch in 1637, and eventually fell to the English in the eighteenth century. Surrounded on three sides by water, it was accessible by a drawbridge over a moat. I had to walk across the stone courtyard inside its high walls —today used by Ghanaian police cadets for drills—and climb the narrow winding steps to the auction room in a wing facing the ocean. Here in this high-ceilinged barnlike structure, thousands of Africans captured inland and driven to the coast by other Africans were sold to European traders for the slave markets in the Americas. Watching the auction through peepholes cut in the wall were the African chiefs who were growing rich and powerful from the lucrative trade in human flesh. They concealed themselves from their victims in a small cubicle above and to the rear of the auction area so that captives who managed to escape would never know the identity of their captors.

I had to follow in my imagination the movement of the captives as I walked through the dark, muggy dungeons, tunnel-shaped rooms, and small courtyards where they were stored awaiting shipment; I retraced their footsteps as they were herded along the black passageways under the cover of night, out through a small opening in the wall, onto the rocks above the sea, and down into the waiting canoes, which transported them to slaveships anchored offshore and to an unknown destination. Projecting myself backward in time, I tried to feel the bewilderment, the anguish, and the terror of this agonizing ordeal, which marked the introduction of Africans into America.

The young Ghanaian guide who glibly recited these historic events as he led me about could not possibly know how immediate these happenings were to me or the tumultuous emotions I felt at that moment. Tropical Africans, for whom American slavery is little more than a legend (or a political weapon), would hardly understand the shock I felt listening to a local chief tell how his great-grandfather and grandfather used to catch and sell slaves and how his grandfather often wondered what happened to those he sold. I was too numbed to tell this chief that I am only two generations removed from slavery, that my own grandmother was born a slave, and that I had seen its scars on her personality.

These experiences have left me deeply shaken, perhaps as much by the casual manner in which facts of the slave trade are related without embarrassment or feeling as by the facts themselves. I have a profound new respect for those unknown African forebears who survived the horror of that ordeal, but am filled with an unexpected bitterness when I realize the extent to which many Africans themselves participated in the slave trade, drew their wealth from it, and continued to carry it on after it was outlawed by England and the United States. I am forced to realize that the cruel exploitation of human victims by the most brutal methods is not the monopoly of any one race or nation. Thus, when I hear an African leader speaking to a world audience and demanding "restitution" for the wrongs done to the African peoples, his rhetoric leaves me unmoved. I cannot help thinking how difficult it would be to apportion blame for the wrongs done to Americans of African descent. The chain of responsibility touches too many places and peoples, including the African slave traders.

I am beginning to understand that I am the product of a new history which began on African shores but which has not been shared by Africans, a history accompanied by such radical changes in a new environment that over time it produced a new identity. For me, the net gain of coming to Africa has been to reexperience imaginatively this break in continuity as well as to gain an appreciation for the peoples and cultures who remained on the African side of the historical divide. The veil of mystery has been removed and Africans are no longer faceless peoples. They have emerged as individuals who may be kind or cruel, honest or thievish, industrious or lazy, arrogant or gentle, as the case may be. And in this knowledge of real people, lingering ghosts of the past have been exorcised. I can face all the contradictions of my American background without ambivalence and return to my country with renewed determination to claim my heritage.

In the years that have passed since I first recorded those searing impressions, nothing has dimmed the impact of the lessons I learned in Ghana. Generation after generation of the best of Africa's youth—those with straight backs, those with good teeth, those with strong hearts—were shipped in manacles across the terrible sea. Some jumped overboard, others died of disease or of overpowering grief. But those who made it were champions, and the American Negro was born out of their will to survive.

CHAPTER 28

Teaching in Ghana

Two months after my arrival in Ghana, the electorate approved the new constitution, which was said to incorporate some features of the American presidency as well as the parliamentary system, adapting both to the Ghanaian custom of paramount chieftancy. The result made Ghana a republic but without the separation of powers familiar to Americans. Western writers described Ghana's government as "authoritarian," a government of one-party rule. Members of the Convention People's Party, which had been in power for almost ten years, publicly declared that "the CPP is the government and the government is the CPP." Significantly, in Accra only 40 percent of the voters turned out, and 30 percent of those who cast their ballots voted against Kwame Nkrumah's party. Following the April plebiscite, there were public threats of "purges" and charges of disloyalty among Ghana's civil servants. Dr. Nkrumah also frightened the academic community by making a speech in which he declared that academic freedom was not to be used to cloak hostility to government policies.

Although the masses of people were likable and friendly, a growing uneasiness and fear among civil servants and intellectuals was apparent to any foreigner. Ghanaians, afraid to express their opinions to other Ghanaians for fear of losing their jobs, talked freely to foreigners who had no stake in the government. Even foreigners were warned to be careful of their statements, however, and I was told I might be deported if I wrote an article for publication in the United States that, in the opinion of the Ghana government, was critical of its policies.

Coupled with the political turmoil and the confusion of a society in transition, the magnitude of the academic task I faced at the law school seemed overwhelming. The faculty was small, the curriculum limited. Our group consisted of the director, John Lang from England; a retired judge from Tanganyika; a former antigovernment senator from the Union of South Africa, now in voluntary exile; an English-trained Ghanaian; and myself, supplemented by one or two lecturers from the local bench and bar. We had no faculty meetings and no unified approach to the problems of legal education in Ghana. We had the almost impossible task of developing lawyers in a country where the bar had not functioned as a professional group; where the statutes were antiquated and in a hopelessly confused state; where no professional legal journal existed in the whole of sub-Saharan Africa which might facilitate academic discussion; and where we had no casebooks or textbooks and had to develop our materials as we went along. Our library facilities were extremely limited and our students worked full time, usually as civil servants or grade school teachers, attending school in the evening. They depended more on lecture notes than on independent research for their training.

We could expect little help from the local judicial system. At the lower levels were lay magistrates, who were not legally trained. At the higher levels were judges without clerks or court stenographers, who had to hear a case and take notes at the same time. They had no transcripts before them when reviewing evidence, and no written briefs were submitted to them. They did not write their opinions but, following English custom, delivered their "judgments" orally. Since African customary law existed alongside English law, although it was not codified and varied from place to place, there was the additional problem of discovering and applying this law in a given case.

I was not the only woman on the faculty—our lecturer in criminal law was Senior Magistrate Annie Baeta, whose courtroom was a model for criminal-trial practice—but I was the only American, and this placed me in an unenviable position. I had been assigned to teach constitutional and administrative law in part because the faculty preferred to have an American deal with politically controversial issues. When I began to teach, the new constitution was barely two months old, and there were no judicial precedents in Ghanaian law for its immediate interpretation. I would be strictly on my own trying to develop in my students an appreciation for the Anglo-American legal system as applied to Ghanaian institutions in a country rapidly moving toward the suppression of freedom of expression and other civil liberties inherent in Western constitutionalism.

My dismay increased when I examined the records of my prospective students and discovered how little preparation they had for the rigorous demands of law as I had studied it in the United States. The overwhelming majority had never gone to college, and their secondary school education included no political and social science or government. Their studies were limited to mathematics, general science, geography, religious instruction, English literature, the history of the British Empire, and, occasionally, Latin.

Given their meager academic backgrounds, the lack of teaching materials, and the prickly political situation in Ghana, I hardly knew where to begin in constructing my course. I had only a small collection of miscellaneous books I had brought with me. Aside from a set of United States Supreme Court Reports sent to the law school by Peter Weiss, an American lawyer, the school library had few helpful materials. My immediate problem was to devise a course that would bridge some of the gaps in the students' knowledge, introduce them to basic principles of government and of written constitutions, and supply them with research materials from texts not easily available to them.

I finally put together a set of lecture notes in outline form which combined elementary concepts of government with a comparative study of principles of constitutional law as they evolved respectively in Britain and the United States, then attempted to identify their influence on the constitutional development of Ghana. The outline began with definitions of a state, the functions of a government, the nature and scope of constitutional law, and moved from there to a discussion of such constitutional theories as separation of powers, parliamentary sovereignty, judicial review, and the rule of law. Each topical item was followed by summary statements and excerpts from various scholarly texts—an English view, an American view, and, whenever possible, quotations from a constitutional authority in India and Pakistan. The lecture notes were accompanied by a set of cases and materials drawn from a wide variety of sources.

Fortunately, I found a loyal friend and ally at the law school in Joyce Markham, who worked as secretary to the director. Joyce was a high-spirited, quick-tongued young woman from Chicago whose family had migrated to Liberia in 1951, when she was a teenager just out of high school. She had lived in Ghana since 1953, married a Ghanaian, and taken out citizenship. Her husband was a close associate of Dr. Nkrumah and she had worked in his office when he was prime minister, but she could not suppress her critical view of the trend of events and allowed no one to step on her rights. Joyce volunteered to assist me, and in her capable hands the mass of material was mimeographed on legal-size paper and bound with bright-blue covers. When the job was completed, I had an impressive document, tailored (I hoped) to the special needs of my class.

On the first day of the term, I nervously faced several rows of young men whose impassive expressions gave me no hint of their reaction to the unique experience of having a woman professor from the United States. They expected a lecture and looked surprised when I distributed the blue-bound lecture notes and explained that I had prepared them in advance for study at home. Having been trained in the lecture method, they looked even more amazed that they must be prepared to come to class and discuss the issues outlined and that lectures would be used only to fill in gaps. At the next session I introduced another innovation by having them rearrange their tables and chairs in a square, seminar style, so that they faced one another and could carry on informal discussions.

Our progress was slow at first; the students were unused to expressing their opinions and needed reassurance. To encourage the widest possible participation, I never rejected a student's offering, however stumbling or unclear it seemed. We would struggle with it until I recognized the point he was trying to make, then I would rephrase it for the benefit of the class, asking him if this was what he meant. Often, when my opinion was asked, I would not answer the question specifically; instead I would outline the principles from which to proceed, in an effort to encourage the students to answer it for themselves. As the students warmed up to the discussion method, I timed the explosive issues so as to leave them with a provocative question at the end of the class period. This technique paid off handsomely. Classes ended in an uproar as the students clattered down the steps and stood in the schoolyard for an hour or more arguing a point, sometimes becoming so excited they switched from English to their own vernaculars. The next step was teaching them to support their arguments with judicial authority based upon their own independent research, so we held classes in the law library. John Lang demonstrated how to look up a problem in the available English digests and reference works and I duplicated the process with American sources.

When we took up the Rule of Law, which included the concept of human rights, the idea struck me that a review of United States Supreme Court decisions on civil rights would demonstrate the growth of a written constitution through judicial interpretation as well as give Ghanaian students a needed perspective on the American race problem. I lectured on sixteen cases, beginning with the infamous *Dred Scott* case of 1857, in which a divided court held that the descendants of Africans were not citizens within the meaning of the U.S. Constitution and had no right to sue in the courts, and in which Chief Justice Roger B. Taney observed that blacks were regarded "as beings of an inferior order . . . and so far inferior that they had no rights which a white man was bound to respect." From this degraded constitutional position I traced the long struggle of American Negroes for recognition of their rights as full citizens, through the "separate but equal" doctrine of *Plessy,* which upheld state-enforced racial segregation, to the overturning of this doctrine in the school desegregation cases of 1954, and finally to the Court's ringing pronouncement in 1958, at the height of the Little Rock crisis, that the constitutional rights of Negro children "are not to be sacrificed or yielded to the violence and disorder which have followed the actions of the Governor and the Legislature" of the State of Arkansas. My lectures presented the historical background of each case and described the political and social atmosphere of the more recent decisions. I showed the students a copy of the voluminous brief in the 1954 cases, pointing out the hundreds of hours of labor involved in preparing these cases for argument, the authorities amassed, and the teamwork of dozens of lawyers, white and black, who worked voluntarily and without compensation to vindicate the rights of the Negro plaintiffs. I also read excerpts from the majority opinions, or dissents which opposed racist views of the majority, emphasizing that throughout the civil rights struggle in the United States, courageous voices had spoken out for the rights of all human beings. The students were so fascinated with this presentation that they insisted upon extra class time to complete the review.

By coincidence, two weeks later Professor Fowler V. Harper of the Yale Law School arrived in Accra under the auspices of the U.S. State Department to give a series of lectures to our students on civil liberties in the United States, the role of the U.S. Supreme Court, separation of powers, and judicial review. I had never met Professor Harper but had studied his textbook on torts as a first-year law student, and I was delighted to hear him clinch some of the points I had just made in class. He also showed a television film reenacting several of the same cases I had presented and using identical quotations from the opinions. He expressed surprise and pleasure when he discovered how conversant some of my students were with the issues and heard the cogent questions they raised in discussion. In fact, the coincidence was so striking that it looked as if Professor Harper and I had collaborated in advance and that I had consciously primed my students for his visit. It was one of two high points in my course. The other was having the students meet and hear my former professor at Howard Law School, Judge William H. Hastie of the U.S. Court of Appeals for the Third Circuit. At my invitation Judge Hastie, who was on his way home from a conference of the International Commission of Jurists in Lagos, stopped over in Accra to lecture to my class. The students were thrilled to have personal contact with two distinguished American legal scholars, and as their professor, I received compliments for the favorable impression they made on their visitors.

My greatest reward, however, came on the last day of the term from Joseph Musah, the youngest member of the class. Musah was from the

Northern Region and spoke of the poverty of his people and how little opportunity for education they had been given in the past. He told me that if he was successful in being admitted to the Ghana bar, he would be the first lawyer from his district. He added that Ghanaian students had been led to believe that American education was inferior, but that through my constitutional law class, which was the first course at the law school taught by an American, he and his classmates had come to change their views. "We used to accept without questioning whatever the lecturer told us," he said. "Through your class we have now learned to inquire."

Looking back, I see the sixteen months I spent in Ghana as a roller-coaster existence, charged with the excitement of tumultuous events on an awakening continent. Accra was the gateway to Africa south of the Sahara, a nerve center of African nationalism and a political seismograph registering every tremor of the struggle for black nationhood. It combined the attributes of a capital city—intense political maneuverings, intrigues, rumors, and counterrumors—with the intimacies of a small town. During those years, Accra was the site of numerous international conferences; one continually rubbed shoulders with foreign delegates as well as diplomats, and felt "the winds of change" at close range.

Living in Accra during the Congo crisis was like living with a bomb that might explode at any moment. The actual fighting was several hours from Accra by air, but President Nkrumah's deep involvement with Patrice Lumumba brought the war close to us; its military and political repercussions were part of our daily lives. When the airlift of U.N. troops to the Congo began, the transport planes stopped in Accra to refuel, and I could stand in my yard near the airport and watch the huge USAF Globemasters, barely airborne, lumber past just above my roof before turning southward over the Guinea Gulf. Later, when U.N. Secretary General Dag Hammarskjöld made the first jet trip to Accra en route to the Congo and stopped to confer with President Nkrumah, we watched his plane come in over the flat plain of Accra for a landing on the unfinished jet strip and stop just twenty feet from the end of the runway. In January 1961, when Mr. Hammarskjöld cut short his mission to the Union of South Africa to return to U.N. headquarters in New York because of the Lumumba crisis, the Pan American jet carrying him and his aide (who was later killed with him in a plane crash) stopped at Accra to take on passengers, including Judge Hastie, who had just completed his lectures to my classes, and Dr. Horace Mann Bond, president of Lincoln University and a member of the international commission on the University of Ghana. Several of us from the American colony were at the airport to see them off. We watched the plane taxi down the runway ready for takeoff, then suddenly turn and taxi back again. Seconds later, a violent tropical thunderstorm with tornado-like winds broke over us and raged for more than an hour. Successive bolts of lightning struck the power station and the auxiliary unit, and we huddled in darkness between rapid flashes of eerie light, staring at the ghost-like plane on the tarmac. When the torrential rains stopped and the plane finally took off, a Ghanaian friend said, "The gods are angry."

Relations between Ghana and the United States deteriorated as the Congo situation worsened, and Americans living in Accra were exposed to continuous, shrill denunciations of American foreign policy. The government-controlled press contemptuously referred to Dr. Ralph Bunche as a "stooge of U.S. imperialism" and soon began applying the same phrase to American Negroes generally. Once he became president, Mr. Nkrumah moved quickly to suppress all dissent. Because I was teaching a course in constitutional law, which necessarily dealt with the workings of the Ghana government, I was in a sensitive position, especially when some of my students began to raise pointed questions about the authoritarian direction of the Nkrumah regime. My suspicion that the government was interested in what was going on in my class was confirmed one day when I arrived to find six uniformed members of the Criminal Investigation Department sitting in my classroom. I spent some anxious moments during the next hour but conducted the discussion in my usual manner, as if the C.I.D. members were guests. They did not return, and when I heard nothing from official sources I concluded the government had been unable to find anything offensive in my teaching.

Nevertheless, this open display of government surveillance warned me just how precarious my situation was. (After I left, the American lawyers who followed me to teach in Accra were unceremoniously deported overnight.) Shortly after this incident, Fowler and Miriam Harper, having completed an African tour, returned to Accra on their way back to the United States. They spent several days with me as my houseguests and their observations confirmed my own anxieties. Professor Harper's assessment of Ghana's political future was pessimistic. He was convinced that Nkrumah was embarked on the road to dictatorship and that my approach to constitutional law represented a threat to authoritarian rule. He said he was impressed with my teaching ability but felt that in the current political atmosphere my talents were being wasted. Because Professor Harper felt Nkrumah was simply waiting for a chance to get rid of me, he suggested I return to the United States and come to Yale for my doctorate in law. He spoke warmly of Yale's graduate program and said the law school would be delighted to have me.

The thought of going back to school at my age had not occurred to me. I told Professor Harper I was too old to undertake additional study, and besides, I was not interested in doing so unless there was the possibility of a breakthrough for women on law school faculties.

He responded that my objections on the grounds of age were nonsense. He also pointed out that Yale Law School already had two women on its faculty, and he assured me he would do everything in his power to support me. "At least you should give it a try," he said, and as soon as he got back to New Haven he had the school registrar send me the necessary application forms. Somewhat dubious over Professor Harper's optimism, I nevertheless filled out the forms and mailed them back. Fortunately, I had little time to brood over my situation. A project developed that absorbed most of my energies for the remainder of my stay in Ghana.

For some time I had been discussing the urgent need for published works on Ghana law with a colleague, Dr. Leslie Rubin, a former senator in the South African parliament who had chosen self-exile rather than remain in a country that practiced *apartheid*. He was now senior lecturer in law at the University College of Ghana. Dr. Rubin had been in touch with Sweet & Maxwell, London publishers who were interested in putting out a series of books on law in Africa, including a volume on Ghana. In view of the worsening political situation, both Professor Rubin and I felt we would be unable to stay in the country much longer, but we also felt we could leave behind a significant contribution to legal education in Ghana if we collaborated on a textbook that would serve as a convenient reference for teachers, students, lawyers, judges, and government officials. Our joint effort, the first book in the series, was published in late 1961 under the title *The Constitution and Government of Ghana*. Dr. Rubin and I had left the country before the book appeared, but it was so well received that it went into a second and revised edition in 1964.

With about half the manuscript completed by spring vacation in 1961, I was so drained by the strenuous working schedule and continued attacks of malaria that my local physician urged a change of climate. I spent two weeks in Europe, flying to Holland to meet my friends Caroline Ware and Gardiner Means, who were returning from a lecture tour in Yugoslavia. I had not realized how bound I was to my own culture until the plane landed and, for the first time in thirteen months, I felt the bracing air of the north temperate zone and saw the pink faces of Europeans, who reminded me of home in the United States. That night I slept blissfully under a blanket, relishing the cold temperature.

The vacation was a sparkling interlude of incredible timing and happy coincidences. In Holland, we were houseguests of Professor and Mrs. J. M. Romein, a delightful couple and the embodiment of World War II history. Professor Romein was one of Dr. Ware's two coeditors of Volume Six of *History of Mankind—The Twentieth Century*, a UNESCO project. Mrs.

Romein had been consulted by the finder of Anne Frank's diary, written while Anne was in hiding in Amsterdam before she was discovered by the Nazis and perished with her mother and sister in a Nazi concentration camp. I had worked on a case involving *The Diary of a Young Girl* in 1958, when our firm defended Anne Frank's father, Otto, in a civil suit charging breach of contract in connection with the dramatized version of the book, and I shared Mrs. Romein's deep interest in this international classic, which she had been instrumental in first bringing to public attention.

Our arrival in Holland also coincided with the opening session of the International Court of Justice and the swearing in of Philip Jessup as the new United States judge on that tribunal. I had known Lois Jessup ever since we worked together on the Stevenson campaign in 1956, and I had studied international law under Philip Jessup at Columbia University before leaving for Ghana. The previous summer, when he visited Ghana, I had driven him and his party sightseeing around Accra and we had laughed over how he had to stuff his long legs into my little Karmann Ghia. To be present at The Hague on this important occasion and see him take the oath of office along with new judges from Poland and Japan was an unexpected thrill. Afterward we listened to Dean Acheson and James Hyde from the United States, both formally attired in striped pants and tail coats, argue the opposing sides of a dispute between Thailand and Cambodia over the ownership of an ancient temple.

From Holland, Skipper, Gardiner, and I flew to England, for two days in London. I delivered the partially completed Ghana manuscript to Sweet & Maxwell while Skipper conferred with her English publishers on the UNESCO work. Then for my benefit we had a lawyer's holiday. We went to hear the arguments in a criminal appeal before the Lord High Justice's Bench. We wandered through Temple Inn and the Inns of Court and, on impulse, walked unannounced into a lawyer's chambers and had a pleasant chat with the surprised occupant. We saw the Speaker's procession in the House of Commons and in the House of Lords we sat in the balcony reserved for members of the Commonwealth Parliamentary Association and watched the investiture of a new peer, done with all the colorful pageantry of British tradition. We also managed to see on successive evenings the long-running play *The Mousetrap* and a musical, *King Kong,* performed by a South African Coloured troupe.

Gardiner then flew back to the United States and Skipper and I spent several days visiting American friends in Warwickshire and Essex and touring Shakespeare country before going on to Paris, where Skipper had conferences scheduled at UNESCO headquarters. We managed to get about on Skipper's quite literal translation of French, the most memorable example being the directions we received when we were looking for the proper entrance to the law courts. According to Skipper, we were told to "penetrate the interior and attend to the séance." I left her in Paris, flying out of Orly airport just hours before a bomb exploded there, an act of terrorism connected to the Algerian struggle. In Rome, where I changed planes and had a layover for several hours, I spent the time visiting Saint Peter's basilica and wandering about the ruins of the Colosseum.

Several weeks after returning to Accra, I received a cable from the Yale Law School, telling me of my admission to graduate study and the award of a five-thousand-dollar fellowship for the coming school year. Professor Harper had lost no time in opening the way for me. The news meant I would have to scramble to complete all assignments, since I would not be returning to Ghana after my summer leave. Earlier that year I had met Keith Highet, a young American graduate of Harvard Law School who was in Ghana on a year's grant from the Maxwell School at Syracuse University. Keith had originally been assigned to the attorney general's office in Accra, but he had not been given any work to do and was thoroughly frustrated. I persuaded him to transfer to the law school and let him teach some of my classes. We hit it off well, and he was delighted to have contact with students. Toward the end of the term he took over more of my school load so that I could devote additional time to finishing up my chapters of the textbook.

Just before I left Ghana in June, Keith Highet and I found ourselves drawn into a government controversy. Together we played a behind-the-scenes role in an unsuccessful legal effort to halt the trend toward absolute rule. Eight members of the party opposing the Nkrumah regime had been arrested and detained under the Preventive Detention Act of 1958, which empowered the chief executive to order the detention of any citizen of Ghana for a period up to five years if satisfied that the person was acting in a manner prejudicial to the security of the state. The detainees had retained Dr. J. B. Danquah, the most distinguished lawyer in Ghana, to represent them. Dr. Danquah, a venerable, scholarly man, was known as the doyen of Ghana's independence. It was he who had persuaded Kwame Nkrumah to return to the country and assume leadership in the struggle against England, and he was universally loved and respected. After Nkrumah took power and embarked upon repressive policies, Danquah broke with him and became part of the opposition.

Dr. Danquah brought habeas corpus proceedings on behalf of his clients in the detention case and, as part of his argument, wanted to attack the constitutionality of the Preventive Detention Act. He was not familiar with American constitutional law but had been talking with one of my most devoted students, Kwaku Baah, and was convinced that the "American lawyers" had the expertise to present the strongest argument on this point in his brief. So he sent Kwaku Baah under cover of night to appeal for our assistance.

Keith and I believed an argument could be made that Nkrumah's flagrant use of the Preventive Detention Act to crush all opposition to his policies violated a provision of the new constitution that required him upon assumption of office to declare solemnly his adherence to certain fundamental principles, including freedom of speech and assembly and the maintenance of freedom and justice. Dr. Nkrumah himself and the government white paper issued before the plebiscite had declared that the new constitution contained safeguards against oppression. It was worth testing this constitutional provision to determine whether the people had been cynically misled by these reassurances.

We had to work fast; Dr. Danquah's request came on the weekend just hours before he would have to present his argument to the Ghana Supreme Court Monday morning. By Sunday evening we had typed up the last page of the point on the constitutional issue, but then we faced the problem of how to get the draft across town to Dr. Danquah without attracting attention. Fortunately for us, it was during the rainy season and the day's torrential downpours had left the streets deserted. Kwaku and I took a roundabout route to Dr. Danquah's house, driving through floods so deep that once or twice the car sank into invisible potholes and we had to take off our shoes and wade in pools of water up to our knees to lift it out again.

I was back in the United States when the Supreme Court of Ghana rendered its decision rejecting Dr. Danquah's argument and dismissing his clients' appeal. The Court held:

> [The declaration] to which every President must pledge himself . . . does not represent a legal requirement which can be enforced by the courts. . . . The declarations, however, impose on every President a moral obligation, and provide a political yardstick by which the conduct of the Head of State can be measured by the electorate. The people's remedy for any departure from the principles of the declaration is through the use of the ballot box, and not through the courts.

Two weeks after the court rendered its decision, Dr. Danquah himself was arrested under the Act. He was released after about a year, but was rearrested and died in prison. When Nkrumah's rule was finally overthrown in 1966, I recalled Joyce Markham's impassioned declaration to me before I left Ghana: when the coup came, she said, she wanted to be among the first to help tear down Nkrumah's statue in the public square. By the time that happened, however, Joyce and her family had already fled to Tanzania.

CHAPTER 29

Civil Wrongs and Rights

L EAVING Ghana, I was anguished by my students' sadness at seeing me depart and by the vast needs I was leaving behind. At the same time I felt a tremendous sense of relief to be going home.

I had been back in the United States hardly a month before my contentment ended with a sharp jolt of reality. I was in New Haven looking for an apartment so I could get settled before fall classes began at Yale, and my introduction to the city was a sickening reminder that racism flourished on the edge of a liberal university campus. Friends had thoughtfully arranged to have Marjorie Ulman, an experienced member of an interracial committee, meet me and take me around to see available apartments. We finally found one within my budget on Howe Street near the campus, and Mrs. Ulman was delighted because she and her husband were friends of the rental agent. When we arrived at the rental office, however, the agent turned me down cold. He said he had nothing against me personally, but he simply could not risk renting an apartment to a colored person.

One is never really prepared for those sudden, ruthless psychic blows, which, although rendered without physical violence, are no less in violation of what is sacred to the individual—human dignity. The invisible wounds from racial indignities generate an inner rage which festers under the surface, often unrelieved until it explodes in indiscriminate violence against white people. I was angered and hurt, of course, but Marjorie Ulman was devastated. She had not expected a crude form of racial bigotry from a friend, and the personal rejection she felt cemented a bond of understanding between us. I admired the principled stand she took in that

344

situation. Difficult as it was for her, and notwithstanding her friendship, she filed a complaint against the real estate agent with the local antidiscrimination agency. I found an apartment on Dixwell Avenue close to campus, but it was a long time before the bitter aftertaste of that experience disappeared.

When classes at Yale began, I developed all the anxieties of an older woman returning to school and surrounded by bright, mostly male, law students less than half my age. For a time I was nearly overwhelmed and had to lecture myself to keep from becoming discouraged. I would have to accept the fact that many of these students had certain advantages as part of their birthright which gave them an edge I could never hope to duplicate. What was important was that I come to class prepared to the best of my ability, and if it took me three times as long as they required to cover an assignment, I should consider the extra time spent as *my* investment in the equalizing of opportunity.

Once over the initial panic, I began to enjoy being a student again and having my mind stretched in Myres S. McDougal's classes on law and social policy, F. S. C. Northrop's heady lectures on legal and ethical philosophy, and Thomas Emerson's course on political and civil rights. It was a good time for me to be at Yale. I got to know some of the younger law students, whose ranks included the new generation of civil rights activists, among them Heywood Burns, Eleanor Holmes (Norton), Inez Smith (Reid), Marian Wright (Edelman), and Clarence Laing. Most of these future leaders were fresh from student sit-in demonstrations and marches against racial segregation in the South, and I was especially glad that my own earlier activism gave me credibility among them and won their respect.

There were some fifty students in our graduate program, about half of whom came from foreign countries and represented fifteen or more nationalities. The largest proportion were from Asia, Africa, and Latin America. Mary Ellen Caldwell and I were the only women. She had earned her master's degree at Yale a year or so earlier and was then appointed lecturer in charge of the orientation of foreign students. In time, Mary Ellen and I became good friends and gave one another moral support as we struggled with our feeling of isolation in an almost entirely male domain. At the end of my first year, I was appointed tutor of law, to work with Mary Ellen and Assistant Dean Charles Runyon in the orientation program. My specific assignment was to help foreign degree candidates who had language difficulties, assisting them with the mechanics of writing term papers and theses in English. This assistance was especially important to Asian and African students trained under the English tutorial system.

We also took groups of foreign students on field trips, visiting industrial plants and Wall Street, and observing trial procedures in local, state, and federal courts as well as the operations of large law firms in New York. On one of these trips my old law firm, Paul, Weiss, Rifkind, Wharton & Garrison, played host to a group of students. They joined the legal staff at its bimonthly luncheon and were welcomed by U.S. Ambassador to the United Nations Adlai Stevenson, a former member of the firm, who attended the luncheon especially to greet them. Later we toured the firm's offices and held small seminars with leading partners who directed various departments.

My work in Ghana began to bear fruit. Three of my former students completed the program at the Ghana School of Law in the year after my departure and won fellowships for further study in the United States. One spent a year at Harvard University; Joseph Musah, the young man who had "learned to inquire," was coming to Yale for a specialized program; and Kwaku Baah, my devoted student assistant, received a fellowship from Northwestern University.

Kwaku Baah's situation was desperate. His role in openly assisting Dr. Danquah in the preventive detention case had brought him under government suspicion and he was in grave danger of being arrested before he could leave the country. In fact, as I learned later, he miraculously escaped arrest only because of an "error" at the security office. A good friend who worked as a typist there conveniently failed to include his name on the official list of persons to be detained. He was safe only until the error was discovered and corrected, but he had no funds to leave Ghana, and Northwestern University had not included travel expenses in its grant. He could take advantage of his fellowship only upon reaching the United States.

Kwaku sent me an urgent appeal for assistance. I showed his letter to Fowler Harper, who remembered him as the kind of "gutsy civil libertarian" so badly needed in Africa if the rule of law was to prevail over chaos and violence. There was no time to arrange a loan, so I gambled with my own scholarship funds, underwrote his boat passage with the American-Israeli Shipping Company, and then sent out a round-robin letter to a list of my friends and acquaintances to raise five hundred dollars to cover his boat ticket and funds to get him to Chicago.

The response was astounding. In all, I received over $2,600 from 135 contributors—enough to cover Kwaku's travel expenses and give him a clothing allowance (he arrived with one light summer suit and his few belongings in a small battered suitcase). The additional funds allowed me to assist a young student from India with his college tuition and to help both Kwaku Baah and Joseph Musah continue their education for a second year. Kwaku eventually got his master's degree, and remained in the United States until the Nkrumah regime was overthrown. He then returned to Ghana, was elected to Parliament, and served as under secretary of the interior in the Busia government. Joseph Musah eventually became general counsel of the state-owned Ghana Insurance Company.

During my four years at Yale, two major developments absorbed my energies. One was the civil rights issue, which became so pressing by 1963 that I switched my doctoral research from a study of constitutional guarantees of human rights in the organic documents of the new African states to our own domestic problem, and I ultimately wrote a dissertation entitled "Roots of the Racial Crisis: Prologue to Policy." The second development was the emerging issue of women's rights, on which I spent most of my free time in voluntary research.

I had been interested in the rights of women since the early 1940s and in isolated instances had challenged sex-based discrimination, but it was not until President Kennedy issued an executive order in December 1961 creating the President's Commission on the Status of Women that I had an opportunity to participate in a detailed study of women's position in American society. The twenty-six-member commission of distinguished women and men was chaired by Eleanor Roosevelt until her death on November 7, 1962. It would be concerned with "barriers to the full realization of women's basic rights" and was directed to "review progress and make recommendations as needed for constructive action." Its final report to the President was to be submitted by October 1, 1963.

The creation of the President's Commission on the Status of Women (PCSW) was the most significant and exciting development affecting women in decades: no such concentration on women's problems by prominent people had ever occurred before. I avidly followed the early stages of the body's work through Dr. Caroline Ware, a Commission member who had prepared a stimulating working paper, "Women Today—Trends and Issues," for the Commission's initial discussion.

Dollie Lowther Robinson, a friend and neighbor of my Brooklyn years, was working in the Women's Bureau of the U.S. Department of Labor at the time, and at her urging, I was invited in the spring of 1962 to serve on the Committee on Civil and Political Rights, one of seven study committees set up by the PCSW to assist it in formulating policy in particular fields. Our committee was assigned to review and make recommendations on "differences in legal treatment of men and women in regard to political and civil rights, property rights, and family relations." The other six committees were to deal with education, federal employment, home and community, private employment, protective labor legislation, and social insurance and taxes.

I look back on this experience as an intensive consciousness-raising process leading directly to my involvement in the new women's movement that surfaced a few years later. Through the work of the President's Commission, upwards of two hundred able women (and a number of sympathetic men) from many professions and from all sections of the country were brought together in Washington for meetings over an eighteen-month period, and out of these associations developed a new strength and increasing pride in being a woman. An important by-product of the Commission's existence was that like-minded women found one another, bonds developed through working together, and an informal feminist network emerged to act as leaven in the broader movement that followed.

The fourteen-member Committee on Civil and Political Rights was a high-powered group of eleven women and three men chaired by Commission member Edith Green of the U.S. House of Representatives and cochaired by another Commission member, Marguerite Rawalt, a tax attorney with the Internal Revenue Service and a former president of the National Federation of Business and Professional Women's Clubs. Because of our subject matter, seven of our members were lawyers, and we had the full-time professional services of Mary O. Eastwood, a highly capable young attorney on loan from the Office of Legal Counsel, Department of Justice. The legal contingent was balanced by the heads of four national women's organizations and top officials from two international unions. I hit it off immediately with Judge Florence K. Murray of Rhode Island, whose views paralleled my own, and, among the organizational representatives, developed a close working relationship with Sophie Yarnall Jacobs, president of the National Council of Women, U.S.A.

Our committee had been carefully selected to reflect a wide range of experience and expertise, because it had to deal with the most controversial issue to come before the PCSW—the proposed Equal Rights Amendment to the United States Constitution, which had been introduced in every session of Congress since 1923 and was increasingly a source of bitter debate. The amendment provided that "Equality of rights under the law shall not be denied or abridged by the United States or by any State on account of sex." Controversy over the proposed amendment had divided women's groups, and one of the chief reasons for the formation of the President's Commission on the Status of Women was to find an alternative. In fact, according to Katherine Ellickson, the PCSW's executive secretary, the original proposal for the Commission that was submitted to the White House began:

The appointment by the President of a commission on women in our American democracy would substitute constructive recommendations for the present troublesome and futile agitation about the equal rights amendment.

The Commission would help the nation to set forth before the world the story of women's progress in a free, democratic society, and to move further towards full partnership, creative use of skills, and genuine equality of opportunity.

Ellickson, who with Esther Peterson, then head of the Women's Bureau, U.S. Department of Labor, and Evelyn Harrison, a high official of the U.S. Civil Service Commission, had developed the concept of the PCSW, later described its beginnings in a memo dated January 1976, now held by the Walter P. Reuther Library at Wayne State University. She wrote:

> In opposing ERA, we wanted to preserve protections currently afforded to families through support laws. We also feared the abolition of state protective labor laws which could usually be secured only for women. We thought that the Equal Rights Amendment would wipe out these still-needed protections and that off-setting gains to be derived from it were problematical since the all-male Supreme Court would still have to interpret each particular situation, as under the Fourteenth Amendment.

This view was widely held among women's groups and liberal and labor organizations at the time. The National Women's Party and the National Federation of Business and Professional Women's Clubs, both of which ardently supported the ERA, were minority voices. Although Marguerite Rawalt was the lone member of the PCSW who strongly advocated the amendment, her presence on our committee along with the current national president of the Business and Professional Women ensured that the issue would be thoroughly debated.

I had not been involved in the heated controversies over the ERA and was not actually opposed to the amendment, although I thought it had little chance of getting through Congress in the near future. However, I found myself at the center of the debate when the Committee requested me to prepare for its information and consideration a memorandum entitled "A Proposal to Reexamine the Applicability of the Fourteenth Amendment to State Laws and Practices Which Discriminate on the Basis of Sex *Per Se.*" The Committee felt I was the logical person to make this inquiry because of my academic background in civil rights cases under the Fourteenth Amendment. When I undertook the study, I had no idea where my research would lead me and certainly did not anticipate that the resulting memorandum would play a strategic role in the formulation of Commission policy. Yet, knowing the strong opposition to the ERA within the Commission, and doubting that it would receive congressional approval, I was eager to explore a constitutional alternative.

While researching the memorandum at Yale that summer, I saw Mrs. Roosevelt briefly when she came to the campus to speak to a group of foreign students. We had not visited with one another since my return to the United States, and she invited me to come to lunch at Val-Kill Cottage on July 14. Since she was having a picnic lunch for U.N. families from India and Haiti and could fit in a few more people, I was able to bring my brother Raymond, his wife, Margaret, and their three children, Robert, Marcia, and Michael, for a memorable afternoon in Mrs. Roosevelt's presence.

It was the last time I saw Mrs. Roosevelt. A small incident during the luncheon should have alerted me to what was to come. Mrs. Roosevelt presided at the buffet tables inside the cottage until all the children and adults had been served and had gone outdoors to eat. I had lingered in a sitting room to talk with her uncle, David Gray, when she brought in her plate and joined us. While we sat there chatting, Mrs. Roosevelt asked me casually, "Pauli, if you're going into the next room for anything, would you please bring me a glass of lemonade?"

In all the years I had known Mrs. Roosevelt, this was the first time she had ever asked a personal favor of me, and I was so delighted to perform even so small a service and pleased that she felt close enough to me to request it that I did not realize the significance of that moment. Joseph Lash wrote later that Mrs. Roosevelt really began feeling unwell in mid-July of that year. My first inkling of her illness came in a note she wrote me on August 29, saying: "I have had a miserable summer and spent a week in the hospital. Now, however, I am slowly getting stronger and learning not to be impatient with my progress. All lectures, except dinner speeches, are being cut down, so I am really trying to lessen my work load from now through December." It was the last letter I received with Mrs. Roosevelt's own signature. Even then, her determination to carry on left me unaware of the seriousness of her condition.

When our committee met at the end of the summer, my preliminary report impressed some Commission members who were present, and it was arranged that I would present my tentative findings to the full Commission when it convened on October 1. I arrived that morning expecting Mrs. Roosevelt to chair the session, only to learn that she was ill and would not be there. My report was well received, and Kitty Ellickson urged me to complete the study as soon as possible so that it could be reproduced and circulated among Commission members. I was so distressed over Mrs. Roosevelt's illness that I wrote her a note, and this time Maureen Corr, her secretary, wrote back that "Mrs. Roosevelt is still in the hospital." I began to suspect the worst some days later, when newspapers reported her release from the hospital and enigmatic news bulletins began to appear stating such things as "Mrs. Roosevelt is resting comfortably." I telephoned Miss Corr, who could tell me only that Mrs. Roosevelt's condition was the same, and I remember that she asked me to pray.

By this time I knew that Mrs. Roosevelt was dying, although no one dared use the word. She had filled the landscape of my entire adult life as she had done for millions of my generation, and it was unthinkable to associate her with death. As First Lady of the World, she belonged to humanity, an extension of ourselves. Yet in this crisis those of us outside her intimate family circle had no way of showing our love for one who had given us so much. I kept a private vigil as others must have done during those final days, and the only way I knew how to serve her was to pour myself into completing the memorandum, following her example of "doing the things at hand." It became my memorial to her last public service, and I have always believed Mrs. Roosevelt's spirit suffused that effort and shaped the final product. I think her death had the same effect upon all of us who worked with the President's Commission on the Status of Women under her leadership. We transformed our mourning into redoubled efforts to carry forward with distinction the task she was unable to finish.

I remember the day of Mrs. Roosevelt's funeral as appropriately somber, with low-hanging dark clouds and intermittent heavy rains. A great light had gone out of the world, and even nature was weeping. Renee Barlow came up to New Haven, and we picked up her sister Doris in Hartford, driving through the gloom to Hyde Park, where we joined a sorrowful graveside gathering in the Rose Garden and said our last farewell. For the remnant of the New Deal stalwarts standing in the Rose Garden that afternoon, it was the passing of an era.

Three weeks later I completed and turned in my proposal for renewed litigation under the Fourteenth Amendment. The memorandum presented a comprehensive analysis of judicial decisions on cases involving legal distinctions based on sex, and it stressed the need for a reexamination by the courts, in light of present-day knowledge and conditions, of state laws and practices that discriminated solely on the basis of sex. The U.S. Supreme Court had not reviewed its position since 1908, when it announced the doctrine of "sex as a basis for legislative classification," which I suggested had become as pernicious as the racial doctrine of "separate but equal," now overruled by that Court.

In urging the pursuit of litigation under the Fourteenth Amendment, the memorandum was nevertheless careful not to disclaim the ultimate need for an equal rights amendment. It had seemed to me that given the absence of broad public support for the ERA at the time, the Fourteenth Amendment approach was a practical intermediate step. If successful, it might achieve on a case-by-case basis the same objectives as ERA supporters envisioned, but if the courts failed to respond favorably, then the case for the ERA was unassailable.

Our committee, having approved the substance of my proposal, recommended litigation under the Fifth and Fourteenth amendments in its report to the Commission. Mary Eastwood and I had the delicate task of wording the recommendation, especially its reference to the ERA, in language that Marguerite Rawalt could accept, thus enabling the Committee to reach a consensus. We spent hours with her, struggling over phraseology, and finally settled on a sentence that read: "In view of this constitutional approach, the Committee does not take a position in favor of the proposed equal rights amendment at this time." Marguerite was unhappy with the compromise, but she realized that the words "at this time" left the ERA issue open for future reassessment and gave her some leverage when the report reached the Commission.

When this crucial point was considered by the Commission, the language of our committee recommendation was adopted almost verbatim. In its final report, *American Women,* the Commission declared in part:

> Equality of rights under the law for all persons, male or female, is so basic to democracy and its commitment to the ultimate value of the individual that it must be reflected in the fundamental law of the land. The Commission believes that this principle of equality is embodied in the 5th and 14th amendments to the Constitution of the United States. . . .
>
> Since the Commission is convinced that the U.S. Constitution now embodies equality of rights for men and women, we conclude that a constitutional amendment need not *now* [emphasis supplied] be sought in order to establish this principle. But judicial clarification is imperative in order that remaining ambiguities with respect to the constitutional protection of women's rights be eliminated.
>
> Early and definitive court pronouncement, particularly by the U.S. Supreme Court, is urgently needed with regard to the validity under the 5th and 14th amendments of laws and official practices discriminating against women, to the end that the principle of equality become firmly established in constitutional doctrine.

The word "now," like the earlier addition of "at this time," was inserted to meet Marguerite Rawalt's argument, thus averting a complete repudiation of an equal rights amendment. The "carefully worded compromise," as Ellickson described it, permitted the Commission to issue a unanimous report while preserving, however slightly, the ERA option which came to the forefront in the following decade. Far from being mutually exclusive, both approaches were actively pursued and bore fruit as the women's movement gained momentum. On November 22, 1971, the United States Supreme Court struck down for the first time a state statute discriminating against women on the ground that it violated the Equal Protection Clause of the Fourteenth Amendment. And four months later, on March 22, 1972, Congress passed and sent the proposed Equal Rights Amendment to the states for ratification.

As I look back more than twenty years later, none of us in 1963 could have foreseen that the ERA would emerge as one of the foremost issues of the women's movement or that it would fail of ratification by only three states. Watching the history of this amendment, I have felt that the effort to reawaken interest in litigation under the Fifth and Fourteenth amendments was not entirely misplaced. While the U.S. Supreme Court has not yet ruled that sex is a "suspect classification" requiring "rigid scrutiny" by the courts—as it has done with regard to racial classifications—women have nevertheless won a number of significant victories from that court.

As we wound up our committee work on the status of women in the summer of 1963, a controversy arose over the issue of the sex-based discrimination practiced by leaders of the great March on Washington for Jobs and Freedom. I was shocked to learn that A. Philip Randolph, veteran labor chief and acknowledged leader of the March, had accepted an invitation to speak at a luncheon of the National Press Club on August 26, two days before the March, over the protests of newspaperwomen. At that time, women were excluded from membership in the Press Club and could attend events there only by sitting in the balcony. I was also incensed to discover that no woman had been invited to serve on the delegation of Negro civil rights leaders scheduled to meet with President John F. Kennedy on the day of the March. After these matters were aired in the press, Mr. Randolph issued a statement that March leaders "are definitely committed to the equality of women." Although Dorothy Height, who headed the National Council of Negro Women, was finally asked to join the White House delegation, Mr. Randolph went ahead with his speech at the segregated all-male Press Club. On the whole, Negro women were accorded little more than token recognition on the March program, and not a single woman was invited to make one of the major speeches on August 28—a significant difference between the March of 1963 and the Anniversary March of 1983.

That day, as I was swept along in the waves of marchers, I was reminded of the Negro spiritual "In Dat Great Gittin' Up Mornin'." It combined my childhood images of a jubilee and Judgment Day. I marched twice: the first time with my niece Bonnie Fearing Alexis and Patricia

Roberts Harris, my friend of Howard University student days, under the banner of the Washington chapter of the American Civil Liberties Union; the second time with my parish delegation from Saint Mark's-in-the-Bowery, New York City. When Bonnie and I reached the Lincoln Memorial close behind the March leaders, we reversed ourselves and walked back toward the Washington Monument to witness the miracle of the oncoming multitudes. I fell in line a second time when the Saint Mark's delegation appeared. Bonnie, who had been ten years old during my student activist days at Howard, was now married and the mother of three small children. Although she was ill on the day of the march, she said to me, "I owe it to my children to march today."

Later that week Pat Harris and I had lunch together in a downtown restaurant to celebrate the twentieth-anniversary year of our restaurant sit-ins as students in 1943, an effort that sparked the successful campaign led by Mary Church Terrell to desegregate places of public accommodation in the nation's capital.

On October 11, 1963—the anniversary of Mrs. Roosevelt's birth—the President's Commission on the Status of Women and its consultative committees presented the reports of the Commission's work to President Kennedy. It was a joyous occasion, recognized in front-page stories in the *New York Times* and other leading newspapers and celebrated at a reception at the White House. Eleven days later, President Kennedy's life was snuffed out by an assassin's bullet.

If my proposal on the constitutional position of women helped the President's Commission to sustain a moderate position in 1963, I played an entirely different role some months later on the crucial issue of equal opportunity for women in private employment. The Commission's cautious pronouncement in this area was outstripped through what has been called a legislative "fluke," in which I became involved shortly after the PCSW had completed its work and disbanded. Even before our deliberations ended, my friend Thacher Clark Anderson, counsel for the New York State Division of Human Rights, had alerted me to the need for including "sex" in fair employment practices legislation, and he anticipated that New York would adopt such a provision at its next legislative session. I tried to have the issue considered by the Committee on Civil and Political Rights but learned that it was not within our jurisdiction but within that of the Committee on Private Employment. We had felt it was important enough, however, to recommend that it be included among areas for further study and appropriate action, calling attention to the need for affirmative legislation on both federal and state levels "to remove discrimination in the private sector, including discrimination in employment."

The report of the President's Commission itself did not deal with a legislative approach but limited its attention to private employers holding federal contracts. While it agreed that the governing principle in private employment should be "equality of opportunity for women in hiring, training and promotion," it opposed the inclusion of the word "sex" in the existing Executive Order 10925 prohibiting discrimination based on race, creed, color, or national origin in employment under federal contracts. The report declared: "We are aware that this order could be expanded to forbid discrimination based on sex. But discrimination based on sex, the Commission believes, involves problems sufficiently different from discrimination based on the other factors listed to make separate treatment preferable." The report was silent on the need for enforceable legislation of broad coverage.

The picture was suddenly changed by a surprising development in Congress. During the closing hours of debate on February 8, 1964, Representative Howard W. Smith, a Virginia Democrat, who chaired the House Rules Committee, introduced an amendment to H.R. 7152 to include the word "sex" as a prohibited ground of discrimination in Title VII, the Equal Employment Opportunities title of the omnibus Civil Rights Bill. Some observers thought Representative Smith's quixotic action was intended as a joke. The amendment had not been considered when Title VII was reviewed in committee and consequently had no legislative history. At the time, only the states of Wisconsin and Hawaii had fair employment statutes that included the word "sex" (although New York State would adopt such a provision in 1965). The President's Commission on the Status of Women had opposed its inclusion in an executive order, and during the brief House debate Representative Emmanuel Celler read a letter from the secretary of the U.S. Department of Labor, quoting the Commission's statement in *American Women* together with a further statement by Esther Peterson, assistant secretary of labor, who had also served as executive vice-chair of the PCSW, which read: "In view of this policy conclusion reached by representatives from a variety of women's organizations and private and public agencies to attack discrimination based on sex separately, we are of the opinion that to attempt to so amend H.R. 7152 would not be to the best interest of women at this time." Representative Edith Green of Oregon, who had also been a member of the Commission, strongly opposed the amendment, arguing: "It will clutter up the bill and it may later . . . be used to help destroy this section of the bill by some of the very people who today support it." However, the amendment was vigorously supported by Representative Martha Griffiths from Michigan, and in the end, to almost everyone's surprise, the sex provision was adopted by a vote of 168 to 133. Next day the entire Civil Rights Bill was passed and sent to the Senate.

Though immersed in my doctoral research at Yale, I was keeping abreast of events affecting women through the informal network that had begun during the PCSW's existence and included, among others, Catherine East, executive secretary of the newly established Interdepartmental Committee and Citizens' Advisory Council on the Status of Women (created by President Kennedy, shortly before he was assassinated, to follow up on PCSW proposals); Mary Eastwood, who was assigned to represent the attorney general on the Interdepartmental Committee; and Marguerite Rawalt, who sat on the Citizens' Advisory Council. I was overjoyed to learn of the House action, particularly because, as a Negro woman, I knew that in many instances it was difficult to determine whether I was being discriminated against because of race or sex and felt that the sex provision would close a gap in the employment rights of all Negro women. My cohorts in Washington were equally pleased, because of the potential coverage of large numbers of the more than twenty-four million women then in the nation's work force.

Our enthusiasm changed to alarm in early April, when Senate Republican leader Everett M. Dirksen announced his intention to seek a series of amendments to Title VII, including the elimination of the word "sex" adopted by the House. Senator Dirksen's opposition to the provision increased the danger that it would be dropped during the inevitable political trade-offs, because his support was crucial to mobilizing enough votes to impose closure and defeat the anticipated Senate filibuster against the bill.

At this point our little network began to consult frantically by telephone. We hardly knew what strategy to pursue. We had no national organization of sufficient power and expertise in employment matters to lobby effectively for the sex amendment, and its lack of official support from the Women's Bureau in the U.S. Department of Labor was a formidable barrier to successful passage. Few people outside official Washington were even aware of the issue, and most of the knowledgeable women who supported the amendment were federal employees, restricted in their political activities. None of us immediately involved was a major public figure and so our influence was extremely limited. Furthermore, little time remained to publicize the issue and mobilize favorable opinion. We had to act on the spot, with almost no hope that we would achieve success.

Since I could act freely, being outside the government, and could also present an argument as a victim of both race and sex discrimination, I was asked to prepare a "Memorandum in Support of Retaining the Amendment to H.R. 7152 (Equal Employment Opportunity) to Prohibit Discrimination in Employment Because of Sex." It was a strongly worded document, pointing to the historical interrelatedness of the movements for civil rights and women's rights and the tragic consequences in United

States history of ignoring the interrelatedness of all human rights. It argued that the inclusion of the "sex" amendment would strengthen the main purpose of the bill and reduce the bitter tensions that would result from the exclusion of so large a category as women workers. It declared: "A strong argument can be made for the proposition that Title VII without the 'sex' amendment would benefit Negro males primarily and thus offer genuine equality of opportunity to only *half* of the potential Negro work force." A further argument was made that the amendment would buttress the recently enacted Equal Pay Act of 1963, and in answer to the PCSW position that a separate program was necessary to eliminate employment discrimination against women, the memorandum asserted:

> This view betrays an undue caution in dealing with the near-revolutionary problem of human rights today. The "uniqueness" of the nature of the discrimination on the basis of sex is largely fictitious and cloaks both timidity and paternalism. There are few, if any, jobs for which an employee's sex could be considered relevant. . . . A sound national employment policy must establish the principle of equal opportunities for all. Implementation through administrative means involves the working out of standards of merit and of bona fide occupational qualifications which apply to *individuals* and do not blanket an entire sex. This does not require studies in advance but the application of the principle to various case situations.

The completed memorandum was rushed to Mary Eastwood and Marguerite Rawalt, who were able to get it reproduced and distributed quickly. We managed to get copies to Attorney General Robert F. Kennedy, Vice-President Hubert Humphrey, Senators Margaret Chase Smith, Everett M. Dirksen, and a few others on Capitol Hill. Marguerite was from Texas, knew Lady Bird Johnson personally, and hoped to enlist her support, so I sent Mrs. Johnson a copy of the memorandum, with a covering letter asking her to discuss the matter with the President.

Our first hopeful response came two weeks later, in a letter from Senator Margaret Chase Smith informing me of her actions during a Senate Republican conference.

> Senator Dirksen, the Republican Minority Leader upon whom much of the fate of the Civil Rights Bill rests, originally offered an amendment to strike the word "sex" from the Bill as passed by the House. . . . I stood up and opposed and argued against his amendment. In doing so, I marshaled so much Republican opposition to it that Senator Dirksen decided not to introduce his amendment.

This was followed by a letter from Bess Abell, Mrs. Johnson's social secretary, acknowledging on her behalf my "convincing and persuasive" memo and telling me: "I have checked this matter out and I am pleased to advise you that as far as the Administration is concerned, its position is that the Bill should be enacted in its present form."

We were jubilant when the historic Civil Rights Act of 1964 became law on July 2, and Title VII contained the "sex" amendment intact. Marguerite Rawalt wrote me enthusiastically: "To you comes a real measure of credit for the ultimate successful passage of Title VII of the Civil Rights Bill with its protection for women in employment. The prompt meeting of the threatened amendment by Senator Dirksen was crucial, and your memorandum and your thinking was really fine. I do think we can take a share of the credit."

We had apparently created enough of a furor to inspire the belief that an incipient women's rebellion was in progress and that killing the sex provision would provoke a nationwide protest. Although only a handful of women were involved in the legislative maneuvers, the strong response of working women to Title VII after it went into effect fully justified our efforts. The Equal Employment Opportunity Commission later reported that in its first year of operation, 33.7 percent of complaints filed with EEOC alleged sex discrimination. Yet, from the outset, there were strong indications that unless a powerful watchdog organization of women came into being, the sex provisions of Title VII would not be enforced.

CHAPTER 30

The Birth of NOW

THE Yale University commencement of 1965 was the high point of my
legal career, for it brought the great thrill of walking across the platform
to receive the degree of Doctor of Juridical Science from Eugene V.
Rostow, dean of the law school. That it happened at all seemed miraculous.
In January, six months before my graduation was scheduled, the faculty
adviser in charge of my dissertation, my friend Fowler Harper, died of
cancer. Fowler and Miriam had been my "family" in New Haven, and his
death was a great personal blow. It also created an academic problem. My
dissertation was about two-thirds completed, but I faced the difficulty of
finding another member of the faculty committee that evaluated my work
who would be willing on such short notice to take over the job of guiding
me through to completion. For a while it looked as if I would have to wait
at least another year to get my degree.

One of my warmest friends in New Haven was Ruth Calvin Emerson.
I had known her before coming to Yale, and she had since married Thomas
Emerson, professor of civil and political rights at the Yale Law School.
Ruth was herself a graduate of the law school, and with her support I
mustered the courage to approach Tom Emerson about becoming my
adviser. Despite his heavy academic load and the many outside demands
upon his time and energies, he agreed. One of my greatest pleasures
during our academic association was watching Tom's steady progression
toward active support of feminism. To Ruth's delight, he became the
foremost constitutional authority advocating the proposed Equal Rights
Amendment.

When my dissertation was approved and commencement finally arrived, it was a celebration of "firsts" as well as an important personal milestone. Although four generations of my immediate family had been deeply involved in public school education, I was the first member to earn a doctorate and the first to be awarded a degree from a major university. Also, as far as anyone could tell, I was the first Negro—male or female— to be awarded the J.S.D. from Yale Law School. This achievement had come so late in my career that none of my older relatives was alive to share in it, but feeling a deep need for historical continuity, I invited as my special guest for commencement my former high school teacher Mary Fisher Morris, who forty years earlier had taught me fundamentals of sentence structure through Latin grammar and had encouraged me to use my writing talent. Miriam Harper gave me a big graduation party, and the day ended with a joyous gathering of family and friends from out of town as well as scores of people I had come to know at Yale and in New Haven.

Once this day of triumph was over, I faced the somber reality that my years of academic toil had merely provided the formal credentials needed for teaching law; I still lacked the indispensable contacts I had to have to gain admission into an almost exclusively male preserve. Without a sponsor to make the crucial preliminary contacts, I was unlikely to receive serious consideration when applying for an academic appointment. Fowler Harper, my sponsor at Yale, was dead, and I was still, in 1965, a few years ahead of the upheaval that would begin to open up law school faculties to women. It was true that these faculties were becoming more receptive to Negro men: a Negro male graduate with an LL.M. from Yale was immediately accepted on the faculty of another law school, and a few years later he became its dean. But teaching jobs were not readily forthcoming to women of any race. Despite Yale Law School's enormous prestige and its reputation for successfully placing graduates holding its higher degrees, I was an embarrassment. Ironically, holding the doctorate placed me in the position of having a higher law degree than most of those who would pass upon my candidacy. That, combined with my age and professional experience, doomed me to being "overqualified" for available lower-entry-level positions—instructor, assistant professor, associate professor—and yet no law school faculty was prepared to offer me a full professorship in the field of my competence.

My predicament as a freshly minted J.S.D. without prospects of an academic job pointed to a more widespread problem. I belonged to the class of unattached, self-supporting women for whom employment opportunities were necessary to survival. We were the ones most victimized by a still prevalent stereotype that men are the chief breadwinners and women work to supplement their husband's income.

For the next twelve months I supported myself chiefly by writing a monograph entitled "Human Rights U.S.A.: 1948–1966" for the Women's Division of the Methodist Church, on a contract negotiated by my old friend Thelma Stevens. During this period I pursued so many job leads which failed to materialize that I finally stopped actively looking for a law school teaching job.

But if my professional status and economic position remained precarious for some time after I finished Yale, it was a highly productive period for me. My intense involvement with the early stirrings of the resurgent feminist movement called on all my professional skills and kept me so busy I had no time to become demoralized. In 1965 and 1966, Title VII was the principal issue that fueled the movement, especially among business and professional women, as we battled against public attitudes ranging from ridicule to disregard of the new law. The Equal Employment Opportunity Commission (EEOC), charged with administration of the statute, was one of the chief offenders in that respect. A warning of what women might expect came shortly after the law went into effect, on July 2, 1965. EEOC Chairman Franklin D. Roosevelt, Jr., declared in his first public statement that "the whole issue of sex discrimination is terribly complicated," and indicated that the Commission had not yet come to grips with most of the problems involved. Along with this lukewarm approach, Chairman Roosevelt announced the appointment of his seven key aides who would head the EEOC staff, giving a further clue to official indifference toward women's issues. All seven appointees to the staff were men, and not one of them had functioned on the President's Commission on the Status of Women or any of its study committees that had canvassed sex-based discrimination in employment. The prevailing attitude of the EEOC staff (with a few exceptions) seemed to be that of its executive director, Herman Edelsburg, who stated some months later at New York University's Annual Conference on Labor that the sex provision of Title VII was a "fluke" and "conceived out of wedlock." The newly appointed EEOC deputy general counsel had recently published a lengthy law review article on Title VII, offering an unduly restrictive interpretation of the sex provision as a prohibited ground of discrimination.

Only two of the EEOC's five commissioners responded sympathetically to representations made by women's groups: Richard Graham, a Republican appointed for a term of one year, who had been given responsibility for reviewing cases of sex discrimination, and Aileen Clarke Hernandez, the lone female member of the Commission, an honor graduate of Howard University and a former official of the International Ladies' Garment Workers' Union, with extensive experience in the administration of the California fair employment practices law. No pressure group existed to press for implementation of women's employment rights under the statute, and members of our feminist network who had fought to keep the word "sex" in Title VII were powerless to do more than sound an alarm.

Three weeks after the EEOC began to function, I wrote Marguerite Rawalt and Mary Eastwood, warning that unless we developed some fast coordinated action, we would lose the little we thought we had gained. I pointed out that the Illinois Chamber of Commerce was reported to have called for a repeal of the sex provision. "What will it take to arouse the working women of this country to fight for their rights?" I asked them. "Do you suppose the time has come for the organization of a strong national Ad Hoc Committee of women who are ready to take the plunge?" Marguerite wrote back immediately that my letter gave her a marvelous springboard. "I am in complete agreement that we need fast coordinated action," she said, adding that it was time for a strong national committee of dedicated women and that she was ready to volunteer and expected to have more time in the not far distant future.

The idea of a national civil rights organization for women was beginning to circulate within our network, although none of us had any clear ideas as to the form it would take. Catherine East, staff officer of the Interdepartmental Committee, was quietly laying the groundwork for such a national organization. She acted as a clearinghouse for information which flowed through her office, and she built up a special mailing list of key women around the country whom she kept informed through periodic mailings of reports, memoranda, clippings, summaries of court actions, administrative decisions, and new legislation affecting the status of women. Almost any evening, weekend, or holiday, one could find Catherine East toiling away in her tiny office at the U.S. Department of Labor, making frequent trips to the Xerox room to reproduce data for the packets she sent out to her small constituency. During those years Catherine was our most reliable source of information.

In the absence of organized group actions, we had to rely upon maximizing our individual efforts. Mary Eastwood and I coauthored a law review article entitled "Jane Crow and the Law: Sex Discrimination and Title VII," setting forth ways in which the Fifth and Fourteenth amendments and the sex provisions of Title VII could be interpreted to accord women equality of rights. We equated the evil of antifeminism (Jane Crow) with the evil of racism (Jim Crow), and we asserted that "the rights of women and the rights of Negroes are only different phases of the fundamental and indivisible issue of human rights." Published in the *George Washington Law Review* in December 1965, at a time when few authoritative legal materials on discrimination against women existed, our article broke new ground and was widely cited.

That fall I moved back to New York from New Haven and rented an apartment at 245 East Eleventh Street, on the corner of Second Avenue, overlooking the churchyard of Saint Mark's-in-the-Bowery, the parish church to which Renee Barlow and I had belonged since before I went to Africa. Saint Mark's could no longer afford to employ a professional choir as it had done in the late 1950s, and Renee soon recruited me to sing in the volunteer choir. Returning to New York was like coming home again to renew my spiritual resources and get a fresh start. Smokey, my constant companion for thirteen years, had died of a heart ailment in January, and I had brought home from the dog pound a replacement I alternately called Doc and Black-and-White-Together-We-Shall-Overcome, in recognition of his spectacular black-and-white markings. Doc, a large floppy-eared mixed breed, with a clumsy gait and traces of Saint Bernard ancestry, seemed to realize I had saved his life and showed his gratitude by being a fiercely protective watchdog. I felt perfectly safe walking him on a leash through the streets of the lower East Side at night. One of our favorite hikes took us to visit Renee and her mother, who lived in Peter Cooper Village at Twenty-third Street and East River Drive. Mrs. Barlow, then in her mid-eighties, welcomed these visits, for she was virtually housebound and increasingly isolated from human contact except when Renee's friends came.

Shortly after returning to New York, I was appointed to the national board of directors of the American Civil Liberties Union, a post I held for the next eight years as the ACLU developed into one of the most effective advocates of women's rights, particularly through constitutional litigation. In fact, it was through the ACLU that I played a part in the first judicial victory for the proposition that the Fourteenth Amendment forbids state action which arbitrarily discriminates on the basis of sex. As soon as I became a member of the ACLU board I was asked to help write the brief in *White* v. *Crook,* a civil rights case then pending before a three-judge United States District Court in Montgomery, Alabama.

The case was the first of its kind, a double-barreled challenge of the constitutionality of all-white, all-male juries in Lowndes County, Alabama. (This was the county where Viola Gregg Liuzzo and Jonathan Myrick Daniels, an Episcopal seminarian, were murdered during the civil rights campaign for voter registration in 1965, and in both cases attempts to convict the accused slayers were unsuccessful.) ACLU attorneys were representing the plaintiffs—Negro men and women residents of Lowndes County joined by the Episcopal Society for Cultural and Racial Unity—in a suit charging that the systematic exclusion by jury officials of Negro men, and the statutory exclusion of all women, black and white, from jury service, constituted a violation of the Equal Protection Clause of the Fourteenth Amendment. The United States Department of Justice intervened as plaintiffs in the action. Judge Dorothy Kenyon, vice-chair of the American Civil Liberties Union, and I were assigned to write the section of the ACLU brief that dealt with exclusion from jury service on the basis of sex. A prepublication copy of the law review article Mary Eastwood and I had written supporting the argument was made a part of the appendix of the brief.

At the time, three states—Alabama, Mississippi, and South Carolina— had statutes limiting jury service to men, and at least twenty-four states and the District of Columbia treated men and women differently under their jury laws. The President's Commission on the Status of Women had strongly recommended appropriate judicial and legislative action to achieve equal jury service in all fifty states, a situation already in effect for federal juries by virtue of the Civil Rights Act of 1957.

We could hardly contain our joy on February 7, 1966, when the federal court ruled unanimously in favor of the plaintiffs with respect to both racial and sexual bias. On the issue of exclusion of women the court declared:

> Jury service is a form of participation in the processes of government, a responsibility and a right that should be shared by all citizens, regardless of sex. The Alabama statute that denies women the right to serve on juries in the State of Alabama therefore violates the provision of the Fourteenth Amendment that forbids any State to "deny to any person within its jurisdiction the equal protection of the law." The plain effect of this constitutional provision is to prohibit prejudicial disparities before the law. This means prejudicial disparities for all citizens—including women.

The principle announced seems so obvious today that it is difficult to remember the dramatic break the court was making with scores of previous judicial decisions. Mary Eastwood and I were ecstatic that the ruling was in accord with the position we had urged in our law review article. Our only regret was that we had no opportunity to have the issue passed on by the United States Supreme Court, because the attorney general of Alabama announced he would not appeal the lower court's decision. Nevertheless, *White* v. *Crook* signaled a turning point in the law.

Of all the lawyers who worked on that case, it was a supreme triumph for white-haired, seventy-eight-year-old Dorothy Kenyon, a stalwart survivor of the earlier women's movement who had been devoted to the "Cause of Women" since her youth. Admitted to practice law in 1919, she had battled her way in a male-dominated profession, disarming her male colleagues with amusing witticisms to win their support of her point of view when her brilliant logic failed. *White* v. *Crook* was her first victory

in a number of attempts to have the equal protection clause of the Fourteenth Amendment judicially applied to cases of sex-based discrimination.
She had flown down to Montgomery to appear personally before the court
and argue the point herself. The decision was a vindication of her years
of effort, all the more significant because by the time the United States
Supreme Court decided the landmark case of *Reed* v. *Reed* in 1971, she
was too ill fully to enjoy the victory. Judge Kenyon died of cancer a few
weeks after the *Reed* decision was announced.

Just about the time I was packing to leave New Haven for New York,
I began what was to be a productive association with Betty Friedan, then
chiefly known as the author of *The Feminine Mystique*. On October 12,
1965, I spoke on Title VII at a conference held by the National Council
of Women of the United States at the Biltmore Hotel in New York City.
Most of my talk was a straightforward legal analysis of issues arising from
sex-based discrimination in employment. At the end I touched on some
political implications, pointing out that the historical significance of the sex
provision of Title VII was comparable to that of the Nineteenth Amendment because, if vigorously enforced, it would give women the opportunity of advancing in accordance with their abilities and interests. Then I
added:

> But there is reason to believe that it will not be adequately enforced unless
> the political power of women is brought to bear. In the case of the Nine-
> teenth Amendment, the organized resistance came in advance of the law.
> In the case of Title VII, the resistance is just beginning to be organized.
> It should not be necessary to have another March on Washington in order
> that there be equal job opportunities for all. But if this necessity should
> arise, I hope women will not flinch from the thought.

As one who had participated in the 1963 March for Jobs and Freedom,
I did not think my closing statement was unusual, but apparently the fact
that the audience was made up for the most part of white upper-middle-
class women gave it dramatic value in the eyes of a *New York Times*
reporter. In any case, the prominently placed report that appeared next
day in the *Times* was headlined PROTEST PROPOSED ON WOMEN'S JOBS;
YALE PROFESSOR SAYS IT MAY BE NEEDED TO OBTAIN RIGHTS. To my great
embarrassment, the news story erroneously identified me as "a woman
Professor of Law at Yale," but I suppose the gratuitous label gave the
statement extra clout. At any rate, Betty Friedan, who had not attended
the conference, read the news account and immediately tracked me down
by telephone in New Haven. We arranged to get together for talks as soon
as I was settled in the city.

As I recall, Betty Friedan was interviewing people for a second book, but our subsequent meetings and telephone conversations quickly moved beyond a personal interview and began to focus upon what was happening to women, particularly the shoddy treatment we were getting under Title VII, and what we should be doing about it. I put Betty in touch with Mary Eastwood, Catherine East, Marguerite Rawalt, EEOC attorney Sonia Pressman (Fuentes), and other members of the feminist network in government, and she later acknowledged the influence of this "underground network of women" who nudged her steadily on toward action. To varying degrees, each of us who had worked with government-sponsored agencies on women's issues knew their limitations, so we stressed the need for an independent national civil rights organization for women comparable to the NAACP, an organization that would have enough political power to compel government agencies to take seriously the problems of discrimination because of sex. In expressing this idea to Betty Friedan, I recall how timid I was, how modest were my expectations, and how anxious I was to avoid competing with established women's groups. I said wistfully how wonderful it would be "if we only had a network of about five hundred key women around the country who could spring into action whenever issues directly affecting women arise in Washington." Catherine East was more decisive in her approach. She said later that she saw Betty Friedan as the only woman who at that time had name recognition enough to organize a national group, and she set out to persuade Betty to take the initiative in bringing such an organization into being.

By the time the Third National Conference of State Commissions on the Status of Women convened at the Washington Hilton Hotel in June 1966, Betty Friedan was just about convinced that a new action group should be set up. Sponsored by the Interdepartmental Committee and Citizens' Advisory Council on the Status of Women and bringing together prominent women commission members from virtually every state, the conference seemed the logical setting in which to test the idea among a broad cross-section of women. As a writer-observer covering the conference, Betty was in a position to sound out leading representatives from state commissions around the country. I was to speak on the panel "Sex Discrimination—Progress in Legal Status," held on the final morning of the conference, and other members of our network were there to support Betty in exploring possibilities.

By June 29, the second day of the conference, there were enough rumblings of dissatisfaction among activists in attendance to suggest that the time was ripe. Betty was encouraged to invite a few women who might be interested in organizing a new group to join an informal discussion in her hotel room that evening, the only opportunity we would have for a meeting before the closing sessions next day.

Some fifteen women met in Betty Friedan's room at about ten o'clock. Many of us were strangers to one another; I knew only five of those present —Betty herself, Mary Eastwood, Dorothy Haener of the Women's Department of the United Automobile Workers, Catherine Conroy of the Communications Workers of America, and Kathryn Clarenbach, chair of the Wisconsin Commission on the Status of Women. Everyone present felt the general frustration over the issue of women's employment rights under Title VII. Each conference participant had been furnished with a copy of Congresswoman Martha Griffiths' angry speech of June 20, delivered on the floor of the House, in which she charged "The whole attitude of the EEOC toward discrimination based on sex is specious, negative and arrogant." Working women were outraged over a guideline issued by the EEOC in April, permitting employers to advertise jobs open to both sexes in segregated "Help Wanted, Male" or "Help Wanted, Female" newspaper columns in blatant contradiction of Title VII's prohibition of any want ad expressing a preference or limitation based on race, religion, sex, or national origin. Griffiths found the Commission's interpretation of the statute "nothing more than arbitrary arrogance, disregard of law, and a manifestation of flat hostility to the human rights of women." Conference delegates were also angry over the impending expiration of EEOC Commissioner Richard Graham's term on July 1 and the strong rumors that he would not be reappointed. Since he was the one male member of the Commission who had shown sensitivity in dealing with issues of sex bias in employment, Commissioner Graham's imminent departure was seen as calamitous. Our only differences were over strategies to meet what we all saw as an ominous situation.

But those differences were deep. The discussion quickly developed into a heated debate over the need for a new organization. Kay Clarenbach, the commissioner from Wisconsin, and Catherine Conroy of the Communications Workers union, in particular questioned the idea and argued that the issues which immediately concerned us could be handled through the existing machinery of state commissions. Kay suggested that since the theme of the conference was "Targets for Action," it would be appropriate for conference delegates to adopt strong resolutions at the closing luncheon next day, urging the enforcement of the sex provisions of Title VII and the reappointment of Commissioner Graham. Those of us who felt the time had come for action independent of government sponsorship could make little headway against the state commission approach. Tempers flared and we wrangled until after midnight without resolving the basic disagreement. The meeting finally broke up after we agreed— some of us halfheartedly—to Kay's proposal that she draft the resolutions and bring them before the entire conference the following day.

I left Betty Friedan's room that night thoroughly discouraged; it seemed to me that we had fumbled a major opportunity to begin mobilizing women nationally to press for their civil rights. I was so depressed that I seriously considered leaving for New York immediately after my panel presentation next morning, without attending the closing luncheon. But I had not reckoned with the persistent power of an idea whose time had clearly come, and I had not anticipated the radicalization of Kay Clarenbach and Catherine Conway when their plans for moderate action through existing channels were frustrated. In the morning, when Kay approached conference officials to arrange to introduce her resolutions, she was told that "government commissions cannot take action against other departments." Kay and Catherine were so outraged by this rebuff that they had an immediate change of heart. By noon, word had been passed that we were going ahead with the new organization.

During the luncheon about twenty of us gathered at two tables near the rostrum, and while conference dignitaries were making speeches just above our heads, we carried on whispered conversations and set in motion a temporary body to be called the National Organization for Women. Betty Friedan hastily scribbled its purpose on a paper napkin: "to take the actions needed to bring women into the mainstream of American society now . . . in fully equal partnership with men." We urged others at the luncheon to join us in a brief meeting to form the new organization.

Before the conference ended that afternoon, twenty-eight women had signed up and paid five dollars each for immediate expenses. A telegram bearing the names of the twenty-eight founding members went to the White House, urging the reappointment of Richard Graham to the Equal Employment Opportunity Commission, and night letters were sent to each EEOC commissioner, urging that the discriminatory guideline approving sex-segregated "help wanted" ads be rescinded. Kay Clarenbach was named temporary coordinator of NOW, and along with Caroline Ware, I was elected to a "temporary coordinating committee" of six to assist Kay over the summer in developing the framework for a permanent organization. The birth of NOW had happened so quickly and smoothly that most of the delegates left the conference unaware that a historic development in the women's movement had begun. Three months later, at an organizing conference held in Washington on October 29 and 30, 1966, thirty-two of us set up the permanent organization of NOW, never dreaming that within less than two decades it would have more than 200,000 members and become a potent force in American politics.

CHAPTER 31

A Stumbling Block to Faith

INEVITABLY, my growing feminist consciousness led me to do battle with the Episcopal Church over the submerged position of women in our denomination. Challenging inequalities in religious life was much more difficult than challenging similar inequalities in the secular world, because church practices were often bound up with questions of fundamental faith, insulating them from attack. An aura of immutability surrounded the exclusion of women from the clergy, reinforced by a theology which held that an exclusively male priesthood was ordained by almighty God. Other privileges enjoyed by males—lay participation in the liturgy and governance of the church—carried the weight of centuries of custom.

As a child growing up in the church, I knew that I could never be privileged to carry the cross or serve at the altar as an acolyte. Only boys were permitted to do so. I grudgingly accepted these limitations, suppressing my resentments and serving in the capacities open to me—as choir member, Sunday school teacher, member of the Altar Guild, and occasional organist. I was vaguely aware that women did not serve on vestries or other governing bodies of the church, and I responded to this lack of representation when I became an adult by a studied indifference to church organization. I confined myself to attending worship services and remained aloof from parish life. My feelings toward the church were ambivalent: I could neither stay away entirely nor enter wholeheartedly into Christian community.

Since worship was a tremendously important part of my devotional life, my first overt protest against the sexism of my church came on the issue of the full participation in the liturgy of lay women. Now that I was living across the street from Saint Mark's, I liked being close to my church home and able to run over for occasional weekday prayer services. Saint Mark's had an upbeat congregation, more willing than many churches I had attended to experiment with new ideas. Its rector, the Reverend Michael Allen, was sympathetic to an expanded role for women in the church and under his leadership, the congregation, after two years of discussion, voted to elect women to the vestry for the first time in the history of the parish. Renee Barlow was one of two women elected, and since Renee's feminism was as thoroughgoing as mine, if less obvious, for the first time I felt fully represented in the governance of the congregation and began to take more interest in parish affairs.

Actually, my protest was triggered by the small steps already being taken toward having both sexes participate more fully in all church activities. Renee casually mentioned to Michael Allen that it would be nice to have a woman lay reader, and shortly afterward he asked a woman to read the Epistle at the early morning Thanksgiving service. Often at a weekday evening service when only a few people were present, Michael would appoint a woman or a teenage boy or girl to read the Bible lesson. Men were invited to serve on the Altar Guild and join in the United Thank Offering, both of which were formerly women's activities.

These innovations only whetted my desire to help do away with other restrictions, for they served to emphasize the male domination of the most elaborate and solemn service of the week—the Holy Eucharist on Sunday morning. Women were virtually invisible as participants except as members of the choir. Only males wore the colorful vestments and processed to the altar—the thurifer swinging the incense, the crucifer carrying the cross between two torchbearers, the subdeacon and acolytes handling the sacred vessels and serving the priest at the high altar.

I do not know why this familiar spectacle suddenly became intolerable to me one Sunday morning in March 1966. I doubt that Rosa Parks could explain why on December 1, 1955, she rebelled against the segregation she had endured all her life. I remember only that in the middle of the celebration of the Holy Eucharist an uncontrollable anger exploded inside me, filling me with such rage I had to get up and leave. I wandered about the streets full of blasphemous thought, feeling alienated from God. The intensity of this assault at the deepest level of my devotional life produced a crisis in faith. I had been taught all my life to revere the church and its teachings; now I could only condemn the church as sinful when it denied me the right to participate as fully and freely in the worship of God as my brethren. If the present church customs were justified, then I did not belong in the church and it became a stumbling block to faith.

That afternoon I wrote a letter to Michael Allen and the members of the vestry, trying to put into words the pain and turmoil I felt:

> I could not take Communion this morning because . . . I was rebellious and resentful and had a grievance against my brothers in the Church.
>
> Throughout the services, I kept asking myself: Why is not one of the candle bearers a little girl? Why cannot the crucifer be a girl or woman? Why cannot the vestmented lay reader be a woman of the church? Why cannot women and men, boys and girls, participate equally in every phase of Church activity?
>
> If, as I believe, it is a privilege to assist the priest in the solemn Eucharist, to hold the candles for the reading of the Gospel, to be the lay reader at the formal churchwide 10:30 service, why is this privilege not accorded to all members without regard to sex? Suppose only white people did these things? Or only Negroes? Or only Puerto Ricans? We would see immediately that the Church is guilty of grave discrimination. There is no difference between discrimination because of race and discrimination because of sex. I believe . . . that if one is wrong, the other is wrong.

My letter requested the vestry to initiate discussion with a view toward opening every office and activity in connection with the worship services to both sexes equally, and should bars to this equality be imposed by the diocese or other church hierarchy, to take appropriate steps to request the removal of these barriers.

The letter was discussed and referred to the Commission on Worship, an advisory body to the rector, which held a meeting and invited interested members of the congregation to attend and express their views on the proposal. I was surprised to discover that no church law existed that barred women from functioning as lay readers, acolytes, or other servers; these matters were within the discretion of the rector, who controlled the form of worship, and they had been determined by custom. I also discovered that much of the opposition to the idea came from other women. One said, "I'm a traditionalist; we've always done it this way." Another objected because she felt "if women start doing these things, the men won't be as active as they are now and we're so glad to have the men doing something." The conventional patriarchal view came from the twenty-six-year-old curate, who declared that "the Church is like the family; the father always sits at the head of the table and carves the roast," although he conceded that the mother carves the roast when the father is away. Nothing was settled at that meeting; it was clear that further discussions would have to be held; but a beginning had been made and Michael Allen suggested that meanwhile we might begin to think about what vestments a woman lay reader might wear if we decided to take that step.

Similar changes were beginning to come about in other congregations. We had no Episcopal Women's Caucus in the 1960s to exert organized pressure for change, but here and there individual women who felt as I did were speaking out. As in secular life, linkages were being formed, and although we did not define what was happening to us, as we reached out to one another we were finding authentic ministries among ourselves years before they were validated by the official church. In some respects the women's movement was also an ecumenical religious movement, and the term "sisterhood" had religious as well as political meaning.

I sent a copy of my letter to Catherine East, a Unitarian, who promptly passed it on to her colleague Morag Simchak, an active Episcopalian who worked in the U.S. Department of Labor and had responsibility for administering the Equal Pay Act of 1963. Morag wrote me immediately, saying, "I am in complete agreement with your position, and reactions, in this area," and asking permission to send the letter on to Frances Young, director of the Division of Women's Activities at the Episcopal Church Center in New York. (Ironically, it developed that Frances Young was also a member of Saint Mark's, but she had been out of town a great deal and we had never met.) Morag's letter was the beginning of our close collaboration over the next twelve years as we worked together in the early phases of NOW and within the Episcopal Church for the seating of women as lay delegates to the General Convention and for their ordination to the priesthood. Morag, a native of Scotland, then in her fifties and the mother of three young adults she had reared largely by herself, was a seasoned fighter for human rights. She had worked in the European underground during World War II before coming to the United States, and she was a remarkable blend of fragile elegance, religious devotion, and tough-minded political savvy. Our bond was so deep that when I was ordained a priest in 1977, Morag was one of my lay presenters. Twenty months later she succumbed to cancer, and in accordance with her final wishes I was Celebrant of the Holy Eucharist at her memorial service at Saint Alban's in Washington, D.C.

In 1966 I was concerned only with the position of women as lay Christians, not with their admission to the clergy. But the explosive issue of women's ordination was already being raised within the church. I was not aware of it at the time, but in October 1966 (the same month I attended NOW's conference in Washington to organize a permanent structure), a Committee to Study the Place of Women in the Ministry filed a progress report of major significance. The Committee, authorized by the House of Bishops in 1965 and appointed by the chief executive of the Episcopal Church, the presiding bishop, reported that "the place of women in the

Church's ministry demands the facing of the question whether or not a woman should be considered eligible for ordination to any and all Orders of that Ministry." This question had been given "new urgency," the report declared, by various factors which "require a fresh and unprejudiced look," and it warned against "uncritical acceptance of beliefs, attitudes, and assumptions that have been inherited from the past and strongly persist at the present time."

If in 1966 anyone had spoken of a "call" to the ordained ministry with reference to me, I would have reacted with a feeling akin to terror. At the time, I would even have protested the idea of a lay ministry, for like many people who compartmentalize human experience into separate spheres labeled sacred and secular, I associated ministry with a holiness I could never attain, worldly as I am, and I shrank from any identification with the concept. But in the turbulent decade between the filing of that committee report and the action of the General Convention of the Episcopal Church in September 1976 approving the ordination of women to the priesthood, my own life was undergoing profound changes which nudged me closer to the vocation I dared not acknowledge.

For the next two years I maintained my apartment in New York as a permanent residence while working elsewhere. In the fall of 1966, I spent seven months in Washington as a consultant to the Equal Employment Opportunity Commission. The following year I accepted a position in Columbia, South Carolina, as part of the new administration of President Benjamin F. Payton at Benedict College, a small, private, Baptist-related liberal arts institution which began in 1867 on a former slave plantation. My function was to develop educational plans and programs geared toward innovative approaches that would help close the educational gap between Negro college students and their white counterparts.

Before leaving for South Carolina in the summer of 1967, I had an experience that foreshadowed a deeper involvement in human suffering quite apart from societal oppression, and although I attached no religious significance to it at the time, in later years I recognized it as a step in preparation for a ministry to those in life crises of catastrophic illness, bereavement, or death. In June, cancer struck Renee Barlow without warning. She had just been appointed personnel officer at the Executive Council of the Episcopal Church, and she had been on her new job less than a week when a lump was discovered in one breast during a routine physical examination required of all new employees. Further tests confirmed a diagnosis of malignancy and immediate surgery was recommended.

Renee reacted to the blow with her characteristic courage, but she was determined not to let the nature of her illness be known beyond one or two trusted friends. In those days people spoke of cancer in hushed tones as if it were leprosy, and she feared that if people in the personnel field got wind of her situation her chances of future employment would be severely damaged. A single woman of fifty-three who depended solely upon her own earnings to support herself and her increasingly fragile eighty-seven-year-old mother, Renee dreaded the specter of a protracted illness and unemployability. Not even her mother was told of the true situation; Mrs. Barlow had already lost two daughters to cancer, and Renee was determined to spare her the shock of learning that a third daughter, and the one upon whom she most relied, was also stricken. When she made arrangements to enter Harkness Pavilion at Columbia-Presbyterian Medical Center, she let Mrs. Barlow believe that she was having corrective surgery for a long-standing condition of varicose veins.

As one of the close friends in whom Renee confided, I volunteered to stay with Mrs. Barlow at night during Renee's hospitalization and to bring Mrs. Barlow firsthand information on her daughter's progress. Under the most favorable conditions it would have been a difficult role, because I am no good at dissembling, but in this case I had to cope with unexpected complications. Renee underwent a radical mastectomy requiring blood transfusions and extensive skin grafting. I could share none of these details with the anxious Mrs. Barlow, and had to parry her questions with the lame explanation that the "repair of the varicose veins" had gone as well as could be hoped for. While the surgeon reported optimistically that he believed all the malignancy had been removed and that radium treatments would not be necessary, this news was all but canceled out by a series of postsurgical complications which came near to being fatal. Renee was stricken with a severe case of hepatitis acquired through blood transfusions, and her weakened condition was aggravated by pneumonia. The medical staff was so preoccupied with pulling her through this crisis that little attention was paid to the place on her thigh from which flesh had been removed for the skin grafting. It became infected and developed into a festering wound which stubbornly refused to heal.

Renee barely survived these afflictions, which kept her in the hospital three months. For days she was so ill she was hardly aware of my presence when I visited her. I kept a silent vigil, powerless to ease her suffering yet hoping that somehow just by being with her, without words, I was communicating support. Because of the confidentiality of the situation, I could not share my anxieties over her illness with anyone, and found the worst part of my mission was having to face Mrs. Barlow each night, knowing that she was eager for the word that Renee would be coming home soon. I would leave the hospital so depressed that I would have to walk the streets with Doc on a leash, trying to muster the courage to assume a false cheerfulness or at least not to betray my own concern when I arrived at the Barlow apartment. As days passed and Renee's release was delayed, I had to concoct an explanation that the "varicose veins" were healing more slowly than anticipated and they didn't want her to risk infection by walking too soon. It was a stern test of my own faith, trying to assure Mrs. Barlow that all would be well when the opposite seemed true.

I had to leave for South Carolina in late July, but at least Renee had recovered enough before my departure to take a short walk with me along the hospital corridor. The Episcopal Church held her job open for her, and by mid-September she was able to return part time and gradually increase her hours to full time. That Christmas, when we took a holiday trip together to Jamaica, she had regained much of her old gaiety, but a new element had entered our friendship. I now shared with her the burden of a knowledge she had withheld from most of her friends and from her mother—the threat of recurring cancer. In the years that followed, Renee seldom referred to her Damoclean situation, but underneath her light-hearted banter was an urgency to live fully each day granted to her and a deepening of her natural gift for helping others. She would say, "The time is now," and I would find myself caught up in her spirit of celebrating the small blessings of life in the midst of uncertainty. Since she was a few years younger than I, her battle against cancer was a constant reminder of my own mortality, an encounter that forced me to think more deeply about the ultimate questions of human destiny.

The most important consequence of my stay in South Carolina during the school year 1967–68 was the gradual exorcism of long-buried childhood terrors of lynching and other forms of racial brutality. Although I had not lived in the South for forty years, I had not conquered the special feeling of unease that assailed me whenever I traveled below Washington. It was now three years since the passage of the 1964 Civil Rights Act, and contrary to my initial apprehensions, I did not experience a single humiliating incident while I was there. The tradespeople of downtown Columbia were courteous and friendly and some of them showed genuine interest and community pride in Benedict College as an educational institution.

My greatest surprise came when I ventured into the backcountry. Maida Springer visited me one weekend and we drove through desolate country to a rural community across the state line in Georgia, where the National Council of Negro Women was having a special program to promote a self-help sewing project. On the long journey over almost deserted roads, the only eating place we saw was a small diner near a crossroads filling station. Driven to find rest room facilities, we stopped and went in, not knowing what to expect. I asked for the ladies' room and the proprietor pointed to a door. When I came out, Maida was seated in a booth looking at a menu and two glasses of water had been placed on the table. We ate a good meal, and as we were leaving after paying our bill, we heard the characteristically friendly southern leavetaking: "Come see us agin!"

Evidence of a new era extended even to Mississippi, the state I had vowed I would not even *fly over* at an altitude of forty thousand feet. Ironically, my first assignment upon arrival at Benedict College was to attend a late-summer educational conference at a small Negro boarding school near Columbus, Mississippi. To my astonishment, reservations had been made for me at a motel near the school grounds, and when I appeared I was shown to my room without hesitation. Later, when the conference was over, five of us—three whites and two Negroes—hazarded entering a cafeteria on the main street of Columbus, where we were served with no more excitement than curious stares from the white customers.

That conference was memorable to me because I met and talked with Fannie Lou Hamer and because a small flurry of excitement developed reminiscent of earlier civil rights struggles. Mrs. Hamer's presence and the fact that the gathering was interracial guaranteed the possibility of surveillance on the part of some local whites. Conference leaders were on the alert. The school buildings, reached by a long, narrow lane, were clustered on a hill, which sloped down to the county road skirting the school grounds. When the headlights of a stream of cars moving slowly and close to one another along the road below stopped, everyone who had an automobile on the premises was asked to drive at once to the front of the building in which we were meeting. The dozen or more cars were parked side by side, facing downhill toward the lane and the main road, and their high-beam headlights were turned on. No one could enter the lane or drive up the hill without moving into the full glare of our improvised floodlights. The procession of cars down below soon moved on, and although everyone on the grounds stayed up late that night, keeping an eye on the road, nothing further happened to arouse suspicion.

Yet if my own experience that year symbolized the changing South, there were grim reminders that racial violence smoldered beneath the surface, ready to flare up at any moment. A shock went through our own campus in February 1968 when, thirty-five miles away, three black students were shot to death and more than thirty people were wounded by police officers in a disturbance on the campus of South Carolina State College in Orangeburg. The violence grew out of student protests against a segregated local bowling alley in a shopping center only a few blocks from the school, and the evidence indicated that the students were fired upon as they were fleeing from the police on the school campus. Two months later, the assassination of Dr. Martin Luther King, Jr., shocked the nation and the world. Anticipating trouble, Benedict College sent its students home for Easter vacation. A curfew was declared in Columbia, and armed units of the South Carolina National Guard set up stations within a few yards of the school gate. Fortunately, the curfew was lifted and the National Guard withdrawn before the students returned to school, thus avoiding a violent confrontation comparable to those that erupted in many cities in the aftermath of Dr. King's death.

By strange coincidence, when the shattering news of Dr. King's slaying came over the radio on the evening of April 4, 1968, I happened to be reading the final chapters of *The Autobiography of Malcolm X* and had just finished a passage written shortly before Malcolm's own assassination in 1965. Malcolm had observed:

> Sometimes, I have dared to dream to myself that one day, history may even say that my voice . . . helped to save America from a grave, possibly even a fatal catastrophe.
>
> The goal has always been the same, with the approaches to it as different as mine and Dr. Martin Luther King's non-violent marching, that dramatizes the brutality and the evil of the white man against defenseless blacks. And in the racial climate of this country today, it is anybody's guess which of the "extremes" in approach to the black man's problems might *personally* meet a fatal catastrophe first—"non violent" Dr. King, or so-called "violent" me.

The prophetic power of Malcolm X's reflection was staggering. I had not been a passionate admirer of Dr. King himself because I felt he had not recognized the role of women in the civil rights movement (Rosa Parks was not even invited to join Dr. King's party when he went abroad to receive the Nobel Peace Prize), but I was passionately devoted to his cause. Beneath the numbness I felt after that fatal evening was the realization that the foremost advocate of nonviolence as a way of life—my own cause—was stilled and those who had embraced Dr. King's religious commitment to nonviolence were called upon to keep his tradition alive and to advance the work for which he gave his life.

With the college closed during the week following Dr. King's death, I flew to New York and kept vigil at my television set on the day of his funeral in Atlanta. I did not know until some time later that I had, in a way, been part of one of the many public tributes to the fallen leader. Sarah Dalkowitz Kaplan, friend of my student days at International House in New York, who was now living in Seattle and teaching high school history, wrote me and enclosed a column by Emmett Watson, writer for the *Post-Intelligencer,* describing a memorial service for Dr. King held on

Sunday, April 7. Sarah was among nearly ten thousand people of all races and faiths who marched hand in hand to Seattle's Memorial Stadium, where the governor and other notables spoke and where thousands of voices joined in the moving chorus "We Shall Overcome." Emmett Watson reported further that "Olivia Cole, a tall, beautiful actress with the [Seattle Repertory Theatre] gave a reading from "The Dark Testament" which brought the crowd to its feet in tribute to its eloquence." Sarah continued the story: "Pauli, when did you do it? . . . Your stirring words echoed across the fields—up into the stands for an unforgettable experience for so many. . . . Next day the Seattle Repertory Theatre office was flooded with calls—the library had calls too—'What had she read?' 'Who wrote it?' 'Where can we find a copy?' " The following week, in answer to the many inquiries, Emmett Watson headed his column "Dark Testament" and reprinted those passages Olivia Cole had read at the memorial service. Written twenty-three years earlier, the poem began, "Freedom is a dream," and the closing lines seemed prophetic of Dr. King's life and message:

> Then let the dream linger on.
> Let it be the test of nations,
> Let it be the quest of all our days,
> The fevered pounding of our blood,
> The measure of our souls—
> That none shall rest in any land
> And none return to dreamless sleep,
> No heart be quieted, no tongue be stilled
> Until the final man may stand in any place
> And thrust his shoulders to the sky,
> Friend and brother to every other man.

Although I never met Olivia Cole (who later starred in the television drama *Upstairs in the White House*), her taped recording of "Dark Testament" enabled my friend Morris Milgram, who had long admired the poem and who had read it to audiences around the country, to find a publisher. In 1970 Silvermine Publishers, Inc., brought out a small volume of my poetry, with "Dark Testament" as the title poem.

The academic year at Benedict College was modestly successful. We developed several innovative programs, including a reading center, a pilot math developmental project, and the beginnings of a mathematics laboratory. Our reading center and other remedial efforts produced encouraging results. According to California achievement tests given in September and again in February and May, some first-year students made a leap of four years, four months; some advanced more than three years, and some, two or more years in reading. The median jump in reading of those for whom test scores were available was 1.7 years, or twice the normal rate of growth. We also received a grant from the U.S. Office of Education for a year of cooperative interinstitutional planning with Allen University, a school supported by the African Methodist Episcopal Church and located across the street. Our most exciting proposal won a grant from the Ford Foundation for a 1968 six-week summer institute for teachers of freshman English from six or seven Negro colleges in South Carolina. Dr. Anna Hedgeman, continuing consultant at the institute, reported later that it was a highly creative, stimulating experience, and she believed that the interchange of ideas and the discovery of new approaches to the teaching of first-year English could be a significant turning point in the higher education of Negro youth in South Carolina.

These developments were encouraging, and I derived satisfaction from having drafted proposals that attracted government and foundation funds to finance Benedict College's special educational projects. At the end of the school year, however, I resigned my post and returned to New York, convinced that my talents lay in having direct contact with young minds in classroom situations, and that I was misplaced in a purely technical, administrative job.

I had barely arrived home when, for the second time in two months, the nation reeled under the impact of the assassination of a national public figure—the gunning down of Robert F. Kennedy in California on June 5. I recalled my brief contact with Attorney General Kennedy some years earlier, when I served on a delegation of civil rights activists led by James Farmer and we went to see him in an effort to get the Department of Justice to enter an important housing discrimination case. The park authority of Deerfield, Illinois, had taken over land areas which were being developed into an interracial housing project by Morris Milgram's open housing corporation, and while the takeover seemed obviously motivated by an official determination to prevent Negro occupancy in the Chicago suburb of Deerfield, the lower courts upheld the local authorities and the United States Supreme Court refused to review the case. I reminded Mr. Kennedy of the riots of World War II and told him that if the Negro community could not obtain elbow room in which to spread out, the frustrations would again explode into riots. The attorney general was less sensitive to the complexities of the racial problem then than he became in later years; the Department of Justice ignored our pleas and the Deerfield case was one more of the many provocations that ignited racial explosions and ultimately led to the March on Washington in August 1963.

Coming on the heels of Martin Luther King's slaying in April, this second tragedy was almost too much to bear. For nearly a decade the lives of Dr. King and Robert F. Kennedy had been linked together in the bitter civil rights struggle, and only a few weeks earlier Kennedy had attended Dr. King's funeral. His death deepened the gloom that had settled over me, for nonviolence now seemed more discredited than ever before.

Two unexpected developments that summer saved me from being overwhelmed by despair. One was a cable from Geneva, Switzerland, sent by Rena Karefa-Smart on behalf of Dr. Eugene Carson Blake, the general secretary of the World Council of Churches, inviting me to participate as a resource person with co-opted staff status in the Fourth Assembly of the World Council of Churches meeting from July 4 to 20 in Uppsala, Sweden. I would be involved in the work of the subcommittee created by the World Council's Department of Church and Society, "to work on priorities and details of the Council's effort to contribute in the post-Uppsala period to the elimination of white racism from European civilization and from those societies influenced by it." The cable arrived less than ten days before I would have to leave for Sweden and was followed by a letter apologizing for the short notice and explaining that organizers of the Assembly had only recently agreed to include "Racism" as a major issue on the agenda of the 1968 meeting. I had serious reservations about going because I was skeptical about the institutionalized church, but the urgency of the appeal and the immediacy of the event gave me little opportunity to do more than make a decision on the spot. I accepted.

In the middle of my frantic preparations for going overseas, a second development competed for attention. Morris Abram, the newly designated president of Brandeis University, who had become a partner in Paul, Weiss, Rifkind, Wharton & Garrison after I worked there, telephoned out of the blue, asking me to consider joining the Brandeis faculty in the fall. Brandeis University, like other predominantly white educational institutions at the time, was feeling the repercussions of the Black Power movement and the new depths of anger and frustration that followed Dr. King's martyrdom. Afro-American societies on predominantly white college campuses began to demand courses in African and Afro-American history and culture as well as the appointment of more black faculty members. Faced with growing black militancy at the outset of his administration, President-elect Abram apparently thought I could be a valuable asset in helping to ease tensions. At his request, I squeezed in a hurried visit to Brandeis four days before leaving for Uppsala, and held exploratory discussions with the dean of faculty, Peter Diamondopoulos, and faculty members Lawrence H. Fuchs, Ruth Schacter Morgenthau, William Goldsmith, and Jacob Cohen about the possibility of an interdisciplinary program that would offer courses in Afro-American studies during the coming school year. The discussions were pleasant, but no conclusions were reached and I had to leave for Sweden before further negotiations could take place.

Uppsala turned out to be one of those peak experiences seldom duplicated in a lifetime. Never before 1968 (or since) had I been privileged to see so many religious leaders, scholars, and international public figures assembled at one place; nor had I seen people of such diverse origins and backgrounds attempting to surmount differences in style of worship as well as cultural, political, and national barriers in order to find common ground in relating the teachings of the Christian faith to world problems of war and peace, hunger and poverty, economic development, racial conflict, and the worldwide revolution in human rights.

The Fourth Assembly of the World Council of Churches had been in preparation ever since the WCC last met, in New Delhi seven years before, and the Uppsala meeting was said to be one of the largest gatherings of Christendom since the writing of the Nicene Creed in A.D. 325. For eighteen days the normal routines of secular life were suspended and we lived in the intensely devotional atmosphere of a self-contained ecumenical community of more than 2,700 people—a small city within a city —made up of men, women, and children of many cultures, races, and nationalities, coming from every continent and drawn together by a common faith to work and worship for a time under the Biblical theme "Behold, I make all things new."

The WCC has been described as a kind of "United Nations of Christendom," and indeed the Fourth Assembly combined the characteristics of a vast religious retreat and an international political congress. Almost every denomination of the Protestant Church was represented—235 member churches sent more than 700 official delegates—and many nonaffiliated churches sent observers. The Eastern Orthodox delegations from the Soviet Union, East Germany, Serbia, Bulgaria, and other Eastern regions contributed the largest single bloc, and official delegations came from almost every area except mainland China and South Africa. Some thirty-five Roman Catholics came as invited observers. They participated in the discussions and some were elected to WCC commissions.

Less than half the voting delegates were lay persons and only 9 percent were women. In addition to voting delegates, more than four hundred people attended as advisers, fraternal delegates, youth representatives, observers, spouses, and guests. A staff of 330 (including forty co-opted staff members like me) carried on the day-to-day work of the Assembly; 345 young stewards, mostly college students from many countries, served the Assembly as messengers, clerical assistants, waiters and waitresses, houseworkers who prepared our breakfasts and cleaned our rooms, and performers of other functions, for which they received a small daily stipend. The Assembly events were covered by a media corps of about 750.

We were rigidly screened (our badges of identification were as impor- tant as our passports) and were housed all over the city of Uppsala, but most of us stayed in new high-rise student apartments close to the univer- sity and to the main headquarters of the Fourth Assembly. To facilitate our transportation to meetings and activities, which were spread over a wide area, a corps of fifty-odd uniformed women bus drivers of the Women Motorists' Association of Sweden (an organization of eleven thousand or more members) worked as volunteers and drove the chartered buses that picked us up at the airport and made continuous rounds to all Assembly buildings and dormitories from 7:00 A.M. until midnight. My feminist heart thumped with pride when I boarded the bus at the airport and glimpsed a woman's handbag draped over the driver's railing.

From early morning until late at night, we were kept busy with a crowded agenda, which featured daily prayer services, study groups, com- mittee meetings, lectures, discussions, dramatic and cultural presenta- tions, sightseeing trips, and the nightly plenary sessions held in a huge gymnasium building, where the delegates were seated at rows of tables on the main floor and staff members, advisers, visitors, and guests sat in assigned seats in the balconies. I had never traveled as far north as Sweden and was entranced by the long midsummer twilights that lingered until dawn and brought back the wonderment of my childhood, when I read stories about "the land of the midnight sun." I was also deeply impressed by the thoughtfulness of the people of Uppsala and surrounding areas, who spared no effort to extend every courtesy and service, a thoughtfulness typified by the little plastic spoon which was attached to a bottle of medi- cine I bought in an apothecary.

Uppsala had been chosen for this mammoth religious gathering be- cause it was the scene of one of the pioneer ecumenical councils through which the groundwork for the World Council of Churches, founded in 1948, was laid. The closing sessions of the 1925 Stockholm Conference on Life and Work had been held in this university and cathedral city. Uppsala was also Dag Hammarskjöld's town. The late secretary general of the United Nations had grown up there in the castle when his father was governor of the province; he had attended the university and in 1925 was one of the young stewards who served at the Stockholm Conference, where, as one of the speakers at the Assembly recalled, he "thus got his first introduction to the problem of management of an international as- sembly, not realizing that this would become his chief task in his later years." Killed in a plane crash in 1961 while on a peace mission seeking to arrange a cease-fire in the Congo civil war, Dag Hammarskjöld was buried in his family's cemetery plot up the hill from the university, and many of the Assembly participants made a pilgrimage to his grave.

Dr. Martin Luther King, Jr., had been scheduled to set the tone of the Fourth Assembly by preaching the sermon at the open service held on July 4 in the seven-hundred-year-old cathedral of the Church of Sweden. The circumstances of his death cast a shadow over that awe-inspiring event. I sat in the balcony of the cathedral and thought how much Dr. King's origins, his life, and his work were symbolic of the Christian hope for human freedom and reconciliation which motivated this international assembly. Solemnity and pageantry combined to produce ecumenical worship at its best. The delegates, led by five of the six WCC presidents, marched in procession through the streets from the university to the cathedral. At the head of the column walked the Archbishop of Canterbury, Michael Ramsey, and Archbishop Iakovos, head of the Greek Orthodox Archdiocese of North and South America. The delegates, many of whom wore elaborate ecclesiastical vestments, brilliantly colored national dress, or academic robes and hoods, marched by countries alphabetically and by churches within each country. At the cathedral, the king of Sweden entered first to begin the formal ceremony, as trumpeters in red and gold sounded a fanfare. He was followed by the column of delegates.

Dr. D. T. Niles of the Methodist Church, Ceylon, who preached in Dr. King's place, memorialized the fallen leader as one of "God's sign-bearers" who "carry convincing testimony of some aspect of His working." At a plenary session, the entire Assembly stood for a minute of silence "in memory of two great Christian leaders who had lost their lives in the search for peace, love and harmony between men—Dr. Dag Hammarskjöld and the Rev. Dr. Martin Luther King." Later, as three of us climbed the hill to visit Dag Hammarskjöld's grave, we came upon a little green square named for Martin Luther King, Jr.

Several days after the Assembly began, I went to the deeply moving ecumenical High Mass at the cathedral, attended by more than three thousand people. We followed the service in four languages and sang the familiar hymns in our own tongues, knelt together at the many altars, and reenacted the ritual of the Feast of Love. It was reported that some of the Roman Catholics present defied the restrictions of their church and joined in the celebration of the Holy Communion.

A stirring moment for me came when I shook hands with Dr. Martin Niemöller, the Protestant clergyman who had spoken out for freedom in Hitler's Germany and spent eight years in a Nazi concentration camp as a result. He chaired the meeting on "White Racism: Chaos or World Community," in which the principal speakers were the author James Baldwin and the United Kingdom representative to the U.N., Lord Caradon. And there was that moment of disappointment on Human Rights night when tributes were paid to several people who had labored in the United Nations to develop an international standard of human rights, but no one—not even the delegates from the United States—mentioned the contribution of Eleanor Roosevelt, who had chaired the U.N. commission that drafted the Universal Declaration of Human Rights.

The Working Party on Racism, for which I was a resource person, was composed of WCC staff members and advisers to church delegations who had a special interest in seeing that the issue of racism was raised in the appropriate committees and that the Assembly adopt recommendations for future action toward its elimination. The group met daily under the direction of Rena Karefa-Smart, an American from the African Methodist Episcopal Zion Church and a volunteer staff member of WCC stationed in Geneva, where her husband, John Karefa-Smart, a physician who was a native of Sierra Leone, was attached to the World Health Organization. The warm friendship we began continued when Rena and John later settled in the United States and Rena completed her doctorate at Harvard Divinity School before joining the faculty of the Howard University School of Religion.

My work at Uppsala culminated in the drafting of a Background Statement on White Racism, which was finished and reproduced just in time to be distributed at the closing business session of the Assembly. Although the delegates were too preoccupied with taking action on pressing issues of world peace and economic development to consider the document, we were successful in getting portions of our statement incorporated in the Report of the Committee on Church and Society adopted by the Assembly, which charged the newly elected Central Committee "to undertake a crash program to guide the Council and the member churches in the urgent matter of racism." Our effort laid the groundwork for the Central Committee to authorize WCC sponsorship of an international Consultation on Racism to be held in London in May 1969.

Women's issues had been neglected on the Assembly agenda, but a lively Women's Caucus kept them from being ignored altogether. One of the truly exciting moments of the conclave came during elections, when a few determined women from third world countries, led by High Court Justice Annie R. Jiagge of Ghana (whom I had known in Accra) and Josefina Phodaca-Ambrosia, an attorney and president of the National Council of Women of the Philippines, abetted by me and by John and Rena Karefa-Smart and a few others, challenged the male-dominated organizational structure. When the patriarch of the Serbian Orthodox Church, one of the nominees proposed by the nominating committee for the six-member Praesidium, declared that he would refuse to sit if a woman was elected to that body, the women rose up in their wrath and decided to make a floor fight. Several delegates expressed strong objections to the fact that no woman had been nominated for the Praesidium. They were told that while the desirability of nominating a woman had not been overlooked, the committee, taking all other factors into account, had not found it possible to include a woman in its list. A motion to substitute the name of Birgit Rohde of the Church of Sweden for that of Presiding Bishop Johannes Lilje of the Evangelical Lutheran Church of Germany was finally put to the voting delegates by written ballot. Mrs. Rohde lost by 339 to 284, with three abstentions. Women were elected to seven seats on the 120-member central committee, the governing body between assemblies, and four women were named to the 135-member Commission on Faith and Order, concerned with questions of unity of the churches. Women also sought to have included in every major document wording that could be utilized to strengthen their position during the next seven years.

Our unsuccessful fight in 1968 prepared the ground: when the Fifth Assembly met in Nairobi in 1975, two women were elected to the WCC Praesidium—Justice Annie Jiagge of the Evangelical Presbyterian Church in Ghana and Dr. Cynthia Wedel of the Episcopal Church, U.S.A. Yet by the time of the Sixth Assembly, which convened in 1983 at Vancouver, British Columbia, a retreat from the upsurge of feminism at Nairobi seemed to have occurred. Justice Jiagge publicly expressed her deep disappointment over female underrepresentation. Noting that fewer than 30 percent of the delegates were female, she lamented, "When it comes to naming members of the central committee, 50 percent should be women, but we won't even get a third." And Dr. T. B. Simatupang of Indonesia, another member of the Praesidium, told the press "the next central committee will have less female participation than the present one."

Uppsala fired me with a renewed determination to return to the United States and proclaim through my own life and work the universal sisterhood and brotherhood I experienced during those eighteen days, however transitory and incomplete that expression of solidarity may have been. I was encouraged by the Assembly's forthright denunciation of the evil of racism as a blatant denial of the Christian faith and of our common humanity, and its recognition of how deeply entrenched the twin evil of sexism remained in the structures and much of the theology of institutionalized Christianity. In fact, and perhaps paradoxically, Uppsala furnished both the inspired moments and the frustrating impediments that strengthened my resolve to remove all barriers to my full exercise of the Christian ministry of reconciliation.

CHAPTER 32

My World Turned Upside Down

ABOUT halfway through the conference in Uppsala, I came down with a summer cold and a fever and had to stay in bed for two days, forlornly wishing I were back in the United States and near some friend who could look out for me. Isolated in a high-rise building among strangers, I felt like the "motherless child, a long way from home" of the Negro spiritual, conscious of the pressure to complete the background document for the subcommittee on white racism, yet too miserable to lift my head. In the midst of this minor crisis, a cable arrived from Peter Diamondopoulos, dean of faculty of Brandeis University, offering me a year's visiting professorship in American civilization and politics, to begin in September, and concluding PLEASE CABLE ACCEPTANCE LETTER FOLLOWS. His follow-up letter explained that I would have the dual function of teaching in the American Civilization program (later the American Studies Department) and of helping to plan and develop a program in Afro-American Studies.

Until the cable arrived, I had not given serious thought to teaching at Brandeis, having actually been in the process of moving back into the practice of law when Morris Abram tracked me down earlier in the summer. Now seemed an inopportune time for me to make a major decision about the future, alone and ill in a foreign country without anyone close at hand I knew well enough to consult. The offer would require me to uproot myself once more from New York—a city I loved—with the certainty of only one year of employment. At fifty-seven I was feeling a great weariness of wandering and longed to put down roots somewhere. I dragged myself out of bed and walked the unfamiliar streets, heedless of where I was, trying to weigh the extraordinary challenge presented by the cable from Dean Diamondopoulos.

The name Brandeis held a certain magic for me, evoking the tradition of the "Brandeis Brief," the model for lawyers presenting sociological issues to the courts. Founded in the same year as the State of Israel—1948 —Brandeis University was widely recognized as one of the top liberal private educational institutions in the United States, a center of Jewish learning which was nevertheless nonsectarian in its admission and personnel policies. I also knew that Eleanor Roosevelt had left her imprint on the school, both as a professor and as a member of the board of trustees. Given Brandeis' high academic standards and the temporary nature of the offer, I knew that I would be under tremendous pressure to prove my competence in just two semesters of teaching, in a position as demanding as any I had ever contemplated. Thus I seesawed up and down between apprehension and suppressed excitement.

During my brief visit to the Brandeis campus before leaving for Uppsala, Larry Fuchs, who chaired the committee on the American Civilization program (and later headed the American Studies Department), had been warm and cordial; he spoke confidently of the contribution I could make to Brandeis and suggested that I might develop innovative courses in legal studies designed for undergraduates. At that time such an imaginative concept was so new that few legal scholars had given it more than a passing thought. I found it startling; yet as I mulled over the idea, the need for introducing legal studies into a liberal arts curriculum became evident. It began to seem incredible that college students would spend four years in disciplined study and not have access to the most elementary knowledge of an increasingly complex legal system that profoundly affected almost every aspect of their social relations from birth to death. I reflected that prospective medical students were offered premed courses; why not prelaw courses for those headed for law school or those who wished to consider law as a possible career? The notion of designing and teaching legal studies seized me as a singular opportunity to satisfy my passion for pioneering in a new field, with freedom to make my own tracks, so to speak.

Helping to plan an Afro-American Studies program presented a similar challenge. In 1967 few such programs existed on college campuses, white or black, and the field was wide open for innovators. I visualized an interdisciplinary curriculum, bringing together scholarship in history, law, politics, sociology, psychology, anthropology, economics, and related human sciences to focus upon both the contributions of Negro Americans and the complex issues of white racism in Western civilization. Because I had devoted much of my adult life to independent research on Negro life and history, and had used an interdisciplinary approach in my doctoral dissertation in law, which examined the roots of the racial crisis in the United States, Afro-American Studies was familiar territory if not my area of formal training. Also, in West Africa I had spent nearly two years immersing myself in an intensive study of legal institutions and local customs, and I felt confident I could transmit to American students of whatever color an enthusiasm for the vitality and rich variety of the African peoples I had observed. Aware of the "Tarzan" stereotype of Africa prevalent in the United States, I saw a need to give college students an appreciation for those African customs that had universal relevance. As for Brandeis University itself, I had long admired the Jewish tradition of learning, which predated Western civilization and produced the Holy Scriptures, my earliest model of poetry and historical literature as well as the principal canon of the Judeo-Christian faith. All in all, joining the Brandeis faculty seemed like a thrilling adventure in intellectual endeavor, and in spite of my apprehensions I cabled my acceptance.

Back in the United States a few weeks later, I drove with my fifteen-year-old nephew, Michael Kevin Murray, then a student at the Bronx High School of Science, up to northeastern Maine for a two-week vacation on Yellowhead Island in Machias Bay with Caroline Ware, Gardiner Means, and Mary Norris, a young friend who was completing her senior year at Radcliffe after a time out of school. Sitting on tiny Yellowhead Island, about thirty miles south of Campobello, where Mike and I made a pilgrimage to the Roosevelt summer home, with its memorable photographic montage of Eleanor Roosevelt's hands in various positions, I poured out on my portable typewriter a summation of the previous six years of my life. Suddenly I realized that what I really wanted to do was to write an autobiographical book on Jim Crow and Jane Crow—racism and sexism as they had impinged upon my life. Skipper, Mary, and I began to hold vigorous discussions on the conflict between my desire to write and the positive benefits of teaching at Brandeis. It was a renewal of the conflict that intensified with each career change.

As products of the Harvard/Radcliffe tradition, Skipper, Gardiner, and twenty-five-year-old Mary knew that I would thrive in the intellectual atmosphere of the Boston area, studded with colleges, universities, seminaries, and cultural attractions. They urged me to settle in at Brandeis, achieve tenure, and spend my free summer periods writing the book. With the conflict temporarily resolved, I began eagerly to anticipate the school year ahead, and Mike and I had a rollicking drive back to New York by way of the White Mountains of New Hampshire, the Green Mountains of Vermont, and down into New York State, where we visited the Roosevelt shrine in Hyde Park as a fitting conclusion to our trip and prelude to my new mission.

That September, in the brilliant sunrise of a crisp fall morning, I drove with my dog into Massachusetts, having spent the night in a motel just south of Sturbridge. Feeling like a teenage college freshman on a high adventure away from home for the first time, instead of a fifty-seven-year-old woman with a silver streak in her hair, I arrived at Brandeis University in time for an early breakfast in the students' cafeteria. My VW, like a turtle traveling with its house on its back, was loaded to the ceiling, and the luggage carrier on top held a burden of boxes and cartons covered by a tarpaulin, which had flapped in merry syncopation as I whizzed along the Massachusetts Turnpike. (The VW would be followed shortly by a moving van out of which flowed a half-dozen file cabinets, dozens of cartons of books and papers, and a few household effects. I prayed that no Brandeis official would see me, lest they think I was moving in for life!)

It was a glorious new beginning, and—uncharacteristically for me at breakfast time—I was ravenously hungry. In the cafeteria line, I naively asked for bacon and eggs and was embarrassed by the sharp response, "We don't serve bacon here!" I could have melted through the cracks in the floor. Later, in the faculty dining room, I discovered that the dieticians had thoughtfully provided a beef product that looked indistinguishable from strips of bacon. The encounter foreshadowed my adjustments that first year at Brandeis and, to a less intense degree, my entire five years of teaching in the Boston area—the most exciting, tormenting, satisfying, embattled, frustrated, and at times triumphant period of my secular career.

My venture into American Studies was perhaps my most rewarding involvement. Unfortunately, within less than six months after my arrival, calamitous events short-circuited the positive role I had hoped to play in the development of the Afro-American Studies program. With the opening of the fall semester, the vision of carrying forward Dr. Martin Luther King's dream of the "beloved community" I had brought from my religious renewal in Uppsala receded like a mirage. Across the country, the convulsions of Negro student rebellion spread like a contagious madness on predominantly white college campuses already shaken by earlier white student protests. (The shock waves from these firestorms would reach the black campuses a few years later.) Thrust headlong without preparation into the ferment and caught up in the turbulence that transformed Afro-American/Black Studies into an intensely political issue, I shared the excruciating anguish of the college faculties and administrators, who were forced to cope simultaneously with educational dilemmas and spasms of mutinous confrontation accompanying the enrollment of unprecedented numbers of black students in institutions that had formerly been over-whelmingly white. I was learning again that each step toward equality of opportunity brought its own peculiar set of problems, and my loyalties were divided between professional integrity and racial sympathy. Since the educational problems were embedded in the racial past, I suffered even more; in black-white confrontations, I found myself in the position of my Fitzgerald forebears, whom I had described in *Proud Shoes* as occupying "a no man's land between the whites and the blacks, belonging wholly to neither, yet irrevocably tied to both . . . always at the vital nerve center of racial conflict, stretched taut between strong bonds of kinship and tides of rebellion."

In those early days of innocence at Brandeis—and elsewhere, I suspect —those of us involved at the faculty/administration level were amazingly unanimous in our approach to Black Studies. As scholars, we favored specialization in the field in graduate school and the treatment of Black Studies in an undergraduate curriculum as an integral part of the study of American civilization, emphasizing the impact of Europe and Africa in particular upon the New World experience. I concurred with the late Frank Tannenbaum that the shaping of the New World was a joint enter-prise of Europeans and Africans, notwithstanding the power relationships between the peoples of the two continents. I also held the conviction that racial integration is essentially an experience of mind and spirit and begins with a reinterpretation of our social history to show the interconnected-ness of peoples, emphasizing their common humanity. To have a part in the effort of reintegrating our national heritage, of making whole the American psyche, of bringing into the intellectual currents of our past the significant tributaries of the "Black Experience," was a creative mission of high order, one that in its potential for reconciliation had religious as well as political and social implications.

In my idealism, however, I had overlooked the crucial factor of living experience. While I shared the onerous burdens of inequality of status with all other people of color, in the case of Negro students at Brandeis I brought to my teaching position the outlook of one who had lived through a preceding historical period extending forty years before they were born and which they either knew little about or embraced only in theory. Those forty years of intense personal history separated me from the young black students and gave me a somewhat different perspective on the ubiquitous racial dilemma which now tore at their vitals.

In many respects we seemed light-years apart. They were engaged in a collective search for an acceptable identity, which took the form of pride in *blackness,* grasping the nettle of a term of former humiliation and

converting it into a symbol of personal worth. Their struggle was reinforced by their numbers, through which they were able to provide one
another with mutual support. By contrast, my own quest for identity had
been a long, painful, relatively private search; my youthful rebellions were
individualistic, and I had spontaneously resisted racial injustice without
waiting for others to join me. I had come to my present plateau by small,
positive accretions—periodic recognition of myself as a person of worth
interspersed with desolate periods of suffering, bewilderment, anger,
rage, and self-doubt—often finding myself so hemmed in by suffocating
walls of exclusion that my only safety valve against frenzy was the act of
pouring out my feelings through the written word.

I had chosen to affirm my own identity by anchoring myself firmly in
the immediate American past, which had produced my mixed racial origins with all their Ishmaelite implications—a stance that made both blacks
and whites uncomfortable. From childhood I had been taught that
"Beauty is as beauty does," so the slogan "Black is beautiful" had no
personal meaning for me. I had come to appreciate the beauty of American Negroes in all their rich variety of features, hair texture, and skin tone
—the arresting combination, for example, of gray eyes, red hair, and
nut-brown complexion—revealing the harmonious genetic blending of
several races. As one of an earlier generation of "firsts," when our numbers
were few and we were vulnerable to explicit expressions of racial stereotypes, I had lived with the continual challenge of proving myself. To
survive these initial breakthroughs with dignity, my generation of
Negroes had relied upon such slogans as "Don't get mad, get smart!" or
"Do not judge us by where we are now but from where we have come!"

And while I never denied my identity as a person of color, and took
pride in the achievements of "the race" as my ancestors had done before
me, my strong individualism worked against tendencies toward a too
strong alliance with a racial group to the exclusion of others not so identified. My background and upbringing had been such that I was uncomfortable in any environment that was not inclusive. To thrive, I needed a
society that was hospitable to all comers—black as well as white, women
as well as men, "the lame, the halt, the blind," the browns and yellows and
reds—a society in which individuals were free to express their multiple
origins and to share their variety of cultural strains without being forced
into a categorical mold. Almost from birth I had been conditioned by
religious training to believe that love was more powerful than hate—not
a passive, submissive love but a vigorous love which resisted injustice
without stooping to the level of hating the oppressor. Applying this belief
to the racial problem in the United States, I held to the conviction that

once discriminatory laws and systemic practices were removed, the ultimate resolution of racism would come through one-to-one interracial relationships creating a climate of acceptance.

A new generation of black students, however, many of whom I encountered at Brandeis University that fall, were marching to a different drum-
mer. From the moment I arrived on campus, I was thrown into fundamental philosophical and moral conflict with the advocates of a black ideology
as alien to my nature and as difficult for me to accept as white ethnocentrism. This emerging racial rhetoric smacked of an ethnic "party line" and
made absolutely no sense to me; in turn, some of my most deeply held
values about universal human dignity were considered obsolete by young
black radicals. While not all, nor even a majority, of the Negro students
who attended Brandeis were political extremists, a few highly vocal insurgents were able to silence the views of the studious, serious-minded mod-
erates among them.

Little in my recent academic experiences had equipped me to cope
with a sudden sea change in racial attitudes on the part of those who were
enjoying privileges my generation of civil rights fighters had never known.
I had just come from a year at a Negro institution, Benedict College,
where most of the students were from southern states, many from impoverished rural areas. Frequently they were members of large sharecropper
families and the first from their families to go beyond a high school education. I had felt a spiritual kinship with those students because I had grown
up only two hundred miles away from Columbia, in a semirural environment where making a living was hard and the mark of oppression so harsh
that I had once said of my racial experience, "Don't touch me, I'm full of
slivers!"

The students at Benedict College, unlike their northern counterparts,
seemed grateful for the opportunity to go to college on the work-study
program, and living in the shadow of continued violent repression, they
had shown remarkable restraint in their responses to provocation. When
the three Negro students at South Carolina State College were massacred
—shot in the back—on the Orangeburg campus by state police in 1968,
the students from Benedict College and nearby Allen University accepted
my suggestion, made as vice-president of Benedict, to be creative in their
protest. They planned and held a joint memorial service on the Benedict
campus in the open air near a well-traveled intersection. Marked by dignity and solemnity appropriate to the occasion, the young people used the
service to reaffirm their rights as citizens of the United States. To me,
the most moving moment of the ceremony had been the presentation of
the flags of all the armed services by a uniformed student color guard,
followed by the mournful sound of Taps. The impressive demonstration

was covered by local television and commented upon favorably in the press. Later that day, the governor of South Carolina received a student delegation from both colleges and was visibly impressed by their courteous, intelligent presentation of racial grievances. As one who had grown up in the South, I recognized this tentative overture to future black leaders by a white governor as one of thousands of similar tiny steps in the fragile process of rapprochement developing slowly and painfully between the races in a newborn, almost embarrassed, feeling of mutual respect following the demise of the rigid Jim Crow system.

As their adviser, I had enjoyed the confidence and affection of the Benedict College students during this episode and, for my part, I admired their maturity—a maturity beyond their years—in handling themselves in a racially inflamed situation. Thus at Brandeis I was wholly unprepared for the bellicose postures of their northern counterparts in the peaceful, friendly surroundings of a New England suburban campus. While Dr. King's assassination in the intervening period understandably stirred up the passions of a sorely tried people, it seemed to me that the excessively churlish, racially inspired rhetoric of the more radical black students was misplaced in the comparatively sympathetic atmosphere of Brandeis University.

Far from providing leadership in a new and constructive phase of civil rights, I found myself in a head-on collision with those whom I most wanted to serve. To appreciate my dilemma, one needs to recall the political climate of the late 1960s. In the three years since my graduate student days at Yale, when integration had been the dream many of us believed was about to be realized, a radical turnabout in racial consciousness had occurred, especially among young Negroes. This change of mood followed in the wake of spectacular civil rights victories that had dismantled the system of legalized segregation and brought about comprehensive federal laws against discrimination. But there was a vast difference between laws on the books and the realities of everyday experience. Desegregation of hearts and minds was light-years away from the pronouncements of the Supreme Court and the Congress. Perplexing new issues had arisen, and the answers were more complicated than the mere removal of the old signs "White" and "Colored" or the knocking down of partitions which separated the races in public transportation, those visible symbols of racial degradation. The civil rights victories merely stripped away the outer layers of *apartheid,* exposing the depth and intransigence of a racism that had been several centuries in the making and pervaded the whole of American society in subtle as well as blatant forms.

At one level was the complex issue of communication between black and white individuals. Negroes with finely sensitized antennae, which had been their principal means of detecting hostile or friendly attitudes in the white world, were quick to pick up the nuances of condescension or a patronizing tilt in an otherwise innocent remark. On the other hand, many white people exposed to colored individuals for the first time and anxious not to insult or offend them maintained an embarrassing formality in the most natural of situations or became effusive in their attempts to make their black acquaintances feel comfortable. The results were seldom felicitous and contributed little to a sense of community.

At another level, most Negroes remained in impoverished circumstances, isolated in ghettos and unable to take advantage of the substantial benefits to be gained from the new legislation. A massive, sustained national effort comparable to a domestic Marshall Plan was essential to removing the blight of centuries of oppression—an effort that necessarily entailed painful dislocations and sacrifices on the part of the dominant and heretofore privileged white population. Yet, once the anti-bias laws were passed, the growing indifference of white Americans to the continuing plight of Negroes walled into the decaying inner cities, mired in poverty and unemployment or in the most menial jobs, jobs that were fast disappearing under the impact of a new technology, had turned the bright hopes of millions of black people into disillusionment and despair. For younger, impatient civil rights activists who threw themselves passionately into the movement for Freedom Now in the late 1950s and early 1960s, their efforts had seemed to bring only a harvest of bitterness. After all the jailings, the bombings, the burnings, the killings, the battered bodies and shattered careers, the supreme sacrifices of their youth, the dream was as distant as ever.

The earlier consensus, which had unified church groups, labor and liberal groups, and the major civil rights organizations around the goal of integration, was shattered in the mid-1960s, and interracial coalitions fell apart. Older leaders whose patient toil had made possible civil rights victories up to that time were being discredited and shunted aside by younger, embittered black nationalistic radicals. With the assassination of Martin Luther King, Jr., advocacy of the moral principle of nonviolent resistance to injustice coupled with the promise of racial reconciliation was quickly overtaken by the idea of black liberation by any means necessary and a mood of violent response to racial subjugation, real or imagined. Ghettos in the North and West exploded into the self-inflicted destructiveness of despair. President Johnson's National Advisory Commission on Disorders, appointed in 1967 to review the riots, reported: "This is our basic conclusion: Our nation is moving toward two societies, one black, one white, separate and unequal."

A new phase of the struggle emerged, variously called Black Power,

Black Liberation, and, in its most extreme form, Revolutionary Black Nationalism, profoundly affecting the outlook of thousands upon thousands of people of color who embraced the new movement as a means of survival and self-respect. Emphasis shifted from interracial cooperation to self-determination and a strong identification with the rising African nations and other nonwhite third world peoples. "Black and white together, we shall overcome"—the song that had rallied the old civil rights movement—was discarded by many, who now shouted "Black is beautiful," "Black Consciousness," or "Black Nationhood."

A generation of Negro students, in their infancy when the historic 1954 desegregation decision was handed down by the Supreme Court and whose entire lives were shaped by continuous, overt racial strife, were now entering college, bringing with them a legacy of nearly two decades of unrelieved turbulence. Although fully aware of this unsettling trend, which confused and distorted earlier goals to which I had given my allegiance, I had not had to grapple with it in face-to-face, student-teacher relationships.

The convulsions of my own youth had been more universal, emphasizing the international solidarity of the working classes, the racial component of which had been a fire burning underground with only an occasional spurt of smoke and flame becoming visible. I had fortified my longing to belong with the words of great poets: Walt Whitman, who said, "We shall not convince them by our words, we shall convince them by our presence"; or that poignant line of Langston Hughes, "I, too, sing America"; or the heroic declaration of Claude McKay, the Caribbean poet who wrote in his "America":

> Although she feeds me bread of bitterness,
> And sinks into my throat her tiger's tooth,
> Stealing my breath of life, I will confess
> I love this cultured hell that tests my youth!
> Her vigor flows like tides into my blood,
> Giving me strength erect against her hate . . .

And there was Georgia Douglas Johnson's "Interracial," which ended: "Oh, let's build bridges everywhere/And span the gulf of challenge there."

Then, too, as a veteran of the earlier civil rights movement, I saw no contradiction between racial consciousness and the pursuit of excellence in making my way into the cultural mainstream of life in the United States. Being part of the mainstream had meant to me not the blind imitation of dominant values but a choice of those verities, handed down through centuries of human experience, that enriched the quality of life. Chief among these was the sacredness of the individual, who, in Biblical tradition, is created in the image of God, and from that vision followed my obligation to work with others to transform the planet Earth into a place where each individual would have an opportunity to fulfill his or her highest creative potential.

Cast in this mold, I found it grated upon my sensibilities to hear from young people—beneficiaries of the ongoing effort to create a more open society—that integration was "irrelevant to the problems of the masses of black people," that it was merely the "acceptance of a few token Negroes into white institutions on the white man's terms," resulting in "the loss of black identity and pride in blackness."

"Pride in blackness" ranged from adoption of African dress to flirtation with extreme black nationalism, accompanied by a strong tendency toward separatism and antiwhite feelings expressed in epithets like "Honkie" and "Whitey," and a generally uncivil manner toward white individuals. (Having lived in West Africa and been on the receiving end of arrogance directed at American Negroes, I thought much of this newfound cultural nationalism was misplaced.) For a time, I was living in a world turned upside down; in a complete reversal of goals that had fired my own student activism, some of the young militants were now demanding separate dormitories and cultural centers, from which whites were to be excluded, as well as Afro-American/Black Studies departments controlled by blacks, taught by black professors, and attended exclusively by black students.

As a teacher observing variations of this theme on a predominantly white campus, it seemed to me that such withdrawal into a self-imposed segregation was a symptom of a deep-seated fear of failure in an open, competitive society, a drawing back from the stringent demands of equality at a high academic level, a self-deception that would lead ultimately to isolation and abandonment to the mediocrity of a second-class citizenship which was now partially self-induced. Of the many crosses I had had to bear labeled "the race problem," this was to be the most painful during that ghastly period of readjustment.

CHAPTER 33

Black Politics at Brandeis

LIVING through the tumultuous events of that first semester at Brandeis University in the fall and winter of 1968–69 was at times like rolling backward down a steep incline in a vehicle out of control, unable to brake my perilous descent. I saw Brandeis as my "big chance," and I felt that if I muffed it, I would be discredited as a competent scholar and teacher. I was at the peak of my intellectual powers and my future professional career was at stake. The term began with a complicated classroom situation which threatened to torpedo my reputation and ended with a drama-packed confrontation between a group of militant black students and the school's administration, which burst upon the front page of the *New York Times,* engulfed the Brandeis campus for eleven anxious days, and caught me in the middle. In both situations, I was an incidental victim of the consequences of well-intentioned efforts to increase educational opportunities for Negro youth—efforts that backfired.

Brandeis was not unique in this respect. I would have been in the same predicament as a member of the faculty of Cornell, Swarthmore, Harvard, Yale, Columbia, or Berkeley. We were all caught up in one of those spasms of history that sweep aside all human calculations when escaping social disaster seems to depend less on the wisdom or intelligence of human beings than on the intervention of Providence. To say that the chaotic aftermath of a racial revolution should have been predictable is to apply the understanding of hindsight. What happened at Brandeis that year pointed up the reality that privileged groups voluntarily pursuing change on behalf of those who seek the instant realization of opportunities long denied are sometimes as vulnerable to attack as downright racial bigots forcefully resisting change. In the agony of breaking free from the bondage of past untouchability, its victims flailed at friends and enemies alike.

During the spring and summer of 1968, the university had intensively recruited Negro students under the leadership of its outgoing president, Dr. Abram L. Sachar, who became the school's first chancellor, and Morris Abram, the incoming president, who brought with him an impeccable civil rights record from his native Georgia. By fall, Negro enrollment had increased from 58 to 120 in a student body of 2,600, and financial aid for Negro students had nearly tripled—from $125,000 to $349,000. The college administration had also authorized a concentration (major) in African and Afro-American Studies, to be administered by a committee of faculty and student representatives, and I was appointed one of the faculty members to serve on the committee.

The most ambitious project—and ultimately the most troublesome that year—was a Transitional Year Program (TYP), spearheaded by faculty members Jacob Cohen and William Goldsmith, who had both been active in Upward Bound programs and were especially eager to open the door to a college education for young inner-city males. In aid of its twofold purpose, "to assist the educationally disadvantaged" and "to recruit higher proportions of qualified black undergraduates," TYP offered a year of residence on campus on full scholarship and a curriculum of specially designed remedial instruction to students selected for their intelligence and educational promise. Those who successfully completed the program were admitted to the regular Brandeis undergraduate curriculum. In addition to the three TYP courses required of the enrollees, each TYP student was permitted to take one regular Brandeis undergraduate course, to get a foretaste of normal college work and competition with regularly admitted undergraduates. Given the euphemistic classification "pre-freshmen," TYP students could select the regular course themselves; if they passed it, they would receive college credit. If they failed, the course grade was not recorded and did not prejudice their later candidacy for admission as regular undergraduates. It was a bold, imaginative idea, which would be tested in the crucible of bitter conflict.

The initial TYP enrollment that fall was twenty-six male students— twenty-three of them black. They were in a high-risk category; only thirteen had achieved high school diplomas, and a number were high school dropouts from the seething Roxbury section of Greater Boston. Critics of the program justifiably pointed out that given the generally high scholastic standing of regular Brandeis students, whatever their ethnic background, a wiser approach to implementing equal educational opportunities during this volatile period might have been the recruitment of transfer Negro students from predominantly black colleges in the South, who had been exposed to the discipline of college study and therefore were better equipped to cope with the hazards of competing with educationally advantaged students who were mostly white.

In addition to the educational complexities of the experimental program, the introduction into a small residential campus of an all-male contingent of nonmatriculated, aggressive minority students immediately concerned with flexing their muscles and expressing their "manhood" carried with it built-in tensions. Some of the white women students found the new arrivals intriguing and sought to be friendly. Their overtures created animosity among some of the Negro women students, who already suffered from a dearth of black men to date, and they looked upon their white female counterparts as sexual predators. At times, I observed outbursts that crackled with hostility. The situation was aggravated by the tendency of some of the TYP men to glory in their prowess; in their academic vulnerability they fell back on their sexual attractiveness as an affirmation of their personhood, confusing masculinity with personal worth.

Then there were well-meaning white students who had never had close contact with Negroes as peers and were anxious to increase their understanding of the racial problem. In the dormitories, some black students felt suffocated by hovering white cohorts who plied them with questions that came across as "Tell me in five minutes what it is like to be black." Although these awkwardly expressed attentions revealed a sincere desire to narrow the racial distance, they served merely to arouse impatience and irritability in many black students, who were already under heavy competitive academic pressures to succeed and resented what they perceived as insensitive distractions.

In a setting of general unrest among articulate students preoccupied with the Vietnam War and other societal stresses, this mercurial racial mix was a keg of dynamite waiting for a spark. In my peculiar position as a Negro woman and the only Negro full professor on campus, I was sensitive to these tensions, all the more so because as a new arrival myself I did not know what was expected of me. I also heard complaints from black students that they felt isolated, a feeling I shared because, living off campus in Cambridge, I had fewer opportunities to participate in student activities and to develop the kind of informal relationships that break down student-faculty barriers, as I had been able to do the previous year at Benedict College. In time, I was to discover that the black students suffered in acute form the more general isolation felt by a resident student body with a nonresident faculty. The psychological distance between

Brandeis, set in the hills of Waltham, and the hub of collegiate life in Harvard Square was much greater than the geographical distance of ten miles or less.

What almost defeated me during my first term, however, was an unexpected snarl in the "regular course" feature of the TYP project. I discovered that sometimes the most innovative approaches to remedying wrongs long in the making can create new problems as complex as any they were intended to solve. As academics, we were less attuned to the fact that the issue of equal opportunity in higher education had deep political as well as educational implications, and we lacked comprehensive knowledge of the process by which the most disadvantaged members of a racial caste—literally "untouchables"—could be brought into the academic mainstream. Back in 1954, none of us could have foreseen the consequences of the legal revolution wrought by the United States Supreme Court decision in *Brown* v. *Board of Education,* which ultimately went beyond the public schools and with a ripple effect churned up almost every public and private institution in the United States. A certain complacency had enveloped most northern institutions until the riots exploded in the ghettos in the mid-1960s, followed by more firestorms in the wake of Dr. King's assassination. The reaction to that latest catastrophe was an emergency response without benefit of long-term advance planning—a typical American response. At the time of the *Brown* decision, I had written idealistically: "The Supreme Court has set the example for future conduct by combining moral and constitutional integrity with wisdom of high order. . . . It has indicated an orderly procedure of moving forward with patience and restraint." Now, fifteen years later, I found myself trying to cope with the passions of a new generation of ghetto-bred black youths reacting to the long overdue response of the so-called white establishment, while at the same time I tried to work out a centuries-old problem of deprivation, using the sensitive but imperfect tool of classroom democracy.

Both a victim of and a participant in this hurried response, I arrived at Brandeis in mid-September and, with classes scheduled to begin in two weeks, was asked to undertake a seminar course in the American Civilization program, to be entitled "Law as an Instrument of Social Change" (later streamlined to "Law and Social Change"). It was the first such course to be given at Brandeis, and I had no idea at the time that it would eventually generate a full-scale Legal Studies program with its own director, an interdepartmental faculty committee of twenty-two or more, and at least twelve course offerings. I hurriedly prepared a syllabus geared to the level of senior undergraduates. The course was publicized as a special attraction by word of mouth, by notices posted on bulletin boards in classroom buildings, and by an announcement at the first fall meeting of the Afro-American Students Association. Much like the proprietor of a small novelty store in a shopping mall, I waited nervously to see if the course drew any "customers."

On my first day of class—my first day as a teacher at Brandeis—I faced fourteen students sitting at tables arranged in U-formation, seminar style, in a classroom down the corridor from my office on the second floor of Ford Hall, a building later to acquire prominence when it was taken over by black militants. From their enrollment cards, I learned that the class included eight seniors and two juniors (who had arranged themselves along the sides), and, in the rear facing my desk, four black students from the TYP project!

A more problematic pedagogic situation could hardly have been devised, for I faced the nearly impossible task of bridging the huge gap in educational backgrounds and skills existing between the regularly matriculated third- and fourth-year students and the TYP recruits. All the regular students had strong backgrounds in political science and government, and several were already considering law school. Five of the seniors would graduate with honors in the spring, one with high honors. To make matters worse, the division was racial as well as academic. Except for one woman, a senior, all of the regular students were white. The four black TYP students—Leonard E. Carson, James Graham, Ernest R. Myers, and Joseph Reese—were separated (in academic terms) from their classmates by four to five years of concentrated study and were thrown into an uneven competition with academic leaders from the regular student body. Racial considerations had apparently motivated them to select my course, and no one on the faculty had thought to consult me about the academic prerequisites for such a seminar.

The small class size made each incident loom large, and the classroom atmosphere was made even more combustible by a compulsion on the part of the young black men to exhibit their "macho" in their speech and gestures. As I perceived it, because of my race and gender they assumed a license typical of unruly high school adolescents—from which they were not far removed in age and educational background—and their tendency to dominate the first few class discussions with political rhetoric shocked the more restrained juniors and seniors. When they advanced the Black Power "line," the normally articulate white students retreated into an embarrassed silence. I was torn in several ways: as a feminist I bristled at their macho attitudes; as a scholar I related to the sharp intellects of the advanced students; as a person of color I suffered the pain I knew the TYP students must be feeling with so many odds stacked against them. They were unable to keep up with the rapid note-taking my lectures required or to understand much of the terminology familiar to upper-class members, and they were quickly overwhelmed by the heavy reading assignments essential to the course. The tiny classroom group mirrored the tensions of racial-sexual-class conflicts in the larger society.

Symbolic of the heightened racial consciousness that invaded the classroom was an exchange with one of the TYP students which threatened to disrupt my class on my first day of teaching. I was outlining the content of the course when a young man interrupted me with the question, "Why do you keep saying 'Knee-grows' when you're talking about *black* people?"

The young man's querulous inquiry caught me off guard. I was having my usual first-day jitters, meeting a strange class in a new setting, and his combative manner embarrassed me. I explained that "Negro" was a legitimate usage, a proper noun adopted by scholars and official government publications, and was preferred by many people, including me. What I could not explain—on the spot—was how my own strong feelings about the usage were rooted in a lifetime of experience with varied racial designations. The right to name oneself, as liberation movements have emphasized, is profoundly important to a people or group emerging from subjugation. By 1968 the ground swell had begun for what developed into a largely successful effort to repudiate the capitalized term "Negro" and replace it with the virtually exclusive use of the lowercase "black" to designate persons with any degree of African ancestry.

The instability of relations between the races in this country during more than three centuries is reflected in the long list of designations used for persons of African descent which have gained currency from time to time: "African," "African-American," "Afro-American," "Black," "People of Color," "Colored," "negro," "Negro" (and the feminine forms "negress" and "Negress," recognized in some dictionaries as derogatory). The most recent change, which was accomplished with dizzying speed by clamorous black militants abetted by the electronic media, was symptomatic to me of confused attitudes over questions of identity. As my Howard University friend of the 1940s, Ruth Powell, expressed it, "Pauli, I find it very disconcerting to go to bed one night a Negro and wake up the next morning a 'black.' Nobody gave me any choice in the matter."

The internal controversy over a choice of racial designations had become intensely emotional by the late 1960s and there was very little consensus among those directly involved as to a preferred term. In June 1969, *Newsweek* published the results of a poll (apparently conducted among Negroes) which showed that "Negro" was most liked by 38 percent of those questioned; followed by "Colored People" (25 percent), reflecting an older generation; "Blacks" (19 percent); and "Afro-American" (11 percent). The rest were either uncertain or did not care. When the respondents were asked which term they liked least, "Colored People" was least preferred by 31 percent; "Blacks" by 25 percent; "Negro" by 11 percent; and "Afro-American" by 11 percent.

Despite the clear preference given to "Negro" at the time, and the statement of Dr. James A. Morsell of the NAACP published in the *New York Times* that "Only 'Negro' possesses by reason of wide and continuous usage, a clear, specific and exclusive connotation," aggressive advocates of "black" won the day, partly through manipulation of the media, which facilitated the new trend, and partly through coercive ideological arguments, which silenced opposition. Plausibly, they argued that they were transforming a word of shame and rejection into a term of pride and self-worth. They went further, however, contending that "Negro" was a "white man's term of contempt," notwithstanding that over time it had attained the dignity of a proper noun and, as Dr. Morsell pointed out, "historical circumstances brought into common English use the Spanish term for black, which is 'Negro.' " In diatribes that allowed no room for personal choices, the militants condemned those who continued to use "Negro" as persons who were insensitive or disloyal to the true interests of black people.

I strongly objected to the *exclusive* use of "black" as an official designation for several reasons, even though I gradually came to appreciate the need of many people to strip the term of its derogatory connotation. Not unlike using the word "man" as a generic term for all human beings as well as a term to describe a male human being, making "black" do double duty to describe (the color) and to name (the race) gave the term a confused meaning. It inaccurately described the physical identity of millions of Negro Americans, or people of color, whose characteristics varied from blond Causasian types to almost pure-black African types. The logical consequence of such usage was the paradox in 1983 of the selection of the first black Miss America and her runner-up, followed by letters addressed to Negro newspapers complaining that neither of the young women was representative of black people since both were hardly distinguishable from the white contestants.

In 1968, "black" had political connotations closely allied with the ideology of separatism. It emphasized a black-white polarization that the term "Negro" did not convey, and its projection into settled usage had a disturbing effect, captured in the comment attributed to the late Ethel Waters: "I'm comfortable with being a Negro, and I'm tired of changing my racial identification every few years." Like Ethel Waters, I was born during the era when "Colored" was the prevalent usage, along with the ignominious lowercase "negro," which I passionately hated because the absence of capitalization conveyed the status of a *thing* and not a person. During my college days in the early 1930s I routinely went through my textbooks, using a fountain pen to change the small *n* to capital *N* wherever I encountered the term "negro." My generation of activists was part of a long struggle to elevate the designation to its capitalized form, so that "Negro" became a mark of dignity and respect. That struggle was finally won when textbook writers and newspapers adopted uppercase "Negro" in the late 1930s, and official government publications followed suit in the middle and late 1940s.

The transition among many white Southerners from use of the contemptuous "niggers" to a grudging "nigras" and finally to "Knee-grows" had occurred in my lifetime. I felt that the reversion to lowercase "black" was a self-defeating step and the surrender of a term of dignity that previous generations had fought so hard to achieve. Nothing could dramatize more the symbolic demotion to second-class status, I thought, than the appearance in print of the new designation in a sequence of classifications, as in *Puerto Ricans, Hispanics, Native Americans, blacks, Jews, Chicanos, Orientals,* etc. It seemed to me that the black militants had put themselves in the place where their white detractors wanted them. As time has passed, some black writers, recognizing their predicament, have tried to promote the usage of "Black," with not too much success outside of racial publications. More recently, the nineteenth-century term "people of color" has been creeping back into usage, partly as a reaction against "black" and partly as an identification with third world peoples. For all these reasons, I continued to use the term "Negro" or "person of color" interchangeably with "black."

Determined not to let the matter rest, the student continued his harangue, growing more aggressive. Tension electrified the classroom; it was an awkward moment. My credibility as an instructor was being challenged at the threshold of my performance, and I was unnerved by the quizzical stares of the other students. In a humorless encounter, I was allowing a mere stripling to choose the weapons in a duel that probed my most vulnerable emotions and cast doubt upon my intellectual authority.

Finally, I exploded. "Sir," I said sharply—I did not then even know the student's name—"we live in a nation of democratic institutions, where freedom of expression is a constitutionally guaranteed right. This course is all about the enforcement of the constitutional rights of all people. Your rights end where the other fellow's rights begin, and if you cannot accept this principle you do not belong in this class. Now, you have every right to define yourself as 'black' if you choose, and in deference to your choice I shall try to remember to use that term at least half of the time. But since I have an equal right to define myself as a Negro, I shall expect you to respect my choice when I use that designation the other half of the time." My unorthodox concession broke the tension, and the class tittered in relief. The young man, taken aback, subsided into disgruntled silence, allowing the discussion to resume, but his face told me I had not heard the last of this explosive issue. He had found my forthrightness a challenge. Several weeks later, after a lecture on a court decision involving civil rights, he came up to my desk at the end of the class period, opened his notebook, and announced pointedly, "Dr. Murray, I've been keeping score on you, and I want you to know that today in class you used 'Negro' *twenty-five times* and you used 'black' only *seven times!*" I was compelled to laugh at his enterprising way of continuing the argument and promised to do better, but wondered ruefully how much of the substance of my lecture he had absorbed that day.

Meanwhile I faced another academic crisis when, after a few class meetings, several of the white women—all seniors and obviously super-achievers—came to me privately. They were polite and deferential, but they did not mince words. I was pitching the course to meet the experience level of the pre-freshmen, they said, and my lectures were "too simplistic." They considered the hours spent in the course an investment which they expected to yield profits, and they made it clear that all the seniors might withdraw if I continued in this vein. They also told me they would be willing to act as tutors, partly because they liked me as a teacher and did not want to see me rated unfavorably as a "poor instructor." (During my years at Brandeis, students published a course evaluation based on questions answered by students who had taken the various courses. The responses described the course content and evaluated the instructor. I took those evaluations very seriously and revised and improved my course outlines accordingly.)

The candor of the women left me shaken. I was in an untenable position. Clearly, since the TYP students could fail the course without prejudice, my main responsibility was to the regularly matriculated students, who needed course credit for graduation. Yet it was equally clear that although the work was too advanced for the four young black men, the escalating racial tensions on campus were such that a request to have them withdrawn would certainly provoke heated charges of racial discrimination despite the sound academic basis for the request. My own academic reputation as a new professor was on the line, and I wanted very much to excel. The very presence of these young men was a challenge to one shaped by a family tradition of teaching dedicated to "the advancement of the race." Their needs and concerns not only demanded my best efforts but also sharpened the legal and moral issues of human rights I was dissecting for the class in illuminating the process of law and social change.

Somehow I would have to find a way to give the pre-freshmen extra help in classroom assignments and in their term papers without either lowering class standards or threatening their fragile self-esteem.

It was a tall order. Had I been in British-oriented Africa, my students would have understood the system of tutorials as part of their cultural exposure. I dared not risk the embarrassment American black males would feel if I spoke openly of "tutors." It would only underscore their unequal performance and reinforce their feelings of inferiority, all the more vulnerable because *women* students had volunteered to perform this service to resolve the classroom dilemma. In desperation, I reached back to my own somewhat comparable experience as a new associate lawyer in Paul, Weiss, Rifkind, Wharton & Garrison, unaccustomed to the methods of a highly prestigious law firm. I would introduce the concept of "preceptors," as if it were a normal and expected part of the course. In an elaborate presentation, I told the class we had now reached the point in our work where we could benefit by the "preceptor system," a method used in huge law offices to make the volume of work flow more smoothly. More experienced associates were assigned to guide newcomers on a one-to-one basis, to help them "learn the ropes" more quickly—a kind of coaching process also used in major league sports. I added that preceptorship applied a principle developed in cooperative study in law schools and in preparing for bar exams. (I refrained from disclosing that in the more elementary levels of education, it is known as the "each one teach one" principle.) I then announced that in sharing the work of the classroom assignments, several seniors had volunteered to become preceptors to "lowerclassmen," and invited the pre-freshmen, especially, to take advantage of this resource.

For two weeks nothing happened. The four young men in the rear sat in almost bewildered silence as the juniors and seniors became more excited about the course and reasserted themselves. The transitional-year students were not being ignored, but without a single pointed remark having been made, they realized they were losing face. Then, just as I began to feel an inner despair (because I so much wanted them to succeed), Carson and Myers, whom I had spotted as the most promising of the four, approached me after class and wanted to know more about those "what did you call them—pre—pre-something?" I could have wept with relief. Evidently, they had chewed over the idea among themselves and were intrigued by the novelty of the term and its association with the prestigious legal profession, which was precisely what I had hoped would happen. As if it were merely routine, I put the two young men in touch with two of the senior volunteers and waited for the next move.

It began to work! Not long after that, the seniors reported that the two groups had gotten together and the experiment was developing successfully. For the first time, I learned, a genuine dialogue was developing between black and white students outside class, and they were beginning to talk more freely to one another about some of the sensitive racial issues. In time, such encounters would come to be known as "consciousness raising." For my part, I noticed a more relaxed atmosphere in class and a more comradely spirit in the sharing of notes and cigarettes.

The course allowed me to integrate materials on the life and culture of Negroes in the United States into the framework of law and social change. I often selected cases from the long and bitter struggle of Negro Americans for racial justice to illustrate the legal process and changing concepts in law. Making the past come alive for the whole class, I could see the black students gaining new respect for themselves and their history as I went back to Colonial times and told of the continuous resistance to enslavement through use of the courts during the entire antebellum period. Most of the students were aware of violent slave revolts and of the Underground Railroad for runaway slaves, but they were amazed to learn that the *Dred Scott* case was merely the most famous of hundreds of such legal challenges to slavery, usually made through petitions for freedom brought in the state courts on various grounds, and that black people persisted against numerous hardships in pressing litigation, which sometimes dragged on for ten or twenty years before final disposition.

The wide-eyed excitement I could see on the faces of the entire group as the racial drama in the courts unfolded confirmed my belief that white students needed Afro-American studies as part of our common American heritage every bit as much as black students needed it to build an "acceptable past." And since both races faced the common burden of wiping out the vestiges of racism, I believed it might be more profitable to come together to analyze contemporary issues of race rather than struggle with them separately.

By midterm I was beginning to feel more confident about the seminar as well as my relationship with the TYP students. Larry Fuchs, who guided the American Civilization program, was as proud as a mother hen with a single chick. He told me he had not had so much fun since the days he sponsored a course in international relations taught by Eleanor Roosevelt, and he fancied that he had discovered another outstanding teacher in me. (In fact, two years later he successfully recommended my inclusion in the 1971 edition of *Outstanding Educators of America*.) I began to blossom under his encouraging report that he was "hearing wonderful things" about my course; that one of his bright concentrators (majors) had come to thank him for steering her toward the seminar, that it was the best course she had taken at Brandeis and that it was "pulling together many things" for her.

Most important to my sense of adequacy was a marked change of attitude on the part of the TYP students. They were less defensive in class, seemed to feel more accepted, and were obviously getting a great deal out of the course even though they lacked the formal skills to articulate their accretions of knowledge in writing. When they began following me back to my office after class sessions, to hang about asking endless questions and fingering my books, I knew that I had broken the barrier and was making some progress.

I would never really know whether my experiment had any lasting impact upon those four young men. The delicate learning process nurtured so carefully during that fall was abruptly shattered by powerful events which overtook the school less than two weeks before final examinations were scheduled to begin. Like every other member of the faculty and administration, I was caught by complete surprise in a crisis that exploded without warning.

On Wednesday afternoon, January 8, 1969, my seminar class met as usual in Ford Hall, an old building which housed the university's central switchboard and a $200,000 computer on the first floor, a science lab, one or two classrooms, and several offices, including my own, on the second floor. When the seminar assembled I noticed that all four TYP students were absent. Shortly after two o'clock we heard a commotion in the hallway, then the door opened and someone shouted, "Everybody out! This building is being taken over by black students!" A few minutes earlier, fifteen black students had entered the building, ejected the two telephone operators on duty, commandeered the switchboard, and then sent several of their number upstairs to clear out the rest of the building.

I was one of the few faculty members immediately affected by the takeover, because, as I recall, no other class was being held in the building at the time. All my students except one were in a quandary. Patricia Hill, the only black senior in the class and an honor student, got up immediately and left the room, saying something about "black solidarity." At this point I asked the remainder of the class to decide what they wished to do. Stephen Deitsch, who was vice-president of the Student Council, suggested that we vacate the building, and since the period would normally end in about fifteen minutes, the group voted to follow his advice. I went down the hall to my office, gathered up a few books and papers, locked the door, and made my way downstairs. As I left Ford Hall, I encountered two of my TYP class members standing guard at the entrance. They were obviously embarrassed to see me and one of them said apologetically, "Dr. Murray, I'm sorry I couldn't make it to class today."

By evening, sixty-five Negro students, many of whom were TYP enrollees, had occupied Ford Hall, barricading themselves inside with heavy chains across the outer doors and barring all faculty and administrators from access to the building. The prominence of TYP students in the leadership of the revolt led faculty members who had worked with them to speculate that these young men, filled with anxiety over approaching exams and fearful of making a poor showing, needed to demonstrate their adequacy through exhibiting political clout. They had not presented any list of grievances before the takeover, and their drastic action was explainable only as the contagious influence of black student actions on other campuses.

The previous evening, two faculty members from embattled San Francisco State College had spoken at Brandeis on the controversy over Black Studies at their institution, which resulted in its being closed down in November. One of the speakers reportedly goaded the black students of Brandeis during the discussion period, telling them that if they had any "manhood" they "would shut down the damn campus" to show their solidarity with the black students at San Francisco State and their support of the Black Revolution in the United States. Unable to resist his challenge, the formerly peaceful Brandeis students were precipitated into a spontaneous uprising, so unplanned that they had been in Ford Hall for several hours before they hastily put together a list of ten "non-negotiable" demands, which President Abram later characterized as "startling because so many were existing policy or being implemented." The principal demand was the establishment of an Afro-American Studies Department as a separate discipline, with power to hire and dismiss. Others included year-round recruitment of Negro students under the leadership of a Negro director, immediate action to hire more Negro professors in the various departments, the establishment of an Afro-American center designed by black students, and the establishment of ten Martin Luther King or Malcolm X full scholarships for black students.

The campus was in a state of shock because of the unexpectedness of the takeover. The next few days were harrowing. Communications were almost totally disrupted, since few telephones on campus were independent of the central switchboard the black students controlled in Ford Hall. The faculty had met in emergency session on the first evening of the takeover and voted overwhelmingly to condemn the occupation of the building and to demand that the insurgents vacate Ford Hall. President Abram announced that he would not act under coercion. That same evening, however, five hundred Brandeis students held a mass meeting on campus and voted to demonstrate next morning in support of amnesty for the Ford Hall rebels. Next day, two hundred white students staged a peaceful sit-in to express solidarity with the black students.

Negotiations between the school administration and the Ford Hall group kept breaking down because the members of the black student negotiating committee kept changing and no one seemed to have the authority to speak for the occupying group. By Friday, January 10, President Abram had obtained a temporary restraining order against the defiant students, issued by the Middlesex Superior Court, but he held it in reserve without serving it. Rumors circulated that the state police were poised to invade the campus. Counterrumors spread that extremists inside Ford Hall were threatening to blow up the computer equipment and themselves with it if any attempt was made to eject them by force. Since the building also contained a chemistry lab, this rumor was one to be taken seriously. Some 890 Brandeis students reportedly signed a resolution opposing the use of police force to break up the siege, and President Abram told the press he saw "no need for forcible removal of the black students."

As the crisis continued I felt a deepening sense of isolation. That fall I had been assigned the only office space available, which happened to be in Ford Hall, not regularly used by other faculty members. This meant that I was cut off from the normal give-and-take of my departmental colleagues. My isolation was now intensified because I had no access to my office to prepare for classes or hold conferences with students. In some ways I felt like a hostage, because my office, containing my entire library, electric typewriter, and file cabinets crammed with manuscripts, research notes, correspondence, and other irreplaceable records, was located directly above the computer system and directly beneath the chemistry laboratory that presented the means of destroying the building. One student had told me half-jokingly that in a confrontation they just might burn down my office. I feared that if the rumored threats were carried out, my most cherished possessions would go up in flames. As it was, during the siege the occupying students gained access to my office through an interconnecting door, used it as their headquarters, appropriated personal items, helped themselves to my books and supplies, and left behind notes of their strategy sessions. When I returned to my office after the takeover ended, I could barely suppress my rage over the violation of my privacy, which I considered just short of a physical violation of my person.

I was one of two Negro faculty members then at Brandeis, both of us women, and both of us virtually invisible throughout the crisis, which was a struggle for power between white male institutional heads and black male challengers supported by black women students playing a secondary role. The other Negro faculty member, Frances J. Perkins, an instructor in psychology who directed the nursery school, shared my loneliness and sense of inadequacy. Mrs. Perkins managed to gain admittance to Ford Hall and tried to talk to the rebelling students, who treated her with deference but ignored her advice. We had no real standing with either of the contending parties to the dispute, since no one considered that we might have something to contribute.

For several days after the initial takeover the Brandeis campus was in an uproar. Only about fifty yards separated Ford Hall from the L-shaped complex of administration buildings, and picketers, reporters, small groups of students, and curious onlookers milled about in the space between the two "headquarters" as negotiating teams moved back and forth. The student fracas attracted the attention of the Boston branch of the NAACP, which issued a statement that its representatives had met with the black students on Friday morning, found their demands "just," and "unequivocally" supported their objectives. Bags of food, donated by the Freedom Food Market in Boston's predominantly Negro Roxbury section, were sent in to the demonstrators, and sixty persons from the Boston area joined the occupiers over the weekend. From a second-story window the rebelling students hung a large sheetlike banner which bore a photograph of the slain civil rights leader Malcolm X, with the caption MALCOLM X UNIVERSITY. A four-page "Brandeis Black Bulletin from Ford Hall" was issued, containing a clarification of the list of black student demands and declaring that while "our interest is NOT in occupying a building, destroying property, or getting our pictures in the papers . . . we will use whatever tactics we feel necessary and strategically valid to achieve our ends: the implementation of our ten demands."

By the weekend, the Brandeis community had virtually closed ranks. The Student Council and the Graduate Student Council had voted to oppose the seizure, called upon the black students to leave Ford Hall, urged continued negotiations, and requested President Abram not to use force. Abram had suspended and threatened to expel the sixty-five students inside the building, and the faculty, by a vote of 207 to 12, with 17 abstentions, expressed "complete confidence in and support" of Abram's action and called for a resolution of the controversy consistent with "academic integrity and academic standards at Brandeis." An in-depth report on the crisis appeared on the front page of the Sunday *New York Times,* and similar protest demonstrations by black students were reported at Swarthmore College, the University of Minnesota, and Wittenberg University in Springfield, Ohio.

The Brandeis administration then moved to isolate the students in the communications center by setting up a temporary alternative telephone system, by ostensibly ignoring the occupation, and by carrying on normal school activities while continuing to refuse police intervention and keeping the door open for negotiations. On Monday, the thirteenth, the faculty approved a "legitimate" Afro-American Studies Department on condition that Ford Hall be evacuated. The word "legitimate" reflected the Brandeis faculty's determination not to surrender control of its jealously guarded prerogatives in matters of academic standards. By this time the militance inside Ford Hall had begun to peter out. On Tuesday, in a show of bravado, five black women students invaded the reserve section of the library and pushed some 2,500 periodicals off the shelves. There was a poignant moment later that day when an angry mother appeared outside Ford Hall, pounded on the barricaded doors, calling her son by name, and shouted, "Come out! I've sweated to get you to college, and I don't believe in this black power business!" Morale began to disintegrate among the occupiers. Several of the regularly matriculated students, anxious about final exams, left the building. Finally, on Saturday afternoon, January 18, about four-thirty, following a demonstration of support by some 150 black students from other Boston-area campuses, the last of the sixty-five students who had occupied Ford Hall filed out of the building, many hiding their faces with their hands or with books to avoid being photographed. Complete amnesty had been granted and a committee of black students had examined the building thoroughly to determine what physical damage, if any, had been done during their ten-day stay. Ford Hall was closed and locked, and the Brandeis campus returned to normal.

The students had not won their principal demand, for an autonomous Black Studies department controlled by black students and black faculty. Eighty-five members of the faculty signed a letter, which appeared in the *New York Times*, declaring:

The act of seizing and holding a university building in order to secure "nonnegotiable" demands violates the very character of any university worthy of the name. Force and threat, blackmail and extortion are the death of dialogue, of reason, of the university. . . . Let the university community offer to its black students, and to black Americans generally, its friendship and commitment, its talents and resources. But let it not dare to think that it can help others by destroying its own character. Let us rather offer black students a full share in our common pride as scholars, teachers, students.

Like many Negro educators at the time, I agonized over the movement for Afro-American/Black Studies departments, suffused as it was with militant racial politics. I feared that the insistent demand for an immediate Afro-American Studies Department as a separate discipline without careful advance planning or sufficient faculty risked setting up an isolated, second-rate enclave on the Brandeis campus that would be unable to compete academically with other departments. I had sat on the faculty-student committee appointed to develop the Afro-American Studies program that had met and functioned until its work was disrupted by the Ford Hall incident. Our major difficulty was luring available Negro scholars to teach the recommended courses at Brandeis, since we were competing with other major colleges and universities seeking the same scholars. There were simply not enough Negro scholars at the time to meet the suddenly burgeoning demand for "black studies taught by black faculty" at the undergraduate level. Our committee suffered a bitter disappointment when we thought we had an acceptance from the distinguished poet and author Arna Bontemps to teach Black Literature at Brandeis, only to have him turn us down at the last minute in favor of an offer from Yale that he found more congenial to his own literary research.

Campus politics could be brutal, and in the academic pecking order a discipline whose faculty could not present credentials comparable to those of the faculty members in more traditional departments was treated with derision and contempt. To insist that only black professors could interpret the black experience in the United States and to ignore the interdisciplinary nature of Afro-American studies would foster a spirit of separatism within the university and would relieve white faculty members of responsibility to include materials on Negro life and history in the regular curriculum. During the faculty debate on the issue at the height of the Ford Hall crisis, I had observed the cynicism among some of my colleagues, who voted to approve an Afro-American Studies Department as a matter of expediency, calculating that within a few years such a program would disintegrate from its own inherent weaknesses and the issue would be forgotten.

At any rate, with the new policy to set up a department inaugurated, the committee on which I had served was disbanded and I had very little further connection with the Afro-American Studies program. A black director, Ronald Waters, who was completing requirements for his Ph.D., was appointed in the late spring to head the new venture, and I remained in the American Studies program, which by 1970 had become a separate discipline and achieved departmental status. Retaining my·courses in legal studies, which became highly popular and were responsible for motivating a number of young women as well as young men to enter law school during the next few years (two of my former students became law clerks of a justice of the United States Supreme Court), I also taught a course on the Constitution and civil rights and pioneered a course on Women in American Society.

The supreme irony of my tenure at Brandeis was that while my courses were very popular with white students and attracted some of the brightest minds in the school, only a handful of black students ventured into my classes. The militants who had been most vociferous in their demand for "black faculty" shunned them. At first I thought I was the target of a political boycott, but after being at Brandeis for a while I learned that some black students avoided my classes because I had developed a reputation for rigorous standards of performance. The word was passed around, as expressed in one comment that reached me, "Man, are *you* gonna take her course? They tell me she'll work you to death!"

It was not the radical politics of the militant black students that bothered me most but the intellectual laziness I sometimes encountered in them, for I knew that while massive physical protest might blast open the doors of opportunity, only those willing to engage in the prodigious exertion of the mind that leads to competence would be able to walk through. In time, more black students enrolled in my courses, with mutually rewarding results, but never in large numbers.

In the face of the increasing racial polarization that persisted into the 1970s, I made the lonely choice of remaining part of the academic mainstream while insisting that my unique racial experience be recognized as part of the cultural whole. During that period I found great solace in the companionship of Harold and Viola Isaacs, whom I had come to know in 1960 when they were in Ghana, monitoring the interracial Crossroads Africa project, in which American students spent a summer working and living in African villages. It was a kind of volunteer forerunner of the Peace Corps. Harold, who taught political science at M.I.T., Viola, who was a social worker, and I all shared the same year of birth—1910—and had lived through the same history. We huddled together for psychological warmth at a time when close friendships across racial lines were difficult to sustain. It was a period that Harold Isaacs described, in his *Idols of the Tribe*, as "a convulsive ingathering of people in their numberless grouping of kinds—tribal, racial, linguistic, religious, national." But we were among the "rootless" ones, "the products of social and economic and technological change, of migrations, of cross-cultural mingling," who quested for something "beyond parochial ties" that would connect us more broadly to others: I was soon to find such a connection in the crisis of death. It was a bond that defied all social barriers, dwarfing my other problems as I came to confront the ultimate mystery of human existence.

CHAPTER 34

The Death of a Friend

WHILE the upheavals at Brandeis University alienated me from the coercive feature of the Black Power movement, in time I came to realize that beneath the superficialities and the strident revolutionary rhetoric of many black students of that period, something more profound was taking place. Notwithstanding excesses that were destined to fail, the more enduring result of the black consciousness movement was the transformation of a people robbed of a prideful past, the retrieval of a communal history that had long been ignored, the affirmation of a positive identity after centuries of denigration, and the flowering of racially inspired art, music, literature, and scientific achievement once barriers began to fall.

In later years, trying to put my relation to this development in perspective, I realized that my own resolution of the question of identity had been in seeing myself as the product of a slowly evolving process of biological and cultural integration, a blending of widely diverse strains into a new, whole being. The integration I envisioned promised a stronger and freer America, no longer stunted in its growth by an insidious ethnocentrism. During the black student rebellion at Brandeis, I was too threatened to appreciate the necessary intervening stage of a newly raised ethnic consciousness.

Ironically, my adamant views were effectively challenged not by the black students but by my discerning young friend Mary Norris, who was a keen observer of social currents. Attuned to the student generation of the 1960s, she had gained insights from her contacts with black women schoolmates at Radcliffe, contacts that were less accessible to me, removed as I was by age and faculty position. Mary helped to soften my harsh estimate of what was happening at Brandeis by suggesting that I substitute the words "women," "women's consciousness," and "women's liberation" for "black" and note the parallel stridency and even the calls for separation among some radical, angry feminists within the women's movement. Since I recognized that shrillness of protest in no way lessened the authentic claims of women for equal status, I began to see that much of my barely disguised hostility toward the Black Revolution was in reality my feminist resentment of the crude sexism I perceived in many of the male leaders of that movement.

The early 1970s found me responding alternately to the competing demands of the black movement and the women's movement, often taking the lonely (and unpopular) position of calling for a broad, inclusive expression of feminism at a time when many prominent Negro women felt impelled to subordinate their claims as women to what they believed to be the overriding factor of "restoration of the black male to his lost manhood." As a self-supporting woman, I saw this as a shortsighted view and said, in an article I wrote for Mary Lou Thompson's book, *Voices of the New Feminism,* published by Beacon Press in 1970:

> Reading through much of the current literature on the Black Revolution, one is left with the impression that for all the rhetoric about self-determination, the main thrust of black militancy is a bid of black males to share power with white males in a continuing patriarchal society in which both black and white females are relegated to a secondary status.

Pointing to the triple handicap under which black women labored— race, sex, and economic exploitation—I argued: "black women can neither postpone nor subordinate the fight against discrimination to the Black Revolution. . . . As a matter of sheer survival black women have no alternative but to insist upon equal opportunities without regard to sex in training, education and employment. Given their heavy family responsibilities, the outlook for their children will be bleak indeed unless they are encouraged in every way to develop their potential skills and earning power." I saw the liberation of black women in terms of feminist solidarity across racial lines:

> Because black women have an equal stake in women's liberation and black liberation, they are key figures at the juncture of these two movements. . . . By asserting a leadership role in the growing feminist movement, the black woman can help to keep it allied to the objectives of black liberation while simultaneously advancing the interests of all women.

I also envisioned feminist solidarity achieving a broader objective than would be possible if black women confined themselves solely to the demands of black militancy:

Beyond all the present conflict lies the important task of reconciliation of the races in America on the basis of genuine equality and human dignity. A powerful force in bringing about this result can be generated through the process of black and white women working together to achieve their common humanity.

As I struggled with the racial and sexual conflicts of that period, I clung to the twofold legacy left to the world in the 1960s—the life and work, respectively, of Eleanor Roosevelt and Martin Luther King, Jr. Each in different ways had emphasized the moral and spiritual imperatives of the ongoing struggle for human dignity and had demonstrated the power of love to transcend divisions of race, sex, or class. Pondering the source of their great influence on their times led me to reflect more deeply upon the meaning of the Christian faith.

Yet had anyone suggested in 1972 that within less than a year I would resign my by-now tenured faculty position to enter seminary as a candidate for holy orders in the Episcopal Church, I would have questioned that person's sanity. I had been named Louis Stulberg Professor of Law and Politics in the American Studies Department at Brandeis, and that spring was also a lecturer at the Boston University School of Law, teaching my favorite subject, the enforcement of constitutional rights and liberties. My articles were being published in law reviews and journals of opinion, and I had even found time to begin my memoirs, work postponed since 1968. The burgeoning women's movement absorbed much of my energies, for I was serving on a faculty committee to improve the status of women at Brandeis, on the national board of the ACLU to win support for the ERA, and on the Commission on Women organized by Church Women United and chaired by my good friend Thelma Stevens.

Although I was active in ad hoc groups seeking wider recognition of women's ministries in the Episcopal Church, and strongly supported women's ordination to the priesthood, I had no conscious desire to enter the ordained ministry myself. At the same time I was being drawn into the ferment growing among women I met at what was then the Episcopal Theological Seminary and is now the Episcopal Divinity School in Cambridge. Their passionate commitment to their calling left a deep impression.

The church's slow response to women's appeals spurred me to greater activism. In the summer of 1969, a special convention of the Episcopal Church meeting at South Bend, Indiana, refused to seat a woman as a delegate to the House of Deputies, although she had been duly elected from her diocese in California. The fact that the church excluded women from its national deliberative body while it accepted millions of dollars collected by women through the United Thank Offering so incensed me

that I joined in a telegram of protest signed by six active Episcopal lay-
women and addressed to the presiding bishop, John E. Hines, and the
president of the House of Deputies, Dr. John B. Coburn. In a follow-up
memorandum sent to these officials, I analyzed the system of discrimination against women within the Episcopal Church and pointed to the dire
consequences if women became so alienated that they withdrew their
support from the church. The memorandum created a little flurry in
church circles when Church Women United got permission to reproduce
it and distributed it to five hundred key women in other denominations.

Several months later, in early 1970, I was surprised to receive notice
that I had been appointed to a special Commission on Ordained and
Licensed Ministries to study the issue of women's ministries and make a
report. Along with the letter of appointment, however, the secretary of
the convention sent a communication advising commission members that
since no money had been allocated to finance the commission's work, we
should file a report of "No Progress" and request the 1970 General Convention to provide the necessary funds.

By this time the movement for women's ordination was beginning to
escalate. That spring I attended a weekend conference of forty-five Episcopal women at Graymoor Monastery in New York State, at which we
attempted to formulate a position on the aspirations of women in our
denomination. At least eight or ten of the women were seminary graduates or were attending seminary and actively seeking ordination, among
them the redoubtable Jeannette Piccard, a former balloonist who had
ascended higher in space than any other woman at the time, had earned
a doctorate, and was a consultant to NASA. Then in her seventies, Jeannette told me she had been waiting almost fifty years to fulfill her call to
the ordained ministry. The body adopted a strong resolution calling for
equality of women in every aspect of the life of the church, including
admission to all levels of the clergy. The Graymoor Conference was a
precursor of the Episcopal Women's Caucus, which would later mobilize
wide support for women's ordination.

My involvement with the issue deepened later that spring when I met
the Reverend Henry H. Rightor, a lawyer-priest, then professor of pastoral
theology at Virginia Theological Seminary and an ardent supporter of
women's ordination. The Reverend Rightor, who had also been appointed
to the Commission on Ordained and Licensed Ministries, was a veteran
of general convention politics and knew that such an issue could drag on
for years unless the convention was forced to deal with it promptly. He
proposed that our commission not postpone deliberations but that we
meet at our own expense and produce a report in time for the General
Convention meeting in Houston in October.

We held a one-day meeting on September 19 in Baltimore, during which Henry Rightor and I examined the Constitution and Canons of the Episcopal Church and reported that there was no language in that official document which specifically prohibited the ordination of women as priests. (Obviously, the drafters of the original Constitution had taken for granted that women would never be considered for ordination and so had felt no need to make explicit their exclusion.) This finding led us to assert that there would be no need to invoke the cumbersome procedure of amending the Constitution, a process that would require approval by two consecutive conventions and usually took at least six years to become effective. We argued that a simple resolution concurred in by the House of Bishops and the House of Deputies at a single convention was all that was necessary to remove any doubt about the eligibility of women for ordination. Moreover, the Commission concluded, there was no need to undertake still another review of the issue. The time had come for decision. Our report was brief and to the point; it recommended immediate approval of the admission of women to all levels of the ordained clergy. Henry Rightor volunteered to have copies of the Commission's report reproduced and to attend the Houston convention in the hope of having our recommendations accepted.

It was naive to hope that any effort to overturn a deeply entrenched tradition would be that simple. The General Convention of 1970 bypassed our report, but it did move one step forward by removing language that limited the lowest level of the ordained ministry, the diaconate, to males, thereby opening the way for women to enter the ordained clergy. I was so disappointed over a half-measure intended to keep women in a subordinate category that I stopped going to church. Like many other women on the periphery of organized religion, I began to question the authority of a traditional faith which continued to treat half of its membership as less than fully human. My rejection of the church left me floundering in a wilderness of doubt. At the time, I was living in Boston, next to the Massachusetts Avenue bridge to Cambridge, in an apartment on Beacon Street, and on Sundays especially I used to walk my black Labrador Roy, who had replaced Doc, along the banks of the Charles River, at war with myself because I was not in my accustomed place singing in the choir at Saint James Church over in Cambridge.

I was still in a morass of indecision about the church when calamity struck one of my dearest friends, Irene Barlow, and I was put to a stern test of faith. Over the years, Renee and her mother, Mary Jane Barlow, had remained part of my extended family. Mrs. Barlow was now ninety-three, housebound and very frail, and Renee herself was showing increasing signs of illness.

Because of my experience with my own aging aunts, I felt great sympathy for mother and daughter in their struggle against the encroaching debilities of age. As the years passed I had watched Renee juggle the demands of her busy life to meet her mother's growing infirmity with countermoves designed to make her comfortable: relocation from their walk-up apartment on Second Avenue to a sunny, spacious apartment in Peter Cooper Village overlooking the East River; the employment of a series of paid companions so that Jenny Wren, as we called Mrs. Barlow, would not be alone when Renee was away from home; and numerous projects to keep her busy with useful tasks—mending friends' clothing, shortening skirts, knitting caps, and making dolls and toys for children in the church who had little for Christmas.

During the summer of 1972 Renee celebrated the fifth anniversary of her surgery for cancer. It was an important milestone, and she thought hopefully that she might be out of the woods, but I noticed that whenever she visited me in Boston on a weekend she spent most of her time sleeping. She called my apartment the Murray Rest Home and thought of it as a place where she could get away from constant pressures and be quiet for a few hours. That fall we kept in close touch by telephone, Renee explaining she was calling because there was something wrong with her hand. "I can't type," she said once, and on several occasions she reported she had been trying to reach me, "But I keep getting wrong numbers."

I knew something was terribly amiss, but Renee's casual references gave me no clues. When I stopped over in New York during the Thanksgiving weekend, I was shocked at the way she looked. She told me she had to get away for a little rest and was planning a two-week trip to Montego Bay, Jamaica, where we had spent several winter vacations. Renee had always come back from those trips refreshed and renewed to face the remaining weeks of harsh New York winters. I was relieved to know she would not be traveling alone. Elizabeth Lehmann, a mutual friend, had agreed to go with her. They were to meet in Miami and fly on from there together.

The trip was disastrous. On the plane to Florida, Renee became ill with severe vertigo and was unable to go on. She and Libby had to cancel their plans and return by train. Renee tried to go back to work, but within a few days one leg was dragging and she could hardly walk. Libby, who lived in Philadelphia, came over to give her a hand and called me in desperation. Renee, normally practical in emergencies, was suddenly refusing to call her physician. I had one more week of classes at Brandeis before the semester ended and I would be free to come to New York. Meanwhile Libby and I consulted daily by telephone. Despite our reluctance to assume the prerogatives of Renee's next of kin, we knew someone had to take charge, given Mrs. Barlow's eggshell frailty.

Finally Renee gave in, and on January 10, 1973, she was admitted to Harkness Pavilion at Columbia-Presbyterian Medical Center for observation and tests. I was aghast when I arrived and saw her condition. Her right side was partially paralyzed and her right arm and hand were useless. She could not focus her vision, her speech was slurred, and she could not complete her sentences.

Renee was suffering from a brain tumor, and her physician explained to me that it was so close to vital centers of speech and sight that brain surgery was out of the question. The alternative was to administer heavy doses of steroids to reduce the swelling in the brain, followed by a series of cobalt treatments. Renee had not been informed of the diagnosis, and as her legal representative holding her power of attorney, I was expected to be available to the hospital authorities at all times to give the necessary consents for radical procedures.

This fateful knowledge was a staggering blow. I was stunned not only by the magnitude of Renee's illness but by the awesome responsibility of having to make life-and-death decisions on her behalf. I had no experience in dealing with an extremely ill patient, but over the sixteen years of our friendship, Renee and I had been honest with one another and each respected the other's integrity. Now, in the worst possible crisis, and painful as it might be, I knew I would have to insist that Renee's physicians be candid about her situation, respecting her right to make her own decisions about her future as long as she was able to communicate her wishes.

Renee was probably more aware of the true nature of her illness than any of us close to her realized at the time. Before she went into the hospital she talked with Libby about her youth and spoke of her fiancé, a young medical student, who had died of a brain tumor. Renee had chosen to go on alone, picking up the fragments of her life shattered by an inconsolable loss. Unable to marry the man she loved and have children of her own, she had gone about mothering everyone else. Now, when faced with the same catastrophic illness, she accepted the medical diagnosis with characteristic calm, and her quiet courage throughout her ordeal enabled me to carry on with some semblance of strength.

Over the next ten days Renee made what seemed to be a miraculous comeback, thanks to the steroids. Her speech and vision improved, she was able to sign her own checks and insurance forms and walk with the aid of a metal walker and a nurse's assistance. Her inimitable humor returned and she laughingly referred to the hospital staff and the many friends telephoning from places around the country as her "cast of thousands."

My most immediate problem was trying to persuade Renee's mother to go to Connecticut to stay with her other daughter, Doris Maycock, while Renee was in the hospital. Mrs. Barlow could not be left without constant care, but she had a will of iron. Her fierce determination to stay in their New York apartment, where she was able to do as she pleased, defeated every effort I could make short of risking the shock of telling her the truth about Renee's illness. She clung tenaciously to life, once telling her nurse-companion, "I'm not afraid to die; I just don't want to leave Irene." She yielded only when Renee made the effort to telephone her from her hospital bed and, putting the problem as gently as she could, told her mother there was "pressure on the brain" and she would have to be in the hospital a long time.

Before signing her consent for cobalt treatments, Renee discussed her situation with her physicians and was fully aware of the risks she was taking. As she weighed the matter, she told me, "I've had a good life, and I don't know whether I've got what it takes to fight this thing." It was as close as we came to speaking of death, but I could no more accept the thought of Renee dying than, at the time, I could accept the thought of my own death. I replied, "If we have to go down, we'll go down fighting." I told her I didn't think God intended human beings to be resigned to their fate until they had made every effort, but that when they had done their best, they could leave the outcome to God.

Renee did not tell me she might be paralyzed and lose her sight, although she knew of those risks. I think she wanted to spare me the terrible anxiety of anticipation. In any case, I do not believe I could have accepted the risk for her if it had fallen to me as her legal representative to decide upon cobalt. The treatments began on January 22, her fifty-ninth birthday, a day memorable because it was the day President Richard Nixon announced a cease-fire in the Vietnam War, and later the news was flashed that former President Lyndon B. Johnson had died of a heart attack. That night a blizzard hit New York, and in the midst of the heavy snowfall an electrical storm lighted up the skies like a spectacular display of northern lights.

I rode home from the hospital with one of Renee's medical team, who said it was hoped the treatments would give her a little time—six months, a year, perhaps two years—and that it was also hoped she would "be herself" during whatever time she had left. I clung to this shred of hope, pushing back the reality of a death sentence and helping Renee to plan her convalescence. Anticipating the loss of her hair, she ordered a wig from Lord and Taylor and amused friends who visited her with styling her "new look." She also talked of how she would spend the next few months, when she left the hospital. The treatments had gone so well that her physicians planned to discharge her after the first series, having her return for outpatient treatment. I was sufficiently encouraged by this information to go back to Boston for a few days to take care of my personal affairs, so I could be with her when she left the hospital.

While I was gone Renee had a sudden setback. I rushed to New York on February 5 and found that the tumor had spread to the right side of the brain, partially disabling the left side of her body. Tests also showed a shadow on her lung. Her eyes remained tightly closed and her nurse believed she had lost all sight. She was conscious when awake, was able to call my name and answer "yes" or "no" to questions, and even smiled when I said something humorous, but she kept slipping into a deep sleep. Her doctors had done all medical science could do and she seemed to be resting comfortably without noticeable pain.

The situation was so critical that I telephoned her sister immediately and Doris came down to New York. We stayed in an apartment across the street from Harkness Pavilion, rented to relatives of gravely ill patients, so that we could be close by and also handle the many telephone calls that flooded the hospital switchboard. We were both so shattered by Renee's stillness that we could not look at her without weeping. I would stand by her bed, speak to her, and she would squeeze my hand, then I would have to rush out of the room to a linen closet down the hall, where she could not hear my uncontrollable sobs. Doris had to return to Connecticut after ten days because Mrs. Barlow's health was failing fast, and I was virtually alone with my grief. Renee had once described our friendship as that of two independent spirits who "meshed" in crises and "disengaged" when it was no longer necessary to act as a unit. Now I had to stand by helplessly, our teamwork torn apart by forces neither of us could control. Through all this I had to deal with the many sorrowing people who hung on to the telephone each day, seeking a word of hope or comfort, each one relating to me how Renee had helped them through some crisis in their own lives and each one, like me, refusing to believe that the sturdy, reliable friend they banked upon was dying. I was overwhelmed by the great outpouring of love and gratitude in letters, telegrams, and telephone calls, all the more poignant because Renee was unaware of the enormous response to her lifetime of ministering to the needs of countless others.

For several days I lived in a state of split consciousness. Part of me functioned as a lawyer, organizing Renee's business files and papers in preparation for the administration of her estate by the law firm for which she then worked. The other part of me carried on a dialogue with God, alternately praying, "Thy will be done," and arguing angrily, "It isn't fair, Lord." When I went to the hospital I would sit by Renee's bed, sometimes talking to her as if she were fully present and had all her faculties, although I had heard those dreaded words "brain death." I found myself speaking of the decision she was making with God; that if she went on she would be with all those loved ones who had gone before her; that if she decided to stay with us we would be with her all the way.

Then I went outside and sat in the solarium nearby, thinking about death. I had always been terrified of death and had avoided funerals as much as possible. Now I had to watch death approaching my closest friend, and I could no longer avoid pondering the ultimate mystery of life. All kinds of images were conjured up to help me accept what my mind resisted. Suppose death is a "loving mother" waiting to enfold us in a protective embrace rather than the "grim reaper" that haunted my childhood; or perhaps death is a friend who waits just outside the door until we are ready to go. Why should one fear what is as natural as birth, or what is, perhaps, merely crossing a threshold? I recalled that a friend who was an undertaker's assistant once said there was always peace on the faces of dead people, even those who had died violent deaths. I began to think of the experience of death as a transition in which a person may swing back and forth between two states of being, not quite out of this world and not quite into the next. And, I thought, perhaps those who love the person most can be a hindrance to the process; they may hold on when the one who is dying is ready to die. Knowing nothing of the stages of death and dying described by Elisabeth Kübler-Ross, I was clutching at any theory that would make the thought of Renee's death more tolerable.

Help in coping with the situation came unexpectedly. My college classmate Lula Burton Bramwell, whom I had known since we were freshmen at the Brooklyn Annex of Hunter College, was fighting terminal cancer and the effects of chemotherapy in another hospital across town. On Tuesday, February 20, when Lula's sister Gerry, a brilliant physician, flew in from California to see her, Lula had Gerry talk with me by telephone. Gerry explained that each person who is ill has a lifeline and clinging to that lifeline could go on indefinitely. She thought that I might be Renee's lifeline, and that I had to decide whether I could let her linger in the condition she was now in. Only I could decide that question.

That night Renee's special nurse was called to another room in an emergency. While she was gone Renee grew restless. Her head tossed, her breath came in gasps, and her moans made me cry out silently, "Take her, God, I can't bear to see her suffer this way." No priest was available, so I stood by her bed reading the Twenty-third Psalm, and when I finished I kissed her goodbye and said, "Rest." When I left the hospital that night I knew I could not come back. Her nurse walked me to the elevator and said, "You go out of this hospital and get yourself together. This is *it*, and we don't want you to be here when it happens."

Renee died the next morning around ten o'clock. Time hung like an eternity in the hours before her death; everything in my private world was waiting. When the hospital called, and I knew that her heart had stopped beating, time began to move again. I felt a flood of relief and joy that she was at last released from pain. Although it was bitterly cold outside, I opened all the windows of her apartment to let fresh air blow through, and put on her favorite record—Schumann's Piano Concerto in A Minor—in celebration of the passing of a beautiful spirit. As another friend wrote later of Renee, "she is now making joyful noises to the Lord and delighting those in Heaven with her marvelous wit."

Without knowing it or defining it as such, I had been called upon to minister to my friend in her final hours, and my ministry to her family and friends continued through her funeral and the memorial service held three days later. I helped Doris with all the arrangements, acted as host to Renee's nieces and nephews who came from Connecticut and Massachusetts to attend the private funeral. Renee's memorial service was held on Tuesday, February 27, at Calvary Episcopal Church, where Mrs. Roosevelt had been christened as an infant in the 1880s. The Reverend Thomas F. Pike, who officiated, had been a seminarian at Saint Mark's-in-the-Bowery in 1959, when Renee first joined its congregation. Because Doris had to return to Connecticut immediately after the funeral, and the Reverend Pike had to be out of town until the morning of the memorial service, all the planning and coordination fell to me.

I had never before planned an order of service, and working out numerous details on short notice was more complicated that I had anticipated. Fortunately, Renee's assistant at the law firm, Elsie Lubben, who had worked with me handling her business affairs during her illness, was also an Episcopalian and somehow we managed to secure the speakers, put the service together, and run off copies of the program minutes before it began. There were moving tributes by Lloyd K. Garrison, Peter M. Ward, and N. Beatrice Worthy, representing, respectively, the law firms where Renee had worked and the Personnel Club of New York City, which she had served as vice-president. The service closed with the haunting strains of "We Shall Overcome" sung by the choir as a chorale. The words "We shall live in peace" were a fitting benediction for one whose name, Irene, reflected the irenic quality of her being.

When it was all over, Tom Pike commended me on a beautiful service. I was astonished when he added, "You may not have realized it, but you have been acting as an enabler, a function of a deacon in our church. Have you ever thought of ordination?" Late that afternoon as I drove back to Boston thinking of Tom Pike's words, an exquisite sunset of gold, blue, pink, and aqua filled the western sky. It was as if Renee's spirit was smiling in approval as she bade me farewell.

CHAPTER 35

Full Circle

RENEE'S DEATH changed my life. It was more than the loss of a close friend. In Renee's dying hours I had come face to face with my own mortality. I felt an urgency to complete my mission on earth in the days left to me. From its beginnings, our friendship had centered around the church, and it was in the church that I had found the comforting belief that the living and the dead are bound together in the "communion of saints." For the second time in my life I had been called upon to *be with* a devout Christian whom I loved in the crisis of death and to minister in ways I associated only with the ordained clergy. As I reflected upon these experiences, the thought of ordination became unavoidable. Yet the notion of a "call" was so astounding when it burst into my consciousness that I went about in a daze, unable to eat or sleep as I struggled against it.

In spite of my vigorous advocacy of women's ordination in the Episcopal Church as a matter of principle, my age and, more important, my sense of unworthiness had insulated me against entertaining such a possibility for myself. It had taken a cataclysm, watching my friend in an abyss of suffering, to force my submission and obedience to Divine Will. Now that Will seemed to be leading me into the unknown, on a journey that demanded utmost faith and trust.

In my indecision, I went to the Reverend Alvin L. Kershaw of Emmanuel Church in Boston, which I had begun to attend. After several conversations he assured me I was on the right track. "You and your friend Renee were engaged in a Christian ministry," I remember him saying. "Now that she is gone, you can carry it on for both."

Once I admitted the call of total commitment to service in the church, it seemed that I had been pointed in this direction all my life and that my experiences were merely preparation for this calling. In spite of my own intellectual doubts and the opposition to women's ordination which was widespread within the Episcopal Church at the time, I took the fateful step of applying to the Right Reverend John M. Burgess, bishop of the Diocese of Massachusetts, for admission to holy orders.

In due course Bishop Burgess turned me over to Suffragan Bishop Morris F. Arnold, who supervised candidates for ordination in the diocese. Bishop Arnold put me at ease in our first session by telling me about his maiden speech in the House of Bishops a year earlier during a debate on women's ordination. He had forthrightly told his brethren that the Second Coming of Christ would not necessarily be represented by someone of the same sex or the same race as the First Coming. Bishop Arnold's sympathetic support was a bulwark of strength in the rugged days that followed. In June 1973, when I was accepted as a postulant from the Diocese of Massachusetts, supporters of women's ordination to the priesthood were optimistic that the triennial General Convention meeting at Louisville that fall would approve this historic change in Anglican tradition. In September, however—by which time I had resigned from Brandeis, moved to New York, and entered the General Theological Seminary for a year of training as a special student—the organized opposition had become more vocal and advocates of women's ordination were less hopeful. I had barely begun my studies when the Convention met and voted the issue down.

The Convention's rebuff left women seminarians as well as women who were already ordained deacons with an uncertain future in the church. This continuing barrier had especially serious implications for me as I approached my sixty-third birthday. Having given up my academic career and the financial security it provided, I would be severely handicapped by my age in seeking professional employment after my year of training was completed. No official action would be taken by the church for another three years, when the General Convention would meet again; meanwhile I would be in limbo. To avoid this untenable position (and despite the fact that my academic background did not require me to complete additional formal study), I petitioned the faculty to change my status to that of a regular three-year student and a candidate for the Master of Divinity degree.

Those three years of seminary subjected me to the most rigorous discipline I had ever encountered, surpassing by far the rigors of my law school training. For most people, I think, seminary is an intensely intellectual and emotional experience of living with others in close quarters while dealing with imponderables and the ambiguities of human existence. It brings to the surface hidden doubts about religious faith as well as fears, insecurities, and unresolved problems. One's personality is under the continuous scrutiny of instructors and schoolmates as well as under constant self-examination. In addition to daily devotions and corporate worship, seminarians have to absorb an immense body of learning. Throughout the process they have to satisfy various layers of the church hierarchy not only that they are academically competent but also that the spiritual formation essential to a priestly calling is plainly evident in their bearing.

Women seminarians were in a peculiarly ambiguous position in the mid-1970s. Although we were formally accepted as candidates for a degree and for ordination to the diaconate, we were the center of bitter controversy, the targets of veiled and sometimes overt hostility. Our numbers were few and our presence in a community designed for men only was more tolerated than encouraged. The admission of women to the General Theological Seminary was so recent that the first two women to graduate received their degrees at the end of my first year there. My own situation was especially complex. Not only was I the only Negro woman enrolled, but I felt set apart because I was the oldest student in residence, senior in age and professional experience to most of my professors and several decades older than my classmates, most of whom were white and male and in their twenties, only a few years older than the students I had taught at Brandeis. My legal training was a mixed blessing; while it contributed to clarity of expression, my forensic approach was disturbing in a theological setting. My natural tendency to probe and debate an issue collided with some of the instructors' concepts of being "pastoral," and I soon got a reputation for being "abrasive," a view some professors, believing such a character trait would hinder my ministry, insisted upon expressing in my evaluation report at the end of my first year.

Another complaint, which almost wrecked my seminary career that first year, was that I was "rude" and cut people off in the middle of a sentence when they were speaking in class. I was appalled by this accusation but was at a loss to explain myself until my friend Page Smith Bigelow, a senior, accidentally discovered the real trouble when she borrowed tapes I had recorded in a theology course. After listening to several tapes, Page came to me and said, "Pauli, you are cutting people off because you don't hear them when they drop their voices at the end of a sentence." Tests confirmed that I had a serious hearing loss in both ears, and the deficiency was partially corrected through appliances attached to my eyeglasses. The difference was amazing. With the hearing aids I heard sounds I had not been aware of for years, but I soon learned why so many people who have hearing aids consider them an abomination. The appliances are not yet sensitive enough to tune out background noise, so that turning up the volume to listen to someone speaking magnifies other sounds to a harsh, confusing clatter.

Given my volatile temperament, it was providential that I did not go to the General Convention of 1973. I was too new a postulant to risk a rebuff at the outset of the long road to ordination. By not going I was less battered than the women who went with such fervent hope. This became evident when I attended a weekend conference of women seminarians and deacons shortly after the Convention, to consider future strategy. Many of the women were seething with anger and pain. In one of the small discussion groups, which included Suzanne Hiatt and Carter Heyward, friends from Cambridge who had gone to Louisville, I wanted to talk about next steps, but found they were too furious to listen. Carter burst out, "Pauli, I cannot *hear* what you are saying. Strategy is not where I am at this moment. I'm trying to decide whether to leave this church."

I pleaded with her not to leave. "Do whatever you have to do, Carter," I said, "but let the church put *you* out."

The rawness of these wounds was so distressing that in the closing session I felt compelled to say that the church was losing its authority as a Christian body and that it was no longer speaking with an authentic voice if women were treated as outcasts when they sought to answer God's call to the priesthood. At that session we met jointly with a few key men who supported us, and I was struck by the contrast between each group's approach to the issue. While the women stressed the moral wrong of exclusion from ordination, the male priests were pragmatic and tough-minded, concerning themselves with ways to enlist the support of influential bishops, clergy, and strategic laypersons to ensure victory for the ordination of women at the next general convention, which would meet in Minneapolis in 1976.

I left the conference troubled because I saw no long-range plan of action directed toward the next convention. But action of a different sort was soon forthcoming. In mid-December, five male deacons were ordained to the priesthood at the Cathedral of Saint John the Divine in New York City. At the ceremony five women deacons whose qualifications were identical to those of their brethren—except for their sex—also presented themselves in vestments to Bishop Paul Moore, Jr., for ordination. Women at General Seminary had been alerted that this public "witness" would take place, and several of us attended the service to give our sisters spiritual and moral support.

It was the first of several dramatic confrontations in the Episcopal Church during the next three years as the women's ordination issue rocketed into the news and almost split the church apart. When the women

deacons knelt before Bishop Moore in silent appeal just before the consecration, he told them sadly, "Go in peace, my sisters." Rejected at the altar,
they turned and walked with bowed heads in solemn procession down the
center aisle. No funeral procession could have been more sorrowful. I was
sitting in the second row just beneath the pulpit, and I raced down the side
aisle to join them so they would not be alone, but when I reached the rear
doors of the nave more than half of the congregation was already there.
Almost everyone was crying as we held the women in our arms and let
them sob on our shoulders. Then our "church in exile" went to a building
nearby, where we shared in a joyous agape which had been prepared for
us in place of the Holy Eucharist at the cathedral we had left behind.

The incident had immediate repercussions at General Seminary,
where the community divided into warring camps. Heated exchanges
took place in the corridors and in the refectory. Some male seminarians
condemned the women's action as a scandal. Some who had shown lukewarm support for women's ordination now railed against using a "civil
rights demonstration" tactic which, they felt, had no place in the solemn
liturgy of the church. Others contented themselves with hostile stares at
those of us who supported the women deacons by our presence at the
ordination service. I learned that disputes among the faithful, although
usually fought with polite words, can be as acrimonious in their language
as a street brawl.

At times, when theological arguments were invoked against the ordination of women, I shuttled between faith and inner doubt. These arguments carried the force of a two-thousand-year tribal taboo and were so
deeply embedded in the psyche that on the morning of July 29, 1974,
when I took the train to Philadelphia to attend the ceremony in which
eleven women deacons were ordained priests without the official approval
of their own bishops, I experienced sudden terror. My panic was so great
that I might have left the train at Newark if I had not met two clergy-
women of the United Church of Christ, whose obvious enthusiasm for the
event calmed some of my fears.

In Philadelphia, we joined a throng of two thousand people from many
parts of the country, who crowded into the Church of the Advocate to
witness a dramatic turning point in the struggle for women's ordination.
None of us knew what to expect, although there were rumors that dissi-
dents might try to disrupt the proceedings by seizing upon a rarely used
provision in the order of service, in which the bishop says to the people,
"if any of you know any impediment or crime because of which we should
not proceed, come forward now, and make it known." When this point
was reached in the Philadelphia ordinations, a few male priests fairly
screamed their objections. Their hysterical outburst was received calmly,

and when they had left the church the ceremony continued with customary beauty and solemnity. By the end of the service the joyous spirit that enveloped the congregation swept away all my doubts as to the rightness of the action taken that day. My most cherished memory of the occasion is that of kneeling before the newly priested Jeannette Piccard to receive her blessing.

This ordination was historic in more than one respect. It took place in a church in the heart of the Philadelphia ghetto, and a Negro congregation was the host. Symbolically, the rejected opened their arms to the rejected.

The Episcopal Church would never be the same after the widely publicized and much discussed "Philadelphia Ordinations." The House of Bishops called an emergency meeting and a majority of those present voted to condemn the ordinations as "invalid." Although lively debates among church scholars followed as to whether the ordinations were invalid or merely irregular, the sacramental act could not be rescinded, and the new priests could not be ignored. For many women like me, their existence revolutionized our feelings about the church and its sacraments. When a woman presided at the Holy Eucharist, we felt included in the act more completely than ever before, and were able to enter more fully into this sacred experience. In the days following Philadelphia, some of us met secretly in a small group for a house communion celebrated by one of the Eleven. When the Reverend Alison Cheek, who had been ordained in Philadelphia, became the first woman to celebrate the Holy Eucharist publicly in an Episcopal church in the United States—at Saint Stephen and the Incarnation in Washington, D.C.—my friend Morag Simchak, who attended the service, sent me an envelope containing crumbs of the consecrated bread, reverently wrapped in white paper. Public celebrations like this led to at least two canonical trials in which male rectors were charged with violating their ordination vows by permitting unauthorized persons to exercise priestly functions in their respective parish churches. These trials only fanned the flames of dissension as the church approached its next general convention.

Throughout those turbulent, unpredictable years I felt the steadying influence of seminary professors whose intellectual integrity I respected —theological scholars such as Pierson Parker, James A. Carpenter, Charles P. Price, Henry Rightor, Marianne H. Micks, and others. Their unswerving support strengthened my faith and buoyed my hope.

I had postponed my field work in parish ministry until my senior year and, by getting permission from the General Seminary faculty to study at Virginia Theological Seminary that year, was able to do my field education at Saint Philip's Chapel, Aquasco, in Prince George's County, Maryland. It was the same little mission church my uncle had served as vicar in my childhood fifty years earlier. Some of the infants he had baptized then were now grandparents and leaders of the congregation, and Peter Brooks, who was the oldest communicant, remembered me as a little girl. Members of Saint Philip's had never had a seminarian serve their church before, and they were so pleased to learn that I cared enough to remember and come back to this small rural congregation that they adopted me with pride and affection. Their vicar, the Reverend William A. Jerr, took me under his wing and delighted in coaching me so that I learned to perform liturgical acts with ease.

Working at Saint Philip's was the best possible preparation for ordination. Its white wooden structure held scarcely more than a hundred people, but for me it rivaled the quality of a great cathedral. Knowing that Aunt Pauline, Aunt Sallie, and Grandmother Cornelia had all worshiped there many years before linked me with my past and gave continuity to my spiritual pilgrimage. I remained there through my graduation and ordination to the diaconate, and left only after a tragic fire destroyed the building in November 1976. The morning after the fire, I stood looking at the ruins and at the cardboard sign attached to a scarred railing, on which someone had written: "Jesus wept." I mourned the loss of that small church building as one mourns the loss of a friend. The congregation of Saint Philip's had affirmed my ministry, especially during those months of intolerable uncertainty just before the General Convention met that September in Minneapolis.

My faith had not been robust enough to hazard the possibility of still another rejection in my life, so instead of going to Minneapolis I decided to stay home and spend those fateful days in meditation and prayer. As a result, I missed the excitement when women's ordination was finally approved by the General Convention of the Episcopal Church. I was alone when I learned the result of the vote, but almost immediately afterward I got an amazing telephone call that once more linked my present and past in an almost mystical continuity. Earlier that summer I had received a letter from the Reverend Peter James Lee, rector of the Chapel of the Cross in Chapel Hill, North Carolina. The Reverend Lee wrote that he had read *Proud Shoes* and learned through it of my relationship to the nineteenth-century Smith family of Chapel Hill: how my great-grandmother, the hapless slave Harriet, who was the property of Dr. James Strudwick Smith, had been raped by young Sidney Smith and had borne a daughter, Cornelia; and how Sidney Smith's older sister, Mary Ruffin Smith, had taken her infant niece into her home and church and raised her as a devout Episcopalian. In the parish register of the Chapel of the Cross, the Reverend Lee had found the record of Grandmother Cornelia's baptism.

On the evening of the vote, Peter Lee telephoned me from Minneapolis. "I want to invite you to celebrate your first Holy Eucharist as a priest at the Chapel of the Cross," he told me. "I can think of no more appropriate symbol of what has happened here today than having you preside at the altar in the same chapel building where your Grandmother Cornelia was baptized in 1854." I was so stunned by this proposal that I stammered something unintelligible in reply, but the Reverend Lee cheerfully assured me he would write me all the details. On the same evening, my suffragan bishop from Massachusetts, the Right Reverend Morris F. Arnold, who had ordained me a deacon the previous June, called to emphasize the reality of the event. He told me that he had been thinking of me especially when the vote was being taken and now he was looking ahead to my ordination to the priesthood. He suggested that to spare the expense of my having to return to Boston for ordination in my own diocese, an arrangement could be made to have me ordained at the National Cathedral in Washington, D.C., by the Right Reverend William F. Creighton, bishop of the Diocese of Washington. I was overjoyed at this prospect. Bishop Creighton had endeared himself to women aspiring to the priesthood by announcing his refusal to ordain anyone, male or female, until the General Convention met again and passed on the women's ordination issue. The Convention's approval was to become effective on January 1, 1977, and Bishop Creighton scheduled his ordination ceremony for January 8.

Although I had struggled with doubts throughout my candidacy, the greatest reassurance that I had taken the right step in applying to enter holy orders was the absence of any delay in the process leading to ordination. The timing was providential; even if I had been a man, I could not have been consecrated a priest under the most liberal application of church regulations until December 9, 1976, only a few weeks earlier than my actual ordination. During those few weeks, however, I had to meet a test of pastoral ministry for which my seminary training could not fully prepare me—ministry in the presence of death.

In early December, Adina Stewart Carrington, my friend Maida's mother, who for years had been a second mother to me and whom I called Moms, suffered a stroke, and I rushed to Brooklyn to be with her and with Maida in the crisis. My work among the sick and dying during my pastoral training at Bellevue Hospital could not shield me from the overwhelming sorrow of seeing this vibrant woman, whose home had been filled with laughter, now stricken and unable to speak to me when I entered her bedroom. She could only smile in recognition, as if to say everything was all right now that I was there. For three days Maida and I took turns watching over Moms, as her attending nurse, Maude Fleming, a devoutly religious woman, gently guided us through the subtle changes in Moms' breathing and pulse rate, which signaled her approaching death. When the end came, all three of us were sitting by her bedside reading from the Bible, and as Maida read the Ninety-first Psalm aloud, her mother gave a slight gasp and slipped into eternity.

Mrs. Fleming sent Maida out of the room and pressed me into service to assist her with post-death ministrations, performed with tenderness as if Moms were still alive and could respond to us. Maida had been determined that her mother would die with dignity in the familiar surroundings of her own home. She had succeeded. In death, all pain had vanished from her mother's face, and although she was a woman of eighty, she looked like a beautiful young girl who had fallen asleep. My final test came when I took part in Moms' funeral as a member of the clergy and read the Ninety-first Psalm without letting my voice falter.

Beginning January 1, 1977, the first ordinations of women as Episcopal priests became media events. As each ceremony took place, it was headlined in the news as "the first woman priest in the United States," or "the first woman priest in New York State," or in Virginia or in California. On Saturday, January 8, I was one of three women and three men to be ordained at the same service in which the ordination of two "irregular" women priests was affirmed, all at the Washington Cathedral. The circumstances gave the ceremony unusual prominence.

Several days before the ordination, I was suddenly seized by an agony of indecision, as though I had been assaulted by an army of demons. The thought that the opponents of women's ordination might be right and that I might be participating in a monstrous wrong terrified me. As a sister priest put it later, speaking of herself, "I felt that God might strike me dead before it happened." I have since been told by other priests, male and female, that they faced a similar ordeal just before their ordination, but at the time I thought this ambivalence was peculiar to me, so personal that I dared not speak to anyone about it. I prayed fervently for some sign that I was doing God's will.

January 8 was a bitter-cold, gray morning in Washington, with ice and snow covering the ground, but three thousand or more people packed the Washington National Cathedral, a number of them my relatives and close friends. As was customary, a long procession of vested clergy walked down the aisle, followed by the lay presenters (or sponsors) of the ordinands. Then those of us who were being ordained proceeded to our individual prayer desks, which were arranged in a semicircle around the Great Transept, and the participating clergy and elaborately robed bishops continued up into the chancel. The familiar liturgy moved forward majestically through the presentation, declaration of vows, litany for ordination, sermon, examination, and consecration. I was the last of the six to be consecrated, and was told later that just as Bishop Creighton placed his hands upon my forehead, the sun broke through the clouds outside and sent shafts of rainbow-colored light down through the stained-glass windows. The shimmering beams of light were so striking that members of the congregation gasped. When I learned about it later, I took it as the sign of God's will I had prayed for. Immediately after we were consecrated and vested in our white chasubles, and the words "The Peace of the Lord be always with you" had been spoken, the cathedral throng exploded in a joyous outburst such as one seldom sees at a staid Episcopal service. It was a resounding affirmation of our call to serve God as priests.

Five weeks later, on the weekend of Abraham Lincoln's birthday, I traveled to North Carolina to celebrate my first Holy Eucharist—also the first Eucharist to be celebrated by a woman in that state—at the Chapel of the Cross in Chapel Hill. Family history and religious tradition combined with changing folkways to make it an occasion of high drama, which attracted not only the local media but also Charles Kuralt of CBS—himself a graduate of the University of North Carolina—who came down with his "On the Road" van and television crew from New York to cover the event.

On Sunday, February 13, in the little chapel where my Grandmother Cornelia had been baptized more than a century earlier as one of "Five Servant Children Belonging to Miss Mary Ruffin Smith," I read the gospel from an ornate lectern engraved with the name of that slave-owning woman who had left part of her wealth to the Episcopal Diocese of North Carolina. A thoroughly interracial congregation crowded the chapel, and many more stood outside until they could enter to kneel at the altar rail and receive Communion. There was great irony in the fact that the first woman priest to preside at the altar of the church to which Mary Ruffin Smith had given her deepest devotion should be the granddaughter of the little girl she had sent to the balcony reserved for slaves. But more than irony marked that moment. Whatever future ministry I might have as a priest, it was given to me that day to be a symbol of healing.

All the strands of my life had come together. Descendant of slave and of slave owner, I had already been called poet, lawyer, teacher, and friend. Now I was empowered to minister the sacrament of One in whom there is no north or south, no black or white, no male or female—only the spirit of love and reconciliation drawing us all toward the goal of human wholeness.

Epilogue

PAULI MURRAY died while she was still working with her editor on the final revisions of this book. She had spent the years after her ordination serving what she called her "extended ministry," her own parish in Baltimore as well as churches in Washington, D. C. and Pittsburgh. She held interim posts in a number of Episcopal churches in those cities, and was in constant demand as pastor and preacher. Her health, undermined by years of malnourishment and the demands she made on her frail body, finally gave way, and she died on July 1, 1985.

During her latter years Pauli continued to write, contributing articles to theological publications and, through "confrontation by typewriter," as she put it, challenging newspapers and public officials on a wide range of issues that mattered deeply to her. In whatever time she could spare, she worked on this memoir, drawing on her memory and on her voluminous records—writing, organizing, and rewriting with the same passion for truth that had marked her from childhood. If she had been granted the time, she would have followed this volume with another devoted to her calling as an Episcopal priest.

All who knew Pauli were impressed by the tremendous energy that drove her to achieve excellence in everything she undertook. They felt her total commitment; a commitment that made her always ready to use herself as an instrument to advance whatever cause she was pursuing. They saw her stand firm on principle, pressing through confrontation toward reconciliation by means of reason and disciplined nonviolence. Already she has become a symbol and guiding light to many who never had the privilege of knowing her personally.

For Pauli, differences of culture, appearance, nationality, religion, or any other human circumstance were sources of enrichment, not barriers to human intercourse. She was proud of her mixed ancestry—African, Irish, American Indian, Carolina planter—and she claimed each element fully as part of her rightful heritage. To be treated as a human being and to regard all others as members of the same human family were at the core of Pauli's outlook and effort. As she prefaced her book of poems, *Dark Testament:*

> I speak for my race and my people—
> The human race and just people.

This is her legacy.

CAROLINE F. WARE

Vienna, Virginia

Index